THE ROUTLEDGE COMPANION TO CINEMA AND POLITICS

The Routledge Companion to Cinema and Politics brings together forty essays by leading film scholars and filmmakers in order to discuss the complex relationship between cinema and politics.

Organised into eight parts – Approaches to Cinema and Politics; Cinema, Activism and Opposition; Film, Propaganda, Ideology and the State; The Politics of Mobility; Political Hollywood; Alternative and Independent Film and Politics; The Politics of Cine-geographies and The Politics of Documentary – this collection covers a broad range of topics, including: Third Cinema, cinema after 9/11, eco-activism, human rights, independent Chinese documentary, film festivals, manifestoes, film policies, film as a response to the post-2008 financial crisis, Soviet propaganda, the impact of neoliberalism on cinema, and many others.

This *Companion* foregrounds the key debates, concepts, approaches and case studies that critique and explain the complex relationship between politics and cinema, discussing films from around the world and including examples from film history as well as contemporary cinema. It also explores the wider relationship between politics and entertainment, examines cinema's response to political and social transformations and questions the extent to which filmmaking itself is a political act.

Yannis Tzioumakis is Senior Lecturer in Communication and Media Studies at the University of Liverpool. He is the author and editor of six books, most recently of *Hollywood's Indies: Classics Divisions, Specialty Labels and the American Film Market* (2012). He is also co-editor of the 'Hollywood Centenary' and the 'Cinema and Youth Cultures' book series (both for Routledge).

Claire Molloy is Professor of Film, Television and Digital Media, and Director of the Centre for Human Animal Studies at Edge Hill University. Her recent publications include the books *Memento* (2010), *Popular Media and Animals* (2011), *Beyond Human: From Animality to Transhumanism* (2012) and *American Independent Cinema: Indie, Indiewood and Beyond* (2013).

Contributors: Stephen Baker, Scott L. Baugh, Warren Buckland, Michael Chanan, Felicity Collins, John Corner, Sean Cubitt, Paul Dave, Stephanie Hemelryk Donald, Philip Drake, Dimitris Eleftheriotis, Gregory Frame, Armida de la Garza, Nurith Gertz, Kenneth W. Harrow, Douglas Kellner, Anthony Killick, Geoff King, Yosefa Loshitzky, James Lyons, Ewa Mazierska, Ruth McElroy, Betsy A. McLane, Jacqui Miller, Toby Miller, Panayiota Mini, Petar Mitric, Claire Molloy, Lúcia Nagib, Gary Needham, Brian Neve, Rob Nilsson, Deirdre O'Neill, Lydia Papadimitriou, Anat Pick, Brad Prager, Steve Presence, Peter C. Pugsley, Luke Robinson, Lee Salter, Katharine Sarikakis, Ian Scott, Eleftheria Thanouli, Leshu Torchin, Yannis Tzioumakis, Marijke de Valck, Janet Wasko, Michael Wayne.

THE ROUTLEDGE COMPANION TO CINEMA AND POLITICS

Edited by Yannis Tzioumakis and Claire Molloy

Routledge
Taylor & Francis Group
LONDON AND NEW YORK

First published in paperback 2019

First published 2016
by Routledge
2 Park Square, Milton Park, Abingdon, Oxon OX14 4RN

and by Routledge
52 Vanderbilt Avenue, New York, NY 10017

Routledge is an imprint of the Taylor & Francis Group, an informa business

British Library Cataloguing-in-Publication Data
A catalogue record for this book is available from the British Library

Library of Congress Cataloging-in-Publication Data
Names: Tzioumakis, Yannis, editor. | Molloy, Claire, editor.
Title: The Routledge companion to cinema and politics / edited by Yannis Tzioumakis and Claire Molloy.
Description: London ; New York : Routledge, 2016. | Includes bibliographical references and index.
Identifiers: LCCN 2015049692 | ISBN 9780415717397 (hbk) | ISBN 9781315678863 (ebk)
Subjects: LCSH: Motion pictures--Political aspects.
Classification: LCC PN1995.9.P6 R68 2016 | DDC 791.43/6581--dc23
LC record available at http://lccn.loc.gov/2015049692

ISBN: 978-0-415-71739-7 (hbk)
ISBN: 978-1-138-39168-0 (pbk)
ISBN: 978-1-315-67886-3 (ebk)

Typeset in Goudy
by Book Now Ltd, London

Yannis Tzioumakis would like to dedicate this book to
Julia Hallam
A great scholar, colleague and friend

Claire Molloy would like to dedicate this book to
B.B.

CONTENTS

FIGURES

CONTRIBUTORS

Stephen Baker is the co-author (with Greg McLaughlin) of *The Propaganda of Peace: The role of the media and culture in the Northern Ireland Peace Process* (Bristol: Intellect Books, 2010) and *The British Media and Bloody Sunday* (Bristol: Intellect Books, 2015).

Scott L. Baugh is Associate Professor of Film/Media Studies at Texas Tech University. He specializes in multicultural American cinema with emphases in Latina/o and Latin American cultural expression. His books include *Born of Resistance* (with Víctor A. Sorell, 2015), *Latino American Cinema* (2012), and *Mediating Chicana/o Culture* (2/e, 2008).

Warren Buckland is Reader in Film Studies at Oxford Brookes University. His most recent publications are *The Routledge Encyclopedia of Film Theory* (co-edited with Edward Branigan, 2014), *Hollywood Puzzle Films* (ed. 2014), and *Film Theory: Rational Reconstructions* (2012).

Michael Chanan is a seasoned documentarist, writer and Professor of Film & Video at the University of Roehampton. His last book is *The Politics of Documentary* and most of his films over the last 15 years have either been academically funded or no-budget video blogs, available at mchanan.com and putneydebater.com.

Felicity Collins is Reader/Associate Professor at La Trobe University. She has published widely on Australian screen culture and since the 1990s her work has focused on settler colonial screen culture. She is the author of *Australian Cinema after Mabo* (with Therese Davis), and *The Films of Gillian Armstrong*. She is writing a monograph on television and the Blak Wave, and editing the *Wiley-Blackwell Companion to Australian Cinema* (with Susan Bye and Jane Landman).

John Corner is Visiting Professor in Media and Communication at the University of Leeds. He has written widely on media and cultural theory, media history and documentary. His most recent books are *Theorising Media* (2011) and *Political Culture and Media Genre* (with Kay Richardson and Katy Parry, 2012).

Sean Cubitt is Professor of Film and Television at Goldsmiths, University of London and Professorial Fellow at the University of Melbourne. His current research is on political aesthetics, media technologies and their environmental impacts, and media arts and their history. His most recent book is *The Practice of Light* (2014).

Paul Dave is a Reader in Film and Cultural Theory at the University of Teesside. His current research is in the area of historical materialist approaches to culture and his most recent book, *British Cinema: Romanticism and Historical Materialism* is forthcoming from Pluto Press.

Stephanie Hemelryk Donald is Professor of Comparative Film and ARC Future Fellow at the University of New South Wales. Recent books include *Inert Cities* (2014) with Christoph Lindner. She is currently writing a monograph on migrants, childhood and film for IB Tauris (2017), and co-editing a book on Childhood, Film and Nation for Bloomsbury (2016).

Philip Drake is Professor in Film, Media and Communications at Edge Hill University. He has published widely in film, media and urban studies since 1997, most recently the co-edited collection *Hollywood and the Law* (BFI/Palgrave Macmillan, 2016). He is currently also academic principal investigator on an AHRC NESTA Digital R&D for the Arts funded research project on VOD digital film distribution with Film London and We Are Colony.

Dimitris Eleftheriotis is Professor of Film Studies at the University of Glasgow. An editor of *Screen* and of the *Journal of Greek Media and Culture*, he has published broadly on international film and film theory and history. Currently preparing a monograph on Film and Cosmopolitanism, his most recent book is *Cinematic Journeys* (2010).

Gregory Frame is Lecturer in Film Studies at Bangor University. His research focuses on the politics and ideologies of popular audiovisual culture. His first book, *The American President in Film and Television: Myth, Politics and Representation*, was published in September 2014.

Armida de la Garza is Senior Lecturer in Digital Humanities and Screen Media at University College Cork, Ireland. She is a Member of the Lingnan Centre for Film Studies Advisory Board and co-editor of the *Transnational Cinemas* journal. She is interested in research on screen media and their relation to culture, industry and education. She has published on a variety of topics, ranging from the links between documentary and diaspora, to Realism in Latin American cinema.

Nurith Gertz is a Professor Emerita of Hebrew literature and film at The Open University of Israel and currently heads the Department of Culture Creation and Production at Sapir Academic College. Her recent books include: *Captive of a Dream: National Myths in Israeli Culture* (Vallentine Mitchell, 2000); *Holocaust Survivors, Aliens and Others in Israeli Cinema* (Am Oved, 2004, in Hebrew); *Palestinian Cinema: Landscape, Trauma and Memory*, with George Khleifi (Edinburgh University Press & Indiana University Press, 2008).

Kenneth W. Harrow is a Distinguished Professor of English at Michigan State University, where he specializes in African cinema and literature. His latest book is *Trash: African Cinema from Below*.

Douglas Kellner is George Kneller Chair in the Philosophy of Education at UCLA and author of many books on social theory, politics, history, and culture, including *Camera Politica: The Politics and Ideology of Contemporary Hollywood Film* (co-authored with Michael Ryan) and

Cinema Wars: Hollywood Film and Politics in the Bush-Cheney Era. His website is at http://www.gseis.ucla.edu/faculty/kellner/kellner.html

Anthony Killick is co-founder of the Bristol Radical Film Festival in 2012, co-director of the Liverpool Radical Film Festival and programmer at the Liverpool Small Cinema. He is also a researcher looking at film festivals, urban development and social movements at Edge Hill University, UK.

Geoff King is Professor of Film Studies at Brunel University London. His main research interests are contemporary American independent and Hollywood cinema. Recent publications include *Indie 2.0: Change and Continuity in Contemporary American Indie Film* (2014) and *Quality Hollywood: Markers of Distinction in Contemporary Studio Film* (2015).

Yosefa Loshitzky is Professorial Research Associate at SOAS, University of London. She is the author of *The Radical Faces of Godard and Bertolucci* (1995), *Identity Politics on the Israeli Screen* (2010), *Screening Strangers: Diaspora and Migration in Contemporary European Cinema* (2010) and the editor of *Spielberg's Holocaust: Critical Perspectives on 'Schindler's List'* (1997).

James Lyons is Senior Lecturer in Film Studies at the University of Exeter. He has published widely on American film and television. His forthcoming book is on performance and risk in American independent documentary.

Ewa Mazierska is Professor of Film Studies at the University of Central Lancashire. She has published over twenty monographs and edited collections on European cinema, representation of work and Marxism in film. Her most recent book is *From Self-Fulfilment to Survival of the Fittest: Work in European Cinema from the 1960s to the Present* (2015).

Ruth McElroy is Reader in Media and Cultural Studies at the University of South Wales where she is director of the Centre for Media and Culture in Small Nations. She is editor of *Contemporary British Crime Drama* (Ashgate, 2016) and with Caitriona Noonan is writing *Mobile Fictions: Television Drama Production from Dr Who to Game of Thrones* for Palgrave Macmillan.

Betsy A. McLane is the author of *The New History of Documentary Film*, 2nd edition (2012). She was Project Director of The American Documentary Showcase for the Bureau of Education and Cultural Affairs of the US Department of State, and is Director Emerita of the International Documentary Association. She is currently researcher/interviewer for the Academy of Motion Pictures Arts and Sciences Oral History Program.

Jacqui Miller is Principal Lecturer in Film History at Liverpool Hope University. She is a film historian with a specialism in the relationship between cinema, culture and history. She has published widely on film history and crime fiction. Her most recent publication is on film adaptations of Patricia Highsmith's Ripliad.

Toby Miller is Emeritus Distinguished Professor, University of California, Riverside; Sir Walter Murdoch Professor of Cultural Policy Studies, Murdoch University; Profesor Invitado, Escuela de Comunicación Social, Universidad del Norte; Professor of Journalism, Media and Cultural Studies, Cardiff University/Prifysgol Caerdydd; and Director of the Institute of Media and Creative Industries, Loughborough University, London. His adventures can be scrutinized at www.tobymiller.org.

Panayiota Mini is Assistant Professor of Film History at the University of Crete. She has published articles on Greek cinema and Soviet cinema with an emphasis on issues of film form and ideology. She is the author of *The Filmic Form of Pain and of Aching Recollection: Takis Kanellopoulos's Modernism*, forthcoming from the National Bank Cultural Foundation, Athens.

Petar Mitric is PhD Fellow at the University of Copenhagen. His research focuses on cultural Europeanness and the policy framework that regulates European co-productions. His most recent publication explores the membership of the post-Yugoslav region in the European co-production fund Eurimages.

Claire Molloy is Professor of Film, Television and Digital Media, and Director of the Centre for Human Animal Studies at Edge Hill University. Her recent publications include the books *Memento* (2010), *Popular Media and Animals* (2011), *Beyond Human: From Animality to Transhumanism* (2012) and *American Independent Cinema: indie, indiewood and beyond* (2013).

Lúcia Nagib is Professor of Film and Director of the Centre for Film Aesthetics and Cultures, University of Reading. Her single-authored books include *World Cinema and the Ethics of Realism* (2011) and *Brazil on Screen: Cinema Novo, New Cinema, Utopia* (2007). Her edited books include *Theorizing World Cinema* (with Chris Perriam and Rajinder Dudrah, 2011), *Realism and the Audiovisual Media* (with Cecília Mello, 2009) and *The New Brazilian Cinema* (2003).

Gary Needham is senior lecturer in Film and Television Studies, Nottingham Trent University. He is the author of *Brokeback Mountain* (2010) and co-editor of *Warhol in Ten Takes* (2013), *Queer TV* (2009), and *Asian Cinemas* (2006). He is an editor of the journal *Film, Fashion, and Consumption* and series editor with Yannis Tzioumakis of the Routledge Hollywood Centenary. He is currently working on *Factory Girl/Factory Films: Edie Sedgwick and the Films of Andy Warhol* for Bloomsbury.

Brian Neve is Honorary Fellow (formerly Reader) in film and politics, University of Bath. He has specialized in American film and politics, and his most recent book is *The Many Lives of Cy Endfield: Film Noir, the Blacklist and* Zulu (2015).

Rob Nilsson is a film director/writer/producer as well as a poet and painter. Films done in his Direct Action style have won numerous prizes, including at Cannes and Sundance, been featured in retrospectives, in theaters and on television worldwide. *From a Refugee of Tristan da Cunha* (2007) is a collection of his poetry and *Wild Surmise* (2013) is his book on cinema.

Deirdre O'Neill is lecturer, film maker and the co-ordinator of Inside Film. She is the co-director of *Condition of the Working Class*.

Lydia Papadimitriou is Reader in Film Studies at Liverpool John Moores University. She has published extensively on different aspects of Greek cinema, and is currently researching on documentary, film festivals and distribution. She is the author of *The Greek Film Musical* (2006), co-editor of *Greek Cinema: Texts, Forms and Identities* (2011), and the Principal Editor of the *Journal of Greek Media and Culture*.

Anat Pick is Senior Lecturer in Film Studies at Queen Mary, University of London. She is author of *Creaturely Poetics: Animality and Vulnerability in Literature and Film* (2011), and co-editor of *Screening Nature: Cinema Beyond the Human* (2013). Anat has written widely on animals, ethics and film. Her new book project is entitled *Vegan Cinema: Looking, Eating, Letting Be.*

Brad Prager is Professor of Film Studies and German Studies in the Department of German & Russian at the University of Missouri. He is the author of three monographs including, most recently, *After the Fact: The Holocaust Documentary in the Twenty-First Century* (2015). He is the co-editor of *Visualizing the Holocaust: Documents, Aesthetics, Memory* (2008) and several other books.

Steve Presence is a Research Associate in the Centre for Moving Image Research at the University of the West of England (UWE), Bristol. He is the founder and co-director of the Bristol Radical Film Festival and convenor of the Radical Film Network (RFN), an international infrastructure for politically engaged film culture (www.radicalfilmnetwork.com).

Peter C. Pugsley is Head of Media and teaches Asian Screen Media at the University of Adelaide. He has published widely on the cinemas of Asia, including the recent books *Morality and Sexuality in Asian Cinema: Cinematic Boundaries* (2015) and *Tradition, Culture and Aesthetics in Contemporary Asian Cinema* (2013).

Luke Robinson is Lecturer in Film Studies at the University of Sussex. He has written on Chinese-language cinema and film culture, and is the author of *Independent Chinese Documentary: From the Studio to the Street* (2013).

Lee Salter is a Senior Lecturer in Media and Communications at the University of Sussex. His research covers a range of different subjects, from the Bolivarian Revolution to the uses of technologies by activists. His most recent book is *Digital Journalism* (2011). He is also a filmmaker, collaborating with Michael Chanan on *Secret City*, Liz Mizon on *The Fourth Estate* and again with Michael Chanan on his current project, *Money Puzzles*.

Katharine Sarikakis is Professor of Media Governance in the Department of Communication at the University of Vienna. She leads the *Media Governance and Industries Research Lab* and is the vice-chair of the Communication Law and Policy Division of the International Communication Association and the founding and twice elected Chair of the Communication Law and Policy Section of the European Communication Research and Education Association.

Ian Scott is Assistant Associate Dean and Senior Lecturer in American Studies at the University of Manchester. He has written extensively on representations of politics in Hollywood movies, including a second edition of *American Politics in Hollywood Film* (2011). His new book, *Dramatic History: The Cinema of Oliver Stone*, co-authored with Henry Thompson, will be published in 2016 by Manchester University Press.

Eleftheria Thanouli is an Associate Professor in Film Theory at Aristotle University of Thessaloniki. She is a specialist in the fields of film narratology, digital cinema and world cinema. Her most recent book is *Wag the Dog: A Study on Film and Reality in the Digital Age* (2013).

Leshu Torchin is Senior Lecturer in Film Studies at the University of St Andrews. The author of *Creating the Witness: Documenting Genocide in Film, Video, and the Internet* (2012), she researches and has published on the subject of human rights, genocide, activism, and film.

Yannis Tzioumakis is Senior Lecturer in Communication and Media Studies at the University of Liverpool. He has published widely in the field of American independent cinema studies and his most recent book is *Hollywood's Indies: Classics Divisions, Specialty Labels and the American Film Market* (EUP, 2012).

Marijke de Valck is Associate Professor in the Department of Media and Culture Studies at Utrecht University. She is a specialist in film festival studies and author of *Film Festivals: From European Geopolitics to Global Cinephilia* (Amsterdam University Press 2007). She co-founded the Film Festival Research Network and is co-editor of the book series Framing Film Festivals for Palgrave MacMillan.

Janet Wasko is the Knight Chair in Communication Research at the University of Oregon in Eugene, Oregon, USA. Her research and teaching focuses on the political economy of media, especially the political economy of film, as well as issues relating to democracy and media. She currently serves as the President of the International Association for Media and Communication Research.

Mike Wayne is a Professor in Screen Media at Brunel University. His book *Political Film* (2001) explored the theory and practice of Third Cinema. He writes widely on Marxist cultural theory and has recently published *Red Kant: Aesthetics, Marxism and the Third Critique* (2014).

ACKNOWLEDGEMENTS

This Companion took approximately four years to complete and there were many people who contributed in different ways to its realisation and to whom we would like to express our gratitude.

First and foremost we would like to thank Natalie Foster, senior commissioning editor for Film, Media, Culture and Television Studies at Routledge, for inviting us to edit this Companion. We had previously worked with Natalie, having edited (together with Geoff King) *American Independent Cinema: Indie, Indiewood and Beyond* (2013) for Routledge, and we were extremely happy to extend our collaboration to this project. As always, Natalie helped us immensely, especially with the administrative part of the task in hand, and her experience and advice have been invaluable as has been her patience and understanding when we asked for a bit of extra time to complete the job. She was a sheer pleasure to work with!

Our greatest thanks also extend to Sheni Kruger, editorial assistant at Routledge for being hugely supportive and extremely efficient with the details of the project. Contracts, minutiae about the volume's production, publicity, and a whole host of other issues were all handled with great competence and patience by Sheni. We would also like to thank Mel Pheby, a marketing officer at Routledge, for designing publicity material for the volume and Jef Boys and Richard Cook of Book Now Publishing Services for copyediting it. And of course, we would like to say a big thank you to photographer Simon Norfolk whose "Bullet scarred outdoor cinema at the Palace of Culture in the Kharte Shar district of Kabul" photograph decorates beautifully and poignantly the cover of the volume.

More than anything this book owes its existence to the 48 contributors who entrusted us with their work on aspects of the complex relationship between cinema and politics and who wrote the different section introductions, highlighting particularly important issues and themes, and bringing the chapters together. We would like to say a massive thank you to all of you, for contributing to this volume and for being so collegial and generous throughout the long process of putting it together. In that process, we feel we made lots of new good friends and this was for us as important as was the academic aspect. We hope that you will be happy with the final result.

Yannis would like to extend his thanks to a number of people who have always supported his work in general and this volume in particular: my parents, Panayiotis and Christina Tzioumakis, my brother Leonidas Tzioumakis and his family (Patroula, Christina and Ilias), my close friends Rigas Goulimaris, Harris Tlas, Annalies McIver, Maria Goulimaris and Harris Papadopoulos, Panayiotis Koutakis and his family (Dimitra, Fenia, Ioanna and Roxanne), Paul Shaughnessy, Yolanda Akil-Perez, Alkisti Charsouli, Litsa Kitsou and David Oswald. I would also like to say thank you to my wonderful colleagues in the Department of Communication and Media at the University of Liverpool for sharing my admin responsibilities for a full year when I was on research leave and for being such fantastic people to work with: Kay Richardson, Peter Goddard, Katia Balabanova, David Hill, Les Roberts, Georgina Turner, Rudi Palmieri, Beatriz Garcia, Simeon Yates and Jordana Blejmar. As the now former Head of the School of the Arts, Stephanie Hemelryk Donald was an inspiration, an extremely supportive boss and a contributor to the collection. Thank you Stephie! Big thanks also to Rachael Walker, technician in Liverpool's School of the Arts, for helping me with enhancing the quality of many of the images that appear in this Companion.

I would like to say my last 'thank you' to four people whose help and support were the most important in making this massive volume possible: my co-editor Claire Molloy, a true expert in cinema and politics and a long-time friend and collaborator. We managed to navigate through some difficult times during the production of this Companion and we both came out on the other side wiser and stronger. Thank you for all your hard work and dedication to the project; my wife Sian Lincoln and my son Roman Tzioumakis. As always, Sian was amazingly supportive, especially during the last of the four years this project took to complete when editing and other work intensified considerably. As for Roman, he was a tiny toddler when this volume started in 2012 and now stands a school boy approaching his sixth birthday! He was always ready to take his dad away for a break from the project when he needed one. Thank you both so much!

Finally, I would like to say the biggest thank you and dedicate this book to a wonderful friend, mentor, colleague and world-leading film studies scholar who has been a very influential figure in my life and career, Professor Julia Hallam. Julia, who is retiring in 2016 after an amazing 30-year academic career, offered me my first part-time job in Higher Education back in 1998, and nine years later as the Head of Communication and Media she was instrumental in bringing me to the University of Liverpool as a full-time member of staff. Since then, she has been a great influence in my life and career, which I can honestly say would be very different if I did not benefit from her generosity, friendship, collegiality and support in the last 20 years. So this book is for you Julia! Enjoy your hard-earned retirement!

Claire would like to thank Nina Parkinson, Chris Parkinson, Richie Parkinson and Lou Parkinson who have supported me throughout. Also, special thanks to Ian Eccles, Logan and Trinny. I'm grateful to the many colleagues at Edge Hill University who have supported me and this volume in various ways, especially Paddy Hoey, Phil Jackson and Carol Poole. Sincere thanks go to my co-editor Yannis whose friendship, patience, generosity, understanding and collegiality are beyond measure. Finally, to those I had to say goodbye to during the time it took for this book to come to fruition, thank you for your friendship, time, encouragement, love and the good memories left behind.

INTRODUCTION

Claire Molloy and Yannis Tzioumakis

In June 1869, U.S. Patent 90,646 was granted to Thomas Edison. The patent was for an electric vote recorder which could speed up and replace the lengthy process of roll call voting. However, the possibility of utilising this technology was summarily rejected by a Congressional committee; a technology such as this would prevent filibustering. While Edison's first patent would prove to have little impact on political decision making and discourse, the same cannot be said for his later inventions which shaped a history of cinema. Telegraphy sat behind the shared lineage of both the ill-fated vote recorder and the vastly more successful motion picture technologies that followed, tying the two inextricably together; an intersection of the political and the cinematic. Of course, such linkages between cinema and politics are various and extend far beyond the early and perhaps inauspicious technological relationship noted above. Elizabeth Ezra stresses a more overt relationship between the two in early cinema, writing about the films of George Méliès and noting that in France "the mass diffusion of 'expert' opinions in print was quickly complemented by the use of film as a medium of political expression" (Ezra 2000: 70), and elsewhere the early intervention of film into the sphere of politics can be well illustrated by the now infamous examples of D. W. Griffith's *The Birth of a Nation* (1915) and later in Leni Riefenstahl's *Triumph of the Will* (1935). Fast forward to 2013 and U.S. President Barack Obama's visit to DreamWorks to address studio executives; there he described Hollywood and the entertainment industries as "an engine for the economy", "part of our American diplomacy" and, later in his speech, stated that through the global distribution of entertainment products "we have shaped a world culture" (PBS NewsHour 2013). What these few examples demonstrate is an enduring connection between cinema and politics where films continue to play a role in the dissemination of political messages, shape the collective memories of past events and inform political agendas.

This volume has been conceived as a timely intervention in debates about the relationship between cinema and politics, especially when notions of what constitutes political engagement are being reconsidered in an era of networked environments, the promotion of online activism and an acknowledgement from both academia and industry that films have the potential to play a role in shaping the contours of social change. Films are the centrepieces of environmental, social issue and human rights campaigns, driving audiences toward social networking sites which encourage various forms of activism. At the same time, cinema remains central to the formation and transformation of geopolitical discourses, imagining new geographies and connecting (or separating), in complex ways, the concepts of boundaries and territories with ideas about nation and identity. These multiple contact points between politics and cinema have, for many academics, been cause for lengthy consideration, not least because, as Susan Buck-Morss proposes in her monolithic account of Walter Benjamin's critique of cultural production and consumption, "the tendency of mass media is to render the distinction between art and politics meaningless" (Buck-Morss 1989: 140). The collapse of this boundary both aestheticises mass politics *and* has the potential to politicise art, a phenomenon that led Benjamin to point out the dualistic possibilities of mass culture for both emancipation and manipulation (Buck-Morss 1989: 142). His argument was expressed in the oft-cited *The Work of Art in the Age of Mechanical Reproduction* where Benjamin argued that film held the promise of liberation, that was a technology of democratisation able to reach a mass audience and raise political consciousness. In the "Afterword" to his essay, Benjamin proposed:

> Fascism leads logically to an aestheticization of political life. The violation of the masses, which in a leader cult it forces to their knees, corresponds to the violation exercised by a film camera, which Fascism enlists in the service of producing cultic values.
> *(Benjamin 2008: 36)*

Politicised art could however act as a counter to Fascism where film actively cultivated criticality in audiences (Benjamin 2008: 35).

This optimism for the revolutionary possibilities of film was not shared by Benjamin's contemporaries. Critical of Benjamin's "bipolar categories", which held that the emancipatory potential of film was best illustrated by Soviet montage, Theodor Adorno argued that such categorisation made it "impossible to distinguish between a conception of art that is free of ideology to its core and the misuse of aesthetic rationality for mass exploitation and mass domination" (Adorno 1997: 77). While the historical specificity of Adorno's critiques (and those of other scholars attached to the Frankfurt School) of the culture industry articulated concerns about capitalism, the consumption of standardised cultural goods and the passivity they engendered in mass society, other anxieties about the influence of cinema on moral standards forced regulatory control measures to be instituted in the United States in the form of the Production Code, or Hays Code as it became known. Philip Drake makes this point in his introduction to Part I of this volume where he makes mention of the Payne Fund studies which informed the shaping of the Hays Code and included Herbert Blumer's *Movies and Conduct*, published in 1933, and Charles C. Peters' (1932) "The Relation of Motion Pictures to Standards of Morality", in addition to ten further studies that sought to address the relationship between social values and motion pictures. From the early twentieth century onwards, the ability of film to reach, and potentially influence, mass audiences has continued to be inflected in regulation and policy. Anxieties about the effects of cinema are intrinsically bound up with forms of censorship, both moral and political, while faith in the utility of film as a means of mass manipulation has led to cinema being employed as a weapon of ideological expansion in the arsenals of governments and totalitarian regimes. The histories of propaganda and persuasion in wartime and peacetime continue to raise important questions about the relationship between the state, cinema and citizenship (and Part III of this Companion is dedicated to them), including asking what constitutes propaganda; what the limits and challenges of what can be termed 'propagandist' are; how we should assess the intent and reach of partisan messages; and the extent to which entertainment can be employed as a means of political communication and mass persuasion.

The scope of the chapters included in this *Companion to Cinema and Politics* provide a mapping of the multiple and complex interactions between the two and, as the range of this collection illustrates, these entanglements are numerous. Part I of this book includes a selection of approaches that illuminate how we can think critically about these relationships. As with any volume of this type, the range of ideas represented in this opening part is necessarily selective and makes no claim to providing a comprehensive account of all of the scholarly approaches that can be applied to the interactions between cinema and the sphere of politics. Many other perspectives, concepts and critical positions are illustrated across the remaining seven parts (see for instance, Douglas Kellner's "diagnostic critique", which uses cinema to "gain critical historical knowledge of the past and present", in Part V, Political Hollywood, or Ruth McElroy's discussion of small-nation cinema in Part VII, the Politics of Cine-Geographries). The chapters in this opening part do, however, give a strong sense of the various ways in which the topic of cinema and politics has been and can be addressed. Additionally, there is a series of cross-cutting themes that are discussed in these opening chapters and which re-emerge across the collection. For instance, the dynamics of capitalism are variously addressed by Toby Miller, Mike Wayne and Janet Wasko; ideological practices, imperialism, control, ownership and technology figure as important thematic concerns across Part I, many of which Warren Buckland highlights in his overview of *Screen* theory, while Sean Cubitt looks to the present moment and beyond, attending to the contemporary global environmental crisis, an issue also raised by Miller.

The opening part, moreover, provides a cue to the way in which this is book has been conceived. One way to organise a volume such as this is to adopt an historical trajectory, yet such an approach to organising the material presents its own difficulties, especially in terms of deciding what form of periodisation is appropriate. Instead, the eight parts of the Companion are organised in such a way as to allow historical case studies to sit alongside discussions of recent political and social transformations and their relationship to cinema. Following the critical approaches of Part I, the second group of chapters moves from large-scale frameworks to focus on films as individual acts of resistance and opposition. Part III opens with a bridging chapter from activism to propaganda with the remaining chapters taking up the relationship between state and cinema. Partly in answer to the themes of partisan messages and nationalism that are examined in Part III, the chapters included in Part IV explore the ways in which film intersects with the politics of mobility, which is here adopted as an umbrella term that encompasses diverse but related themes such as cosmopolitanism, migration, displacement and trauma. The chapters in Part V shift the focus of the collection to Hollywood cinema, conceived here as a global mainstream with Part VI taking up the issue of alternatives and opposition to that mainstream. The chapters in Part VII of the book re-expand the focus beyond the United States to look at non-Hollywood cinemas, national identity and geopolitics. Part VIII then continues the international perspective of the previous part to explore different iterations of political documentary. While chapters on documentary appear across the Companion, the decision to include a part on Documentary specifically acknowledges the long history of complex associations between politics and documentary filmmaking and explore in more detail questions pertaining to the format's conventions and its role as an instrument for political critique. The authors of the chapters and Part introductions include academics (many of whom are leading scholars from across the broad field of cinema and politics), filmmakers, festival organisers and those that straddle the worlds of academia and filmmaking as hyphenate academic-filmmakers (Mike Wayne, Deirdre O'Neill, Michael Chanan and Lee Salter). The decision to go beyond scholarly interventions in the debates represented in this volume and to include practitioners is intended to reflect a richer engagement with the overarching subject matter, to examine the extent to which filmmaking is, itself, a political act, and to explore relationships between politics and entertainment, and to attend to associations between the extra-textual and the textual.

Some of the Part introductions make unapologetic reference to the realities of the contemporary moment, identifying how the chapters can be understood as a response to current concerns. The global economic crash in 2007/8 brought into focus the failures of neoliberal economic principles and the ensuing 'austerity politics' that have been pursued by some governments and which permeate through current discourses on migrancy, which Stephanie Donald regards in this volume as a subset of mobility, "a heavily politicised concept in action, encompassing the complex conditions of departure, arrival, settlement, and identity formation". While the development of neoliberalism and its impacts, in the global sense, have been uneven (a point borne out by the various chapters in this volume), its central tenets of deregulation, privatisation, de-unionisation of the labour force and the dismantling of the welfare state, underpinned by the drive towards supposedly free market competition and an ever freer movement of capital, goods and resources find their ideological parallel in notions of globalisation unhindered by political interference, greater consumer choice, individualism, individual responsibility and entrepreneurialism. How the economic, policy and ideological dimensions of neoliberalism play out both in relation to cinema in general and to particular films is discussed by contributors across the parts of this volume.

Although not addressing the subject of neoliberalism directly, Janet Wasko argues in her chapter on political economy that analyses of "communication in total social context" are "crucial" in that "their study helps to dispel some common myths about our economic political system, especially notions of pluralism, free enterprise, competition and others". The extent to which cinema and filmmaking practices have been shaped by and responded to neoliberal forces is specifically highlighted in Lydia Papadimitriou's chapter on documentary filmmakers' responses to the financial crisis and austerity in Greece. Her discussion makes apparent the failures of neoliberalism in the context of international financial dependence, bringing to the foreground its devastating social impacts and argues that the films themselves "were not just *about* the crisis, but they were products *of* the crisis". In contrast with the effects of neoliberal economic crisis on films and filmmakers in Greece, Stephen Baker's argument draws on neoliberalism as an organising frame to understand the on-screen constructions of post-conflict Northern Ireland identity, which has necessitated to large degree an effacement of the tensions of the country's political past. In his chapter, Baker points towards the economic "benefits" of cultural production that capitulates to a neoliberal agenda but, he argues, these "come at the cost of a politically engaged cinema" and he warns that, "the aspiration to full membership of the global free-market render a politically engaged cinema both apparently irrelevant and undesirable".

This conundrum also lies at the core of Petar Mitric and Katharine Sarikakis' discussion of European cinema and policy and the success or failure of films when neoliberal logic dictates that "consumers determine the market". Their argument brings to light the tensions between "two conflicting philosophies", one that underpins state support for national filmmaking and the other that revolves around the neoliberal financial incentives "introduced to bring additional investment into the film industry", the consequences of which, they point out, are that "in an attempt to ensure more audience for, and visibility of, their films, European national cinemas increasingly sacrifice their long-standing emphasis on auteurism and autonomy in favour of more "'predictable' commercial successes". Over the thirty or so years that have seen neoliberalism come to dominate world politics, class structure and inequality have been rendered opaque, "masked", as David Harvey reminds us by "a lot of rhetoric about freedom, liberty and personal responsibility" (Harvey 2011: 10). Deirdre O'Neill explores what happens to working class subjectivity under such conditions in her account of the Inside Film project where she finds that initially

> students struggle to make sense of the discrepancy between the way in which society treats them, the way in which they are represented in the media, the demands society makes on them and the impossibility of meeting those demands precisely because of the way they are treated.

If we consider that neoliberal logic reconfigures the citizen in the image of the individual consumer, as Toby Miller asserts, and encourages policy that substantially weakens or even closes down the opportunities for critical political engagement through film, it becomes vital to turn attention to counter-hegemonic practices and the spaces in which alternative or oppositional views might be flourishing. Besides O'Neill, a number of contributors explore how such practices can and have been articulated and in what spaces (see especially chapters by Presence, Nilsson and Robinson, among others).

Commentators from different fields, including festival directors, academics, film producers, directors and documentary filmmakers, suggest that audiences for politically themed films have changed and grown over the last decade. Facilitating this change, there has been an increase in distribution channels which include subscription services such as Netflix, advertising-supported sites such as SnagFilms, free streaming sites such as freedocumentaries.org, and specialist channels on YouTube and Vimeo. A prolific producer and distributor, Participant Media is one example of a contemporary media company that has created campaigns to accompany the social issue films it produces and distributes while organisations such as BritDoc and Sundance now actively support the funding, development and distribution of political films. These channels do indeed open up opportunities for audiences to engage with social issue films, especially documentaries, all of which Betsy A. McClane argues "include politics, whether personal or governmental". Yet many of these films also sit at the more commercial end of the spectrum having budgets that while not comparable with a Hollywood blockbuster, operate in a different economic sphere to the no- or zero-budget filmmaking that might be associated with activist films. Political documentaries such as those by Michael Moore discussed by McLane and *GasLand*, the focus of the chapter by Claire Molloy, in this volume are a case in point, coming from an independent sector which has recently witnessed a revitalisation of politically oriented filmmaking following more than a decade when, Yannis Tzioumakis points out in his chapter on indie filmmaking, filmmakers "traded a strongly articulated political consciousness for a much more 'commercial' outlook that quickly found a name, and arguably an identity, under the label 'indie' cinema".

Alternatives to theatrical release via online and subscription-based distribution channels have offered independent films generally and politically themed documentaries specifically, opportunities to reach audiences that were previously unavailable. Parallel to this point, cheaper, lighter digital technologies have enabled a new generation of independent political filmmakers to document their personal experiences of conflict, state-building, activism and crisis. In China, digital technologies have enabled a new documentary film culture to flourish (see Luke Robinson's chapter in this volume), finding distribution opportunities through regional television broadcasters, while lightweight cameras have allowed filmmakers to document recent events in the Middle East and North Africa. In his chapter on video-activism, Steve Presence emphasises how "today's radically altered technological context" has altered significantly "contemporary video-activist culture" and in their account of making the, initially, "zero-budget" documentary *Secret City* (2012) Michael Chanan and Lee Salter talk about the distribution strategy for the film which, they argue, demonstrates "the potential of the web to discover an 'audience-in-waiting' that is not served by broadcast media or conventional film distribution – nor the expense of marketing". New technologies have opened up the playing field in relation to production and distribution but this should not be taken to imply that a new utopian era of media democratisation is at hand. Indeed, tensions around this topic are most apparent in Part VII, 'The Politics of Cine-Geographies', where Ewa Mazierska notes that the authors "point to the contradictory effect of the development of technology on the position of cinema" whereby the "digital shift" can be seen to both "democratise the process of film production" as well as "strengthen the hegemonic position of high-budget films in the world market". While none of the authors in this volume expresses what Toby Miller refers to as "cybertarianism", the fantasy that "everyone and no one is a cultural producer in the traditional, quasi-institutional sense, just as everyone is simultaneously an unpaid worker and a paying customer" it is of note that the technological advances which have changed the terrain for activist and oppositional filmmakers may indeed simultaneously benefit Hollywood and sustain forms of inequality.

What also emerges from a number of chapters in this Companion is a problematisation of 'activism' and filmmaking, something which Anthony Killick alerts us to in his introduction to Part II when he refers to the term as an "empty signifier" due to "the contemporary landscape of video activism" which "is formed by the shifting relation between cultural production and domestic as well as geo-politics, with video activists carving their way through in as best a way they can according to their relative prohibitions". It is therefore tricky to conceive of activism as signifying a specific form of resistance or as having involvement in a common set of counter-hegemonic practices, a point which Luke Robinson makes clear in his chapter on documentary in China when he writes, "activism in China does not always manifest in the form of direct legal contestation with the authorities. Indeed, the severity of the potential response to such behaviour means many groups avoid such direct challenges to state power", which means that few of the films or filmmakers he focuses on "conform to the standard Euro-American blueprint of political filmmaking, that of activist documentary". Steve Presence, on the other hand, draws attention to the struggles faced by oppositional filmmakers in Britain who by "making work available for free" are unable to support themselves financially with many having to find "a balance between less overtly political work that is paid or grant-funded, and more radical video-activism that is often produced and shared for free". By way of illuminating a stark comparison, the American filmmaker Josh Fox, although labelled an "activist" and responsible for bringing "anti-fracking propaganda" messages into the public sphere, also sits within an especially privileged enclave, with a network of influential connections that extend to the Hollywood 'A' list (see Molloy's chapter in this volume). The structure of this Companion calls attention to the complexities of definitions of not only "activist", but also "alternative" and "oppositional". While there are Companion parts with these terms in their titles, the aim here is not to attempt to pin down any absolute conception of what they might mean (and therefore chapters that deal with such practices, much like the engagement with neoliberalism, are to be found across the volume) but instead to represent the range of practices and the richness of the debates that surround them.

For instance, Marijke de Valck takes up the issue of what is meant by "alternative" in relation to film festivals. Here she argues that "when described as alternative, film festivals are foremost regarded in relation to Hollywood". In support of this, she proposes that

> while film festivals are part of the spaces and opportunities for alternative forms of filmmaking that have always existed – spaces where marginal voices could be heard

> and counter discourses were created and sustained – they also foster relations with the mainstream and produce new power relations of their own.

The documenting of revolutions, protests and demonstrations has had an impact on the international festival circuit, fuelling a growing transnational interest in films that critique political regimes or reference the Arab Spring. *Tahrir 2011 – The Good, the Bad and the Politician* (Ayten Amin and Tamer Ezzat), a film about the Egyptian revolution, premiered at the Venice Film Festival in 2011 (where three films by Syrian filmmakers were also screened) and was also included in the 'Mavericks' section of the Toronto Film Festival the same year. At Cannes, in 2012, the screening of two feature films dealing with events in the Middle East (*Le Serment de Tobrouk* [Bernard Henri-Lévy and Marc Roussel] and *Baad el Mawkeaa* [Yousry Nasrallah]) received widespread attention while, amongst others, the International Festival of Mediterranean Film and the Berlin International Film Festival have both devoted special programmes to Arab Spring films. In addition to festival audiences, Middle East filmmakers, many of whom are active in protests and civil resistance campaigns, have suggested that their films offer audiences in post-revolutionary regions opportunities to consider alternative political perspectives not currently represented in mainstream media. Indeed, in her chapter on Israeli film, Nurith Gertz draws attention to the ways in which some filmmakers are re-imagining an historical past and future by drawing on the aesthetics of European and American cinema in ways that "corrects, amends and modifies it according to new ethical perceptions". Gertz reflects on how the quest for an alternative history is, amongst other things, "a substitute for the cultural memory of historical traumas", with the connected themes of trauma and memory reappearing across this Companion, centralised in Lucia Nagib's chapter on *The Act of Killing* (2012) and critiqued in Felicity Collins' chapter on Blackfella Films and Prager's chapter on Holocaust documentaries.

For many authors in this volume, like de Valck, alternative and oppositional practices derive their definitional and symbolic weight from being situated outside the mainstream or in relation to some manifestation of Hollywood, either in institutional, ideological or aesthetic terms. Mike Wayne's discussion of Third Cinema in the opening part examines the critiques and filmmaking practices that developed in the 1960s as a response to Hollywood and its international commercial imitators. Here he argues that "cinema contributes to the struggle for liberation by intervening in what turns out to be one of the most important fronts: the front of consciousness, culture and identity", a point which Deirdre O'Neill takes up in Part II in her chapter on film and working-class subjectivity which demonstrates how contemporary praxis can be informed by the principles of Third Cinema. Indeed, many authors across this volume point towards the influence of Latin America (Wayne, O'Neill, Baugh, de la Garza), which Mike Wayne refers to as the "epicentre" of Third Cinema, as a model of oppositional cinema, with Armida de la Garza arguing, in her chapter in Part VII, 'The Politics of Cine-Geographies', that despite arguments to the contrary, a strand of Latin American cinema "remains political in the former utopian sense, namely concerned with broad social transformation, dealing with issues of citizenship and the nation-state".

The issue of citizenship and related concepts of 'nation' and 'transnationalism' resonate across this volume, not least because as Ruth McElroy observes in her chapter on minor cinema, "even as globalisation is seen to be dissolving the force of nations, our world continues to be shaped by the distinctly modern notion of the 'nation' and by the power structures in which nations and nation-building are embedded". Kenneth Harrow discusses this in his chapter on African film and globalisation and cautions that "the turn to transnationalisms as categories that define contemporary world cinema risks reinscribing the same old position of dominance to Hollywood, or 'Western' cinema". Allied to this, notions of otherness connect with questions of transnational encounters, a point which Dimitris Eleftheriotis explores in his chapter that argues for cosmopolitan empathy as "as an ethical way of relating to media representations of the lives, experiences and histories of strangers", noting that "a similar dynamic is offered as a fundamental condition for the politically effective use of empathy". Cosmopolitanism, he points out "focuses on our relationships with each other as citizens of the world as well as on the ways we individually and collectively relate to the world".

While not necessarily interchangeable as terms, "Hollywood" has come to signify "the mainstream" with the footprint of Hollywood writ large across the global market, which leads Brian Neve to state in the introduction to Part V that "no study of the relationship between contemporary film and politics can avoid separate and distinct treatment of the role of Hollywood". Overtly political filmmaking has been considered largely a marginal activity, something that takes place beyond mainstream practices in U.S. cinema, which continues to be primarily concerned with producing and distributing entertainment. On the periphery of popular cinema, political discourse was a strong feature of American independent filmmaking although, as already mentioned, characteristic of a 'pre-indie' era. Indeed, accusations of American cinema becoming gradually depoliticised have been levelled at a post-1980s independent sector which became more interested in box office profits and commercial success than with the political concerns which were considered to inform earlier films such as *Northern Lights* (Hanson and Nilsson, 1978) and the so-called 'LA Rebellion' films of the late 1970s and early 1980s. One reason for this perceived shift was that the studios co-opted or acquired independent companies and, in doing so, the opportunities for producing or distributing politically engaged or challenging films were lessened considerably (though not disappeared completely). This would seem to point to an effacement of political engagement by the Hollywood entertainment product, certainly in the form of critique or challenge to dominant ideology. Douglas Kellner argues that this is not the case and that a film such as *The Day After Tomorrow* "can be seen as a socially critical film in that it puts climate change and environmental devastation in a political context related to dangerous effects of human beings on the environment and incompetent political regimes". He points to Roland Emmerich's use of the "conventions of the disaster film to dramatize the dangers of climate change and global warming, ignored by the Bush/Cheney administration, providing a vision of ecological catastrophe mutating into social apocalypse".

Sean Cubitt, in his chapter on the "Ecopolitics of Cinema", however, argues that to suggest that individual films "communicate ecopolitical ideas is to miss the point: such communication is always" he argues "complicit in the circulation of capital". In the case of ecocriticism, Cubitt proposes, it "has to aim beyond celebrations of green themes and condemnation of anti-ecological movies towards a global understanding of the ecological aspects of all forms of film and every kind of cinematic practice". The capitalistic enterprise of Hollywood does not preclude the integration of political messages and rhetoric into entertainment intended for a global marketplace. Its treatment of politics has sustained and advanced "war on terror" rhetoric which, as Ian Scott argues in his chapter on "Spectacle vs Narrative: Action Political Movies in the New Millennium", has been woven through superhero franchise blockbusters such as *The Dark Knight* trilogy, as well as the *Bourne* series and the *National Treasure* franchise. Gregory Frame in his discussion of the *Why We Fight* series of films, produced by Frank Capra as part of the World War II US propaganda strategy, acts in some sense as a corrective to the notion that Hollywood is a mindless capitalistic monolith, reminding us that even at a time when films were used specifically to influence the public consciousness some of those involved expressed anxieties about the manipulation of the American people.

While it is to be expected that a volume about politics and cinema should engage with propaganda as a core theme, this is not a collection about this type of political cinema, nor is it only about the 'politics of film', although each of these topics is well represented in the volume. *The Routledge Companion to Cinema and Politics* instead is about the various material, textual, institutional, economic and ideological dimensions of cinema and film criticism that intersect with the political. As editors we do not claim that this is a comprehensive volume that addresses all dimensions of the complicated relationships between cinema and politics – something like this would be impossible within the confines of one book. Instead, we suggest that this is a collection that takes on the ambitious task of reflecting on the multiple ways in which cinema is involved in the distribution of power, where it connects with, sustains or challenges modes of governance, and its relationship to the lives of citizens (both human and non-human) and the environment.

Bibliography

Adorno, T. (1997) *Aesthetic Theory*. London and New York: Bloomsbury.

Benjamin, W. (2008) *The Work of Art in the Age of Mechanical Reproduction*. London: Penguin Books.

Blumer, H. (1933) *Movies and Conduct*. New York: The Macmillan Company.

Buck-Morss, S. (1989) *The Dialectics of Seeing: Walter Benjamin and the* Arcades Project. Cambridge and London: MIT Press.

Ezra, E. (2000) *George Méliès: The Birth of the Auteur*. Manchester: Manchester University Press.

Harvey, D. (2011) *The Enigma of Capital and the Crises of Capitalism*. London: Profile Books.

PBS NewsHour (2013) "President Obama Addresses Economic Agenda at DreamWorks"; online https://www.youtube.com/watch?v=kkBggtF5t3w (accessed 2 December 2015).

Peters. C. C. (1932) "The Relation of Motion Pictures to Standards of Morality", in *Journal of Educational Sociology*, 6: 251–255.

PART I

Approaches to cinema and politics

INTRODUCTION

Philip Drake

Film has since its beginnings been political, and the emergence of film and cinema studies can itself be understood as a political project, legitimating film as worthy of scholarship. In arguing that film – both as a technology and cultural form central to the project of modernity – needed to be understood not just in terms of aesthetics but through its articulation with politics and ideology, academic research placed questions of power, identification, and representation at the center of the discipline. Over a century has passed since the release of D.W. Griffith's *Birth of a Nation* (1915) – still one of the most controversial films ever made – and the centrality of film to the twentieth century produced early studies such as those by Herbert Blumer and the Payne Fund Studies in the 1930s exploring movies and social conduct, and the culture industry critiques of the Frankfurt School. It also provoked the use of propaganda films during the World Wars, led to the production of films in the 1950s and 1960s that powerfully documented the post-colonial experience across Africa and Latin America, and consolidated the economic and symbolic power of Hollywood as the global popular cinema.

The chapters in this first part set out a range of theoretical frameworks, introducing critical approaches and key concepts that have shaped this history, and that engage with issues of national and global identity, the ongoing impact of advanced capitalism and new technologies, the global distribution of power and economic dominance, the regulatory forces and boundaries which comprise and construct the conditions within which film intersects with politics, and the explanatory force of approaches and modes of analysis to these issues. They raise key questions and overlapping concerns, for instance, over the relationship between market concentration, economic dominance, and plurality, over the cultural importance of cinema and how it might be regulated, over the relationship between film and dominant ideology, and of the need to understand how externalities, such as ecological footprint and unequal conditions of creative labor, create spill-over effects effaced by late capitalist modes of production, with their over-arching emphasis on consumption.

In "The Dialectics of Third Cinema," Mike Wayne outlines the theoretical and political principles of Third Cinema, paying attention to its exponents in Latin America during the 1960s and 1970s. He argues that the radical politics of Third Cinema was crucially fused with an appreciation of the aesthetic dimension of film and from there, of the importance of cultural politics and struggle. Yet he also views Third Cinema as defined as emerging out of a "dialectical" relationship (of influence and critique) with commercial, state and art cinema (so-called First and Second Cinema). In doing so, he suggests that Third cinema – often mixing documentary and fiction – contributes to the struggle for liberation by intervening in consciousness, culture, and identity, engaging with the political in terms of representation, working practices, and as a wider critique of the film industry and of cultural, political, economic, and military forces.

Cultural diagnosis is also an important theme in Toby Miller's chapter. In "Geopolitics and Cinema" he traces Hollywood's global influence not only on film form but on understandings of cinema itself, demonstrating an ongoing centrality in a supposedly decentered world, and emphasizing that cultural resistance to it will come from the exercise of citizenship rights rather than the advent of an "Asian century" or "cybertarian" technological freedom. In doing so, Miller outlines what we might consider an ethics of cinema, advocating greater attention to the hidden geopolitics of production and consumption.

Developing this theme, Sean Cubitt's chapter on "Ecopolitics of Cinema" provides a critique of what neo-classical economics terms "externalities," those factors not part of idealized models of competitive markets and, as in the case of other kinds of market failure (such as monopoly, oligopoly) requiring intervention or regulation. Cubitt argues that the "toxic soup" of ever increasing entropy, energy use, and alienation from production requires a new eco-cinema to invent new modes of cinematic mediations addressing "free-floating desires, excluded migrants and indigenous peoples, and non-human agents of technology and natural processes." He reminds us that cinema, together with the technology that provides it, is a material practice, and that non-human as well as human actors need to be included in an expanded sense of the political and in the pursuit of common good.

The analysis of dominant cinema by film studies scholars, as Warren Buckland's chapter, "The Politics of Form: A Conceptual Introduction to '*Screen* Theory'" outlines, paid close attention to form and the creation of meaning. His chapter focuses on what became known as "*Screen* Theory," from the influential British journal published at that time by the British Film Institute and indebted to continental European theory and writing in French film journals such as *Cahiers du cinema* which, in the 1950s and 1960s, redefined film style and authorship as political issues. Buckland outlines how "*Screen* theorists" of the 1970s employed Saussurean semiotics, Lacanian psychoanalysis, and Althusserian Marxism to develop a dual agenda: first, to critique the ideology perpetuated by mainstream cinema; and second, to promote a political modernist avant-garde cinema. In using Althusserian concepts to understand ideology, such as interpellation, as well methods of symptomatic reading, such scholars offered a sophisticated analysis of cinema's ideological work, the cinematic apparatus, and political potential of the "counter cinema." This analysis was influential not just in the academic development of film studies, but also in British institutions, notably on the early years of Channel 4 television.

Janet Wasko, in her chapter "Revisiting the Political Economy of Film," presents an overview of the study of the political economy of film, tracing its roots in classical political economy through its application to media and communications. In doing so, she strongly argues for the continued relevance of political economy approaches to understanding media power (what she calls "cultural capitalism"), and continued engagement with the politics of economy/economics. Her discussion also offers a comparison of "new" approaches that study media industries and, she argues, have so far failed to engage with questions of media power whilst misrepresenting political economy as either economistic or top-down. Citing numerous examples of studies engaged with institutions, individuals, processes and conditions of labor – as well as critiques of the regimes that underpin film (such as intellectual property law) – she underlines the continued importance of a political economic approach in critically understanding film and media industries dominated by large commercial enterprises and capitalist markets.

Each chapter in this part unfolds layers of tension and contradiction that characterize the understandings and engagements of film and politics. They collectively offer a range of approaches to re-evaluate the political character of film and media histories, texts, experiences, communities, and institutions. In doing so, they also illuminate the political underpinnings of film and media theories, and shed light on the ways in which these approaches might offer a political means to counter hegemonic, oppressive, or unethical practices through a range of critical or counter-cultural responses. As film has increasingly moved online, and the audio-visual industries have become ever more central to global cultural life, so ways of understanding film and politics continue to evolve. The chapters presented here share a conviction that film, and the understanding of film, is necessarily political. This requires film theory and analysis to rise to the political challenges of the present and future, and not only to develop new scholarly knowledge but also to inform policy and practice, to critique the politics of film but also to aim to change it for the better.

1
THE DIALECTICS OF THIRD CINEMA

Mike Wayne

Introduction

Third Cinema is an appropriate place to begin an anthology on the intersection of politics and cinema. The term refers to a body of filmmaking practice and a series of manifestoes and essays by the filmmakers themselves that emerged in the 1960s. Territorially, its epicentre was Latin America, although important examples of Third Cinema were also produced in Africa and Asia. This tri-continental context was not of course accidental. For Third Cinema was powerfully marked by the political context of the struggle for decolonization and national liberation from the remnants of European settler colonialism and the even more powerful forces of North American Imperialism. The term 'Third Cinema' was coined in 1969 by Fernando Solanas and Octavio Getino to define, in a non-prescriptive manner, a cinema that was emerging out of this struggle and which other writers/filmmakers had called a Cinema of Hunger (Glauber Rocha), a Revolutionary Cinema (Jorge Sanjinés), an Imperfect Cinema (Julio García Espinosa) and a nationalist, realist, critical and popular cinema (Fernando Birri). For Solanas and Getino, Third Cinema emerges as a critique in theory and practice of First Cinema (mainstream, commercial cinema, both Hollywood and its national imitators around the world) and Second Cinema. Second Cinema is the cinema of institutionalized national culture, the cinema of authorial expressivity, the cinema of the middle class, the cinema of psychological crisis or, in its more outward facing, externally orientated 'realist' modes, the cinema of poverty as a great *moral* question (rather than a question of socio-economic relations), and sometimes the cinema of poverty as aesthetic beauty as in Margot Benacerraf's gorgeously shot, and for that very reason, problematic, Venezuelan documentary, *Araya* (1959).

For Solanas and Getino, the prerequisite to imagine and produce a cinema that breaks with the two existing dominant models of cinema, was the Tri-continental movements of the masses that were demanding change:

> [T]he revolution does not begin with the taking of political power from imperialism and the bourgeoisie, but rather begins at the moment when the masses sense the need for change and their intellectual vanguards begin to study and carry out this change *through activities on different fronts*.
>
> (*Solanas and Getino 1997: 35, original emphasis*)

So cinema contributes to the struggle for liberation by intervening in what turns out to be one of the most important fronts: the front of consciousness, culture and identity. It is this focus in fact that means Third Cinema is not merely the subordination of film to a pre-existing political programme or ideology. Third Cinema is orientated towards the everyday life of the people struggling for change, it is, as the Argentinian director Raymundo Gleyzer, killed by the military after the 1976 coup, put it, a "cinema of the base" (Gutierrez 2004). The *aesthetic* dimension of Third Cinema is as important as the political. Third Cinema was characterized by Robert Stam as the conjoining of the two avant-gardes: the political and the artistic, a rare coming together indeed (1998). Stam was specifically discussing Solanas and Getino's film *The Hour of the Furnaces* (1968) and in that context, the artistic vanguard that meets the political is indeed the avant-garde. But the avant-garde is only one specific aesthetic strategy and not all of Third Cinema can be said to draw on the resources of European modernism. The key feature of Third Cinema is that as a politically questioning cinema it is also more than merely an instrumentally political cinema. Some aesthetic dimension – where the medium itself poses questions concerning the role of perception, consciousness and culture in the struggle for change – is as essential to it as an ambition to intervene in the struggle for political change. Birri described the new Latin American cinema in a way that underlines the importance of the aesthetic dimension to Third Cinema and why that aesthetic dimension is itself deeply political. It has, he writes, "a poetics of the transformation of reality … it generates a creative energy … to modify the reality upon which it is projected" (Birri 1997a: 96). This modification may occur because consciousness has been invited to modify its relationship with existing practices, and from that, perhaps, eventually, develop new practices. This aesthetic dimension means that the great Third Cinema films are simultaneously uniquely *singular* and at the same time saturated with the need to communicate truths about social, political, economic, cultural and military domination.

Third Cinema, as a cinema of liberation must pose this aesthetics and politics of transformation at several different levels. They are:

1 At the level of representation – the films themselves, who is represented and how (textual strategies) and with what tacit intention and effects?
2 At the level of working practices – how a production group works, its internal structures and what scope there is to break down hierarchical modes of working and develop collaborative models. Crucially how does the production group – especially the 'intellectual vanguards' as Solanas and Getino call them, relate to the people the film is about? What feedback mechanisms or possibilities of participation exist and how are these balanced against the exigencies to actually produce a 'finished' film? Here there is a whole deeply complex set of issues regarding the relationship between middle-class professionals and their relationship with groups who have not had the cultural and educational benefits of their upbringing. Many, although not all of the Third Cineastes came from such middle-class backgrounds, and if Third Cinema is a cinema that involves a break with the traditional institutional home of the middle-class filmmaker-artist – Second Cinema – then that must involve a continual process of critical self-reflection on the part of those filmmakers. Third Cinema filmmakers were indeed aware of this, more so than most Western filmmakers had been hitherto, but the difficulty and complexity of this question may be signposted by just noting that the very concept of 'vanguards' that Solanas and Getino invoke above, both artistic and political, has come under intense critique in the last thirty years, first with post-modernism and second with new digital technology facilitating and promoting more spontaneous and apparently more leaderless revolt.

3 At the broader level of the industry within which the working practices of a production operates – what is the relationship of a production to the industry in terms of its structures of production and practices of distribution and reception? Apart from fairly brief moments, such as Soviet cinema in the 1920s and Cuban Cinema in the 1960s and early 1970s, when, on both occasions the energies of a popular revolution were still coursing through the new institutions of cinema set up by the state, Third Cinema has been very largely a de-institutionalized cinema, sometimes even a guerrilla cinema, shot on the run from a state that would like to shoot the filmmakers. This de-institutionalized cinematic practice has brought it into conflict with states and has made its viability vis-à-vis the dominant cinemas of One and Two, highly problematic.
4 At the level of the wider cultural, political, economic and military forces at play – what is the relationship of Third Cinema to the concepts and realities of nation, class, race, gender and imperialism?

The posing of political questions by Third Cinema around these four levels is reason enough to return to Third Cinema. But there are other reasons as well. For Third Cinema comes out of the context of decolonization to teach us, here in the West, some crucial lessons regarding the bloody history of our states and the rapacious business interests they defend, which our own education systems and dominant media, routinely hide. The 'moment' of the first wave of Third Cinema more or less ended (with the exception of some significant individual filmmakers, such as Patricio Guzman or, until his death in 2007, Ousmane Sembéne) in the mid-1970s. For that was the period in which coups and ensuing military dictatorships around the world became the favoured means by which the dominant classes in the developing world, and the business and political class in the West, put a stop to the rising aspirations of the masses for radical change. The outcome of that story also forms the prelude to and foundation of our current historical context, one that includes the West as well, namely the rise of neo-liberal capitalism. The 1973 coup in Chile which overthrew the democratically elected Marxist President Salvador Allende, provided the opportunity to test-run the neo-liberal policies that had been developed by the North American Chicago School economists, through the barrel of a gun (Klein 2008). These experiments in privatization, deregulation and opening economies up to international competition and business interests, were then imported into both America and the UK during the 1980s and subsequently exported the world over through powerful supra-national institutions such as the European Union, the World Bank, the International Monetary Fund and various trade treaties. This is why anyone interested today in the possibilities of a political cinema that contests this global trajectory, will find a return to Third Cinema instructive and inspiring.

Writings

The Third Cineastes were writers, thinkers and advocates of cinema and its role within the struggle for liberation. The strong division between critics and filmmakers which we are used to in the West, was not for them. For the Cuban filmmaker Tomás Gutiérrez Alea, "solid theoretical judgment" is a must for the filmmaker because they are "immersed in a complex milieu, the profound meaning of which does not lie on its surface". Filmmakers cannot simply go out in the world '"with just a camera and their sensibility". They need to "promote the theoretical development of their artistic practice" (1997: 109–10). For Fernando Birri in his essay "Cinema and Underdevelopment" the task was to develop a cinema that "awakens consciousness; which clarifies matters … which disturbs, worries, shocks …" (Birri 1997b: 86).

Tomás Gutiérrez Alea elaborates on this in his important, but largely under-appreciated essay "The Viewer's Dialectic". Film for Alea ties emotional engagement to "the *discovery* of something" (1997: 120) by capturing fragments of reality (as images) and reordering and sifting those fragments to create new relations and associations that produce a rupture with our habitualized responses to the everyday environment (122–3). Getino and Solanas concur. Third Cinema does not passively illustrate a situation: "it provides *discovery through transformation*" (Solanas and Getino 1997: 47). At the same time, this is a cinema that rejects the bifurcation of cinema-going into distinct markets. Birri castigates commercial cinema and what he calls the cinema of expression – referring to the Argentinian art cinema which had been established in the 1940s and 50s. The former abandons any cultural goals, the latter abandons the mass audience. The commercial cinema dominated the market back in the 1960s as it does today and the commercial cinema is in turn dominated by Hollywood. "Of about 500 films shown in 1962, 300 were in English, and most of them North American, while some 30 were Argentinian" (Birri 1997b: 91). When one country or region is able to get its media (film, television, radio, music, etc.) into another country or region to the extent that that country or region has difficulty producing and/or circulating its own media in those forms, then we have what is called media imperialism. Understandably in the context of decolonization, media imperialism was often seen as leading to or fostering cultural imperialism. This implies that the media of the dominating country carry with them values, norms, beliefs and perspectives that start to break down and disassemble the *cultural* values of the country whose media are so dominated. As Herbert Schiller notes:

> U.S. films and TV programs are the chief fare of national systems in most countries. News programs, especially CNN, offer U.S. perspectives, sometimes the only perspective provided, to world audiences. U.S. recorded music, theme parks, and advertising now comprise a major part of the world's cultural environment.
>
> *(2001: 160)*

Such concerns about cultural imperialism were subsequently critiqued on the basis that audiences were not passive dupes of media imported from elsewhere, that unequal trade flows were in any case evening up in some media, such as television, with the development of cable and satellite, and national cultures were always more mixed and heterogeneous than the nationalist-orientated critiques of media and cultural imperialism suggested (see Tomlinson 1991). However, the Third Cineastes were not petty nationalists. Their goal was social and political consciousness of the political and economic conditions of the nation. They were well aware that cultural identities did not neatly line up with national borders artificially drawn up, usually by colonialists of yesteryear. They were also intensely aware of how diverse their nations were. The Latin Americans needed no lessons from western cultural theorists on hybridity and *mestizo* culture. Neither were they against cultural exchange, but instead they were demanding a fairer basis for exchange. Tomlinson argues that the discourse of domination that the cultural imperialism theses use does not square with the fact that "plenty of people in the 'undeveloped world' are enthusiastic about the cultural products of the West" (Tomlinson 1991: 94).

Birri encountered the same argument in the 1960s, formulated as "the spectator's right to choose .... But this free-market sophism omits one small detail: that for an audience to choose a film, it must first be exhibited, which generally does not happen with national films" (Birri 1997b: 91). Nor did the Third Cineastes see their audience as dupes. How could they when their audiences were engaging in mass social movements of protest and revolution? But the capacity for audiences to indigenize cultural materials from elsewhere and transform their meanings into the cultural frameworks relevant to them, rather than have such media-cultural products break down their own cultural frameworks, is likely to be best protected if cultures not only receive but also *produce*. The right to be a cultural producer, and to have access to your own national market, is fundamental to the protection of cultural rights. If a society lacks a productive capacity of its own in a given media and perhaps across many media, then it is reasonable to argue that its ability to sustain a cultural identity rooted in its own immediate conditions of existence and thus also its ability to transform foreign media in ways that still connect with those conditions on the terms decided by the social audience, may be harmed. Today Cubans have a great love of classic Hollywood cinema. But they also have the productive capacity to produce their own cinema. Thus the presence of Hollywood in Cuban film culture means something very different than when, as is often the case, Hollywood dominates foreign markets and thus cuts off access of local producers to their own audiences.

Given the situation that Birri confronted in the 1960s, he argued that filmmakers must embrace low-budget production in order to make it easier to recover costs and attract small capital independent of the state, with its tendency to censor. Birri saw low-budget production as a way of transforming "technical limitations into new expressive possibilities" (1997b: 92). Similarly, Garcia Espinosa over in Cuba argued for what he called 'imperfect cinema'. The term imperfect cinema was meant, at one level, to be ironic and playful. Aesthetically it is counterpoised to the 'perfect' cinema of the west, technically polished, resource rich, complete as a narrative in every way. The problem with such 'perfection' in the aesthetic is that it is closed to the spectator. Perfect cinema is a cinema happy with the world as it is and thus against this model 'imperfect cinema' is far more preferable. In part this involves a riposte to big budgets and overconsumption, so that a cinema of the oppressed has the infrastructure that enables it to democratically engage with the real-life conditions of the people it represents. Imperfect cinema revels in and bears the marks of its difficult conditions of production because this brings it closer to the people it is trying to represent. Espinosa's argument finds an echo in Adorno's musings on the possibilities of film in the context of the New German Cinema in the 1960s escaping the apparently all-powerful influence of commodified cinema: "works which have not completely mastered their technique, conveying as a result something consolingly uncontrolled and accidental, have a liberating quality" (1981–2: 199). But for Espinosa (and this is the thrust of Adorno's point as well) 'imperfect cinema' was never a hymn to 'bad' filmmaking, only a rejection of the dominant models that unquestionably make their standards, the universal ones.

There is another dimension to Espinosa's argument that is rarely discussed. On the one hand he argues for a partisan and committed cinema. But this 'committed' cinema, when measured against the utopian injunction for art to transcend immediate social interests and overcome social divisions, must recognize itself as an 'imperfect cinema'. At this ethical level of the argument, Espinosa means the term 'imperfect' quite literally, judged against the normative standard of an art free of social division. Espinosa insists that the aesthetic must be committed to advancing the social interests of the excluded majority (or minorities without power). At the same time he recognizes that this relationship is problematic – it speaks of divisions (including those that structure access to filmmaking) that have yet to be overcome. It is indicative in representatives who speak on behalf of or instead of others, both political cadres and filmmakers speaking for the people. This critical reflection on the role of the filmmaker and intellectual was widespread amongst the Third Cineastes despite the vanguardist politics of the time. Birri invited the shanty-town dwellers of his first documentary *Tire Dié* (1960) to view a rough cut of the film and give him feedback on it and he toured with the film outside the established venues of exhibition. Jorge Sanjinés, who worked with the indigenous people of Bolivia, wrote of the need to break down the bourgeois ideology of the artist, to work collaboratively and to integrate the people who the filmmakers are attempting to represent, into the filmmaking process itself:

> Today there are many group efforts and collective films, and, what is very important, there is the participation of the people who act, who come forward, who create directly, determining the form of the film in a process where the immutable script is disappearing or where the dialogue, during the act of filming, spontaneously issues from the people themselves and from their prodigious capacity.
>
> (*Sanjinés 1997: 62–3*)

Espinosa wonders if the conditions for overcoming the division between elite artists/intellectuals and the broader population can be laid with the universalization of college-level education, a reduction of the working day and evolution of film technology that cheapens production and dissemination technology that facilitates distribution (Espinosa 1997: 72). Of the three, only the technological conditions have been met today.

The ritualized gesture

Hanoi Martes 13 (1968) by Cuban documentary filmmaker Santiago Alvarez was shot in Hanoi during the Vietnam War. The film is a symbol of solidarity across two continents between two countries in their shared struggle against North American Imperialism. In the film Alvarez alternates between charting the everyday life of the North Vietnamese in Hanoi and the surrounding countryside interspersed with their preparations to defend themselves against the aggression of North America. This structure culminates in a shot of what appears to be some sort of live theatrical performance: we can hear singing on the soundtrack but the visual track shows a hand making a Buddhist gesture as part of the performance. The film then cuts to an explosion which visually and aurally takes us to another location – the American bombing which the film has been preparing us for, has begun. After a sequence showing the battle between the airplanes and anti-aircraft fire and ground-to-air missile replies by the North Vietnamese, the raid finishes and Alvarez's camera surveys the damage, the death and the destruction. The camera settles on the remains of a Buddhist statue in the rubble: the hand again is making the Buddhist gesture, the Vitarka Mudra (a symbol of teaching and reason). The message is clear: the North Americans want to destroy a peaceful culture and a way of life that has been conveyed through everyday rituals (fishing, rice cultivation, eating, cycling, taking photos in the park, etc). This is emblematic of a good chunk of Third Cinema: exploring confrontation through the ritualized gesture; that is the gestures of life that become pregnant with social meaning. The aesthetic dimension that Birri noted was central to Third Cinema, here isolates one gesture in particular (the Buddhist one) as a symbol of everything that has gone before. Brecht called this the *gest* (1978: 198–201).

The same ritualized gesture pregnant with social meaning is there at the conclusion of Birri's *Tire Dié*, as the train, that symbol of modernity and communication enters Santa Fe chased by shanty-town kids risking life and limb in a well-rehearsed encounter between the middle-class Argentinians and those that have been excluded from 'progress'. The ritualized gestures of the Argentinian middle class in their leisure and business activities are mercilessly satirized in Solanas and Getino's *The Hour of the Furnaces*. Even their cemetery is a site of interrogation, for the statues and tombs are rituals frozen in stone that act to extend (and thus reinforce) their order from earth into heaven. Another form of interrogating the ritualized gesture is the (re)use of the products of mass culture – the ritualized gestures embedded in a pre-existing piece of film, a photograph, a piece of music, which the viewer can then think about in new ways, and rethink their relationship to this type of material, thanks to its recontextualization in a Third Cinema text. Alvarez uses this technique in *Hanoi Martes 13* to get us to rethink uncritical media coverage of the US President Lyndon Baines Johnson. He uses this technique more extensively in films such as *Now!* (1964) and *LBJ* (1968).

In trying to explore these questions of cultural politics, the thinker who informed the work of the Third Cineastes most directly was probably Frantz Fanon, the African revolutionary originally from Martinique, who went on to join the Algerian revolutionary struggle against the French colonizers. Fanon identifies three typical cultural positions that are taken up by the colonized in the struggle for decolonization, and with suitable modifications, these positions correlate to the positions marked out by First, Second and Third Cinema. Although these three positions may be characterized as three phases through which the colonized can go through – and which Fanon himself did go through at a biographical level – they are best viewed not as a linear process which a people go through once and for all but rather a triangle of positions which a struggle may revolve through according to circumstances and social interests. The main social interests at play in Fanon's argument are the colonialists, the native middle class, who after independence transform themselves into a new bourgeoisie, the intellectuals and the people, themselves divided between urban workers and the peasant rural workers. When the colonialist colonizes, taking land and resources and dismantling the communities and institutions of the colonized, they always also attack the culture of those they dominate. For the culture is the last front of resistance to the colonizer, less tangible than land and resources and more powerful as a way of retaining identities, value systems and consciousness that is differentiated from the colonizer. This is a threat which the colonizer seeks to break down: the destruction of the distinct life-world of the dominated becomes paramount so that the colonizer can say that before their arrival there was merely "barbarism, degradation, and bestiality" (Fanon 1963: 211). Within the force-field of colonial power, the cultural traditions of the people solidify into a formalism "which is more and more stereotyped" (236). Lacking the capacity to innovate, it freezes, becomes inert, even though at the same time, it is taken by the colonialists as "a refusal to submit" (237). The middle class and the intellectuals, however, adopt the first position on offer within these power relations: that of assimilation to the culture of the colonizer.

Later, however, a fraction of the intellectuals break away from this position and adopt a second strategy of survival. Their training and profession is more removed from the direct economic interests which keep the native middle class more or less permanently tied to assimilation. This fraction of a class fraction turns to the frozen culture of the people in an attempt to recover a cultural identity that existed before the arrival of the colonialist. This strategy plays an important role in the struggle for decolonization, building up the resources for the coming struggle: "it was with the greatest delight that they discovered that there was nothing to be ashamed of in the past, but rather dignity, glory, and solemnity" (Fanon 1963: 210). But Fanon is critical of this recovery of tradition because it is purely defensive and above all static, fixed and not profoundly grounded in the movements of change, not profoundly grounded in the *historical* dimension of culture. Instead there is a turn to "customs, traditions, and the appearances of ... [the] people", but this becomes a "banal search for exoticism" (221). This return certainly has an impact on the colonizers, who fear this recovery of lost cultures because it undoes their work of domination – but that in itself is not for Fanon reason enough to uncritically endorse this second position. Instead he criticizes it as a mirror opposite of the "unqualified assimilation" (222) of the middle classes and intellectuals which characterizes the first position. It is a superficial engagement with the culture of a people which the intellectual now endorses and thus betrays an outsider position that often accumulates no more than "a stock of particularisms" (223). The intellectual "wishes to attach himself to the people; but instead he only catches hold of their outer garments. And these outer garments are merely the reflection of a hidden life, teeming and perpetually in motion" (223–4). Thus the intellectual misses "a much more fundamental substance which itself is continually being renewed" and instead, intellectuals satisfy themselves with "mummified fragments which because they are static are in fact symbols of negation and outworn contrivances" (224). This second position correlates to a significant chunk of Second Cinema – where exploring the culture of the people comes to be characteristic of a national cinema differentiating itself from commercial cinema or Hollywood domination. But the culture of the people tends to be viewed by film-makers insufficiently engaged with the culture, as residual, exotic and always to be seen in the rear-view mirror of history. However, only on the surface does tradition appear to be fixed and static. In reality, the meanings of traditions are continually undergoing change and in the context of a revolutionary struggle of national liberation – even more so. Tradition at that point becomes "fundamentally unstable" and "shot through by centrifugal tendencies" (224). This is what Fanon calls the third position – one which correlates closely with Third Cinema. It is the fighting stage, the combative stage. This is the stage where there is a heightened awareness of the relationship between culture and the struggle for change. Now everything is open to question, nothing can be taken for granted. This is the "zone of occult instability" (227) which Fanon recommends the struggle and particularly the intellectuals, to enter, because that is where they will find the people in their real life.

Dialectics of cinema

Fanon's grasp of the dialectics of culture and its relationship with broader political struggles helps us think the typologies of First, Second and Third Cinema as having a dialectical relationship. These categories refer to cinematic practices that are constantly aware of each other and are in a continual process of dialogue, critique and appropriation. The categories refer to a spectrum of possibilities within each type of cinema rather than a fixed homogeneous list of pre-determined characteristics. With Fanon, even the dominant culture that demands assimilation in the context of colonial power, has within it critical sub-currents that Fanon drew upon to critique colonialism (Marx and Hegel for example). Likewise First Cinema, the cinema of commerce, profits, the cinema dominated by Hollywood globally, has critical currents within it that are attuned to the themes of Third Cinema: imperialism, political authoritarianism and capitalist class power (Wayne 2001).

In *Three Kings* (Russell 1999) set as the first Gulf War between America and Iraq in 1991 comes to a close, Mark Wahlberg plays American soldier Troy Barlow who is captured by Iraqi troops. In a key scene Troy is having wires attached to him for some electric-shock torture. In an ordinary First Cinema film, this sort of scene is used to turn the Arab into the Other – an evil, irrational, hate-filled figure who threatens the innocent and the heroic. Yet in *Three Kings*, a Third Cinema moment occurs when the Other now talks back and starts asking some hard questions as to why exactly American troops are in the Middle East. Troy's interrogator asks "What is the problem with Michael Jackson?" before going on to answer a bemused Troy by linking Jackson's well-known surgery that changed the structure of his face and complexion of his skin to a racist United States, which then plays itself out in imperialist adventures abroad. This linking of culture to politics and subversion of the usual frameworks of ideology through which American stars are presented in Hollywood film, shows *Three Kings* to be in some sort of dialogue with Third Cinema.

Nor should we assume that Third Cinema and its themes and strategies are only relevant to contexts involving the struggle against colonial and imperial power.

Andrew Nichol's science fiction film *In Time* (2011) may be read as a blockbuster version of the film Sergei Eisenstein never made, despite plans, namely a film based on Marx's *Das Kapital* (Eisenstein 1976). *In Time* imagines a future where people are genetically coded to drop dead at 25 unless they have time on their genetic clock. The majority literally have little time on their clock, living day to day while prices, controlled by the elites are constantly rising. Meanwhile the rich have hundreds of years available to them and can theoretically live forever. This is virtually a popular culture version of Marx's critique of how a ruling class controls the labour time of the working class and accumulates the fruits of their labour as its own surplus (Wayne 2012).

Of course, with First Cinema films, there are problems in the strategies deployed. That is why they are First Cinema films, but equally, in all cases, a dialogue is going on with the thematic concerns and strategies of Third Cinema. Although a prime motivating force for the development of Third Cinema in Argentina in the 1960s was a deep dissatisfaction with a thoroughly incorporated Second Cinema sponsored by the state, Second Cinema cannot be reduced to these specific circumstances. Like First Cinema it is instead best understood as a spectrum of possibilities that vary according to historical circumstances and personnel. There are plenty of examples of Second Cinema being pushed right to the borders of its own category and opening up a dialogic 'trade' in ideas and concerns with Third Cinema. Werner Herzog's *Aguirre, Wrath of God* (1972) is clearly cognizant of the revolutionary films of the same period as it savagely attacks the madness of colonialism and the hypocrisy of the Church with its tale of Spanish conquistadors searching for the mythical El Dorado. There are times when the film blurs its fictional register with documentary modes, thus destabilizing any complacent sense the viewer may have that this is a story that belongs solely in the sixteenth century. This mixing of documentary and fiction is a recurrent one in Third Cinema. It is a way of opening up the fictional "hermetic structures that are born and die on the screen" (Solanas and Getino 1997: 41–2) to history, while at the same time the fictional register within documentary works to remind audiences that this is a story told from a point of view: it has a subject(ivity) attached to it. This mixing of registers can also be found in the Second Cinema film *The Motorcycle Diaries* (Walter Salles 2004), a biopic based on Che Guevara's diaries that recounted his journey through Latin America with his friend Alberto Granado. The film may be viewed as the story of someone undergoing a journey of political awakening and the film itself travels in the direction of Third Cinema as a result. The documentary style register which the film draws on here and there reminds the viewer again, that this is not a story that exists only in the past, but that the difficulties and injustices that Che encountered back in the 1950s were also discovered by the filmmakers in the course of making the film in the 2000s. Thus Third Cinema is best understood as the dialectical synthesis, that is, the critical sifting and reconfiguration of First and Second Cinema according to the needs of contemporary struggles.

Conclusion

As a critical category Third Cinema remains crucial to understand those examples of First and Second Cinema that are pushing against the limits of these cinematic practices by engaging with the themes and strategies of Third Cinema. Those themes and strategies associated with the first wave of Third Cinema in the 1960s and 1970s left their indelible mark on world cinema. Their grasp of cultural politics and its shaping within the force-field of brute power remains exceptionally sophisticated. Their poetic-political use of the cinematic form is virtually unparalleled. The Third Cineaste challenge to cinema at the level of production practices helped forge new modes of working, new goals for distribution and exhibition and new ways of thinking about what the experience of cinema could be. Their attempt to develop alternative modes of distribution and exhibition for example is now becoming more and more possible with the development of digital media and the internet. This has helped revive a growing alternative film culture as what Solanas and Getino called parallel circuits of exhibition now open up in multi-purpose spaces. Cafes, libraries, museums, community centres, clubs, independent cinemas and so forth are now increasingly venues where a film culture is being watched and discussed that is outside First or Second Cinema and outside the corporate news information media. The documentary genre has been the big winner here. From Michael Moore's *Capitalism, A Love Story* (2009) through to low-budget guerrilla filmmakers on the front line of revolutionary struggles and insurrections around the world, from Greece to Egypt. Third Cinema, despite premature obituaries, is not dead. It will continue to emerge in new and changing forms, tied to the specificities of the struggles it is exploring, as long as the political-ethical imperative for those struggles exists: that is as long as capitalism and its offshoots in imperialism continue to exist.

Bibliography

Adorno, T.W. (1981–2) "Transparencies on Film" *New German Critique*, 24/25, pp. 199–205.

Alea, T. (1997) "The Viewer's Dialectic" in Martin, M.T. (ed.) *New Latin American Cinema, Theory, Practices and Transcontinental Articulations*, Vol. 1. Detroit, MI: Wayne State University Press, pp. 108–133.

Birri, F. (1997a) "For a Nationalist, Realist, Critical and Popular Cinema" in Martin, M.T. (ed.) *New Latin American Cinema, Theory, Practices and Transcontinental Articulations*, Vol. 1. Detroit, MI: Wayne State University Press, pp. 95–98.

Birri, F. (1997b) "Cinema and Underdevelopment" in Martin, M.T. (ed.) *New Latin American Cinema, Theory, Practices and Transcontinental Articulations*, Vol. 1. Detroit, MI: Wayne State University Press, pp. 86–94.

Brecht, B. (1978) *Brecht on Theatre* (John Willet, ed.). New York: Hill & Wang.

Eisenstein, S. (1976) "Notes for a Film of 'Capital'" *October*, 2, pp. 3–26.

Espinosa, J. (1997) "For an Imperfect Cinema" in Martin, M.T. (ed.) *New Latin American Cinema, Theory, Practices and Transcontinental Articulations*, Vol. 1. Detroit, MI: Wayne State University Press, pp. 71–82.

Fanon, F. (1963) *The Wretched of the Earth*. New York: Grove Press.

Gutierrez, B.F. (2004) "*Raymundo* (Review)" *Moving Image*, 4(2), Fall, pp. 119–123.

Klein, N. (2008) *The Shock Doctrine*. London: Penguin Books.

Sanjinés, J. (1997) "Problems of Form and Content in Revolutionary Cinema" in Martin, M.T. (ed.) *New Latin American Cinema, Theory, Practices and Transcontinental Articulations*, Vol. 1. Detroit, MI: Wayne State University Press, pp. 62–70.

Schiller, H. (2001) "The Global Information Highway: Project for an Ungovernable World" in Trend, D. (ed.) *Reading Digital Culture*. Oxford: Blackwell, pp. 159–171.

Solanas, F. and Getino, O. (1997) "Towards a Third Cinema: Notes and Experiences for the Development of a Cinema of Liberation in the Third World" in Martin, M.T. (ed.) *New Latin American Cinema, Theory, Practices and Transcontinental Articulations*, Vol. 1. Detroit, MI: Wayne State University Press, pp. 33–58.

Stam, R. (1998) "The Two Avant-gardes, Solanas and Getino's *The Hour of the Furnaces*" in Grant, B.K. and Slonioski, J. (eds) *Documenting the Documentary: Close Readings of Documentary Film and Video*. Detroit, MI: Wayne State University Press, pp. 254–268.

Tomlinson, J. (1991) *Cultural Imperialism: A Critical Introduction*. London: Continuum.

Wayne, M. (2001) *Political Film: The Dialectics of Third Cinema*. London: Pluto Press.

Wayne, M. (2012) *Marx's Das Kapital for Beginners*, Hanover. NH: Steerforth Press.

2
GEOPOLITICS AND CINEMA

Toby Miller

Sometimes capitalism doesn't feel very advanced, does it? At least not in a positive sense, given the part it has played in environmental destruction, animal brutality, war, discrimination, inequality, and exploitation. We can say with some certainty, however, that capitalism has been with us a long time, that it has changed and expanded its nature and reach, and that it remains both laden with crisis and blessed with success.

The last century and a half of capitalism has been characterized by the global military, cultural, and commercial power of the United States. Some say those times are over, because we occupy a multipolar world with equally powerful economic actors in the European Union and China, while new media technologies are breaking down old forms of dominance. This chapter argues against those positions. They might be true one day. They aren't now.

Of course, there is an ongoing debate about how new and comprehensive global exchange is – whether we are witnessing a return to the *status quo ante* of a century ago, prior to the era of state-based economic nationalism. For the massive protectionist walls constructed after the Great War were in stark contrast with earlier, freer exchange. The remarkable obsession of the last hundred years with controlling and systematizing immigration, citizenship, and the division of labor, in ways that militate against human freedom of movement while facilitating mobility of investment, are strikingly different from the past (Hirst *et al.* 2009). The work of the General Agreement on Tariffs and Trade, its successor – the World Trade Organization (WTO) – and various regional, multilateral, and bilateral agreements to dismantle, or at least regularize, such protections has done much to create a global economy, but questions remain about how genuinely new this is.

It is certainly true that the political economy of culture is more thoroughly international than ever, due to the ability to transmit entertainment and information fulsomely and rapidly via satellite, cable, and air. Such exchange is accelerating remarkably with the advent not only of new forms of communication but deregulated markets in meaning, as television and musical texts in particular rocket around the world at the speed of a Google search: world trade in the culture industries increased from $559.5 billion in 2010 to $624 billion in 2011 (United Nations Conference 2013). Intellectual property remains a limiting factor, but state restrictions on the ownership and control of the media are in long-term decline.

Amongst the media industries, cinema has always been an international capitalist enterprise, thanks to the export of both texts and technologies. At the same time, film has transcended the market, via home movies and the *avant garde*, and drawn on mixed models, from state-supported cinemas to film schools. Such forms of life are as much artisanal and amateur as they are industrial and institutional. And while people buy tickets and subscriptions to watch movies inside the corporate market, they also do so via piracy, sharing, satellite, and broadcast television, paying in kind via their consciousness and their time rather than as consumers.

This chapter is principally concerned with Hollywood, perhaps the most powerful cultural industry the world has seen in terms of its wealth, reach, and influence. I'll trace its connection to geopolitics and economic, theoretical, political, and technological threats to its dominance.

Los estados pinche unidos

In 1820, the noted British essayist Sydney Smith asked: "In the four quarters of the globe, who reads an American book? or goes to an American play? or looks at an American picture or statue?" (1844: 141). Three decades later, Herman Melville opposed the US literary establishment's devotion to all things English. He contrasted its Eurocentrically cringing import culture with the need to "carry republican progressiveness into Literature, as well as into Life" (1850).

Unsurprisingly, the US became an early-modern exponent of anti-cultural imperialist, pro-nation-building sentiment and developed its cultural and communication capacities by rejecting intellectual-property regimes. By the turn of the twentieth century, decades of protectionism and an increasingly large and affluent population had created robust culture industries. Overseas expansion soon became necessary because of a saturated domestic market, so the US government and Hollywood discarded their opposition to global policing of copyright (Miller *et al.* 2005; T. Miller 2010b; J. Miller 2011; Maxwell and Miller 2011).

The semiosis of Hollywood texts began to matter, as both messengers and signals of the nation's importance. By the 1930s, the film industry's peak association referred to itself as "the little State Department," so isomorphic were its methods and ideology with US policy and politics. This was also the era when the industry's self-censoring Production Code appended to its bizarre litany of sexual, racial, and narcotic prohibitions and requirements two items requested by the 'other' State Department: selling the US' way of life around the world, and avoiding negative representations of any "foreign country with which we have cordial relations" (Powdermaker 1950: 36).

Once the Cold War was underway, the CIA's Psychological Warfare Workshop employed future Watergate criminal E. Howard Hunt, who clandestinely funded the rights purchase and film production of George Orwell's anti-Soviet novels *Animal Farm* (1954) and *1984* (1956) (Cohen 2003). Producer Walter Wanger trumpeted this meshing of what he called "Donald Duck and Diplomacy" as "a Marshall Plan for ideas . . . a veritable celluloid Athens," because the state needed Hollywood "more than . . . the H bomb" (1950: 444, 446). Industry head Eric Johnston, fresh from his prior post as Secretary of Commerce, saw himself dispatching "messengers from a free country." President Harry Truman agreed, referring to movies as "ambassadors of goodwill" (quoted in Johnston 1950; also see Hozic 2001).

To US Cold Warriors like the professional anti-Marxist Ithiel de Sola Pool (1983), cultural conservative Daniel Bell (1977), and National Security Advisor Zbigniew Brzezinski (1969), communications technologies guaranteed US cultural and technical power across the globe. And today, former Secretary of State Henry Kissinger's consultancy firm advises that the US must "win the battle of the world's information flows, dominating the airwaves as Great Britain once ruled the seas" (Rothkopf 1997: 38, 47). Ex-National Intelligence Council chair Joseph Nye has promulgated the embarrassingly penile metaphor "soft power" to describe the use of culture as propaganda (2002) and the State Department has established "regional media hubs" to forward its project of *Leading Through Civilian Power* (2010: 60–61).

But today, the US appears to be perennially in crisis. Everyone seems certain that an Asian century is succeeding the American one. Hollywood is also said to be diminishing in importance (more money is made in electronic games, and more films are made in Nollywood and Bollywood). But the reality is – sorry – that the military might, economic importance, environmental impact, and cultural influence of the US have never been greater (Miller 2010a). China and India have many leading software engineers in addition to huge armies of labor, but they lack the domestic venture capitalists, the military underpinnings to computing innovation, and the historic cross-cultural appeal of more established cultural powers.

The contemporary era may one day be known as an Asian century. But it is worth remembering:

- Many Asians choose to live in the US.
- US ties to massive and growing economies in Latin America are profound and deepening.
- Its links with Europe continue to develop.
- It has massive new military bases across Africa and the Arab world.
- Its currency is the world's reserve.
- It has most of the world's wealthy and powerful people.
- What *goes on* in the US remains the topic of governmental, military, commercial, financial, academic, media, and popular fascination everywhere in a way that is not true of any other country.
- Every child in school in China is required to learn English.

US languages, forms of life, consumerism, imperialism, and screen texts proliferate as never before, and attempts to suggest otherwise are absurd. This is, so far, a second American century, and Hollywood both indexes and perpetuates the fact.

The Motion Picture Association of America (2014), the peak body representing the major studios, notes that Hollywood receipts around the world "reached $36.4 billion in 2014" – a record. China has been moved effortlessly into the center of the industry's overseas sales, its reserve army of productive labor now matched by a reserve army of audience labor: "more middle-class movie-goers are being minted every day." Hollywood box office in China increased 34 percent in 2013, "the first international market to exceed $4 billion" (Anon 2013b). Hollywood pictures drew the highest audiences for films on television in twenty-seven nations across all continents in 2009, while fully 80 percent of TV programming for children outside the other white-settler colonies and China comes from the US (Siwek 2011; Best *et al.* 2011; Boyd-Barrett 2006; Anon. 2009; Osei-Hwere and Pecora 2008: 16, 19; Götz *et al.* 2008).

The global market is, of course, affecting where and what Hollywood produces. The opportunity to draw on the New International Division of Cultural Labor (NICL) is at play here, as state subsidies and skilled and pliant labor are available across the globe (Fröbel *et al.* 1980; Hjort 2013; Miller *et al.* 2005). And international audiences favor texts based on expensive, visceral spectacle rather than the culturally specific genres of sports or comedy.

Blockbusters, which are now staples among the few movies actually produced by the majors, generally draw on already-popular, ensemble, multi-generic formats with international appeal. So "[e]ighteen of the all-time 100 top-grossing movies (adjusted for inflation) were sequels, and more than half of those were released since 2000" (Davidson 2012). Such movies minimize character development, narrative complexity, and dialog. They are driven by the global *lingua franca* of testosterone, adventure, and multiculturalism. Profits can be sky-high, but immense investment is needed. In 2005, average expenditure on a fiction feature film by a major studio was $96 million – a four-fold increase in two decades (Organisation for Economic Co-operation and Development 2008: 16).

The desire to spread the risk of blockbusters internationally is a corollary. As a consequence, Hollywood is in full exploitative flight, drawing on the NICL as part of its restless search for free money (Grantham 2011):

> finance in the US and international film industry [i]s filled with soft money from Europe[:] co-producing (co-financing) US pictures directly (as happened in Germany), or by bringing US or international production to Europe by using the co-production structure in the case of the UK model. In both cases the extent of money diversion was considerable. In 2000 alone ... approximately $3 billion or 20 per cent of the entire US expenditure in film and video production was sourced from media companies and private equity film funds listed on the German "new economy" stock exchange Neuer Markt. ... Even after the Neuer Markt's collapse in 2000/2001, German private equity continued to flow into the US industry, with German film funds raising EUR 2.3 billion in 2002, EUR 1.76 billion in 2003 and EUR 1.5 billion in 2004.
>
> (*Morawetz* et al. *2007: 436)*

Co-production is also part of a restless quest for the Asian market (meaning China and India) (Rasul and Proffitt 2012: 567). In 2009, Steven Spielberg received over $800 million from the Indian company Reliance Big Pictures (Ganti 2012: 344). Such localization is not a loss of power, but a strategic and tactical means of opening new markets. LA rarely loses control of the NICL.

'Smaller' Hollywood pictures also need global funders. Their average cost in 2005 was over $39 million for films produced by project-based firms affiliated with the majors (Organisation for Economic Co-operation and Development 2008: 16). Here, too, financing is frequently achieved through co-production, this time via cultural policies originally designed to counter Hollywood hegemony:

> Begun as a tool of resistance to the dominance of U.S. films, [European] film funds were initially designed to support "high quality" movies that provided an artistic voice for domestic auteurs, an outlet that could not be supported by the mass market. . . . In the past two decades, discourse has begun to support public film policy that, instead of supporting individual local auteurs, favors the grooming of a local film industry workforce and foreign direct investment into local facilities. . . . In this way, public film support, particularly in Europe, shifted to encourage foreign productions to shoot on location domestically and to partner with local production companies
>
> *(J. Miller 2011: 1019)*

So Hollywood's story seems to be one of renewal. But what of the resistance mentioned above? How does Hollywood's international impact sit with the powerful geopolitical denunciations of US economic and screen power presented by dependency theory and cultural-imperialism critique?

Dependencia and cultural imperialism

Given their experience of the Monroe Doctrine since 1823, it is no surprise that Latin Americans created a theory of dependent development in the 1940s. They argued that attempts to move from agrarian to industrial societies had foundered because developed nations in Western Europe and the US exploited cheap labor and raw materials elsewhere through multinational corporations (MNCs) that expropriated surplus profit to their metropolitan headquarters, thereby preventing the formation of local capital. These radical critics of capitalist modernization thought the transfer of technology, politics, and economics had become unattainable, because MNCs united business and government to regulate cheap labor markets, produce new consumers, and guarantee pliant regimes (Reeves 1993: 24–25, 30).

Dependency theory gained adherents across the Global South over the next three decades in reaction to the unreconstructed institutional narcissism of the US, which ignored the fact that developed societies at the world core had become so through their colonial and international experience, both by differentiating the metropole from the periphery and importing ideas, fashions, and people (Prebisch 1982; Cardoso 2009).

But despite the power of this critique, it never attained hegemony in policy debates. Formal *political* postcoloniality rarely became *economic*, apart from some Asian states that pursued permanent capitalism, known as Export-Oriented Industrialization, and service-based expansion. And after the capitalist economic crises of the 1970s, even those Western states that had *bourgeoisies* with sufficient capital formation to permit a welfare system found that stagflation undermined their capacity to hedge employment against inflation (Higgott and Robison 1985).

Historic policy renegotiations conducted by capital, the state, and their rent-seeking intellectual servants in political science and economics saw anxieties over unemployment trumped by anxieties over profits, labor pieties displaced by capital pieties, and workers called upon to identify as stakeholders in business or customers, not combatants with capital (Martin 2002: 21; Miller and O'Leary 2002: 97–99). These reforms redistributed income back to *bourgeoisies* and metropoles: reactionaries favored individual rights in the economic sphere of investment, but not other *fora*. Today's privileged citizens are corporations, and people are increasingly conceived of as self-governing consumers (Anon. 2004).

The outcome has been disastrous. In the two decades from 1960 to 1980, most of the Global South was state-socialist, or had a significant welfare system. Per capita income during that period increased by 34 percent in Africa and 73 percent in Latin America, while the standard deviation of growth rates amongst developing economies from 1950 to 1973 was 1.8. In the decades since these political economies shifted to neoliberalism, the corollary numbers disclose a drop in income across Africa of 23 percent and an increase in Latin America of just 6 percent, while the standard deviation of growth has climbed to 3.0, because of China and India's successes. In 1997–98, the richest 20 percent of the world's people earned seventy-four times the amount of the world's poorest, up from sixty times in 1990 and thirty times in 1960, while 56 percent of the global population made less than two dollars a day. In 2001, every child born in Latin America immediately 'owed' $1,500 to foreign banks, as if this were part of original sin. For a tiny number, that would amount to a few hours of work once they attained their majority. For most, it would represent a decade's salary (Ocampo 2005: 12–14; United Nations Development Program 2004; Sutcliffe 2003: 3; García Canclini 2002: 26–27).

But the neoliberal dream has endured. US Trade Representative Robert Zoellick announced to the WTO in 2001 that compliance with trade liberalization was an acid test of attitudes to terrorism, and the US Government's 2002 *National Security Strategy* referred to a "single sustainable model for national success: freedom, democracy, and free enterprise." Identical *nostra* animated the next Administration (Holland 2005; The White House 2002, 2010).

Nevertheless, on the cultural front, nineteenth-century US critiques of cultural imperialism as per Melville still resonate (elsewhere) in everyday talk, cultural and telecommunications policy, trade unions, international organizations, public diplomacy, anti-Americanism, and post-industrial service-sector planning (see Schiller 1976, 1989; Beltrán and Fox de Cardona 1980; Dorfman and Mattelart 2000). They are exemplified by Armand Mattelart's stinging denunciation of external cultural influence on the Global South:

> In order to camouflage the counter-revolutionary function which it has assigned to communications technology and, in the final analysis, to all the messages of mass culture, imperialism has elevated the mass media to the status of revolutionary agents, and the modern phenomenon of communications to that of revolution itself.
> *(1980: 17)*

A latter-day cultural-imperialism thesis turned Melville's original argument *volte face*. It said that the US, which had become the globe's leading media exporter, was transferring its dominant value system to others, with a corresponding diminution in the vitality and standing of local languages, traditions, and national identities. Lesser, but still considerable, influence was attributed to older imperial powers, via their cultural, military, and corporate ties to newly independent countries.

The theory attributed US cultural hegemony to its control of news agencies, advertising, market research, public opinion, screen trade, technology transfer, propaganda, telecommunications, and security (Primo 1999: 183). In addition, US involvement in South-East Asian wars and its adherence to the Monroe Doctrine in the Americas led to critiques of interventions against struggles of national liberation and targeted links between the military-industrial complex and the media, pointing to the ways that communications and cultural MNCs bolstered US foreign policy and military strategy, which in turn facilitated corporate expansion.

During the 1960s and 70s, cultural-imperialism discourse found a voice in public-policy debates through the Non-Aligned Movement and the United Nations Educational, Scientific and Cultural Organization (UNESCO), where the Global South lobbied for a New World Information and Communication Order (NWICO). UNESCO set up an International Commission for the Study of Communication Problems to investigate North–South flows and power. It reported in 1980 on the need for equal distribution of the electronic spectrum, reduced postal rates for international texts, protection against satellites crossing borders, and media systems that would serve social justice rather than capitalist commerce (Mattelart and Mattelart 1998: 94–97).

But UNESCO soon ceased to be a critical site for NWICO debate. The US and the UK withdrew from the Organization in 1985 because it denounced Zionism as racism and supported state intervention against private-press hegemony, and the three decades since have seen UNESCrats distance themselves from NWICO in the hope of attracting these countries back to the fold. The US rejoined in 2003 in time to make noises about the Organization contemplating a convention on cultural diversity that might sequester culture from neoliberal trade arrangements – the wrong kind of globalization, as it might be democratically rather than plutocratically driven. The US argued that texts were not culture, which it defined as the less commodifiable and governable spheres of religion and language. Then the Organization recognized Palestine as a state in 2011, and the US again refused to pay its dues (Gerbner 1994: 112–13; Gerbner *et al.* 1994: xi–xii; State Department 2011).

NWICO was in any event vulnerable, due to its inadequate theorization of capitalism, postcolonialism, class relations, the state, and indigenous culture, in addition to its complex *frottage* – a pluralism that insisted on the relativistic equivalence of all cultures and defied chauvinism, but rubbed up against a powerful equation of national identities with cultural forms. NWICO denied the potentially liberatory and pleasurable nature of different takes on the popular, forgot the internal differentiation of publics, valorized frequently oppressive and/or unrepresentative local *bourgeoisies* in the name of maintaining and developing national cultures, and ignored the demographic realities of its 'own' terrain. For example, alternatives to Hollywood funded under the sign of opposition to cultural imperialism frequently favored exclusionary, art-house-centered hegemons who privileged 'talent' over labor, and centralized authority over openness. As mentioned above, this led not only to public subvention of indolent national *bourgeoisies*, but permitted oleaginous Gringos to fund offshore production through the NICL via proxy locals (Miller *et al.* 2005; J. Miller 2011).

The ongoing power of Hollywood is not only germane to changing geopolitics. It is part of the existing fabric of that geopolitics, as we showed in the *Global Hollywood* project (Miller *et al.* 2005). The state is intimately involved in Hollywood hegemony and *vice versa*, buttressing the ideology and might of the US. It has geopolitical effects on the young, on animals, and on the environment. Consider this finding from the World Health Organization:

> From 2008 to 2010, 14 nations or their sub-units awarded an estimated US$ 2.4 billion to producers of 93% of the 428 films, mainly developed by companies based in the United States, which achieved top box office status in Canada and the United States. Half of these films featured tobacco imagery. Over three years, subsidized with US$ 1.1 billion in tax credits, these films delivered an estimated total of 130 billion tobacco impressions to theatre audiences worldwide.
>
> *(2011: 8)*

As per the findings enumerated above and others, Hollywood appears to take vast amounts of money from MNCs to assist in the mindless addiction of new generations to dangerous drugs (Polansky and Glantz 2009). And a horrendous history of the animal abuse discloses systematic barbarism (Anon. 2013a).

Hollywood also does environmental violence. The first major scholarly study of the industry's despoliation, conducted on behalf of Los Angeles' Integrated Waste Management Board from 2003 to 2005, concluded that motion-picture production generated more conventional pollutants than any other industry in the city, thanks to its massive use of electricity and petroleum and release of hundreds of thousands of tons of deadly emissions each year. In California as a whole, film- and television-related energy consumption and greenhouse-gas emissions (carbon dioxide, methane, and nitrous oxide) are about the same as those produced by the aerospace and semiconductor industries (Corbett and Turco 2006). Then there is the entire question of Hollywood's global carbon footprint and deliberate despoliation of the environment for textual purposes (Maxwell and Miller 2012).

Technology and cybertarianism

But let's explore the counter-argument that decenters Hollywood and the US, based on the notion that a new era of geopolitics has been radically transformed not only by Asia's cheap, pliant labor and emergent, nationalistic middle classes, but by technology. Is today's world transmogrified by innovative cultural and communications technologies that tame and change Hollywood?

There is nothing novel about this venerable utopianism. New media are routinely regarded as signs of progress that can transcend nation-states, moving history towards a common humanity. In 1935, Rudolf Arnheim predicted that television would bring world peace. By enabling viewers to share simultaneous global experiences, from railway disasters, professorial addresses, and town meetings to boxing bouts, dance bands, carnivals, and aerial mountain views – a spectacular montage of Athens, Broadway, and Vesuvius – TV could surpass the limitations of linguistic competence and interpretation to show each spectator that "we are located as one among many" (Arnheim 1969: 160–63). It would bring an end to chauvinism and imperialism.

This reads remarkably like today's neoliberal prelates celebrating the boundless potential of new as opposed to middle-aged media: Facebook predictably features "Peace on Facebook," which will "decrease world conflict" through inter-cultural communication, while Twitter self-effacingly describes itself as "a triumph of humanity" (Anon 2010: 61). *Time* magazine exemplified this love of a seemingly immaterial world when it chose "You" as 2006's "Person of the Year," because "You control the Information Age. Welcome to your world" (Grossman 2006). On the liberal left, the *Guardian* is prey to the same touching warlockcraft: someone called "You" headed its 2013 list of the hundred most important folks in the media.[1] Rupert Murdoch was well behind, at number eight.[2]

The comparatively cheap and easy access to making and distributing meaning afforded by internet media and genres is thought to have eroded the one-way hold on cinema that saw a small segment of the world as producers and the larger segment as consumers. New technologies supposedly allow us all to be consumers and producers (prosumers) without the say-so of gatekeepers. The result is said to be democratized media, higher skill levels, and powerful challenges to old patterns of expertise and institutional authority (Graham 2008; Ritzer and Jurgenson 2010). But again, this idea is older than it appears, and entirely unrelated to the internet. The concept of the prosumer derives from the right wing of US politics in Ronald Reagan's time (Toffler 1980).

Cybertarian discourse takes one or several of the following tacks:

- Because of new technology and consumption, concentration of media ownership and control no longer matters – information is free, thanks to multi-point distribution and destabilized hierarchies.
- Consumers are sovereign and can transcend class and other categories.
- Young people are liberated from media control.
- Creative destruction is an accurate and desirable description of economic innovation.
- Marxist political economy and ideology critique deny the power of audiences and users and the irrelevance of boundaries.
- Cultural-imperialism critiques miss the creativity and resilience of national and sub-national forms of life against industrial products.
- Media-effects studies are inconsequential – audiences outwit corporate plans and psy-function norms.

In cybertarian fantasies, everyone and no one is a cultural producer in the traditional, quasi-institutional sense, just as everyone is simultaneously an unpaid worker and a paying customer. And indeed, Hollywood sometimes does tremble in the face of what has happened over the last twenty years to middle management in the recorded music industry, thanks to file sharing, MySpace, and YouTube (remember Artist & Repertoire [A&R] people who used to hang around music venues looking and listening for hipness to describe next day in the office? They're on the scrapheap, displaced by direct marketing to corporations by artists).

But therein lies the key for Hollywood not only to survive but to prosper. Fans write zines that become screenplays. Interning grad students in New York and Los Angeles read scripts for producers, then pronounce on whether they tap into audience interests. Precariously employed part-timers spy on fellow spectators in theaters to see how they respond to coming attractions and report back to moguls. End-user licensing agreements ensure that players of corporate games online sign over their cultural moves and perspectives to the very companies they are paying in order to participate (Miller 2014).

Intellectual correctives to cybertarian fantasies are thankfully at hand. File under history. Orwell described and criticized such media-centric utopias a decade after Arnheim (i.e., seventy years ago) in ways that resonate as a startling riposte to the claims made for social media:

> Reading recently a batch of rather shallowly optimistic "progressive" books, I was struck by the automatic way in which people go on repeating certain phrases which were fashionable before 1914. Two great favourites are "the abolition of distance" and "the disappearance of frontiers". I do not know how often I have met with the statements that "the aeroplane and the radio have abolished distance" and "all parts of the world are now interdependent."
>
> *(1944)*

So what might the digitization of production and post-production do to Hollywood's dominance? Will this brave new world destabilize the most successful culture industry in history and reshape the globe?

According to the Organisation for Economic Co-operation and Development (2008: 10), new film technology will make for:

- integrated production and post-production;
- redefined and relocated duplication;
- new means of distribution;
- closer integration of film and TV.

Hollywood hegemons will probably gain from reduced costs of duplication and distribution, despite the apparent risk of easier market entry by competitors. The costs of production and distribution have long protected them by restricting new entrants, because the labor-intensive nature of film production, whether on- or off-camera, necessitates major financing (Organisation for Economic Co-operation and Development 2008: 77). Perhaps most importantly, the cost of broadband in the Global South is 40.3 percent of average individual Gross National Income (GNI). Across the Global North, by comparison, the price is less than 5 percent of GNI per capita (International Telecommunication Union 2012: 4). Geopolitics won't change thanks to the newer media unless material inequalities change, too.

Conclusion

We find ourselves in the midst of global economic and environmental crisis. Today's dominant explanatory and policy models are largely insensitive to unequal wealth, influence, status, and carbon use. They don't measure up to critical theories of dependent development, underdevelopment, unequal exchange, world-systems history, center–periphery relations, cultural imperialism, postcolonialism, and environmental impact (Kavoori and Chadha 2009; McPhail 2009). Such counter-discourses struggle against the institutional force, hegemonic media status, and academic endorsement of dominant forms. Across the Global South, vigorous and inventive tactics and strategies, based on these vibrant critiques of structured domination in communications, provide a sharp reminder that there *is* another way (Bycroft 2011; Kapur and Wagner 2011; Bolaño 2012).

This chapter has implicitly and explicitly excoriated dreamers. That said, utopias must be part of our deliberations – or what's a heaven for? But they must be couched as citizenship rights, not entrepreneurial fictions, and grounded in appropriate historical and theoretical narratives. The United Nations rightly calls for "two-way communication systems that enable dialogue and that allow communities to speak out, express their aspirations and concerns and participate in the decisions that relate to their development (quoted in United Nations Development Program 2009).

How can these aims be achieved? A clear-headed analysis of unequal exchange of cultural textuality, technology, environment, and labor should be our starting-point – not fantasies about Asian centuries or technologically-driven transformations. Cybertarianism is the latest technological determinism – reinvented with retreads each time it is rolled out; seemingly new, but relying on the built-in obsolescence of gadgets and theories that imbue historical forgetfulness and fealty to capital.

Hollywood continues to fill screens, minds, waterways, bodies, air, and soil with ideological messages and toxic material by-products and product placements. Its status as a coeval agent of US imperialism remains clear and must be identified as such as a preliminary to serious change.

Notes

1 See http://www.theguardian.com/media/2013/sep/01/you-them-mediaguardian-100–2013 (accessed 1 October 2015).

2 See http://www.theguardian.com/media/series/mediaguardian-100–2013–1–100 (accessed 1 October 2015).

Bibliography

Amin, S. (1997) *Capitalism in the Age of Globalization*, London: Zed.

Anon. (2004) "There's a Word for That" *Economist*, 6 November, p. 14.

Anon. (2009) "The Money Shot" *Economist*, 15 August, p. 57.

Anon. (2010) "A Cyber-House Divided" *Economist*, 4 September, pp. 61–62.

Anon. (2013a) "Last Week We Almost F–king Killed King in the Water Tank" *Hollywood Reporter*, online, http://www.hollywoodreporter.com/feature/index.html (accessed on 1 October 2015).

Anon (2013b) "A Tale of Two Tinsel Towns" *Economist*, online 23 February, http://www.economist.com/news/business/21572218-tale-two-tinseltowns-split-screens (accessed on 1 October 2015).

Arnheim, R. (1969) *Film as Art*, London: Faber and Faber.

Bell, D. (1977) "The Future World Disorder: The Structural Context of Crises" *Foreign Policy*, 27, Summer, pp. 109–35.

Beltrán, L. and Fox de Cardona, E. (1980) *Communicacíon dominada: Estados Unidos en los medios de América Latina*, Mexico City: Instituto Latinoamericano de Estudios Transnacionales/Editorial Nueva Imagen.

Best, S., Kahn, R., Nocella II, A. and McLaren, P. (eds) (2011) *The Global Industrial Complex: Systems of Domination*, Lanham: Lexington Books.

Bolaño, C. (ed.) (2012) *Comunicación y la crítica de la economía política*, Quito: CIESPAL.
Boyd-Barrett, O. (ed.) (2006) *Communications, Media, Globalization and Empire*, Eastleigh: John Libbey Publishing.
Brzezinski, Z. (1969) *Between Two Ages: America's Role in the Technotronic Era*, New York: Viking Press.
Bycroft, M. (2011) *Energy for Radio: A Guide for Practitioners*, CAMECO Practice Series 2, Aachen: Catholic Media Council.
Cardoso, F. H. (2009) "New Paths: Globalization in Historical Perspective" *Studies in Comparative International Development* 44(4), pp. 296–317.
Cohen, K. (2003) "The Cartoon That Came in from the Cold" *Guardian*, online, 7 March, http://www.theguardian.com/culture/2003/mar/07/artsfeatures.georgeorwell (accessed 1 October 2015).
Corbett, C. J. and Turco, R. P. (2006) *Sustainability in the Motion Picture Industry*, report prepared for the Integrated Waste Management Board of the State of California, online, http://personal.anderson.ucla.edu/charles.corbett/papers/mpis_report.pdf
Davidson, A. (2012) "How Does the Film Industry Actually Make Money?" *New York Times*, online, 26 June, http://www.nytimes.com/2012/07/01/magazine/how-does-the film-industry-actually-make-money.html?r=0 (accessed 1 October 2015).
de Sola Pool, I. (1983) *Technologies of Freedom*, Cambridge, MA: Harvard University Press.
Dorfman, A. and Mattelart, A. (2000) *Para leer al pato Donald: Comunicación de masa y colonialism*, Mexico City: Siglo Veintiuno Editores.
Fröbel, F., Heinrichs, J. and Kreye, O. (1980) *The New International Division of Labor: Structural Unemployment in Industrialised Countries and Industrialisation in Developing Countries* (Peter Burgess, trans), Cambridge: Cambridge University Press.
Ganti, T. (2012) "No Longer a Frivolous Singing and Dancing Nation of Movie-Makers: The Hindi Film Industry and its Quest for Global Distinction" *Visual Anthropology*, 25(4), pp. 340–65.
García Canclini, N. (2002) *Latinoamericanos buscando lugar en este siglo*, Buenos Aires: Paidós.
Gerbner, G. (1994) "Unesco in the U.S. Press" in Gerbner, G., Mowlana, H. and Nordenstreng, K. (eds) *The Global Media Debate: Its Rise, Fall, and Renewal*, Norwood, NJ: Ablex, pp. 111–21.
Gerbner, G. Mowlana, H. and Nordenstreng, K. (1994) "Preface" in Gerbner, G., Mowlana, H. and Nordenstreng, K. (eds) *The Global Media Debate: Its Rise, Fall, and Renewal*, Norwood, NJ: Ablex, pp. ix–xii.
Götz, M., Hoffmann, O., Brosius, H-B., Carter, C., Chan, K., Donald, St. H., Fisherkeller, J., Frenette, M., Kolbjørnsen, T., Lemish, D., Lustyik, K., McMillin, D. C., van der Molen, J. H. W., Pecora, N., Prinsloo, J., Pestaj, M., Ramos Rivero, P., Mereilles Reis, A. H., Saeys, F., Scherr, S. and Zang, H. (2008) "Gender in Children's Television Worldwide" *Televizion*, 21, pp. 4–9.
Graham, M. (2008) "Warped Geographies of Development: The Internet and Theories of Economic Development" *Geography Compass* 2(3), pp. 771–89.
Grantham, B. (2011) Podcast, online, 5 May, http://culturalstudies.podbean.com/2011/05/15/a-conversation-with-bill-granthamon-hollywood-and-the-law (accessed 1 October 2015).
Grossman, L. (2006) "You – Yes, You Are *Time*'s Person of the Year" *Time*, online, 13 December, http://content.time.com/time/magazine/article/0,9171,1570810,00.html (accessed 1 October 2015).
Higgott, R. and Robison R. (eds) (1985) *Southeast Asia: Essays in the Political Economy of Structural Change*, London: Routledge & Kegan Paul.
Hirst, P., Thompson, G. and Bromley, S. (2009) *Globalization in Question*, 3rd edition, Cambridge: Polity Press.
Hjort, M. (ed.) (2013) *The Education of the Filmmaker in Africa, the Middle East, and the Americas*, New York: Palgrave Macmillan.
Holland, J. (2005) "Disarming Trade" *AlterNet*, online, 20 December, http://https.alternet.org/story/29718/disarming_trade (accessed 1 October 2015).
Hozic, A. A. (2001) *Hollyworld: Space, Power, and Fantasy in the American Economy*, Ithaca, NY: Cornell University Press.
International Telecommunication Union (2012) *Measuring the Information Society: Executive Summary*, Geneva: International Telecommunication Union.
Johnston, E. (1950) "Messengers from a Free Country" *Saturday Review of Literature*, 4 March, pp. 9–12.
Kapur, J. and Wagner, K. B. (eds) (2011) *Neoliberalism and Global Cinema: Capital, Culture, and Marxist Critique*, New York: Routledge.
Kavoori, A. and Chadha, K. (2009) "The Cultural Turn in International Communication" *Journal of Broadcasting & Electronic Media*, 53(2), pp. 336–46.

Martin, R. (2002) *Financialization of Daily Life*, Philadelphia: Temple University Press.
Mattelart, A. (1980) *Mass Media, Ideologies and the Revolutionary Movement* (Malcolm Joad, trans), Brighton: Harvester Press/Atlantic Highlands: Humanities Press.
Mattelart, A. and Mattelart, M. (1998) *Theories of Communication: A Short Introduction* (Susan Gruenheck Taponier and James A. Cohen, trans), London: Sage.
Maxwell, R. and Miller, T. (2011) "'For a Better Deal, Harass Your Governor!': Neoliberalism and Hollywood" in Kapur, J. and Wagner, K. B. (eds) *Neoliberalism and Global Cinema: Capital, Culture, and Marxist Critique*, New York: Routledge 19–37.
Maxwell, R. and Miller, T. (2012) *Greening the Media*, New York: Oxford University Press.
McPhail, T. (2009) "Introduction to Development Communication" in McPhail, T. (ed.) *Development Communication: Reframing the Role of the Media*, Malden, MA: Blackwell/Wiley, pp. 1–20.
Melville, H. (1850) "Hawthorne and His Mosses" *The Literary World*, online, 17 and 24 August, http://www.eldritchpress.org/nh/hahm.html (accessed 1 October 2015).
Miller, J. L. (2011) "Producing Quality: A Social Network Analysis of Coproduction Relationships in High Grossing Versus Highly Lauded Films in the U.S. Market" *International Journal of Communication*, 5, pp. 1014–33.
Miller, P. and O'Leary, T. (2002) "Rethinking the Factory: Caterpillar Inc." *Cultural Values* 6(1–2), pp. 91–117.
Miller, T. (2007) *Cultural Citizenship: Cosmopolitanism, Consumerism and Television in a Neoliberal Age*, Philadelphia: Temple University Press.
Miller, T. (2010a) "Preface: Why Do First-World Academics Think Cultural Imperialism Doesn't Matter When So Many Other People Disagree?" in Frymer, B., Kashani, T., Nocella II, A. J. and Van Heertum, R. (eds) *Hollywood's Exploited: Public Pedagogy, Corporate Movies, and Cultural Crisis*, New York: Palgrave Macmillan, pp. xv–xix.
Miller, T. (2010b) "Holy Trinity: Nation, Pentagon, Screen" in Roosvall, A. and Salovaara-Moring, I. (eds) *Communicating the Nation: National Topographies of Global Media Landscapes*, Göteborg: NORDICOM, pp. 143–61.
Miller, T. (2011) "The Media-Military Industrial Complex" in Best, S., Kahn, R., Nocella II, A. J. and McLaren, P. (eds) (2011) *The Global Industrial Complex: Systems of Domination*, Lanham: Lexington Books, pp. 97–115.
Miller, T. (2014) "Life as a Prosumer in the Post-Industrial Economy" *The Australian*, online, 25 March, http://www.theaustralian.com.au/higher-education/opinion/life-as-a-prosumer-in-the-postindustrial-economy/story-e6frgcko-1226863075431 (accessed 1 October 2015).
Miller, T., Govil, N., McMurria, J., Maxwell, R. and Wang, T. (2005) *Global Hollywood 2*, London: British Film Institute/Berkeley: University of California Press.
Morawetz, N., Hardy, J., Haslam, C. and Randle, K. (2007) "Finance, Policy and Industrial Dynamics – The Rise of Co-Productions in the Film Industry" *Industry and Innovation*, 14(4), pp. 421–43.
Motion Picture Association of America (2014) *Theatrical Market Statistics 2014* http://www.mpaa.org/wp-content/uploads/2015/03/MPAA-Theatrical-Market-Statistics-2014.pdf (accessed 1 October 2015).
Nye, J. S. (2002) "Limits of American Power" *Political Science Quarterly* 117(4), pp. 545–59.
Ocampo, J. A. (2005) "Globalization, Development and Democracy" *Items and Issues* 5(3), pp. 11–20.
Organisation for Economic Co-operation and Development (2008) *Remaking the Movies: Digital Content and the Evolution of the Film and Video Industries*, Geneva: Organisation for Economic Co-operation and Development.
Orwell, G. (1944) "As I Please" *Tribune*, online, 12 May, telelib.com/authors/O/OrwellGeorge/essay/tribune/AsIPlease19440512.html (accessed 1 October 2015).
Osei-Hwere, E. and Pecora, N. (2008) "Children's Media in Sub-Saharan Africa" in Pecora, N. and Osei-Hwere, E. and Carlsson, U. (eds) *African Media, African Children*, Gothenburg: NORDICOM, pp. 15–27.
Polansky, J. and Glantz, S. A. (2009) *Taxpayer Subsidies for US Films with Tobacco Imagery*, San Francisco: Center for Tobacco Control Research and Education, UC San Francisco.
Polansky, J. and Stanton A. G. (2009) *Taxpayer Subsidies for US Films with Tobacco Imagery*, San Francisco: Center for Tobacco Control Research and Education, UC San Francisco.
Powdermaker, H. (1950) *Hollywood: The Dream Factory: An Anthropologist Looks at the Movie-Makers*, Boston: Little, Brown and Company.
Prebisch, R. (1982) *The Crisis of Capitalism and the Periphery: 1st Raúl Prebisch Lecture*, Geneva: United Nations Conference on Trade and Development.

Primo, A. (1999) "The Paradoxical Brazilian Views Concerning American Media Products" in Kamalipour, Y. R. (ed.) *Images of the U.S. Around the World: A Multilateral Perspective*, Albany: State University of New York Press, pp. 179–95.

Rasul, A. and Proffitt, J. M. (2012) "An Irresistible Market: A Critical Analysis of Hollywood-Bollywood Coproductions" *Communication, Culture & Critique*, 5(4), pp. 563–83.

Ritzer, G. and Jurgenson, N. (2010) "Production, Consumption, Prosumption: The Nature of Capitalism in the Age of the Digital 'Prosumer'" *Journal of Consumer Culture* 10(1), 13–36.

Rothkopf, D. (1997) "In Praise of Cultural Imperialism" *Foreign Policy*, 107, pp. 38–53.

Schiller, H. (1976) *Communication and Cultural Domination*, New York: International Arts and Sciences Press.

Schiller, H. (1989) *Culture Inc.: The Corporate Takeover of Public Expression*, Oxford: Oxford University Press.

Siwek, S. E. (2011) *Copyright Industries in the U.S. Economy: The 2011 Report*, Washington, DC: International Intellectual Property Alliance.

Smith, S. (1844) *The Works of the Rev. Sydney Smith*, Philadelphia: Carey and Hart.

State Department (2010) *Leading Through Civilian Power: The First Quadrennial Diplomacy and Development Review*, online, http://www.state.gov/s/dmr/qddr/ (accessed 1 October 2015).

State Department (2011) "State Department on Palestinian Admission to UNESCO," online, 31 October, http://translations.state.gov/st/english/texttrans/2011/10/20111031170111su0.1734082.html (accessed 1 October 2015).

Sutcliffe, B. (2003) *A More or Less Unequal World? World Income Distribution in the 20th Century*, Amherst, MA: Political Economy Research Institute Working Paper Series, 54.

The White House (2002) *The National Security Strategy of the United States of America*, online, 17 September, http://state.gov/documents/organization/63562.pdf.

The White House (2010) *National Security Strategy*, online, May, https://www.whitehouse.gov/sites/default/files/rss_viewer/national_security_strategy.pdf.

Toffler, A. (1980) *The Third Wave*, New York: William Morrow.

United Nations Conference on Trade and Development (2013) "Trade in Creative Products Reached New Peak in 2011, UNCTAD Figures Show," online, 15 May, http://unctad.org/en/pages/news details.aspx?OriginalVersionID=498&Sitemap_x0020_Taxonomy=UNCTAD%20Home (accessed 1 October 2015).

United Nations Development Program (2004) *Human Development Report 2004: Cultural Liberty in Today's Diverse World*, online, hdr.undp.org/en/media/hdr04_complete.pdf (accessed 1 October 2015).

United Nations Development Program (2009) *Communication for Development: A Glimpse at UNDP's Practice*, online,http://www.undp.org/content/undp/en/home/librarypage/democratic-governance/civic_engagement/communication-for-development-a-glimpse-at-undps-practice-.html (accessed 1 October 2015).

Wanger, W. (1950) "Donald Duck and Diplomacy" *Public Opinion Quarterly*, 14(3), pp. 443–52.

World Health Organization (2011) *Smoke-Free Movies: From Evidence to Action*, 2nd edition, Geneva: World Health Organization.

3
ECOPOLITICS OF CINEMA

Sean Cubitt

The first step for any ecopolitical understanding of cinema and film is to understand cinema's intricate belonging to the planetary ecology, including the environmental politics of the naked humanity produced by global trade, from mineral extraction (Maxwell and Miller 2012) to recycling (Gabrys 2010; Grossman 2007). Communication in its vast variety is the core of human activity, from trade to war, sex to language. But communication is a special instance of a wider and more primal phenomenon, mediation. In the natural universe, everything is a medium, and everything mediates with and through everything else. This is the central tenet of ecological thought: an ecology comprises the mutual mediations of matter and energy, order and entropy, through complex and evolving relations. Communication distinguishes itself from mediation by its separation of roles, a separation which then converts mediations into messages. The evolution of consciousness, collective or individual, human or otherwise, was probably the initiating moment of this communicative split. Certainly the history of consciousness can be traced as a history of communication: human-to-human, and human-to-world. Only in the rise of the recording media of the nineteenth century do we first begin to catch a hint of the possibility of another mode of communication: world-to-human. In the twenty-first century, we confront a human world entirely composed of communications, to the point both of Baudrillard's (2005) nightmare scenario of the disappearance of reality, and of the absolute exclusion of 'nature' from participation in communication. Thus the fundamental question posed by ecopolitical critique of cinema is whether it can use its position in the mediations of ecology to critique the condition of contemporary communication.

This is an unabashedly aesthetic question. Jodi Dean challenges such priorities in the political philosophy expounded in her *Communist Horizon*:

> Some activists and theorists treat aesthetic objects and creative works as displaying a political potentiality missing from classes, parties and unions. This aesthetic focus disconnects politics from the organised struggle of working people, making politics into what spectators see. Artistic products, whether actual commodities or commodified experiences, thereby buttress capital as they circulate political affects while displacing political struggles.
>
> (*Dean 2012: 13*)

This is a serious accusation from a scholar and activist who is far from ignorant of contemporary communications. There are internal contradictions in her argument (she goes on to argue that the "common form – including its images, slogans, terms and practices" [Dean 2012: 14], surely, that is, the communicational aesthetic, of the Occupy movements mark them out from this aesthetic Leftism), but they do not diminish the power of her challenge. To respond that individual films like *An Inconvenient Truth* (Guggenheim, 2006) or *The Day After Tomorrow* (Emmerich, 2004) can communicate ecopolitical ideas is to miss the point: such communication is always, following Dean, complicit in the circulation of capital, and implicitly in converting political motivations into psychological effects like anxiety.

The Brechtian turn of cine-semiotics in the 1970s gave vanguard media artists a political platform for formal experiment. In opposition to films which both in ideological content and formal properties support the established systems of ideas, wealth and power, Comolli and Narboni's influential *Cahiers* essay "Cinema/Ideology/Criticism" defines a political avant-garde which proposes that "only action on both fronts, 'signified' and 'signifiers' has any hope of operating against the prevailing ideology. Economic/political and formal action have to be indissolubly wedded" (Comolli and Narboni 1971: 32).

Could political content be conveyed in the apolitical form of narrative realist cinema? For many of the environmentally conscious vanguard film artists documented in Scott MacDonald's *Garden in the Machine* (2001) the answer was clearly no: but with regard to Dean's challenge, though they were artists, they did begin to mark a shift in consciousness from the humanist presumption (what might be seen by a human observer) of dominant forms of realism. In tune with the anti-humanist bias of much ecological politics of the period, notably Arne Naess' (1989) deep ecology, the anti-humanism of Louis Althusser (Althusser *et al.* 1971) that informed so much of cine-semiotics and the avant-garde film sector encouraged a certain rigorous cyberneticism in the landscape films of Chris Welsby (for example *Sky Light* [1986], a response to the fallout from Chernobyl), quite unlike the muscular backwoods Romanticism of works like Stan Brakhage's *Dog Star Man* (1963). The elegiac tone of later media artworks like Bill Viola's ghostly visions of the Joshua Tree National Park in *The Passing* (1991) and Mary Lucier's expanded cinema installation *The Plains of Sweet Regret* (2007), with its haunting account of the North Dakota landscape abandoned in the expansion of agribusiness, belong, however, to a different strand of ecopolitics, perhaps most familiar from the revisionist westerns of Sam Peckinpah. Much of Peckinpah's *The Wild Bunch* was shot in the province of Coahuila, an area dominated by coal mining, and nowadays by massive maquiladora factories building GM and Chrysler vehicles for export across the Rio Grande that separates it from Texas: his elegy for the horse and the nomadic outlaw culture is matched by the account of a landscape soon to be deeply transformed. The Rio Grande is listed as 'impaired' by the International Boundary and water Commission (http://www.ibwc.state.gov/CRP/riogrande.htm), the result of salinity arising from excessive water extraction for agriculture, bacteria due to untreated sewage from the slums of Ciudad Juarez and the other maquiladora cities, and chemical pollutants, especially from Laredo on the Texan side of the border (IBWC 1994), conditions which still obtain: a 2013 Texas government report mentions excessive levels of "residual chlorine, methylene chloride, toluene, arsenic, cadmium, chromium, copper, lead, mercury, nickel, selenium, silver, zinc, chlordane, *p,p'*-DDE, dieldrin, gamma-BHC (lindane), total PCBs, and cyanide" (Texas Commission on Environmental Quality 2013). Many of these metals are specifically associated with 'offshore' chip fabrication and computer manufacture in the free trade zones along the Mexican border. Peckinpah and Lucier, two wildly disparate filmmakers, meet over this toxic soup to recall a lost way of life in a disappearing environment.

To answer Dean's challenge requires investigation into the ambitions of ecopolitical cine-critique. As feminist film theory began in analyses of sexism, expanded into women's films, and arrived at a platform for understanding films and cinema of all kinds and promoting women's participation at all levels, so ecocriticism has to aim beyond celebrations of green themes and condemnation of anti-ecological movies towards a global understanding of the ecological aspects of all forms of film and every kind of cinematic practice. Since cinema has been widely perceived to be the privileged medium of modernity, ecocritical analysis should give us a powerful insight into the construction of concepts of humanity, of nature and of technology, especially but not exclusively communications technologies, as the privileged mediator between the two. Jonathan Beller's powerful analysis of *The Cinematic Mode of Production* (2006) moves on from Doane's (2002) position on the organisation of time to argue that splitting flow into segments, as film does, became the mode of commodification in the twentieth century. We might add that in the twenty-first, the scanning principle in electronic imaging ensures that the same logic extends not only to the objects communicated but to the arithmetic counting of each point (pixel) in each frame, organising them in the rigid grid which, in spreadsheets and databases, has become the true diagram of the contemporary political economy. This position of mastery through control over the flow of light, sound and time, and their conversion into surfaces in imaging technologies, is not so much a reflection of an underlying political economic principle, but the principle itself. In other words, Beller's argument points towards the aesthetic as the increasingly central concern of capital in the twentieth century, a concern which reaches a new level of generality in the standardisation of digital imaging in distribution and display, and increasingly in production, in the twenty-first century.

Much debated, the transition from analogue to digital cinema has been a decades-long process starting with the introduction of magnetic and later digital sound in the 1970s. The argument that the transition spells the end of cinema's privileged indexical relation to reality (including 'nature') misses the point that scientific instruments have for far longer used arithmetic tools to give their account of natural processes (Galison 1997), so that we are witnessing not an end of realism but a change to the mode of account we give of it. Where early modern accounts of the world bent towards nature as the model for all processes, the emergent science of the seventeenth century and the industrial revolution employed the metaphor of a machine. In our time, the computer gives us our preferred metaphor, the world appearing as bits in thrall to algorithms which, like software, perform it as measurable or perceivable reality. These changes correspond to changes in the meaning of 'environment' over the centuries, from late mediaeval enclosures and colonial land seizures that made land inhuman, through the industrial revolution's factory environments, to today when knowledge is in process of being alienated from its knowers as an environment of data which surrounds us but is no longer ours. So it is that 'nature' as an alienated surrounding of the human moved from wilderness to machine to expression of arcane, self-operating formulae. Contemporary films like *Prometheus* (R. Scott, 2012) recap all three successive alienations. A set of narrative tropes – among them the predestination story of the *Matrix* trilogy (Andy and Lana Wachowski, 1999–2003), the reprogrammable world story of *The Adjustment Bureau* (Nolfi, 2011), the delusion/simulation theme in *Inception* (Nolan, 2010) and the artificial intelligence paranoia narrative of *Eagle Eye* (Caruso, 2008) – mark out a world composed of data where humans are either masters of programming the world, or are programmed by it. This is the status of environmentalism today: we either program 'nature' to our liking, or are programmed by it, passive victims of processes over which we have no control.

Ecocriticism cannot therefore ignore the human–machine relationship in addressing that between human and nature, and indeed in exploring what human 'nature' is under changing circumstances. This too forms part of the ecology of cinema, which must take into account the changing nature of the audience. If, alongside most cinema historians, we date cinema (as opposed to film) from the first projections, the ecopolitical question concerns the nature of the public as it has evolved through the twentieth and twenty-first centuries. Early film criticism, like early sociology, focused on the crowd. By the 1960s, in the era of cine-semiotics, the question concerned 'the subject': an individual consciousness formed in the address of cinema to isolated persons in the dark of the film theatre. In the era of the 'affective turn' in film theory (for example Bruno 2002), the audience is conceived of in the mass mobilisation of desires symbolised by the immense LED billboards of Times Square, Piccadilly and the Ginza. The unit of social and political life, political philosopher Ernesto Laclau asserts, is neither individual nor group (society, class or other such category) but what he calls 'demand', requests or claims that mobilise people to become groups and, in extreme moments, a people (Laclau 2005: 72–4). Groups do not pre-exist demands: demands constitute people as both individuals and as workers, women, Black, American, anti-immigrant, rioter or environmentalist. This is the constitution of the public in the twenty-first century, as addressed not only in the streets but in the micro-flows of affect and spectacle that structure audio-visual culture, and the delivery mechanisms of both large screens and the personal screens of computers and mobile media where much film is viewed today. The strange quandary for ecopolitical film is that it therefore must pursue the mobilisation of demand at the level not of communities or individuals but of desires.

At the same time, as Dean has been swift to point out, Laclau attempts to build a political system without class. The great alliances of peasants and proletarians, he suggests, no longer make sense. The thesis is supported by the theorists of Communisation, who argue that the working class has no identity today, because production, the factory sector that produced the very idea of the modern worker, is now a diminishingly small part of the global economy (Théorie Communiste 2011). From an ecopolitical perspective, however, class has not disappeared but perseveres in the form of a global division of labour. Mines and factories are no longer the prerogative of the 'industrialised' nations as they were in the nineteenth and twentieth centuries. Today's global exploitation has moved them to the former colonies of the developing world. There a working class still exists, on a massive scale, as do the old peasant classes, explaining the continuation of the communal crowd in events like the mass demonstrations in Tahrir and Taksim Squares. On the other hand, deprived of this role, the old working class of the metropoles are no longer required for production but for destruction. The cyclical crises of capital since the 1970s have been driven by over-production, itself a product of the falling rate of profit. By transferring debt to the poor, and making that debt the engine for consumption, the old metropolitan working class becomes the new consumer class, marked by obesity, anxiety and spiralling debt. On the one hand, this is mobilised through media splintering communities and individuals into free-floating desires; on the other, it divides the global poor between metropolitan workers demanding the productive jobs exported to the developing world, and developing nation workers demanding the levels of consumption enjoyed by their First World peers. Ecological thinking thus finds itself facing the political in the form of a global ecology of over-production in the sweatshops of the South and over-consumption in the North, each envying the other's equally unsustainable economies.

In a world in which land, technology and knowledge have become environmental, in which the public is constituted by free-floating desires, and where those desires are marshalled, to the extent that they are organised at all, around unsustainable economics, we confront the resulting thesis: that politics (rather than economics, from which it was ripped in the history of liberal thought: Foucault 2004) is the terrain on which struggle must happen; that the unit of politics is no longer human communities or individuals; and that the division of production from consumption powers an all-consuming machinery of over-production and over-consumption which is effectively suicidal, not only of humans but of their planet. Politics, we might then say, concerns the mobilisation of affect, the raising of demands, at some organisational level higher than that of consumer desire, with a view to producing the good life for all. This in turn raises two questions: who is the 'all', and what constitutes a good life?

Chantal Mouffe (2005) and Jacques Rancière (1999), two political philosophers with very different methods and agendas, agree on the second of these questions: what passes for politics today is not about the good life, but only about managing the existing state of (economic) affairs. True politics, on the other hand, is precisely the open, public debate about how we should live. For Mouffe, where such debate does not occur, for example when an argument that the good life requires adherence to a religious worldview is excluded, it returns in the form of violence. Rancière (2006) takes the view that all politics arises from a challenge made when those governed but with no voice in rule – slaves, the poor, women – demand a place in the debate over how they should live. Today migrants are ruled with no voice in ruling. The same is true of what we call nature: we take responsibility for stewardship over nature, or simply exploit it, without seeking to give nature itself a political voice. The question concerning the good life therefore leads us directly to the question concerning who constitutes the 'all' of politics.

The role of the State is to manage the free flow of desire by ensuring, as indeed most advertising does, that singular desires can be organised into 'lifestyles', identities that can be channelled into predictable consumer choices and predictable socio-cultural behaviours: "What the State cannot tolerate in any way, however, is that the singularities form a community without affirming an identity, that humans co-belong without any representable condition of belonging" (Agamben 1993: 86). The challenge posed by the confluence of desires outside the disciplined channels of lifestyle and identity is doubled over if and when those identities include or 'co-belong' with non-human identities. It is here that ecocritical thinking opens onto the mobilising properties of cinema, which is itself what Latour (2005) would call an 'actor-network', a hybrid, complex organisation of human and technological elements into a single assemblage.

The absurdity of thinking a politics which would include natural phenomena like oceans and jungles has precursors in the shock and ridicule that greeted the idea that slaves or women could form part of the polity. A more significant precursor is the role of the market as political agency. In many respects the opposite of an environment, the market operates by exclusion, including only economic data, and excluding what are known as 'externalities', things which are not included in economic accounting, such as development refugees, poisoned landscapes, and abandoned homes and workplaces. Environments, including those constituted by technologies and data, are treated both as raw materials and as dumping grounds external to accounts. The market recognises only the abstract generation of wealth. Generating wealth in the era of semiocapital (Berardi 2012) is more and more the business of manipulating symbols: brands, lifestyles and the economic data deployed in derivatives markets; and it is conducted more and more not only by human speculators but by algo-trading at inhuman speeds by computers. In short, the market is cyborg: a non-human machine of immense proportions in which human functionaries, no matter how highly paid for their lack of human principle, are merely bio-chips. This cyborg entity, no matter how inhuman, has massive agency in the political affairs of people. The principle of non-human participation in politics is therefore already well-established. The participation of humans, especially indigenous and migrant humans, is far less assured, and clearly marks the first great challenge to political life in the twenty-first century. The second, in which the political elites are also failing, is the challenge of introducing the planetary environment into the polity.

Both because cinema is itself a hybrid composite of human and non-human, and because it operates at the level of affect and desire, it is ideally suited to work politically to engage the non-human world in human affairs. It faces a number of challenges in this enterprise, however. The best-intended films have to face the problem of film's own environmental footprint. Promotional materials and DVD extras for Terrence Malick's *The New World* (2002) emphasise not only the pursuit of authenticity in reintroducing native crops to the stretch of the Chickahominy River where it was filmed, but the meticulous efforts to restore all traces of the production after it wrapped. Like any analogue film, *The New World*, shot on 65 mm stock, relied on petroleum products for the celluloid base and silver for the photosensitive halides; it required petroleum-fuelled generators and transport. More oil and silver, and more energy, would have to be consumed in post-production and distribution, along with paper products for posters and press releases. Digital distribution requires rare minerals like indium for the indium–tin oxide silvering of the DVD, and yet more energy to power online and broadcast delivery to machines themselves composed of many metals and oil-derived plastics whose manufacture, as noted above in the Rio Grande case, have tainted the locales where it is conducted. There have been experiments with wind- and solar-powered cinema, and with carbon-neutral filming: *Syriana* (Gaghan, 2006), *The Day After Tomorrow* and *An Inconvenient Truth* purchased carbon-offset credits to the value of the emissions released in filming. But there has never been, and cannot be, a film production with no ecological effects.

Moreover, over its century of existence, film has become dominated by the aesthetics of communication. On the one hand, this implies a division between producers and audiences; on the other a distinction between the objects and media of representation. Cinema cannot escape the conditions of the historical era in which it is made: this is the source of its relevance, but also of its inability to escape the constraints of the alienations that have produced the very possibility of communication in the twenty-first century. In this film is thoroughly dialectical. On the one hand, it bears, in the form of light and light pollution as well as urban, rural and wilderness settings, the marks of the natural environment, while on the other, the apparatus is premised, through lens technology and framing for example, on a reduction of these features to humanly perceptible form, and to codes of representation first established at the beginning of Renaissance perspective. In this tradition, a human figure is always the centre of attention wherever it appears, and where it does not the appeal is constantly to human emotion. Pliny tells the tale of Zeuxis' painting of grapes, so convincing that birds flew down to peck at them. This is one of the last instances when realism has praised itself for a non-human communication. Communication has a history not because it is carried along by changing technologies, but because it is always an expression of the distinction we make between humans and the worlds they occupy.

The constitution of audiences as communities, individuals and desires, and of the world as land, technological second nature and as data appears as a complex interweaving of pure and hybrid forms in cinema history. Community and land appear in their purest communication in indigenous films like *Atanarjuat* (Kunuk, 2001) and *Ten Canoes* (de Heer and Djiggir, 2006), especially when shown among the peoples with whom they were made; much the same might be said of films like Darcy Lange's *Documentation of Bradford Working Life, England* (1974) and indeed the Lumières' *Workers Leaving the Lumière Factory* (1896) in terms of the congruence of subject, medium and audience. But typically films crisscross between terms: communities as data (Reggio's *Koyaanisqatsi* [1982]), desire as landscape (*Picnic At Hanging Rock* [Weir, 1975]). As we have already noted of *The Wild Bunch*, many films operate in nostalgic mode, recreating lost communities and landscapes and the relations between them, lost rugged individualism and the social relations that spawned them, as an act of mourning. Others construe making community as a vindication of the self, like *Groundhog Day* (Ramis, 1993), reversing the hero as a product of community in films like *Le Crime de Monsieur Lange* (Renoir, 1936). Most films concerned with the datascape of the present are more paranoid, even when, as in *Source Code* (D. Jones, 2011), all's well that ends well. Here the cinema opens up on the vertigo of the present, the gnawing sense that beneath the surface there lie neither gods nor reasons but purposeless emptiness.

Dean's challenge to aesthetic Leftism brings us then to a more complex account of the ecology of communication. Film responds, as it were, automatically to natural processes, including light but also other forms of radiation (Schuppli 2011): it is therefore aesthetically as well as materially linked to the environment. The means through which this automatism is achieved is technical: in this it employs the embodied skills of generations of workers whose ideas and practices it embodies. As presently constituted, both the environmental imbrication and the ancestral forms of labour condensed into the technology are both enslaved, forced to undertake work on behalf of human and often corporate-cyborg masters. Where the cause of migrants and indigenous people might be best served by handing over power to produce and, even more important, distribute their own audio-visual works, the challenge for eco-cinema is to find ways to hand control over the cinematic apparatus to non-human agents. Unsurprisingly, experiments in this vein have come from the artistic vanguard, as in some other of Chris Welsby's landscape works (for example *Wind Vane II*, 1975, where camera movement was driven by microclimatic differences in wind speed and direction), Michael Snow's *La Région Centrale* (1971) with programmed zooms and near-spherical panning, and hint.fm's data live-streaming data visualisation *Wind Map* (2012: http://hint.fm/wind/).

These and other works for the gallery and other recognisably art-based venues remain open to Dean's critique that, "displacing political struggles from the streets to the galleries" (Dean 2012: 13) the institutional formation of the art-world defuses their political potential, in much the same way that clicking to sign a petition is a symbolic act, not a political one. If, as Berardi (2009a) argues, we live in the era of an economy deriving its greatest wealth from symbol manipulation, manipulating symbols is only ever a substitute for genuine political action. And there is the perpetual refrain that art does not reach the people for whom politics matters most. Comolli and Narboni, interested as they were in the political potential not only of cinema but of film theory and criticism, outlined another mode of political film, one made within the commercial cinema and for it, which nonetheless dislocate the smooth operation of ideology: "if one looks beyond its apparent formal coherence, one can see that it is riddled with cracks: it is splitting under an internal tension which is simply not there in an ideologically innocuous film" (Comolli and Narboni 1971: 33).

The ecopolitical internal contradiction appears in road movies such as *Vanishing Point* (Sarafian, 1971) with its incomparable tagline: "The Chase. The Desert. The Shack. The Girl. The Road Block. The End." Prized by car buffs for the featured Dodge Challenger Magnum muscle car, and unabashed by its Bataillean economy of petrol-driven waste, *Vanishing Point*'s absurdist career through the deserts of Colorado, Utah, Nevada and California gives an extraordinary vision of wilderness, of the closeness of the locals to the land, and of the alienation of the driver, whose claustrophobic vehicle is constantly juxtaposed with the open horizons around it. The Christian and to a limited extent natural mysticism of the film sits easily enough with the existential angst of the lead character; but the film pushes the mythology of the car as symbol of freedom celebrated by Chuck Berry to the point where freedom and alienation become identical. The desert through which he speeds is both an image of his soul and of its purification, of what has been lost to the automobile and what preserves itself beyond it. Here too, however, Dean is harshly critical: "Any 'sense' it makes, any meaning or relevance it has, is up to the spectator (perhaps with a bit of guidance from curators and theorists)" (Dean 2012: 14). The hermeneutic moment, dearly prized by film and media theorists who read in it evidence of autonomy under the ideological or discursive regimes of power, is either impotently personal, or only available under the tutelage of an untrusted class of interpreters. The challenge of defining a political aesthetic capable of disrupting and, better still, overcoming, the aestheticisation of politics (Benjamin 2003) remains.

We can outline how such a political aesthetic of cinema might work in four modes: (1) the communication of political content; (2) formal innovation as a way of smashing open normative discursive formations to allow new modes of perception and thought; (3) mobilising the point of consumption rather than that of production; and (4) working at the level of the new crowd. The first merely repeats the structures of command that have dominated cybernetic reason since Shannon and Weaver (1949). The second stands condemned of elitism, and the combination of the two in the formal contradictions of the apparently coherent but ideologically fractured film described by Comolli and Narboni of being either merely idiosyncratic individualism or controlled by a professional class of interpreters. The third has been a part of radical film making from Vertov's Agit-prop train through the workers' film vans of the 1930s (Macpherson 1980) to the village film screenings organised by Anand Patwardhan for his works on communal violence, the Bhopal catastrophe and the Indian and Pakistani race for nuclear weapons. As in the case of indigenous films, however, these practices depend on the existence of communities prior to the screening, where, as we have seen, there are no pre-existing communities, only those constructed by the State and the market as lifestyles and identities. All three concern themselves exclusively with the human sensorium, humanly recognisable realities, human concerns. Therefore eco-cinema finds itself with the task of inventing new modes of cinematic mediations based on the insight that the new crowd is composed of neither communities nor individuals but three apparently incompatible elements – free-floating desires, excluded migrants and indigenous peoples, and non-human agents of technology and natural processes – further driven by the rift between the over-producing and over-consuming poors of South and North.

Berardi writes:

> When things, bodies and signs become a part of the semiotic model of the economy, wealth can only be experienced in a mediated, reflected and postponed way [. . .] wealth is no longer the ability to enjoy things, bodies and signs in time, but the accelerating and expansive production of their loss, transformed in exchange and anxiety.
>
> *(Berardi 2009b: 82)*

In an age when the total knowledge of the data environment, stored in vast, secured and impenetrable server farms, replaces the Absolute knowledge which Hegel saw as the legacy of Enlightenment, "What does not belong to a codified domain is not socially recognizable or relevant, although it still exists in the domain of irrelevance, of residuality" (Berardi 2009b: 73). Either these externalities, as we have been referring to them, explode in the rage of populations, and the storm surges and nuclear cataclysms of abrupt climate change and Three Mile Island, Chernobyl and Fukushima, or they fester in the slow violence (Nixon 2011) of creeping toxicity and the gradual diminution of life through air, light and noise pollution.

The ecopolitical aesthetics that critical film theory pursues will come from more than one front. The tactics developed in the first three of our four modes of political cinema, communicative, formal and activist screenings, will continue because we cannot surrender the ground to commerce and rule, and because we have to work, as Orwell (1969) had it, "inside the whale", dirtied by contact because without it we cannot make media at all. But above all we need to develop a cinema that addresses the excluded migrants and indigenous and the poors of North and South at the level not of identities but of desires and demands, of "what belongs most essentially to human beings [. . .] communication, the creation of mental states, of feelings and imagination" (Berardi 2009b: 84). Ecocritics, however, have to challenge Berardi's analysis on two counts: that communication must not be understood as the passing of messages from senders to receivers but as a special condition of mediation, the universal interconnection of everything that underlies ecological thinking, and that therefore a reconceived communication, along with mental states, feelings and imagination, are not exclusively human. In the formal experiments, the internally contradictory popular films, the documentary and realist communiqués in the manner of *Food, Inc.* (Kenner, 2008) and the history of activist film screening strategies, we have the bases for building a future cinema whose objective would be to overcome the distinctions that disfigure us. Reflecting on the recent history of urban uprisings in the *banlieux* and *cités* of Paris, Badiou writes:

> The State has no other major task except to prohibit, by all possible means, including violent ones, any connection, even limited, between the popular youth of the 'cities' and the students, between the students and the mass of ordinary salaried workers, among the latter and the newly arrived proletarians, and even, despite its apparent naturalness, any connection between the popular youth and the proletarian newcomers, between sons and fathers.
>
> *(2012: 22)*

In this perspective there is no more urgent task than to overcome the identities that divide us. Badiou limits his analysis to human actors in the European capitals. Ecopolitical cinema must move beyond that limitation to enfranchise a new communicative dispensation grounded in the mobilisation of repressed desires for a good life, the externalised environments, including the alienated forms of ancestral labour in technology and the increasingly alienated forms of human knowledge in databanks, the poor and the marginalised. Ecology is intrinsically global. The imagination of cinema as a global language is at least as old as Griffith. It has still not been realised, because its ambition has been limited. Politics begins when ambition soars.

Bibliography

Agamben, G. (1993) *The Coming Community* (trans. M. Hardt), Minneapolis: Minnesota University Press.

Althusser, L., Balibar, E., Establet, R. and Rancière, J. (1971) *Lire le capital*, 2nd edition, Paris: Maspéro.

Badiou, A. (2012) *Philosophy for Militants* (trans B. Bosteels), London: Verso.

Baudrillard, J. (2005) *The Intelligence of Evil or the Lucidity Pact* (trans. C. Turner), London: Verso.

Beller, J. (2006) *The Cinematic Mode of Production: Attention Economy and the Society of the Spectacle*, Lebanon, NH: Dartmouth College Press/University Press of New England.

Benjamin, W. (2003) "The Work of Art in the Age of its Technological Reproducibility: Third Version" in Eiland, H. and Jennings, M. W. (eds), *Selected Writings, Vol. 4, 1938–1940*, Cambridge, MA: Bellknap Press/Harvard University Press, pp. 251–283.

Berardi, F. 'B.' (2009a) *Precarious Rhapsody: Semiocapitalism and the Pathologies of the Post-Alpha Generation* (trans. A. Bove, E. Empson, M. Goddard, G. Mecchia, A. Schintu and S. Wright), London: Minor Compositions.

Berardi, F. 'B.' (2009b) *The Soul at Work: From Alienation to Autonomy* (trans. F. Cadel and G. Mecchia), New York: Semiotext(e).

Berardi, F. 'B.' (2012) *The Uprising: On Poetry and Finance*, New York: Semiotext(e).
Bruno, G. (2002) *Atlas of Emotion: Journeys in Art, Architecture, and Film*, London: Verso.
Comolli, J.-L. and Narboni, P. (1971) "Cinema/ Ideology/ Criticism", *Screen* 12(1), Spring, pp. 27–36.
Dean, J. (2012) *The Communist Horizon*, London: Verso.
Doane, M. A. (2002) *The Emergence of Cinematic Time: Modernity, Contingency, the Archive*, Cambridge, MA: Harvard University Press.
Foucault, M. (2004) *The Birth of Biopolitics: Lectures at the Collège de France 1978–1979* (edit. M. Senellart, trans. G. Burchell), Basingstoke: Palgrave Macmillan.
Gabrys, J. (2010) *Digital Rubbish: A Natural History of Electronics*, Ann Arbor: University of Michigan Press.
Galison, P. (1997) *Image and Logic: A Material Culture of Microphysics*, Chicago: University of Chicago Press.
Grossman, E. (2007) *High Tech Trash: Digital Devices, Hidden Toxics, and Human Health*, Washington, DC: Shearwater.
IBWC (1994) *Binational Study Regarding the Presence of Toxic Substances in the Rio Grande/Rio Bravo and Its Tributaries Along the Boundary Between the United States and Mexico*, International Border and Water Commission.
Laclau, E. (2005) *On Populist Reason*, London: Verso.
Latour, B. (2005) *Reassembling the Social: An Introduction to Actor-Network Theory*, Oxford: Oxford University Press.
MacDonald, S. (2001) *The Garden in the Machine: A Field Guide to Independent Films About Place*, Berkeley: University of California Press.
Macpherson, D. (in collaboration with Willemen, P.) (1980) *Traditions of Independence: British Cinema in the Nineteen Thirties*, London: BFI.
Maxwell R. and Miller, T. (2012) *Greening the Media*, Oxford: Oxford University Press.
Mouffe, C. (2005) *On the Political*, London: Routledge.
Naess, A. (1989) *Ecology, Community and Lifestyle: Outline of an Ecosophy* (trans. and rev. D. Rothenberg), Cambridge: Cambridge University Press.
Nixon, R. (2011) *Slow Violence and the Environmentalism of the Poor*, Cambridge, MA: Harvard University Press.
Orwell, G. (1969) *Inside the Whale and Other Essays*, Harmondsworth: Penguin.
Rancière, J. (1999) *Disagreement: Politics and Philosophy* (trans. J. Rose), Minneapolis: University of Minnesota Press.
Rancière, J. (2006) *Hatred of Democracy* (trans. S. Corcoran), London: Verso.
Schuppli, S. (2011) "The Most Dangerous Film in the World" in Le Roy, F., Wynants, N., Hoens, D. and Vanderbeeken, R. (eds) *Tickle Your Catastrophe! Imagining Catastrophe in Art, Architecture and Philosophy*, Amsterdam and Ghent: Academia Press.
Shannon, C. E. and Weaver, W. (1949) *The Mathematical Theory of Communication*, Urbana: University of Illinois Press.
Texas Commission on Environmental Quality (2013) *Rio Grande Toxic Substances Study Summary*. http://www.tceq.texas.gov/waterquality/monitoring/riosum.html. Accessed 22 March 2015.
Théorie Communiste (2011) "Communization in the Present Tense" (trans. endnotes) in Noys, B. (ed.) *Communization and its Discontents: Contestation, Critique, and Contemporary Struggles*, New York: Minor Compositions/Autonomedia, pp. 41–58.

4

THE POLITICS OF FORM

A conceptual introduction to '*Screen* theory'

Warren Buckland

Theoretical training

The '*Screen* theorists' of the 1970s (those associated with the journal *Screen*: Stephen Heath, Colin MacCabe, Laura Mulvey, Peter Wollen, amongst others) employed Saussurean semiotics, Lacanian psychoanalysis and especially Althusserian Marxism to develop a materialist knowledge of the ideology perpetuated by mainstream cinema. One key idea behind the Marxist theory of ideology is that ideology conceals the contradictions of capitalism, such as the irresolvable conflicts of inequality that exist between different social classes: "ideology has the precise function of hiding the real contradictions and of reconstituting on an imaginary level a relatively coherent discourse which serves as the horizon of agents' experience" (Nicos Poulantzas, quoted in Larrain 1979: 46). *Screen* theorists analysed this ideological process of concealment in mainstream cinema by examining the way the imaginary impression of a coherent filmic discourse is produced.

The obverse side of *Screen* theory's ideological critique of mainstream cinema was its promotion of a political modernist avant-garde cinema, an oppositional cinema that does not function as a vehicle for dominant ideology, but instead reflexively investigates its own materiality, contradictions and conditions of production. By exposing rather than concealing contradictions, this political cinema deconstructs the impression of a coherent filmic discourse that ideology sets up. Key to both dimensions of *Screen* theory was the politics of form, an analysis of the immanent structure of film and its political ramifications, rather than a promotion of the political content of film. Many *Screen* theorists ended up criticizing films with political content (because these films continue to employ dominant, naturalistic practices of filmmaking) and promoted formalist, avant-garde practices with very little content but with a revolutionary critique of dominant ideology.

But where did this agenda come from? In this chapter I construct one historical narrative tracing the various disciplines that established *Screen* theory's agenda. Many historical narratives can be constructed; this one privileges the Marxist philosophy of Louis Althusser and his insistence on an uncompromising 'theoretical training' (*formation théorique*) in order to make ideological critique effective. More specifically, this chapter focuses on Althusser's two theories of ideology (as a system of representation, and as a practice) and his concepts of interpellation and symptomatic reading, and three concepts developed within *Screen* theory: the cinema's ideological impression of reality, the cinematic apparatus and the political avant-garde. The chapter ends on *Screen* theory's engagement with Brechtian distanciation, and a few comments on the institutions that in part disseminated the *Screen* agenda and supported non-mainstream cinema, such as The British Film Institute (BFI), the Independent Film Makers' Association (IFA) and the early years of Channel 4. In regards to Channel 4, Rod Stoneman noted that "Carrying the unwieldy framework of seventies *Screen* theory into the practice of British broadcasting has involved a curious journey leading to some strange connections" (1992: 128), some of which will be briefly explored in the final paragraphs.

Ideological practice

Althusser's work was instrumental in shifting French philosophy away from Jean-Paul Sartre's existential philosophy of individual consciousness, free will and lived experience, and towards their impersonal, underlying social and economic conditions of possibility. For Althusser, lived experience and consciousness are not direct, free, unmediated and pre-constituted, but are constructed and filtered through humanist ideology, which (like all ideologies) conceals its own mediatory function.

Of primary importance to Althusser in criticizing ideology and the humanist illusion of the pre-constituted subject was the concept of 'practice'. For Althusser, the term 'practice' names a process of production (or transformation) of raw material into a product (1969: 166). He identified within the social totality four practices: economic, political, ideological and theoretical (scientific). Theoretical practice is a process of transformation that has scientific knowledge as its product. Knowledge is not based upon pre-given, naturally occurring objects, but is the result of a process of theoretical transformation. The raw material of theoretical practice is not, therefore, reality itself but ideological representations, concepts and facts. This raw material (which Althusser calls Generality I) is general and abstract, and is transformed by theoretical practice (Generality II) into a specific, concrete product, scientific knowledge (Generality III) (1969: 182–93). Generality II consists of the methods and basic system of concepts of the theory that determine the problems capable of being posed and the way they are to be resolved. Althusser emphasized that there are no similarities between the concepts of Generality I (which are ideological) and Generality III (which are scientific). Generality III is not a simple inversion of Generality I (i.e., is not in negative identification with it) but involves a complete transformation, which Althusser highlighted by calling it (following Gaston Bachelard) an 'epistemological break'. In effect, Althusser proposed the theoretical transformation of ideology into knowledge.

Althusser initially defined ideology as a system of representations: "ideology is a system (with its own logic and rigor) of representations (images, myths, ideas or concepts, depending on the case) endowed with a historical existence and role within a given society" (1969: 241). In his seminal essay "Ideology and Ideological State Apparatuses" (1971: 127–86), Althusser developed a second theory of ideology – of ideology as a practice. He posited the individual as a mere support of ideological practice, which works to position and define the role of the individual within the overall social totality (without the individual having any conscious knowledge of the workings of ideological practice). Here Althusser defined ideology not simply as a system of representations imposed upon the individual's pre-existing consciousness, but as a practice that constitutes, by means of the imaginary, the individual's consciousness and their relation to their conditions of existence. In effect, for Althusser, ideology is not a false consciousness of the individual's relation to his/her conditions of existence because there is no 'true', direct experience of these conditions for ideology to falsify.

Althusser's first definition of ideology – a system of representations with a logic and function of its own, opposed to science – conforms to an empiricist theory of representation. But Althusser's later definition of ideology as a practice that constitutes (interpellates) individuals as subjects challenges this empiricist theory. Althusser argued that the imaginary relation is constant, or universal; we cannot escape it. Our access to reality is always mediated through the imaginary and through ideology. Paul Hirst adds:

> The imaginary modality of living is necessary because men's conditions of existence can never be given to them in experience. [. . .] There can never be any true or false *consciousness* because there is no basis for a correspondence between the experience of the subject and his social relations.
>
> (1979: 32–33)

The imaginary is constant because it forms the basis of the individual's relation to the world, and constitutes that relation as a narcissistic orientation towards reality. For Althusser, the only escape from the imaginary and ideology is through Generality III, which does not interpellate individuals as subjects. There is a stark dichotomy in Althusser – between a pre-constituted identity falsified by ideological representations, and no subjectivity within theoretical practice.

The impression of reality

Within the context of Althusser's two theories of ideology, the journals *Cahiers du cinéma* and *Cinéthique* developed a political critique of mainstream cinema, and attempted to define the function of an alternative, materialist (modernist) filmic practice. They defined as their 'object' of analysis the ideological illusions perpetuated by mainstream films and attempted to produce a scientific knowledge of those illusions. Both journals therefore conceived their work as a theoretical practice (Generality II), although *Cinéthique* was far more militant than *Cahiers*. Both French journals had an immense influence on the British journal *Screen*, which translated many of their key essays in the 1970s.

Furthermore, as all three journals operated within the framework of semiotics, their analyses were always directed (at least in principle) towards the specificity (or relative autonomy) of filmic ideology. They defined the specificity of filmic ideology in terms of its impression of reality. *Cahiers du cinéma*:

> Once we realize that it is the nature of the system to turn the cinema into an instrument of ideology, we can see that the film-maker's first task is to show up the cinema's so-called 'depiction of reality'. If he [sic] can do so there is a chance that we will be able to disrupt or possibly even sever the connection between the cinema and its ideological function.
>
> (*Comolli and Narboni 1971: 30–31*)

Cinéthique:

> [Film] produces its own ideology: the impression of reality. There is nothing on the screen, only reflections and shadows, and yet the first idea that the audience gets is that reality is there, as it really is. [. . .]
>
> If one understands that ideology always presents itself in the form of a body of ideas and pictures of reality which people spontaneously accept as true, as realistic, it

is easy to see why the cinema, by its specific nature, plays such a privileged role in the general ideological process. It reinforces the impression that what looks realistic must be real, and thus reinforces the ideology it reflects. It presents it as true, by virtue of its self-evident existence on the screen.

(*Fargier 1971: 136–37*)

Screen:

> The real [is] not an external object represented in the text but the relation between text and reader which reduplicated or cut across the subject's relation to his or her experience. Classically, realism depended on obscuring the relation between text and reader in favour of a dominance accorded to a supposedly given reality, but this dominance, far from sustaining a 'natural' relation, was the product of a definite organisation which, of necessity, effaced its own workings.
>
> (*MacCabe 1976: 24*)

Film produces or constructs reality rather than simply copies a pre-existing reality and, like all ideological practices, it conceals its own process of construction, presenting that construction as natural and pre-given. Underlying the specific ideology of mainstream cinema, the impression of reality, is an empiricist epistemology, for what is directly seen on screen is presented as real, even though it is fabricated by the cinematographic apparatus. And it is in this presentation of a fabricated reality as a pre-existing reality that the editors of *Cahiers*, *Cinéthique* and *Screen* located the ideological function of the cinematographic apparatus. This necessitated a theoretical practice to emphasize the instrumentality that fabricates the reality on screen.

In his essay "On Screen, In Frame: Film and Ideology", Stephen Heath (1976) defined film is a signifying practice. The outcome of Heath's study of film as a signifying practice is to identify the role of the subject in process in the production of filmic meaning, which implies that the inscription of the subject position is not complete, but is an ongoing process, which he described in terms of the concept of suture. Each particular spectator is formally represented in filmic discourse via an abstract universal subject position, an empty position inscribed in the film that each spectator comes to occupy. When a particular spectator does successfully occupy this subject position, he or she is sutured into the film, creating an impression of coherence. But this impression is regularly shattered, especially when the spectator perceives the frame, which leads him or her to experience the emptiness of the universal formal subject position and his or her split from it. At that moment, the spectator is no longer sutured into the film. The film then works (typically via a new shot) to resuture the spectator back into the subject position by trying to eliminate the gap that opens up between the spectator and the image.

In his series of six articles "Technique and Ideology", first published in *Cahiers du cinéma* in 1971–72 (see Comolli 2014), Jean-Louis Comolli defined the various practices that constitute mainstream cinema – consisting of film as a signifying practice, but also economic, ideological and technological practices. Following Althusser's theory, Comolli developed a materialist history of the cinema, which involved taking conventional film history as the raw material (Generality I) to be turned into a materialist history (Generality III). This transformation of conventional film history had multiple effects: first, Comolli did not reduce film to one dominant practice (as in the base/superstructure model), but conceived these practices as semi-autonomous and in conflict with one another. Second, when outlining the various practices, he did not simply focus on the immediately visible part, but also the invisible parts. For example, technological practice does not just refer to the camera, to lenses, and so on, but also to the less noticeable parts of technology, such as the scientific research that invents them and the manufacturing processes that turn them into concrete objects. Third, he argued that technology is not neutral, but is infused with ideology. For example, cinema's 'quest' for greater realism, which André Bazin praised in the use of deep focus in the films of Welles and Wyler, is simply a sign of cinema's conformity to dominant ideology. The ideological demand for greater realism influences the technological development of deep focus lenses; the technological development is not free of ideology, but is an integral part of film as an ideological signifying practice. And fourth, Comolli's definition of film as a signifying practice also entails conceiving film as a discourse articulating meaning for someone. The spectator therefore becomes a necessary support in the film's production of meaning, for his/her position is defined (as is the case with the theory of suture) as the place where meaning is realized. Comolli formulated the concept of film as a signifying practice as a necessary component of a materialist history of the cinema.

The cinematic apparatus

Like Comolli, Jean-Louis Baudry (1974, 1976) analyzed cinema explicitly within Althusser's definition of 'practice', and also examined the processes of ideological transformation effected by the cinematographic apparatus (rather than the filmic text). For Baudry, the cinematographic apparatus as a practice consists of two transformative processes: transformation of the camera's raw material (the profilmic events) into a finished product, a series of discontinuous images inscribed on a strip of film; and transformation of the projector's raw material (the series of discontinuous images) into a finished product, the 'impression of reality', the projection on screen of the light, continuity and movement seized from the profilmic events. But just as Althusser described the relation between Generality I and Generality III as discontinuous, so for Baudry the process of transformation effected by the cinematographic apparatus between the profilmic events and the impression of reality is total (the cinema therefore puts into parenthesis the world's real existence in order to constitute the impression of reality). Rather than automatically reproduce the profilmic events, the cinematographic apparatus transforms them into an imaginary reality, but represses this process of transformation in an attempt to pass itself off as a neutral recording apparatus. It was in this process of transformation and repression that Baudry located the work of ideology. And it is within the context of a discontinuous relation between the profilmic events and cinematographic apparatus that a description of the impression of reality in the cinema requires an analysis of the relation between film and spectator. For Baudry, the impression of reality is fabricated by the cinematographic apparatus itself, in much the same way as the psychic apparatus fabricates virtual images such as dreams and hallucinations; the impression of reality is an imaginary effect, the result of the illusory continuity of filmic space, which constitutes an illusory continuity of consciousness, a transcendental, psychic unity, in the spectator. Baudry took the seminal step of explaining this illusory fabrication of psychic unity (produced by means of an illusory spatial unity on screen) in terms of the experience of the infant at the mirror phase (see Lacan 1977), for both experiences involve the constitution of a psychic unity via a continuous spatial image. The comparison of these two experiences is more than just a metaphor, according to Baudry, for he emphasized that both situations equally involve the individual's immobility and a corresponding precocious maturation of visual organization.

Avant-garde cinema

At its most extreme, *Screen* theory conceived avant-garde filmmaking as a theoretical practice. This means that avant-garde films do not merely oppose the ideology of the mainstream, that is, invert the dominant ideology, because this would mean that the avant-garde is simply the imaginary, mirror image of dominant cinema, is in negative identification with it. Instead of a simple inversion or opposition, the avant-garde needs to effect an epistemological break with ideology (Generality I), to produce a filmic practice that generates materialist (scientific) knowledge (Generality III). The definition of the avant-garde as the inverse of dominant cinema therefore remains within the terms of the dominant, for it simply refuses its ideology, rather than undermines it from within. Anthony Wilden has argued that "Positive or negative identification with or against the Other as the oppressor (or whatever) is politically and psychologically dangerous, for it entails an implicit 'self-definition' in relation to the code of values defined by that Other" (1980: lv). He goes on to argue that

> dissent must transcend the status of negative identification. *In short, all dissent must be of a higher logical type than that with which it is in conflict.* It will thus not make the Hegelian error of trying to reduce real and material differences to identity, for this is to be caught up in the endless mirror-game from which there is simply no escape.
> *(1980: lvii; emphasis in the original)*

His definition of dissent – it must be "of a higher logical type than that with which it is in conflict" – is also a definition of an epistemological break (the break takes the place of inversion/opposition). Wilden concludes that "this is hardly an easy task" (lvi).

In retrospect, we can see that the *Screen* theorists defined the avant-garde in terms of a simple imaginary, binary opposition to dominant cinema. In setting up an opposition between dominant and avant-garde cinema, Heath (1976) classified films as either a cinema of realism (representation, illusion) on the one hand, versus a nonrepresentational, anti-illusionistic modernist cinema; of unreflexive/reflexive practice; acquiescence to dominant ideology/resistance to dominant ideology; a cinema that constructs coherent, centered subject positions/a cinema of decentered, fragmented subject positions.

Earlier, in 1972, Peter Wollen symbolized this conflict in terms of a table of seven oppositions:

Narrative transitivity	Narrative intransitivity
Identification	Estrangement
Transparency	Foregrounding
Single diegesis	Multiple diegesis
Closure	Aperture
Pleasure	Unpleasure
Fiction	Reality

(Wollen, 1972: 6)

This schema, and Wollen's elaboration of the seven oppositions, is one of the most precise representations of the *Screen* theorists' conceptualization of the avant-garde. But, like all *Screen* theory, it is also governed by the imaginary logic of negative identification. Nonetheless, there are formulations that briefly go beyond negative identification. Under the pleasure vs unpleasure heading, Wollen notes the following, and ends up reinforcing the difficulty, expressed by

Anthony Wilden, of transcending the binary logic: "A revolutionary cinema has to operate at different levels – fantasy, ideology, science – and the articulation of these levels, which involves different modes of discourse and different positions of the subject, is a complicated matter" (15).

Politically active British avant-garde filmmakers, such as Peter Gidal and Malcolm LeGrice, were more successful in adopting Althusser's science/ideology opposition in order to transcend the ideological illusionism of classical film. Peter Gidal is a practitioner as well as theorist of structural/materialist films, a form of counter or avant-garde film movement developed in Europe, the USA, but especially Britain in the sixties. Gidal's uncompromising formal experiments in film (*Key*, *Clouds*, *Film Room 1973*, *Condition of Illusion*) are matched by the radical political aims of his theoretical writings (1975, 1989). He initially used theories of French structuralism (structural linguistics, structural anthropology and semiotics), and, most importantly, added 'materialism' to his definition of structural film – meaning not simply the physical material (the specific qualities/limitations of a medium) but more significantly materialism in the sense developed in the Marxist theory of dialectical materialism. Gidal constructs a dialectical theory of film, a theory that conceives film in terms of the interaction of two opposing terms, consciousness and material, in which the material, although primary, is inseparable from the process of knowing it. From this dialectical materialist definition Gidal identified structural film's political agenda – to present the film material and process unfettered by naturalism or ideology.

In his 1975 essay "Theory and Definition of Structural/Materialist Film", he downplayed the value of French theories in theorizing structural/materialist film: "Advanced (mainly French) theory (not necessarily directly concerning film) is either not capable of dealing with film or else posits retrograde, illusionist, post-Bazinian manifestations of such" (1975: 193). Rather controversially, he goes on to say:

> The lamentably derivative watered-down [film theory] regurgitated by the editors of *Screen* is merely importation from at most three Paris sources, which though at moments useful is not directed correctly, is not made to interact with avant-garde film practice in this country (or any other).
>
> (*Ibid.*)

Nonetheless, Gidal's structural/materialism operates within Althusser's structural account of dialectical materialism, for the structure of a structural/materialist film is not perceived instantaneously, but gradually and indirectly, through its effects. A structural/materialist film does not aim to create a coherent gestalt; it does not aim to present the impression of a unified, coherent experience, but a heterogeneous experience.

Symptomatic reading

In 1969, Jean-Louis Comolli and Jean Narboni published their essay "Cinema/Ideology/Criticism" in *Cahiers du cinéma* (translated in *Screen* in 1971). This essay employs Althusser to specify film's relation to ideology. The authors identified seven categories (symbolized into the categories [a] to [g]) that identify how dominant cinema's form and content relate to ideology. To give just a few examples: category (a) films promote the dominant ideology on both form and content; category (c) films contain a subversive form but reactionary content; category (d) films contain reactionary form but radical content; and category (e) films are "films which seem at first sight to belong firmly within the ideology and to be completely under its sway, but which turn out to be so only in an ambiguous manner" (1971: 32). In general, Comolli and Narboni identify film form, especially form that draws attention to film's artificiality, as key to understanding film's relation to ideology.

Category '(e)' films were identified via Althusser's formulation of symptomatic reading. In the opening of *Reading Capital* (Althusser and Balibar 1970), Louis Althusser noted that, when Marx analyzed the works of political economy by Adam Smith and David Ricardo, he did not simply read meaning from the surface of their written texts. Instead, he adopted a reading strategy that also focused on their blind spots – not what the economists left out, but more significantly what of necessity cannot (without sounding contradictory) be stated in their texts.

By focusing on what cannot be stated in the texts of Smith and Ricardo, Marx reconstructed the underlying logic – the constitutive presuppositions – that makes their texts possible. More generally, Marx reconstructed the boundaries that determine what can and cannot be thought within classical economics. The boundary is the framework (the 'problematic', in Althusser's terms) that establishes the internal limits to a way of thinking. For Marx and Althusser, the unthinkable – what cannot be thought within a particular framework or problematic – is just as significant as what can be thought.

Crucially for Althusser, the unthinkable is not simply what is outside the text; it is the invisible inside the text:

> The invisible is defined by the visible as its invisible, its forbidden vision: the invisible is not therefore simply what is outside the visible [...], the outer darkness of exclusion – but the inner darkness of exclusion, inside the visible itself because defined by its structure. [...] In other words, all its limits are internal, it carrie[s] its outside inside it.
>
> (*Althusser and Balibar 1970: 27–28*)

This second type of reading is not, therefore, a reading limited to what is manifest in a finished text, nor is it about what was simply left out. Instead, the object of this second type of reading is what necessarily must be excluded or repressed from the surface text in order to constitute it as coherent and non-contradictory. But the repressed cannot be abolished; it leaves symptoms (gaps or lapses) in the text. In a well-known passage in *Reading Capital*, Althusser called this second type of reading symptomatic:

> Such is Marx's second reading: a reading which might well be called 'symptomatic' (symptomale), insofar as it divulges the undivulged event in the text it reads, and in the same movement relates it to a different text, present as a necessary absence in the first. [...] what distinguishes this new reading from the old one is the fact that in the new one the second text is articulated with the lapses in the first text.
>
> (*1970: 29*)

In 1970, the editors of *Cahiers* employed Althusser's philosophy in order to subject John Ford's *Young Mr. Lincoln* (1939) to a symptomatic reading, that is, read it as a category (e) film (translated in *Screen* in 1972). Like all texts, *Young Mr. Lincoln* was made within an ideological framework or problematic that delimits what is and what is not possible to say within its fictional world. On the surface, the film appears to represent dominant ideology – more specifically, it aims to establish a myth around Lincoln as a perfect Republican president – but symptoms disrupt this ideological message. Texts are overdetermined, that is, have multiple causes, some explicit, others intangible (the structuring absences) that conflict with the explicit causes, producing ruptures or symptoms in the text. These are the 'objects' of a symptomatic reading. The editors emphasized that they are not reading *Young Mr. Lincoln* in terms of its social history, for that history is not present as a pre-existing fixed context. Nor do they read the surface text looking for some pre-existing hidden subtext. The *Cahiers* editors followed Althusser in emphasizing that reading symptoms involves analyzing the film's form and boundary (which constitute it as a coherent text and determine what it can and cannot say) in order to actively reconstruct its intangible political/historical/sexual meanings, the meanings the film attempts to repress.

The editors work their way through the film (which occasionally sounds like a traditional thematic-auteur analysis) to eventually privilege two structuring absences – eroticism and politics. Politics and Lincoln's desire, they argue, are repressed from the film's surface, replaced by morality and the Law. Lincoln represents the Law of the Symbolic order and its moral code. He is depicted as a powerful figure of Law and the Symbolic, that is, a representative of society's prescribed social rules via his castrating (or threatening) stare; he has the phallus (the symbol of power), as the editors put it. However, the film also presents Lincoln as castrated, that is, as weak. He is the phallus, according to the editors of *Cahiers*. Lincoln can only represent the Law by renouncing what cannot be stated in the surface of the film, his Oedipal desire. He retreats to a position outside the Symbolic order, in a pre-Oedipal (desexualized) stage, which makes his Symbolic power paranoid. (See Buckland 2013 for more detailed exposition and a critique of the *Cahiers* reading of *Young Mr. Lincoln*.)

Brecht

One of the key theoretical links between *Screen* theory, as outlined above, and the work of Brecht, is that form is not regarded as a neutral dimension of an artwork. Both Brecht and the *Screen* theorists make the artwork's form a political issue. For playwright Brecht, a play must draw the audience's attention to its form in order to challenge and render strange its naturalism, or impression of reality, which does not represent nature and culture in a neutral universal manner, but is ideological, suppressing social contradictions and representing the interests of the ruling class – as is the case with 'dramatic theatre'. Drawing the audience's attention to form challenges the play's naturalism, creates a gap between artwork and reality, which in turn draws attention to its ideological contradictions – as in epic theatre. (Wollen's table of oppositions is influenced by Brecht's opposition of dramatic to epic theatre.) In theatre, Brecht achieved this change of perception and political consciousness via the *Verfremdung*/distancing effect, which exposes the artificiality of dramatic theatre via actors directly addressing the audience, or by questioning their characters, or via simplified set design, or via the use of written captions (such as stage directions) to interrupt the action. Rather than encourage the audience to identify emotionally with the characters in the story and passively accept the story's naturalism, Brecht encouraged the audience to critically reflect on the reality portrayed in naturalistic theatre.

Colin MacCabe (1974) applied Brecht's theory to a new theoretical object, the 'classic realist text', and outlined how the classic realist text operated in both novel and film. He then employed Brecht to define revolutionary filmmaking. MacCabe defined the classic realist text formally: not as a relation between text and a pre-given external reality, but within the text – as a hierarchy between object language (the realm of characters) and metalanguage, the realm of the narrator, which guarantees the truth and meaning of the object language. The reader or spectator of the classic realist text is aligned with the narrator in this position of omniscience. MacCabe defined revolutionary films as those that subvert the metalanguage's dominance over the object language, thereby rupturing the film's sense of realism or naturalism as well as the spectator's position of omniscience. He cites *Tout va bien* (Godard and Gorin, 1972), which consists of multiple contradictory character discourses competing against each other, with no unitary, omniscient narrator confirming their truth or falsity for the spectator. The conflicts in the film remain unresolved and therefore incomplete; the spectator is no longer able to absorb a pre-existing meaning, but must become more active and productive when engaging with the film. (However, it is possible to argue that, in the end, the film does present the discourse of the workers as the locus of truth – reinforcing Marx's notion that the working class are the universal class in that their particular interests represent the interests of society in general. Non-Marxists would simply see the film as privileging the opposite class that dominant ideology privileges – that is, the film operates as the mirror image of dominant ideology.)

The BFI, IFA and Channel 4

> Much independent UK media production in the early 1980s came out of a dialogue with the theoretical work of *Screen*.
>
> (*Nash 2008: 2*)

The *Screen* theorists' Althusserian agenda of theoretical training did not remain entirely within the institutional context of academia. In February 1985, Colin MacCabe took up the post of Head of Production at the British Film Institute. Christophe Dupin notes that: "Although the appointment of radical theoretician Colin MacCabe as new Head of Production generated a lot of scepticism in the press and among independent film-makers, MacCabe himself immediately announced his intention of continuing his predecessor's feature film policy" (2012: 211). Dupin goes on to list some of the films MacCabe oversaw: "The first projects he oversaw were [Derek Jarman's] *Caravaggio*, Peter Greenaway's *A Zed and Two Noughts* and Terence Davies's *Distant Voices, Still Lives*, three important British art films (and film-makers) of the 1980s" (2012: 211). MacCabe also executive produced other important British art films, including *Young Soul Rebels* (1991) and *The Long Day Closes* (1992), as well as a number of significant documentaries for television.

In 1989, MacCabe became Head of the BFI's Research and Education department as well, where he instigated an overhaul of the BFI magazine *Sight and Sound* (which was relaunched with a new editor, Philip Dodd, in 1991); he also set up the BFI's MA programme; and overhauled BFI Publishing. Unsurprisingly, he relinquished his Head of Production role, and remained in Research and Education until 1998.

Whereas MacCabe worked within the national institution of the BFI, other filmmakers and educationalists worked within more independent, small-scale organizations. The Independent Film Makers' Association (IFA) was set up in 1974 to promote radical filmmaking completely divorced from the finance, production, distribution and exhibition practices of the mainstream film industry, although they campaigned for and received funding from the BFI and lobbied for airtime from the new Channel 4 (which began broadcasting in November 1982) to show independent avant-garde film. In terms of the latter, the first Chief Executive of Channel 4, Jeremy Isaacs, appointed IFA members Alan Fountain, Caroline Spry and Rod Stoneman to commission independent films, political documentaries and community programmes, and many IFA members were able to show their films on late-night TV in programmes such as *The Eleventh Hour* (1982–89) and *Midnight Underground* (1993–97).

Screen also underwent a change in editor (Mark Nash) and editorial policy in the early 1980s, and shifted its focus in part to contemporary independent British film and television, and to film production, distribution and exhibition, rather than limiting itself to autonomous theory and textual analysis. It published several essays on Channel 4, including Stoneman's "Sins of Commission" (1992). Stoneman notes the time lag in the formation of Channel 4, in which "some sections of a dissident cultural intelligentsia [moved] into television (several from the *Screen*/BFI penumbra), carrying the values of late sixties radicalism into the broadcasting of the Thatcher years" (1992: 133). He concludes (in 1992) that, in terms of developing progressive and creative cultural forms on television, Channel 4 had barely scratched the surface. At the time of writing (2014), political filmmaking (especially documentary filmmaking) still has a strong presence in Britain, although less of it is commissioned by Channel 4 or other television channels, due to the general decline in television viewing and the rise in alternative digital media. Chris Jury spells out what is rapidly becoming self-evident in the contemporary media landscape:

> The last major wave of political film-making in Britain happened in the 1980s with the cooperative movement, Channel 4 and the IFA. But much has changed since then.
>
> Near universal access to the medium and distribution of film on the internet is changing the world. Such a communications revolution has not been witnessed since the invention of the printing press and the spread of mass literacy. The social and political power of this is only just becoming evident as we witness the so-called Twitter Revolutions of the Arab Spring and the rapid spreading of activist creative film 'memes' across the world through Facebook, Twitter and emerging social media forums.
>
> *(Quoted in Lezard 2014)*

Bibliography

Althusser, L. (1969) *For Marx*, London: Allen Lane.

Althusser, L. (1971) *Lenin and Philosophy and Other Essays*, New York: Monthly Review Press.

Althusser, L., and Balibar, E. (1970) *Reading Capital*, London: Verso.

Baudry, J.-L. (1974) "Ideological Effects of the Basic Cinematographic Apparatus", *Film Quarterly* 28(2), pp. 39–47.

Baudry, J.-L. (1976) "The Apparatus", *Camera Obscura* 1, pp. 104–126.

Buckland, W. (2013) "Symptomatic Reading in Althusser, *Cahiers du cinéma*, and Žižek", *Jump Cut* 55 [Online]. Available at: http://ejumpcut.org/currentissue/Buckland-Lincoln/index.html (accessed 1 October 2014).

Comolli, J.-L. (2014) *Cinema against Spectacle: Technique and Ideology Revisited*, edited by Daniel Fairfax, Amsterdam: Amsterdam University Press.

Comolli, J.-L., and Narboni, J. (1971) "Cinema/Ideology/Criticism", *Screen* 12(1), 27–38.

Dupin, C. (2012) "The BFI and Film Production: Half a Century of Innovative Independent Film-making", in Nowell-Smith, G., and Dupin, C. (eds) *The British Film Institute, the Government and Film Culture, 1933–2000*, Manchester: Manchester University Press, pp. 197–218.

Editors of *Cahiers du cinéma* (1972) "John Ford's *Young Mr. Lincoln*", *Screen* 13(3), pp. 5–44.

Fargier, J.-P. (1971) "Parenthesis or Indirect Route", *Screen* 12(2), pp. 131–144.

Gidal, P. (1975) "Theory and Definition of Structural/Materialist Film", *Studio International*, 190, pp. 189–196.

Gidal, P. (1989) *Materialist Film*, London: Routledge.

Heath, S. (1976) "On Screen, in Frame: Film and Ideology", *Quarterly Review of Film Studies* 1(3), pp. 251–265.

Hirst, P. (1979) *On Law and Ideology*, London: Macmillan.

Lacan, J. (1977) "The Mirror Stage as Formative of the Function of the I as Revealed in Psychoanalytic Experience", in *Écrits: A Selection*, London: Tavistock, pp. 1–7.

Larrain, J. (1979) *The Concept of Ideology*, London: Hutchinson.

Lezard, T. (2014) "Lights, Camera, Action ... Radical Film Festival to Star at Tolpuddle" [Online]. Available at: http://union-news.co.uk/2014/03/lights-camera-action-radical-film-festival-star-tolpuddle/ (accessed 10 October 2014).
MacCabe, C. (1974) "Realism and the Cinema: Notes on Some Brechtian Theses", *Screen* 15(2), pp. 7–27. [Republished in MacCabe 1985, pp. 33–57.]
MacCabe, C. (1976) "Theory and Film: Principles of Realism and Pleasure", *Screen* 17(3), pp. 7–28. [Republished in MacCabe 1985, pp. 58–81.]
MacCabe, C. (1985) *Theoretical Essays: Film, Linguistics, Literature*, Manchester: Manchester University Press.
Nash, M. (2008) *Screen Theory Culture*, Basingstoke: Palgrave Macmillan.
Stoneman, R. (1992) "Sins of Commission", *Screen* 33(2), pp. 127–144.
Wilden, A. (1980) *System and Structure: Essays in Communication and Exchange*, 2nd edition, London: Tavistock.
Wollen, P. (1972) "Godard and Counter Cinema: *Vent d'Est*", *Afterimage* 4, pp. 6–17.

5

REVISITING THE POLITICAL ECONOMY OF FILM[1]

Janet Wasko

In the late 1970s, Thomas Guback wrote an essay entitled "Are We Looking at the Right Things in Film?" in which he argued that the study of cinema focused overwhelmingly on criticism and theory, with a dash of a theoretical history (Guback 1978). Guback's main point was that film studies typically neglected the analysis of cinema as an economic institution and as a medium of communication. In this paper, Guback described an 'institutional approach' to film, which looked very much like a political economic approach to the study of communication. At the time, this approach was distinctly identified in communication scholarship, but was much less common within film studies. While some things have changed in film/media studies over the course of the last 40 years, it might be argued that some of Guback's concerns are still quite valid.

Defining the political economy of media/communications tradition: classical political economy

Many of the descriptions of political economy of communication or media begin with a discussion of the general study of political economy, drawing on eighteenth century Scottish enlightenment thinking and its critique in the nineteenth century. For Adam Smith, David Ricardo, and others, the study of economic issues was called political economy and was grounded in social theory. Smith defined political economy as the study of "wealth" (material goods) or the allocation of resources in society, and was concerned with "how mankind arranges to allocate scarce resources with a view toward satisfying certain needs and not others" (Smith 1776). Further, political economy focused on the production, distribution, exchange, and consumption of wealth and the consequences for the welfare of individuals and society. More specifically, political economists studied one arrangement for the allocation of resources – they studied capitalism as a system of social production.

Classical political economy evolved as capitalism evolved, adding Marx and Engels' historical materialism and class analysis in the nineteenth century, and emphasizing a radical critique of the evolving capitalist system through a moral stance in opposition to the unjust and inequitable characteristics of that system. During the last half of the nineteenth century, however, there was a fundamental shift in the study of economic issues, as the focus changed from macro- to micro-analysis, emphasis was placed on individual rather than societal concerns, and the methods used came from the social sciences rather than from moral philosophy. These changes were represented in the basic shift in the name of the discipline – from political economy to economics.

The person responsible for the name change, William Jevons, suggested that economics was the study of "the mechanics of utility and self interest . . . to satisfy our wants to the utmost with the least effort . . . to maximize pleasure is the problem of economics" (Jevons 1970). As a more recent economist has explained: the "neo-classical economists made a sharper distinction than their predecessors had done between the explanation of What Is, in an economic system and the consideration of What Ought To Be . . ." (R. D. Collison Black, quoted in Jevons 1970).

Although neo-classical economics prevails today, political economy has survived in different forms. In communication studies, radical, critical or Marxian political economy has been applied to the study of communication and has been recognized as a distinct tradition. In *The Political Economy of Communication*, Vincent Mosco has defined this version of political economy as "the study of the social relations, particularly power relations, that mutually constitute the production, distribution and consumption of resources" (Mosco 1996: 25). He explains that political economy is about survival and control, or how societies are organized to produce what is necessary to survive, and how order is maintained to meet societal goals. Mosco further delineates four central characteristics of critical political economy, which are helpful in understanding this approach:

1. *Social change and history:* Political economy continues the tradition of classic theorists, uncovering the dynamics of capitalism – its cyclical nature, the growth of monopoly capital, the state apparatus, etc.
2. *Social totality:* Political economy is a holistic approach, or, in concrete terms, examines the relationship among commodities, institutions, social relations, and hegemony, exploring the determination among these elements, although some elements are stressed more than others.
3. *Moral philosophy:* Critical political economy also follows the classical theorists' emphasis on moral philosophy, including not only analysis of the economic system, but discussion of the policy problems and moral issues which arise from it. For some contemporary scholars, this is the distinguishing characteristic of political economy.
4. *Praxis:* Finally, political economists attempt to transcend the distinction between research and policy, orienting their work towards actual social change and practice, or as Marx pointed out: "The philosophers have only interpreted the world, in various ways; the point is to change it" (Marx 1845/1945: 2).

Mosco's model draws strongly on the work of British political economists Graham Murdock and Peter Golding, who distinguished critical political economy from mainstream economics: it is holistic, historical, centrally concerned with the balance between capitalist enterprise and public intervention, and "goes beyond technical issues of efficiency to engage with basic moral questions of justice, equity and the public good" (Golding and Murdock 1991: 18–19)

These explanations set the stage or provide the grounding for applying political economy to the study of media and communication.

Political economy applied to media/communication

The academic study of communication has not always embraced economic analysis, much less a political economic approach. During the 1940s and 1950s, communication scholars focused primarily on individual effects and psychologically oriented research, with little concern for the economic context in which media is produced, distributed, and consumed.

In the 1950s and early 1960s, former FCC economist and University of Illinois professor, Dallas Smythe urged scholars to consider communication as an important component of the economy and to understand it as an economic entity. In 1960, he presented one of the first applications of political economy to communication, defining the approach as the study of political policies and economic processes, their interrelations, and their mutual influence on social institutions (Smythe 1960). He argued that the central purpose of applying political economy to communication was to evaluate the effects of communication agencies in terms of the policies by which they are organized and operated, or to study the structure and policies of communication institutions in their social settings. Smythe further delineated research questions emanating from policies of production, allocation or distribution, and capital, organization and control, concluding that the studies that might evolve from these areas were practically endless.

In the 1970s, Murdock and Golding defined political economy of communication as fundamentally interested in studying communication and media as commodities produced by capitalist industries (Murdock and Golding 1974). Their article "For a Political Economy of Mass Communications" represented "a ground-breaking exercise . . . a conceptual map for a political economic analysis of the media where none existed in British literature" (Mosco 1996: 102). A later work placed political economy within the broader framework of critical and Marxian theory, with links to the Frankfurt School, as well as to other critical theorists (Murdock and Golding 1979).

Political economy draws upon several disciplines – specifically history, economics, sociology, and political science. And, while some may question whether or not a specific methodology is involved, the study of political economy draws on a wide range of techniques and methods, including not only Marxist economics, but methods used in history and sociology, especially power structure research and institutional analysis.

Because historical analysis is mandatory, the approach is able to provide important insight into social change and movement. Political economy becomes crucial in order to document communication in total social context. Interrelationships between media and communication industries and sites of power in society are necessary for the complete analysis of communications, and their study helps to dispel some common myths about our economic and political system, especially the notions of pluralism, free enterprise, competition, and others. Through study of ownership and control, political economists analyze relations of power and confirm a class system and structural inequalities. Given its focus on economic and political analysis, political economy becomes necessary grounding for ideological readings and cultural analysis. And through identification of contradictions, political economic analysis provides strategies for intervention, resistance, and change.

Major themes

To further understand political economy and its application on media, it may be useful to consider specific examples of the issues that political economists examine, as well as samples of research from this approach. Because a wide range of themes pertaining to communication and media have been addressed, it is nearly impossible to completely trace the rich history and wide range of communication scholarship that draws on a political economic tradition. Still, the following sections identify some of the general themes that are fundamental to political economists researching the media.

Historical studies

Most political economic media research incorporates historical analysis, for it is essential to document change as well as continuity. Many notable historical studies have focused on the development of media and its relationship to concepts such as democracy, free speech, and others, in addition to historical overviews of specific media, including radio, film, television, and telecommunications.

Media as business

A good deal of political economic media research has focused on the evolution of mass communications/media as commodities that are produced and distributed by profit-seeking organizations in capitalist industries, or in other words, media as business. The trends that Murdock and Golding identified in 1974 have expanded and intensified, not only within traditional media industries but also across industrial divisions into newly converged businesses.

It is clear that the general process of marketization has moved rapidly around the world during the last few decades. Communication and information have become key components of this marketization process but have also developed as significant industries. In many countries, public media institutions have been privatized, along with other public institutions, opening additional markets for growing transnational media and entertainment conglomerates. In addition, new communication and information systems, such as the Internet, are developing as commercialized space, contrary to promises of public access and control. This commercialization process – including the growth of advertising and public relations – has been accompanied by an ever-expanding consumer culture, thus prompting the term "cultural capitalism" as a descriptor for the current period (see Murdock and Wasko 2007).

Analysis of media as business has involved various concepts, including but not limited to the following:

- *Commodification/commercialization:* Increasingly, media and communication resources have become commodities – products and services that are sold by profit-seeking companies to buyers or consumers. In addition, more and more of the media landscape is filled with commercial messages and the privatization of media outlets continues.
- *Diversification:* As media companies have expanded, new lines of business have been added in a process of diversification. While media industries often begin with a relatively large number of differentiated companies, these industries today are typically dominated by huge media/entertainment conglomerates that are involved in a wide range of diversified activities.
- *Horizontal/vertical integration:* As media corporations have grown larger and more profitable, they often have added companies that are in the same line of business, thus integrating horizontally. Not only have such companies expanded their range of businesses, but with new distribution technologies and deregulated markets, media companies have integrated vertically by adding companies in the same supply chain or at different stages of production.
- *Synergy:* There is also the potential for the various businesses owned by these large diversified conglomerates to work together to more effectively market products, thus producing a synergy that maximizes profits and decreases risk.
- *Concentration:* Of course, one of the major issues pertaining to the media business is the level of competition in various markets. While a competitive market is the avowed goal

of capitalism, there is an inevitable tendency for markets to become concentrated, due to any number of factors (as identified by Murdock and Golding, 1974, and elsewhere). This is especially significant for media markets, where the provision of news and public information is vital for informed citizenship and where the provision of diversified entertainment can facilitate cultural and personal development. It is obvious that in many situations (such as in the United States or in the global market for blockbuster films), a handful of conglomerates dominate the media landscape. By documenting the actual level of competition (or lack of competition), political economic media research challenges the myth of the competitive marketplace under late capitalism. Political economists also are keenly interested in the consequences of such media concentration. For example, much attention has been focused on the influence of concentration on the availability and quality of news, as well as the 'blockbuster complex' and the homogenization of content in cultural industries.

Media and labor

Since the 1970s and 1980s, there has been a steadily growing body of work aimed at understanding the role of labor in the media. Studies of labor, media, and the working class were gathered by Mosco and Wasko (1983), and later by Sussman and Lent (1998). More recent work that has addressed media and labor issues includes Kumar (2008), McKercher and Mosco (2007), Mosco and McKercher (2008), and Maxwell (2015).

Media and state relations

Even though studies of ownership patterns and the dynamics of corporate control are essential, political economic analysis is much more than merely identifying and then condemning those who control media and communication resources. To understand the media's role in society, it is essential to understand relationships between media power and state power, as well as the media's relationships with other economic sectors. While it is often assumed that corporations simply seek relief from government intrusion, it is crucial to understand how the state supports the economy and corporations in various ways. To cite only one example, the US motion picture industry relies on the US government for clearing barriers to foreign markets, as well as in tracking and punishing copyright offenders, both in the Unites States and elsewhere. This relationship involves the film industry's lobbying arm, the Motion Picture Association of America (MPAA), which regularly attempts to influence government policies affecting the industry and its members (for more detail, see Guback 1969; Pendakur 1990).

Schiller and Smythe's work paved the way for a range of issues and themes that focus on media–state relations. Smythe's (1957) early work on the electromagnetic spectrum pointed to the state's role in allocating communication resources and protecting corporate interests. Schiller's *Mass Communication and American Empire* (1969/1992) provided an important analysis of the US government's use of communication resources, especially for military purposes. Meanwhile, other aspects of state policy have also been explored, particularly pertaining to support of the corporate interests in areas such as regulation, intellectual property, and many others. Bettig's (1997) work on intellectual property is an especially good example. Meanwhile, regulation and policy have been the focus of work by many of the previously mentioned researchers, as well as Hills (1986), Streeter (1996), and Calabrese and Burgelman (1999).

Media and democracy

Political economists also have discussed media developments specifically in relation to the public sphere, public citizenship, and democracy. While acknowledging the powerful role that capital plays in media developments, researchers have argued that these issues have a direct bearing on citizenship and public participation. These themes have characterized some of the work of Murdock, Garnham, and McChesney, as well as many others, such as Robert Hackett, Andrew Calabrese, and Cinzia Padovani.

Political economists of communications have investigated these themes and concepts, examining them at various levels of analysis with studies of specific commodities, individual corporations and media industries, as well as national and global media systems. Only a few examples have been cited here, but see Mosco (1996, 2009) for more extensive and detailed overviews of the wide range of work done in the study of the political economy of media.

Political economy of film

The political economy of film must incorporate those characteristics that define political economy generally, as discussed previously, i.e. social change and history, social totality, and moral grounding and praxis. Fundamentally, the political economy of film must understand motion pictures as commodities produced and distributed within a capitalist industrial structure. As Pendakur notes, film as a commodity must be seen as a "tangible product and intangible service" (1990: 39–40). Similar to industrial analysts, the approach is most definitely interested in questions pertaining to market structure and performance, but a political economist analyzing these issues more often would challenge the myths of competition, independence, and globalization, and view the film industry as part of the larger communication and media industry, and society as a whole. For instance, the US film industry is not only important because its films are popular worldwide. Indeed, that is only the tip of the iceberg. Rather than celebrate Hollywood's success, political economists are interested in how US films came to dominate international film markets, what mechanisms are in place to sustain such market dominance, how the state becomes involved, how the export of film is related to marketing of other media products, what the implications are for indigenous film industries in other countries, and what political/cultural implications may stem from the situation.

Most importantly, the political and ideological implications of these economic arrangements are relevant, as film must also be placed within an entire social, economic, and political context and critiqued in terms of the contribution to maintaining and reproducing structures of power. Indeed, the focus on one medium or industry, such as film, may be seen as antithetical to political economy's attempt to go beyond merely describing the economic organization of the media industries. The political economic study of film must incorporate not only a description of the state of the industry, but as Mosco explains, "a theoretical understanding of these developments, situating them within a wider capitalist totality encompassing class and other social relations (offering a) sustained critique from a moral evaluative position" (Mosco 1996: 115).

Some of the key distinctions between political economy and other models is the recognition and critique of the uneven distribution of power and wealth represented by the industry, the attention paid to labor issues and alternatives to commercial film, and the attempts to challenge the industry rather than accepting the status quo.

Examples of studies representing political economy of film

While perhaps not as recognized as other approaches, the political economy of film is represented in a wide range of research. Some classic economic studies fit much of the above description, but were not explicitly identified as political economy. For instance, Klingender and Legg's *Money Behind the Screen* examined finance capital in the film industry in 1937, tracing studio owners and their capitalist backers (Klingender and Legg 1937), while Mae Huettig's study of the film industry in the 1930s documented the power inherent in the various sectors of the industry (Huettig 1944).

Guback's work, especially those studies focusing on international film markets, represents ideal examples of political economy of film. *The International Film Industry* presented primary documentation about how the US domination of European film industries intensified after 1945, with the direct assistance of the US government (Guback 1969). Guback followed this classic study with several articles documenting the international extension of US film companies in the 1970s and 1980s, especially emphasizing the role of the state in these activities (see in particular Guback 1976). In another article, Guback defended a nation's right to resist Hollywood's domination and develop its own film industry based on economic and cultural factors (Guback 1989). Finally, Guback's in-depth outline of the US film industry in *Who Owns the Media?* represents a strong critique of Hollywood structure and practices, as opposed to the other industrially oriented articles in the volume (Guback 1982).

Pendakur's study of the Canadian film industry employs a radical political economy of film, but also incorporates industrial organization theory to examine the market structure of Canadian film. He argues that

> Marxian political economy's concern with power in class societies and its emphasis on a dialectical view of history help explain how the battle to create an indigenous film industry has been fought in Canada, in whose interests, and with what outcome.
> *(1990: 39)*

Pendakur (1998) and Wasko (1998) have examined labor issues in film, adding to the growing literature documenting the history of labor organizations and workers in the US film industry. Meanwhile, Miller *et al.* (2001/2008) attempted to reframe the discussion of global Hollywood in terms of a new international division of cultural labor (NICL). The authors outline Hollywood's global dominance in political economic terms, analyzing the strategies that the US film industry has used to "Americanize" the production, distribution, and exhibition of film.

Wasko's other contributions include *Movies and Money* (1982), which presented the historical development of relationships between Hollywood and financial institutions, and *Hollywood in the Information Age* (1994), which examined continuity and change in the US film industry relating the introduction of new technologies during the 1980s and early 1990s. In addition, Wasko *et al.* (1993) examined the on-going commercialization of film, by focusing on growth of product placement, tie-ins, and merchandising activities in film marketing. More recently, *How Hollywood Works* (2003) employs a political economic analysis to explain the process of production, distribution, and exhibition of Hollywood film commodities.

Meanwhile, many other scholars have taken a political economic approach in looking at various aspects of film. Nicholas Garnham incorporated an analysis of the "Economics of the US Motion Picture Industry" to exemplify the production of culture in his collection, *Capitalism and Communication* (Garnham 1990). Aksoy and Robins' study of the motion picture industry also is a good example of a study that focuses on issues on concentration and globalization, and draws fundamentally on political economy (Aksoy and Robins 1992) Another similar example is Prindle's *Risky Business: The Political Economy of Hollywood* (1993), while a rare example of political economy used to analyze Hollywood outside of film or media studies is Hozic (2002). A reviewer of the study noted that Hozic "examines the political economy of film through the lens of geography, adding the dimension of space to the dimensions of power and wealth" (rear cover of Hozic 2002).

Despite these various studies, it still might be argued that political economy is much less common in film studies than in communication research. If so, then why? It is possible that Guback's explanations in the essay mentioned at the beginning of this chapter are still relevant. He argued that one of the reasons that there is so much textual film analysis is the relatively easy access to film texts to study. In other words, scholars depend on the material that is available for study, whether film texts or industry-supplied information. Even though more popular media attention now centers on the film or entertainment industry through stories and programs (such as *Entertainment Tonight*), including stories that explore film production and box office numbers, it is mostly coverage generated by the industry itself and hardly critical.

Indeed, it is sometimes still a challenge to find reliable and relevant data about the film industry on which to base a critical analysis. For instance, where can one find accurate production figures beyond the rumor mill, as reported in *Variety* or other trade publications? The preoccupation with box office receipts that has developed recently often draws attention to the mystical accounting methods used by Hollywood to determine profit and loss for specific films. Other areas also remain mired in mystery, as well; for instance, where is it possible to find accurate or meaningful figures on stock ownership of film companies or the corporations that own them?

The type of information that is available tends to lend itself especially well to congratulatory coverage of the industry's triumphs. But it also might be argued that much scholarly writing on the industry is not critical, anyway, resisting any criticism of the status quo, and basically supportive of the way things are. Even when information is available, the commercial and profit-motivated goals of the industry are assumed, and rarely questioned.

On the other hand, one might also wonder why film is less often included in much of the work in political economy of communication. While film appears in general overviews of communication or media industries, it seems to receive less careful analysis than other forms of media or communication (Jowett and Linton 1980). One obvious reason may be the academic fragmentation that still sometimes separates film studies from media and communication studies, in university organizational charts, certain professional organizations, and scholarly journals. Of course, one explanation is that film studies typically has been based in the humanities, while communication and media studies tend to draw more on the social sciences. Beyond this fragmentation, though, there also may be different perceptions of film's importance for communication scholars. Film still often represents 'only entertainment,' thus not as worthy of scholarly attention as news and information programming, or computer and information technologies.

These oversights need to be addressed if we are to understand film in its actual social context. These days, film must be considered as part of the larger communications and media industry. More than ever before, distribution outlets such as cable and satellite services link news, information and entertainment programs; and sometime in the future, it seems likely that there will be further links via new digital and multimedia forms. It is no longer novel to observe that news is looking more like entertainment, with new forms evolving and assuming the shape of infotainment, docudramas, and other formats.

But importantly, these activities are, more than ever, under the same corporate ownership. Films are produced by the same companies that are involved with other media and communications activities, and it is no secret that fewer and fewer giant corporations control these activities. These transnational corporations have diversified into all areas of the media, sometimes attempting to maximize profitability by building synergy between their corporate divisions. For some of these companies, film plays a key role in these synergistic efforts, as corporations such as the Walt Disney Company build product lines which begin with a film, but continue through television, cable, publishing, theme parks, merchandising, etc. These days, companies like Disney not only distribute products to these outlets, but also own the outlets. In addition, it may be useful for communication scholars to look more closely at the international expansion of the US film industry to better understand the historical evolution of current globalization trends. While the expansion of global markets may be relatively new for some media, the US film industry developed global marketing techniques as early as the 1920s and continues its dominant position in international media markets today.

Political economy of media and media industry studies

Despite the broad definitions discussed previously, the study of political economy of communication is still often considered narrow and deterministic, accused of focusing primarily on the economic or on the production side of the communication process, and neglecting texts, audiences, and consumption. Another common misconception is that political economists are concerned only with ownership and control questions.

Over the years, political economists have defended their theoretical positions and research from extreme and inaccurate accusations, but also have attempted to respond to reasonable criticism of the approach (compare Murdock and Golding 1974; Murdock 1995). Some of this discussion has taken place in the flurries of theoretical debates between political economy and cultural studies (for instance, Garnham 1995; Grossberg 1995).

More recently, during the 1990s, a number of approaches emerged in Media Studies building on the work of a few film scholars while asking questions similar to those explored by political economists. These 'new' approaches have fallen under various rubrics, including creative industries, convergence culture, production culture, production studies, cultural economy, and media industry studies. These developments are well represented by the growth of Media Industry Studies and the founding of the SCMS Media Industry Studies Scholarly Interest Group, which has continued to rapidly increase in popularity.

The explications of these 'new' approaches have often included a rejection of political economy as a viable framework for studying the media. Certainly, the choice of a theoretical framework is up to the researcher and a political economic perspective is only one of the lenses that can be used to understand media. However, these 'new' approaches often present political economic approaches in a distorted and inaccurate manner. These misrepresentations may be especially obvious given the previous history and discussion presented in this chapter.

In their edited collection devoted to Media Industry Studies, Holt and Perren (2009) state that they intend to provide a framework for the 'new field': "While the world does not necessarily need another field of study, one has indeed emerged" (2009: 2). In another example, Havens *et al.* (2009) have outlined an approach called 'critical media industries studies.' They argue that this was part of Cultural Studies from its very beginning but was eclipsed by textual analysis and reception studies. Consequently, scholars have used various phrases to describe middle-range studies of the managerial and production employees working in media operations. They seek to unify these various studies under the umbrella of critical media industries.

The increased attention to institutional and economic dimensions of the media is appreciated. These 'new' approaches claim to draw on existing theoretical frameworks, such as cultural studies and political economy. However, most often, the theories, methods, and findings of political economy are ultimately rejected. Some of the accusations have to do with the level of analysis and which media are studied:

> Critical political economy approaches, which predominantly and consistently focus on the larger level operations of media institutions – and, *with few exceptions, emphasize news production* – have been a favored paradigm among many media scholars looking to add an industrial dimension to their research.
>
> (*Havens* et al. *2009: 235, emphasis added)*

A neglect of entertainment and/or cultural media is thus claimed to limit "the usefulness of many political-economic theories and perspectives, which are based on the industrial analysis of news" (Havens *et al.* 2009: 236).

The analysis of political economy of the media, according to Havens *et al.*, represents a consistent

> focus on the larger level operations of media institutions, general inattention to entertainment programming, and incomplete explanation of the role of human agents (other than those at the pinnacle of conglomerate hierarchies) in interpreting, focusing, and redirecting economic forces that provide for complexity and contradiction within media industries.
>
> *(2009: 237)*

Overall, the claim is that political economy is "reductive, simplistic, and too economistic" (Hesmondalgh 2009: 237). Thus, the new critiques have joined the old ones, adding elements of misrepresentation in addition to ideological positioning and red-baiting.

Conclusion

As noted previously, issues related to economics, industrial structure, and policies of film and television are finally attracting more attention through the growth of 'new' fields – media economics, media industry studies, production cultures, etc. Meanwhile, political economy represents a distinct approach to studying media and communication, which has grown dramatically during the last few decades. However, the approach has not received as much recognition within cinema studies. When it does, it is still often misrepresented and/or rejected. This is unfortunate as the political economic approach offers an insightful and critically important lens by which to view media, which is still dominated by commercial enterprises and capitalist principles that need to be understood through critical and unidealized analysis.

Note

1 This chapter is based on the following previous publications: "The Study of the Political Economy of the Media in the Twenty-First Century" *International Journal of Media and Cultural Politics*, 10(3), 2014; "Understanding the Critical Political Economy of the Media" in Cliff Christians and Kaarle Nordenstreng (eds), *Communication Theories in a Multicultural World*, New York: Peter Lang, 2014; "Critical Crossroads or Parallel Route?: Political Economy and New Approaches to Studying Media Industries and Cultural Products" (with Eileen Meehan), *Cinema Journal*, 52(3) Spring 2013; "The

Political Economy of Film" in Toby Miller and Robert Stam (eds) *A Companion to Film Theory*, Oxford: Blackwell, 1999, 2004.

Bibliography

Aksoy, A. and Robins, K. (1992) "Hollywood for the 21st Century: Global Competition for Critical Mass in Image Markets" *Cambridge Journal of Economics* 16(1), pp. 1–22.

Bettig, R. (1997) *Copyrighting Culture: The Political Economy of Intellectual Property*, Boulder, CO: Westview.

Calabrese, A. and Burgelman, J. (eds) (1999) *Communication, Citizenship and Social Policy*, Boulder, CO: Rowman & Littlefield.

Garnham, N. (1990) *Capitalism and Communication: Global Culture and the Economics of Information*, London: Sage Publications.

Garnham, N. (1995) "Political Economy and Cultural Studies: Reconciliation or Divorce?" *Critical Studies in Mass Communication* 12(1), pp. 62–71.

Golding, P. and Murdock, G. (1991) "Culture, Communication, and Political Economy" in Curran, J. and Gurevitch, M. (eds) *Mass Media and Society*, London: Edward Arnold, pp. 15–32.

Grossberg, L. (1995) "Cultural Studies vs. Political Economy: Is Anybody Else Bored with This Debate?" *Critical Studies in Mass Communication* 12(1), pp. 72–81.

Guback, T. (1969) *The International Film Industry: Western Europe and America Since 1945*, Bloomington, IN: Indiana University Press.

Guback, T. (1976) "Hollywood's International Market" in Balio, T. (ed.) *The American Film Industry*, Madison: The University of Wisconsin Press, pp. 463–486.

Guback, T. (1978) "Are We Looking at the Right Things in Film?" Paper presented at the Society for Cinema Studies conference, Philadelphia, PA.

Guback, T. (1982) "Theatrical Film" in Compaine, B. (ed.) *Who Owns the Media? Concentration of Ownership in the Mass Communications Industry*, White Plains, NY: Knowledge Industry Publications, pp. 179–249.

Guback, T. (1989) "Should a Nation Have Its Own Film Industry?" *Directions* 3(1), pp. 489–492.

Havens, T., Lotz, A., and Tinic, S. (2009) "Critical Media Industry Studies: A Research Approach" *Communication, Culture & Critique* 2(2), pp. 234–253.

Hesmondalgh, D. (2009) "Politics, Theory, and Method in Media Industries Research" in Holt, J. and Perren, A. (eds) *Media Industries: History, Theory, and Method*, Malden, MA: Wiley-Blackwell, pp. 245–255.

Hills, J. (1986) *Deregulating Telecoms: Competition and Control in the United States, Japan and Britain*, London: Frances Pinter.

Holt, J. and Perren, A. (2009) "Introduction: Does the World Really Need One More Field of Study?" in Holt, J. and Perren, A. (eds) *Media Industries: History, Theory, and Method*, Malden, MA: Wiley-Blackwell, pp. 1–16.

Hozic, A. (2002) *Hollyworld: Space, Power, and Fantasy in the American Economy*, Ithaca, NY: Cornell University Press.

Huettig, M. D. (1944) *Economic Control of the Motion Picture Industry*, Philadelphia, PA: University of Pennsylvania Press.

Jevons, W. S. (1970) *The Theory of Political Economy*, Harmondsworth: Penguin.

Jowett, G. and Linton, J. M. (1980) *Movies as Mass Communication*, Beverly Hills, CA: Sage Publications.

Klingender, F. D. and Legg, S. (1937) *Money behind the Screen*, London: Lawrence & Wishart.

Kumar, D. (2008) *Outside the Box: Corporate Media, Globalization and the UPS Strike*, Urbana: University of Illinois Press.

Marx, K. (1845/1945) *Ludwig Feuerbach and the End of Classical German Philosophy*, Moscow: Progress Publishers.

Maxwell, R. (ed.) (2015) *The Routledge Companion to Labor and Media*, New York: Routledge.

McKercher, C. and Mosco, V. (eds) (2007) *Knowledge Workers in the Information Society*, Lanham, MD: Lexington.

Miller, T., Govil, N., McMurria, J., and Maxwell, R. (2001/2008) *Global Hollywood*, London: BFI.

Miller, T., Govil, N., McMurria, J., Maxwell, R., and Wang, T. (2008) *Global Hollywood 2*, London: BFI.

Mosco, V. (1996) *The Political Economy of Communication: Rethinking and Renewal*, London: Sage Publications.

Mosco, V. (2009) *The Political Economy of Communication*, 2nd edition, London: Sage.
Mosco, V. and McKercher, C. (2008) *The Laboring of Communication: Will Knowledge Workers of the World Unite?*, Lanham, MD: Lexington.
Mosco, V. and Wasko, J. (eds) (1983) *The Critical Communications Review. Vol. 1: Labor, the Working Class and the Media*, Norwood, NJ: Ablex.
Murdock, G. (1995) "Across the Great Divide: Cultural Analysis and the Condition of Democracy" *Critical Studies in Mass Communication*, 12(1), pp. 89–95.
Murdock, G. and Golding, P. (1974) "For a Political Economy of Mass Communications" in Miliband, R. and Saville, J. (eds) *Socialist Register*, London: Merlin Press, pp. 205–234.
Murdock, G. and Golding, P. (1979) "Capitalism, Communication and Class Relations" in Curran, J., Gurevitch, M., and Woollacott, J. (eds) *Mass Communication and Society*, Beverly Hills, CA: Sage Publications, pp. 12–43.
Murdock, G. and Wasko, J. (eds) (2007) *Media in the Age of Marketization*, Cresskill, NJ: Hampton.
Pendakur, M. (1990) *Canadian Dreams and American Control: The Political Economy of the Canadian Film Industry*, Detroit, MI: Wayne State University Press.
Pendakur, M. (1998) "Hollywood North: Film and TV Production in Canada" in Sussman, G. and Lent, J. A. (eds) *Global Productions: Labor in the Making of the 'Information Society'*, Cresskill, NJ, Hampton Press, pp. 213–238.
Prindle, D. F. (1993) *Risky Business: The Political Economy of Hollywood*, Boulder, CO: Westview Press.
Schiller, H. I. (1969/1992) *Mass Communication and American Empire*, Boston, MA: Beacon.
Smith, A. (1776/1937) *An Inquiry into the Nature and Causes of the Wealth of Nations*, New York: Random House.
Smythe, D. W. (1957) *The Structure and Policy of Electronic Communications*, Urbana, IL: University of Illinois Press.
Smythe, D. W. (1960) "On the Political Economy of Communication" *Journalism and Mass Communication Quarterly* 37(4), Autumn, pp. 563–572.
Streeter, T. (1996) *Selling the Air: A Critique of the Policy of Commercial Broadcasting in the United States*, Chicago: University of Chicago Press.
Sussman, G. and Lent, J. A. (eds) (1998) *Global Productions: Labor in the Making of the "Information Society"*, Cresskill, NJ: Hampton.
Wasko, J. (1982) *Movies and Money: Financing the American Film Industry*, Norwood, NJ: Ablex Publishing.
Wasko, J. (1994) *Hollywood in the Information Age: Beyond the Silver Screen*, Cambridge, MA: Polity Press.
Wasko, J. (1998) "Challenges to Hollywood's Labor Force in the 1990s" in Sussman, G. and Lent, J. A. (eds) *Global Productions: Labor in the Making of the "Information Society"*, Cresskill, NJ, Hampton Press, pp. 173–190.
Wasko, J. (2003) *How Hollywood Works*, London, Sage Publications.
Wasko, J., Phillips, M., and Purdie, C. (1993) "Hollywood Meets Madison Ave.: The Commercialization of US Films" *Media, Culture and Society* 15(2), pp. 271–293.

PART II

Cinema, activism and opposition

INTRODUCTION

Anthony Killick

The flippancy with which terms like "activism", "social change" and "human rights" are espoused and equated, in scholarship and activist circles, may lead us to believe that they are interchangeable and self-justifying. In fact, such terms are empty signifiers. They can only be qualified by the end/s to which they attach themselves. Even those activists working towards something as specific as "long-term social change" need to recognise that this is also the goal of neo-liberalism and its harbingers. Indeed, that the vacuity of such terms leaves them open to appropriation by the incentives of capital is well evidenced in our contemporary age of 'lifestyle activism' and 'social entrepreneurship'. As Harvey notes, "we live in a world, after all, where the rights of private property and the profit rate trump all other notions of rights one can think of" (2012: 3).

Historically speaking, film and video activists have been acutely aware of the socio-political aims toward which they are working. The question of the extent to which the aims, aesthetics and methods of video activism corroborate with those of dominant institutions has been at the forefront of a politically conscious praxis. However, since the 1970s the downfall of the classical Marxist narrative and its replacement by a Thatcher/Reagan-inflected liberal pluralism has had a drastic effect on popular ideas regarding political legitimacy, action and protest. At the same time, the proliferation of cheaper filmmaking, distribution and exhibition technologies does not in itself make video activism a more viable tool of opposition, insofar as these developments occur under the spatial, temporal and financial command of neoliberalism. Thus the contemporary landscape of video activism is formed by the shifting relation between cultural production and domestic as well as geo-politics, with video activists carving their way through in as best a way they can according to their relative prohibitions.

As the chapters in this part show, video activism has taken many forms, and been utilised in the pursuit of numerous causes, with varying degrees of efficacy. It is within and through networks that collaborative projects begin to take shape and struggle to influence wider political developments. This is crucial to understanding cultural production, particularly, as Scott Baugh notes, throughout Latin America since the turn of the century. Baugh's chapter on contemporary Latin American media co-operatives contrasts these 'new' cinemas with those of the militant New Latin American Cinema that emerged in the late 1960s. Here, we see how the movement responded to a changing political situation over the course of decades. Baugh's discussion on the role of indigenous media again shows how control over the means of cultural production becomes key to constituting subjectivity, and in the Latin American context, sovereignty.

Anat Pick's chapter on animal rights films shows how video activists have shot and exhibited undercover footage to expose the conditions of abattoirs to a meat-consuming public. Framing normalised mass slaughter as a "war against nonhuman animals", Pick alludes to a society in which barbarism is hidden in plain sight. Thus exposure via animal rights films must be accompanied by a new "politics of seeing" that seeks not only to recognise but extend animal rights.

Steve Presence highlights the ways in which the culture of video activism has been altered since the 1990s, resulting largely from political and technological developments to which radical video activists have had to adapt. Here 'radical' describes an anti-capitalist political avant-garde that encompasses a number of organisations which, over the past couple of decades, directed their efforts toward issues around environmentalism and globalisation. Presence's discussion of Reel News presents a shift in orientation to include more class-conscious practices, raising important questions about alternative funding models for media that strive to exist as far as possible outside of the 'market'.

This tendency towards subverting restrictions is both necessary and ideologically permissible (if not desirable) to many video activists. It transpires not only in film production and exhibition, but in the extension of the means of cultural production to disenfranchised groups. As Deirdre O' Neill notes in her chapter on filmmaking as a radical pedagogical tool, this can facilitate a transcendence of the discursive regime advanced by the mainstream media, particularly in relation to the working class. O'Neill's Inside Film project gives prisoners and ex-prisoners the means with which to constitute their own subjectivities (as opposed to having representations of their own lives imposed on them from above) via an examination of the world through film production. Her chapter describes the project's roots in a Marxist analysis of class relations and the development of a praxis inspired by the radical strategies of Third Cinema. This emphasis on pedagogy highlights the multi-faceted applications of counter-hegemonic cultural production and the search for effective modes of resistance to the detrimental effects of capital.

Leshu Torchin's analysis of the "Kony 2012" campaign video made by the non-governmental organisation, Invisible Children, highlights a form of video activism that has in many ways suffered those effects, oriented as it is towards consumerism and visual hyperbole. Nevertheless, the initial success of the campaign in attracting huge amounts of attention to a single issue warrants further analysis. Torchin looks at the relations between testimony, advocacy, mimesis and the type of activism the "Stop Kony" campaign sought to inspire, developing in her analysis some ideas of how public spheres can be built and connected to each other.

As well as being one of the primary mediators of the world, film has the capacity to alter physical and mental space. Thus video activists are key players in a hegemonic struggle. At the same time, the applications of video activism are as multifarious as the shifting socio-political contexts in which praxis develops. However, this does not mean that we should err on the side of a vacuous pluralism that risks neoliberal colonisation. Rather, it is essential, both in theory and practice, to engage in the kinds of discussion presented here so as to maintain a properly democratic opposition.

Bibliography

Harvey, D. (2012) *Rebel Cities: From the Right to the City to the Urban Revolution*. London & New York: Verso.

6

"NEW" NEW LATIN AMERICAN CINEMA MANIFESTOES

Scott L. Baugh

The *levantamiento* (uprising) of June 1990 in Ecuador, figured alongside the solstice festival *Inti Raymi* honoring the Inca sun god, represents a watershed moment not only for Latin American Indigenous political movements but for multiculturalism across the Americas leading into the twenty-first century. Initiated by the pacific occupation of Santo Domingo Cathedral in Quito, thousands of protestors throughout the country rallied for over a week in organized protests – parading the streets, blockading traffic, sitting-in at public spaces, and vocalizing statements of rights and justice. Clashes with police resulted in incarcerations and some injury, but the protests were almost entirely diplomatic and non-violent in aim and action. Within days, "*16 Puntos*," a sixteen-point plan, was delivered to then-President Rodrigo Borja, a call to reconstitute "economic development" issues like territorial ownership and land usage, conservation and preservation of natural resources, taxation, legal citizenship, trade, and privatization of public services specifically with Indigenous perspectives and claims in consideration (CONAIE 1991 [1990]: 41). The body of this uprising, CONAIE (Confederation of Indigenous Nationalities of Ecuador), a pan-Indigenous group formed four years prior, grew from the events and, from hemispheric meetings, launched the larger-scale *Declaration of Quito* (1990), which emphasizes communication networks, syncretic knowledge and beliefs systems, and the incorporation of traditional information with modern technology. These documents advance the movement's aggressive agendas for Indigenous representation and renewed autonomy and sovereignty; they aim at radically progressive realignments of State policies and bureaucracies; they acknowledge complex negotiations among levels of independence and inter-relatedness communally, nationally, and globally; and they fuse crucial symbolic, cultural, political, and economic aspects of American identity in the charge of democratic and humane pluralism; yet, in spite of restive qualities, the documents also engender conciliation and reciprocal exchange, communication, and coordination.

That the uprising implemented and benefitted from these collateral documents, their manifestoes, is likely not terribly surprising. A manifesto serves as a public pronouncement of principles, objectives, and more, especially surrounding the political aspects of an organization's activities. They can report the past, discern the present, and project the future. They frequently disclose and address alternatives to the canon and mainstream and thereby invite change. Rather than strictly limiting, manifestoes may range 'political' issues – from State bureaucracy and institutional enforcement of governance and citizenship, commerce, social justice, and human rights to the daily-lived cultural transformations and identifications, some pointed and mundane and others sweeping and symbolic, that can transcend any discrete conceptions of politics, nation, law, ideology, property, and economy. Manifestoes maintain a long-standing and significant tradition within Latin American political culture – and this is never truer than in the politics surrounding Latin American cinema and cultural production since the late 1960s. What may prove surprising, however, is that select contemporary organizations and their manifestoes stand in distinction from those of previous generations that have been characterized largely by militant rhetoric and defiant postures. These contemporary organizations emphasize cooperation, sustainable resourcefulness, and diversity even as they extend a significant political-arts legacy in Latin America.

Organizations like CONAIE and their complementary manifestoes offer a useful point of departure from which to examine this significant shift in Latin American cultural production at the turn to the twenty-first century. Reassessing the renowned New Latin American Cinema and then reappraising its political-arts project, this chapter attests to the profound but too frequently overlooked emergence of cooperative multicultural media in Latin America. The rise of coalitional media networks throughout Latin America resituates knowledge bases, which propose revolutionary alternative development models that afford identity and autonomy for traditionally disenfranchised citizens and institute progressive forms of American cultural citizenship leading into the twenty-first century. In their challenge to prevalent developmental models, these contemporary media organizations override the encumbrances of neoliberalism and provide for reasonably limited sovereignty and agency. The force of these revolutionary turns resides in coalition-building initiatives within and among independent but inter-related organizations that intervene on state-sponsorship restrictions and corporate-capitalist values dictated by 'first-world order' regimes but do so precisely through conciliatory methods rather than traditionally understood (and mainstream media sensationalized) militancy and oppositional politics. The intertextual relationships among Latin American cinema, its makers and audiences, and correlative manifestoes avouch the arrival of coalitional networks, cooperative informatics, and differential cultural identities across a range of vital political issues. Like their 'New Latin American Cinema' predecessors, representative contemporary media cooperatives in Latin America privilege the role manifestoes have played in the formulation of 'new' Latin American cinemas.

New Latin American Cinema's establishment

The 1967 Latin American Cinema festival in Viña del Mar, Chile, officially pronounced a cinema culture – through films and manifestoes especially, but also festivals, journals, schools, archives, state-sponsored institutions, and more – politically committed in theory and practice to a militant rhetoric of cultural nationalism and oppositionality: New Latin American Cinema (NLAC) proceeds as an anti-establishment (Aufderheide 1991: 63–64; Pick, 1993: 13–21). Addressing one of the formative films of the movement, *The Hour of the Furnaces* (1968) directed by Fernando Solanas and Octavio Getino, Robert Stam definitively describes "two avant-gardes" – one formal and based on artistic innovation, the other political and infused with "Third World radicalism," "connoting political as well as cultural militancy" – that converge aesthetics and politics as a "model for cinematic practice"; the model's "charging" with "a precise revolutionary signification" derives largely from its invocation of camera-as-gun imagery (1981: 151–152). Solanas and Getino's landmark manifesto, "Towards a Third Cinema" (1969), equally emphasizes militancy inextricably linked to the hope for a "transforming world-view" and the need to reimagine "the System" of world relations (1997: 47, 42–43).

Militancy figures into the revolutionary quality of NLAC, its perturbations awakening consciousness, *la conciencia*, in and from cultural productions, expressedly in Latin American films and manifestoes of the period (Burton 1978). The pan-Latin American movement's successes were dedicated, in spite of national, regional, and communal distinctions, to common "struggles" across the continent for "cultural, political, and economic autonomy," distinguished "by comparison to the standard or dominant" models, thus maintaining a "tenacious, albeit often problematic, unity" (López 1988: 93–96; King 1990; Rich 1991). Histories relate the backstory of Latin American cinema – the earliest trends followed European traditions; the arrival of sound entered select cinemas into a "golden age"; and several national industries emerged in competition with but also adopting and extending the aesthetics, corporate mechanisms, and capitalist machinations of Hollywood over periods of growth and decline concurrent with their regional and national economies and political stability, particularly in Mexico, Brazil, and Argentina, and across international co-productions. Countercultural and political shifts there and in Cuba, Chile, Bolivia, Colombia, Venezuela, and elsewhere in the 1950s and 1960s drew attention to relatively radical expressions in film and film culture (Burton 1986). Out of this late-1960s context was born the NLAC. The movement opposed not only the aesthetics and industry of mainstream cinema. More fundamentally, NLAC reacted against the very bases of the world-system political economy – whereby richer 'first-world' countries are considered 'developed'; poorer 'third-world' countries function as labor, resource suppliers, and consumers in the world market; 'developing' countries are thereby 'dependent' upon the system; and valuations, literal and figurative, are skewed toward Eurocentric values and particular notions of 'modern' industrialism. Countries are supposed to 'evolve' into development, and decades forward through the close of the twentieth century, into the twenty-first century, generations of neoliberalism across the Americas have prioritized corporate privatization and capitalist trade, and enforced dominant models of economic development to determine, among other things, community and individual cultural citizenship and identity. Certainly the most pervasive themes and clearest objectives of NLAC films and manifestoes dispute precisely these reigning notions of 'development' and the 'dependency' they dictate, momentous battles fought and won, and this may prove NLAC's legacy to be carried forward by later generations of alternative political-art cinema.

An established body of scholarship rightly points to what Zuzana Pick describes as the "continental project" of the NLAC, organizing the relatively diverse collection of fiction and nonfiction, feature and short-program, large- and small-gauge films, later some television and video too, in strategic coordination with their primary means of "promoting their work more widely," their political manifestoes, around militant agendas armed and mobilized by a "consciousness of underdevelopment" (Pick 1993: 18; *Hojas* 1988; Martin 1997). Alongside Solanas and Getino's "Towards a Third Cinema", the manifesto complement to *The Hour of the Furnaces*, leading figures of the NLAC include:

- Fernando Birri's "Cinema and Underdevelopment" (1967);
- Julio García Espinosa's "For an Imperfect Cinema" (1970);
- Glauber Rocha's "The Aesthetics of Hunger" (1965);
- With the collective *Ukamau* (Aymara for "the way it is"), Jorge Sanjinés's "Problems of Form and Content in Revolutionary Cinema" (1979);
- Tomás Gutierrez Alea's "The Viewer's Dialectic" (1982).

With the 1987 New Latin American Cinema festival, held in Havana, Cuba, commemorating the twentieth anniversary of the groundbreaking Viña del Mar meeting, anxiety and quiet doubts among veterans of the movement met disaffection from newcomers, and debates ensued over the viability of NLAC (Aufderheide 1991; *Nuevo* 1988). Witnesses of this festival were left to wonder if the continental project could revive itself, must reinvent itself, or accept its own demise. Presenting at this meeting, Julianne Burton offers one of the keenest insights: debates of this sort are "a natural if not inevitable part of the process of institutionalization of the New Latin American Cinema" (1988: 5). Corresponding with the late-1980s and 1990s contexts, the radical political-aesthetic experiments that voiced anti-establishment consciousness-building sentiment in late-1960s milieu grew into the "institution" of NLAC, an alternative establishment hampered by its own contravening militancy.

Ironic 'developments' in Latin American Cinema

Amid the recession and failings of NLAC's militant rhetoric as consequent of its "consciousness of underdevelopment" – as well as the liberating forces provided extensively by that militancy – the movement found itself at a crossroads, if not at cross-purposes, and marched in different directions. A host of filmmakers associated with the formative period continued filming and writing manifestoes into the 1980s and forward, trying to stabilize a later period of NLAC. Akin to Glauber Rocha's "ever more extreme and contradictory polemics" by the late 1970s (quoted in Burton, 1978: 54–55), his prophetic political stance that "revolutionary truth lies within the minorities" contests his own characterization of his art as "full of enthusiasm, faith, and militancy" and of the Brazilian Cinema Novo as a synthesis of popular cinemas – and neverminding his 1965 manifesto "Down with Populism" (quoted in Marcorelles, 1978; Burton, 1986: 105–114). Jorge Sanjinés' *Ukamau* projects, the films *La Nación Clandestina* (1989) and *Insurgentes* (2012) and manifesto "The Integral Sequence Shot" (1989), for example, represent an aim to reach back to militant, oppositional strategies but may also suffer due to their isolation from and inaccessibility to contemporary audiences in a thoroughly globalized marketplace (Wood 2012).

A segment of formative NLAC figures adopts increasingly commercial and conventional tendencies, exemplified by the period's "New Mexican Cinema" – seen in the range of films like Jomi García Ascot's *En el Balcón Vacío* (1961) to Paul Leduc's *Reed: Mexico Insurgente* (1970) and in *El Grupo de Nuevo Cine*'s 1961 manifesto (Treviño, 1979). Arguably, some post-1980s NLAC cultural production reaches mainstream expectations through closer affinities to film conventions and genres, critical schools, industrial mechanisms, and cultural traditions than pre-1980s indicated. And individual 'stars' detracted some attention from the collectivism of the continental project and thwarted new pledges. Across the diversity of Latin American cultural production since the 1960s, "Third Cinema" does not equate to "'Third World' Cinema," as Paul Willemen emphasizes, but rather enacts political-aesthetic explorations in cinema (1989). Had NLAC "Third Cinema" *developed*, itself, into an avant-garde institution, an alternative to Second Cinema's art film and auteurism? Like *Nuevo Cine Mexicano*, the "Manifesto for a Popular Cinema" (1975), compiled by Cineclub Macunaíma from Nelson Pereira dos Santos' interview comments, also teases out complicated notions of commercialism within Latin American media. Full departures from his 1969 work, Solanas' *Sur* (1988) and its accompanying book-length manifesto *La Mirada* (1989) may replace political context with social allegory but more fully explore theoretico-aesthetic extensions of Latin American arts to world cinema schools. Getino's post-1980s writing largely turns to industrial standards across production and distribution mechanisms and platforms, converting NLAC interests into mainstream-corporate currency (1988; 1990; 1996). And Birri's 1986 manifesto "For a Filmmaker of Three Worlds in the Year 2000" (1996) as well as his 2000–2001 lectures at Stanford University (2007) conjoin the "*Nueva Nueva Cine Latinoamericano*," the "New New Latin American Cinema," with state-sponsored institutional settings, expressedly Cuba's EICTV, the International School of Film and Television, which he co-founded with Julio García Espinosa and Gabriel García Márquez. Ana M. López succinctly surmises: "the ideals and practices of the New Latin American Cinema have become the norm for the continent," "no longer necessarily a marginal cinema" (1988, 114–116) by the last decade of the twentieth century.

To Nestor García Canclini's (1997) famous and vexing question, "will there be a Latin American Cinema in 2000?," most recent cinema scholarship effectively attempts to reconcile the paradoxical relationship between NLAC's initial anti-establishment militancy and the alternative establishment it has become (Nagib 2003; Alvaray 2008; Schroeder Rodríguez 2012); to a great extent, scholarship looks to a cinema in the pattern of global commercialism and mainstream traditions. Withal, B. Ruby Rich warns, judging Latin American cultural production by a "fixed" political-aesthetic relationship based on the militancy of NLAC "early classics" condemns the political art and artists as "victim[s] of a stereotype" (1991: 5). Patricia Aufderheide smartly points to the "ideological ambition" of "grassroots video in Latin America" that echoes NLAC's legacy (2000), and the argument only gains profundity as accessibility to emerging networked media and technologies increases. If the effectiveness of NLAC's militancy declined by the late 1980s, what may prove the continental project's likeliest heir to a radical political-arts agenda through the 1990s and turning to the twenty-first century, this chapter argues, is a body of alternative media emphasizing greater diversity and sustainability in its cooperative strategies and coalitional organizations.

A dimension of twenty-first-century Latin American Cinema

In a groundswell of activity since the late 1980s, media organizations throughout the Americas have taken up activist causes initiated by the NLAC through current and emerging information-communication technologies (ICTs), and manifestoes serve key functions programmatically in articulating and directing political, cultural, and figurative components of these latest network technologies around their revolutionary call. Like the formative NLAC, this contemporary body of work combines politics with aesthetic innovation into transformative processes that detour hegemonic forces. It is creatively resourceful and diverse – predominantly short-program non-fiction but with notable reaches into features and fiction, epistolary, animation, *memoria*-ritualistic, and other experimental or nontraditional modes. Even more than NLAC, it experiments with multimedia and draws special strength from electronic and digital options, especially around current video and internet and promises of mobile telephony and broadband technologies. Whereas some later NLAC borrows from and converts to the mainstream for commercial advantage, contemporary media initiatives provocatively integrate convention and tradition without jeopardizing communal, localized, and ancestral information and expression. Mobility and supranationality of the media programs complicate conceptions of community beyond essentialistic categories of race, ethnicity, or nationality even as they draw networked strength to relatively divergent goals; furthermore, finances take advantage of various government, corporate, commercial, non-profit, and individual resources commensurate with circumstance and availability (Himpele, 2004: 354; Córdova and Schnell, 2005; Ranucci and Burton, 1990). Still, reconceptualizing 'development' and breaking Western dependency has remained of paramount concern across these ages of Latin America cinema. Extending the

NLAC legacy, these media organizations uphold complicated notions of independence (especially practically around finances) alongside pluralist political topics, multicultural aesthetics, and collectivist dynamics: the hallmark quality of this latest "new" Latin American Cinema's continental project amplifies these equally radical cooperative strategies in coalitional organizations, forming and representing social solidarity and, crucially, aiming for greater diversity and sustainability through networks and syncretic knowledge bases.

With strongholds in northern Brazil, southern Mexico, Bolivia, Colombia, and Ecuador, the cooperative media organizations typically cross national boundaries and provide a number of different products and services according to the needs of the communities and individuals they serve without succumbing to capitalist-commercial restrictions. And of no small importance, like their NLAC counterparts, many contemporary media initiatives promote themselves through manifesto declarations and reports. With CONAIE, among the exemplary stand:

- Lilith Video Collective, 1983–1994, founded by Jacira de Melo, Marcia Meireles, and Silvana Afram, with "Broadcast Feminism," the collective's interview with Julianne Burton and Julia Lesage (1988);
- *Vídeo nas Aldeias* (VNA) (Video in the Villages), started in 1987 as a project under a Brazilian NGO, and the *Um Olhar Indígena* (*Through Indian Eyes*) exhibition catalog (Corrêa 2004), including complementary manifestoes by co-directors Vincent Carelli and Mari Corrêa and Ashaninka video artist Isaac Pinhanta;
- *TV dos Trabalhadores* (Workers' TV) and "The Third Age of TV" by the group's founders, Regina Festa and Luiz Fernando Santoro (1991);
- CEFREC (Cinematography Education and Production Center), its founding coordinator Iván Sanjinés, son of Jorge Sanjinés, and CAIB (Bolivian Indigenous People's Audiovisual Council), its president Jesús Tapia, first partnering in 1996 and over subsequent years co-producing *The National Indigenous Plan for Audiovisual Communication* (CEFREC-CAIB 2013 [2006]);
- CMCM, the Center for Mayan Women Communicators – shorthanded "*Nutzij*," Maya-Kaqchikel for "my word," – and its 2000 director's report by Fermina Chiyal Jiatz;
- Aligned with early-1990s Zapatista/EZLN movements, the Chiapas Media Project (*Promedios de Comunicación Comunitaria*) (CMP/*Promedios*) and the manifesto-report "Outside the Indigenous Lens" (2008 [2006]) by its founding director, Alexandra Halkin;
- *Ojo de Agua Comunicación* collective's "*Plan Rector 2012–2014*" (2013), updating and referencing its 2000–2001 "*Plan de Trabajo*" ("Work Plan");
- *Somos@telecentros* and its telecenter network "Declaration" for the 2003 WSIS (World Summit on the Information Society);
- Chasquinet Foundation and its "State of the Art" proclamation (2002);
- *TICBolivia* network and its *Programme* (2005).

Additionally, Sami Pilco's production company especially effectively balances support from a range of collateral organizations with a stridently independent creative spirit. An Ecuadorian national who proclaims ethnic-cultural identification with *Puruhá de Cacha*, Sami Ayriwa Pilco Janeta has held administrative roles that broach political spheres, from reorganizing communication procedures for CONAIE in 2002 to serving as National Director of Educational Television for Ecuador in 2003. Pilco's projects merge mass broadcasting, commercial enterprise, artistic expression, and political demonstration, and sponsorship reaches from UNESCO's Ministry of Education and Culture (MEC), the non-profit *Fundación Futuro* and *Grupo Futuro*, and the private Banco Pichincha of Ecuador. Among numerous award-winning short-program experimental media projects since 2000, Pilco co-produces through Ecuador's public television ECTV *Ñukanchik Muskuy/Nuestra Sueños* (2009–present), "Our Dreams," a public-affairs series which enhances talk-show format conventions with a breadth of indigenous perspectives, dialects, music, communication forms, and aesthetics. Clarifying issues like territorial rights, gender roles, oil drilling and logging in protected lands, and water use, the shared "dreams" equally invoke personal-communal and ancestral knowledge bases and the alternative epistemologies necessary to access them. Alongside fellow organizations, Sami Productions highlight sustainable development models, alternatives to the mainstream, for wide audiences. Episodes air across the Americas through TeleSUR and DirecTV and over the internet as streaming media. As early as 2000, Pilco outlined the parameters of net-based political-art media projects in "*La Red de Internet*," a manifesto statement also serving as her graduate thesis. Through the trope of 'the network,' her manifesto mirrors and articulates the 'networked independence' of her media projects as well as their potential for providing differential American cultural identification and consciousness building by taking advantage of emerging ICTs and redefining modern development.

Even a quick glance at this list of a dozen examples, organizations and their manifestoes, reveals increased diversification – particularly a much greater involvement of women and multi-ethnic indigenous organizations and across multimedia platforms – matching and surpassing the NLAC. There is an even greater complexity in the various 'networks' of independent and collaborative ventures; interrelationships continue to exist among organizational-group dynamics and individual leadership, and sponsorship and support draw from private, state, and NGO sources. Perhaps a moral to this story is that the revolutionary knowledge within minorities can cycle through moments of reception and acceptance, with grudging stops and starts, reaching its varied audiences in turns to established truths. The Latin American cultural production narrative hinges from the crisis of confidence in institutionalized NLAC leadership to upstart organizations gathering funds, resources, and creative energy by the 1980s; through the 1990s, when video and local-access television provided alternative outlets for media artist-activists previously overlooked or removed from consideration, thus crossing racial, ethnic, gender, and communal restrictions and increasing diversity; into the first part of the twenty-first century, when the internet and collateral figurative networks allow untold access across producers and audiences with varying perspectives and worldviews, not the least of which emphasizes responsibility to multiculturalism, egalitarianism, social justice and human rights, environmental concerns, and ecological sustainability.

Almost fully neglected in mainstream cinema studies, the use of emerging media and technologies, including particularly internet and analog and digital video production, in Latin America has been a subject of discussion mostly within visual anthropology, which emphasizes racial/ethnic factors across world cultures and defines the body of work "*indígena*," "indigenous," acknowledging bureaucratic and neocolonialist impulses in invoking such a category (Wortham 2004; Wilson and Stewart 2008: 2, 12–17; Salazar and Córdova 2008: 39–40). Foundational scholarship on Indigenous media and their organizations has taken into account concerns in ethnography/autoethnography around outsider/insider cultural distinctions, self-reflexive anthropological methods, and the role of advocacy (notably in the practical form of state and NGO funding), allying significant aspects within the politics of representation and the importance of self-representation to sovereignty among Indigenous communities (Prins 1989; Weinberger 1992; Ginsburg 1994, 1999). These discerning issues in cinematic-ethnographic representation, referencing the documentary tradition, arrive with the 'observational' cinema of the 1960s and 1970s – accentuating the portability of lightweight film equipment and ease of synch-sound – and grow in complexity with greater accessibility and lessening expense associated with analog and digital video equipment since the 1980s, noted by Pamela Wilson and Michelle Stewart (2008: 3–4). In her landmark study, Freya Schiwy reads a process of "indianizing" cinema that Indigenous expressions employ to recover ignored or forgotten indigenous information and integrate it with contemporary lived experience; of paramount importance, these strategies emphasize the use of emerging media as a "technology of knowledge" in order to include local and ancestral knowledge like myths, rituals, dreams as "modes of knowing" and storytelling, song, weaving, housekeeping, and other acts of "transmitting social memory" (2009: 8–15). Many recent Indigenous cinema projects pivot from "*video indígena*" to "*comunicación de lucha*," "social struggle," and activist media more broadly conceived, Erica Wortham proves (2013: xiii, 9–14, 220). The initiatives themselves more emphatically concern their networks, their diversification and sustainability, their syncretism and consciousness-transformative processes over strictly Indigenous character, and there are clear advantages in reading this movement through its cooperative informatics and coalitional strategies.

Contemporary Latin American cinema takes up the challenge left off by NLAC films and filmmakers, replacing militant rhetoric with formal and thematic conciliation and consolidation, self-reflexively appropriating "stock codes of Hollywood film" in measured response to geopolitical systems of exploitation and colonization (Schiwy, 2009: 11–13). Nothing short of a paradigmatic turn, cooperative media initiatives propound a shift in logic based on conjoining distinct bases of Indigenous and non-Indigenous knowledge and decolonizing modes of expression (Harrison 1989: 78–84, 62–64; Whitten and Whitten 1988: 25–33). It would be beyond the aim of this chapter to attempt to exact the positioning of these Indigenous concept models and their hybrids – moreover, admittedly, to do so necessarily may reinstall a stamp of Eurocentric values and discourses. Still, as delineated in the manifestoes and cultural production, contemporary cooperative media initiatives oscillate among their influences and invent differential identities rather than adhere strictly to traditionally defined national or ethnic/racial limits. Progressive literacies can detect the distinct and distinctly complex condition in which contemporary Latin American media arts have been made and help overcome traditional-cultural barriers.

Conclusions: The sun also rises

In the years following the 1990 uprising, *levantamiento indígena de Inti Raymi*, revolutionary organizations throughout Latin America ushered America past its quincentenary of Columbus's voyages, recognizing in those centuries struggles against imperial domination. By 2000, CONAIE leveraged some influence in national and regional governance in Ecuador and Bolivia, not least of which included the check and resignation of President Jamil Mahuad and promotion of the Pachakutik political party, *pachakutick* referencing a Quechua concept for social revolution mirroring the Earth's and sun's movements in tandem to bring forth new days (Becker 2010). As historian and cofounder of NativeWeb Marc Becker explains, *pachakutick* as both cultural concept and government apparatus stresses a philosophy of *sumak kawsay*, an "alternative development model" based on reciprocity, solidarity, egalitarianism, and the welfare of all humans (2011: 1–2, 26–28). As part of this age of social activism, the NLAC's late-1980s decline and the rise of cooperative media initiatives into the twenty-first century reflect on-going processes of decolonization for community-based organizations throughout Latin America, their cultural production and manifestoes making this clear. If NLAC's "consciousness of underdevelopment," Ana M. López argues, demands a revision of the very "categories" "normally utilized to construct film historical discourses" (1988: 96–97), cooperative media and coalitional strategies offer a wider range of epistemic bases and differential senses of consciousness. Reflecting on the "modernist critique of modernity" found at the hinge-point of late-1980s Latin American cinemas, Pick argues that the "convergences and divergences" demand a social inquiry by "breaking away from the predominantly ethnographic model" (1993: 16). Valerie Alia (2010) suggests that these coalitional relationships, seen in the inner- and inter-workings of contemporary media initiatives throughout Latin America, deal less with fixed aesthetics or strict national or racial-ethnic categories of indigenous authorship and more with a "fluid" and "changing" act of moving across space, a "new media nation," created by pan-indigenous political artwork and the media tools used to create them. Not an actual "destination" – some thing or place one may align with either the teleology of industrial modernity and world-system developmentalism or the anti-establishment agendas of the NLAC – the utility of contemporary emerging-media initiatives allows "the right to travel freely," and in virtual realms, imaginary networks, like cinema spectatorship and the information pathways of the internet (Alia 2010 13–14), retracing the sun's enlightenment across the Americas and the globe.

Media and mediamaking can recognize Indigenous worldviews, as Juan José García richly describes them, "loaded with symbols, codes"; he continues, they are "loaded with what we up there in the sierra call *comunalidad*. What are its elements? Principally, collectivity, language, facial features… the intimacy of a family" (qtd. in Wortham 2013: 12). Diverse viewerships benefit from the inclusion of syncretic knowledge and belief systems, expressed figuratively and embodied literally in operations and messages of multicultural-media organizations throughout Latin America – *nutzij, um olhar Indígena, ojo de agua, comunalidad, chasquis, ñukanchik muskuy, sumak kawsay, pachakutick*. Beyond trite symbolism or marketing motifs, these complex concepts fuse highly significant multicultural influences and multi-discursive codes, and they warrant closer scrutiny in scholarship on twenty-first-century Latin American cultural production; they offer Indigenous categories of knowledge to be placed alongside better-known non-Indigenous information in our analyses and construction of cinema discourse. In addition to greater internet usage/penetration and affordable access throughout the Americas, trends in mobile-cellular telephony, mobile-broadband technologies, digital television, and web-based TV and radio broadcasting reflect potential riches and enrichment. As the sun rises and sets and rises again, the latest age of Latin American Cinema takes advantage of multicultural initiatives within and among independent but inter-related organizations and their conciliatory methods and objectives. Progressive literacies and open access to the intertextuality among Latin American Cinema, its makers and audiences, and correlative manifestoes emphasize the significance and value of coalitional networks, cooperative informatics, and differential cultural identities across a range of vital political issues. Within a revolutionary shift in Latin American cultural production, the rise of networks of cooperative media resituates knowledge bases and discloses development models that afford identity and autonomy for traditionally disenfranchised citizens. This latest "new" Latin American Cinema reflects these larger political, economic, social, and cultural shifts and facilitates greater diversification and sustainability at the turn to the twenty-first century.

Note

I would like to acknowledge, first, the artists and organizations I have encountered in my research; specifically I extend my gratitude to Sami Pilco for sharing her materials and insights. Unless otherwise noted, translations are by the author (c/s). I would also like to thank Regina Harrison and Lisa Warren for sharing materials for this project and Marc Becker for reading an early draft of this chapter.

Bibliography

Alia, V. (2010) *The New Media Nation*, New York: Bergham.
Alvaray, L. (2008) "National, Regional, and Global: New Waves of Latin American Cinema," *Cinema Journal* 47.3, pp. 48–65.
Aufderheide, P. (1991) "Latin American Cinema and the Rhetoric of Cultural Nationalism," *Quarterly Review of Film & Video* 12.4, pp. 61–76.
Aufderheide, P. (2000) *The Daily Planet*, Minneapolis: University of Minnesota Press.
Becker, M. (2010) "The Children of 1990," *Alternatives* 35, pp. 291–316.
Becker, M. (2011) *¡Pachakutick!*, Lanham, MD: Rowman.
Birri, F. (1967) "Cinema and Underdevelopment," in Chanan, M. (ed.) *Twenty-five Years of the New Latin American Cinema*, London: British Film Institute, pp. 9–12.
Birri, F. ([1986] 1996) "*Manifiesto por un Cineasta de Tres Mundos, en el 2000*," *El Alquimista Poetico-Político*, Madrid: Spanish Ministry of Culture, pp. 26–35.
Birri, F. (2007 [2000–2001]) *Soñar con los Ojos Abiertos: Las Treinta Lecciones de Stanford*, Buenos Aires: Aguilar.
Burton, J. (1978) "The Camera as 'Gun': Two Decades of Culture and Resistance in Latin America," *Latin American Perspectives* 5.1, pp. 49–76.
Burton, J. (1986) (ed.) *Cinema and Social Change in Latin America*, Austin: University of Texas Press.
Burton, J. (1988) "*El Próximo Tango en Finlandia: Cine-Medios y Modelos de Transculturation*," *El Cine Latinoamericano en el Mundo Hoy*, Mexico City: UNAM, pp. 81–88.
Burton, J. and Lesage, J. (1988) "Broadcast Feminism in Brazil: An Interview with the Lilith Video Collective," in Schneider, C. and Wallis, B. (eds) *Global Television*, Cambridge: MIT Press, pp. 225–229.
Carelli, V. (2004) "*Moi, un Indien*," in Corrêa, M., Carelli, V. and Bloch, S. (eds) *Um Olhar Indígena*, Olinda: Centro Cultural Banco de Brasil, pp. 21–32.
CEFREC-CAIB (2013 [2006]) *The National Indigenous Plan for Audiovisual Communication*, http://www.sistemadecomunicacionindigena.org (accessed in July 2013).
Chasquinet Foundation (2002) "*Estado del Arte de los Telecentros de América Latine y el Caribe*," *Somos@-telecentros*, http://www.tele-centros.org/estarte (accessed in July 2013).
Chiyal Jiatz, F. (2000) *Centro De Mujeres Comunicadoras Mayas, Nutzij*, Sololá: ACMCMN.
Cineclub Macunaíma (1988 [1975]) "*Manifesto por un Cinema Popular*," *Hojas de Cinema*, Vol. 1, Mexico City: Fundacion Mexicana de Cineastas, pp. 141–145.
CONAIE (1990) *Declaration of Quito*, http://www.nativeweb.org (accessed in July 2013).
CONAIE (1991 [1990]) "*16 Puntos*," in Field, L. "Ecuador's Pan-Indian Uprising," *NACLA Report on the Americas* 25.3, p. 41.
Córdova, A. and Schnell, M. (2005) "Resources for Indigenous Film and Video," *Cultural Survival* 29.2, np.
Corrêa, M. (2004) "*Video das Aldeias*," in Corrêa, M., Carelli, V. and Bloch, S. (eds) *Um Olhar Indígena*, Olinda: Centro Cultural Banco de Brasil, pp. 33–39.
Corrêa, M., Carelli, V., and Bloch, S. (2004) (eds) *Um Olhar Indígena: Mostra Vídeo nas Aldeias /Through Indian Eyes: Video in the Villages Exhibition*, Olinda: Centro Cultural Banco de Brasil.
Festa, R. and Santoro, L. (1991) "*A Terceira Idade da TV: o Local e o International*," in Novaes, A. (ed.) *Rêde Imaginária*, São Paulo: Companhia das Letras, pp. 179–195.
García Canclini, N. (1997) "Will There Be a Latin American Cinema in the Year 2000? Visual Culture in a Postnational Era," in Stock, A. (ed.) *Framing Latin American Cinema*, Minneapolis: University of Minnesota Press, pp. 246–258.
García Espinosa, J. (1997 [1970]) "For an Imperfect Cinema," in Martin, M. (ed.) *New Latin American Cinema*, Vol. 1, Detroit: Wayne State University Press, pp. 71–82.
Getino, O. (1988) *Cine Latinoamericano: Economía y Nuevas Tecnologías Audiovisuales*, Buenos Aires: Legasa.
Getino, O. (1990) *Impacto del Video en el Espacio Audiovisual Latinoamericano*, Lima: FNCL/IPAL.
Getino, O. (1996) *La Tercera Mirada: Panorama del Audiovisual Latinoamericano*, Buenos Aires: Paidós.
Ginsburg, F. (1994) "Embedded Aesthetics: Creating a Space for Indigeneous Media," *Cultural Anthropology* 9.3, pp. 365–383.
Ginsburg, F. (1999) "Shooting Back: From Ethnographic Film to the Ethnography of Media," in Miller, T. and Stam, R. (eds) *A Companion to Film Theory*, New York: Blackwell, pp. 295–322.
El Grupo de Nuevo Cine Mexicano. (1988 [1961]) "*Manifesto del Grupo Nuevo Cine*," *Hojas de Cinema*, Vol. 2, Mexico City: Fundacion Mexicana de Cineastas, pp. 33–34.

Gutierrez Alea, T. (1997 [1982]) "The Viewer's Dialectic," in Martin, M. (ed.) *New Latin American Cinema*, Vol. 1, Detroit: Wayne State University Press, pp. 108–131.
Halkin, A. (2008 [2006]) "Outside the Indigenous Lens: Zapatistas and Autonomous Videomaking," Wilson, P. and Stewart, M. (ed.) *Global Indigenous Media*, Durham, NC: Duke University Press, pp. 160–180.
Harrison, R. (1989) *Signs, Songs, and Memory in the Andes*, Austin: University of Texas Press.
Himpele, J. (2004) "Gaining Ground: Indigenous Video in Bolivia, Mexico, and Beyond," *American Anthropologist* 106.2, pp. 353–354.
Hojas de Cinema (1988), 3 vols, Mexico City: Fundacion Mexicana de Cineastas.
King, J. (1990) *Magical Reels*, London: Verso.
López, A. (1988) "An 'Other' History: The New Latin American Cinema," *Radical History Review* 41, pp. 93–116.
Marcorelles, L. (1978) "*Le Nouveau Cinéma Brésilien*," *Le Monde*, 30 March, np.
Martin, M. (1997) (ed.) *New Latin American Cinema*, 2 vols, Detroit: Wayne State University Press.
Nagib, L. (2003) (ed.) *The New Brazilian Cinema*, New York: I.B. Tauris.
El Nuevo Cine Latinoamericano en el Mundo Hoy (1988), Mexico City: UNAM.
Ojo de Agua Comunicación (2001) "*Plan de Trabajo: Tres Años*," Oaxaca: Ojo de Agua.
Ojo de Agua Comunicación (2013) "*Plan Rector 2012–2014*", http://www.ojodeaguacomunicacion.org/images/archivos_pdfs (accessed in July 2013).
Pick, Z. (1993) *The Latin American Cinema*, Austin: University of Texas Press.
Pilco, S. (2000) *La Red de Internet*, Bergen, Norway: University of Bergen.
Pinhanta, I. (2004) "*Você Vê o Mundo do Outro e Olha para O Seu*," in Corrêa, M., Carelli, V. and Bloch, S. (eds) *Um Olhar Indígena*, Olinda: Centro Cultural Banco de Brasil, pp. 12–20.
Prins, H. (1989) "American Indians and the Ethnographic Complex: From Native Participation to Production Control," in Flaes, R. (ed.) *Eyes across the Water*, Amsterdam: Het Spinhuis, pp. 80–90.
Ranucci, K. and Burton, J. (1990) "On the Trail of Independent Video," in Burton, J. (ed.) *The Social Documentary in Latin America*, Pittsburgh, PA: University of Pittsburgh Press, pp. 193–208.
Rich, B. (1991) "An/other View of Latin American Cinema," *Iris* 13, pp. 5–27.
Rocha, G. (1965) "The Aesthetics of Hunger," in Martin, M. (ed.) *New Latin American Cinema*, Vol. 1, Detroit: Wayne State University Press, pp. 59–61.
Rocha, G. (1993 [1965]) "Down with Populism," in Chanan, M. (ed.) *Twenty-five Years of the New Latin American Cinema*, London: British Film Institute, pp 15–16.
Salazar, J. and Córdova, A. (2008) "Imperfect Media and the Poetics of Indigenous Video in Latin America," in Wilson, P. and Stewart, M. (eds) *Global Indigenous Media*, Durham, NC: Duke University Press, pp. 39–57.
Sanjinés, J. (1979) "Problems of Form and Content in Revolutionary Cinema," in Martin, M. (ed.) *New Latin American Cinema*, Vol. 1, Detroit: Wayne State University Press, pp. 62–70.
Sanjinés, J. (1989) "*El Plano Secuencia Integral*," *Cine Cubano*, 125, pp. 65–71.
Schiwy, F. (2009) *Indianizing Film*, New Brunswick: Rutgers University Press.
Schroeder Rodríguez, P. (2012) "After New Latin American Cinema," *Cinema Journal*, 51.2, pp. 87–112.
Solanas, F. (1989) *La Mirada*, Buenos Aires: Puntosur.
Solanas, F. and Getino, O. (1997 [1969]) "Towards a Third Cinema," Martin, M. (ed.) *New Latin American Cinema*, Vol. 1, Detroit: Wayne State University Press, pp. 33–58.
Somos@telecentros (2003) "Declaration of *Somos@telecentros* at the World Summit on the Information Society," *Other Side of the Divide*, RedISTIC, pp. 38, http://resources.ethnosproject.org (accessed in July 2013).
Stam, R. (1981) "*The Hour of the Furnaces* and the Two Avant-Gardes," *Millennium* 7–9, pp. 151–164.
TICBolivia (2005) *The TICBolivia Country Programme*, La Paz: International Institute for Communication and Development.
Treviño, J. (1979) "The New Mexican Cinema," *Film Quarterly* 32.3, pp. 26–37.
Weinberger, E. (1992) "The Camera People," *Transition* 55, pp. 25–54.
Whitten, D., and Whitten, N. (1988) *From Myth to Creation*, Urbana: University of Illinois Press.
Willemen, P. (1989) "The Third Cinema Question," in Willemen, P. and Pines, J. (eds) *Questions of Third Cinema*, London: British Film Institute, pp. 1–29.
Wilson, P. and Stewart, M. (2008) (eds) *Global Indigenous Media*, Durham, NC: Duke University Press.
Wilson, P. and Stewart, M. (2008) "Introduction: Indigeneity and Indigenous Media on the Global Stage," in Wilson, P. and Stewart, M. (eds) *Global Indigenous Media*, Durham, NC: Duke University Press, pp. 1–35.

Wood, D. (2012) "Andean Realism and the Integral Sequence Shot," *Jump Cut* 54, np.
Wortham, E. (2004) "Between the State and Indigenous Autonomy: Unpacking *Video Indígena*," *American Anthropologist* 106.2, pp. 363–368.
Wortham, E. (2013) *Indigenous Media in Mexico*, Durham, NC: Duke University Press.

Further reading

Aufderheide, P. (2000) *The Daily Planet*, Minneapolis: University of Minnesota Press.
Martin, M. (1997) (ed.) *New Latin American Cinema*, 2 vols, Detroit, MI: Wayne State University Press.
Schiwy, F. (2009) *Indianizing Film*, New Brunswick, NJ: Rutgers University Press.
Wilson, P. and Stewart, M. (2008) (eds) *Global Indigenous Media*, Durham, NC: Duke University Press.
Wortham, E. (2013) *Indigenous Media in Mexico*, Durham, NC: Duke University Press.

7

ANIMAL RIGHTS FILMS, ORGANIZED VIOLENCE, AND THE POLITICS OF SIGHT

Anat Pick

Documentary and fiction films in a wide variety of genres and styles address the treatment of nonhuman animals and carry pro-animal messages. In this chapter I focus on a number of traditional and new media formats promoting awareness of animal issues: films produced by animal welfare organizations, including footage shot undercover by animal activists, and feature-length animal rights (AR) documentaries. Undercover footage is an important tool of animal advocacy but has recently come under attack in the US and elsewhere by so-called 'ag gag' laws like the Animal Enterprise Terrorism Act. The contemporary prominence of AR films is part of the growing popularity of social justice and activist documentaries in the last fifteen years or so. Other moving-image work, from features to animation and artists' film and video certainly warrant discussion for the ways they negotiate the violent predicament of billions of animals who live and die by human hands. My focus on 'activist animal documentary' is partly a matter of expediency. I limit myself here to the most explicit and widely seen animal advocacy films. My concern is with what Susan Sontag (2003) called, in her last book on the photography of atrocity, "regarding the pain of others," and with the political and ethical ramifications of these acts of seeing. Building on recent theorizing on organized violence against animals and on the politics of visibility, I am also interested in the regulation and codification of vision on which the representation of atrocities committed against animals depends. In this sense, documentary's chronicling and evidentiary functions make it a useful case study, as much for its advantages as for its limitations.

Because political film deploys a range of traditional and new media, and because documentaries are produced across increasingly convergent media platforms (such as CNN's film division CNN Films, or the Discovery Channel), I include examples from film, television, and the Internet. Each format has its own potential, methods, and reach, yet each relies on similar assumptions of what Timothy Pachirat (2011) has called a "politics of sight" – exposing hidden realities to bring about political change – to fulfill its goals effectively.

Killing well: *Slaughter House 1930–1939*

In 1940, the Council of Justice to Animals and Humane Slaughter Association produced a film promoting the use of the bolt gun in so-called humane slaughter in Britain. Laconic in tone, the film is a series of set pieces demonstrating the killing of pigs, sheep, and calves with and without the use of the bolt gun. In place of a soundtrack or voiceover, a title card precedes each act of killing. Two men standing at the mouth of an open shed carry out each kill. Despite its title, there is no real sense in the film of an operational slaughterhouse; the footage demonstrates killing as visible evidence to inform and persuade the British public of the moral imperative of humane slaughter practices.[1] A closing intertitle encourages viewers to get involved by either donating to the organization or handing out leaflets.

In stark contrast to Georges Franju's poetic meditation on slaughter, *Blood of the Beasts/ Le Sang des bêtes* (1949), empiricism and utilitarianism govern this British counterpart. The film's sole aim is to show viewers that the 'dreadful but necessary task' of killing animals for food ought to be accomplished humanely by eliminating animal suffering through the use of the 'mechanical killer.' The role of the camera as the observer is to yield incontrovertible evidence that substantiates the filmmakers' claim.

But the evidentiary authority of *Slaughter House 1930–1939* is mitigated at once by the film's opening intertitle that instructs viewers on how to interpret the images they are about to see. "In any form of slaughter," reads the card,

> there *must* be a certain amount of "reflex" of the muscles, or after activity. This should not be taken to indicate pain. So long as the animal has been rendered unconscious before being stuck with a knife it *cannot* feel.
>
> (*Emphasis in the original*)

Anticipating the difficulty to distinguish visually between a reflex and a response, between involuntary and conscious animal activity, the film also anticipates the blurry boundary between humane and inhumane killing, between, that is, necessary and unnecessary suffering. The prompting of the title card unwittingly undermines the validity of cinematic observation – the camera's capacity to show conclusively the profilmic events. In its limited claim of protecting animals from 'unnecessary suffering,' then, the legitimacy of limitless power over nonhuman animals is tacitly reinforced.

By focusing exclusively on the animals' 'after activity,' moreover, the film precludes viewers seeing the animals' activities *before* they are struck. The animals' reactions in the fleeting moments before the killing work begins are bracketed off and the possibility of considering them is rendered irrelevant. It takes another kind of gaze, an unguided and unguarded eye, to recognize in the short intervals that remain in the edit the expressions of individual animals as they pull back or show signs of struggle before being hoisted, cut open, and bled.

The moral obligation to distinguish between 'humane' and 'inhumane' slaughter depends precisely on correct interpretation of the footage. Without the titles, however, the acts of killing recorded by the camera would be virtually indistinguishable, necessitating the film's cautionary note to disregard the movements of the stunned animals as anything other than involuntary and unconscious. Paradoxically, the film's scientific pretensions (the instantaneous rendering unconscious of the knocked animal, the circumventing of consciousness by an advanced technology of killing) supported by the objectivity of the cinematic apparatus are undermined by the need to verbally interpret the visual material.

The interplay between the surface and depth of animal life on which hinges the imperative to not cause pain does not quite sidestep the problem with which the Council of Justice refuses to grapple, but which the difficulty to tell apart reflex from response (expression of pain, or, perhaps, resistance) implies: the fundamental question of the morality of killing animals for food. The volatility of the boundary between interior life and observable behavior unsettles the assumption of 'dreadful but necessary,' anxiously inserted into the film to secure the

Council's ethical remit and assuage the collective conscience, on which the film's conservative welfarist arguments rest.

Beyond this moral conundrum, *Slaughter House 1930–1939* demonstrates the complexity of making visible as a political strategy. In this way, the epistemological and strategic questions of documentary film encounter the problematic of the 'politics of sight' in the battleground over political transparency. In *Every Twelve Seconds*, Pachirat defines the politics of sight as "organized, concerted attempts to make visible what is hidden and to breach, literally or figuratively, zones of confinement in order to bring about social and political transformation" (2011: 236). *Slaughter House 1930–1939* promotes undisputed, if not universally applied, welfare standards in industrialized slaughter, methods that, it must be noted, enhance the efficiency of slaughter by eradicating any resistance on the part of the animals during 'processing.' The film exemplifies the challenges that animal advocacy films face: the balance between showing unpleasant realities and transforming the audience. The goal of animal rights films is to motivate change. Change, it is assumed, is brought about by illuminating and informing a largely ignorant audience. And yet, as I have just explained, in the very act of showing, *Slaughter House 1930–1939* participates in the work of concealment and suppression that helps normalize public perception in relation to slaughter.

Over 50 billion land animals are killed each year worldwide for food.[2] This vast enterprise of killing is a major battleground of the politics of sight. The stakes of making killing visible are high in a political climate that aggressively targets animal and environmental activists as 'extremists' and 'domestic terrorists.' As indictments under the raft of ag gag and the Animal Enterprise Terrorism Act indicate, activists are poised against powerful state and corporate entities that strive to keep the activities of animal industries beyond public scrutiny.

The war waged these days against animal and environmental activists over what can and cannot be seen is couched in the defensive post-9/11 rhetoric, and in the US it comes in the legislative package of the Animal Enterprise Terrorism Act that covers a range of activities deemed hostile to businesses that use animals, especially those activities involving making publicly visible the conditions in animal agriculture and animal testing facilities. Both sides of the Act share an understanding of the political, economic and affective stakes of transparency. But the war over what can and cannot be seen is part of another war, whose very immensity makes it almost invisible: the war against nonhuman animals.

Media activism and the politics of visibility

In 2014, Mercy for Animals (MFA) released a video shot undercover in a turkey hatchery in North Carolina owned by the Butterball company. The video depicts "birds having their sensitive toes and beaks cut and burned off without any painkillers, workers callously throwing and dropping these fragile animals, and sick or injured birds being thrown into a pit to be ground up alive" (MFA n.d.b). The video followed earlier investigations in 2011 and 2012 at other Butterball facilities in Hoke County that resulted in the successful prosecution of a number of the company's workers (see MFA n.d.a).

Efforts by MFA and similar organizations like People for the Ethical Treatment of Animals (PETA) to shed light on the violent practices of animal businesses bear witness to the routine atrocities that befall animals in agriculture, biomedical research, hunting, entertainment, and sports. Revealing what goes on behind closed doors, or walls, is intended as a catalyst for legislative reforms of the conditions of animals used for a host of human purposes. In the face of the imbalance of power between animal producers and processors and their critics, activists seek to draw attention to the cruelties that even the most 'humane' uses of animals entail, which animal users generally want to keep hidden.

Carrie Packwood Freeman and Scott Tulloch (2013) describe this strategy as "reverse Panopticon." In "Was Blind and Now I See: Animal Liberation Documentaries' Deconstruction of Barriers to Witnessing Injustice," Freeman and Tulloch argue that in animal activist films the correlation between vision, power, and knowledge is appropriated by advocates who harness the powers of surveillance for the purpose of animal liberation:

> Through undercover footage, the marginalised ideology and discourse of animal rights asserts itself through the gaze and directly challenges the powerful and vested interests that activists oppose. The traditional panopticon is about maintenance of order and discipline; the reverse-panopticon form of these films aims at discursive disorder … inviting all viewers willing to bear witness.
>
> (*Freeman and Tulloch 2013: 115*)

The industry's response to MFA's 2011–12 investigation was standard. Butterball reiterated that animal welfare was a priority and that rogue employees will not be tolerated. To the latest release, Butterball responded somewhat differently. It launched an internal investigation by its Animal Care and Well-Being Advisory Council, which found, predictably, that no violations took place. The company's official statement dismisses the cruelty allegations:

> While experts agree the video does not depict any wilful acts of negligence or mistreatment, Butterball does proactively search for continuous improvement opportunities and will provide additional training and education to hatchery associates on animal care and well-being policies to include proper poult handling, transferring methods and management of facility equipment.
>
> (*Butterball 2014*)

Council member, animal scientist Joy Mench, confirmed that "[t]he undercover hatchery video I reviewed did not depict any animal mistreatment" (quoted in Butterball 2014). Butterball's strategy has apparently shifted from attempting to conceal the mistreatment of turkeys to embracing transparency and disputing the meaning of the footage.

The case raises important questions about what it means to see, when visible evidence alone is insufficient. What looks like repeat welfare violations becomes 'continuous improvement opportunities' in commercial Newspeak. Yet even where violations were deemed 'egregious' by the mainstream media, individual workers, mainly nonwhite, migrant and poor, were singled out for blame. In the 2014 footage, visible cruelty was redefined as standard practice, raising the stakes for consumers and the media. Ultimately, Butterball seems to be saying, MFA's 'revelations' are nothing of the sort. Mirroring recent debates on America's detainee torture program, what *appears* as excessive cruelty is recast as 'standard operating procedure.' It now behooves animal advocacy organizations, consumers, and the mainstream media to contemplate the relationship between the 'standard' and the 'egregious' in an industry that has effectively collapsed the distinction between the two. The question has far-reaching implications for both the exposers of cruelty and those, like the *Daily Mail* or the *Huffington Post*, quick to condemn it. What would it mean to widely acknowledge standard practice as flagrantly cruel?

The act of seeing, the Butterball case suggests, is steeped in ideologies that do not only filter but determine the seen. How we see, or what we know, is not simply a matter of the availability of visible evidence. Since the same footage can be viewed as constituting cruelty and as standard practice – indeed, since much of the cruelty *is* standard practice – the question is not *what* but *how* we see. This is a challenge to which all media campaigns for animal liberation must rise. Taken to its logical extreme, Butterball's tactics may be understood as a final gesture of concealment – when visibility itself becomes the cloak of unseeing. No longer "absent referents" (Adams 2010), sentient beings violently rendered into disposable pieces of meat feed a transparent regime in which everything is permissible.

The repugnance that the disclosure of the unacceptable is designed to generate, Pachirat claims, relies on the initial concealment that underwrites civilized sensibilities: repugnance is partly constituted through concealment. In Norbert Elias' *The Civilizing Process* (1939), the theoretical backbone of *Every Twelve Seconds*, Elias argues that modern societies increasingly expand the frontiers of repugnance by removing from sight acts of organized violence (Pachirat 2011: 249–251). The push for transparency "paradoxically relies on the very distance and concealment they seek to counteract for the emotive engine that is implicitly or explicitly assumed to generate their transformational power" (252). Reversing such sanitizing gestures of concealment risks undoing the very sensibilities of pity and repulsion that are the centerpiece of the politics of sight. What if, to repeat the adage adopted on both sides of the debate, slaughterhouses having glass walls would *not* turn most people vegetarian?

We can take further Pachirat's reading of Elias, and wonder if instead of moving people away from animal products, glass-walled abattoirs would gradually recalibrate perception to render the mass killing of animals both visible and palatable. The recent popularity of television programs featuring celebrity chefs who slaughter, cook and eat animals onscreen attests to such a reframing of vision that remakes the repugnant into the acceptable. The BBC's *Kill It, Cook It, Eat It* (2007–) or Hugh Fearnley-Whittingstall's *River Cottage* deploy the politics of sight to combat the 'disconnect' most people have with what, or who, they eat. Chefs like Fearnley-Whittingstall and Jamie Oliver are vocal critics of intensive farming. Although their 'neo-carnivorism' is both gendered and nostalgic, it has been hailed by proponents of 'humane meat' and some animal welfare organizations. Whether or not such transparency is possible in mass-produced meat is questionable, but the link between making visible and making acceptable, on any scale, remains the same.

The paradoxical nature of the politics of sight means that seeing alone is not enough. At stake is not seeing but the "field of perception" (Butler 2009: 66). Establishing what Spinoza (1677/1992) might have called an *adequate* context of vision – righting perception – is thus a primary task of animal rights films. One way of distinguishing between more or less successful animal activist films is the degree to which they disclose, not only the horrors that befall animals, but the contexts that make these horrors unnoticeable.

What, then, is the adequate context for discussing animals in the field of vision? First and foremost it is the context of relentless power in which all forms of animal use, including the most benign (like pets or animal sanctuaries) are imbued. I want to briefly consider two examples of AR films that attempt to convey the depth and breadth of domination that impacts animals at every turn: Victor Schonfeld and Myriam Alaux's *The Animals Film* (1981) and Liz Marshall's *The Ghosts in Our Machine* (2013). Of the two, Marshall's film specifically names the political framework for viewing images of animals: the frame of war.

The war on animals

Extending her analysis of vulnerability and ethics in *Precarious Life* (2004), Butler's *Frames of War* explores the "selective and differential framing of violence" (2009: 1) that determines which lives are perceived as grievable and which not. "[W]hether and how we respond to the suffering of others," Butler says, "how we formulate moral criticisms, how we articulate political analyses, depends upon a certain field of perceptible reality having already been established." She continues:

> This field of perceptible reality is one in which the notion of the recognizable human is formed and maintained over and against what cannot be named or regarded as the human – a figure of the non-human that negatively determines and potentially unsettles the recognizably human.
>
> *(64)*

In the case of animals, the perceptual frame – not least Butler's own – has been placed in such a way as to exclude the lives of animals from the field of the precarious, the grievable, and the violated. Animals' lives are disposable precisely in their designation as nonhuman in a tautology that reads grievable life *as* human life. Discussing images of suffering, Butler explains that

> it is precisely as human animals that humans suffer. And in the context of war, one could, and surely should, point to the destruction of animals, of habitats, and of other conditions for sentient life, citing the toxic effects of war munitions on natural environments and ecosystems, and the condition of creatures who may survive but have been saturated in poisons.
>
> *(75)*

Butler's discussion of the framing of grievable and ungrievable lives betrays the very framing she critiques. Despite her insistence that the human is not a property or an essence and that precariousness exceeds the human, Butler is unwilling to perceive systematic violence against animals that bears the hallmarks of war (killing, confinement, torture, rape, occupation, destruction of territory, etc.) as war. Animals are accidental victims of war, but this does not even afford them the cynical status of 'collateral damage.'

The realities of mass domination of animals are unframed so as to become imperceptible. In the following sections, I turn to the theme and images of war as potentially transformative for the appreciation of the state and scale of organized violence against animals.

War as substructure: *The Animals Film*

In their book *Zoopolis* (2011), Donaldson and Kymlicka posed a number of important questions relating to people's reluctance to accept animal rights. They write:

> A central task for the movement is to figure out why ART [animal rights theory] remains so politically marginal. Why is the general public increasingly open to welfarist and ecological reforms … while remaining implacably resistant to animal rights? Having acknowledged that animals are living beings whose suffering matters morally, why is it so hard to take the next step and acknowledge that animals have moral rights not [sic] be used as means to human ends?
>
> *(Donaldson and Kymlicka 2011: 5)*

There are no easy answers to Donaldson and Kymlicka's questions. The authors insist that a new moral framework for seeing animals is needed. It entails a nuanced and overtly political notion of animal rights not content with securing basic negative rights (the right to life and to liberty), which acknowledges animals' political place in democratic societies in a radical extension of liberal political theory. *Zoopolis* stands in stark contrast to the current state in which animals find themselves, which prompts Dinesh Wadiwel to ask a similar question, whose answer is markedly darker:

> how else can we explain the complete impotence of ethics, 'humane' thinking, and the rights framework before these horrors, without recourse, to understanding how *victory in war leads to an intoxication of power that guarantees a total and unending defeat of the losers through other means*? It is a victory so absolute that it becomes merely everyday, apparently lacking in any resistance, without politics. This is violence that, to use Hannah Arendt in another context, is so utterly 'banal' that it is only barely perceptible.
>
> (*Wadiwel 2009: 289 author's emphasis*)

Wadiwel's recognition of war and the intoxication of power as the locus of our relation to animals casts doubts on *Zoopolis*' liberal political salves. In "The War Against Animals," Wadiwel calls war "the substructure of relationality between human and non-human animals" (2009: 290). The framework of war, claims Wadiwel, is uniquely adept at explaining the scale and ferocity of humans' domination of other animals.

Victor Schonfeld and Myriam Alaux's *The Animals Film* is an exhaustive anthology of the spoils of war interminably wrested from nonhuman animals. It is a suffocating compilation of animals' subjection to violent economies of domination and exploitation, including the cinema. War is not mentioned in Schonfeld and Alaux's film, except, ironically, in the sections on military testing, where, in an allegorical loop, the animal 'stand-ins' for prisoners of war point back to their own imprisonment in the battle between humans and animals. The omission of a war on animals in *The Animals Film* is hardly surprising. For, as Wadiwel explains, the war against animals is too pervasive to be seen. But the sheer scope of atrocities that the two-hour long film lays bare in footage of the pet industry, factory farming, blood sports, and animal experiments, interspersed with vox pop interviews, film clips, Julie Christie's indicting narration, and Robert Wyatt's unnerving score, spells out the horrors of war for its nonhuman victims.

Although *The Animals Film* is not rendered from the perspective of nonhuman animals, the film's relentless parading of human orchestrations of violence makes it difficult to sustain a human perspective with its narratives and rationalizations of animal use. The result is an outsider's gaze – a defamiliarization whose essence is horror. War, and the horrors of war, is the logical conclusion of Schonfeld and Alaux's analysis, even if they do not explicitly say so. But if war and the permutations of war are an overwhelming reality for animals, how does one make visible reality itself?

Picturing war: *The Ghosts in Our Machine*

Organized violence against animals threatens to drive to despair, enrage, and debilitate its witness. The subject of Liz Marshall's *The Ghosts in Our Machine*, the photographer Jo-Anne McArthur, is a witness of war: "I feel like I'm a war photographer," McArthur says in the film's opening sequence, "and I'm photographing history, I'm photographing changes in history right now in terms of animal rights and where it's going." Here, war provides an explicit backdrop, and the now familiar fallout of war for the photojournalist, PTSD (post-traumatic stress disorder), is also introduced at the outset. "I have a lot of nightmares," McArthur tells the three Redux Pictures agents who politely refuse to publish her photographs because, "I mean, this is still, like, a PG society for a lot of magazine [sic] here in the US, or PG13, you know …" 'Difficult images' of animals are deemed unpublishable by consumer magazines. The media's preferred examples – Fox News' "Grand Canyon investigating squirrel-kicking video" (Anon. 2014) or *The Daily Mail*'s reporting on a cat boiled alive in a microwave – are exceptional cases that mask the unexceptional violence animals suffer as a matter of course.

A project like McArthur's, expansive in scope and inclusive of all branches of animal use, proves too challenging for mainstream media, whose consumers – us – benefit from the subjugation of animals. In the introduction to her book *We Animals* (2013), eventually picked up by the dedicated publisher Lantern Books, McArthur insists she does not seek to accuse or alienate. She wants to reach out to a wide range of people, to raise awareness and inform. As she puts it: "I can't spend a lot of time thinking why, why, why are we like this because, I don't have an answer and there's not an easy one, so my job is to take the pictures" (Jo-Anne McArthur 2013). McArthur's choice to eschew pictures of individual perpetrators refocuses attention on the institutional violence against animals – the machine of the film's title – that turns individual animals into ghosts. This is our machine, our war machine, from which we all benefit.

The Ghosts in Our Machine does not distinguish between 'better' or 'worse' animal use. The film's contention is that animals have inalienable rights to life, liberty, and flourishing and this means "animals have moral rights not be used as means for human ends" (Donaldson and Kymlicka 2011: 5). Unlike *Slaughter House 1930–1939*, this is not a welfarist moral framework: the film rejects outright the idea that human needs, however seemingly urgent or noble, necessarily outweigh the rights of nonhuman animals. Thus the distinction between animal use in medical research, for fur or food is irrelevant. The complaint in one review that the film fails to distinguish between legitimate and illegitimate forms of animal use misunderstands the film's espousing of the inviolable rights of animals (Harris 2013). It also misses the film's underlying contention about war. If, as Wadiwel suggests, victory in war categorically sanctions the use of animals for *any* human purpose, then justifiably self-serving purposes (discovering cures for sick human children – the standard of 'necessary' harm) and patently spurious ones (fashion or the pleasures of the palate) are hardly distinguishable. 'Victor's justice' legitimates the use of animals as such and explains the failure thus far to significantly improve the lives of animals in our society. Restriction on methods of use, as in the case of the bolt gun examined earlier, do not challenge the self-given right to use animals. This is McArthur's (and Schonfeld's and Alaux's) proper subject: her work attests to the systematic and widespread harming of animals that has no limits.

Animal rights films, whatever their formal properties, must find ways to articulate the fundamental conditions and mechanisms of humans' crushing power over nonhuman animals. Only once the 'field of perception' – the visual frame – has been adjusted to account for the "violent forms of relationality" (Wadiwel 2009: 289) that underwrite our contact with animals, could the rights and wrongs of specific cases of instrumentalization – 'single issue' matters – be considered.

As the success of *Blackfish* (Cowperthwaite, 2013) illustrates, single-issue films can be powerful. They might even lead to legislative changes. Film can also have unforeseen consequences and affect people in unexpected ways, opening our eyes and minds to new ways of seeing. Moments, gestures, or fragments in film are not wholly subsumed by narrative. But single-issue films are misleading if they fail to address the power dynamic that naturalizes extreme forms of violence against animals, which Wadiwel and McArthur believe warrant the title of war.

The backdrop against which images of animal cruelty are seen is one in which eating animals is not only legitimate but culturally encouraged. Melanie Joy (2010) has coined the term 'carnism' to describe the ideological smokescreen that labels certain animals (and not others) as food. AR films are produced and viewed in a carnist society and are therefore swimming against the current of public opinion. To reach the unconverted, AR films have a number of options: they can shock (*Earthlings* [Monson, 2005]); tell personal stories of human and nonhuman animals (*Peaceable Kingdom* [Stein, 2004]; *Vegucated* [Miller Wolfson, 2011]; *Maximum Tolerated Dose* [Orzechowski, 2012]); present arguments in favor of veganism and animal rights from a variety of standpoints such as environmentalism, health, and social justice (*Forks Over Knives* [Fulkerson, 2001]; *Food, Inc.* [Kenner, 2008]; *Cowspiracy: The Sustainability Secret* [Andersen and Kuhn, 2014]).

With Butler's *Frames of War* and Sontag's *Regarding the Pain of Others* in mind, McArthur's war photography produces some interesting tensions. First, the orchestrated assault on animals is not widely considered as war, so the claim that AR documentaries chronicle the atrocities of war is a challenge and a provocation. Second, Sontag points out that "in a system based on the maximal reproduction and diffusion of images, witnessing requires the creation of star witnesses" (2003: 30). But, as a young female photojournalist, McArthur is no Robert Capa or Don McCullin, her risky excursions to procure images from the frontline (a remote fur farm in Sweden, or monkey farms in Cambodia and Laos) hardly garner the epithets of "bravery and zeal" attributed to Capa by the *Picture Post* in December 1938 (Sontag 2003: 30). Not just species but gender, too, makes a difference. Furthermore, if most images of human atrocity, like those of Buchenwald or Dachau, are taken after the event (Sontag 2003: 74), the war on animals is continually waged and, unlike genocides taking place in faraway continents, its participants and beneficiaries are us.

McArthur never questions the efficacy of showing. She admits she does not fully understand the phenomenon she is capturing on camera. Her activity is depicted as one of vocation, and there is something to be said for the literal naiveté with which she doggedly pursues her mission. The personal narratives at the core of *The Ghosts in Our Machine* – McArthur's and some of the animals she photographs – edge seeing towards witnessing as an ethical, not only an evidence gathering, act. *The Ghosts in Our Machine* documents the documentarian; it does not question the act of seeing as a political strategy. Its uncomplicated participation in the politics of sight sets it apart from other, more critical, inquiries into the act of looking at animals in the context of power, films like Nikolaus Geyerhalter's *Our Daily Bread* (2005), Nicolas Philibert's *Nénette* (2010), or Leanne Allison and Jeremy Mendes' interactive online documentary *Bear 71* (2012). These films question looking, and the technologies of sight, in the wider context of biopower. Activist films rarely interrogate the act of seeing as a political strategy because seeing *is* their political act. This is their strength and their weakness.

There is a moment in *The Ghosts in Our Machine* that complicates the politics of sight. The film's decision to include the voice of animal scientist, slaughterhouse designer (and Butterball council member) Temple Grandin seems a bizarre one in a film whose protagonist's vegan ethics opposes the killing of animals for human purposes. Grandin's lone dissenting voice is heard at the outset, amidst recordings of animal advocates (including Jonathan Balcombe, Lori Marino, Antoine Goetschel, and Vandana Shiva). Although animals can feel pain and are conscious, Grandin says, they are not people. Towards the end of the film, Grandin's voice is featured again over sketches of her slaughterhouse facilities and footage of cattle passing through some of the plants she designed.

Grandin wants slaughterhouses to have glass walls so that people could see how a well-designed slaughterhouse is morally unproblematic. What do we see when we look at the images of industrialized slaughter guided by Grandin's voiceover that assures us these are images of morally appropriate killings? Is the decision to include Grandin intended to highlight the logical, moral, and practical absurdity of her position, or is it a genuine counterpoint to McArthur's ethics? The difficulty to provide a clear-cut answer to these questions demonstrates the ambivalence of the politics of sight that champions transparency as the guarantor of social transformation. If Grandin is right, then live slaughter via video stream (the updated version of a glass-walled abattoir) will normalize the mass killing of animals. This hypothetical is reminiscent of Butterball's response to MFA's 2014 investigation. Rather than encourage concealment, make visibility itself an instrument of not seeing.

McArthur's activism extends beyond photography to education and outreach. Seeing her speak in schools as part of the humane education project of We Animals provides hope for the future. The sequences shot at Farm Sanctuary are glimpses of this alternative future (while failing to question the sanctuary's own dynamics of benign domination). They provide respite for McArthur, as well as the viewer, from the more difficult scenes. But the barriers to transformation seem almost insurmountable. Late in the film McArthur says she believes people are innately compassionate. As *Slaughter House 1930–1939* clearly shows, compassion for animals arises within an overdetermined context of violence. Moreover, the moral capacity for compassion can itself be seen as part of an exceptionalist humanist discourse that reinforces differences between humans and other beings. Compassion becomes a moral distinction that bypasses the need to challenge the structures that overpower animals, and blinds us to the reality of war.

Seeing as a mode of empowerment for political change certainly has a place in critiques of oppression. It is difficult to conceive of political change that does not resort, in one form or another, to visibility. But the politics of sight requires reflexivity and nuance cognizant of the ideological mechanisms that govern sight. Films that attend to such mechanisms of seeing are not activist films in any straightforward way because activism tends to favor making visible over asking how visibility comes about.

Coda

The political constructions of seeing are the subject of Hans Christian Andersen's tale "The Emperor's New Clothes," in which clever swindlers convince a vain but insecure sovereign that the clothes they are pretending to weave are made of material visible only to those worthy of office. Fearing exposure as unfit to rule, the emperor, his advisors and subjects publicly declare they can see the nonexistent garments. An allegory on the spectral trappings of power and on the entry of sight into the political field, Andersen understands that the act of seeing is subject to complex posturing born of the strategic requirements that generate and maintain political hierarchies. The point is not that those in the radius of ideology pretended to see what they knew was not there, but that sight itself becomes something bartered and fictitious that can turn the invisible into the seen. In the social realm, Andersen suggests, we all function as if we can see what we know is not there. "The Emperor's New Clothes" is not, then, simply a story about cowardice and conformism. It is a clever rendering of a politics of sight, the process of something – even the unseen – becoming visible in the social realm. At the end of the tale, a child, the not-yet-initiated into the network of power relations, proclaims the emperor is naked, bringing about a change in the power dynamic and a readjusting of sight. When it comes to animals, we are like the emperor and his cronies. Unlike the tale, calls by animal liberationists, often dismissed as childlike, rarely lead to a shifting of the visual frame.

There is another interpretation of the story, which returns us to the subject of animals and war. In this reading, human power and those who maintain it rely precisely on the disavowal of nakedness – the fact of our animal bodies – as the original site of struggle between humanity and animality. If the origins of human exceptionalism are rooted in not seeing our naked animality, then Andersen's story is really about the foundational moment of the repression of human animality that gives birth to politics. In this sense, politics itself has always been a politics of sight.

Visibility is an insufficient tool in the hands of filmmakers and animal advocates when it fails to see itself as an ideological (not only a biological) effect. Thinking through the intricacies of looking, then, is essential to the flourishing of oppositional filmmaking in solidarity with nonhuman animals.

Rebecca Solnit (2004) has written about the importance of a politics that does not see too clearly, that embraces ambiguities and doubts and leaves room for the inscrutability of the future. For Solnit this inability to see, or foresee, is hopeful and creative, allowing for possibilities that transcend the injustices of the present. An uncritical politics of sight assumes that we already know what seeing entails: that once an injustice is made visible, it will be recognized as such. Seeing the injustices committed against animals demands redefining the conditions of vision so that cruelty may emerge in its absolute routineness. But it also bears remembering that the unwavering chronicling of injustice is an integral part of imagining what a different world might look like.

Notes

1 The film can be viewed online on the British Pathé website, under "Early Animal Rights Film: Slaughter House 1930–1939," http://www.britishpathe.com/video/slaughter-house-footage/query/documentaries
2 Animal Equality estimates the number is above 56 billion land animals, http://www.animalequality.net/food. According to the Humane Slaughter Association, in the UK alone, 2.6 million cattle, 10 million pigs, 14.5 million sheep and lambs, 80 million fish, and 950 million birds are killed each year for food, http://www.hsa.org.uk/faqs/general#n1, accessed 9 November 2015.

Bibliography

Adams, C. J. (2010) *The Sexual Politic of Meat*, New York: Continuum.

Anon. (2014) "Grand Canyon Investigating Squirrel-Kicking Video" in Fox News, online, 6 August, http://www.foxnews.com/us/2014/08/06/grand-canyon-investigating-squirrel-kicking-video/ (accessed 1 September 2015).

Butler, J. (2004) *Precarious Life: The Power of Mourning and Violence*, London: Verso.

Butler, J. (2009) *Frames of War: When is Life Grievable?*, London: Verso.

Butterball (2014) "Butterball Responds to Undercover Hatchery Video," online, 3 June, http://www.butterballcorp.com/press-releases/butterball-responds-to-undercover-hatchery-video/ (accessed 9 November 2015).

Donaldson, S. and Kymlicka, W. (2011) *Zoopolis: A Political Theory of Animal Rights*, Oxford: Oxford University Press.

Elias, N. (2000/1939) *The Civilising Process*, Oxford: Blackwell.

Freeman, C. P. and Tulloch, S. (2013) "Was Blind and Now I See: Animal Liberation Documentaries' Deconstruction of Barriers to Witnessing Injustice" in Pick, A. and Narraway, G. (eds) *Screening Nature: Cinema Beyond the Human*, Oxford: Berghahn, pp. 110–126.

Harris, S. J. (2013) "*Ghosts in Our Machine* Review," online, 8 November, http://www.rogerebert.com/reviews/the-ghosts-in-our-machine-2013 (accessed 15 August 2014).

Joy, M. (2010) *Why We Love Dogs, Eat Pigs, and Wear Cows: An Introduction to Carnism*, San Francisco: Conari Press.

McArthur, J. A. (2013) *We Animals*, New York: Lantern Books.

McArthur, J. A. (n.d.) We Animals Humane Education Program, http://humaneeducation.ca (accessed 27 August 2014).

Mercy for Animals (n.d.a) "Butterball Abuse", in Mercy for Animals, online, http://www.butterballabuse.com/ (accessed 10 November 2015).

Mercy for Animals (n.d.b) "Butterball, North Carolina, 2014", in Mercy for Animals, Undercover Investigations online, http://www.mercyforanimals.org/investigations (accessed 10 November 2015).
Pachirat, T. (2011) *Every Twelve Seconds: Industrialized Slaughter and the Politics of Sight*, New Haven, CT: Yale University Press.
Solnit, R. (2004) *Hope in the Dark: The Never-Surrender Guide to Changing the World*, Edinburgh: Canongate.
Sontag, S. (2003) *Regarding the Pain of Others*, London: Penguin.
Spinoza. B. (1677/1992) *Ethics: With the Treatise on the Emendation of the Intellect and Selected Letters* (Samuel Shirley, trans.), Indianapolis: Hackett.
Wadiwel, D. (2009) "The War against Animals: Domination, Law, and Sovereignty," *Griffith Law Review* 18(2) pp. 283–297.

8

REEL NEWS IN THE DIGITAL AGE

Framing Britain's radical video-activists

Steve Presence

Introduction

This chapter explores Reel News, a radical left video-activist collective based in London. Since 2006, Reel News has released a bi-monthly newsreel on progressive movements and campaigns in Britain and around the world, and has become the longest-running radical newsreel in British film history. However, along with much of the rest of contemporary oppositional British film culture, Reel News and the video activist community of which it is a part have largely escaped scholarly attention. In fact, the last book-length study to get anywhere near our current moment was Margaret Dickinson's edited collection, *Rogue Reels: Oppositional Film in Britain*, 1945–90 (1999). Petra Bauer and Dan Kidner's *Working Together: Notes on British Film Collectives in the 1970s* (2013) is a valuable, more recent addition but, as its subtitle suggests, Working Together focuses on the so-called 'golden age' (Kidner 2013: 18) of radical film in Britain – a moment that passed more than forty years ago.

Given the absence of research on contemporary developments one could be forgiven for thinking that oppositional film in Britain today is all but non-existent (save for the work of auteur filmmakers such as John Akomfrah or Adam Curtis). On the contrary, politically and aesthetically radical film culture in Britain is in a state of rude health. Long-standing production and exhibition organisations such as Amber in Newcastle, Leeds Animation Workshop and London Socialist Film Coop have been joined by more recent companies and collectives such as Migrant Media in Coventry or Global Faction and Neontetra Films in London, with the latter also running the London Labour Film Festival. Arts organisations such as Bristol Expanded and Experimental Film and Vivid Projects in Birmingham, curators such as the Otolith Group and filmmakers such as Luke Fowler or Andrea Luka Zimmerman constitute a politically engaged aesthetic avant-garde. The political avant-garde, meanwhile, is catered for by a plethora of organisations ranging from DiY film clubs and cooperatives to annual festivals and volunteer-run, not-for-profit cinemas – see, for instance, London's Exploding Cinema, Manchester Film Coop, Liverpool Radical Film Festival, The Cube Microplex in Bristol or the Star and Shadow cinema in Newcastle.

In focusing on Reel News, this chapter concentrates on just one aspect of contemporary radical film culture – video-activism. I have written about the range of organisations involved in British video-activist culture elsewhere (Presence 2015). Here, I want to outline how the culture as a whole has been influenced by certain key technological and political developments that have occurred since the period covered in Dickinson's book, before zooming in to discuss Reel News in detail. Exploring the organisation's history, politics and practical strategies, the chapter shows how these contextual shifts shaped its development, and offers in the process a profile of one of Britain's most exciting video-activist organisations to date.

The internet and digital technologies

One of the most significant factors distinguishing contemporary video-activist culture from the period covered in Dickinson's book is today's radically altered technological context. Described as a "technological revolution" (Castells 2000: 28), the growth of the internet and digital technologies has fundamentally transformed the ways in which information, knowledge and culture are produced and shared in the twenty-first century. Indeed, for Castells, the production, distribution and consumption of information has become "the new material, technological basis of economic activity and social organisation" (14).

This shift in the productive forces of society has rendered the production and distribution of digital information a major site of economic, political and cultural struggle. New forms of peer-production have proved potentially more productive than conventional, proprietary relations of production (Wikipedia is only the most obvious of numerous examples) and, though not necessarily free from exploitation, are also not dependent on capital or wage labour. Several commentators have thus argued that this technological context constitutes "a profound challenge to the whole concept of scarcity on which capitalist political economy depends" (Wayne 2003: 47) and, having sown the seeds of a sharing economy, even heralds the end of capitalism itself (Mason 2015). Others, however, point to the increased reach and flexibility of capital in the digital era and its ability to exploit a global labour market; to inequalities of access to the internet and connected technologies; and the emergence of new forms of commerce (often based on unpaid labour), power and surveillance derived from mass data collection. Leaving aside debates about its macro socio-political consequences though, such a transformative and uncertain technological context has also created a range of affordances and challenges for contemporary video-activists.

File-sharing and proprietary online platforms such as YouTube and Vimeo have vastly increased the potential audiences for oppositional filmmaking and created an immense archive of potential footage, for example. Yet mainstream culture and politics are almost as dominant online as they are off it. Prominent illegal file-sharing sites, such as The Pirate Bay and Kickass Torrents, are dominated by Hollywood entertainment, for instance, while sites dedicated to sharing radical material, such as OneBigTorrent, remain relatively obscure. Similarly, with so much content competing for attention on commercial video-sharing sites it is difficult both for video-activists to distinguish themselves and for audiences to locate their work. Again, as in conventional media, those with the most resources are most able to stand out.

Furthermore, although it is potentially easier than ever before to find and view video-activism online, making work available for free makes it harder for oppositional filmmakers to earn a living from their work. Developing strategies for financially stability in this context is thus essential. For many video-activists, this has meant striking a balance between less overtly political work that is paid or grant-funded, and more radical video-activism that is often produced and shared for free. For example, Undercurrents (1994–), one of Britain's best-known video-activist organisations, subsidises its more radical work with commissions for commercial activities and funding for work as an access organisation with disadvantaged groups in Swansea. Other organisations, such as Camcorder Guerrillas (2003–) in Glasgow or the Brighton-based SchMOVIES (2004–14) (the descendant of the 1990s video-activist collective, Conscious Cinema) have developed similar models. As we will see, Reel News is especially interesting in this regard, having developed a funding strategy that enables it to solely produce radical video-activism.

Direct action and anti-globalisation

In the 1990s, Britain's video-activists were largely aligned with the direct action community which, beginning with the Poll Tax revolt at the start of the decade, was characterised by a series of vibrant campaigns centred around particular issues: road-building; live-exports; GM foods; fox-hunting and so on. As the decade wore on, these initially distinct struggles increasingly overlapped and developed a heightened awareness of their shared national and international interests. By the end of the 1990s, many of those involved in direct-action campaigns earlier in the decade were part of an international anti-globalisation movement,[1] which identified capitalism as a primary cause of global injustice and inequality. Characterised by a series of large, globally coordinated anti-summit protests that explicitly targeted some of capitalism's key global institutions, this period consolidated an internationalist anti-capitalist current among many British activist networks.

In Britain, the global Carnival Against Capitalism on 18 June 1999 marked the beginning of this new wave of anti-capitalist protest. J18, as it was known, was followed by N30, the infamous 'Battle in Seattle' on 30 November 1999, when five hundred thousand activists successfully shut down four days of World Trade Organisation meetings despite extraordinarily high levels of police brutality. In 2000, prominent anti-capitalist protests took place in Washington, London, Prague and Nice, and in Davos and Genoa in 2001. The global justice movement generated a significant body of British video-activism: the spectacular tactics displayed at the protests were suited to visual media; there was much excitement about the potential of the internet as an alternative media source (Indymedia, the international network of radical media organizations (discussed below), began at N30 in Seattle); and many felt that the global nature of the movement was potentially revolutionary.[2]

However, Genoa was the last big demonstration of the anti-globalisation movement. The ferocious response of the police – who shot and killed one protestor and seriously injured many more following a raid on the Indymedia Centre – confirmed what many already knew: that anti-summit protests were becoming increasingly dangerous events, marked by the extreme violence of militarized police forces and taking place at a date and location necessarily chosen by the state. The shockwave of Carlo Giuliani's death at the Genoa protests stalled the movement, which was then effectively halted by the events of 9/11 four months later. Following George Bush's abstract declaration of 'war on terror' and the UK and US' joint-invasion of Afghanistan in October, anti-war activism became the key imperative for the left.

The anti-war movement, climate change and the Latin American left

Unlike the anti-globalisation movement, the anti-war movement failed to generate any substantial video-activism. Partly, this was down to the differing kind of politics and protest tactics adopted by the Stop the War Coalition, a broad alliance of socialist groups which quickly became the dominant anti-war voice in the UK. In contrast to the anarchist-oriented politics of the anti-globalisation movement and its theatrical, experimental tactics, Stop the War adopted more mainstream tactics designed to appeal to the widespread demographic that opposed the war. Though popular (the 2003 anti-war marches were some of the largest ever recorded), the marches failed to grasp the imagination of video-activists and the dismissive response of those in power left many disillusioned with that form of protest. The lack of anti-war video-activism was also a result of exhaustion in video-activist organisations and the uncertain technological context in which they were operating. As Paul O'Connor, co-founder of Undercurrents, one of the most established video-activist groups in the 1990s, explains,

> in the early 1990s with the roads protests it was all kinds of local. But by the end of that decade it was a worldwide movement. So people were going off to summits, Prague, Genoa and all that . . . I think we realised that we just couldn't sustain it . . . Indymedia was out there and things were going online and you were thinking 'great, we're going to have videos on the web'. [But] video on the web didn't take off for another four, five years.
>
> (*O'Connor, quoted in Presence 2011a*)

With VHS fast becoming obsolete and web video not quite viable, there was no reliable distribution platform for anti-war video-activism and the few attempts at newsreel production were unsuccessful. Instead, most anti-war films produced at the time were feature films such as *Not in My Name I, II and III* (Platform Films, 2002–4), *Breaking the Silence: Truth and Lies in the War on Terror* (Pilger, 2003) and *Letter to the Prime Minister* (Guest, 2005).

In contrast to the anti-war demonstrations, which were for the most part peaceful and within the parameters of the law, the radical environmentalist movement in the UK largely maintained the traditions of direct-action and broadly anarchist modes of organising that characterised the movement in the 1990s. Partly as a result of this continuity, radical video-activist groups like Undercurrents and visionOntv, the London-based aggregator of video-activism, found a natural affinity with climate activists, providing media support with projects like Climate Camp TV in the mid-2000s (which broadcast live news updates and reports from within the camps) and at anti-fracking sites today.

Another significant influence on Britain's video-activists was the grassroots struggles and electoral successes in various Latin American countries – the so-called 'Latin American Left Turn' (Cameron and Hershberg 2010). This influence was partly derived from the anti-globalisation movement's emphasis on non-Eurocentric perspectives, which both celebrated and was shaped by various movements and campaigns, such as the Zapatista uprising of 1994 or the election of Hugo Chavez in 1998. While election successes attracted most attention from the mainstream media, it was grassroots movements and their attempts to develop forms of popular democracy adequate to them, such as the People's Global Action (PGA, 1998–) or the World Social Forum (WSF, 2001–) that had most effect on video-activists in Britain. visionOntv, for instance, adopted the Hallmarks of the PGA as its organisational principles. Reel News, meanwhile, was especially influenced by the workers' cooperatives in Argentina that emerged in the wake of the protests that toppled Fernando de la Rua's government in December 2001. It is to that organisation that we now turn.

Reel News

Prior to founding Reel News in 2006, Shaun Dey had accrued almost fifteen years' experience of video-activist production working with various radical filmmakers in Britain and abroad. Consequently, Reel News is well connected to contemporary video-activist culture and organisations such as visionOntv, SchMOVIES and Camcorder Guerrillas, and is familiar with the recent history of British video-activism, acknowledging key 1990s groups such as Undercurrents, Despite TV and Conscious Cinema as 'trailblazers' of the movement and as influences on its own work. Like those earlier groups, Reel News is a newsreel for the radical left but, having already released its bi-monthly newsreel for nearly a decade, it has already outlived its predecessors by some time. Reel News is also distinct from both its recent predecessors and contemporaries by virtue of its explicit class consciousness and its distinctive (in the UK) funding model: Reel News is funded solely by donations and subscriptions to its newsreel, and performs none of the more commercial, less overtly political activities adopted by many other advocacy-based film organisations. For these reasons, Reel News is unique in the history of British video-activism.[3]

Reel News' distinctive ideological perspective derives from the trade-unionist background of those involved in the collective (Dey is currently its only full-time member but the 'immediate circle' consists of seven people – three video-activists, a designer, a still photographer and two activists who help connect the groups to campaigns – with more assisting on the periphery of the organisation). According to Dey, "not just me but the other people involved in Reel News are all or have been activists and in trade-unions", and these roots in the labour movement are the source of the organisations' ideological outlook. He continues:

> I think what we bring to it is more of a class edge, to be honest. Because of where we come from. I suppose it's that old Marxist idea that power, real working class power, is withdrawing your labour, because without that the whole thing can't function. So I suppose we're always looking for how to galvanise that at that level.
>
> *(Dey, quoted in Presence 2011b)*

Dey was thus acutely aware of the absence of class when watching Undercurrents' newsreel in the 1990s:

> That was more about social and community struggles with direct-action going on … I was always thinking 'yeah this is good, you can get inspiration and often results from this but the most serious direct-action you can imagine is a mass strike'.

A former activist for the public sector trade union, Unison, Dey quit his job to return to education in the mid-1990s, just prior to the development of the alter-globalisation movement. Studying lens-based media at Camberwell Art College in London, Dey used his experience to support a number of student protests and occupations, and focused his own research on student radicalism and the relationship between art, culture and working class politics. Graduating from the course in 1999, this art education and trade-unionist background meshed with the political context of the emergent alter-globalisation movement, and motivated Dey to start making his own work:

> that's where it all started really, in 1999. Then the next thing that happened was J18 and Seattle … [what] stood out of all that for me, apart from obviously this new movement that was happening, was that kids were getting hold of all this new technology

> that was available, digital technology, and actually reporting on their own struggle. I remember for J18 they put it live up on the net. And it was completely unheard of … I looked at that and thought, 'that's what I should be doing'. So I came out of Camberwell, got myself a video camera and went to the Prague World Bank/IMF protest. So it was all that that led to me doing all this now. It was the synthesis of my trade-union background and the arts school background and thinking that the obvious thing to do is to carry on going to protests and getting involved in disputes but with a camera in my hand.
>
> *(Dey, quoted in Presence 2011b)*

Following the Prague demonstration, Dey attended the G8 summit protest in Genoa the following year, working as part of the burgeoning Indymedia movement. After Giuliani's killing, some Colombian activists remarked on the tragedy of the event but pointed out that people were killed in the same struggle every day, telling him: "'if you really want to see what the fight against neoliberalism is about then you should come to Latin America'". Following the death of his father, Dey used his small inheritance to purchase some equipment and travel to Argentina, where he arrived two weeks after the 2001 uprising that toppled Fernando de la Rua's government. In Argentina Dey met Rick Rowley and Jackie Soohen from Big Noise Films, one of the most prominent oppositional film collectives in the US (*This is What Democracy Looks Like* (Friedberg and Rowley, 1999), *Fourth World War* (Rowley 2003), *Dirty Wars* (Rowley 2013)), and together they worked with Argentinean Indymedia for six weeks.

Working with Indymedia in Europe and Big Noise in Argentina was a significant influence on Dey, as was Argentinian oppositional film culture. For example, Indymedia activists at the summit protests in Prague and Genoa practised the pooling of their footage, from which anyone could then make their own edit – a practice Reel News would later replicate. Argentina Indymedia operated similar practices, and when Big Noise arrived Dey worked closely with them and Argentinian filmmakers to produce "short, sharp, functional films" from the pool of footage they had shot together. While the practical skills Dey learned in this period were invaluable, it was also here that he saw the value of screening those films in public:

> there would be a big assembly every Sunday where all the popular assemblies would come together – you'd get about 5000 people in this park – and they would not only be filming it but they would also show footage on a big screen at the end of all the things that had happened over the last few days. That was when I started to see the potential of video as a really useful tool for a movement.
>
> *(Dey, quoted in Presence 2011b)*

Returning to Britain, Dey produced a short film about Argentina, six hundred copies of which were distributed through *International Socialism*, the quarterly journal associated with the Socialist Workers Party (SWP). He continued with this model for a few years, producing films sporadically and releasing each one as a separate project, working on building sites in the meantime to supplement his income.

Frustrated by a process in which more time was spent working to pay for the films than actually making them, Dey began to consider the possibility of producing video-activism full-time. Accompanying a trade-union delegation to Bolivia in 2006, he stopped off again in Argentina and revisited the factories under workers' control. This experience was decisive, and directly inspired Dey and some of his colleagues to found a newsreel when they returned to Britain:

> it was meeting the women of Brukman's that really got conversations going amongst a few of us, because they sat down and told us the whole story. From the reason they occupied in the first place – most of them didn't have the bus fare to get back home because they were owed so much money by the owner – to going through this nine-month struggle where they were living on nothing . . . . And we were sitting there with them and they were running the place. And you think 'fucking hell, if these people who we're sitting with who had nothing, can go through all that suffering and all that hardship and then run an entire factory, then surely we can get a newsreel off the ground'.
>
> (*Dey, quoted in Presence 2011b*)

Developing a sustainable funding model for a radical newsreel was their most significant challenge, however, especially given Reel News' decision not to adopt any of the typical approaches used by other groups: applying for funding; offering training; or selling footage to the media.

Although this means that 'money is the main problem' for Reel News, financial difficulties are outweighed by the political independence they afford. With no need to moderate its rhetoric to appeal to more liberal funding sources, Reel News is the most outspoken of contemporary video-activist groups. The organisation's website, for instance, proudly declares that

> Reel News is completely independent and non-aligned. We are completely against sectarianism in all its forms, anti-capitalist in outlook, against the anti-trade-union laws and in favour of mass collective action in the workplace and on the streets to change society.
>
> (*Reel News 2012*)

Another reason for not applying for funding is more practical: the demands of regular newsreel production mean Reel News must dedicate all of its time to making films, not working on applications to fund them. Having discussed with Hamish Campbell and Richard Hering their drawn-out experience of applying for funding for visionOntv, Dey notes that "they spent a year doing that and didn't make any films . . . [T]he way Reel News works, I'm not in a position to not be making any films". In any case, funding opportunities for such an overtly political project are few and far between, and Dey is reluctant to take on the paperwork that funding applications require: "to be honest whenever I look at a funding application form I just get completely miserable. Because you're thinking 'how do I wrangle what I'm doing into this' or 'how do I lie about that'".

With regards to training, despite Reel News' informal policy that it will train anyone who wants to learn and Dey's belief that political filmmakers have a responsibility to pass on their skills, he argues that this role is better left to other, more technically proficient groups such as Spectacle (a London-based, anarchist-oriented production company run by former Despite TV video-activist, Mark Saunders). Although Dey is certainly capable of offering training to new filmmakers, his reluctance to do so comes from a self-effacing attitude derived from his "punk attitude to filmmaking" and a sense that, because the production values of the films are less important than the political motivations for making them, they have little to offer aspiring filmmakers. Uninterested in making films for posterity, Dey describes Reel News' work as "throwaway" filmmaking, designed to be used in the moment as campaign tools for whichever organisation the group is working with at that time.

Political reasons also underpin the policy of not selling footage to mainstream news sources. Television news companies tend only to be interested in the kind of footage Reel

News has if it includes political violence, such as clashes between police and protestors. Aside from not wanting to contribute to the way in which the media already focuses on violence against property or the police to the detriment of the political issues that cause it, Dey also argues that "without 100% editorial control I wouldn't trust what they were going to do with it". Citing well-known examples from the miners' strike and Poll Tax riots as well as the BBC's unauthorised (and misleading) use of Reel News' footage,[4] taken from YouTube, in October 2013, Dey is adamant that he would not consider selling footage to the media.

While the incident with the BBC might have prompted other organisations to adopt a stricter approach to its intellectual property, since 2010 Reel News has in fact made all of its work available online for free, alongside an option for audiences to pay for it. Due to differing opinions among the group about what the consequences of this move would be, the first time this practice took place was during the Copenhagen Climate talks in December 2009, when it was deemed useful for those present at the talks to have access to the material immediately. As a result, the rushes were placed online at the end of each day's shooting before being sold on DVD as *Reel News 22: System Change Not Climate Change* (2010). Similarly, when the student movement against fee increases began in Britain in late 2010, the feeling within the organisation was that making the footage of the various protests freely available online could help build the movement. As a result, Reel News had an increasing number of visitors to its website and its work was distributed widely, with campaigners able to access and share films of the protests and demonstrations with which they were involved almost as soon as they had taken place. Moreover, contrary to the risk that this would erode Reel News' ability to generate income from its work, subscriptions and sales of its DVD have been steadily growing ever since.

Conclusion

Despite its growth in recent years, analysis of the contemporary political avant-garde in Britain is a notably absent from scholarship on British film culture. Of course, video-activism is just one facet of that avant-garde and Reel News is just one among many organisations that constitute contemporary video-activist culture. Nevertheless, I hope this chapter has gone some way towards demonstrating the extent to which the historical record of oppositional film in Britain is in need of updating. Twenty-five years have passed since the period covered in *Rogue Reels* and, as we have seen, many significant changes have taken place in that time which have transformed radical film culture and the social and political contexts from which it emerges and which it attempts to engage.

And yet, as the case of Reel News demonstrates, while the spectacular expansion of grassroots filmmaking in the digital era has resulted in a contemporary video-activist culture that is in many ways unrecognisable from that of the 1990s, today's dominant video-activist organisations are intimately bound-up with that earlier period and cannot be understood in abstraction from it. To be sure, the next generation of video-activists will be influenced by those organisations and the struggles and campaigns in which they are involved. From Occupy and the *indignados* to migrant solidarity movements, campaigns against fracking and the struggles against austerity in Greece, Spain and the UK; these movements are the soil from which tomorrow's video-activists will grow, just as the direct action campaigns and the anti-globalisation movement forged groups like Reel News. Recovering the history of such organisations is thus essential if we are to understand both the nature of our contemporary video-activist culture and the various directions it may take in the future.

Notes

1 There is a variety of names for this movement (other prefixes include 'anti-capitalist', 'global democracy' and 'global justice'), each of which has advantages and drawbacks that have been discussed elsewhere (for example, see Graeber 2002). Although 'alter-globalisation' perhaps more accurately indicates that the movement's target was global capitalism, rather than globalisation *per se*, I have opted for the less clumsy 'anti-globalisation' here.

2 Key films from the anti-globalisation movement include *J18: The First Global Protest Against Capitalism* (Undercurrents, UK, 1999) *Revolting in Prague: IMF Protests 2000* (various, UK, 2000), *Behind the Barricades* (Guerrillavision, UK, 2000), *Suits and Savages: Why the World Bank Won't Save the World* (Conscious Cinema, UK, 2002) and *Globalisation and the Media* (Undercurrents, UK, 2002).

3 Submedia.tv is a Montreal-based anarchist production collective which is also funded exclusively by its supporters and, like Reel News, is similarly outspoken about its ideological orientation.

4 A BBC report on the peaceful strike at Grangemouth petrochemical plant in Scotland was illustrated with Reel News' footage of conflict between police and demonstrators at a protest against blacklisting in London, six months previously.

Bibliography

Bauer, P. and Kidner, D. (eds) *Working Together: Notes on British Film Collectives in the 70s*, Southend-on-Sea: Focal Point Gallery.

Cameron, M. A. and Hershberg, E. (eds) (2010) *Latin America's Left Turns: Politics, Policies, and Trajectories of Change*, London: Lynne Rienner.

Castells, M. (2000) *The Rise of the Network Society*, 2nd edition, Oxford: Blackwell.

Dickinson, M. (ed.) (1999) *Rogue Reels: Oppositional Film in Britain, 1945–90*, London: BFI.

Graeber, D. (2002) "The New Anarchists" *New Left Review*, 13, January-February 2002, online, http://newleftreview.org/II/13/david-graeber-the-new-anarchists (accessed 17 October 2015).

Kidner, D. (2013) "There and Back Again" in Bauer, P. and Kidner, D. (eds) *Working Together: Notes on British Film Collectives in the 70s*, Southend-on-Sea: Focal Point Gallery, pp. 17–18.

Mason, P. (2015) *Post-capitalism: A Guide to Our Future*, London: Allen Lane.

Presence, S. (2011a) Interview with Paul O'Connor, Swansea, 19 May, unpublished.

Presence, S. (2011b) Interview with Shaun Day, Swansea, 19 November, unpublished.

Presence, S. (2015) "The Contemporary Landscape of Video-Activism in Britain" in Mazierska, E. and Kristensen, L. (eds) *Marxism and Film Activism: Screening Alternative Worlds*, Oxford: Berghahn Books, pp. 186–212.

Reel News (2012) "About" *Reel News*, online, http://reelnews.co.uk/about/ (accessed 7 October 2012).

Wayne, M. (2003) *Marxism and Media Studies*, London: Pluto.

9

FILM AND THE POLITICS OF WORKING CLASS REPRESENTATION

The Inside Film project

Deirdre O'Neill

This chapter is concerned with questions of subjectivity and representations as they relate to the working class in theory and in practice. It explores (albeit briefly) the way in which a radical pedagogic film project grounded in the experiences, class location and everyday realities of the working class can provide a starting point for a critical engagement with and a materialist understanding of how society is organised. The Inside Film project is an attempt to situate theoretical considerations, film-making practices and pedagogic practice within a dialectical relationship to working class experience in ways that blur the boundaries between theory and practice. The refusal to draw rigid lines between the theoretical and the practical and the insistence on radical film-making as a fusing of thought and action is an attempt to resist the division between intellectual and manual labour that Marx considered a socialist society would eradicate. It is for this reason the project insists on the importance of both a critically applied theoretical knowledge of film-making as well as the practical activity of making films.

The Inside Film project works with a specific group of people (prisoners and ex-prisoners) in a particular set of circumstances (in prison or on parole) in the United Kingdom. It explores how film can be used within a pedagogic, overtly classed context as a means of fostering a critical engagement with society in ways that more traditional academic subjects are unable to do. Over a period of three to four months the Inside Film students script, storyboard, act in, shoot and edit their own films. Before this practical work takes place we provide the students with historical and theoretical frameworks within which to make sense of their own practice. Our work insists on the importance of self-representation for the working class and argues for the recognition of working class culture, values and attitudes as distinct from those of the middle and upper classes. Representations of working class people are often predicated on a presupposed set of experiences that manifest visually as generalised stereotypes. These representations fail to contextualise lives exposed to myriad situations of exploitation and oppression or the extent to which (the often criminalised) responses to exploitation and oppression are linked to the social and economic environment within which they occur.

The hypothesis of this research – that it is possible to utilise film as a radical pedagogic tool – is dependent for its outcomes on a paradigmatic Marxist understanding of class as a theoretical and practical model adequate to the conceptualisation and practice of a class-based radical pedagogy. This project and the research it has generated assume there is an ontological category that can be identified as the working class (Charlesworth 2000: 7) and during the course of this chapter that category is utilised in different ways. The overarching paradigmatic use of the category is a utilisation of the Marxist model of class that is at 'base' a socio-economic one premised on the division of labour wherein the working class sells their labour to the bourgeoisie who own the forces of production:

> Our epoch, the epoch of the bourgeoisie … has this distinctive feature: it has simplified the class antagonisms. Society as a whole is more and more splitting up into two great hostile camps, into two great classes directly facing each other: bourgeois and proletariat.
> (*Marx and Engels 1967: 80*)

This binary division of the two classes situates both classes within the structurally determined relations of production associated with capitalism as a system. According to Marx this polarisation of two opposing but interlocking classes produces not only struggle but also conflict generated by the antagonistic and alienating nature of the capitalist system. The experience of struggle and conflict is one shared by the working class as a whole and therefore unites them as a class. This is true even if they are not conscious of themselves as a class. Consciousness of class is not necessary in order to experience class. More than thirty years of neoliberalism has dramatically restructured the working class while the category has all but been erased from public discourse. This has led to the removal of class as an analytical framework with the explanatory power to account for the individual and social pathologies we are currently witnessing in contemporary society. According to David Harvey, this reconfiguration of the way in which the working class is constructed (or not) within neoliberal discourses does not mean that class does not exist, on the contrary: "Masked by a lot of rhetoric about individual freedom, liberty, personal responsibility and the virtues of privatisation, the free market and free trade, it [neoliberalism] legitimised draconian polices designed to restore and consolidate capitalist class power" (2011: 10).

The rhetoric of neoliberalism has become entrenched over the last thirty years and while I would argue that the Marxist binary model is still a theoretically viable one (particularly if we consider the working class globally) practically the examination of the present condition of the working class and its relationship to education and the media demands a more nuanced exploration of the concept. Marx did not allow for the growth of a professional middle class. This class stands between the working class and the capitalist class but belongs to neither; it would be productive for our purposes to view this class as an intermediate one, caught as it is between capital and labour. The middle classes are obviously not members of the capitalist class but, while they do not own the major means of production, they do not occupy the same relations to capital and the means of production that members of the working class do. They are differentiated from the working class by their cultural and educational 'capital' (Bourdieu 1996) and this means that their experience of capitalism is very different from the working class. Indeed, within the production process, as supervisors, or outside it, as teachers, lawyers, doctors, social workers, psychologists, media workers, politicians, etc. they are typically in positions of authority in relation to the working class (Wright 1978: 63). Therefore the second way in which this work deals with class is the stratified tripartite system combining Marx's binary model of class with a more 'sociological' examination of the differences within classes.

Within this conceptual system of class categorisation my approach insists on negotiating the power relations that result in the working class and the middle class living significantly different lives and experiencing the world in comprehensively different ways. While acknowledging there are diverse fractions within the working class and that quite recently there was what has been theoretically configured as an 'affluent working class', the prisoners and ex-prisoners that Inside Film works with are, generally speaking, those members of the working class who have received a limited education; if they are or have been employed, the work they do is often unskilled, low paid and low status with few financial or career prospects. They do not own property, nor do they have any savings, and their inadequate income, which fails to provide for even the basic necessities of life, makes crime appear an attractive option. Among this section of the working class I include the increasing numbers of the working poor and the unemployed. It is the experiences of these members of the working class that are more likely to be distorted and silenced by a privileged middle class increasingly subservient to the demands of the corporate neo-liberal agenda. The privileged access of the professional middle classes to the forces of knowledge dissemination is controlled in ways that legitimise existing structural inequalities and consolidate their own interests. The cultural appropriation and resulting distortion of the experiences of the working class by those in positions of power within the media effectively condemns them to marginalisation and silence and prevents them from playing a participatory role in the public sphere.

As I indicated previously, class here is not purely an economic category. This work treats it as a multivariate relational category that considers economic, social, cultural and political aspects of the formation and experience of class. This allows us to recognise the ideological role of orthodox pedagogic practices in the delivery of consensus and the reproduction of the neoliberal order, one that continues to denigrate, marginalise and silence the experiences of the working class.

We live at a time when our lives are constantly mediated and this creates the conditions for a project such as Inside Film to highlight the effects of a mainstream media wedded to neoliberalism because the participants have direct experience of the distortions, contradictions and lies that sustain the capitalist system. Unlike most films with working class life as the subject matter, the people making these films are not the middle class graduates of film schools and unpaid internships for whom the life they film is nothing more than another subject to be studied before they move onto the next project. While working class life is organised in order to increase the profit margins of a small powerful elite, the potential to transform the relations of production and replace them with a fairer more equal system will always exist. This is was the trajectory Marx envisaged when he claimed that capitalism would be its own gravedigger (Marx and Engels 1967: 94).

Initiating a change in working class subjectivity can trigger the potential to bring about the conditions necessary to challenge the social relations of capitalism. This challenge can then begin the process that will eventually transform them. In the pursuit of this aim an engagement with the methodological and theoretical systems currently in circulation in relation to the concept of working class subjectivity is crucial, in order to better understand the ways in which they are constituted within the ideological framework of the capitalist order (Meszaros 2010: 13). I want to attempt to conceive of the ways in which the constitution of these methodological and theoretical systems constructs, not a *collective* working class subject aware of its potential power to demand changes leading to the transformation of society, but an *individualised* subject impoverished and trapped by the lack of a theoretical understanding of its place within the totality of capitalism. The chapter will also consider the part played by pedagogical practices (both radical and mainstream) in the construction of subjectivities. Following on from this, the chapter will conclude by considering the connection between subjectivity and representation. As means to underpinning and reinforcing the theoretical aspects of this chapter the discussion will reference the pedagogical practices of Inside Film and discuss one of the films produced by the students who take part in the course.

Working class subjectivity

Subjectivity cannot be separated from the conditions under which it comes into being or the material ways in which it manifests itself. Our sense of self develops through personal, environmental and institutional social interactions, interactions directly influenced by our historically determinate class positions. Therefore it appears irrational in the extreme not to acknowledge that working class people will develop subjectivities that differ in significant ways from those of people whose subjectivity is formed under privileged conditions. Marx has made clear that this applies to both the way in which we think and the way in which we act, even our biological drives cannot escape the influence of our class position, as Marx's visceral example illuminates:

> Hunger is hunger; but the hunger that is gratified by cooked meat eaten with a fork and knife is a different hunger from that which bolts down raw meat with the aid of hand, nail and tooth. Production then produces not only the object but also the manner of consumption, not only objectively and subjectively. *Production thus creates the consumer*.
>
> (*Marx 1973: 92, my emphasis*)

It is critical that attempts such as the Inside Film project (or any other counter hegemonic project) whose aim is to expose the ways in which working class people and the culture of the working class are represented negatively for political and ideological purposes, takes this into account.[1] It is only through an exploration of how the working class is socialised differently that we can begin to consider how capitalism universalises and presents as eternal the historically specific and socially determined structures of society; structures, which in our present moment have embedded within them the ideological tropes of individualism and competition that embody the logic of a neo-liberal system, often leading to the destruction of social bonds. This aim of exposing the political, historical and ideological contingency of these structures can be achieved by engaging in an analysis of the often unexamined ongoing *process* of adaptation to these structures and how this process of adaptation contributes to the construction of subjectivity. The systemic ideological institutions of contemporary capitalism, the family, academia, education, religion, government and the media, are the conduits through which representations are both organised and circulated, universalising and reinforcing the perspectives and values of the privileged. The range and force of these representations penetrate into all areas of life and are by necessity profound and far reaching.

Not surprisingly these representations often translate into a contradictory working class subjectivity, opposed as they are to the structural reality of working class lives. The relationship between the social and the subjective is for working class people often an incoherent one. Many of the Inside Film students struggle to make sense of the discrepancy between the way in which society treats them, the way in which they are represented in the media, the demands society makes on them and the impossibility of meeting those demands precisely because of the way they are treated. This circular formulation produces a state of ongoing conflict exacerbated by the lack of an explanatory framework that might offer an insight into the cycle of deprivation, crime and imprisonment. The institutions to which the working class is bound are not able to reconcile these contradictions. They therefore impose different realities which the working class subject cannot hope to understand. As Lichtman points out in relation to institutions, the most important work they carry out consists of:

> Channeling human action in accordance with previously constituted relations of power and meaning. Every significant institution serves the same structure of power – the domination of the productive process by the class with predominant control over its property and forms of accumulation .... The conduit of social structure is the institution, which articulates individual existence through a system of variegated roles.
> *(1982: 27)*

Of course all of this means we have no choice but to engage critically with institutions such as the law, the education system, prisons and the subjectivities they construct. Not simply because it is then possible to demonstrate a 'historical temporality' essential to undermining bourgeois claims of the natural and universal and the eternal, but because a critical engagement is the first step in comprehending class, in the Marxist sense, as a dialectical relationship between our life experiences, the material world that shapes those experiences and our resulting subjectivity.

Externally this relationship is a mutually dependent one between those who have only their labour to sell (even if they are not actively selling it the relationship still holds) and the owners of the means of production. It is the existence of this relationship and the surplus it generates in the form of profit that the continuation of capitalism is dependent upon. Therefore, subjectivity or our *sense* of who we are and where we belong, is, in a capitalist society, determined by our classed responses to our experience of that society. For the working class this can only mean, "knowing the world through a medium and in a manner that emerges from conditions of deprivation and symbolic impoverishment ..." (Charlesworth 2000: 6). Therefore if this is our experience of the world, if this is what we know of the world, then, logically, it follows that our subjectivity will correspond to those experiences.

The social relations through which our subjectivity is formed and through which our understanding of the world takes shape are the social relations necessary to the reproduction of capitalism. This of course is not the end the matter; if it were, the charges of determinism often levelled against Marx would hold true. Tensions and contradictions between the life experiences of social actors and the precepts of capitalism have a destabilising effect on conceptual appraisals of the self and the environment in which the self exists. This can bring to the fore antagonisms, which result in the search for alternative appraisals – what Marx would have considered to be *class conflict*. Any change (transformation) in subjectivity demands 'knowing' the world differently, but this 'difference' requires action upon the external world in ways that recalibrate how we see the world. According to Marx it is only by acting in the world that we can begin to change it and through this action, change ourselves, "by thus acting on the external world and changing it; man [sic] at the same time changes his own nature" (1961: 177). This is the central, most significant aspect of Marx's notion of praxis. In the process of acting upon objective reality there is a resulting transformation of subjectivity. Praxis in this sense meant by Marx involves critical knowledge that can be tried, tested and applied to practical activity and it is the unity of thought and action or theory and practice that creates the conditions for change. One, without the other, is meaningless.

To act upon the world in order to bring about effective change requires comprehension of the need to act upon the world and a consideration of the most effective strategies to bring about that change. Marx does not dictate a universal model for his understanding of praxis. On the contrary, his insistence on a unification of theory and practice acknowledges the historically dynamic process of change that must of necessity exclude any attempt to provide a determinate theory of praxis. Integral to Marx's consideration of praxis is a dialectical conception of the relationship not only between theory and practice but also between society and the individual at different historical moments.

Film as praxis

Here I would like to discuss one of the Inside Film student films, *Who Am I?* (2007). This film was made in HMP Wandsworth[2] and will, I hope, demonstrate some of the issues I have raised in this discussion so far. Using the documentary form, the film is constructed around questions of subjectivity that explore not only class, but gender, race and religion. Operating on three different but connected levels, the subjective, the national and the international, the film dramatically undermines the preconceived assumptions produced by the mainstream media in relation to the working class by posing questions from the perspective of a group of working class men serving prison sentences. The questions the film asks attempt to demonstrate connections between the personal actions of individuals with actions carried out by the rich and powerful globally, making links between the struggle of young black men to survive (or not)[3] on the streets of the United Kingdom and the war in Iraq.

It situates these questions within the context of consumer capitalism, drawing attention to the ways in which advertising and celebrity serve the purpose of distracting us from the criminal activities of politicians and world leaders while punishing those whose options for survival are extremely limited. It uses direct address with questions being asked straight to camera, an overt challenge to the viewer of the film not to ignore the issues it is dealing with (Figure 9.1). Formally the film takes an unconventional approach, mixing a series of dramatic vignettes with montages of found material drawn from print and television news.

The group who made this film had never made a film before; indeed the majority of them had never picked up a film camera before.

Figure 9.1 *Who Am I?* The masked hoodie challenges media perceptions that construct his sense of self.

Their knowledge of film was limited to the dominant film product that is readily and easily available and has a near monopoly in commercial cinemas and on the television. Their ideas about the kind of film that they wanted to make were influenced by a workshop on Third Cinema run by one of the project volunteers, a university academic. Third cinema is a low-budget, politically motivated cinema that grew out of the anti-colonial struggles taking place across South America and Africa during the 1960s and 70s. It was clear to the students almost immediately that the anger and frustration they wished to convey would lose some of its power if it were situated within the dominant form of film-making and that it could be represented more effectively in this unconventional form. Budget and time restraints meant that the amount of subjects they wished to cover such as war, crime, violence, consumerism, celebrity, drug dealing, etc. could not be achieved using conventional continuity editing strategies. The radical strategies of Third Cinema, which they had discussed at length, with its insistence on an 'Imperfect Cinema' (Espinosa 1979: 24–26) allowed them the freedom to reject the conventions of dominant film-making practices such as narrative linearity, continuity editing, and spatial and temporal logic and think about film more in terms of its potential for analysis and critical engagement. This model of film-making is less preoccupied with technical and formal accomplishments and more concerned with political and social interventions which hold out the "possibility for everyone to make films" (24).

Who Am I? attempts to explore the complex interactions between the media, politics, economics and history and to reveal the role their constitutive discourses play in constructing a sense of identity. Implicit within its excavation of the often concealed complexities of identity formation is how the media-constructed positions offered to us to make sense of our lives are based on political strategies whose ideological function it is to avoid and displace the question of class.

The students who made *Who Am I?* produced a film that posed not just the question of who we are but who we want to be and in doing so demonstrated the complexities involved in answering these questions. These complexities are highlighted by a short sequence of a man sitting in front of a computer screen typing. He is dressed in a shirt and tie and is strongly coded as an office worker. He swivels round in his chair and staring directly at the screen asks "Am I what you see?". As the chair straightens in front of the camera the man's shirt is replaced by a red tee-shirt emblazoned with the words 'anti-capitalista'. At this point he says "or am I what I want to be?". The filmmakers do not offer any answers to these questions but appear to be suggesting that under certain circumstances we have choices and those choices include denying who you are in order to live a life of quiet desperation, working in an office and conforming to the demands of a capitalist society or of making choices that could be considered revolutionary. This is underlined by the choice of the red tee-shirt and the Spanish translation of 'anti-capitalist' connoting as it does the revolutionary potential of Latin America and, of course, one of the origins of Third Cinema. At the same time, the two questions the actor poses draw attention to the disjuncture between the real "am I what you see?" and the actual "or am I what I want to be?" The distinction raised between the real and the actual (Bhaskar 2008: 6) invites us to confront the system of beliefs and rationalities that justify the mechanism of capitalism, suppress the experience of the working class and contribute to their systemic subordination.

The debates that accompanied the making of the film and the struggle to make positions clear and to justify the raising of these questions meant that the students involved, both as individuals and as group members, were being called upon to examine their own position in society and the ways in which that position relates to members not only of their immediate group but other people who would see the film. One of the most interesting aspects of the process of making this film was how much their experiences, not only of being in prison but of their lives before prison coincided, how the conditions that had shaped them were recognised by other members of the group. The film itself and the process of making the film both demonstrate the existence of a working class subjectivity different from the subjectivity of more privileged members of society but, in the absence of any recognition that this is indeed the case, it is only through a process of radical education, democratic participation and critical engagement that an awareness of that subjectivity can be initiated. The working class inhabits specific ways of being and develops specific modes of knowledge but the universalising strategies of capitalism construct these differences as aberrations. *Who Am I?*, informed by an analysis of politics, class and film-making, articulates the resulting feelings of alienation.

Theorising class

The working class is inseparable from capitalism, indeed the very existence of capitalism is dependent upon it, but the alienation of the working class due to the miserable conditions they often suffer creates a position for them that is distinct from the more privileged members of society (Charlesworth 2000: 74). This is not merely a local phenomenon but a global one. The socially determined position occupied by the global working class results in subjectivity formed out of a habitus of degradation, exploitation, poverty and exclusion. Bourdieu's concept of habitus is one that allows some purchase on the generationally reproduced cycle of deprivation and poverty. The spatial, social and symbolic sites into which we are born means we inherit our relationship to the world:

> The relationship to the social world is not the mechanical causality between a 'milieu' and a consciousness ... when the same history inhabits both habitus and habitat, both dispositions and position, history in a sense communicates with itself, is reflected in its own image. History as 'subject' discovers itself in history as 'object ... in which a body, appropriated by history, absolutely and immediately appropriates things inhabited by the same history'.
>
> *(Bourdieu 1981: 306)*

Thus we are born into a class position we feel powerless to change not least because we often do not attempt to change it considering it to be natural. This state of affairs has intensified over the last thirty years as the collective historical knowledge and instances of social and political resistance of the working class are ignored or marginalised. This is why, as Balibar has pointed out, "it is important to have at our disposal instruments of analysis which are not neutral but comparative" (2002: 62). Film can be such an instrument of analysis. Films are records of the past and the present and as such can be a vehicle for comparing both. Films can reveal the lives of the poor and compare them to the lives of the rich. Radical pedagogic practices can also be utilised comparatively by refusing neutrality, as Balibar demands, and therefore can expose the differences between the state-sanctioned education and one with a liberatory potential.

In contrast to Bourdieu, theorists such as Laclau do not consider class as an aprioristic identity. On the contrary, Laclau considers contemporary society to offer a proliferation of subject positions, all of which contribute to the diluting of antagonisms and militate against classed identity and working class hegemony (2005: 86–87). According to Laclau, structural changes that have taken place in the capitalist system have resulted in working class subjectivity no longer being linked to working class identity, in fact, working class identity is no longer the primary marker of identity. To reinforce his argument he claims that there has been a "drastic fall in the working class and [there has been an] emergence of a social stratification quite different from that on which Marxist class analysis was based" (Laclau 2000: 206).

It is not difficult to see how this example of academic theorising reinforces a 'retreat from class' as an analytical framework through which to make sense of the world. It is true to say that there has been a restructuring of capitalist working practices over the last generation and working class industries and organisations have become weakened and demoralised, while the people themselves have found it harder to organise as mass unemployment and falling wages have put enormous pressures on the struggle to survive and the left wing groups that offered the possibility of building a unified working class movement have been marginalised (Callinicos 2006: 138). While there has been some agreement with Laclau's theorisation of the changes in capitalism since Marx's time, attention has also been drawn to the problems in his conclusion that this would necessarily lead to a weakening of classed subjectivity.

On the contrary, as some theorists have argued it would perhaps be more apposite to conclude that it has strengthened class allegiances (Thoburn 2007: 87). It has also been pointed out that Laclau does not take into account Marx's claim that it is the *position* of the worker in relation to the forces of production that defines class position (Callinicos 2006: 144). The globalisation of capital has highlighted not the differences but the similarities in the national and global working class, and it is possible to imagine this awareness of their positioning within the mode of production (a connection Laclau dismisses) will result in a class that develops a primary subjectivity with the potential to create a movement intent on overthrowing capitalism. Therefore class is not just one subject position among many other subject positions all of which are in a continuous state of flux but "*the definitive* subject position" (Meyerson 2001: 2). Laclau's reduction of working class subjectivity to numbers and changing structures fails to consider the ways in which consciousness is formed and shaped through the daily experience of poverty, unemployment and marginalisation. What may have declined is class-consciousness, but not consciousness shaped by class. The Occupy movement, the anti-capitalist protests, the anti-war movement and the marches against gentrification (to name a few) demonstrate a sustained and ongoing critique of the neoliberal paradigm. While these campaigns and protests may not necessarily declare themselves as working class, there is, in their existence, a consciousness shaped by and made aware of the destructive nature of the present neoliberal order.

For both Marx and Engels (1989: 118, 121, 123) and for Lukács (1971: 262) it is only through the development of cognitive powers that a radical subjectivity able to perceive capitalism as a historically specific set of relations will begin to emerge. The barrier to the perception of this consideration is the reification that takes place under capitalism. Reification refers to the social relations of capitalism, and the way in which the private monopoly of wealth, both social and economic, is naturalised to appear as an attribute of things rather than historically shaped social relationships.

According to Marx, the modes of production under capitalism encompass not simply an economic model but are irrevocably connected to the social and the cultural and to the theoretical concepts that organise and justify them. The capitalist mode of production does not allow for direct relationship between the producer and the means of production. Rather the workers, divorced from a direct relationship between production and existence, must sell their labour to the capitalist who pays them to produce whatever commodity is required. Any surplus value that is produced is appropriated by the capitalist as profit. The selling of labour in the market place for financial remuneration is the mediating factor between production and existence. Therefore the workers' lives and the choices they (are forced to) make are mediated by capital (Burton 1997: 175). Understanding this relationship leads to a recognition of the way in which subjectivity is shaped by the socio-economic realities of lived experience.

Conclusion

What is the nature of subjectivity under capitalism? I have tried to answer this question here but feel it still needs to be posed as the question continues to present us with a problem; subjectivities formed under capitalism are distorted by the experience of capitalism. Wayne refers to them as "crippled" (2003: 185). What then does this mean for our conception of film as a radical tool or for our hypothesis that a critical pedagogy can begin to transform subjectivity? One of the most important aspects of the Inside Film project involves separating what it means to be working class from the ideologically loaded distortion of middle class norms, that is, clarifying the specificity of working class experience and the mode of living of the working class. As Lebowitz has argued in relation to the working class: "Given the differences in the specific conditions of their individual production (as well as the separation that capital itself produces), there is a definite material basis for seeing themselves as separate" (2003: 179).

This movement towards a subjective mode of knowledge that can exist alongside the internalisation of the logic of capitalism allows for both an objective knowledge of capitalist totality but also a subjective knowledge of how one is situated within that totality. This subjective knowledge provides insight into how that totality affects us as individuals belonging to a particular class at a specific historical moment and involves a complex engagement with both the particular and the general, an engagement that can only develop though praxis. This matrix of knowledge for the Inside Film students comes into being through the productive activity of making films. Making films encompasses a total experience. Tasks are not divided into specialised and hierarchical units, rather the students' work on the film together. The Inside Film project insists on the collaborative nature of film-making, one that fosters collaboration and not competition.

Wayne has posited the notion of a 'subjectless subject' to describe the way in which the agency of all human actors is powered by the internalisation of the social and economic relations of capitalism. Agency in this model is not agency at all but is rather the acting out of the logic of capitalism which has "emptied them [people] of authentic autonomy, power and free will …" (Wayne 2003: 184). This internalisation has the effect of reconciling the contradictions and antagonisms of capitalism mentioned before so that they are conceived of as individual failings, with the result that many people strive to reconcile themselves to the demands of the status quo. It is only when they are externalised and viewed as systemic problems that these contradictions and antagonisms can begin to play a dynamic role in the construction of a radical subjectivity that disrupts the hegemonic order. This process demands something other than agency. Although agency is a prerequisite of change it is not of itself sufficient, meaningful change will only come about if agency is linked to critical engagement.

This is not to claim that film can of itself change the ways in which society is ordered but it can in no small measure actively contribute to creating the conditions to bring about change (Eagleton 1976: 10); it can (literally) reframe pre-existing knowledge and construct a position from where the working class can narrate their own lives.

Notes

1 Recently, I was invited to talk about the Inside Film project at an academic conference, screening the film under discussion here – the feedback afterwards was that people found the talk of class too

challenging and that after a long day listening to conference papers they did not want to discuss the subject.

2 HMP Wandsworth is a Category B men's prison in South West London. It is the Largest Prison in the UK.

3 I say 'or not' because one of the young men involved in the making of this film was shot dead a couple of years ago over a drug debt of £50.

Bibliography

Balibar, E. (2002) *Politics and the Other Scene* (C. Jones, J. Swenson and C. Turner, transl.), London: Verso.

Bhaskar, R. (2008) *Dialectic: The Pulse of Freedom*, London: Routledge.

Bourdieu, P. (1981 [2015]) "Men and Machines" in Knorr-Cetina, K. and Cicourel, A. V. (eds) *Advances in Social Theory and Methodology: Toward an Integration of Micro and Macro Sociologies*, 2nd edition, Routledge: London, pp. 304–317.

Bourdieu, P. (1996) *Distinction: A Social Critique of the Judgment of Taste*, London: Routledge.

Burton, J. W. (1997) *Violence Explained: The Sources of Conflict, Violence and Crime and Their Prevention*, Manchester: Manchester University Press.

Callinicos, A. (2006) *The Resources of Critique*, Cambridge: Polity Press.

Charlesworth, S. J. (2000) *A Phenomenology of Working Class Experience*, Cambridge: Cambridge University Press.

Eagleton, T. (1976) *Marxism and Literary Criticism*, London: Routledge.

Espinosa, J. G. (1979) "For an Imperfect Cinema" *Jump Cut*, 20, pp. 24–26.

Harvey, D. (2011) *The Enigma of Capital and the Crises of Capitalism*, London: Profile Books.

Laclau, E. (2000) "Structure, History and the Political" in Butler, J., Laclau, E. and Zizek, S. (eds) *Contingency, Hegemony, Universality: Contemporary Dialogues on the Left*, London: Pluto Press, pp. 182–212.

Laclau, E. (2005) *On Populist Reason*, New York: Verso.

Lebowitz, M. A. (2003) *Beyond Capital: Marx's Political Economy of the Working Class*, Basingstoke: Palgrave.

Lichtman, R. (1982) *The Production of Desire: The Integration of Psychoanalysis into Marxist Theory*, New York: The Free Press.

Lukács, G. (1971) *History and Class Consciousness: Studies in Marxist Dialectics*, (R. Livingstone, transl.), London: Merlin Press.

Marx, K. (1961) *Capital Vol. I*, (S. Moore and E. Aveling, transl.), Moscow: Foreign Languages Publishing House.

Marx, K. (1973) *Grundrisse*, London: Penguin.

Marx, K. and Engels, F. (1967) *The Communist Manifesto*, London: Penguin.

Marx, K. and Engels, F. (1989) *The German Ideology*, London: Lawrence and Wishart.

Meszaros, I. (2010) *Social Structures and Forms of Consciousness, Volume 1 The Social Determination of Method*, New York: Monthly Review Press.

Meyerson, G. (2001) "Rethinking Black Marxism: Reflections on Cedric Robinson and Others" *Cultural Logic*, 3(2), online, http://clogic.eserver.org/3-1&2/meyerson.html (accessed 17 October 2015).

Thoburn, N. (2007) "Patterns of Production: Cultural Studies after Hegemony" *Theory, Culture and Society* 24(3), pp. 79–94.

Wayne, M. (2003) *Marxism and Media Studies: Key Concepts and Contemporary Trends*, London: Pluto Press.

Wright, E. O. (1978) *Class, Crisis and the State*, London: New Left Books.

10

KONY 2012

Anatomy of a campaign video and a video campaign

Leshu Torchin

On 5 March 2012, the organisation Invisible Children posted their video *Kony 2012* online where it subsequently went viral. The thirty-minute advocacy video received approximately 112 million views in the period of six days, surpassing former records set by Susan Boyle on *Britain's Got Talent*, Rebecca Black's "Friday" and even "David After Dentist" (Visible Measures Blog 2012). The video trended on Twitter and Facebook where it was shared and the story reached major international news outlets. The enthusiastic response was followed by an almost equally enthusiastic backlash, as the euphoria generated by possibility of online participation turned to criticism and controversy. It is tempting to critique the campaign for its naive and offensive tropes, its misinformation, its questionable goal of military intervention and its narcissism. It is even tempting to attribute the dissolution of Invisible Children in 2014 to these factors. However, such dismissal might be premature. The oscillation between these two poles of celebration and condemnation – whether in response to the possibilities of online activism or to entertaining advocacy – is a persistent one. But this binary risks obfuscating what can be learned from such campaigns. *Kony 2012* offers an occasion for thinking about the benefits and limitations of video advocacy as it moves online. Through an analysis of the video and its epiphenomena, this chapter outlines the practices and pitfalls of video in online advocacy more broadly.

Background: Invisible Children and online advocacy

When Invisible Children produced and uploaded *Kony 2012*, it was by no means their first foray into activism or filmmaking. Founded in 2004, the nongovernmental organisation Invisible Children (IC) made it their mission to call attention to the conflict around the Lord's Resistance Army (LRA) in Northern Uganda and in particular to the human rights abuse of conscripting child soldiers. Between then and the upload of *Kony 2012* IC produced and screened numerous documentaries to schools and universities in the US and beyond, building a core constituency and networks of engagement. Their student base was active, particularly in realms of fund-raising and event-planning to which this typically affluent demographic was well-suited (Finnegan 2013: 32). Meanwhile, IC engaged not only in filmmaking, but also in decision-maker advocacy, rehabilitation programmes, and, through a partnership with Resolve, the LRA Crisis Tracker, which mapped and aggregated data in order to publicise the crisis. With regional partners, IC developed the Early Warning Radio Network, which alerted communities as well as NGOs and security organisations to violence in the area.[1] Moreover, their alignment with the Obama administration's position on Uganda resulted in significant impact on public and foreign US policy (Titeca and Sebastian 2014). Whatever one might say about IC and its student activists, the engagement was neither as fleeting nor as superficial as the eventual criticisms of 'clicktivism' (Drumbl 2012) would suggest.

Produced as centrepiece for the "Stop Kony" campaign, *Kony 2012* features IC co-founder Jason Russell as its key protagonist and voiceover narrator along with a cast characters with varying degrees of input. These include: Russell's 5-year-old son Gavin; his Ugandan friend Jacob; Luis Moreno Ocampo, the Chief Prosecutor of the International Criminal Court (ICC); John Prendergast of ENOUGH – an anti-genocide human rights organisation; two Ugandan politicians; Invisible Children's Country Director Jolly Okot; the enthusiastic participants in Invisible Children campaigns, and in some ways – global citizenry, as the foregrounding of social media (Twitter, YouTube and Facebook) as method and aesthetic might suggest. The "Stop Kony" campaign had a seemingly straightforward mission: Stop Joseph Kony, Ugandan warlord and leader of the LRA by apprehending him and bringing him to justice at the International Criminal Court, where he has already been indicted. Clearly, arrest and prosecution are not the tasks of the audience; rather, as Russell explains in voiceover, the goal is to make Kony 'famous', a process that will lead to his capture.

As naïve as this plan may sound, this is the very sort of Enlightenment-style thinking that underpins much human rights work: if people know, they will act accordingly (Cohen 1996; Keenan 2004; Torchin 2012). This model is based on the assumption that exposure results in knowledge, rational thought, deliberation and response. This faith in a relationship between revelation and justice is embedded in the names, slogans and mission statements of a host of organisations. For instance, Human Rights Watch, for example, investigates and publicises violations, reporting on their findings in order to mobilise a range of responses, from the shame of the perpetrators to the outrage of their public, while WITNESS's name and logo ("See it. Film it. Change it.") further underscores visuality's value.

This tenacious formulation requires intervention if one is to better understand the relationship between images and action. Exposure does not automatically lead to justice. Pushing a button does not automatically lead to regime change. But it is unlikely that anyone, even Invisible Children, is actually labouring under that belief.

As I have written elsewhere (Torchin 2012), testimony provides a useful model and method for fleshing out the territory between seeing and doing. This first-person narration of suffering, after all, has been deployed in numerous transformative scenarios: in Christian martyrdoms, where the performance of suffering bears witness to the truth of Christ and ushers in utopia; in therapy (Felman and Laub 1992); and in politics, such as in the Latin American genre of *testimonio*, which "records the cry against oppression" (Peters 2001: 714) and endeavours to "[set] aright official history" (Yúdice 1996: 44).

Meanwhile, the function and efficacy of the testimony rests on its deployment of generic codes, characterisations and recognisable tropes to translate distant suffering into an immediate cause for concern. Equally important, if not more so, is to consider the conditions of the testimonial encounter, or the contexts of production, exhibition and circulation of the text, and in the case of *Kony 2012* to view this video as one highly visible component of a much larger campaign (Torchin, 2006, 2012). There is a dynamic relationship between these two aspects that accelerates and deepens as we move into the online world.

The viral 'success' of *Kony 2012* was due in part to practices long building among activists. Since the founding of YouTube in 2005, NGOs, advocacy organisations and coalitions have established channels in order to exploit the Internet's capacity for radically extending witnessing and promotion of information. Here, they can bypass the restrictions of mainstream news media and post videos where they may be shared and circulated among communities bound by shared interests. Such advocacy potential led to the founding of "Citizen Tube" in 2007, a political video platform where not-for-profit organisations were invited not to broadcast themselves, but broadcast their cause (Torchin 2012: 196–215).

Even in this new field, *Kony 2012* signalled a change, as the runtime of this advocacy video significantly exceeded the typical lengths of those found online. Many run the length of a Public Service Announcement or Public Information Film – 30, 60 or 90 seconds to correspond with usual timeslots allowed to advertisers. And like adverts, they contain basic information and a brief directive. Some videos, particularly those intended to be circulated within a young adult age group, run three to four minutes, as slide shows with image macros (photographs with textual information) are set to music associated with the well-meaning (for instance, Gary Jules's "Mad World", John Lennon's "Imagine" or anything with Bono). As they grow longer, they are nonetheless constrained by the former parameters of the platform sticking around the nine-minute mark – the original cap of a YouTube video length. In cases of streaming video, highlight reels are posted. Despite greater liberties to post longer videos, short running times can be crucial in a context where a small screen competes for attention with many others – on the computer and off (Caldwell 2005: 15–19; Torchin 2012: 196–215).

Even so, the longer video may not have been a liability given shifts in consumption practices that cater to long-form viewing. After all, IC's target audience viewed most audio-visual media on phones, tablets, laptops and desktop computers.

Kony 2012: the text

The video's runtime allows for a lot of information and the development of a clear narrative. It opens with a prologue that praises social media, observing that the world is connected unlike ever before and that these connections have benefited interpersonal relationships, community building and social change. Jason Russell articulates this sentiment as a montage of technologically facilitated human interaction takes place. From there *Kony* launches into a section that could be called "The Story of Two Boys". Russell introduces himself and his son Gavin in a section that has baffled many who tuned in to watch a film about Uganda and instead found an extended sequence of a caesarean birth followed by home video horseplay. During the birth sequence, Russell explains that this is the start of all human life. This secures the focal point of identification in the white, American, male body. Or rather, two bodies. In the YouTube home movies sequence, we learn of Gavin's love of filming and being a star, highlighting the father–son prominence as image-maker and subject. Audio-visual media is the start of life and human connection, and the theme persists throughout the video.

The next boy introduced is Jacob, Gavin and Jason's friend in Uganda. His introduction once again highlights the function of social media in the social world. "Who is this?" Russell asks his son, as they look at his photograph pasted to a refrigerator door. As Gavin answers, the camera pulls back, revealing this interaction to be taking place on a video that plays on Russell's Facebook timeline. A cursor stops the video and navigates the timeline, moving further back in time to play additional video clips, highlighting both the personal element of the story and Russell's clear agency: he is the centre of activity as he is imbued with the power to navigate space and time as he moves back to Uganda, in 2003, where he first met Jacob. The goal is double: Jacob provides the entry point into the issue under discussion and offers emotional resonance as counterpoint to Gavin's privilege.

In the first encounter, Jacob tells of his brother's murder and speaks of his worry and fear of abduction. Other snippets articulating this fear follow, as images of speaking individuals give way to a wide shot of bodies huddled on the ground of a shelter, and Russell's breathless shock at the magnitude and length of this crisis. He returns to Jacob, combining interviews that share Jacob's wish for education and his despair, before Jacob breaks down in tears and the film fades to black. In the darkness, Russell promises him all will be ok. It is this suffering Russell promises to alleviate – it is here that he makes his promise to help.

This reliance on the testifying body – whether the masses on the floor or Jacob's personal voice – is a mainstay of the human rights display, which relies on the forging of an encounter between suffering subject and witness. Social documentaries have often relied on testifying bodies to articulate a problem, one that will ostensibly be fixed by the viewer or producer of that film in what Brian Winston has termed, "The Tradition of the Victim" (1988). Jacob's helplessness is underscored by the film's refusal to grant him much in the way of testimony. The statements are cobbled together, with almost all interrupted by Russell's prodding. It is as if the goal is to reduce the boy to tears, to produce a spectacle of suffering. Meanwhile, the other children appear as predominantly mute, whether in the huddled crowds or in the highly stylised re-enactments of abduction that follow later in the film. In both image and speech, the children receive little opportunity to demonstrate agency or voice, which is unsurprising as this segment receives less than a minute compared to the detailed introduction to Gavin, which takes two to three minutes.

This is the dark side of human rights discourse: the human rights subject must show him or herself as the bearer of human rights, but also – simultaneously – as one whose rights (including dignity) have been stripped away (Hesford 2011). Trauma erodes or assaults the dignity, humanity and rights of the subject – and the performance of trauma perpetuates this loss. Through this encounter, what Luc Boltanski called a "politics of pity" emerges as a spectator encounters an "unfortunate" and experiences a moral obligation to act (1999). At the same time, this encounter positions one as abject other whilst endowing the spectator with agency and the capacity to bestow rights. These dynamics, which apply to the spectator of *Kony 2012* are on display in the video, as Jacob breaks down weeping, becoming nonverbal and fading into the darkness where Russell promises to make things better. Such are the limitations of a victim-based politics, particularly here as they reanimate the ugly tropes of Africa in Crisis and White Man's Burden or the White Saviour complex. It reinforces ideas of helplessness and the need for Africa to be guided by the White-West. This strategy, particularly as deployed in the film, reduces the endangered community to mute victims as it maintains power and agency in the body of white men.

Narratively, this encounter precipitates Russell's own trajectory of action. Following the promise, the video delivers a montage of Russell as activist, wielding a camera and addressing crowds. According to the voiceover, this story has "led me to here and the movie you're watching", thereby hailing the spectator into this movement. The invitation is explicit. This project "is not just about Jacob, or me, it's also about you", he states, shifting into the first person plural with the claim that this is the year "we change the course of human history".

An outline of aims and directives ("I'm going to tell you exactly how we're going to do it") concretises what might otherwise stay in the abstract. A montage of young people putting up "Stop Kony" posters and protesting at the US Capitol delivers the first glimpses of the plan. These placards resemble an election campaign poster. With its bold type of "Kony 2012: One Thing We Can All Agree On", the image situates itself within the political, and potential for (American) democratic action.

This peek at the future is interrupted when Russell restarts the story of the LRA and of his activism. Gavin makes an appearance as Russell seeks to explain the situation to his young son in the simplest of terms. This exchange is one of the more problematic ones in the film, and not simply because of the questionable parenting on display. He pitches the narrative and the politics to a five-year-old when the target audience, the IC constituency of high-school and university students, is older and more capable of comprehending something more complex. As a result, Russell fundamentally redraws the terrain, transforming it into a ready-to-comprehend battle of good versus evil. At the same time, such simplicity is easily distilled into 140 characters and shared. The framing of the issue lends itself to memification – reproducability and spreadability. When the LRA Conflict is filtered through the figure of one man, Joseph Kony, apprehending him and prosecuting him seems like an achievable goal. This section, much like its prologue or the short interview with Jacob, provide repetition and consumable data to accommodate the challenges of attention in viewing, and to supply soundbites to be repeated and transmitted by the listener.

The second explanation develops his points – however slightly – with its brief interviews with Ugandan politicians, Santo Okot Lapolo and Norbert Mao, as well as American human rights activist John Prendergast, onetime Director for African Affairs of the National Security Council and co-founder of the Enough Project. These excerpts support the claims of urgency, provide invitation to intercede and ultimately serve to legitimate Russell's goals – despite Lapolo's disturbing human rights record (Diebert 2012). Alongside this institutional reinforcement, Russell presents the obstacles he faced: without financial or policy-based interests, intervention was unlikely.

These impediments feed the dramatic arc of activism, as IC and its publicity strategy are shown to overcome these challenges. Russell decides the solution is to "show the movie [*Invisible Children*] to everyone". His voiceover avers its success as he states, "Awareness turned to action". The video supports this claim, with a depiction of the tours of schools and university campuses and with montages of youth attending screening events and joining demonstrations. The embodied meets the virtual, as Facebook emerges as an expression of community building through page building – its growth represented in the climbing numbers as well as repeated shares and invitations. The sequence of mounting activism concludes with Obama's promise to commit troops and the celebration of Invisible Children groups worldwide. As Russell tells the viewer (mistakenly) "For the first time the government took action because the people demanded it".

Ostensibly pushing the naïve sentiment that awareness leads inevitably to action, this sequence in fact offers much more. The activity shown on-screen or with screens (the film exhibitions, the Facebook groups, the YouTube posts) is in a dynamic relationship with activity off-screen. Here, publicity is only one component of a larger campaign, used to support such activities including direct services, lobbying and capacity building. Whatever one may think of Invisible Children, they developed a nationwide network of student activists focused on what was then one of the lesser-discussed issues in Central Africa – an issue whose prominence has grown in recent years. Covertly, this sequence models one of the key principles of video advocacy outlined by WITNESS Programme Manager Sam Gregory: video complements other forms of activism. It is not the sole arrow in the advocate's quiver (Gregory 2012a, 2012b).

This success story may activate what Jane Gaines (1999) has called "political mimesis", which refers to the sensuous link formed between on-screen and off-screen bodies that encourages personal affiliation and replication of the struggle. These sequences of youth activists burgeon with possibility, promise and excitement as they direct their energies into public demonstrations and advocacy projects. It is frustrating that there is no such encouragement of affiliation with the African bodies on screen, whether in terms of the activists on the ground or in the figure of Jacob. Yet, this limited field of representation is, as Melissa M. Brough observes, in keeping with both Invisible Children's overall strategy and a trend in Western humanitarian culture to cultivate "the sex appeal of America as donor/consumer" (2012: 180). Situating the video within a broader field of commodity activism, which unites consumer and popular culture with advocacy, one can see how it is the consumer who is hailed, and whose idealised self is projected as possibility.

The video deploys images of past genocides, including that in Rwanda, to remind the viewer of other atrocities that took place on the world stage to sluggish or minimal intervention. The gesture emphasises the obligation that comes with awareness. Here, multiple political emotions come into play: pity – that sentiment which intends to foster moral obligation to the subject and shame – no longer reserved for the perpetrator, but extended to the bystander. These recollections warn of failed promises. It is at this point that Russell outlines the plan and breaks down how it will work, each offering a step and a player: Kony is to be captured by Ugandan military, who must be supported by the US government, which will act only if they believe the citizenry cares, which can happen only if people know his name.

To promote this core awareness, IC planned the action of Cover the Night, when, on 20 April, people would cover their towns with posters to help put Kony's name everywhere. The video outlines this plan and the visualisation of the chain reaction: a young man puts up a poster. The wall collapses to reveal another wall, whose embedded television screen broadcasts images of a demonstration. This wall collapses onto another, this time showing Congress in action. The domino effect continues until only one thing is left standing: A fantasy mock-up of the *New York Times* declaring "Kony Captured". An action is connected to a distinct outcome. Even as exposure leads to action, the trajectory is not seamless: postering is an activity linked to other projects and other screens.

Cover the Night is not the sole advocated activity. Russell also provides instruction on how to apply pressure to culture makers and policy makers. He provides the list of 20 individuals seen as useful public spokespeople for the campaign. And celebrities are lightning rods for attention: they can help make noise and get attention in a crowded media ecosystem. The names provided also come with twitter handles – a mode of direct address which has the benefit of not only reaching the person, but also of being seen by those who follow that person. The video does not end with the celebrity. Rather, it encourages the audience to send messages (and in effect lobby) those who have the authority to implement policy or apply pressure to those who do create policy.

This campaign is predominantly American as suggested by the list of political names, and by the iconography of the posters. Here we see something that suggests the bipartisan nature of the campaign as the Republican Elephant and the Democrat Donkey come together in a Venn diagram resulting in peace. The poster, with its party-based imagery and a slogan of "Kony 2012" highlight the US election cycle. This is a period many citizens and organisations leverage to help set agendas. And in this case, Cover the Night becomes an agenda-setting mechanism within a larger campaign. Although the US-centric perspective possibly impedes a truly transnational movement, it is a shrewd decision.

The film concludes with some immediate practical instruction: to sign a pledge; to purchase an action kit; to sign up for the TRI to Rescue Joseph Kony's Child Soldiers campaign – a commitment to donate $3 per week to IC; and to share the video. These directives give the excited viewer a space to channel his or her energies, harnessing the excitement to activity, and they hew to Gregory's second principle for video in an advocacy campaign: "Storytelling should be Audience-Oriented and Should Provide a Space for Action" (Gregory 2012b).

The social life of video or, the context for the text

In the case of Invisible Children and *Kony 2012* one can see Gregory's principles come together along with the aforementioned recommendation that video and publicity function as components of a larger campaign. The video has clearly identified its audience, and for the most part, makes its pitch to that audience: students likely to be near a chapter of Invisible Children's robust network and impressive presence on campuses in the US and beyond. Invisible Children has employed such strategic narrowcasting from its start, centring on, as Amy Finnegan has observed, "affluent, Christian, and largely female activists to 'save Africa' from itself" (2013: 31). Continuing, Finnegan notes that this demographic is well matched to the kind of "'non-wave making activism' that centres on fundraising, event planning, and supporting mainstream policies toward Africa" (ibid.). A narrative that places agency within the male bodies might seem counterproductive given this largely female base, but, as Finnegan notes, they "often profess fascination with the Invisible Children male protagonists [and] feel a deep-seated compassion for the African children and an urgency to respond and do something" (ibid.).

Meanwhile, Cover the Night provided just the opportunity to build on the excitement and contribute to capacity building. It was a real-life activity intended to bring together local Invisible Children chapters and potential new members, as students on campus sought to organise the event. The planning meetings leading up to the major event, as well as the event itself, could supply occasions to invite interested participants into a broader structure of sympathy outside the text of the video. For savvier groups, this could also provide an occasion to invite local media, and extend the reach of the campaign and reinforce its messages.

For some, the seeming failure of Cover the Night reads as a failure of the video or of the campaign. But this may actually be more of an issue of the unpredicted and unprecedented viral success of the video; in a manner, it was too successful. The video was released on 5 March with a plan for Cover the Night to take place on 20 April. Clearly they anticipated six weeks as the time needed to build the trajectory of awareness to action. However, that plan was met with real-world challenges: there were not enough Action Kits available to meet the demand, leading to backlog and highly publicised frustrations with the operation. Meanwhile, the critiques proliferated and the backlash against the campaign came swiftly and hard.

However, the crisis faced does not suggest the futility of a social media campaign but rather it raises questions of how activists negotiate the speed and reach of these new media, particularly when assessing the timeline of a campaign. Sam Gregory sees this as a lesson in "the importance of building momentum through in-person screenings" – something formative in the development of Invisible Children until then – because these are still crucial and useful to "creating strong collective nodes of activism [that] allow responsiveness to questions that come up about choices of advocacy and dialogue" (Gregory 2012b). Such practices as outlined by Gregory indicate why viral video may be entirely desirable within programmes that are better served not by broadcasting, but by narrowcasting, a form of niche marketing that speaks directly to its target audience.

The wider dissemination and viral spread gave rise to numerous critiques of the work. There were those who found the 'slick', 'Hollywood' aesthetics of the video to be instantly damning. Yet, that is not necessarily antithetical to the production of an advocacy video. Although there has been a longstanding discomfort in the combination of politics and entertainment, with mass culture seen to pose a threat to the political potential of the public sphere and dismissive scepticism lingering in hybrid-terms like "charitainment" or "slacktivism", popular culture is not at odds with advocacy. Liesbet Van Zoonen (2005) and Henry Jenkins (2006), for instance, explore the ways entertainment culture offers opportunities to exercise citizenship typically associated with entertainment as places where one can exercise or entertain citizenship. Andrew Cooper (2008) treats celebrities as significant figures in international diplomacy. A move away from the expected sobriety of an advocacy piece does not necessitate an ineffective or self-cancelling outcome.

In the case of *Kony 2012*, the aesthetics seemed to speak to the core constituency and target audience, particularly with the use of Facebook and YouTube, which reflected on the immediate modes through which audiences would encounter the film and then share it. Moreover, these platforms serve as sites for the construction and performance of self, and here, a performance of the humanitarian self, which works within IC's "logic of neoliberal consumer capitalism and identity branding" (Brough 2012: 188). These platforms, both as represented in the film and as imagined in use, can function to articulate the relationship of the user to the world, and of the humanitarian to the person in need.

Such a focus contains a pernicious narcissism, wherein the self provides the filter for perceiving the world. And here, we can see a quality of social media life that represents the perception of the world through expressions of the self. While Russell's navigation through the Facebook timeline may appear an innocuous segue strategy, it establishes his place as the centre of the world, not only as explorer and navigator, but also as narrator and saviour of the others on his wall. It aggrandises Russell – and the identifying viewer – and unites this solipsistic approach to the world with the "politics of pity", generating a "narcissism of pity" whereby the emotion generated by the encounter creates a glorified humanitarian agent empowered to bestow aid upon the victimised subject. Such an imperialist mentality reaffirms problematic tropes and power dynamics. The sequence wherein Russell explains the situation to his son may be most representative of this practice.

The drastic simplification of European saviours for an Africa in crisis, while emotive, obfuscated the complexity of what was happening on the ground, and at times relied on misinformation. At the time of the video's release, the Lord's Resistance Army had ceased to be the threat to safety and security it had posed earlier, and Joseph Kony was no longer in Uganda. Such facts brought into question the necessity of empowering the Ugandan military, particularly in light of the terrible human rights record of the government in power, one of the video's own interviewees, and the army that was fighting the LRA.

A campaign film, its critiques and the public sphere

The success of this video allowed not only the critiques, but also the responses to the flaws to come to the fore. The digital platform of distribution and exhibition offered up a discursive space for people to debate the merits of the video and the campaign, and to speak back to it. Such activity fits neatly with Michael Warner's (2005) centrality of speech in the formation of publics, as well as Craig Calhoun's suggestion that we "think of the public sphere as involving a field of discursive connections" with clusters "organized around issues, categories, persons, or basic dynamics of a larger society" (1992: 37). Pierre Levy's idea of the virtual agora, where communities use knowledge space as "a site of collective discussion, negotiation and development" (1997: 13) enhances this awareness of the Internet's potential as public sphere, and the capacity of this campaign to generate a number of publics.

In this case, the prominence of the video provided an occasion both to clarify the political conditions, and, more importantly, for Ugandan voices to come to the fore. Al Jazeera online produced "The Kony Debate" as a page that combined additional reportage and clarification with links to Ugandan activists, in particular "Uganda Speaks", a collective of Ugandan bloggers and filmmakers who provided reports from the field, and who later released their own film about the LRA, bringing more local voices into the discussion. And while mainstream media aggregated the dissenting voices, less formally curated spaces also offered a platform as video bloggers and Ugandan journalists appeared on YouTube to speak back and respond to *Kony 2012*.

Invisible Children was also interrogated as newly aware audiences inquired about the financial management and Evangelical ties of the organisation. And again, the online space where the video was released provided a platform for these debates and discussions. Blogger and communications specialist Jed Sundwall (2012) noted that although the organisation and its campaign was beset by many problems, corruption in the ranks was not one of them as the allocation of funds both fit the organisation's mission (to raise awareness through film) and was commensurate with that of other charities. Meanwhile, IC kept the conversation going, offering answers to critiques on their website, and even asking people to tweet their questions to @Invisible with the hashtag "#AskICAnything".

The question of the organisation's Evangelical ties is particularly sticky, especially as IC obfuscated their proselytizing mission and links to the religious organisation, The Fellowship (Troutfishing 2012). Such potential ties become all the more unsettling when one considers Evangelical lobbying for fundamentalist values that ostensibly led to the introduction of the Anti-Homosexuality bill in the Ugandan government (Hunter and Sharlet 2010). Indeed, both organisations have been seen as closely aligned with the government under President and Fellowship member Yoweri Museveni. Such discussion regarding these ties, appearing in many blogs such as *Daily Kos*, *Talk to Action* and *Truth Wins Out* produced a public discussion about the organisation, its ambitions and the risks of supporting even the most seemingly innocuous or well-meaning component of their work (Besen 2012; Wilson 2012).

Yet is essential not to condemn Christianity within activism. Although alarming when tied to ugly principles, religion and advocacy work have longstanding ties, and this has even been the case within early Protestant evangelical movements and human rights or humanitarian activism. Missions around the world have provided a transnational infrastructure for sharing testimony and administering aid in cases of the Abolitionist movement or the coordinated effort to end the persecution of Christian Armenians in Turkey at the turn of last century (Torchin 2006). Moreover, faith-based networks are prominent today in the in humanitarianism, human rights and environmental justice. That said, Invisible Children maintained equivocation around their partners or their missionizing aims, which came under scrutiny within the new public and blogosphere that this highly visible campaign provoked into view. Indeed, amidst the spreadability came an opportunity for "drillability", a term Gregory (2012b) develops to address the ways a campaign can open issues beyond the core message; even when unintentional, the campaign and its videos remained productively drillable.

Conclusion

In this chapter, I have explored some of the concrete practices around crafting and deploying testimony within an advocacy campaign. Despite the seeming damp squib of Cover the Night 2012 and the backlash Invisible Children received for *Kony 2012*, it is essential to remember that this is one component of a wide-ranging and deeply entrenched campaign that offers lessons in how to build sustained engagement by complementing online media with other forms of action. Moreover, it offers an occasion to consider the ethical dimensions of representational strategies and prompts us to ask how one can engage an audience without resorting to excessive simplification, or a narcissism of pity that engages politics of victimisation and occludes local agency and voice. The phenomenon of *Kony 2012* – its success and the backlash – offers a useful reminder of the changing landscape of online media, which amplify the speed and reach of a message and its response. How does one manage the distribution and exhibition of a video in a field of increasingly spreadable media? What emerges throughout, however, is that there is potential for the activation of witnessing publics through media and within media domains, but that content and context must be actively and rigorously considered.

Note

1 LRA Crisis Tracker's website can be found at http://www.lracrisistracker.com/.

Bibliography

Besen, W. (2012) "Invisible Children and the Barnabas Group", *Truth Wins Out*, 10 April, online, http://www.truthwinsout.org/blog/2012/04/24158/ (accessed 15 October 2015).

Boltanski, L. (1999) *Distant Suffering: Morality, Media and Politics* (G. D. Burchell, transl.), Cambridge: Cambridge University Press.

Brough, M. (2012) "'Fair Vanity': The Visual Culture of Humanitarianism in the Age of Commodity Activism" in Mukherjee, R. and Banet-Weiser, S. (eds.) *CommodityActivism: Cultural Resistance in Neoliberal Times*, New York: New York University Press, pp. 174–94.

Caldwell, G. (2005) "Using Video for Advocacy" in Gregory, S. G., Caldwell, G. Avni, R. and Harding, T. (eds.) *Video for Change: A Guide for Advocacy and Activism*, Ann Arbor, MI: Pluto Press, pp. 15–19.

Calhoun, C. (1992) "Introduction: Habermas and the Public Sphere" in Calhoun, C. (ed.) *Habermas and the Public Sphere*, Cambridge, MA: MIT Press, pp. 1–50.

Cohen, S. (1996) "Government Responses to Human Rights Reports: Claims, Denials, and Counterclaims", *Human Rights Quarterly* 18(3), pp. 517–543.

Cooper, A. (2008) *Celebrity Diplomacy*, Boulder, CO: Paradigm Publishers.

Diebert, D. (2012) "How Invisible Children's Kony 2012 Will Hurt – and How You Can Help – Central Africa", *Huffington Post*, 9 March, online, http://www.huffingtonpost.com/michael-deibert/how-invisible-children s-k_b_1334410.html (accessed 15 October 2015).

Drumbl, M. (2012) "Child Soldiers and Clicktivism: Justice, Myths, and Prevention", *Journal of Human Rights Practice* 4(3), pp. 481–485.

Felman, S. and Laub, D. (1992) *Testimony: Crises of Witnessing in Literature, Psychoanalysis and History*, London: Routledge.

Finnegan, A. (2013) "The White Girl's Burden", *Contexts* 12(1), pp. 30–35.

Gaines, J. (1999) "Political Mimesis" in Gaines, J. and Renov, M. (eds) *Collecting Visible Evidence*, Minneapolis: University of Minnesota Press, pp. 84–102.

Gregory, S. (2012a) "Kony 2012: Juggling Advocacy, Audience and Agency When Using #Video4Change", *WITNESS Video4Change Blog*, online, https://blog.witness.org/2012/03/kony-2012-juggling-advocacy-audience-and-agency-when-using-video4change/ (accessed 15 October 2015).

Gregory, S. (2012b) "Kony 2012 Through a Prism of Video Advocacy Practices and Trends", *Journal of Human Rights Practice* 4(3), pp. 1–6.

Hesford, W. (2011) *Spectacular Rhetorics: Human Rights Visions, Recognitions, Feminisms*, Durham, NC: Duke University Press.

Hunter, B. and Sharlet, J. (2010) "Bob Hunter and Jeff Sharlet: An Exchange", *Harper's Magazine*, 19 November, online, http://harpers.org/blog/2010/11/bob-#hunter-and-jeff-sharlet-an-exchange (accessed 15 October 2015).

Jenkins, H. (2006) *Convergence Culture: Where Old and New Media Collide*, New York: New York University Press.

Keenan, T. (2004) "Mobilizing Shame", *South Atlantic Quarterly* 103(2/3), pp. 435–449.

Levy, P. (1997) *Collective Intelligence: Mankind's Emerging World in Cyberspace* (R. Bononno, transl.), Cambridge, MA: Perseus Books.

Peters, J. D. (2001) "Witnessing", *Media, Culture and Society* 23(6), pp. 707–723.

Sundwall, J. (2012) "The problems with the Problems with Kony 2012, and other Problems", *Manso* (blog), 10 March, online, http://manso.jed.co/post/19066683169/the-problems-with-the-problems-with-kony-2012 (accessed 15 October 2015).

Titeca, K. and Sebastian, M. (2014) "Why did Invisible Children Dissolve?", *Washington Post*, 30 December, online, https://www.washingtonpost.com/blogs/monkey-cage/wp/2014/12/30/why-did-invisible-children-dissolve/ (accessed 5 October 2015).
Torchin, L. (2006) "*Ravished Armenia*: Visual Media, Humanitarian Advocacy, and the Formation of Witnessing Publics", *American Anthropologist* 108(1), pp. 214–220.
Torchin, L. (2012) *Creating the Witness: Documenting Genocide on Film, Video, and the Internet*, Minneapolis: University of Minnesota Press.
Troutfishing (2012) Report Ties Invisible Children/KONY 2012 To 'The Family': Extensively, *Daily Kos*, 5 April, online, http://www.dailykos.com/story/2012/04/05/1080853/-New-Report-Ties-Invisible-Children-To-The-Family-Extensively (accessed 15 October 2015).
Van Zoonen, L. (2005) *Entertaining the Citizen: When Politics and Popular Culture Converge*, Oxford: Rowman and Littlefield.
Visible Measures Blog (2012) "Update: Kony Special Video Campaign Tops 100 Million Views", 12 March, online, http://www.visiblemeasures.com/2012/03/12/update-kony-social-video-campaign-tops-100-million-views (accessed 15 October 2015).
Warner, M. (2005) *Publics and Counter Publics*, New York: Zone Books.
Wilson, B. (2012) "KONY 2012, Invisible Children, and the Religious Right: The Evidence", *Talk to Action*, 12 April, online, http://www.talk2action.org/story/2012/4/16/223727/559 (accessed 15 October 2015).
Winston, B. (1988) "The Tradition of the Victim in the Griersonian Documentary" in Rosenthal, A. (ed.) *New Challenges for Documentary*, Berkeley, CA: University of California Press, pp. 269–287.
Yúdice, G. (1996) "Testimonio and Postmodernism" in Gugelberger, G. M. (ed.) *The Real Thing: Testimonial Discourse and Latin America*, Durham, NC: Duke University Press, pp 42–57.

PART III

Film, propaganda, ideology and the state

INTRODUCTION

Claire Molloy

At the beginning of the twenty-first century, critical engagement with the concept of propaganda appeared to have waned to the extent that Nicholas J. O'Shaughnessy has described it as, "relegated beyond the marginal to the irrelevant" (2004: 1). Consigned primarily to historical accounts of early Soviet cinema and twentieth century American, British and German wartime activity, propaganda was considered to have little contemporary currency in the face of communications and audience theories that were thought to better describe a more complex and nuanced media environment and its agents. All of this was to change, however, after the September 11 attacks as the ideological stakes were ramped up, and public and academic interest in propaganda reignited. More than a decade later, the 'power of film', its practices of manipulation and the potential for mass persuasion have continued to be debated, the discussion accelerated by internet sharing activities and the rise and reach of social media. In the mid-2010s, training and execution videos attributed to IS, controversial videos about the migrant crisis such as *With Open Gates: The Forced Collective Suicide of European Nations* (2015) or about the geopolitical role of Russia such as *I, Russian Occupier* (Zhurov, 2015) and a number of recent, high-profile Hollywood films such as *American Sniper* (Eastwood, 2014), *The Hunger Games: Mockingjay Part 1* (Lawrence, 2014), *The Hunger Games: Mockingjay Part 2* (Lawrence, 2015), *The Interview* (Goldberg/Rogen, 2014) and many others, kept the issue of propaganda in sharp focus and in the public consciousness. While much news media coverage has continued to employ the term propaganda in a disparaging sense, academic engagement with the concept of propaganda has sought to revise such narrow definitions and give consideration to its various complexities. The chapters in this part contribute to the expansion of thinking about the topic in relation to film and the associated connections between state and ideology.

The first chapter in this part, which focuses on the anti-fracking film *GasLand* (Fox, 2010), acts as a bridge between this and the topic of the previous part, activism. Like other recent films of its type, which have the intention of mobilizing action and support, *GasLand* was able to capture the wider media and public attention and, in doing so, was perceived as a threat to the oil and gas industries and a dominant state discourse which supported fossil fuels. With the film often branded as 'anti-fracking propaganda' and 'cinematic propaganda', the first chapter in this part seeks to enlarge the connotations of the term propaganda beyond its pejorative associations and embrace the form of cinematic persuasion evident in *GasLand* through an examination of the film's visual style and the propagation of its message.

The next two chapters explore the topic of propaganda in relation to more familiar areas of academic focus: that of US World War II and Soviet propaganda films, respectively. Gregory Frame's analysis of the *Why We Fight* series of films, produced by Frank Capra, explores the complex context from which these films emerged, attentive to the anxieties about the manipulation of the American public. Tracing out the relationship between Hollywood and the US propaganda strategy, Frame analyses the thematic threads, methods, techniques and functions of the films, which, he argues, were not simply to demonize an enemy but also to mobilize support for a particular envisioning of Americanism. This analysis makes apparent the extent to which this group of films reflected Capra's views and the delicate balance that had to be achieved between presenting an enemy as powerful and therefore a cause for public concern and, at the same time, a force that could be defeated. The third chapter in this part argues for a more nuanced view of propaganda that can take account of the multiplicity of ways in which film can incorporate a variety of propagandist elements and begins from the standpoint that persuasion and the influence of public opinion is not fundamentally 'evil'. Looking across three films, *Mother*, *The Girl with the Hat Box* and *The Tractor Drivers*, Panayiota Mini explores the uneven terrain of Soviet propaganda, which had to respond to various societal changes. Stressing the influence of American cinematic techniques, Mini's analysis of *Mother* identifies how these common stylistic devices were combined with Eisensteinian montage to engage audiences. Following from the previous chapter on the US *Why We Fight* series, it is interesting to note that Mini isolates aspects of the influence of American filmmaking in *The Girl with the Hat Box* and *The Tractor Drivers*, exploring the diverse ways in which these were deployed.

Moving from the post-revolution environment of Soviet cinema in the 1920s and 1930s to the re-envisioning of a 'post-conflict' Northern Ireland identity, the fourth chapter in this part explores how films have disavowed political commentary in favour of, what Stephen Baker refers to as, the 'propaganda of peace' in service to a neoliberal agenda and principles. Baker's critique of the lack of a politically engaged film culture traces the transformation of Belfast's on-screen image across a range of films. In doing so, he argues for a broader conception of propaganda that can take into account the 'persuasion for peace', which Baker contends is shaped by hegemonic social forces in concert with the state. This state of affairs naturalises the connection between peace and the neoliberal 'free market' and has resulted, as Baker points out, in the rapidly expanded use of the region as a prime film and television location. The cost of this expansion has been political disavowal at a time, Baker argues, when a politically engaged cinema is needed.

The final chapter in this part also explores national self-image, in this case through the lens of British film policy and its relationship between government intervention and the project of constructing national identity. Like Baker, Paul Dave examines this theme in relation to the shift towards a neoliberal agenda and the cultural and creative industries discourses which have supported it. Using Shane Meadows as a case study, Dave argues for a reorientation of film policy that is attentive to the notion of a creative democracy, suggesting this could be achieved with a move away from cultural politics in service to neoliberal capitalism and a move towards a 'politics of culture'.

Bibliography

O'Shaughnessy, N.J. (2004) *Politics and Propaganda: Weapons of Mass Seduction*, Manchester: Manchester University Press.

11

PROPAGANDA, ACTIVISM AND ENVIRONMENTAL NOSTALGIA

Claire Molloy

Introduction

A brief survey of internet search term trends reveals that searches for the term 'fracking' showed a dramatic increase from 2011 onwards, with strong regional interest in the United States and the United Kingdom (Google Trends 2015). The upsurge in key search queries for 'fracking' and 'what is fracking' followed the release of the film *GasLand* (Fox, 2010), a feature length documentary made and narrated by Josh Fox, the founder of the film and theatre production company International WOW Company. There is little doubt that Fox's film had an impact on the international public debate about hydraulic fracturing, a process for recovering natural gas from underground rock formations that involves pumping fracking fluids, a combination of water and proppants, at high pressure to fracture the rock and release the gas from underground reservoirs. *GasLand* followed the filmmaker's journey to discover the impacts of this process on the landscape and communities across the western United States. Interviews with citizens revealed a catalogue of questions about the safety of the process and the health problems which, Fox suggested in the documentary, were directly attributable to hydraulic fracturing. The film met with criticism from the gas industry and some scientists – labelled in various quarters as anti-fracking propaganda – and was used widely by activists and grassroots groups to mobilise action in communities across the US and Europe. Using personal and archival footage, fragmented landscape shots and imagery of domestic water supplies set alight, this chapter argues that the film's use of environmental nostalgia and spectacle constructs a form of positive cinematic propaganda and it examines the film's reception and the channels of information flow by which the film's anti-fracking message was propagated.

Documentary response to the oil and gas 'crisis'

In the wake of the National Energy Policy Development Group (NEPDG) chaired by Dick Cheney and established by George W. Bush in 2001, a slew of films about oil and gas emerged that responded critically to a new 'energy crisis' discourse. In May 2001 the NEPDG produced *National Energy Policy*, a 169-page report which set out the context and recommendations to address what it termed as "the most serious energy shortfall since the oil embargoes of the 1970s" (NEPDG 2001: viii). The report identified three key challenges: the promotion of energy conservation, repair and modernisation of the energy infrastructure and increasing energy supplies "in ways that protect and improve the environment" (NEPDG 2001: ix). On the last point, the report claimed that although renewable and alternative fuels offered a way forward in the future, their potential for meeting the United States' energy needs was "still years away" and for that reason existing practices had to be maintained and energy production be expanded (NEPDG 2001: x). The basis for concern, the report claimed, were the estimated increases in US oil and gas consumption over the next two decades – 33 per cent and 50 per cent, respectively – that would, given the (then) current rates of production, require America to import two-thirds of its oil. This, the report continued, would lead to a problematic "condition of increased dependency on foreign powers that do not always have America's interests at heart" (NEPDG 2001: x).

Such concerns were exacerbated by the 'peak oil' discourse, an event predicted to occur when consumption would outstrip maximum oil production. Global dependence on oil and the anticipated and actual increase in domestic demand thus had major geopolitical and economic implications. In 2014, the US Energy Information Administration reported that domestic energy production had met 84 per cent of energy demand in 2013 (EIA 2014). Noting that national consumption had increased continually since 2005 and that 82 per cent of overall energy consumption was fossil fuels, the EIA listed natural gas as the largest domestically produced energy resource, with renewable energy accounting for only 10 per cent of US energy consumption. Critics of the 'fracking boom' pointed out that tax incentives were offered to the fossil fuel industry which had the benefits of political allies and lobbying muscle, while the case for sustainable renewable energies was sidelined or ignored. As an op-ed in *The New York Times* argued:

> Let's face it: a large part of our political class, including essentially the entire G.O.P. [The Republican Party], is deeply invested in an energy sector dominated by fossil fuels, and actively hostile to alternatives. This political class will do everything it can to ensure subsidies for the extraction and use of fossil fuels, directly with taxpayers' money and indirectly by letting the industry off the hook for environmental costs, while ridiculing technologies like solar.
>
> (*Krugman 2011*)

Documentary films such as *The End of Suburbia: Oil Depletion and the Collapse of the American Dream* (Greene, 2004), *Escape from Suburbia: Beyond the American Dream* (Greene, 2007), *Fuel* (Tickell, 2008), *Blind Spot* (Doring, 2008), *Split Estate* (Anderson, 2009), *Haynesville: A Nation's Hunt for an Energy Future* (Kallenberg, 2009), *Houston, We Have a Problem* (Torre, 2009) and *Crude Independence* (Hutton, 2009) addressed variously the issues of peak oil, increasing US energy consumption, the localised impacts (and, in a minority of cases, the benefits) of US energy production, and the need for alternative and renewable energies. In 2010, *GasLand* was released, focusing specifically on the impacts of hydraulic fracturing on the lives of individuals, communities and the American landscape. *GasLand, Part II*, a sequel to *GasLand*, premiered at the Tribeca Film Festival in 2013, the same year *FrackNation* (McAleer, McIlhenney and Siegeda, 2013), a rebuttal to Fox's original film, was released. Furthermore, after the Deepwater Horizon oil spill in April 2010, films such as *Dirty Energy* (Hopkins, 2012), *The Big Fix* (Tickell and Tickell, 2012) and *The Great Invisible* (Brown, 2014) dealt with the relationship between politics and oil, safety, corporate greed and the immediate and lasting impacts of the spill, reported at the time to be the worst in US history. Other documentaries to explore the relationship between politics, power and fossil fuels include: *The Oil*

Factor: Behind the War on Terror (Brohy and Ungerman, 2005), *Crude Impact* (Wood, 2006), *Out of Balance: ExxonMobil's Impact on Climate Change* (Bardosh, 2006), *Blood and Oil* (Earp, 2008) and *Greedy Lying Bastards* (Rosebraugh, 2012). Many of these films also addressed the impact of fossil fuels and energy production and consumption on landscape, the environment and climate change, the latter of which had been propelled as an issue onto the public agenda in no small part by *An Inconvenient Truth* (Guggenheim) in 2006.

This notable trend for documentaries about oil and gas included films which had the aim of functioning as a call to action. In this regard, *GasLand* presents itself as an important case study; a film which has acted as the centrepiece for campaigns against fracking and, significantly, despite focusing on localised situations in the US, has been used also as a tool to inform and mobilise grassroots action elsewhere, including the UK and Australia. Indeed, the impact of the documentary outside the US was made apparent when British newspaper *The Guardian* quoted the communications advisor to Cuadrilla, a UK-based shale gas company, who commented on growing resistance to fracking in the UK: "*GasLand* really changed everything. Before that, shale gas was not seen as routinely controversial" (Harvey 2011). At the same time, the film attracted criticism as commentators aligned its aesthetic qualities with claims that Fox did not present a scientifically accurate account of fracking to label the film as "anti-fracking propaganda". One geoscientist argued,

> *Gasland* the movie should be evaluated not as if it was a scientific analysis or even as a work of journalism, but rather as a highly skilled piece of propaganda. Unfortunately, most of the viewers of this movie will see it as a fact-based documentary, and of course that is the genius of Fox's work.
>
> (*Duncan 2014*)

Elsewhere *GasLand* was "credited with spreading hysteria about the practice of hydraulic fracturing" (Markay 2012) and as "cinematic propaganda" promoted by "anti-fracking Hollywood" (BSEEC 2012).

It is important to consider that at the time of the film's release there was a relative void of information about fracking specifically. *GasLand* offered communities and individuals a viewpoint on hydraulic fracturing processes that stood in stark contrast to the industry discourse. In 2011, a year after its release, *The New York Times* foregrounded the film's influence on public debate in America, claiming that "the documentary *Gasland* brought the term 'hydraulic fracturing' into the nation's living rooms" (Soraghan 2011). Furthermore, such was the public response to the film in the UK that public relations trade news reported on the crisis management strategy undertaken to counter the film's impact noting that Cuadrilla Resources was put under major public scrutiny following the UK launch of *GasLand* (*PR Week* 2011). In Australia, community action groups organised well-attended screenings of the film, despite industry claims reported in the mainstream Australian media that there were substantial geological and regulatory differences between America and Australia which made *GasLand* irrelevant in the latter. One spokesperson for the energy industry contended, "it is difficult to comprehend how an American movie-maker who does not understand the NSW [New South Wales] or Australian regulatory environment, let alone the local geological conditions, can make these baseless claims about the local industry" (Galvin 2010). Yet, the authority granted to the film by activist groups and the potential for it to mobilise action was apparent in the promotion for screenings.

Activist films have a dynamic relationship with audiences and, given their aim to respond to the specificities of a particular moment or political situation, have a certain shelf life. In other words, their contemporaneity with specific issues or concerns is necessarily a characteristic of their existence as an activist film. As Mazierska and Kristensen contend, "A given political film can activate the audience shortly after it was made, but usually not twenty or fifty years later" (2015: 14). The need to function as a timely intervention also means that

> filmmakers therefore try to react to events promptly, acting as journalists rather than auteurs who patiently wait for inspiration and take time to polish their works. This is one reason why documentary films are a privileged type of political or activist film. (*Ibid.*)

It is then of little surprise that the majority of films about gas and oil since 2001 have been low-budget independent documentaries that have utilised film festivals to garner attention, have had limited theatrical exhibition, tending instead towards television, grassroots screenings, online platforms and social media to reach audiences. While the majority adopt an investigative journalistic approach and a style which has less 'commercial polish', *GasLand* opts for a different aesthetic approach. Despite using some conventions of investigative journalism with the viewer firmly placed in the position of detective, uncovering the evidence against fracking with the filmmaker, its visual style is considerably more polished than other similar documentaries. Specifically, *GasLand* utilises a visual style that incorporates images of unspoiled nature that work with the personal recollections of the filmmaker to create a strong sense of environmental nostalgia. On the one hand, this enables the film to make the point about the negative impact of fracking extremely clearly as it equates it with the destruction of the natural landscape. On the other, such environmental nostalgia allows the film to have universal appeal as the 'idyllic landscape under threat', harnessing the potent connotations of vulnerable 'nature-spaces' which I define elsewhere as "objects of discourse with differing symbolic resonances *and* physical places that are acted in and upon" (Molloy 2013: 182). The meanings of nature-spaces are therefore never fixed; they change over time, always open to physical reconfiguration and ideological management.[1] Despite the landscape being subject to human management and therefore change through, for instance, farming, tourism, fishing, hunting and so forth, *GasLand* succeeds in producing a very specific type of nature-space that serves the narrative's message. In the following section I discuss how the visual style of *GasLand* constructs the landscape as a vulnerable nature-space in need of protection.

GasLand, spectacle and evironmental nostalgia

In *GasLand*, Fox offers a persuasive account of the vulnerability of nature that could be delocalised and utilised in campaigns outside the US. Personal accounts of people affected by fracking are combined in sequences with the spectacle of water being set alight, visually reinforcing the dangers of the fracking process in ways that can be immediately grasped by an audience. While the personal stories of health problems included in the film are vital to engaging an audience's sympathy for Fox's message, the impacts on personal health cannot be made easily apparent, and without expert corroboration from, for instance, a doctor, are open to challenge. Images of burning water in the domestic home, however, provide shocking visible evidence of something dangerous and alien. The spectacle of water being set alight allows the viewer the privilege of verifying the authenticity of the personal accounts and the dangers posed by the fracking process. Moreover, throughout the film, images of water are used as important signifiers, indicative of the health of the landscape and those that inhabit it. Clean, healthy water is contrasted with the unhealthy contaminated water of fracked areas.

GasLand opens with a surreal image of the filmmaker wearing a gasmask, holding a banjo, walking backwards into the frame, the background to which is a fracking site in front of a ridge of mountains and wide blue sky. Fox's narration is slow, almost lethargic. He claims "I'm not a pessimist; I've always had a great deal of faith in people, that we wouldn't succumb to frenzy or rage or greed, that we'd figure out a solution without destroying the things that we love". The opening narration sets the tone for the film; a personalised yet general position statement that utilises emotive tropes (greed versus the destruction of something loved) which is difficult to contest. The film's title, *GasLand* interrupts the narration, followed by a short clip of the start of a meeting of the Chesapeake Subcommittee on Energy and Minerals which cuts sharply to an image of a car driving through a snow storm, a forest and beside a glittering lake accompanied by a haunting soundtrack as the film cuts back to the subcommittee meeting and one of the speakers extolling the benefits of fracking. The imagery moves back and forth between handheld close-ups of the subcommittee speakers refuting the environmental and health issues claimed to be associated with fracking, and wide sweeping landscape shots, some of which are images of the fracked landscape from the vantage point of a car.

This opening sequence sets up a visual opposition between the pro-fracking establishment and the landscape; the soft, often motion-blurred imagery of snow, mountains, lakes and forest, is in stark contract with fracked landscape, and the hard lighting of the committee room filled with white middle-aged men in suits. All of this is visually prefixed in the pre-title sequence by the gasmask-wearing, banjo-playing Fox, an intriguing image of the filmmaker which was subsequently used in the marketing and promotion of the film. Fox, as the narrator, introduces himself by name to the audience accompanied by images of his driving in the snow. Initially introducing the beginning of the story with an image of Dick Cheney, Fox then corrects himself and says "er, no, maybe I'll start with a different beginning". Switching the mode from that of a documentary on the oil and gas industry to a personal journey narrative, we are shown a red timber house hidden behind trees, which Fox identifies as his home. He gives a very short account of his family life and the building of his home accompanied by personal video footage and photographs. This is followed by archival footage of Pete Seeger singing "This Land is Made for You and Me" with Fox explaining how he discovered the importance of the interconnected natural waterways. Brief accounts of Richard Nixon's introduction of the Clean Air Act, Safe Drinking Water Act and Clean Air Act in 1974, 1972 and 1970, respectively, is referred to by Fox as an "era of environmental progress". A brief description of the technological progress being made at the time is then contrasted with Fox's idyllic and sheltered upbringing in the house in the woods. The narration leaps forward to 2009 and Fox's receipt of a letter from a gas company telling him his home was on top of the Marcellus shale formation and an offer to lease his land to the company in return for a signing bonus for almost $100,000. Using contrasting personal and archival footage, Fox explains that after 2005 the oil and gas industries were exempt from the Safe Drinking Water Act, the Clean Air Act, the Clean Water Act, the Superfund Law and various other environmental regulations. A map of areas in the US being fracked and an explanation of the fracking process are followed by a calculation of the amount of chemically infected water used and the stark warning from Fox "and now they're coming east". Images of the green landscape and sparkling waterways provide the emotive visual context for Fox's claim, "From 1972 until now – my whole life – all this has been protected". Using personal and pubic archival imagery (home videos and news footage), this sequence constructs the sense of an authentic history of a landscape which has been personally loved and state-protected. The notion that this protection has been provided for a 'whole lifetime' functions as a rhetorical device to expand the sense of longevity, despite it being a period of less than forty years (at the time of the film's release).

Fox's slow style of narration is gentle and sleepy, paralleling the apparent blissful tranquility of his childhood, upbringing and home surroundings. This style is clearly adopted for the purposes of the narration as we are, in the sequence following the film's exposition segment, introduced to the business-like tone Fox uses when asking for interviews with industry experts; invitations that are repeatedly refused. What is especially important about the sequences in which Fox is shown as being unable to secure an interview with industry experts are the sense of intrigue they construct. While footage of the refusals for interviews might otherwise be considered redundant, in this narrative they give the impression that something is being purposefully withheld. The viewer is then placed in the position of verifying the evidence placed before them. This includes the factual information provided by Fox, the personal accounts offered by people affected by fracking and the visual spectacle of burning water, all of which are contextualised by the construction of an imagined vulnerable landscape.

Throughout *GasLand*, montages move the audience through landscapes usually via car, sometimes on foot, giving little more than an impressionistic flowing sense of the natural landscape space, punctuated by longer shots for moments of visual contemplation. By contrast, the shots of fracking in the landscape, while often handheld and shifting between sharp focus and blurred, are from a fixed point. The visual effect is a subtle contrast between the flow of natural space and the static brutalised fracked landscape. Nostalgia for an authentic landscape, in other words an unfracked landscape, is communicated through the references to Fox's own happy childhood which frame the narrative, as well as through the poetic flowing visuals and references to how things used to be. The narrative is split into two distinct eras, the 'authentic' landscape before fracking and the unhealthy, technologically scarred, corporate fracked landscape after 2005. Despite the various interviews with individuals affected by fracking and the health problems that had plagued communities close to fracked areas, these individual stories are secondary to the story of the American landscape which is positioned by Fox's narration and the visual style of the film as the victim in this account of the fracking industry. Although the film follows Fox's own journey, the audience is constantly reminded to identify with the impact on the landscape, the loss of an authentic natural space and nostalgia for an imagined pristine landscape.

It is this thematic return to the notion of an authentic landscape and the variety of fragmented imagery – trees, snow, sun on water, backlit leaves, mountains, sky and so forth – which, despite retelling the experiences of individuals in small American towns, delocalises the landscape and opens up the film for appropriation by other communities. This fragmented impressionistic landscape could, at times, be elsewhere, certainly not specific to any particular American state or region. The signifiers of the authentic unfracked landscape are highly symbolic of a timeless unidentifiable pristine nature, one that is littered with references to an undisclosed actual place in time and space. Coupled with the framing of the personal narrative which uses signifiers of childhood memories, and the collective memory of political change signified by the references to Nixon's introduction of legislative change which Fox refers to as an "era of environmental progress", *GasLand* evokes the language of nostalgia.

In their discussion of *An Inconvenient Truth*, Murray and Heumann discuss the ideological power of environmental nostalgia and identify characteristics in *An Inconvenient Truth* which *Gasland* shares. Murray and Heumann note that *An Inconvenient Truth* opens with historical memories, one of which is personal to Al Gore – the river, the Gore family farm and the green landscape – and the 'universal historical memory' of images of Earth from Apollo Eight and Apollo Seventeen in 1968 and 1972. They argue, "Gore's personal memories not only add to his credibility by drawing empathy from his audience; they also serve as powerful environmental messages that connect tightly with the science on display in his slide show" (2009: 198). The collision of the personal and the public is central to evoking the environmental nostalgia that is able to engage an audience.

They note the importance of universal signifiers, for example images of trees which they regard as "reminders of a natural world we seem ready to preserve", and after discussing the limits of nostalgia which, they suggest, accumulated much negative criticism from postmodern scholars, Murray and Huemann argue for the recuperative power of nostalgia (202–203). For them, environmental nostalgia can be positive if it is able to convey a sense of hope for the future:

> Gore looks to a past [...] to demonstrate the destruction to which we have already contributed but which we now have the chance to overcome. Gore does not play the role of an apocalyptic prophet [...] He serves as a personal example and a conveyer of hope.
> (203)

In this respect, despite their use of propaganda conventions and rhetoric and in spite of the criticism they have attracted for their use of science, Murray and Huemann suggest that films "including Gore's *An Inconvenient Truth*, may inspire ecological action because they reveal much about the current state of environmental politics" (205). They add that "the messages from films [...] can also offer hope as they move audiences to action" (ibid.).

Murray and Huemann's argument that nostalgia functions as a powerful rhetorical device when combined with a discourse of hope could be also applied to *GasLand*. In much the same way as *An Inconvenient Truth*, *GasLand* also collapses the private and the public to evoke a form of shared environmental nostalgia. However, *GasLand* does not end with a message of hope, but one of a shared problem and the possibility for collective resistance. The end of the film returns to Josh Fox's home and the land surrounding it, depicted as lush, green clean, healthy and fertile. Fox explains that the Frack Act is making its way through congress. In his narration, he says:

> I don't know what's going to happen around here. I don't know if all of this is going to be destroyed. I don't know what's going to happen around the rest of the United States, whether all the friends I've made on this trip will get some relief. I guess in large part that's up to you. One thing I've found deep inside is a love for this whole country.

Fox then explains that the stream that runs through his property is part of a bigger waterway that flows through other states and regions and he claims that "my backyard wasn't my backyard anymore. It belonged to everybody else too". He ends the narration saying that fracking is planned for North Africa and Europe, "and it's possible that gasland might stretch a little bit further than my backyard, into yours". The final image is a close-up of clean running water; a moment for the audience to contemplate the evidence they've been witness to.

Distribution, exhibition and campaign

It would be inaccurate to assume that *GasLand* and the accompanying social media campaign led directly to mass public reaction against fracking. While the film may indeed have been key to opening up the public debate, anti-fracking sentiment was expressed and propagated through the news media and other networks of information flow following its release. Writing in *Variety* and echoing similar sentiments in the critical discourse elsewhere (for instance, see Kohn 2010; Nusbaumer 2010), the reviewer remarked that hyphenate writer-director Josh Fox's documentary *GasLand* "may become to the dangers of natural gas drilling what *Silent Spring* was to DDT" (Koehler 2010). In the review, Koehler claimed the film to be a

> rare example of cinema art that is also an organizing tool, the pic has a level of research, gutsiness and energy that should generate sensational response everywhere it plays. Distribs with a social conscience have a gem to buy, if they dare.
>
> (*Ibid.*)

Premiering at Sundance in January 2010 where it won the Special Jury Prize, *GasLand* had only minimal theatrical distribution through Fox's own International WOW Company, opening in September 2010 on two screens and grossing domestically \$30,846 from a five-week run (Box Office Mojo). Although the theatrical box office was slim, it was not insignificant when set against the production budget of a mere \$32,000 (Box Office Mojo). In terms of its reach, more important for the film was a deal with HBO, which saw *GasLand*'s US television premiere in June 2010 and an estimated HBO television audience of over one million in America and Latin America (Impact Field Guide).

GasLand was distributed on DVD and digital platforms in December 2010 through the Docurama division of New Video, which was acquired in 2012 by Cinedigm, an independent content distributor to Wal-Mart, Target, iTunes, Netflix, Amazon and the cable television Video on Demand platform. Following New Video's acquisition by Cinedigm, *GasLand* became available on Netflix in 2012. Early promotion for the DVD release by New Video continued to emphasise the film's potential to mobilise action, the authorial importance of Fox and the social responsibility of the distributor, quoting Vice President of Acquisitions, Mark Kashden saying, "*GasLand* is much more than documentary film. It's a compassionate call to action and great storytelling [...] New Video will play a vital role in bringing Josh's message to the widest possible audience" (New Video 2010).

The New Video press release hinted at the distributor's role in a wider campaign that accompanied the film. In this sense, the formal routes of distribution worked alongside with the strategic campaign which sought to raise awareness about fracking as an issue, mobilise and strengthen localised action by connecting the film's audiences with relevant organisations, and lobby against fracking. The film was the centrepiece with the website and social media playing vital roles in promoting the campaign's key strategic aims. Fox posted regularly on the film's official Facebook page with details of upcoming screenings, personal experiences and grassroots action in the US and beyond, and developments in US fracking legislation. The website included details about the making of the film, a fracking FAQ, a call to action and a list of suggested actions that could be undertaken by individuals, while a tracker was regularly updated with the number of actions taken. In addition, the website offered information about upcoming screenings and a blog which covered international as well as domestic fracking stories. Fox also toured the film across America in more than 180 towns. The screenings aimed to function as a call to action for activist and community groups, often conducted in coordination with grassroots, environmental and national organisations as well as colleges and universities, and were followed by a director's Q&A session. Fox also travelled further afield with the film, making personal appearances in Australia and across Europe.

Reception

Critical reception and marketing and promotional discourses for the film drew attention to the filmmaker's activist credentials, an identity which was further strengthened by his appearing in person at grassroots screenings. A review in *Indiewire* claimed that "Josh Fox's *GasLand* is the paragon of first person activist filmmaking done right" (Kohn 2010); *The Sydney Morning Herald* noted Fox's alignment with "local campaigners" and praised the film's evidentiary basis, the reviewer writing:

> *GasLand* is an angry film but its director, Josh Fox, is far from being a tub-thumper. He has set out to systematically investigate methods used in the US for producing natural gas – a supposedly pure form of energy – and the evidence he has unearthed is devastating.
>
> (*Hall 2010*)

Less favourable reviews such as those in the *Washington Post* and *New York Times* were critical of the film as a piece of investigative journalism and, by extension, Fox's credibility as a journalist. Both reviews made comparisons between Fox and Michael Moore, with the *Washington Post* review also describing Fox as "a banjo-plucking, horn-rimmed-hipster filmmaker in his late 30s" and the film's style as demonstrating his "failings as an amateur journalist" (Stuever 2010) and *The New York Times* review stating that "Mr. Fox shows a general preference for vivid images – bright red Halliburton trucks, beeping but unidentified scientific instruments – over the more mundane crossing the t's and dotting the i's of investigative journalism" (Hale 2010).

The impact of *GasLand* can be understood through the industry response to the film, which was swift in its organisation of a debunking discourse designed to counter the film's claims and dispute Josh Fox's credibility. Despite labelling the film anti-fracking propaganda, as anticipated, this debunking discourse focused primarily on the film's "factual inaccuracies" and much less on the film's potent (and manipulative) aesthetics of environmental nostalgia for a pristine landscape. Prior to the HBO premiere, the Independent Petroleum Association of America's (IPAA) PR operation, Energy In Depth, released *Debunking GasLand*, a document that set out the industrial concerns about the film. In its introductory paragraphs, *Debunking GasLand* questions Fox's credentials, noting that he is an "avant-garde filmmaker and stage director", accuses the film as displacing accuracy in favour of simplicity, and exaggeration in place of evidence, identifying the potential reach of the film (HBO's 30 million US subscribers) as a key issue (Energy In Depth 2010: 1). It then goes on to describe *GasLand* as "politics at its worst, art at its most contrived, and contradictions of fact found around every bend of the river" (ibid.). From there, the document proceeds to a breakdown, point by point, of what the industry regarded as the film's factual inaccuracies. In response, the following month, Fox issued a "de-debunking" document titled *Affirming Gasland*, a "point-by-point rebuttal" of the claims made in *Debunking GasLand* (Fox 2010).

The energy industry's debunking discourse on *GasLand* argued against its legitimacy as documentary, introducing the generic classification of the film as a key component of its claims to undermine Fox's authority. Whilst it can argued that, from an academic standpoint and following Bill Nichols (2001), *GasLand* straddles the performative, participatory and poetic modes, or after Toni de Bromhead (1996) that it fulfils the characteristics of detective and poetic storytelling, the debunking discourse proposed that *GasLand*'s "factual inaccuracies" rendered it a work of fiction rather than non-fiction. Writing to the Academy of Motion Picture Arts and Sciences following the film's Oscar nomination in the Best Documentary category, Lee Fuller, executive director of Energy in Depth, called for *GasLand* to be disqualified from the Best Documentary category. The letter to the Academy was accompanied by the *Gasland Debunked* document as evidence for disallowing *GasLand* as a work of non-fiction. Fuller wrote:

> Although we believe the film has value as an expression of stylized fiction, the many errors, inconsistencies and outright falsehoods catalogued in the appendix attached to this letter – and the many more we withheld for sake of brevity – cast serious doubt on *GasLand's* worthiness for this most honored award, and directly violate both the letter and spirit of the published criteria that presumably must be met by *GasLand's* competitors in this category.
>
> (*Fuller 2011*)

Coverage of the industry response to *GasLand* in *Time* magazine noted that there was a similar industry backlash and debunking of activist films *The Cove* (Psihoyos, 2009) and *Food Inc.* (Kenner, 2008) for taking "narrative liberties" (Walsh 2011).

Conclusion

In gaining purchase on the public consciousness, the labelling of *GasLand* as propaganda can be regarded as a rhetorical strategy designed to draw on a widespread acceptance of the term's pejorative associations with the intention of providing a counter to the film's apparent mobilising effects. In this respect, *GasLand* can be regarded as an important node in the construction of fracking as an object of discourse that opened up competing subject positions and reinscribed new limits on what could be said. At the same time, in combining environmental nostalgia with spectacle as evidentiary material, suggesting (by means of the footage of interviews being refused) that experts were withholding information, placing the viewer in the role of detective and leaving the narrative unresolved thereby prompting the viewer to become active in the story's conclusion, *GasLand* constructed a potent and persuasive narrative that closed down opportunities for alternative readings of the situation. The film's poetic style manipulates the visual elements for maximum impact, constructing an imagined vulnerable landscape that is easily delocalised. The ideological function of environmental nostalgia is utilised to rally public support, while the film's moments of visual spectacle are easily highly memorable and present evidence of a shared environmental threat that makes its way into the domestic space. The rhetorical strategies and visual devices do take narrative liberties and the film, I argue, is indeed cinematic propaganda. However, in this case, *GasLand* offers an important opportunity to expand the narrow pejorative status of propaganda to reclaim positive connotations for those films that serve to expose social ills, challenge dominant state discourses, influence public opinion and motivate progressive action at the grassroots level and beyond.

Note

1 For a discussion of how nature-spaces have been variously constructed and reimagined in response to political engagement with the environmental discourse see Molloy (2013).

Bibliography

Box Office Mojo, online, http://www.boxofficemojo.com/search/?q=gasland (accessed 4 July 2015).

BSEEC (2012) "Cinematic Propaganda", online, http://www.bseec.org/cinematic_propaganda (accessed 4 July 2015).

de Bromhead, T. (1996) *Looking Two Ways: Documentary Film's Relationship with Reality and Cinema*, Aarhus: Intervention Press.

Duncan, I. (2014) "Forum: Environmental Impacts of Shale Gas Development, Fact or Fiction? The 'Science' Behind *Gasland*" *EM*, July, online, http://digitaladmin.bnpmedia.com/display_article.php?id=1744569&id_issue=214918 (accessed 4 July 2015).

Energy in Depth (2010) *Debunking GasLand*, online, http://energyindepth.org/wp-content/uploads/2010/06/Debunking-GasLand.pdf (accessed 4 July 2015).

Energy Information Administration (2014) "Domestic Production Satisfies 84 per cent of Total U.S. Energy Demand in 2013", online, http://www.eia.gov/todayinenergy/detail.cfm?id=16511 (accessed 1 August 2015).

Fox, J. (2010) *Affirming Gasland*, online, http://1trickpony.cachefly.net/gas/pdf/Affirming_Gasland_Sept_2010.pdf (accessed 4 July 2015).

Fuller, L. (2011) "Letter to the Academy of Motion Picture Arts and Sciences" 1 February, online, http://energyindepth.org/wp-content/uploads/2011/02/EID_Letter_to_Academy_020111.pdf (accessed 4 July 2015).

Galvin, N. (2010) "Activists Warn Pollution Fears Hold Water Here" *Sydney Morning Herald*, 14 November, online, http://www.smh.com.au/environment/conservation/activists-warn-pollution-fears-hold-water-here-20101113-17ru2.html (accessed 4 July 2015).

Google Trends (2015) online, https://www.google.co.uk/trends/ (accessed 4 July 2015).

Hale, M. (2010) "The Costs of Natural Gas, Including Flaming Water" *The New York Times*, 21 June, online, http://www.nytimes.com/2010/06/21/arts/television/21gasland.html (accessed 4 July 2015).

Hall, S. (2010) "An Inflammatory Expose Warns of the Dangers of Natural Gas Mining" *The Sydney Morning Herald*, 13 November, online, http://www.smh.com.au/entertainment/movies/gasland-20101112-17qfa.html (accessed 4 July 2015).

Harvey, F. (2011) "'*GasLand* Changed Everything' – Fracking Film Battles to Woo English Villagers" *Guardian*, online, 20 April, http://www.theguardian.com/environment/2011/apr/20/gasland-shale-gas-drilling-uk (accessed 10 December 2014).

HBO (2010) *Gasland*, online, http://www.hbo.com/documentaries/gasland/synopsis.html (accessed 10 August 2015).

Impact Field Guide (no date) "GasLand", online, http://impactguide.org/ (accessed 4 July 2015).

Koehler, R. (2010) "*GasLand* May Become to the Dangers of Natural Gas Drilling what *Silent Spring* Was to DDT" *Variety*, online, 25 January, http://variety.com/2010/film/markets-festivals/gasland-1117941971/ (accessed 2 August 2015).

Kohn, E. (2010) "The Toxic Avenger: Josh Fox's *GasLand*" *IndieWire*, 30 January, online, http://www.indiewire.com/article/the_toxic_avenger_josh_foxs_gasland (accessed 4 July 2015).

Krugman, P. (2011) "Here Comes the Sun" *The New York Times*, 6 November, online, http://www.nytimes.com/2011/11/07/opinion/krugman-here-comes-solar-energy.html?_r=0 (accessed 10 October 2015).

Markay, L. (2012) "State Department Promotes Debunked 'Fracking' Propaganda" *The Daily Signal*, 17 February, online, http://dailysignal.com/2012/02/17/state-department-promotes-debunked-fracking-documentary/ (accessed 10 August 2015).

Mazierska, E. and Kristensen, L. (2015) "Introduction" in Mazierska, E. and Kristensen, L. (eds) *Marxism and Film Activism: Screening Alternative Worlds*, Oxford: Berghahn Books, pp. 1–25.

Molloy, C. (2013) "Animals, Avatars and the Gendering of Nature" in Pick, A. and Narraway, G. (eds) *Screening Nature: Cinema Beyond the Human*, New York and Oxford: Berghahn Books, pp. 177–193.

Murray, R. L. and Heumann, J. K. (2009) *Ecology and Popular Film: Cinema on the Edge*, Albany: State University of New York Press.

NEPDG (2001) *National Energy Policy: Report of the National Energy Policy Development Group*, May 2001, online, http://www.wtrg.com/EnergyReport/National-Energy-Policy.pdf (accessed 10 December 2014).

New Video (2010) "*GasLand* Partners with New Video for DVD and Digital Release" (press release 23 September 2010), online, http://www.newvideo.com/pressroom/release/gasland-partners-with-new-video-for-dvd-and-digital-release/ (accessed 4 July 2015).

Nichols, B. (2001) *Introduction to Documentary*, Bloomington: Indiana University Press.

Nusbaumer, S. (2010) "Big Sky Doc Film Fest: *GasLand* Fuel for Justice" *Huffington Post*, 20 April, online, http://www.huffingtonpost.com/stewart-nusbaumer/big-sky-doc-film-fest-emg_b_467605.html (accessed 4 July 2015).

PR Week (2011) "*PR Week* Awards 2011: Issues and Crisis Management" 26 October, online, http://www.prweek.com/article/1100817/prweek-awards-2011-issues-crisis-management (accessed 10 December 2014).

Soraghan, M. (2011) "Groundtruthing Academy Award Nominee *GasLand*" *The New York Times*, 24 February, online, http://www.nytimes.com/gwire/2011/02/24/24greenwire-groundtruthing-academy-award-nominee-gasland-33228.html?pagewanted=all (accessed 4 July 2015).
Stuever, H. (2010) "On HBO, One Man's Journey into a Natural Gas Crisis" *The Washington Post*, 20 June, online, http://www.washingtonpost.com/wp-dyn/content/article/2010/06/20/AR2010062003000.html?sid=ST2010062003687 (accessed 4 July 2015).
Walsh, B. (2011) "A Documentary on Natural Gas Drilling Ignites an Oscar Controversy" *Time*, 26 February, online, http://science.time.com/2011/02/26/a-documentary-on-natural-gas-drilling-ignites-an-oscar-controversy/ (accessed 4 July 2015).

12

BETWEEN 'INFORMATION' AND 'INSPIRATION'

The Office of War Information, Frank Capra's *Why We Fight* series and US World War II propaganda

Gregory Frame

While there is little debate that the United States *required* propaganda films as part of its war effort in order to combat the masterful and dangerous concoctions of the Axis powers and to inspire its people for a war of unprecedented ferocity against an unrelenting and vicious enemy, how these films should be constituted, and by whom, was a matter of significant debate and disagreement. This chapter will address the background to the propaganda produced by the United States during World War II, but will interrogate and analyse perhaps its most famous and sophisticated expression: the *Why We Fight* series. Executive produced by prominent Hollywood director Frank Capra, the series skilfully interwove newsreel footage, enemy propaganda, animated maps and battlefield reportage, into a coherent, dynamic and highly persuasive vision of the world before, during and after World War II.

The picture of the United States' propaganda operations during World War II is a complex one. On the one hand, there was the government's production of films for consumption by civilians at home and abroad, as well as 'orientation' films for troops heading into battle. On the other, there was the government's relationship with Hollywood and the concerted attempt to ensure that the film industry's output supported the war effort. Around the fringes of these operations existed a palpable hesitation about the production and utilisation of propaganda films, and this anxiety coalesced around two factors. First, the idea of propaganda – setting out deliberately to manipulate people through misleading, sometimes inaccurate information – was considered anathema to a nation proud of its democratic ideals and traditions (Koppes and Black 1990: 48). The United States was the only major power without an official propaganda agency prior to World War II. Second, it was widely regarded that films produced during World War I, particularly the popular shorts that demonised the Germans as "oversized marauding ape[s] that indiscriminately kidnapped and slaughtered Belgian women and children" had overstepped the mark (Geiger 2011: 125). These excesses prompted a call for a more streamlined and careful approach to the form during World War II, which led to the creation of the Office of War Information (OWI) by presidential decree in June 1942.

OWI was designed, as Betsy McLane suggests, "to coordinate all government information released to the media and to develop its own means of informing the public" (McLane 2012: 147). A wide variety of propaganda films were produced, aimed at audiences domestic and international, civilian and military. However, chaos continued to be caused by a number of government information divisions competing over similar territory which, taken together, failed to create a coherent and unified war vision. While it was accepted that "controls over the politic and morality of American movies were [...] crucial to the project of establishing national unity", the relationship proceeded in a rather disorganised, *ad hoc* fashion (Geiger 2011: 127). This was because, as Koppes and Black note, "propaganda policy evolved from a typically Rooseveltian melange of caution, indirection, duplication, half-measures and ambiguity" (1990: 50). OWI was meant to take charge of propaganda, but the Office of the Co-Ordinator of Inter-American Affairs (CIAA), devoted to operations in Latin America, retained its independence. OWI itself was separated into branches dealing with foreign and domestic affairs, with the latter branch working closely with Hollywood to produce pictures that would bolster the war effort.

Hollywood, otherwise supportive, nonetheless resisted anything that would impact its business interests. As Thomas Doherty notes of the Washington/Hollywood relationship during the war, "the liaison [...] was a distinctly American and democratic arrangement, a mesh of public policy and business enterprise" (1993: 63). Aside from any conflict with Hollywood studios, OWI also faced hostile opposition from Congress which, consistent in its resistance to Roosevelt's New Deal, attempted to block the unit's funding, citing concerns regarding infringement of free speech. Ultimately, OWI's Domestic Branch "never succeeded in getting a production programme underway", a failure driven by a combination of a recalcitrant Congress and the American people's widespread suspicion of information directed at them by the government (McLane 2012: 48).

The confusion and apparent disorganisation of the United States' propaganda strategy is indicative of a nation experiencing a profound struggle as to how it would deliver films that would galvanise its citizenry and inspire its troops without compromising its democratic ideals. The approach taken, to produce films that would celebrate Americanism rather than vilify its enemies, combated this anxiety: Robert Riskin's work for the OWI's Overseas Bureau, the ambitious *Projections of America* films (of which 26 were produced) aimed to challenge preconceptions of the United States in foreign territories (Scott 2008: 347). Both Riskin and his chief of production Phillip Dunne preferred the subtly persuasive brand of propaganda to the more common aggressive approach: their films were intended to generate sympathy for the 'American way', promoting free speech, free enterprise and equal opportunities. Films such as *Valley of the Tennessee* (Hammid, 1944) and *The Town* (von Sternberg, 1945) were affirmations of Americanism for foreign audiences, the former a paean to the ways in which "American ingenuity and the collective pioneer spirit have translated into social progress and personal empowerment", the latter a reconstruction of Rockwellesque fantasy, an image of Middle America as "clean-cut, industrious, family-oriented, churchgoing" (Geiger 2011: 133). In the worlds created by Riskin's films, the post-war landscape would be as imagined by Roosevelt's famous "Four Freedoms" speech of 1941: "led by the US and characterized by freedoms of speech, of religion, and of freedom from want and fear" (135).

Similarly inspiring films were sought for American troops, ones that offered more than the usual training information. George C. Marshall, Chief of Staff of the US Army, believed that soldiers should not just be shown *how* to fight, but told *why* this particular fight is necessary: for him, "military education was never just a matter of force-fed information and rote recitation but of nurtured incentive and felt commitment" (Doherty 1993: 70). As McLane suggests, it was assumed that servicemen would be "more committed and able fighters if they knew about the events leading up to, and the reasons for, US participation in the war" (2012: 139). The OWI was careful to avoid the terms 'indoctrination' and 'propaganda' (considered 'un-American'), and preferred instead 'orientation' (ibid.) Given this strategy, it is perhaps unsurprising that Frank Capra was employed to produce the series. The films Capra directed in the years before the war, including *Mr Deeds Goes to Town* (1936), *Mr Smith Goes to Washington* (1939) and *Meet John Doe* (1941), are often remembered as shining celebrations of the United States' democracy and economy. In truth, they are more complicated. In all three films, the Capra hero – the ordinary, honest, straightforward individual – is brought in to rescue this system from corruption and greed. In their own individual ways, Capra's films can be viewed as performing acts of rescue for America's democratic and economic systems in the darkest hours of the Great Depression. *Meet John Doe*, in particular, released six months prior to America's entry in to World War II, was a downbeat vision of the ways in which the 'common man' could be overwhelmed by a society manipulated by a deceitful press kowtowing to corporate interests. *Why We Fight* would offer a similar impression of what life would be like if the United States did not stand up for its values, while simultaneously celebrating the courage and heroism of its allies and pointing the way to a brighter, more prosperous and peaceful future.

Why We Fight was an ambitious project that, as Richard Dyer MacCann suggested, sought first to destroy faith in the notion that the United States could remain isolated and unaffected by the wars in Europe and the Far East; second, to create a clear dichotomy between the strong and righteous Allies and the stupid and malevolent Axis; and third, to ensure that the courage and success of America's allies before 7 December 1941 was recognised (1973: 157). What Capra recognised from the beginning, however, was that this intention could not be fully realised or achieved without recourse to techniques used in drama in order to excite the senses, inspire and, in many cases, horrify and disgust. The dazzling array of methods employed, combining existing footage (newsreels, Allied and captured enemy records of battle, segments from fictional films, Nazi propaganda films) with animation, voiceover narration, music and dynamic editing, were put in service of this goal. As Doherty notes of the series' style and composition, "never before had the entire panoply of cinematic devices been put to such concerted and seamless instructional use" (1993: 74).

The series consisted of seven parts: *Prelude to War* (1942), *The Nazis Strike* (1943) and *Divide and Conquer* (1943) covered the years from the end of World War I until American entry into World War II, and constructed the clear dividing lines between the Allies and the Axis. *The Battle of Britain* (1943), *The Battle of Russia* (1943) and *The Battle of China* (1943) saw the series turn its attention to the specific campaigns fought by America's allies, and looked to draw these nations together in common cause, emphasising their beliefs in freedom from tyranny (a debatable characterisation of the Soviet Union at the time) and their bravery and determination to achieve this goal. The final part, *War Comes to America* (1945) examined changing attitudes in the United States as a result of the war. In the rest of this chapter I will address each film in turn but retain the clear demarcation between the films that focus on the 'pre-war' phase of action and those that concentrate on the campaigns (the former has attracted far more critical attention than the latter). I will explore the ways in which the thematic drive of the series – to celebrate the values of freedom and democracy as simultaneously American and universal – is demonstrated and reinforced consistently through its use of film language. In so doing, this chapter will show how *Why We Fight*'s function was not simply to demonise the enemies of these values, but to act as a clarion call to defeat them and build a better world underpinned by a benign vision of Americanism. In this respect, *Why We Fight* offers a less overtly manipulative vision than might otherwise be expected from propaganda. However, its view of the world remains inextricably linked to the ideological preoccupations of Capra, and Hollywood cinema more generally, in this period.

Prelude to War (1942) / *The Nazis Strike* (1943) / *Divide and Conquer* (1943)

Prelude to War establishes the series' themes, style and overall message swiftly and uncompromisingly. Quoting Vice President Henry Wallace, it constructs a clear dichotomy between 'the free world', a gleaming white globe of hope and optimism, and 'the slave world', a black void dominated by authoritarian regimes, violent demagogues and people suffering from collective insanity and mass delusion. Geiger suggests that the film "leaves little room for contemplation", "disallows questioning of images" and "presents audiences with a simple, divided world view" (2011: 136). This is inarguable, although one might question why this is necessarily problematic given the intended audience of the film and its goals: as Joseph McBride suggests, the "'us or them' dialectic gave the films the emotional power Capra sought, simplifying the enormously complex historical and political issues underlying the war into a single, quickly grasped, black-and-white concept" (1992: 468). Capra believed that normal soldiers had little to no understanding of geopolitics and therefore, in order to achieve the stated aim of inspiring the troops through a clear celebration of Americanism and denigration of its enemies, this apparently simplistic approach was the only way (469).

Prelude to War is very keen to emphasise the similarities and common bonds between the Allies despite their various differences in language, culture and systems of government and economy, and its internationalist approach is emphasised in the first few minutes of the film, which seek to historicise and explain America's reasons for intervention not merely as a response to the attack on Pearl Harbor but as a result of the cumulative effect of Axis violence towards Britain, France, China, Czechoslovakia, Norway and Greece (to name but a few), achieved through a rapid montage of battlefield footage. It is underpinned by the greatness of the American system of government which, according to the film, represents the greatest that mankind has achieved, with particular significance afforded to the Declaration of Independence and the figures of George Washington, Thomas Jefferson and Abraham Lincoln. This strategy is entirely in keeping with the series' joint goals of emphasising the need for international cooperation and celebrating American democratic traditions (467).

Every opportunity is taken to contrast this image of tolerance, freedom and democracy with the frightening authoritarianism, imperialism and violence of the Axis powers. However, this does not automatically lead to a demonisation of the people of these nations. While there remains rhetoric that plays clearly on national stereotypes ('Germans had in an inborn love of regimentation and harsh discipline'), great emphasis is placed on the *cessation of thought* in these countries, the film arguing that the peoples of Germany, Italy and Japan were being manipulated by dangerous, devious men pursuing nefarious ends. Capra's films, particularly *American Madness* (1932) and *Meet John Doe* (1941), are often wary of the tendency of the masses to behave irrationally, abandoning their principles when threatened by insecurity and *Prelude to War* is no different. Newsreel images show huge crowds of Italians and Germans mindlessly saluting their Mussolini ('an ambitious rabble rouser') and Hitler ('a forceful demagogue [who] took advantage of postwar chaos'), respectively. Particularly chilling is the lengthy montage of footage of children training, marching and saluting in unison in all three Axis countries. As James Agee notes of this sequence, it is a "virtuoso job of selection and cutting, and the grimmest image of fascism I have seen on a screen" (1975: 156). The intended meaning here is to present the German, Italian and Japanese people as victims of brainwashing by their leaders, striding mindlessly towards oblivion.

Prelude to War establishes animation, which is employed consistently throughout the series, as a fundamental stylistic choice to illustrate the manipulation and imperial ambition of the

Axis powers. Animated telegraph poles, representing the Axis' ability to manipulate their populations through propaganda, transmit 'lies, lies, lies'. Piles of animated coins, representing the Nazi military budget, dominate the screen. In keeping with the dichotomy established by the 'free' and 'slave' world construction at the film's beginning, maps illustrate the conquering of nations by subsuming them beneath a malevolent, almost tumorous black ink. The plan for global domination is outlined halfway through *Prelude to War*, with the final phase being the capture of the United States by Japan and Germany. If one of the series' stated aims was to 'destroy faith in isolation', the depiction of such an alarming present and frightening future is likely to have played a significant part in it, showing the entire globe under the dominion of the *swastika* and the *rising sun*. In the final part of the film, which chronicles Japan's attempt to conquer China, the campaign is introduced by a dagger being driven into the heart of Manchuria, preceded by a steadily rising drumbeat and accompanied by a clap of thunder. It is a dramatic device clearly designed to shake loose any lingering shards of complacency.

The Nazis Strike elaborates on the relentlessness and brutality of the Nazis introduced in *Prelude to War*. Much of the film concentrates on Nazi treachery up to the formal beginning of World War II: the annexation of Austria, the stealthy capture of Czechoslovakia and the conquest of Poland. Richard Barsam argues it is "a highly charged, emotionally told history of the 'maniacal will,' the 'madness,' and the 'insane passion for conquest' of the Nazi leaders" (1975: 152). The film is preoccupied with establishing the Nazis as a formidable, malevolent and terrifying force. In keeping with this reading, it begins with footage from Leni Riefenstahl's *Triumph of the Will* (1935), which Capra described as 'terrifying' in his autobiography; "the ominous prelude of Hitler's holocaust of hate", but "as a psychological weapon aimed at destroying the will to resist, it was just as lethal" (Capra 1971: 328). The expressed intention behind the repurposing of this footage for American propaganda was to divest it of its mythological underpinning: traumatic images of the victims of Nazi violence are superimposed over the militaristic precision of the Nuremberg rally. The goose-stepping soldiers, mindlessly obeying their leader, are made to look ridiculous, undermined by music that would not sound out of place in a Looney Tunes cartoon. As Capra himself stated, "We took their own footage and tried to make it backfire on them" (quoted in Bailey 2004: 127).

However, examining it closely it is clear that the film intended to construct the Nazis as an awesome force not to be underestimated: as Doherty notes, "the enemy soldier should be looked upon as a vicious gangster – skilful, dedicated, and deadly as a cobra" (1993: 75). The use of *Triumph of the Will* is intended to show the Nazis as united, disciplined and, judging by the ominous music that accompanies the film's title at the beginning, a formidable foe. This intention is reinforced by the German-accented voiceover narration early on in the film that looks at the rearming process and the insane, terrifying ideology that lay behind it:

> forget hours, forget working conditions, forget how to think … let the democracies talk about freedom. No freedom here. No labour unions. No overtime. The führer tells you where to work, when to work, how long to work, how much your work is worth. […] We have a sacred mission: today we rule Germany, tomorrow the world.

This foreboding monologue is followed by two rapid tracking shots of saluting Germans superimposed over one another. Accompanied by the repeated chant of "Sieg heil!", the image is visually and aurally overwhelming.

The tendency to present the Nazi war machine as an all-encompassing, unstoppable force risks painting a rather hopeless picture. The conclusion is an emotional one, designed to disturb and terrify: underscored by the second movement of Beethoven's Seventh Symphony, reported to be a favourite of Hitler's, the consequences of Nazi violence are laid bare. The destruction of Poland is made manifest through the relentless rhythm of the music, its minor key lending it a mournful quality, and accompanying images of Polish corpses lining the streets, mothers weeping over dead children. The volume and timbre of the music builds to a crescendo, which further reinforces the overwhelming nature of Nazi devastation. Cannily, the film does not end here but rather with a note of hope: the British declaration of war, which, explored at the very end of the film, is designed to inspire, cited as evidence that "the democracies had convictions on which they were willing to stake their lives". The film then repeats some of the images of displaced, desperate, weeping Polish civilians used only moments prior, this time underscored both by Beethoven and Winston Churchill's inspirational words: "Lift up your hearts, all will come right, and out of the depths of sorrow and of sacrifice will be born again the glory of mankind", before a rousing chorus of "Onward Christian Soldiers" and the Liberty Bell draws the film to its ultimate conclusion. Barsam suggests that this "mood of moral righteousness" detracts from the film's effectiveness, but it is difficult to see how: the repetition of the footage of civilians at the film's end allows it to perform the task of the series overall; to inform *and* inspire (1975: 152). The closing moments of *The Nazis Strike* is intended to fulfil the latter half of the bargain in explicit terms.

Divide and Conquer is the first of the films to look in great detail at military strategy (although the latter part of *The Nazis Strike* did explore this in relation to Poland), and deals primarily with the Nazi conquest of Western Europe and Scandinavia, building towards The Battle of Britain. McLane suggests the film is akin to a classical tragedy, and the comparison is certainly a compelling one: the film begins with the conquering of Poland, moving through German strategy and Hitler's treachery, before chronicling the speed and ruthless efficiency with which the German army overwhelmed Denmark and Norway, detailing French vulnerability to invasion, showing the swift defeats of Holland and Belgium before concluding, in heartbreaking fashion, with the fall of France (2012: 142). The use of combat footage and animation work again in conjunction to present images of Nazi power, with particular care taken to ensure the images, assembled from a variety of sources, appear as though they had originated with this production: as McLane notes, it is "almost as if all of this footage had been shot for these films under Capra's or Litvak's direction" (ibid.). The effect of this assembly is a sense of intensity: the rapidly edited footage of German artillery battering the French lines creates an unremitting din, Nazi strength further reinforced by the figuration of their forces as an enormous phallic arrow piercing the French lines with ease, which fragment and scatter in the face of this potent, ruthless barrage.

Hitler is explicitly compared to John Dillinger, his treachery and backhandedness reinforced at every turn by quotations of his peaceful intentions towards these nations before proceeding to chronicle the brutal bombardment and cruelty towards civilians, particularly children (indeed, the series' tendency to emphasise the suffering of children is amongst its most blunt persuasive techniques). The persuasive strategies here are similar to the previous two films, although this film is slightly more preoccupied with the parade of Nazi ghouls and presenting Hitler at his most theatrical. Importantly, the voiceover narration does not contextualise or translate these speeches, preferring instead to allow the maniacal performances to speak for themselves, including a montage of unquestioning followers saluting their leaders. This renders the footage of Hitler striding into France to secure its surrender before taking a tour of Paris all the more upsetting, underscored first by stunned silence, and then by a mournful trumpet and drumbeat as disconsolate French citizens weep at their new subservience. The surrendering French are not spared any criticism, however: as Barsam suggests, the film presents France as "disillusioned and cynical [...] weary of her own ideals", almost ripe for the plucking by a force as focused and ruthless at Hitler's (1975: 152). It is in this instance that one could agree with McLane's suggestion that the series was "admired on aesthetic and technical grounds but not for its ability to indoctrinate", because *Divide and Conquer* presents a devastating vision of catastrophic defeat by a terrifying foe, but offers little in the way of inspiration (aside from a rather limp suggestion that Charles de Gaulle's army-in-exile would rescue the French people in conjunction with Britain and the United States) (2012: 142).

The Battle of Britain (1943) / *The Battle of Russia* (1943) / *The Battle of China* (1943)

The three films chronicling the efforts of the United States' allies up to, and immediately following, American entry into the war are politically interesting for a variety of reasons, not least because the latter two are poetic and at times beautiful celebrations of two nations that would quickly become enemies of the United States in the years following World War II. All three of these films are designed to inspire by demonstrating that, unlike the first three in the series, the Axis powers were beatable. Although McBride notes that the earlier films, such as *Prelude to War*, may have in fact *increased* the impression of the enemy's strength by the soldiers watching, the films about the battles of Britain, Russia and China all conclude with inspiring words from, and images of, the victorious Allies (1992: 482).

The Battle of Britain is perhaps the simplest of the three films. It begins with the infamous footage of Hitler surveying the spoils of his French conquest, looking up at the Eiffel Tower, the images of the Nazi armies robotically marching through the Parisian streets underscored by an ominous orchestral score as attentions turn to Britain. The image of Britain the film offers is a familiar one: the plucky, stubborn little island in the north Atlantic that refused to yield to Hitler and his plans for world domination. In service of this image, the film consistently juxtaposes the ruthless power of the German forces with the determined British people, memorably figured as little Jonah about to be swallowed by the Nazi whale. The use of familiar British songs like "Land of Hope and Glory" and "British Grenadier" provide defiant counterpoint to the images of German bombardment, and the animations that show the malevolent Nazi forces scorch their way across Europe.

These are the most politically significant elements of *The Battle of Britain*: the fearsome Nazi bombardment, witnessed the previous two parts of *Why We Fight*, is repeated here, but interspersed are British propaganda images to reinforce the pluck and determination in the face of adversity. As Dyer MacCann suggests of the film:

> The outnumbered people and the little air force are the steady heroes of this remarkable moving picture. No thoughtful American could watch this dramatic and terrible story without a sense of wonder and gratitude that this thing could have been done on this little island in 1940.
>
> *(1973: 159)*

In this regard, the film offers us romanticised images of the people of Britain: women scrubbing floors, serving meals, caring for children; men in pubs, tending churchyards. This 'home guard' – the clerk, the butcher, the farmer, the member of parliament – constituted the nation that would resist German conquest at all costs. In the absence of the right equipment, the British would employ 'the weapon of spirit'. Capra's Britain is the stuff of Ealing comedies: we are shown footage of resolute citizens playing harmonicas in underground bomb shelters, making light of the persistent threat of death at the hands of German bombs, Londoners waking up each morning after a night of bombardment to continue life as normal, drinking cups of tea and comparing notes on the previous evening's bombing, a husband and wife returning to their damaged home, the woman dismissing her husband's suggestion she leave for safer terrain. All of these images are designed to reinforce the narrator's suggestion that "Hitler could kill them, but damned if he could lick them", a claim further reinforced by the images of Brits celebrating Christmas in the middle of the Battle of Britain. The carol-singing, when one considers the anti-religious attitudes of Nazism addressed in *Prelude to War*, becomes itself a political statement.

Barsam suggests "*The Battle of Russia* is a tough, fast, informative film", although it is the longest of the series (1975: 153). It is an emotional celebration of the nation that tore the heart out of the German war machine, and is rather more careful in its construction than Barsam's characterisation implies. While familiarity with Britain and the British (or, at least, *stereotypes* of the nation and its people) probably negated the necessity of such a strategy in the series' previous instalment, *The Battle of Russia* emphasises the size ("all of North America and a million square miles to boot"), wealth (gold, silver, copper, tin, manganese and nickel), and diversity (Ukrainians, Armenians, Georgians and Laplanders, to name but a few) of the Soviet Union. The film makes use of other (fictional) films, particularly Sergei Eisenstein's *Alexander Nevsky* (1938) and Vladimir Petrov's *Peter the First* (1937) to celebrate Russian heroes, and emphasise the historical tendency for the country to be invaded though never conquered.

What the film does not do, and scholars of Capra and of documentary have been quick to point this out in postwar studies of the film, is excoriate (or even mention) Soviet communism or authoritarianism. The absence of this criticism caused headaches for Capra and his production team in the anti-communist 1950s: as McBride notes, "Capra felt vulnerable for having made *The Battle of Russia*, which not only had nothing critical to say about the Soviet political system but even went so far as to call the Soviets a 'free and united people'" (1992: 462). The cloud of suspicion that hung over the film after the war ended speaks far more of the atmosphere of paranoia in the United States rather than anything actually in (or not in) the film itself: it is indeed an insistently positive vision of Russian bravery in the face of what appeared inevitable defeat, and a highly selective image of its government and economy, but this is entirely unsurprising. *Why We Fight* intends to emphasise the similarities and continuities between the Allies, and *The Battle of Russia* is no different. As Capra himself stated (having attempted to distance himself from the production of the film in the immediate aftermath of the war, as discussed by McBride (1992: 486–7), "you understand these were our allies. We were fighting a common enemy at the time, not each other. Unless you get into that, you won't understand the simplifications" (quoted in Bailey 2004: 126).

The 'simplifications', as Capra describes them, are in keeping with those of the previous instalment, *The Battle of Britain*. The setpieces of the film are no doubt the siege of Leningrad and the battle of Stalingrad. It is in these sequences that the series' sophisticated use of montage editing comes to the fore to emphasise the Russian grit and determination to resist the Nazi bombardment: German shelling is juxtaposed with Russian manufacturing, welding, smelting, producing their own weapons to counter the unrelenting volley of ammunition headed their way. The editing is rapid, so each German shell is swiftly followed by a shot of Russian military manufacturing. Significantly, the German shelling is impersonal, delivered by enormous guns thrust into the sky, while the film shows us Russian faces working at their machines, creating a sense of identification with the cause. The victory at Stalingrad is rendered all the more powerful by the images of the defeated Germans, who appear addled, exhausted, shuffling to oblivion, one soldier trudging into an icy abyss.

The Battle of China, criticised by Barsam as the "weakest" of the series, does suffer from a trite, patronising tone, but given the fact that it was designed to be seen by American troops who had never been to China, nor met many of its people, this is perhaps unsurprising (1975: 152). At the time, there was some criticism of the film from General Frederick Osborn, to whom Capra was answerable, because the film contained so much material taken from fiction film that did not depict historical events (McBride 1992: 482). Similarly, the sentimental tone of the film was rebuked by the War Department, to which Capra responded,

> I know there are people [...] who claim we have put too much 'emotion' in these films. [...] But my experiences with audiences has [*sic*] long ago taught me that if you want facts to stick, you must present them in an interesting manner.
>
> (*Quoted in ibid.*)

Like *The Battle of Russia*, it emphasises the history of the nation, its civilisation and its achievements: "an ancient culture [...] bigger than Europe and the United States [...] never waged a war of conquest". Again, like the Russians and the British, the Chinese are portrayed as a courageous and defiant people, who employ their ingenuity to resist their invaders and prevent their ultimate defeat. Indeed, the film suggests that it was the Japanese invasion that 'created' the Chinese nation, as it forced the people to band together in a show of collective solidarity.

This is radically juxtaposed by the film's representation of Japan, whose plan for world conquest is laid bare. The film is almost as concerned with demonising the Japanese as it is with celebrating China. Indeed, the film seeks to establish China and Japan as diametrically opposed – where China uses Western manufacturing technology to modernise its nation and improve the lives of its people, Japan employs this for naked military aggression. In its treatment of the Japanese, *The Battle of China* represents the closest the series comes to open racism, for while its attitude towards the Germans often played on national stereotypes of ruthless efficiency and organisation, the Japanese are characterised as "blood-crazed Japs", dehumanised as "the little yellow men". Although the films' previous instalments featured shocking footage of the German bombing of Rotterdam following the Dutch surrender and deeply upsetting images of dead children during the attacks on Stalingrad, the bombardment of Shanghai paints the Japanese as a savage, cruel people. Capra may have balked at the accusation of infusing his propaganda films with 'too much emotion' but *The Battle of China* does occasionally tip the scales of information and inspiration in favour of the latter, skating close to the kinds of 'hate' films produced in World War I that the American government were determined to avoid.

Conclusion: *War Comes to America* (1945)

The seventh and final part of *Why We Fight*, released just two months prior to Japan's unconditional surrender, is also the least considered of the series (perhaps because of its proximity to the war's end). *War Comes to America* provides a satisfying conclusion, drawing together the various strands of the conflict and presenting them entirely through the eyes of Americans, both soldiers and civilians. It charts the changing attitudes Americans took to their participation in the war, shifting from isolationism to internationalism. Like Capra's fiction films, it is a celebration of Americanism, from the first few seconds where Old Glory, billowing proudly in the wind, is underscored by children reciting the Pledge of Allegiance. It makes consistent use of American imagery, particularly the Statue of Liberty, as symbolic of the 'idea' on which the nation is founded: democracy and freedom. Like the films about Britain, Russia and China, the film emphasises the diversity of America's fighting forces ("rich man, poor man, beggar man, thief; doctor, lawyer, merchant, chief") and, as a final blow to isolationism, recalls the birth of the nation on the battlefields of the War of Independence.

In drawing the series to a conclusion in this fashion, the film demonstrates the extent to which *Why We Fight* fulfilled the demand for a coherent and holistic chronicle of the history and context of the war the American government were asking its people to fight, and offers compelling and clear reasons for it. Doherty's suggestion that the films speak "eloquently and calmly" for the hopes of a better world in the future is an instructive one, although it must be remembered that, as indicated by the conclusion of *War Comes to America*, this future is linked, inextricably, with the success and vitality of American ideology. As the series' first instalment had celebrated the Declaration of Independence as a document that could speak for *all* mankind's hopes for a better world, so the series' concluding moments, the American flag billowing in the wind and the Statue of Liberty standing proud and tall, offer visual figuration of that which the seven films had sought to reinforce throughout: this is not only a fight against tyranny and persecution, but a fight *for* liberty, tolerance, and the 'American way'.

Bibliography

Agee, J. (1975) "Prelude to War" in Glatzer, R. and Raeburn, J. (eds) *Frank Capra: The Man and His Films*, Ann Arbor: The University of Michigan, pp. 155–6.

Bailey, G. (2004) "Why We (Should Not) Fight: Colonel Frank Capra Interviewed" in Pogue, P. (ed.) *Frank Capra Interviewed*, Jackson: University Press of Mississippi, pp. 124–31.

Barsam, R. (1975) "Why We Fight" in Glatzer, R. and Raeburn, J. (eds) *Frank Capra: The Man and His Films*, Ann Arbor: The University of Michigan, pp. 149–56.

Capra, F. (1971) *The Name Above the Title*, New York: Macmillan.

Doherty, T. (1993) *Projections of War: Hollywood, American Culture and World War II*, New York: Columbia University Press.

Dyer MacCann, R. (1973) *The People's Films: A Political History of US Government Motion Pictures*, New York: Hastings House Publishers.

Geiger, J. (2011) *American Documentary Film: Projecting the Nation*, Edinburgh: Edinburgh University Press.

Koppes, C.R. and Black, G.D. (1990) *Hollywood Goes to War: How Politics, Profits and Propaganda Shaped World War II Movies*, Berkeley and Los Angeles: University of California Press.

McBride, J. (1992) *Frank Capra: The Catastrophe of Success*, London: Faber & Faber.

McLane, B.A. (2012) *A New History of Documentary Film*, London: Bloomsbury Academic.

Scott, I. (2008) "*Why We Fight* and *Projections of America*: Frank Capra, Robert Riskin, and the Making of World War II Propaganda" in Rollins, P. and O'Connor, J. (eds) *Why We Fought: America's Wars in Film and History*, Lexington: University Press of Kentucky, pp. 242–58.

13

STRIVING FOR THE MAXIMUM APPEAL

Ideology and propaganda in the Soviet cinema of the 1920s and 1930s[1]

Panayiota Mini

Soviet cinema has often been described as propagandistic. And rightly so. Some of the most famous Soviet films, the silent montage works of Sergei Eisenstein, Vsevolod Pudovkin, Alexander Dovzhenko, and Dziga Vertov, were openly pro-Bolshevik, as they were products of a "highly politicised" society (Taylor 1979a: 15).

This recognition of its propaganda quality is not intended to disparage Soviet cinema. As Welch states, "propaganda in and of itself is not necessarily evil" (2003: xix). Instead of being equated with malicious content, propaganda should be regarded as "a deliberate attempt to influence public opinion through the transmission of ideas and values for a specific persuasive purpose that has been consciously devised to serve the self-interest of the propagandist, either directly or indirectly" (ibid.). In the Soviet case, after the October 1917 Revolution, the Bolsheviks made no secret of their reliance on propaganda in influencing the people (Reeves 1999: 43). They explicitly gave cinema a prominent role in this task. Perhaps more revealing than V.I. Lenin's famous dictum that "of all the arts for us the most important is cinema" (quoted in Reeves 1999: 48) is Leon Trotsky's 1923 description of cinema as

> the best instrument for propaganda, technical, educational, and instructional propaganda, propaganda against alcohol, propaganda for sanitation, political propaganda, any kind of propaganda you please, a propaganda which is accessible to everyone, which is attractive, cuts into the memory and may be a possible source of revenue.
>
> *(Ibid.)*

Soviet propaganda addressed such a wide range of issues, as Trotsky suggests, because the Bolshevik principles were new to the people. The state needed to instill in a huge population fresh ideas about the world and particular doctrines. During the Civil War (1918–21), and especially under the New Economic Policy (NEP, 1921–9), this endeavor was further complicated as the Bolshevik ideas were in a state of flux, generating heated debates under the relative pluralism of NEP. In the 1930s, Soviet ideology lost its pluralism; ideological orthodoxy was consolidated and hardened under Joseph Stalin (Gill 1988).

All these changes affected Soviet cinema. The film companies that operated in NEP's market economy transmitted new ideas through different kinds of film. In addition to didactic documentaries, two categories of fiction film production appeared: avant-garde and popular entertainment. The former, to which the montage films belonged, were overt works of propaganda which were not commercially successful but which mythologized the past, while substantiating a distinctive, revolutionary style. The latter were money-making genre films, with comedies constituting the lion's share and dealing with mainly contemporary issues. In the mid-1930s, Socialist Realism was declared the only acceptable aesthetic doctrine, under which the Party's ideological orthodoxy was narrativized through primarily traditional techniques. In both periods, the filmmakers' efforts involved appropriations of American film techniques that had proven popular with audiences.

This chapter will explore the political messages and formal methods of the Soviet cinema of the 1920s and 1930s through three films: Pudovkin's montage film *Mother* (*Mat'*, 1926), Boris Barnet's everyday-life (*bytovaia*) comedy *The Girl with the Hat Box* (*Devushka s korobkoi*, 1927) and Ivan Pyr'ev's *kolkhoz* musical *The Tractor Drivers* (*Traktoristy*, 1939). The analyses will unpack each film's key ideologies with a view to refine the often crudely applied term 'propaganda' to montage cinema (*Mother*); explore how propaganda works in a film largely considered as mere entertainment (*The Girl with the Hat Box*); and examine how propagandistic elements operate in a Socialist Realist film in its original version (*The Tractor Drivers*), that is, before its alteration ('restoration') in the post-Stalinist era. Influenced by some fine ideological readings of Soviet film form (Bordwell 1990: 234–273; Kepley 1995), my analyses will also consider how these films gave ideology an artistic shape. As Soviet society and ideologies changed, so did the ways in which directors used film form for propaganda purposes.

The background

The first propaganda Soviet films were newsreels and *agitki*, short and medium-length agitational films designed during the Civil War to instruct the soldiers, peasants and civilians on political, military, industrial and health issues (Taylor 1979b: 56–57). Produced by the government, these films found a large audience thanks to the famous agit-trains, which carried propaganda materials, including films, to remote places (Taylor 1979b: 52–63); after Lenin's Cinema Nationalization Decree (27 August 1919) this type of production was also shown in the newly nationalized movie-theaters. The newsreels, the *agitki* and the agit-trains greatly contributed to training important future montage filmmakers in the art of propaganda. For instance, Eisenstein and Grigori Kozintsev were active in agit-train work, Vertov relied on the agit-train circuit for the making and distribution of his newsreels, while as a student of the State Film Institute, Pudovkin participated as an actor, writer, or assistant director in five *agitki* (Leyda 1983: 157–159).

The State Film Institute was established in 1919 in Moscow by the Commissariat of Enlightenment. During the early 1920s, the Institute became primarily known for Lev Kuleshov's experimental Workshop. Kuleshov sought to identify cinema's essence in order to find the appropriate form for Soviet films. He concluded that cinema's essence is montage, by which a filmmaker could transmit precise messages and create illusionary realities. Crucial to Kuleshov's conclusions was his familiarity with American films, which were being massively imported during NEP, as their commercial success helped the state to accumulate capital (Kepley 1994: 71–77). The American montage, Kuleshov argued, resulted in a clear and dynamic cinema that had a great impact on the spectators. Among Kuleshov's students who collaborated on his research and projects, including the comedy *The Extraordinary*

Adventures of Mr. West in the Land of the Bolsheviks/Neobychainye prikliucheniia mistera Vesta v strane Bol'shevikov (1924), were Pudovkin and Barnet.

After 1925, Pudovkin and Barnet went to work for Mezhrabpom-Rus', a semi-independent film company, second in importance only to the government-owned Sovkino. In Mezhrabpom-Rus', Pudovkin and Barnet made their directorial debuts with Kuleshovian projects – Pudovkin with the comedy *Chess Fever/Shakhmatnaia goriachka* (1925) and Barnet with *Miss Mend* (1926, co-directed with Fedor Otsep) – to be followed by his solo film *The Girl with the Hat Box*. Mezhrabpom-Rus' assigned these directors different pictures as well. Pudovkin shot a documentary on Ivan Pavlov's experiments, *Mechanics of the Brain/Mekhanika golovnogo mozga* (1926), and *Mother*, while Barnet made *Moscow in October* (*Moskva v Oktiabre*, 1927), commemorating the tenth anniversary of the 1917 revolution. With *Mother*'s huge critical success, Pudovkin came to specialise in revolutionary pictures (*The End of St. Petersburg/Konets Sankt-Peterburga*, 1927; *Storm over Asia/Potomok Chingiskhana*, 1928). In contrast, Barnet's *Moscow in October* was deemed a failure, so he returned to lighter works.

Mother

Mother constituted Mezhrabpom-Rus' anniversary film of the 1905 revolution on a par with Eisenstein's *The Battleship Potemkin/Bronenosets Potemkin* (1925) shot for Sovkino. *Mother* was based on Gorky's titular novel (1907/1922). The novel focuses on Nilovna Vlasova, the mother of worker Pavel, and on her consciousness-acquisition process from an ignorant woman into a committed socialist. Halfway through the novel, Nilovna marches in a May Day demonstration, where she holds the red flag. When Pavel is sent to prison for his political activities she moves in with the intellectuals Nikolai Ivanovich and Sophia, and travels from the city to villages where she distributes illegal publications. At novel's end, the police beat her to death in a railway station, as she is trying to smuggle copies of the speech that Pavel had delivered during his trial.

In *Mother*, Gorky, inspired by some incidents in Somov in 1902, actually alluded to the events surrounding the Bloody Sunday of January 1905 in St. Petersburg. The novel's plot echoes theories of God Building, a Bolshevik heresy that perceived religious fervor as capable of being converted into the energy required for building socialism (Read 1979: 77–89). Nilovna undergoes such a conversion. Gorky renders her consciousness acquisition as a process in which socialist principles replace religious beliefs (Scherr 1988: 44–45). In addition, Gorky stresses the intellectuals' participation in Russia's transformation and the people's enlightenment. Pavel becomes enlightened through books, Nilovna teaches herself how to read and converts the people by distributing leaflets and books, and workers are arrested for possessing forbidden books.

The film that the Soviet spectators saw in October 1926 differed from Gorky's novel. Pudovkin and his scenarist Nathan Zarkhi had drastically altered the novel to make it fit the 1920s Bolshevik explanation of 1905 (Mini 2002) as this derived from Lenin's *Lecture on the 1905 Revolution* (1917). According to Lenin, the 1905 revolution, which in terms of its demands represented Russia's democratic revolution, originated in Russia's biggest factories where the proletariat was most class-conscious, and it spread thanks to mass strikes. Thus, concerning its means of struggle, that is, the strike, and its participants, Russia's *bourgeois* revolution was actually *proletarian* (Lenin 1951: 9–10). Furthermore, regarding the intellectuals, Lenin dismissed their notion of education as something that imbues the masses "with bourgeois prejudices" (14). For Lenin, the fate of the 1905 revolution "could and would [have been] decided only by an armed struggle" (26), an explanation to which he later added that the 1905 revolution was the "dress rehearsal," without which the victory of the 1917 revolution "would have been impossible" (1920/1971: 521).

To tell their story in proper Bolshevik logic, Pudovkin and Zarkhi deleted all Gorkian situations pertaining to religion, the peasants, the intellectuals' activism, and Pavel's and Nilovna's conversions to socialism through reading. In the film, the single protagonist in the making of history is the working class. To this class and its main representative, Pavel (Nikolai Batalov), the film opposes the Black Hundreds – an historical group of reactionaries absent in the novel – who lure Pavel's father to be against an impending strike. The strike is being designed by socialists, who circulate guns, not books as in Gorky's novel. In contrast to Gorky's workers, who either ignore or criticize Pavel's call for strike, Pudovkin's working class acts in solidarity with the strikers but is prevented by the Black Hundreds' scheming from offering real assistance.

After the death of Pavel's father, the mother (Vera Baranovskaia) believes a colonel's false promises and betrays her son, a situation absent in Gorky's novel. The film then focuses on her consciousness-raising. Pudovkin's heroine does not teach herself how to read. She acquires consciousness through personal experience – her confrontation with tsarist duplicity at Pavel's trial where Pavel is sentenced to exile. As a result, she joins the cause and notifies the imprisoned Pavel of an escape plan during the May Day demonstration. The film's last section unfolds on May Day. Contrary to Gorky's hero who refuses to flee, Pudovkin's Pavel overpowers his guard and gains his freedom. At the same time, the working class stages a demonstration, during which the mother picks up the red flag, while the ice melts in a nearby river. After some suspenseful scenes in the prison and the river, Pavel joins the demonstration. Both he and his mother are killed by the state troops. The film ends with shots of factories and of the Kremlin topped with the red flag.

By ending the film with the May Day demonstration, Pudovkin accomplishes important propaganda objectives. As May Day is the most significant day of the working class and its strikes, Pudovkin associates the 1905 revolution exclusively with this class and its struggle. Furthermore, and as Karaganov argued, May Day, with its bright sun and melting ice blocks symbolizes the rebirth that is to follow the 1905 tragedy (1983: 72–74). Pudovkin's imagery of the thaw also propagates the Bolshevik idea of the 'uninterrupted revolution,' according to which the transition from the democratic to the socialist revolution of 1917 did not require an entire historical period, as orthodox Marxism had claimed. Stalin emphasized Lenin's depiction of "the bourgeois-democratic revolution and the socialist revolution as (…) a single and integral picture of the sweep of the Russian revolution" ([1924]/1939: 39). In *Mother*, the concluding images reinforce this interpretation of the revolution's phases. The streams produced by the thaw lead seamlessly from 1905 to the next stage: socialism. The film's last shots illustrate a historical law. Superimposed shots of factories foretell the inevitable, according to Marxism, strengthening of capitalism and proletarian reaction. The shots of the Kremlin flying the red flag suggest the completion of the democratic revolution by the dictatorship of the proletariat (Figure 13.1).

To endow their film with the maximum appeal, Pudovkin and Zarkhi converted Gorky's loose plot into a tight family drama. They devised a betrayal and an apotheosis alluding to D.W. Griffith's *Way Down East* (1920) (Karaganov 1983: 73–74) and Kuleshov's *By the Law/Po zakonu* (1926). Moreover, from Gorky's novel they selected a number of conflicts to enhance the drama. In the novel, these conflicts do not always concern the Vlasov family. In the film, however, all conflicts are connected to the Vlasovs. Thus, the film registers ideology as an engaging American-like drama, in which the father chases his son and is killed; the mother betrays her son; and the son escapes from prison at the very last minute only to die in his mother's arms.

Pudovkin also used cinematic rhythm to reach his spectators. He believed that the spectator should be "gradually engrossed by the developing action, receiving the most effective impulse only at the end" (Pudovkin 1974: 46). When writing this, Pudovkin had in mind the rhythm of American films, primarily those of Griffith, which peaked in the crosscutting between remote actions. The significance of crosscutting, said Pudovkin, lay in its creation

Figure 13.1 The Kremlin flying the flag at the end of Vsevolod Pudovkin's *Mother* (1926).

of suspense that draws in the spectator "by the constant forcing of a question, such as [...]: Will they be in time?" (77). In this respect, Pudovkin sprinkled tension throughout *Mother*, saving the most exciting scene for the end, where he brought together shots of Pavel – first in the prison and later in the river – and of the demonstration. The spectators are cued to side with Pavel, as they leap mentally from one place to another, witness the obstacles that block Pavel's escape from prison, and worry about his survival.

Pudovkin's stylistic devices are ideologically motivated. By applying his knowledge of American continuity editing, he used unobtrusive shot/reverse shots, eyeline matches and cuts on action in a few serene scenes, where the participants share views (as when the mother visits Pavel in prison). In all other scenes, Pudovkin revised the continuity editing techniques, producing a disjunctive style, or used the radical montage that Eisenstein had presented in *Strike/Stachka* (1925). As a result, Pudovkin accentuated what he called "plastic materials," images which clearly conveyed a film's ideas (Pudovkin 1974: 54–59). During a fight between Pavel and the father, for example, Pudovkin's self-conscious shots stress a hammer, a ubiquitous Bolshevik symbol (Figure 13.2), while *Mother*'s climax constitutes the most notable example of Eisensteinian montage. A profusion of shots depicts the attack against the workers and Pavel's death. When the mother holds the banner, jump cuts and striking camera angles from below lionize her, and when she is killed, each shot consists of only a few frames. The film ends with the ideologically motivated association of factory chimneys, the walls of the Kremlin, and the red flag on top.

Pudovkin's combination of art and propaganda led the Soviet reviewers to praise *Mother* effusively (Mini 2002: 169, 240). As Il'ia Trauberg (1926) wrote:

> The spectator cannot oppose this persuasion; he [sic] is shaken and conquered [...]. He [Pudovkin] developed an exact and tireless rhythm, he commanded the film

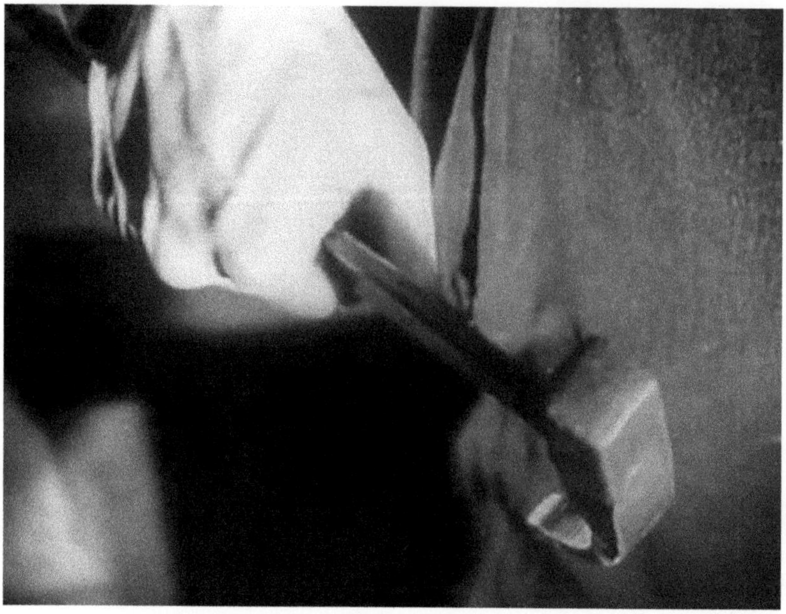

Figure 13.2 Vsevolod Pudovkin's cut directs attention to a hammer, a Bolshevik symbol, in *Mother* (1926).

apparatus to think, and he compelled us to study every moment of the action like a wonderful theorem of art.

The Girl with the Hat Box

The international acclaim that followed the domestic release of *Mother* and other montage films obscured the importance of less radical silent Soviet pictures, including those by Barnet (Christie 1985: 74–77). Beginning in the 1980s, however, a critical appreciation of Barnet's output took place, commenting on a need for their examination within their original context (e.g. Christie 1985). Such an examination of *The Girl with the Hat Box* reveals that instead of departing from Kuleshov's principles as some scholars have claimed (e.g. Zorkaia 2000: 196) or being apolitical (see below), this film actually conveyed Soviet theses, strategically embedding them in a Kuleshovian form.

The Girl was solicited by the Commissariat of Finance as a propaganda picture for the state bonds (Kushnirov 1977: 52). Although Barnet's project did not bear the ideological weight that the anniversary film *Mother* did, its mission was still important. The state bonds had been first issued in 1922 as part of a program aiming at monetary stability, and by the mid-1920s they "had become the principal mode of financing budget deficits" (Millar 1974: 1). To make the bonds attractive the government often relied on lotteries, which proved successful. In February 1927, the popular response to the first mass subscription bond exceeded all expectations, and from March to December 1927 five more bonds were issued (Millar 1974: 1–8). Mezhrabpom-Rus' contributed to the popularity of the bonds. In 1925–6 it produced no fewer than thirteen newsreels for lottery draws (Deriabin 2011) and within three years released three fiction films on this topic: Iakov Protazanov's *The Tailor from Torzhok/Zakroishchik iz Torzhka* (1925), *The Girl with the Hat Box*, and Leonid Molchanov's *The Unpaid Letter/Neoplachennoe pis'mo* (1927).

The Girl tells the story of Natasha (Anna Sten), a young milliner who lives on the outskirts of Moscow and works for a hat store in the city, and Il'ia (I. Koval'-Samborskii), a young peasant who has just arrived in Moscow and has nowhere to stay. After some amusing squabbles in their first encounters, Natasha and Il'ia enter into a fake marriage, which entails Il'ia staying in the room that the store owners, Madame Irène and her husband, have falsely registered to Natasha to acquire extra space for themselves. Soon, Madame Irène's husband reimburses Natasha with a bond instead of money, but when the bond wins 25,000 rubles, he tries to trick her into giving it back to him. With Il'ia's intervention the bond remains with Natasha. Natasha and Il'ia unite, welcoming Fogelev (Vladimir Fogel), a train station cashier who also loves Natasha, as a friend.

Although Valentin Turkin and Vadim Shershenevich's literary script mentions the bond early on (Deriabin 2011), Barnet tactically invokes it in the last half of the film. Barnet allows the spectators to become absorbed into a story where two characters develop genuine feelings for each other. It is only then that the bond comes into the picture. Thus, the couple's union appears to be devoid of self-serving interests (Kushnirov 1977: 60–61). To dissociate the romance and particularly Il'ia's intentions from such interests, the plot also presents him asking for a divorce when Natasha's bond wins. It is Natasha who negates his petition and the couple stay married. The state bond secures a good future for two people who deserve it. Unlike the union of Natasha and Il'ia, the marriage of Natasha's petit-bourgeois employers is portrayed as based on hypocrisy and economic exchange.

In addition, *The Girl* reflects important Soviet attitudes towards sex, marriage, women, and peasants. Peasantry was one of the thorniest issues after the mid-1920s. Stalin and his chief ally at the time, Nikolai Bukharin, argued that Soviet economy ought to rely on the peasant-worker bloc and that backward peasants could gain consciousness through their rapport with the working class. Different, however, was the opinion of Trotsky's United Opposition, which distrusted the peasants and argued that the Soviet economy would recover instead through deals with foreign countries. *The Girl* narrativizes the leadership's position. Il'ia appears naïve and backward, yet trustworthy and likable. He is also clumsy. He drops his books, scrubs himself when he gets up and acts like an embarrassed child in front of Natasha (Figure 13.3). Despite his backwardness, Il'ia has admirable qualities. He protects Natasha when her employers try to exploit her, siding with the working girl instead of the bosses. His carrying books shows his eagerness to learn. He starts his day with gymnastics (Figure 13.4), as Soviet hygiene dictated.[2] His desire for cleanliness, however awkward, is another good habit that the film's petit-bourgeois characters lack. Instead of washing themselves and exercising in the morning, they smoke cigarettes, a habit deemed unhealthy and unbecoming for a Soviet person and opposed by Bukharin himself (Starks 2008: 182).

Natasha, the city girl, is an energetic, modern woman. More educated than Il'ia, she pulls the strings of their relationship. She also educates Il'ia (and the film's spectators) on the simple procedure of registering a marriage and on a woman's equal say in the preservation or dissolution of a union. Furthermore, the film's final shot suggests a new way of marital life: a love trio. Fogelev, who has just beaten the bourgeois boss, stands between Natasha and Il'ia, who whisper something to him and kiss his cheeks. Fogelev cheerfully looks at them; Natasha and Il'ia kiss one another, and Fogelev frowns and turns his back. The finale leaves open the possibility of a *ménage a trois*, an important topic in the Soviet discourse on sex and marriage. This topic had just caused a controversy due to Abraam Room's *The Third Meschanskaia/ Tret'ia Meshchanskaia*, al. *Bed and Sofa* (1927) (Graffy 2001: 17–20, 58–59, 73–75). In Room's film, one of the three protagonists had also been played by Fogel, who bore the same name (Fogelev) that he has in Barnet's comedy.

Figure 13.3 Il'ia as an embarrassed child in front of Natasha in Boris Barnet's *The Girl with the Hat Box* (1927).

Figure 13.4 Il'ia starting his day with gymnastics in Boris Barnet's *The Girl with the Hat Box* (1927).

No doubt, the ending of *The Girl* reflects some unresolved issues in Soviet society. Moreover, Il'ia's washing himself seemed open to interpretation. The Central Repertory Committee (Glavrepertkom) detected "an air of hooliganism" in it and asked be deleted, a request that was soon withdrawn (Deriabin 2011). This scene in fact indicates the challenges of film comedies in trying to balance laughter with ideologically correct depictions of Soviet mores (Youngblood 1993). Yet this and other such scenes do not make *The Girl* 'apolitical' or ideologically useless as some reviewers complained (Nedobrovo 1927: 17; V.N. 1927: 3), most likely because of their disapproval of Soviet comedies in general. On the contrary, such scenes demonstrate that in a Soviet film every detail was judged according to political criteria.

Regarding the film's form, Barnet stated that he approached his project as an experiment on the comical depiction of daily life (1927: 10). In this experiment, Barnet employed American cinematic devices, as they had been filtered through Kuleshov's teachings, including chases, fights (Deriabin 2011), and staccato performances. With 'tricks' and gags he exploited cinema's power to create illusion. He created a fast rhythm of 15.5 shots per minute, while apart from some incorrect cuts, Barnet practiced continuity editing in a wealth of elegant cuts. Above all, Barnet relied on Kuleshov's principles: clarity, economy and direction of attention to the important action (Deriabin 2011). In describing the shooting of a scene in which Il'ia and Natasha are in a virtually bare room, Barnet remarked:

> We arrived at a pleasantly surprising fact: we could build scenes that impressed not only by montage, but by the *mise-en-scène* itself [...]. Shooting in long shots was enough: extra objects neither interfered nor diverted attention from the important.
> (1927: 10)

This statement, often interpreted to signal Barnet's departure from Kuleshov, actually means that Barnet considered his teacher's principles on visual economy and spectator guidance to be so strong as to be identified not only in montage, but also in a sparse *mise-en-scène* setting. Barnet's film conveyed ideology through both its topical messages and precise form, becoming one of the most popular silent Soviet comedies (Rollberg 2009: 82).

The Tractor Drivers

A year after the release of *The Girl with the Hat Box*, the transformation of Soviet cinema began. In March 1928, the First All-Union Party Conference of the Cinema resolved, among other things, that Soviet cinema needed to rely on domestic technology and on Soviet films which would be intelligible to the masses. By the early 1930s Soiuzkino had replaced Sovkino and purges of the studios began (Youngblood 1991: 189–191). A highly bureaucratized censorship apparatus halted or delayed film production, dramatically lessening the number of finished films (Kepley 1996: 47–48; Miller 2010), while the films that were completed conformed to the Socialist Realist doctrine. Following the example of the acclaimed *Chapayev* (Georgi Vasilyev and Sergei Vasilyev, 1934), they propagated the Socialist reality in its revolutionary development through easily comprehensible stories centered on 'positive heroes.'

The model for accessible Socialist Realist stories was once more found in American cinema. Soiuzkino's head Boris Shumyatsky envisioned a Soviet Hollywood on the Black Sea (which never materialized) and a "cinema for the millions" substantiated in genre films (Taylor 1983: 451–453). Highly popular among them were Sergei Alexandrov's musical comedies and Pyr'ev's *kolkhoz*, folk musicals. These musicals have now attracted considerable attention from scholars who are interested in their utopian vision (Anderson 1995; Taylor 2007), political significance (Haynes 2013), gender representation (Anderson 1995: 47–48; Haynes 2013), the combination of entertainment and ideology (Taylor 1999), and fairy-tale motifs (Turovskaia 1988: 122–128). Most crucial to the films' propaganda was their contribution to Stalin's personality cult, an aspect missed by most contemporary spectators who are familiar with the films' altered versions, which have been cleared of references to Stalin. This is also the case with Pyr'ev's *The Tractor Drivers*, a Mosfilm and Kiev Kino Studio co-production, the original version of which perpetuates the Stalin cult.

The plot of *The Tractor Drivers* unfolds in a Ukrainian village, where Klim Iarko (Nikolai Kriuchkov), a tank driver who has just been demobilized from the Far East front, arrives in order to meet his ideal girl, the *stakhanovite* tractor driver Mariana Bazhan (Marina Ladynina). In the village, Klim proves his expertise in tractor repair. Soon, the *kolkhoz* chair, Kirill Petrovich, appoints him foreman in the place of Nazar Duma, a loafer whom Mariana falsely presents as her fiancé to discourage potential suitors. By the film's end, Klim has taught the farmers tank operation and helped Nazar to become a conscious worker. Klim and Mariana then get married.

The Tractor Drivers stresses patriotism, a key point of pre-World War II official rhetoric. This theme, which permeates the film, culminates in a cluster of scenes that follows the unearthing of a 1918 German helmet. Holding the helmet, Kirill Petrovich bursts into an enthusiastic speech about "our glorious 1918" and congratulates Klim's initiative to "work, compete and teach his men defense," because, as he says, "A tractor, guys, is a tank. And a tank is … boom!" His phrase is completed by images of tanks running in forests, fields, and waters. The plot moves to an outdoor meeting, where Klim instructs the farmers on tank machinery. After a brief scene, in which Mariana reads a book about the ideal tankman's traits, we return to the meeting, where Klim sings the "March of the Soviet Tankmen."

The powerful "March of the Soviet Tankmen," composed by the Pokrass brothers with lyrics by Boris Laskin, is very effective propaganda. Its chorus refers directly and indirectly to Stalin. Klim sings about the tanks' '*stali*' (steel) and the heroic moment "when we're called to battle by Comrade Stalin/And the First Marshal will lead us in this battle," the First Marshal being Kliment Voroshilov, a Red Army associate of Stalin in 1918, Commissar of Defense since 1934 and a leader of Stalin's Great Purge of 1936–9 ("Kliment Voroshilov" n.d.).[3] Klim's song has a tremendous effect on his disciples. They are captivated by it, including Nazar who undergoes a transformation: in the next scene, he is shown proudly driving a 'Stalinets' tractor and singing the march. A little earlier, in a brief scene, Mariana had read that a tankman should be "enduring, calm, and decisive," adding in an ecstatic tone "and handsome …" Metonymically, her description seems more about Stalin than Klim, because Klim often lacks calmness and decisiveness. Mariana undergoes a transformation: for the first time in the film, she seems overwhelmed by a desire for a man (the ideal tankman whom she describes), a desire that she then lets herself to express for the film's actual tankman, Klim.

These scenes bring together the film's two plot lines, the romance between Mariana and Klim and Nazar's change of character. At the same moment, Mariana and Nazar fall under the influence of Klim, and on a symbolic level of Stalin. The film's double plot structure is reminiscent of Hollywood cinema. Contrary to a canonical American film, however, in which the two plot lines are interdependent (Bordwell 1990: 157–158), in *The Tractor Drivers* they are only loosely connected. The love story and Nazar's improvement are not essentially interdependent. More than by any notion of mutual causality, the two plot lines are brought together by ideological motivation, in this case what we can call a "Stalinist motivation" to differentiate it from the Bolshevik one that had shaped the silent montage films.

In terms of style, the film's most impressive scenes are also ideologically motivated. Nazar's driving the 'Stalinets' tractor occurs in a quasi-baroque setting with fires coming from the earth and fumes filling the air (Figure 13.5). One might argue that generic motivation (Bordwell 1990: 36, 162–163), that is, the musical genre conventions, accounts for this excess. Yet, a similar excess is absent in other musical scenes in *The Tractor Drivers*, which suggests that Stalin's effect on Nazar is actually responsible for this stylistic exuberance. The film's other grandiose scene is the concluding wedding feast. From some windows in the background, Pyr'ev's camera tracks backwards, gradually revealing the wedding couple, Kirill giving a patriotic speech, and the guests sitting in symmetrical rows. When the camera's movement reaches Nazar, he starts singing the "March of the Soviet Tankmen." By the moment he and the guests are singing the chorus, the shot has expanded to include a photograph of Stalin on the top of the hall, decorated with flag-like garlands. In a subsequent shot an officer energetically cries "Comrade Stalin," while a very long shot, showing Stalin's photograph and the guests singing the "March" and raising their glasses to the words "Comrade Stalin," closes the film (Figure 13.6).

The style in the rest of the film is more modest, reminding one of the transparency of the American cinema. Nevertheless, Pyr'ev does not copy his model. He makes a restrained use of shot/reverse shots, some of which are incorrect. Pyr'ev's cuts do not confuse the spectators because he often shoots the characters talking amidst the Ukrainian landscape in long or very long shots. Thus, spectator orientation is maintained and the Ukrainian land acquires the magnitude which Bordwell (2001: 21–23) has identified in the post-1938 Socialist Realist cinema. Furthermore, the rather slow tempo of Pyr'ev's film (5.85 shots per minute, or one-third of those in *The Girl*), evokes a sense of serenity. In this earthly paradise, the characters make

Figure 13.5 Nazar drives a 'Stalinets' tractor in a quasi-baroque setting in Ivan Pyr'ev's *The Tractor Drivers* (1939).

Figure 13.6 The wedding hall topped with a photograph of Stalin at the end of Ivan Pyr'ev's *The Tractor Drivers* (1939).

broad, sometimes clownish gestures and laugh heartily. They look like big children, inspired and protected by a godlike father – Stalin – who is omnipresent, via tractor designations, photographs, and song verses, in the fields, the homes, the *kolkhoz* headquarters, and the wedding hall. The film's original audiences approved of Pyr'ev's propaganda, making *The Tractor Drivers* one of the most popular films of the 1930s (Taylor 2011: 86).

The above three Soviet films, *Mother*, *The Girl with the Hat Box*, and *The Tractor Drivers*, help us to appreciate the various nuances which the notion of film propaganda can encompass and the different ways in which it can work. Film propaganda may adapt the historical past to an overtly political narrative, transmitted through bold cinematic means; it may subtly promote particular state programs and everyday mores, embedding them into an entertaining picture; and it may, both implicitly and explicitly, put a genre film's formal elements into the service of a leader's personality cult. The case studies show that even in highly politicized societies, such as the Soviet one, propaganda does not appear in a uniform manner. As a society changes, filmmakers employ different ways to propagate its ideologies and to endow them with the maximum appeal.

Notes

1 I thank the staff of the University of Wisconsin-Madison Libraries and Anna Stavrakopoulou for assisting me with hard-to-obtain printed sources.
2 The information on Soviet hygiene derives from Starks (2008).
3 In the original film a photograph of Voroshilov appears in Mariana's home. The hero's name (Klim) also reminds one of Kliment Voroshilov.

Bibliography

Anderson, T. (1995) "Why Stalinist Musicals?," *Discourse* 17:3, pp. 38–48.

Barnet, B. (1927) "*Devushka s korobkoi*,"/*The Girl with the Hat Box*, *Sovetskii Ekran*, 12, 19 March, p. 10.

Bordwell, D. (1990) *Narration in the Fiction Film*, London: Routledge.

Bordwell, D. (2001) "Eisenstein, Socialist Realism and the Charms of *Mizanstsena*," in LaValley, A. and Scherr, B.P. (eds) *Eisenstein at 100: A Reconsideration*, New Brunswick: Rutgers University Press, pp. 13–37.

Christie, I. (1985) "Barnet tel qu'en lui-même? ou L'exception et la regle"/"Barnet such as into Himself? or The Exception and the Rule" in Albera, F. and Cosandey, R. (eds.) *Boris Barnet: écrits, documents, études, filmographie*, Locarno: Festival international du film de Locarno, pp. 74–85.

Deriabin, A. (2011) "Commentary," *The Girl with the Hat Box* [DVD], Disc 1, Moscow: Ruscico.

Gill, G.J. (1988) "Ideology and System-Building: The Experience Under Lenin and Stalin" in White, S. and Pravda, A. (eds) *Ideology and Soviet Politics*, Basingstoke: Macmillan, pp. 59–82.

Graffy, J. (2001) *Bed and Sofa: The Film Companion*, London: I.B. Tauris.

Haynes, J. (2013) *New Soviet Man: Gender and Masculinity in Stalinist Soviet Cinema*, Manchester: Manchester University Press.

Karaganov, A. (1983) *Vsevolod Pudovkin*, Moscow: Iskusstvo.

Kepley, V., Jr. (1994) "The Origins of Soviet Cinema: A Study in Industry Development" in Taylor, R. and Christie, I. (eds) *Inside the Film Factory: New Approaches to Russian and Soviet Cinema*, London: Routledge, pp. 60–79.

Kepley, V., Jr. (1995) "Pudovkin and the Continuity Style: Problems of Space and Narration," *Discourse* 17:3, pp. 85–100.

Kepley, V., Jr. (1996), "The First Perestroika: Soviet Cinema Under the First Five-Year Plan", *Cinema Journal* 35:4, pp. 31–53.

"Kliment Voroshilov" (n.d.) [online]. Available: http://en.wikipedia.org/wiki/Kliment_Voroshilov (Accessed on 18 November 2013).

Kushnirov, M. (1977) *Zhizn' i filmy Borisa Barneta*/The Life and Films of Boris Barnet, Moscow: Iskusstvo.

Lenin, V.I. (1951) *Lecture on the 1905 Revolution* [1917], Moscow: Foreign Languages Publishing House.

Lenin, V.I. (1971) "'Left-Wing' Communism: An Infantile Disorder" [1920], *Selected Works*, one-volume edition (New York: International Publishers), pp. 516–591.

Leyda, J. (1983) *Kino: A History of the Russian and Soviet Film*, Princeton: Princeton University Press.

Millar, J.R. (1974) *History and Analysis of Soviet Domestic Bond Policy* (Faculty Working Papers), College of Commerce and Business Administration, University of Illinois at Urbana-Champaign. Available: https://www.ideals.illinois.edu/bitstream/handle/2142/32177/historyanalysiso178mill.pdf (Accessed on 18 November 2013).

Miller, J. (2010) *Soviet Cinema: Politics and Persuasion under Stalin*, London and New York: I.B. Tauris.

Mini, P. (2002) *Pudovkin's Cinema of the 1920s*, Unpublished PhD Thesis, University of Wisconsin-Madison.

Nedobrovo, V.L. (1927) "Ekran: *Devushka s korobkoi*"/The Screen: *The Girl with the Hat Box*, *Zhizn' iskusstva*, 10 May, No. 18, p. 17.

Pudovkin, V.I. (1974) *Film Technique and Film Acting*, Memorial Edition (Transl. by Ivor Montagu) London: Vision.

Read, C. (1979) *Religion, Revolution and the Russian Intelligentsia, 1900–1912: The* Vekhi *Debate and its Intellectual Background*, London: Macmillan.

Reeves, N. (1999) *The Power of Film Propaganda: Myth or Reality?*, London and New York: Continuum.

Rollberg, P. (2009) *Historical Dictionary of Russian and Soviet Cinema*, Lanham, MD: Scarecrow Press.

Scherr, B.P. (1988) *Maxim Gorky*, Boston: Twayne Publishers.

Stalin, J. ([1924]1939) *Foundations of Leninism*, New York: International Publishers.

Starks, T. (2008) *The Body: Propaganda, Hygiene, and the Revolutionary State*, Madison: The University of Wisconsin Press.

Taylor, R. (1979a) *Film Propaganda: Soviet Russia and Nazi Germany*, London: Croom Helm.

Taylor, R. (1979b) *The Politics of the Soviet Cinema 1917–1929*, Cambridge: Cambridge University Press.

Taylor, R. (1983) "A 'Cinema for the Millions': Soviet Socialist Realism and the Problem of Film Comedy," *Journal of Contemporary History* 18:3, pp. 439–461.

Taylor, R. (1999) "Singing on the Steppes for Stalin: Ivan Pyr'ev and the Kolkhoz Musical in Soviet Cinema," *Slavic Review* 58:1, pp. 143–159.

Taylor, R. (2007) "The Stalinist Musical" in Chapman, J., Glancy, M. and Harper, S. (eds) *The New Film History: Sources, Methods, Approaches*, New York: Palgrave, pp. 137–151.

Taylor, R. (2011) "Red Stars, Positive Heroes and Personality Cults" in Taylor, R. and Spring, D. (eds) *Stalinism and Soviet Cinema*, New York: Routledge, pp. 69–89.

Trauberg, I. (1926) "*Mat'*," *Rabochii i teatr*, No. 43, 26 October, p. 17.

Turovskaia, M.I. (1988) "I.A. Pyr'ev i ego muzykal'nye komedii. K probleme zhanra"/I. A. Pyr'ev and his Musical Comedies. On the Problem of Genre, *Kinovedcheskie zapiski* No. 1, pp. 111–146.

V.N. (1927) "Ha ekrane"/On the Screen, *Kino*, 2 May, No. 18, p. 3.

Welch, D. (2003) "Introduction: Propaganda in Historical Perspective" in Cull, N.J., Culbert, D. and Welch, D. (eds) *Propaganda and Mass Persuasion: A Historical Encyclopedia, 1500 to the Present*, Santa Barbara, CA: ABC-Clio, pp. xv–xxi.

Youngblood, D. (1991) *Soviet Cinema in the Silent Era, 1918–1935*, Austin: University of Texas Press.

Youngblood, D. (1993) "'We don't Know What to Laugh at': Comedy and Satire in Soviet Cinema (from *The Miracle Worker* to *St. Jorgen's Feast Day*)" in Horton, A. (ed.) *Inside Soviet Film Satire: Laughter with a Lash*, Cambridge: Cambridge University Press, pp. 36–47.

Zorkaia, N. (2000) "'Ia delaiu stavku na aktera': Boris Barnet v raznye gody"/'I Count on My Actors': Boris Barnet in Different Periods, *Kinovedcheskie zapiski*, No. 47, pp. 186–214.

14

"VICTORY DOESN'T ALWAYS LOOK THE WAY OTHER PEOPLE IMAGINE IT"

Post-conflict cinema in Northern Ireland

Stephen Baker

Introduction

Casting off Northern Ireland's atrocious image and reputation has been a priority for policy makers in the region. Once better known for violent sectarian conflict and a reliance on a substantial subvention from the British exchequer, there is today a determined attempt to present Northern Ireland in a more affirmative light by rebranding it as politically stable, 'open for business' and competitive in the global free market. To this end, film has played a largely complimentary role in the makeover of the region and its citizens. First it aided the transformation of Northern Ireland's image on-screen from one of interminable bloody conflict to a much more pacified and domesticated version. Lately the emphasis has been on marketing Northern Ireland to major global media corporations as an attractive film location, so raising the region's international profile as a site for inward investment and tourism. However, while attempts at image transformation and economic regeneration are welcome, they have come at the cost of a politically engaged cinema that might illuminate, investigate and question Northern Ireland's new dispensation.

All films, as Mike Wayne points out, are political, "but films are not all political in the same way". For instance, films that "address unequal access to the distribution of material and cultural resources" have, for Wayne, a particular claim upon the designation *political film* (2001: 1). On the other hand, what Mas'ud Zavarzadeh refers to as "seemingly innocent films" are political also in the sense that they are deeply ideological. For Zavarzadeh these films establish "an 'imaginary' relation between spectator (the subject) and the world" that helps to reproduce the ruling social order (1991: 1). The distinction between these two types of film is important and instructive when thinking about Northern Ireland, for as this chapter will argue, since the ceasefires and the beginning of the political negotiations that led to the signing of the Good Friday Agreement in 1998, Northern Ireland has appeared in too many seemingly innocent films and not enough determinedly *political* ones. In fact, film in the region has striven to renounce political conviction, in an effort to promote Northern Ireland's interpolation into free-market capitalism after decades of violent civil strife and economic dependency made its full membership of that global community all but impossible. On the surface this appears as good thing; a sign that the region is normalising. However, it comes at a time when Northern Ireland's status as a post-conflict society is in jeopardy, with sectarian divisions deepening, and the region's growing association with global capitalism bringing to the surface social and political tensions that historically have been supressed. Rather than usefully intervene in these political controversies and contribute to the region's democratic processes, film has been hitched to projects that conceive of culture simply as an extension of orthodox economic policy.

Disavowing politics

Film did make a contribution of sorts to the Northern Ireland peace process through the 1990s and into the new millennium with a series of rather banal tales of romantic restoration that seemed to depend upon a disavowal of politics in any form.[1] Among the most remarkable were films that attempted to transform Belfast's on-screen image from one of a "primarily dark and strife-torn maelstrom" (Hill 1987: 147) into a delightful setting for romantic comedy. So, for instance, in *An Everlasting Piece* (Levinson, 2000) and *Wild About Harry* (Lowney, 2000), Belfast's City Hall, once a symbol of unionist power and domination, is divested of its controversial history, charmingly illuminated, and presented as a backdrop against which couples are reconciled and friends celebrate. Similarly, *The Most Fertile Man in Ireland* (Appleton, 2000) takes a signifier of historic political dispute – the Loyalist bonfire – and renders it an image of romantic potential. Bonfires are lit in Loyalist areas on the eve of 12 July, when the Orange Order takes to the streets of Northern Ireland to march in celebration of the Protestant King William's victory over Catholic King James at the battle of the Boyne in 1690. Although frequently a source of sectarian tensions and violence, *The Most Fertile Man in Ireland* transforms the occasion into an idyllic milieu within which a Catholic and Protestant couple fall in love, while illuminated by firelight, surrounded by lanterns and ecstatic friendly celebrants, and to the strains of a sweet, romantic Irish ballad.

However, the image of Northern Ireland as a violent dystopia has not been banished from screen altogether. *Nothing Personal* (O'Sullivan, 1996) and *Resurrection Man* (Evans, 1998) are cases in point that draw variously on the generic conventions of the gangster film and horror to tell tales of violent masculinity, underscored by the romantic failure and the sexual dysfunction of their loyalist protagonists. Elsewhere the image and reputation of republicans has fared better. *The Boxer* (Sheridan, 1997) and *The Mighty Celt* (Elliot, 2005) offer remarkably similar representations of reconstructed Irish republicans returning home to contemporary Belfast, one having been in prison, the other on the run from the authorities. As the films' respective protagonists try to pick up the pieces of their lives, turning their backs on violence and rekindling relationships with old girlfriends, they are confronted by resentful, political hardliners who oppose the peace process and stand in the way of all romantic intentions. In the end the hardliners are dispatched or faced down and the protagonists are reunited with their former lovers, both of whom are coincidently single mothers. The films conclude then, not only with romantic successes but the achievement of a broader domestic intimacy as the men take on paternal roles. In this way both films present a picture of a thoroughly domesticated republicanism in which political ambition has been supplanted by romantic desire and domestic responsibility.

At the heart of the film *Divorcing Jack* (Caffrey, 1998) is a similar validation of domesticated citizenship. A cynical Belfast journalist, Dan Starkey, becomes estranged from his wife after a moment of drunken infidelity. Once thrown out of his home by his furious wife, he finds himself immersed in a darkly comic world of political machinations. He begins to investigate its duplicitous politicians, stupid loyalists and psychotic republicans, but as a consequence his wife is kidnapped. The rest of the film is taken up with Starkey's attempts to expose the political intrigue he has become embroiled in, while simultaneously rescuing his wife. Having achieved both, the final scene sees the couple reconsummate their relationship in their living room at home, away from the 'chaos out there' in what appears to be Northern Ireland's eternally dystopian political sphere.

David Butler points out how public discourse and cultural representation is always potentially contentious in Northern Ireland because, as he puts it, all the signifiers are spoken for by one political persuasion or another (1995: 135). The concept of home is then an attractive proposition in films like *Divorcing Jack* and *The Boxer* since it can be assumed to escape sectarian designation or dispute. *Divorcing Jack* is explicit about this when an American colleague asks Starkey what he prefers to call Northern Ireland – 'Ulster', 'the occupied six counties', 'the North' or 'the province'? Starkey tells him he just calls it 'home', avoiding the political and sectarian associations of the other descriptions. Likewise in *The Boxer* there is a clear validation of 'home' that sets it beyond political controversy, illustrated in a deeply symbolic scene shortly after Danny's release from prison. He returns to where he once lived, which is now a derelict, boarded up flat. To get access he takes a sledgehammer to the bricks that block his front door but his actions attract the concerned attention of British soldiers who ask him what he is doing. Danny states simply that the flat is his home. No further explanation is necessary and indeed throughout the film, when Danny refuses to be intimidated out of Belfast, he evokes the notion of 'home' as an inalienable right.

Politics is likewise refused and domestic probity exalted in *Titanic Town* (Michell, 1998) and *Some Mother's Son* (George, 1996), two films in which mothers are reluctantly drawn into public life by threats to their children. In *Titanic Town*, set in 1970s Belfast, Bernie McPhelimy's well-meaning but naïve efforts to broker a ceasefire between the British army and the IRA brings her to the attention of government officials and the republican leadership, both of whom try to subvert her good intentions for their own ends. Sickened by their politicking and duplicity she stands down from the peace campaign and retreats back into domestic life for the sake of her family. Like Bernie, Kathleen Quigley in *Some Mother's Son* flees a political sphere that appears incomprehensible and double-dealing. Initially a politically disinterested school teacher, Kathleen is drawn into political activism when her incarcerated son joins the hunger strike staged by republican prisoners demanding political status in the early 1980s. She lobbies the British government on her son's behalf but is ultimately repelled by the pedantry and sophistry of both sides in the dispute. In the end she gives permission for her ailing son to be taken off the strike and retires once more into the private sphere.

In both *Titanic Town* and *Some Mother's Son* we are invited to approve of the warm maternal virtues displayed by both women and contrast them with other women whose political convictions damage their domestic life or bring it into disrepute. Bernie's homely propriety and modesty is contrasted with her vociferously republican neighbour who is represented as a foulmouthed slattern, ranting in the street at British soldiers. A more gentle distinction is offered between Kathleen and her friend, Annie, whose son is also on hunger strike. But unlike Kathleen, Annie's strong political convictions prevent her acting upon maternal instinct to intervene and save her son. As in all the other films referred to here, the message is clear: political convictions imperil honourable domestic accord.

There are two incongruities that arise from this sanctification of the home and the demonisation of political conviction and action. The first is that they appear on film in a period of apparent political transformation that would lead to the Good Friday Agreement and the establishment of political and democratic institutions in Northern Ireland. So just at the moment when film might have made a useful contribution to public debate about the quality of the new dispensation in the region, it became politically disengaged. Remarkably, when Northern Ireland's politics were more vexing and belligerent, films about the region were bolder and domestic intimacy was presented in terms that politicised it. Films such as Pat Murphy's *Maeve* (1982), Joe Comerford's *Reefer and the Model* (1987) and *High Boot Benny* (1993), and Thaddeus O'Sullivan's *December Bride* (1990) radically reimagined personal relationships and challenged conservative notions of community and nationhood. The renegades and misfits that come together as 'family' in Comerford's films are provocative alternatives to traditional versions of Irish nationalism, while Thaddeus O'Sullivan's *ménage à trois* in *December Bride* offers an affront to patriarchy and religious, communal conformity. Similarly, *Maeve* challenges and questions the patriarchal assumptions of Irish republicanism, using a radical visual style and disruptive narrative. In the film Maeve's relationships with her father, mother, sister and boyfriend provide the context for an often very intense dialogue about the history and myths of national belonging and gender. Martin McLoone argues that these films (among others) constituted "a cinema of national questioning" (1994: 168). They were "explorations of the many-layered and contradictory nature of identity, explorations at the interface of modernity and tradition, of the particular and the universal" (ibid.). However, it is hard to detect any such qualities in 'ceasefire cinema', when *The Boxer* and *Divorcing Jack* can only recommend 'home' as an anodyne sanctuary from the challenges of Northern Ireland's contemporary politics.

The second problem with this conception is that there is no easy distinction between the domestic and the political. As feminists rightly point out, the domestic sphere, and the gendered values and roles located there, are deeply contested. In this respect Northern Ireland is no different to anywhere else. However, there is also a specifically Northern Irish challenge to the benign view of the home. The Northern Ireland civil rights movement put homes on the political agenda when it campaigned for an end to the sectarian allocation of housing back in the 1960s. More recently the Northern Ireland Housing Executive has recorded "a sharp increase to 411 in 2012/13 in the number of people intimidated out of their homes and accepted on to the Special Purchase of Evacuated Properties (SPED) scheme – up from 303 in 2011/12" (quoted in Nolan 2014: 11). To consider the home as a sanctuary from politics in the context of Northern Ireland is to conceive of it in a highly idealised form.

What accounts for these banal representations of home and domestic intimacy is the figurative and ideological role they play in film. Mas'ud Zavarzadeh argues that ideologically speaking the representation of intimacy is critical to the reproduction of contemporary capitalism because of how intimacy is configured as being beyond the reach of history and culture. Intimates – whether lovers, friends or family members – are assumed to enter into their relationships freely. This freedom is a 'given', transcending all cultural, social and political discourses (1991: 113–114). Intimacy then is a sign of authentic self-hood, which aids the recruitment of people to a dominant economic order where the notion of the 'true', sovereign individual is the cornerstone of a society committed to free enterprise, entrepreneurship and competition.

If intimacy provides ideological sustenance to the prevailing economics of the age, it simultaneously abbreviates public debate. In this respect, Richard Sennett refers to the 'tyrannies of intimacy', which he sees as a contemporary obsession with the self, personality and intimate human relations in western culture that has led to a withdrawal from political and public life. Sennett argues that we now consider public matters more in terms of personal feelings and intimate relations than "codes of impersonal meaning" (1977: 5). Able only to see public concerns in private terms we have lost much of our rational understanding of society. This, Sennett argues, leaves us ill-prepared to think about forces of domination and inequality (339).

The propaganda of peace and post-conflict society

Depoliticising and valorising domestic intimacy in 'ceasefire cinema' has made Northern Ireland and its people imaginable as constituents of the global free market, while simultaneously advancing the truncated public discourse that helps to sustain the system's inequities. This process of political pacification and cultural curtailment are key elements of what Greg McLaughlin and I refer to as "the propaganda of peace", which in the context of Northern Ireland works to persuade a sometimes doubtful public that peace is possible and assure them of the economic dividends that supposedly will accompany political accord (McLaughlin and Baker 2010). This requires a broader conception of propaganda than that typically deployed at times of war by the state, the military or paramilitary organisations. To be sure, the state still plays a definitive role in the propaganda of peace, but it acts in concert with other hegemonic social forces, key among them the local business community and political elites, but also trade unions, the community and voluntary sector, academia and, of course, the media. Persuading for peace is no less propaganda because of its association with civil society and its apparently benign intentions, for it displays a coherent set of ideas and values that seek to mobilise people to act and behave in the interests of power. In short, the propaganda of peace seeks to encourage political accord on terms that are conducive to the neoliberal rationality of the age.

This goes to the heart of what it means to be a post-conflict society. It is not just the absence of violence that defines it. It is the submission of culture and social life to the imperatives of capitalism. As Daniel Jewesbury and Robert Porter (2010) argue, Northern Ireland is subject to a "moralising politics of social and economic development":

> By this we mean that there is a strong connection between the twin narratives of political progress and social-economic development in contemporary Belfast; that post-Agreement Belfast has, to a significant degree, become a story in which the twin moral goods of political progress and privatised, neo-liberal economic development are folded into one another.
>
> (36)

This apparently natural correlation of peace and the global free-market was reiterated by the British Prime Minister, David Cameron, in October 2013 when he spoke of "a new Northern Ireland open for business, ready for investment, strengthening the foundations for peace, stability and prosperity and determined to be defined not by a divided past but by shared future" (Anon. 2013a). In this narrative of combined economic and social regeneration, film production in the region is clearly assigned a role, as illustrated by the announcement in March 2014 by Northern Ireland's Enterprise, Trade and Investment Minister, Arlene Foster, of a planned investment of up to £42.8 million pounds over four years in the region's film, television and digital industries. It is anticipated that this strategy will attract a direct spend of £194 million pounds in the Northern Ireland economy (Anon. 2014). This follows the announcement in January 2014 of plans to expand Belfast's existing studio space in the city's Titanic Quarter by building two new studios at an estimated cost of £14 million. David Gavaghan, the chief executive of Titanic Quarter, claims that the filming of HBO's television series *Game of Thrones*, which is partly shot in Northern Ireland, is driving demand for additional studio space in Belfast (quoted in O'Neill 2014).

While *Game of Thrones* is shot in a variety of international locations, including Malta and Iceland, Northern Ireland secured its place as one of those locations after Northern Ireland Screen (with funding support from Invest NI, a regional agency responsible for developing business and growing the local economy) provided the show's producers HBO with £6.05 million of 'assistance' for the pilot and first two series. The return on that initial investment was an estimated £65 million generated for the local economy, which no doubt played a part in encouraging NI Screen to offer further financial incentives to HBO to film subsequent series of *Game of Thrones* in Northern Ireland, and emboldened Peter Robinson and Martin McGuinness, Northern Ireland's First and Deputy First Ministers, to travel to Los Angeles in a bid to attract more film projects.

A pleasingly blank canvas

No one could accuse Northern Ireland of lacking ambition with regards to film and television production. Indeed, NI Screen's chief executive, Richard Williams, has said that within 10 years he wants the screen industries in Northern Ireland to be second only to London in the UK and Ireland (Anon. 2014). To that end, in 2012 NI Screen produced an impressive showreel that displays the region to spectacular effect through a dynamic montage of film and television clips culled from a range of productions that have used Northern Ireland as a location. Northern Ireland, we are told in the accompanying text,

> is the most compact 5,196 square miles of back-lot in the world – offering myriad stunning film locations from beautiful coastlines to idyllic villages, mountains, glens and loughs, through to urban landscapes and bustling cities with a diverse mix of architectural styles, from Victorian red-brick to 21st century glass and steel.
>
> *(Northern Ireland Screen 2012)*

Film production in the region fits comfortably into a broader strategy that proposes high-profile, global media events as opportunities to market Northern Ireland primarily as an attractive tourist destination. Events such as 2011's MTV European Music Awards, the hosting of the G8 summit in 2013 and the *Giro d'Italia* in 2014 are highly prized for the international exposure they give. As Northern Ireland's Enterprise minister, Arlene Foster put it:

> Capturing the attention of prospective holidaymakers is essential to ensure Northern Ireland stands out from other destinations. In order to attract new and repeat visitors, Tourism Ireland will be seeking opportunities to capitalise on the huge worldwide popularity of HBO's *Game of Thrones* ...
>
> *(Anon. 2013b)*

To this end, in a Baudrillardian example of hyperrealism, the Northern Ireland Tourist Board now invites holidaymakers to "discover the real world" of the *Game of Thrones* by visiting the locations across the region were the series is filmed (Discover Northern Ireland). In effect, Northern Ireland is rendered a tabula rasa – a mere location for economic activity far removed for the cultural lives and experiences of people who live there. As the American actor Bill Murray puts it at the start of the NI Screen showreel: "We're on the biggest set in the world. We're in Belfast". Or similarly, to recall NI Screen's boast, Northern Ireland is "the most compact 5,196 square miles of back-lot in the world". Interestingly, these casual evacuations of the region's historical and social experience effectively complement the rhetoric of property developers looking to profit from Northern Ireland's post-conflict status. Phil Ramsey highlights how Harcourt Developments, the company behind the redevelopment of Belfast's Titanic Quarter, the site of the new film studios, proclaimed glibly:

> Belfast is unique among Western European cities in that more than half of its city centre has yet to be redeveloped, creating a pleasingly blank canvas for regeneration. True, the circumstances that led to this are unfortunate. The violence that plagued the province for 32 years, until peace was declared by the IRA, meant that Belfast was completely underdeveloped and under-regenerated compared to English cities of the same size.
>
> *(Quoted in Ramsey 2013: 176)*

As Ramsey argues, having been wasted by decades of violent conflict, Northern Ireland is seen as ripe for development and capital accumulation, the profits of which are not progressively distributed but serve primarily to deepen inequality in the region. In addition, economic regeneration carries on without any genuine regard for the 'unfortunate' great human cost that has facilitated it in Northern Ireland (177).

This is not a case of special pleading. Many readers situated in other regions will be familiar with the economic and cultural processes illustrated above. In this respect, Northern Ireland's entry into neoliberal globalisation is simply belated, albeit sudden. What does distinguish Northern Ireland is its assumed post-conflict status. This means that the region is simultaneously undergoing what Conor McCabe (2013) has described as a 'double transition' – from violent civil conflict to political accord with a democratic process; and from an economy that was based on broadly social democratic ideals to one dominated by free-market agendas and neoliberal principles. What makes this transition fragile is that the promised 'peace dividend' – the economic reward – that was to accompany the achievement of political stability has never been delivered. In 2014 the Joseph Rowntree Foundation reported that, since 2009, Northern Ireland's household incomes, poverty rates and labour market had all suffered a greater deterioration than those in the rest of the UK (Joseph Rowntree 2014). In effect, the region has finally been exposed to the vagaries of the global free-market just in time to experience persecuting austerity imposed in response to the calamitous consequences of a profligate financial sector.

This economic transition has the potential to threaten peace and reconciliation in Northern Ireland, where historically antagonist communities are left to compete for limited and diminishing resources. Reflecting upon the prospects for war and peace across the world in the twenty-first century, Eric Hobsbawm points out that "the more rapidly growing inequalities created by uncontrolled free-market globalisation are natural incubators of grievance and instability" (2008: 42). As Northern Ireland enters a world of mobile capital and labour, competition for jobs and housing is fuelling racism in the region as well as sectarianism. The region's growing immigrant communities have already suffered a dramatic rise in the incidence of hate crime that has seen Belfast dubbed the race-hate capital of Europe. Meanwhile devolution has made local politicians responsible for legislation on abortion and same-sex marriage, revealing the depth of dispute that exists between conservative and liberal forces in the region. It seems that just as old antagonisms die hard, new battle-lines are emerging in the 'new' Northern Ireland.

A politically engaged film culture would speak to these issues, but this is precisely what the region lacks in any substantial sense. Instead, film is conceived of as an adjunct to tourism; a mere means by which to rebrand Northern Ireland as a site for inward investment and capital accumulation. In an era dominated by the ethics of the free-market it seems that it is almost impossible to conceive of film in any other terms. There are exceptions to the rule but they are rare and usually produced by British television, which still has a residual commitment to public service broadcasting. The BBC's *As the Beast Sleeps* (Bradbeer, 2002), a story of a loyalist gang alienated from the peace process, brings a degree of social realism to the plight of its protagonists, which offers a context for their estrangement and violence. There has also been a series of documentary dramas: Channel 4's *Sunday* (McDougall, 2002) written by Jimmy McGovern about the events of Bloody Sunday in Derry, 1972, provides a damning indictment of the British army's actions on that day, as does Paul Greengrass' *Bloody Sunday* (2002), broadcast on ITV.[2] Paul Greengrass has also co-written *Omagh* (Travis, 2004) with Guy Hibbert, which dramatises Michael Gallagher's investigation into his son's death in the Real IRA bomb that killed 29 people on 15 August 1998. These films, made in the tradition of British television realism, have no counterparts in cinema.

The most intriguing film from Northern Ireland in recent years is BBC Films' *Good Vibrations* (Barros D'sa and Leyburn, 2013), about the life of Terri Hooley, who played a key role in the city's burgeoning punk scene at the end of the 1970s. The film's title comes from the eponymous record shop and label that Hooley established, but is also surely a reference to the emancipating impact of punk on the lives of many young people in Northern Ireland, who were faced with a stifling cultural environment during the so-called Troubles.

The film opens with an idyllic remembrance of Hooley as a boy playing in his garden at home; a brief prelapsarian moment that is brought to a violent conclusion when a sectarian youth shoots an arrow over the hedge at the young Hooley, striking him in the eye. There is little by way of political or historical explanation for this act of sectarian belligerence, save for a rapid montage of documentary images and news footage that depict the region through the decades, marking its deteriorating political situation in the late 1960s and 1970s. However, the sequence barely gives any time to consider the conflict or its roots but simply establishes Northern Ireland as tradition-bound and violently contested. As such, backwardness and sectarian conflict provide a pretext for Hooley's efforts to carve out an alternative to the dismal social life they engender.

Good Vibrations is a paean to the idea of an 'alternative Ulster', a term coined by a Belfast punk band of the era, Stiff Little Fingers. In the film, Belfast is depicted as a terrorised and deserted city of dive-bars defended by security grills and derelict buildings. Stock news footage of bombs exploding, riots, security checkpoints and other documentary images speak for the veracity of this representation of danger and decay. Encounters with paramilitaries are rendered in shades of noir. Elsewhere Hooley's home, the shop and the pub interiors are pictured in a sepia-tinged realism that stands in for historical authenticity. There are moments when the gloom and dread lifts, such as a scene of drug-induced surrealism; sequences of sublime childhood recollection; and occasionally Hank Williams appears in angelic form, as a muse to Hooley throughout. But the key contrast in the film is between the forsaken Belfast streets and the noisy, crowded little bars taken over by Belfast punks, where an alternative Ulster is enacted nightly. In *Good Vibrations*, punk's collective ecstasy is posed as a necessary retort to the sectarian violence that has driven people from public space and crushed the social and cultural life of the city. In this respect, Hooley compares the political urgency of punk in Belfast to what he suggests is its relative superficiality elsewhere. New York, he says, may have the haircuts and London the trousers but 'Belfast has the reason.'

Punk rescues Hooley, not only from Belfast's numbing social environment, but from potential mediocrity and domesticity. Initially he cuts a lonely figure in Belfast as the city's self-proclaimed 'No. 1 DJ', playing to an empty bar, and recounting how his counter-cultural comrades divided along sectarian lines and stayed home as soon as hostilities broke out in the city. His chance encounter with a young woman, Ruth, in the deserted Harp Bar, leads to marriage and the two move out of their respective parents' homes and into a terrace house together. Hooley perseveres as a DJ but is confronted with paramilitary violence and intimidation.

Refusing to be cowed, he conceives of a bold idea, setting his heart on opening a record shop on Belfast's Great Victoria Street, referred to in the film as 'Bomb Alley' on account that it was a regular paramilitary target.

Hooley's optimism and enterprise appear ill-founded in such a ravaged and divided city, but he is presented as possessed of an almost messianic belief in the power of music to transform the social atmosphere in Belfast, and send out the eponymous good vibrations to the beleaguered city. But the shop attracts few customers and Hooley's idealism looks misplaced until his chance encounter with punk in the Pound Bar. The moment is presented as an epiphany during which actor Richard Dormer's performance as Hooley is exceptional. As he pogos in the crowded public house, surrounded by young punks, he experiences a moment of rapture, captured on Dormer's face as it collapses – caught between laughter and sobbing – in a sort of guileless ecstasy. It is a moment Hooley tries to recreate and share with others when he takes the punk bands on tour, 'on the road to Damascus', as he puts it. The religious theme is carried also in the film's frequent reprise of Hank Williams's country hymn, *I Saw the Light*, and again when Hooley tastes success for the first time when John Peel plays The Undertones, *Teenage Kicks* on BBC Radio 1. He walks trance-like into the street, and into the beam of an army helicopter's search light, which for a the moment is transformed into a sublime ray from heaven, at the foot of which Hooley strikes a Christ-like pose while looking up at a heavenly host led by Hank Williams.

This moment of transcendence is fleeting. Figuratively Hooley is brought back down to earth by a series of bust-ups with friends; mounting debts; a vicious paramilitary assault upon him and the news that he is to be a father – a responsibility he is ill-prepared for and shows no aptitude. Indeed shortly after having the baby, Ruth moves out of their home and at the end of the film they break up amicably; she apparently accepting that his commitment to music and its associated lifestyle is incompatible with his role as a husband and father. Hooley's preferred 'family', in any case, are the punk bands and their audience that make a stand against the violent monotony of Northern Ireland's social life. But Hooley's inclusion in this broadly homosocial cadre depends upon Ruth shouldering the weight of the couple's domestic responsibility. In short, she is literally left holding the baby.

If Hooley cuts a poor romantic lead in the film he is depicted as a worse business man. When The Undertones give the Good Vibrations label its bestselling single with the seminal "Teenage Kicks", Hooley relinquishes the rights to the song to a major record company for a derisory figure and the promise of a signed autograph of 60s pop group The Shangri-Las. But as he sees it: "Teenage Kicks didn't belong to me; it belonged to everybody". This disregard for the commercial imperatives and his emersion in an extended, surrogate family of punks is given full expression in the film's climax. To rescue his business Hooley organises a Good Vibrations gig in the relatively grand surroundings of the Ulster Hall, Belfast. In commercial terms the concert is a failure. The hall is packed out but Hooley has let so many people through the doors for free that the event makes a loss. But as he tells his exasperated partner, the night was about more than making a profit: "Money couldn't buy what we've just done". Indeed its real achievement becomes apparent in the final scene of communal solidarity, as Hooley takes to the stage, and accompanied by the Good Vibrations' bands and friends, he gives a rendition of Sonny Bono's anthem to misfits and losers, *Laugh at Me*.

While not a resolutely political film, in the sense that Mike Wayne proposes, neither is *Good Vibrations* banally innocent. Its dénouement of romantic and commercial underachievement flies in the face of the classical narrative conventions of 'feel-good' films. Hooley rejects the soporific domesticity that romantic success implies, instead striving to carve out a public space and identity that is distinct from the atavistic politics and sectarianism that surround him. However, an equally refreshing aspect of *Good Vibrations* is Hooley's cultural entrepreneurship that shows no regard for the commercial imperatives that today's rebranded Northern Ireland is so enamoured by. Indeed by today's standards, Hooley would be deemed a failure. But as his socialist father understands, success depends upon the criteria used to measure it. Having stood for election on twelve occasions and failed to get elected once, Hooley senior can nevertheless boast of having "friends and comrades living all over this city" and to having increased his vote at each election. "Victory", he tells his disconsolate son, "doesn't always look the way other people imagine it".

There is a danger that a post-conflict society anticipates a post-political cinema; that the achievement of constitutional accord and the aspiration to full membership of the global free-market render a politically engaged cinema both apparently irrelevant and undesirable. What need has Northern Ireland of a political cinema when it has achieved a constitutional accord and when film presents a delightful opportunity to market the region on the world stage? Here the confluence of political self-congratulations with economic imperatives and ambitions offers a seemingly cast-iron case for a depoliticised film culture: except that Northern Ireland has no call to be politically complacent. It is riven with residual political antagonisms and confronted with emergent ones, many of which have been given impetus by the region's new political arrangements and its entry into global capitalism. In this context there is a pressing political imperative to strive for a cinema that can speak to these issues.

Notes

1 A more detailed analysis of the films that follow in this section is available in McLaughlin and Baker (2010).

2 For a full discussion of *Sunday* and *Bloody Sunday* see McLaughlin and Baker (2014).

Bibliography

Anon. (2013a) "Investment Conference 'will Bring Hundreds of Jobs to NI'", BBC News Northern Ireland, online, 11 October, http://www.bbc.co.uk/news/uk-northern-ireland-24486093 (accessed 5 October 2015).

Anon. (2013b) "Hike in Visitors to Northern Ireland", UTV News, online, 4 December, http://www.u.tv/News/Hike-in-visitors-to-Northern-Ireland/81ebfbf6-bcf3-4333-890d-d1326b25733d (accessed 5 October 2015).

Anon. (2014) "Northern Ireland Screen gets 50% funding boost", BBC News Northern Ireland, online, 31 March, http://www.bbc.co.uk/news/uk-northern-ireland-26826099 (accessed 5 October 2015).

Butler, D. (1995) *The Trouble with Reporting Northern Ireland*, Aldershot: Avebury Publishers.

Discover Northern Ireland, online, http://www.discovernorthernireland.com/gameofthrones/ (accessed 5 October 2015).

Hill, J. (1987) "Images of Violence", in Rockett, K., Gibbons, L. and Hill, J. (eds) *Cinema and Ireland*, London: Croom Helm, pp. 147–193.

Hobsbawm, E. (2008) *Globalisation, Democracy and Terrorism*, London: Abacus.

Jewesbury, D. and Porter, R. (2010) "On Broadway", in Jewesbury, D. (ed.) *The Centrifugal Book of Europe*, Belfast: Centrifugal, pp. 34–53.

Joseph Rowntree (2014) Joseph Rowntree Report, Monitoring Poverty and Social Exclusion in Northern Ireland 2014, http://www.jrf.org.uk/sites/files/jrf/northern-ireland-poverty-summary.pdf

McCabe, C. (2013) *The Double Transition: The Economic and Political Transition of Peace*, Belfast: Irish Congress of Trade Unions and Labour After Conflict.

McLaughlin, G. and Baker, S. (2010) *The Propaganda of Peace: The Role of Culture and Media in the Northern Ireland Peace Process*, Bristol: Intellect.

McLaughlin, G. and Baker, S. (2014) *The British Media and Bloody Sunday*, Bristol: Intellect.

McLoone, M. (1994) "National Cinema and Cultural Identity: Ireland and Europe", in Hill, J., McLoone, M. and Hainsworth, P. (eds) *Border Crossing: Film in Ireland, Britain and Europe*, Belfast: Institute of Irish Studies/British Film Institute, pp. 146–173.

Nolan, P. (2014) *Northern Ireland Peace Monitoring Report*, Belfast: Community Relations Council.

Northern Ireland Screen (2012) Showreel and text, online, http://www.northernirelandscreen.tv/video/206/northern-ireland-screen-film-locations-showreel-2012.aspx (accessed 1 October 2014).

O'Neill, J. (2014) "Titanic Quarter Belfast to Get two New Film Studios", BBC News Northern Ireland, online, 29 January, http://www.bbc.co.uk/news/uk-northern-ireland-25944177 (accessed 5 October 2015).

Ramsey, P. (2013) "A Pleasingly Blank Canvas: Urban Regeneration in Northern Ireland and the Case of Titanic Quarter", *Space and Polity* 17(2), pp. 164–179.

Sennett, R. (1977) *The Fall of Public Man*, London: Penguin.

Wayne, M. (2001) *Political Film: The Dialectics of Third Cinema*, London: Pluto Press.

Zavarzadeh, M. (1991) *Seeing Films Politically*, New York: State University of New York Press.

15

FILM POLICY AND ENGLAND

The politics of creativity

Paul Dave

Patterns of policy

Historically, British film policy has covered a range of different objectives which can be classified according to the distinctive as well as necessarily overlapping instances of the economic, cultural, social and political (Hill 2004). Whilst the coverage of the first three is familiar in the academic literature, perhaps the last tends to be given less attention. From the perspective of a left politics of film culture this is a pity. For instance, it is common for histories of British film policy to start in the 1920s with its key pieces of protectionist legislation affecting the economics of the industry in the face of Hollywood dominance, thus neglecting earlier legislation such as the Cinematograph Act of 1909. One of the effective but covert political expedients in this earlier act, the first licensing of premises with a view to audience safety in consideration of the fire hazards presented by early cellulose nitrate film stock, was to help smother the emergence of a proletarian counter public sphere constituted by the so-called 'penny gaffs' in areas such as East London with their high immigrant communities (Burrows 2004). Such moments help to remind us that policy combines precisely formulated forms of intervention (here local government licensing) along with that which is much harder to analyse and evaluate: currents of political and ideological pressure. The 1909 Act is the beginning of that stealthy form of ruling class vigilance over a popular cultural form felt to require unique and extra controls – such as local council approval over exhibition. Such concerns speak to a recognition of film's potential political disruptiveness (the incitement to 'disorder'). As Julian Petley sardonically notes, the licensing powers of local authorities survived the end of flammable film stock (Petley 2013).

Whilst politically attentive to film, the state has nevertheless been keen to conform to a treasured national self-image: one of British democratic freedoms. This has historically necessitated maintaining the appearance of a distance between the state and regulation of the industry. Thus, Western Europe's most heavily censored film culture has been characterized by the use of para-state, non-governmental institutions such as the British Board of Film Classification in order to exert discreet, 'arm's length' political pressure in support of the status quo. The careful shadowing by the state of the radical cinema of the inter-war years is a good example of this vigilance (Petley 1986: 44). This politically coercive face of the state is of course only one aspect of its engagement with film policy. Historically, interventions have sought to regulate the economics of the industry in support of commercial film production, and to achieve social aims: see for instance the support for the documentary movement under the Empire Marketing Board in the 1930s and under the Ministry of Information during World War II. As John Hill puts it, this distinctive strand of British film culture represented the "cultivation of film as a vehicle for information, instruction and the construction of citizenship" (Hill 2004: 33). To these older examples of social aims we can add the United Kingdom Film Council's (UKFC) and its successor, the revamped British Film Institute's (BFI), shared objectives of an 'inclusive' and 'diverse' film culture (BFI 2012).

Finally, historically there has been a distinctive cultural component to policy, one which as we will see has recently been expanded and transformed in importance, but which can be traced back to initiatives such as the setting up of the BFI in the 1930s with its mission to archive the national film culture and promote those aspects of film culture which were perceived to be in excess of its purely commercial qualities, including educational initiatives, the provision of forums for evaluative criticism, the fostering of wider distribution and exhibition outlets for distinctively cultural films from outside the national culture, and the small-scale support of cultural film production (Nowell-Smith and Dupin 2012).

Clearly the relationship between these different aspects of policy (economic, social and cultural) is historically mutable; however, this variability is not simply contingent on successive governmental agenda. One way of characterizing it over the post-war period would be in terms of the shift between social democratic and neoliberal state formations. The former attempted to manage the relationship between capitalism on the one hand, and social equality on the other, a concern which, as Jim McGuigan points out, expanded into the related project of fostering cultural inclusion and access (McGuigan 2004). By contrast, a tempting, but misleading view of neoliberalism would be to see it as the abandonment of social and cultural concerns to the indifference and philistinism of the market. Rather it has sought the incorporation of social and cultural policy objectives within a market which is reconfigured as their ideal medium for realization. To this extent the critical point of distinction between the two moments is the neoliberal rejection of the contradiction between capitalism and either social equality or cultural access, a contradiction which the social democratic moment had recognized as a given.

On the level of cultural policy formations, this shift between social democratic and neoliberal frameworks can be roughly mapped onto the difference between the post-war 'arts and culture' paradigm (which accepted the need for cultural state subsidies because of the perceived likelihood of the market failing to provide for recognized cultural values) and that of the post-1980s 'cultural and creative industries' (CI) paradigms which conceptualised commerce and culture entering into new productive partnerships, whereby culture was deemed to be less that which needed protecting from the market and more that which might flourish within it (Dickinson and Harvey 2005). With a historical tidiness, Keynes himself was involved in the institutionalisation of the former immediately after the war; the creative and cultural industries moment is, however, more untidy in its periodisation. Thus, Thatcher's early 1980s pursuit of *laissez-faire* accepted an opposition between the market (which the state was to leave untouched), and 'arts and culture' provision (which might require some – reduced – assistance or patronage). But this kind of opposition was by no means typical of the mature neoliberal approach to cultural policy adopted by the Majorite Tories or New Labour in which the cultural instance was subject to an economic transvaluation which has had important results for film policy and the willingness of the state to actively engage with the film industry. Simply put, within the CI model, culture is viewed as a resource. Thus, in the contemporary 'creative economy', cultural policies rest upon economic justifications (neoliberal accountancy practices quantify the economic value of culture). Equally, in indication of the close co-operation and compatibility of the economic and cultural instances, economic policies can rest on cultural assumptions (for instance the UKFC's Cultural Test of 2007 which set cultural thresholds in exchange for film industry tax relief) (Hill 2012: 337).

With the advent of the Tory-led coalition government of 2010 a largely settled pattern of policy appears to have emerged which dates back roughly to the early 1990s. Before that time, in the early 1980s, commercial subsidies for the indigenous film industry were removed as Thatcher's governments abolished older, protectionist-styled interventions, including the Eady Levy (a redistribution of a proportion of box office takings to producers), the Quota Act (a requirement placed on exhibitors and distributors to handle a minimum percentage of British films) and the National Film Finance Corporation (providing loans for British producers). At the same time, cultural film subsidy was maintained largely through the interventions of the Arts Council, Channel 4 (C4) and the BFI, the latter two responding to lobbying by the Association of Cinematographic and Television Technicians (ACTT), and the Independent Film-Makers' Association (IFA). By such means, pressure in support of a critical and public service view of film culture was sustained. By the early 1990s, under John Major, help for the commercial film sector resumed in the form of tax relief and Lottery funding. From 2000 this arrangement was consolidated and rationalised through New Labour's UKFC which also took on a cultural and social remit, rendering subordinate the BFI and placing an emphasis on the expansion of the regional sector to deliver a spectrum of policy goals. These covered a social inclusion agenda which sought to develop a wider social base for cinema-going by means of distribution and exhibitions strategies, a pledge to encourage diversity in the workforce, along with training and educational initiatives, and a commitment to foster an identifiable sense of national film heritage. As John Newsinger argues, after 2010 this basic mix was maintained; nevertheless, in the context of the coalition's austerity drive there has been a weakening of the regional sector whilst, despite initial fears, support for the mainstream industry remains solid (Newsinger 2012).

State and nation

Before we can evaluate these shifting relations between social, economic and cultural aspects of policy we need to consider the problematic historical relationship of the British 'state' to its 'nation'. Generally, it has been recognized that states can struggle to effectively formulate national film policy. Limitations are imposed by the transnational or globalizing logic of mainstream cinema, and in particular by the dominant power of Hollywood. But equally, the desirability of an uncritical defence of a putatively national culture by the state is problematic given the dangers of the falsely socially homogenised, essentialised or mythified manifestations such national cultural formations can assume (Higson 2000, Wayne 2002).

In the British case this situation contains a further complexity which can be summed up thus: the British state is historically strong, whereas the 'nation' which is its object is neither unified nor, in the case of England, strongly defined in terms of what many would view as authentic traditions of popular sovereignty (Gardiner 2012; Colley 2014). This underlying problem, if unaddressed, can disturb contemporary discussions of the problem of defining an authentic (or 'cultural') national cinema for the purposes of policy intervention. For some, such problems appear to relate to a general condition (Higson 2000). According to a commonplace of contemporary cultural theory, this is the collision between an essentialised project of national identity and the necessary actuality of cultural hybridity which is especially acute in postmodern times. There is a danger that such arguments can act to conceal the historical peculiarities in this particular state–nation relationship. The conjunction of an Englishness which lacks "clarity about boundaries and identity" with a strong imperial state represents such a peculiarity (Colley, 2014: 60; Gardiner, 2012). Indeed the idea of a British 'state-nation', a reversal of the accepted formulation 'nation state', emphasises this historical subordination. That is to say, this Englishness (the hegemonic core of a falsely homogenised Britishness) might be seen less as an 'expression of English arrogance' and national presumption, and instead be viewed in terms of the longevity and dynamism of a strong centralised state projecting a capitalist culture of class and empire in order to offset the missing cultural yeast of popular sovereignty – what Linda Colley describes as a culture of "people-building" (2014: 60–1).

As a context for policy measures this legacy is both a problem and an opportunity. Thus, in its historic hyper-visibility, the Englishness of British cinema is eminently exploitable. Indeed, the strength of 'industrially' defined British cinema (as opposed to a 'culturally' defined one) is dependent in important ways on this mythic and globally recognized culture of Englishness, with all its abstract, idealized and marketable characteristics (Westall and Gardiner 2013). This is a thoroughly profitable cultural resource that the British state seems happy to support through the agency of the UKFC and at global showcase events like the London Olympics (directed by Danny Boyle). The reconceptualisation of culture as an economic resource to be exploited is an important part of the shift at the heart of the CI model of cultural policy. Here, the profitable projection of Englishness has its popular cultural face: Bean, Bond, Potter; its canonical literary tradition: Austen to Forster; its associated imperial kudos along with its fetishised class-system imagery; and finally its self-conscious investment in and studied exploitation of a precious historicity. All these aspects constitute what Andrew Higson refers to as a "surprisingly resilient national stereotypes" (2010: 10). Note these same features are emphasised in Higson's success story account of English cinema in its New Labour/UKFC moment.

It might be argued then that policy aimed fundamentally at supporting industrially British filmmaking is simultaneously, among other things, helping to support a regressive culturally English cinema. Indeed, it is open to doubt, as Newsinger observes, whether such policy meaningfully supports a *national* industry, as opposed say, to say a "cheap outsourced Hollywood assembly plant" with generous tax breaks soliciting 'inward investment' for the UK styled as a global 'creative hub' (2012: 139). Higson, however, argues that an evolving and renewed national cinema is emerging out of such policies after what he sees as the near collapse of the early 1980s (2010: 63). Placing emphasis on the benefits of the Cultural Test of 2007 he also points to the irony that its more substantive national cultural features (for instance the categories of 'content' and 'cultural contribution') were imposed on New Labour by the transnational agency of the European Commission. Equally, he highlights the fact that national film culture renewal can be seen so clearly in the work of directors who seek to 'creatively' reinterpret it and whose reference points are clearly transnational, such as Gurinder Chadha (2010: 63). This account then places significant emphasis on the dimension of contemporary international exchanges and flows, both cultural and economic.

Commerce and culture: cultural industries to creative industries

Claire Monk describes Higson's work cited above on contemporary British cinema since the 1990s as "consensus case studies of Englishness-for-export" and "academic capitulation to market agendas" (Monk 2011: 461). And it does seem that Higson's emphasis confirms the diminishing significance afforded to the older sense of a contradiction between commerce and culture. David Puttnam's statement "strong cultural resistance can best be built on the basis of a firm understanding of the realities of the marketplace" sums up this shift neatly

(Miller 2000: 44). This is a development with a complex genealogy going back to the 1980s when attempts were made through metropolitan socialism (including the initiatives of the Greater London Council, GLC) to explore the opposition between commerce and culture in a socially and culturally progressive direction. The cultural industries strategy sought to overcome the art vs. popular culture dualism through a critique of the traditional left's suspicion of market-based forms of popular culture. This was with a view to supporting forms of independent cultural entrepreneurialism and previously marginalized social voices. As Margaret Dickinson and Sylvia Harvey put it: "The intention was to promote a new kind of popular culture led neither by remote multinationals nor by the limited cultural tastes of the local dominant class" (Dickinson and Harvey 2005: 424).

The argument that Hollywood's popular cultural influence can be viewed as a potentially beneficial or critical aspect of 'cinema in Britain' because of its demotic energies and the contrast it offers with an indigenous class-bound offering, fits with this 'cultural industries' policy moment (Hill 1992; Nowell-Smith 1985). The latter's critique of an older 'arts and culture' agenda, as say manifested in the support of the independent cinema movement of the 1960s and 1970s, was aimed at combating the problem that such cultural formations often displayed a middle-class bias in terms of participation and thus had inbuilt tendency to rely on exclusionary forms of cultural capital, not to mention a relative neglect of the problem of race and racism (Dickinson 1999: 54).

The policies of the GLC were preoccupied with ideas of cultural democracy. However, from the late 1990s, under New Labour, this critical and politically radical edge to policy was subject to a significant transformation within the discourse of 'creativity', which translated the "reconciliatory logic" of New Labour's "social market" idea into policy interventions (Neelands and Choe 2010: 288–9); 'reconciliatory' because the social market (or Third Way) suggests that social (or cultural) objectives can be achieved painlessly via market means (289). Thus, the social and cultural 'exclusions' of the market are lost to sight. The discourse of 'creativity' then represents a particular articulation of the commerce/culture opposition, with a marked insistence on a common core of activity/energy. As the UKFC put it: "Film is a complex combination of industry and culture. Common to both are creativity and commerce" (Newsinger 2009). If the idea of creativity attempts to establish a fundamental identity, however complex, of commerce and culture, it nevertheless remains the case, as I will argue below, that it ultimately subordinates the hopes of a progressive cultural policy to an overriding concern with satisfying dominant industrial interests. And this despite the persistence, in the case of film policy, of social and cultural aims of inclusion and diversity – aims which in the assessment of many have been weakly developed (Hill 2004; Dickinson and Harvey 2005; Newsinger 2009).

Regional film policy

Newsinger's work helps to show that it was in the regions during the New Labour period that the CI model of policy was most vigorously developed and also where the task of supporting a culturally 'national' cinema was principally located – in tacit recognition that the commercial mainstream could not sustain such ambitions (Newsinger 2009). The objective was to build up an industrial infrastructure upon which to sustain a wide range of indigenous film cultural activity. Public subsidy was directed through Regional Screen Agencies (RSAs) to small commercially oriented independent companies (small to medium enterprises, SMEs) for the purpose of encouraging training, outside investment and a network of facilities linked up to local broadcasters. This hive of regional 'creative' activity was then presented as the point at which cultural and economic policy converged generating a virtuous cycle of 'sustainable' film culture.

It is important to note two things at this point. First, that which in the CI model's application to regional policy appears to fit with the neoliberal ideology of the 'creative' spirit of the market – the emphasis on the small scale, lean, competitive, energetically entrepreneurial, and of course successful – is actually dependent on public funds. Indeed, under this regime, references to public 'subsidy' tend to be replaced by terms such as 'investment' (Hill 2010). RSAs, like the UKFC itself, were private companies operating with public money, but with limited public accountability, and they preferred to use the language of commerce.

The second point to note is that the flow of public money into private hands, overseen by industry 'experts', fits with the general eclipsing of the idea of the importance of publicly debatable notions of public interest, separable from trade interests – or rather, it indicates the democratic deficit in the CI model of policy making. This is a point made effectively by Dickinson and Harvey about the UKFC era, and it is one that remains relevant in the present BFI dispensation. Just as private companies benefit from public money disbursed by bureaucratic and professionalized experts on the regional level, so on the national level regular policy reviews are conducted by 'consultation' which necessarily limits democratic discussion in the name of efficiency and superior industry know-how (Dickinson and Harvey 2005).

As Newsinger argues, the CI model has effectively depoliticized the regional film sectors, replacing the idea of film as a cultural practice exemplified by the older regional workshop model which we will consider below. One area where this problem in regional policy can be examined is that of the short film which boomed under the UKFC. The digital short represents a good example of the proposed painless convergence of cultural, social and economic policy objectives within the CI framework. What Newsinger's research illustrates, however, is how it poorly served the objectives of 'access' and 'diversity', social and cultural goals which it was deemed an ideal vehicle for (Newsinger 2009). Indeed, the intention to include groups traditionally marginalized from film culture found itself channelled into the 'institutionalized individualism' promoted by the empowered regional agencies (McGuigan 2004). The short film presented a form whose relatively rapid fabrication and usefulness as an industry entry 'stepping stone' militated against the complex collective productive context and more erratic temporal rhythms of the residual regional workshop culture which arguably was more successful in achieving headway with objectives such as diversity and access.

Despite the rhetoric of a convergence of policy objectives, the economic one of maintaining mainstream commercial objectives remained dominant. Indeed, a key aspect of the CI model has been the fostering of a skilled, regionally based labour pool. Much of what appears to be regional 'regeneration' has been established by an expansion of the sector based on the entrenching of neoliberal labour market practices such as casualisation. Such practices fit with what critics call the New International Division of Cultural Labour whereby more pliant, less protected labour markets are prepared for multinationals and local businesses seeking to reduce labour costs (Miller 2000: 38).

The vigour of this CI entrepreneurial dynamism coincided with the defeat and decline of the older model of the regional workshops. Fundamentally, the workshop principle recognized the exclusionary logics of the commercial mainstream on levels of access/participation and reception/response, logics that remain difficult to meaningfully evade by the voluntarism or 'institutionalised individualism' of the CI model. Along with the stress on collective production came an emphasis on democratic control of projects and a different conception of 'creativity', not reducible, as in the regional digital shorts boom, to eye-catching stylization or even 'innovation' around genre, but seeking to engage with a range of forms (experimental, narrative and documentary) and offering sustained attention to the politics of form. Equally, the workshops operated according to contrasting temporal rhythms which, given their detachment from commercial motives (profit), enabled what Peter Thomas calls "durational and immersive" projects embedded in specific communities. Such practices are opposed to the commodified logic of speed and market distinctiveness in which, for example, short films grab attention as a prelude to feature film production and career advancement (Thomas 2011: 11).

In earlier periods, such as the 1930s and 1960s, a process of reflection and making-do was a feature of politicized film culture in what might be called its incubational stage, and as Dickinson argues, the workshop movement as a whole has strong filiations with these traditions (1999: 31). To take one example, Amber Film Collective from the north-east sought both to engage in such reflective activity (over time reworking social realist traditions in its output), and to retain as much as possible its autonomy through mixed survival strategies, including controlled engagement with the market as well as workshop grants via C4 and other funding bodies.

There has always been in such oppositional projects from which the workshops emerged an aspect of what has become known as DIY counter-culture. According to George McKay, this is an informal, collectively organized culture, in which productive activities are characterized by *lending, giving, helping out* without the necessary expectation of commercial return/remuneration (McKay 1997). Dickinson is referring to the same phenomenon when she cites the "unofficial cottage industry" of 1960s independent film culture relying on practices of mutual borrowing, assistance, working for free on projects where there was no attempt to acquire funding and an implicit denial of market values. This was the pre-existing, enabling tradition for the first workshops (1999: 30–1).

Of course, it might be argued that the labour market casualisation which is at the heart of the CI model has increasingly cynically adopted and deformed this DIY ethic to the advantage of commercial motives through practices such as 'unpaid internships'. But equally, it is interesting to see how this DIY culture re-emerges in explanations of the significance of the work of Shane Meadows, one of the key figures of the regionalization of film production under the CI model. Meadows is a determinedly regional filmmaker whose work helps to us to get a dialectical view of the relationship of policy to left critical ambitions for regional and national film culture, a view which captures such policies' consequences both negative and positive, intended and unintended. Also, Meadows' example will help us to elicit the outlines and possibilities of alternative frameworks for policy.

The case of Meadows

The first thing to consider is the problem of origins. Read retrospectively, Meadows' critical and commercial success which was consolidated in the era of the CI model suggests a mythic vindication of voluntarist entrepreneurialism. To ironise the title of his first feature, this is the Meadows of manic, unflagging, prolific energies, an exemplar perhaps of the nightmarish neoliberal 24/7 work culture discussed by Jonathan Crary (Crary 2013). However, Meadows' short-film exercises (1994–7) cannot be reduced to a sequence of 'calling cards', 'stepping stones' or 'rungs on the ladder' helping him climb out of obscurity. Instead, it might well be argued that the aura of his origins ("a filmmaker who came from nowhere" as Kate Ogborn puts it), conceals some of the residual strengths of the older, workshop paradigm which in practice overlapped with the emergent CI model during this period, before the latter was operationally formalized post-1997/2000 by New Labour's UKFC (Ogborn in Newsinger 2013: 25).

It was through a strong, pre-existing, local context of community access, central to workshop tradition and mediated in Meadows case through the Nottingham-based workshop Intermedia, that the early shorts were made. When Meadows refers to the state giving him his break (money saved from his social security payments funding his early efforts), our attention is drawn to the Headstart scheme run by Intermedia in the 1990s which offered training and access to equipment for the unemployed (Meadows in Newsinger 2009). Such schemes tend to put emphasis on the social aspect of policy (and the accounts Meadows gives of his experiences at Intermedia indicate the community-based/pastoral ethic in operation at the time) (Wilson 2013: 913). However, it is equally true that Meadows remained wary of the independent, theoretically informed leftist film culture which represented the core of the regional workshop movement during the late 1970s and 1980s – he refers to it disparagingly as "elite", "condescending" and "exclusive" and this is a judgement which speaks to the realities of the gradients of class and cultural capital in predominantly middle-class independent film cultures of the time (Meadows, quoted in Wilson 2013: 912).

Notwithstanding this, the fact remains that the local and residual influence of the workshop moment helped Meadows and his collaborators to explore a specific working-class culture of youth. Newsinger makes the important point that much of this activity was reliant on a strong local DIY counter-culture (Newsinger 2009).

Success in short films brought Meadows firmly into the orbit of the CI model; however, the results of this encounter are complex, contradictory and dialectically entangled. On the one hand there was the danger of the mainstreaming of regional material, or what Mike Wayne refers to as the pressure to adapt authentic regional/national representations to transnational logics, a development clearest in the comically inflected regionalism of the social realist tradition during this period (Wayne 2002, 2006). A film like *Once Upon a Time in the Midlands* (Meadows, 2002) in its mainstream casting practices (running counter to Meadows' habitual approach before and after) is in some ways indicative of this trend whereby the regional policies of the CI model acted to drain away indisputably 'homemade' or locally specific cultural energies into product for larger markets.

Equally, however, it remains true, as Newsinger observes, that regional policy under the CI model has offered provincial filmmakers creative freedom and autonomy from London (an explicit concern of Meadows). In this respect Warp Films stands as a representative and tutelary institution for the established director, just as Intermedia did for the beginner. Warp sits in a network of regional funding institutions (co-ordinated, during the UKFC period, by EM Media, the Regional Screen Agency for the area), and has distribution partners (including C4 for broadcasting); it is integrated horizontally (through interests in music and publishing), and it is connected inter-regionally (with co-production links to the north-eastern RSA Screen Yorkshire). This enables access to both private and public funds while giving its directors a degree of local autonomy. *Dead Man's Shoes* (Meadows, 2004) and *This is England* (Meadows, 2006) – perhaps the two most critically successful of Meadows' films – were produced by Warp according to its principles of reduced budgets within "generic niches" (Newsinger 2009). Under such circumstances Meadows' reconnected with his preferred methods, including the use of non-professional actors and improvised production practices.

These two films display the complexity of Meadows' work under the CI model as it reaches beyond the commercialized bleaching-out of regional culture that some have detected in *Once Upon a Time in the Midlands* and offers a revision of the established conventions of what has historically been the dominant form of regional film production, social realism. The key to this complexity lies in the engagement with popular culture. In the earlier 'cultural industries' model of policy, popular culture, with its relationship to mainstream markets, was recognised as a significant preference for working-class audiences seeking to evade the suffocating elitism of British national culture. Hollywood has clearly been important in Meadows' development as a filmmaker. But for Newsinger, his interest in popular genres suggests a historical contrast between the older workshop model and the depoliticizing effects of the CI model – as he puts it, Meadows' reference point is "popular culture not cultural politics" (Newsinger 2009). Whilst Meadows is by no means an explicitly political filmmaker, it is less straightforward to claim that the inclusion of popular genres within social realism necessarily depoliticizes the work. For Newsinger the compromise with 'escapism' or the capitulation to 'entertainment' takes Meadows over the traditionally designated discursive boundary within which the 'moral realism' of social realism maintains itself (Newsinger 2009). However, we might view Meadows' use of popular culture (the humour and farce as well as the generic self-consciousness) differently. The aesthetic extremism available in popular cultural genres, for instance the use of elements of horror, the gangster and western film, black comedy and satire in *Dead Man's Shoes*, helps construct a form of tragic realism which in turn facilitates an exploration of the neoliberal politics of class with its "law and order grand guignol" (Wacquant, quoted in Dave 2011: 39).

Finally, we need to consider an issue closely connected to the affect generated in Meadows' work around 'sociality'. This is a quality which is also related to the importance of popular cultural forms, in this case comedy. The pleasure of sociality is clearly central to Meadows' work, and provides a further explanation of the apparent enigma of his 'origins' which avoids drawing on the competitive individualism of neoliberal ideology that is at the heart the CI model. Critics recognize a fundamental continuity in Meadows' films around the apparent 'belief in community' along with his persistent attention to the 'sociality of the group' (Monk 1999, Newsinger 2009, Dave 2011). This recurring feature appears as a thematic; as a foregrounded element of style (the centrality of improvisation) and as a production practice (DIY with its valorisation of mutuality and collectivity, not just as methods of oppositional cultural practice but as pleasurable ends in their own right). And, of course, it can be pushed back further into the popular cultural experiences of specific, youthful, working-class communities. Indeed, this overdetermination of the motif of sociality gives Meadows' work that peculiarly allegorical, self-referential transparency whereby the diegetic and extra-diegetic realms appear to call each other. Thus, to take one example, the exuberant improvisation in the films is clearly rooted in Meadows' casts' collective experiences of popular culture. As a technique, it accesses commonly held popular cultural repertoires (horror and comedy, for instance) in order to act out the social realist dramas. Popular culture then is not so much an escape from the themes of the films as it is a means of collectively exploring and keeping them close to common cultural experiences.

But we can push this further and argue that this aspect of Meadows' work suggests a grounding in particular cultural values which have a political significance, even if this political significance is not explicitly formulated as such. That is to say, this thoroughgoing interest in the collective – the enjoyment of its potential inclusiveness and enabling mutuality, the 'sense of belonging and access to the social group' that is projected in so many of the films and which seems to persist even in the most extreme and destructive of situations depicted – is reminiscent of what Raymond Williams intended with his normative principle of a 'common culture' (Newsinger 2009; Williams 1989). Common culture has its origins in working-class history with its co-operative institutions and their ethic of solidarity (Eagleton 2000: 120; Dave 2011). However, what Williams meant by a common culture was neither to be restricted to any 'panacea of proletarian culture', nor to designate a culture of uniformity (Eagleton 2000: 121). 'Common' referred to a culture that was to be understood as common in form, but not in content. A common culture is one in which the principles of cultural democracy through which cultural pluralism or diversity can flourish, rest on politically securing the 'means of community' (Williams 1984). In other words, a common culture implies a politics which vigorously acts against, rather than rhetorically deprecates, material structures of exclusion from cultural participation. 'Sociality' is the residual (and anticipatory) trace of that common culture but can only become the context of policy through what would be a fundamental realignment: a moving away from *cultural politics* (whose problem is that it legitimises the nebulous liberalism of cultural difference which is so adaptable to the neoliberal capitalist realism promoted by the fundamentally industrially oriented film policy of recent years), and a moving towards the *politics of culture* (policies informed by the regulative principle of a common culture in which participatory democracy is "the condition of which culture is the product") (Eagleton 2000: 122).

A fundamental reorientation of policy ambitions on the left might be guided by contemporary forms of the "politics of the collectivity" (Gilbert 2006: 192). The ideal of a common culture, in its demand for at least the possibility of general participation in the making of a culture, is closely related to the idea of a creative democracy and thereby converges with recent forms of the "anti-individualist politics of the common" which strike at the competitive individualism, authoritarianism and marketised reason of neoliberalism (191). As Jeremy Gilbert argues, 'creativity' in this kind of politics is theorized as having an inherently social character, just as 'collectivity' is increasingly seen as "inherently productive" (192). This rearticulation of the discourse of creativity (dislodging its limited and regressive 'social market' inflection within the CI model) helps us to get another view of the complexity of the apparent depoliticisation of a filmmaker like Meadows and to fortify those seeking to resist the "reality-generating power of market reasoning" with its deadly insistence on its own inherent superiority over democratic political deliberation itself (McGuigan 2004: 43).

Bibliography

Anderson, B. (2006) *Imagined Communities: Reflections on the Origins and Spread of Nationalism*, London: Verso.

British Film Institute (2012) "Film Forever", online, http://futureplan.bfi.org.uk/launch.aspx?pbid=62b10d3a-080b-4234-93d6-5fffb70b4509 (accessed 5 October 2015).

Burrows, J. (2004) "Penny Pleasures: Film Exhibition in London during the Nickleodeon era, 1906 1914", *Film History*, 16(1), pp. 60–91.

Colley, L. (2014) *Acts of Union and Disunion*, London: Profile Books.

Crary, J. (2013) *24/7: Late Capitalism and the Ends of Sleep*, London: Verso

Dave, P. (2011) "Tragedy, Ethics and History in Contemporary British Social Realist Film" in Tucker, D. (ed.) *Social Realism in the Arts since 1940*, Basingstoke: Palgrave Macmillan, pp. 17–56.

Dickinson, M. (1999) "A Short History: Hope Deferred, 1945–65" in Dickinson, M. (ed.) *Rogue Reels: Oppositional Film in Britain, 1945–1990*, London: BFI, pp. 6–91.

Dickinson, M. and Harvey, S. (2005) "Film Policy in the United Kingdom: New Labour at the Movies", *The Political Quarterly* 76(3), pp. 420–429.

Eagleton, T. (2000) *The Idea of Culture*, Oxford: Blackwell.

Gardiner, M. (2012) *The Return of England in English Literature*, Basingstoke: Palgrave Macmillan.

Gilbert, J. (2006) "Cultural Studies and Anti-Capitalism" in Hall, G. and Birchall, C. (eds) *New Cultural Studies: Adventures in Theory*, Edinburgh: Edinburgh University Press, pp. 181–199.

Higson, A. (2000) "The Limiting Imagination of National Cinema" in Hjort, M. and Mackenzie, S. (eds) *Cinema and Nation*, London: Routledge, pp. 63–74.

Higson, A. (2010) *Film England: Culturally English Filmmaking since the 1990s*, London: I.B. Tauris.

Hill, J. (1992) "The Issue of National Cinema and British Film Production" in Petrie, D. (ed.) *New Questions of British Cinema*, London: BFI, pp. 10–21.

Hill, J. (2004) "UK Film Policy, Cultural Capital and Exclusion", *Cultural Trends*, 13(2), pp. 29–39.

Hill, J. (2010) "Revisiting British Film Studies" in *Journal of British Cinema and Television*, 7(2), pp. 299–310.

Hill, J. (2012) "'This Is for the *Batmans* as well as the *Vera Drakes*': Economics, Culture and UK Government Film Production Policy in the 2000s", *Journal of British Cinema and Television* 9(3), pp. 333–356.

McGuigan, J. (2004) *Rethinking Cultural Policy*, Milton Keynes: Open University Press.

McKay, G. (1997) *DiY Culture: Party and Protest in Nineties Britain*, London: Verso.
Miller, T. (2000) "The Film Industry and the Government: 'Endless Mr Beans and Mr Bonds'?" in Murphy, R. (ed.) *British Cinema of the 90s*, London: BFI, pp. 37–47.
Monk, C. (1999) "From Underworld to Underclass: Crime and British Cinema in the 1990s" in Chibnall, S. and Murphy, R. (eds) *British Crime Cinema*, London: Routledge, pp. 172–177.
Monk, C. (2011) "Review of Paul Dave's *Visions of England: Class and Culture in Contemporary Cinema*", *Journal of British Cinema and Television*, 8(3), pp. 460–3.
Neeland, J. and Choe, B. (2010) "The English Model of Creativity: Cultural Politics of an Idea", *International Journal of Cultural Policy*, 16(3), August, pp. 287–304.
Newsinger, J. (2009) *From the Grassroots: Regional Film Policy and Practice in England*, unpublished PhD thesis, University of Nottingham.
Newsinger, J. (2012) "British Policy in an Age of Austerity", *Journal of British Cinema and Television*, 9(1), pp. 133–144.
Nowell-Smith, G. (1985) "But Do We Need It?" in Auty, M. and Roddick, N. (eds) *British Cinema Now*, London: BFI, pp. 147–158.
Nowell-Smith, G. and Dupin, C. (eds) (2012) *The British Film Institute, The Government and Film Culture, 1933–2000*, Manchester: Manchester University Press.
Petley, J. (1986) "Cinema and State" in Barr, C. (ed.) *All Our Yesterdays: 90 Years of British Cinema*, London: BFI, pp. 32–34.
Petley, J. (2013) "The Censor and the State in Britain" in Bilereyst, D. and van de Winkel, R. (eds) *Silencing Cinema: Film Censorshp Around the World*, Basingstoke: Palgrave, pp. 149–165.
Stoneman, R. (1999), "Sins of Commission" in Dickinson, M. (ed.) *Rogue Reels: Oppositional Film in Britain, 1945–1990*, London: BFI, pp. 174–187.
Thomas, P. (2011) "The British Workshop Movement and Amber Film", *Studies in European Cinema*, 8(3), pp. 195–209.
Wayne, M. (2002) *The Politics of Contemporary European Cinema: Histories, Borders, Diasporas*, Bristol: Intellect.
Wayne, M. (2006) "The Performing Northern Working-Class in British Cinema: Cultural Representation and its Political Economy", *Quarterly Review of Film and Video*, 23(4), pp. 287–297.
Westall, C. and Gardiner, M. (2013) *Literature of an Independent England: Revisions of England, Englishness and English Literature*, Basingstoke: Palgrave Macmillan.
Williams, R. (1984) *Culture and Society: 1780–1950*, Harmondsworth: Pelican.
Williams, R. (1989) *Resources of Hope: Culture, Democracy, Socialism*, London: Verso.
Wilson, J. (2013) "Shane Meadows and Associates: Selected LeftLion Interviews", *Journal of British Cinema and Television*, 10(4), October, pp. 909–924.

PART IV

The politics of mobility

INTRODUCTION

Stephanie Hemelryk Donald

This part references enduring themes of twentieth century politics, all of which are prominent today. Mobility is the key term, pulling together a sliding scale of opportunity and misery: cosmopolitanism, migration, displacement and trauma. Mobility refers here and in the wider world to both human and cinematic phenomena. People and ideas, thought systems and cultures, economic and political systems are all subject to, and dependent on, mobility. Migrancy, here described as a subset of mobility, is a heavily politicised concept in action, encompassing the complex conditions of departure, arrival, settlement and identity formation. Migrancy entails mobility at some point, but the ongoing condition of migrancy does not necessarily entail constant movement between places of origin and arrival. Some are born migrants, some choose it as a cosmopolitan option, whilst many more have continuous migrancy-at-home thrust upon them by resistant 'hosts'.

Thus, much of the debate in and through cinema concerns the physical and imaginary movement of humans around a world scarred by self-inflicted tragedy, but also – and this is exemplified in Felicity Collins' chapter on the Blakwave in Australia – a world that produces moments of redemption and truly radical departures. Mobility produces itself as a state of being that reflects the capacity of cinema itself to move between peoples and across boundaries. Indeed, even the personal and historical relationships essayed on screen may shift in time and space according to the conditions of spectatorship and the forms of representation accorded to their story. Writing this introduction in Europe in August 2015, one cannot but mention that the matter of forced and voluntary migration is enormously relevant. Every night thousands of Syrian refugees walk across borders to escape conflict and grasp at a future. The scenes are starkly reminiscent of European history of the twentieth century. Film-makers will have a wealth of emotional, moral and political subject matter to deploy over coming months and years. But much of what they will inevitably discuss is already in our shared cinematic consciousness, and the sub-themes of this part define the ways in which cinema directs our attention to mobility now.

Mobility in cinema is a topic – what happens when converging movement brings strangers into contact or confrontation – but also a set of formal enablers. The mobile camera creates points of view and radicalized perceptions of personality, narrative, space and time that can up-end political certainties and challenge comfortable ideological sutured positions. The mobile camera creates new subject positions on screen and offers new subjective viewing positions to spectators. In so doing, it also denies certain spectator groups the positions that they are wont to occupy and that they consider therefore a kind of visual birthright. The films and film-makers considered in this part are very concerned with the power of the camera to order and rearrange power on screen in order to question the structures of power and authority in which their work is viewed.

Mobility may also refer to the process of cinematic production and distribution. A film made in Australia will be understood quite differently and with local points of reference, whether those be shameful, forms of pride or simply matters of information. The history of major world events – whether it be a genocidal period of Indonesia history or the genocide of Indigenous peoples worldwide, or the Holocaust of European Jewry – are of note and concern to all of us, but how much more do we feel and how much more carefully do we watch from local spectatorial positions if the film-makers' decisions recruit, ignore, underplay or glorify certain actors and victims at the expense of others and other strategies of narration and perspective?

The mobilities of cinema are enunciated here through four constitutive situations: cosmopolitanism, migration, displacement and trauma. Each stands alone as a major aspect of modern experience. The chapters in this part range widely in addressing these themes, but they share a common interest in how the ethics of such experience is explored on screen.

Dimitris Eleftheriotis is interested in 'cosmopolitan empathy'. His chapter discusses the ways in which film theorists and writers on film and media more broadly engage ethically with a world divided between Self and Other. Eleftheriotis rightly acknowledges Said's vision of a stranger who sees the world clearly, from the outside in and the inside out. That acknowledgement heralds a careful account of how the readability of film is partial and opaque. Performativity is itself variously legible, as much as it is revelatory, and relies on access to codes in history, society, culture, language and performance traditions – inflected and enforced by the local intention of director, actor, cinematographer and writer. The idea of a cross-border empathy, enacted through film (Eleftheriotis makes the argument through a discussion of the enigmatic promises of the close up) is therefore suspect.

Lúcia Nagib is, however, impressed by Oppenheimer's *Act of Killing* (2012), a film that mixes genre, documentary and politics in an extraordinary clarification of how it is to be a killer. The film excludes empathy but allows access to the psycho-pathologies of murderous beings. The core theme is trauma, and the ethics of the director's strategy for discovering, expropriating and revealing the momentous sins of his subjects. Nagib points out that the personal danger in which the director placed himself is key to the ethical character of the film. Not only does he expose himself and his camera to the raw madness of his subjects, but he does so in a political context where they remain the winners, there has been no vengeance and no justice for their victims. There is a different order of ethical parameters when the war remains open and dangerous. The question of mobility is less visible in this chapter, except perhaps to note that as film has travelled back into the art houses and movie theatres beyond Indonesia so different ethical questions have been raised about its treatment of protagonists – killers and survivors both. Is this a film about genocide that plays too outrageously on the fringes of genre? Or is this, and both Nagib and the present writer would agree, a film that explodes the horrible banality and lasciviousness of cultural play outside the borders of morality? The mobility of genre is also then a target and a victim of Oppenheimer's brilliant and disturbing project.

Brad Prager discusses the *Shoah* and film-makers who have tried to deal with pan-continental genocide. Mobility is a buried theme here but I would suggest that his aim is to bring to our attention the limits of our cosmopolitan imagination as film-makers and spectators. Prager guides us through films that have treated the Holocaust as a discreet and unimaginable narrative, a documentation of terror, or a treatise on post-genocidal justice. Prager's choice of films and his focus on the relationship between Israel and the Holocaust, and between the questions of survival, survivors and Palestinian claims to land and freedom test the bounds of what and who is a cosmopolitan and when forgiveness does become possible.

Finally, Yosefa Loshitzky's chapter on the lack of sociality between Palestinian Arabs and Jewish Israelis is explored through the backdrop of films set in multicultural Spain and France. Her outlook is bleak for a rooted cosmopolitanism, seeing that the grounds for political optimism may be effective in a comedy, but fade into realism and incommensurability in a realist drama. The films seek out solidarity but find visual division, even as they attempt to bind souls together through romance and the production of children.

16

COSMOPOLITANISM, EMPATHY AND THE CLOSE-UP

Dimitris Eleftheriotis

Introduction: film and cosmopolitanism

Increasingly film studies turns to cosmopolitanism as a conceptual framework for the study of cinema in its full international dimensions. Monographs and articles that explore various aspects of film and cosmopolitanism (e.g. Nava 2007; Schwartz 2007; Loshitzky 2010; Bergfelder 2011; Eleftheriotis 2012; Stacey 2014) are appearing with accelerating regularity and in 2012 *Screen* themed its annual conference on cosmopolitanism. If anything, such engagement is only surprising in its belatedness, in the noticeable delay in engaging with a term that has been central to other disciplines since the 1990s. Paradoxically this might well be because film is a profoundly cosmopolitan medium. As cultural product and commodity it encounters multiple cultures in its circulation, depends on multi-ethnic groups of creative personnel and utilises transnational channels of marketing, distribution and exhibition. But it is also cosmopolitan in its form, stories, characters and settings, in its presentation of relationships between strangers, in its articulation of difference.

It is the obvious, self-evident nature of the link between cinema and cosmopolitanism that can account for the reluctance with which film studies has come to address the term. I have accounted elsewhere (Eleftheriotis 2012) for these developments and limitations which form the genealogical ground out of which the recent turn to cosmopolitanism surfaces. Cosmopolitanism focuses on our relationships with each other as citizens of the world as well as on the ways we individually and collectively relate to the world. This is also a central concern of the so-called 'ethical turn' in the study of media, summarised very succinctly by Jonathan Corpus Ong:

> This is why the emergence of a significant and forceful agenda of media and morality, I believe, reflects a seismic shift in both the conceptualization of and the application of the word *morality* within the field. Morality here is concerned with the Other. Capital O as Silverstone may be likely to remind us. The Other across media space, the Other represented and representing, the Other invisible in media space, the Other disabled and distorted. And morality here is thus concerned with the status of the cosmopolitan, and how he or she may be constituted (or not) by the work of the media.
>
> *(2009:450)*

Arguably, questions of the relationship with the 'Other' have been at the heart of film theory in the last forty years or so but the shift in conceptual and historical context towards the cosmopolitan is rather recent. The conversation between film studies and cosmopolitanism has not been explicit or overtly theorised but it has made significant progress in a number of areas, which include, among others: ethics in relation to criticism and evaluation with special consideration given to spectatorial positions and empathy as a particular concern (e.g. Landsberg 2004, 2009; Nagib 2011; Stacey 2014); and aesthetics, an area under which questions of cosmopolitan position and disposition are brought together especially in relation to issues of agency and authorship (e.g. Naficy 1996; Marks 2000; Naficy 2001; Suner 2006; Eleftheriotis 2012).

The interaction between the last two categories provides this chapter with its focal point and involves a partial investigation of how ethical approaches mobilise film aesthetics in their argument and inversely, how theoretical approaches around film aesthetics can be brought to bear on ethical discourses. In theorisations of the ways in which cosmopolitan positions might relate to aesthetic dispositions a key dialectic of proximity/distance is often posited (e.g. Anderson 2001; Beck 2007). For example, conditions of displacement, exile, migration, diaspora have been described as engendering a tension, often productive and creative, between physical nearness and cultural detachment of creative agents in such positions. This is a line of thought that goes back to Georg Simmel and his seminal work on the 'stranger' (1964) and has been more recently developed by Edward Said and others who praise in the stranger the potential to "see the whole world as a foreign land", a vision that has the ability to function in a "contrapuntal" way (2001:148). In approaches that champion cosmopolitan empathy as an ethical way of relating to media representations of the lives, experiences and histories of strangers, a similar dynamic is offered as a fundamental condition for the politically effective use of empathy (Landsberg 2004, 2009). Admittedly each discourse places different emphasis on the two sides of the dialectic, with work on the aesthetics of strangeness focusing on the effects of distancing and the discourse on empathy valuing moments of closeness but importantly they both centralise proximity/distance in their critical practice. This dialectic that lies at the heart of both ethical and formal/aesthetic/theoretical approaches to cosmopolitanism in film is key to the investigation of their mutual relationship that follows.

This chapter aspires to facilitate a conversation between on the one hand some of the most apposite aspects of cosmopolitanism, especially around politics and ethics, and theoretical discourses and models of analysis in film studies on the other. The overarching objective is to open up the possibility of infusing political and ethical agendas in film analytics from the prism of cosmopolitanism while interrogating some of the (mis)appropriations of film form and film theory that occasionally surface within the forays into that field of approaches that are primarily philosophical, ethical and political. The next section will address empathy, a concept that has been widely suggested as an ethical and politically useful way of relating to cinematic representations of others. In such approaches the close-up tends to become a privileged empathic tool, an assumption that will be problematised from the perspective of film theory in a critique that will be supported through a close analysis of the credit sequence of Michael Haneke's *Code Unknown* (2000).

Detachment, empathy and the close-up

Before considering empathy itself a sketchy outline of changing attitudes to spectatorial engagement can be instructive. Empathy seems to be replacing a politics of detachment that was inspired by the Brechtian *Verfremdungseffekt* as a privileged analytical tool for evaluating the construction of cinematic encounters. This is very much in line with a shift towards affect, emotion and feeling in film studies and with positive evaluations of the role of the media as agents of prosthetic memory; a detached, intellectual engagement with films and their representations of others is rejected in favour of emotional closeness and the ability to feel what the other feels.

This constitutes a remarkable reversal that has moved the discourse on the value of spectatorial engagement from one extreme to the other. It is useful to revisit some of the key instances of this discursive trajectory not in order to reassert a modernist sensibility but in an effort to contribute to a contextualisation of currently 'in-vogue' paradigms. The positive value attached to critical distance as opposed to emotional closeness has as its most prominent genealogical reference Berthold Brecht's attempt to make the relationship between spectator and spectacle 'strange', a technique of facilitating a better understanding of social and historical forces with an ultimate political objective to change the world. Brecht's *Verfremdungseffekt*, a method with which representation is denaturalised beyond its theoretical and critical implications, has inspired a whole repertoire of textual conventions in cinema that have very much defined a certain type of political modernism.

The various appropriations of *Verfremdungseffekt* are in themselves fascinating: distanciation, alienation, defamiliarisation, making strange, are terms that have been used in descriptions and definitions of the effect. These terms clearly foreground the political desire to turn the figures of cinematic representation into 'unfamiliar', 'alien' and 'strange', in a conscious attempt to infuse distance and difference in the process of spectatorial engagement. The significance of the historical context within which *Verfremdung* came to oppose *Einfühlung* (empathy) cannot be overlooked, and underscores the political value of the ability to stand outside an overwhelming absorption into a consensus. In the terms used to describe *Verfremdungseffekt*, critical detachment is placed in a stark contrast politically and ethically as a way of relating to the world and others to that championed by empathic relationships that seek to overcome otherness through emotional closeness.

The opening-up of critical distance as an attempt to occupy a place that escapes ideology became key to 1960s and 1970s Marxist and psychoanalytic models that sought to discover ways of combating all-encompassing capitalist apparatuses. Althusser's (1969) 'knowledge effect' was in many ways the epistemological equivalent to *Verfremdungseffekt*, the only possibility to resist ideological interpellation. Crucially this was only possible through awareness and rejection of one's positioning by/in the ideological apparatus and in the context of film studies involved a radical refusal to engage with representation in the terms imposed by mainstream films.[1]

This was extensively analysed and theorised within the 'apparatus theory' paradigm that dominated film theory in the 1970s and early 1980s. Work by Metz (1983), Baudry (1999), Heath (1981), de Lauretis and Heath (1980) and others repeatedly criticised the ways in which a certain type of cinema 'draws' the spectator into the world of the film, a world infected by various strands of capitalist ideology. The key mechanism that creates the ideological effect in the cinematic apparatus is identification, distinguished between primary (with the apparatus itself) and secondary (with the characters) but in both cases responsible for the spectator's interpellation. Emotional closeness and attendant spectatorial pleasures solicited by the apparatus through identification became politically suspect in such models with the 'mission' of film theory to deconstruct or destroy them (Mulvey 1975). Particularly critical of identification and emotional proximity were psychoanalytically informed feminist approaches, which suggested that the positioning of the spectator in the cinematic apparatus of mainstream cinema does not just further capitalist ideologies but also patriarchy. Quite striking for the intensity with which identification is attacked is Ann Friedberg's critique: "Here we are left with a question that is unerringly political. Identification enforces a collapse of the subject onto the normative, a *compulsion for sameness*, which under patriarchy, demands critique" (1990: 45) my emphasis.

The clear suggestion here is that identification, disguised as emotional affinity with a film character, is in effect a denial of difference and an appropriation of both the subject and the other in a common ground of sameness and repetition. There followed a series of interventions revising the absolutist nature of such critical positions and offering refined models of identification. Anne Breckon (2013) (who interestingly in the context of the present emphasis on empathy is writing in defence of a 'politics of disgust') offers a succinct summary juxtaposing Friedberg's approach to that of Kaja Silverman's (1996) who was keen to preserve the possibility of 'heteropathic identifications' tracing in the process traditions in film theory that are more sympathetic to emotional proximity. Worth remembering is Silverman's consideration of Sergei Eisenstein's praise of cinema as a tool for constructing revolutionary consciousness in an 'ecstatic spectator' whose identification with exemplary heroes or agents of revolutionary deeds can be transformative (Silverman 1996).

A distinct and particularly influential strand developed around theoretical models of embodied spectatorship. In contrast and opposition to accounts of spectatorship that emerged under the aegis of the 'cinematic apparatus' paradigm and privileged detached visuality, theories of affect and embodiment focus on the relationship between the body of the spectator, the cinematic image and the bodies in the film, foregrounding affective and sensual dimensions and opening up critical possibilities for a reassertion of closeness, at least on the level of theory (e.g. Sobchack 1992; Shaviro 1993; Marks 2000).

This is the theoretical backdrop against which work on empathy has emerged. I will focus this discussion on Alison Landsberg's particular appropriation of the term because of the influence that her work had on the field but more importantly because of the clear political and ethical agenda that informs it. In Landsberg's work (2004, 2009) the ability of the media to provide 'prosthetic memories' (experience of past events that one has not actually lived through) is politically useful when supported by an empathic engagement with the histories and experiences of others:

> These prosthetic memories [m]ight help to condition how a person thinks about the world and might be instrumental in articulating an ethical relation to the other or in advancing egalitarian social values. [L]earning to engage both intellectually and emotionally with another who is radically different from oneself is crucial to the development of empathy, which in turn enables the larger political project of advancing egalitarian social goals through a more radical form of democracy.
>
> *(2009: 222)*

Undoubtedly this is a very compelling (if self-evident) ethical and political case for empathic inter-subjective relations; however, what might be debatable is the way in which empathy is conceptualised and how media representations of others achieve this commendable objective. Landsberg's definition of empathy is set out in clear distinction to sympathy, the former unlike the latter maintaining a balance between the cognitive/intellectual and the emotional, recognising that a 'distance exists' between the 'empathizer' and the 'object of contemplation' (2009: 223) and asserting that identification in sympathy is essentialist whereas empathy recognises alterity (2004: 135). While on the conceptual level Landsberg is keen to qualify her endorsement of identification and there is a considerable volume of literature that elaborates on the important differences between empathy, sympathy and identification (see e.g. Haney 1994; Mellmann 2010; and from a film studies perspective Gaut 2010a, 2010b), when attempting to deploy the concept in the analysis of film caution is thrown to the wind.

Discussing film in particular and despite recognising the theoretical complexity of identification, Landsberg still proposes it as a powerful tool in the construction of empathic relationships as

> it is still the case that films create a preferred vantage point for us as viewers, and sometimes occupying the vantage point requires us to look at the world differently from how we would normally see it, looking as it were, as if through someone else's eyes.
>
> (2009: 224)

Indeed, she proposes that film as a formal system offers a number of techniques that can become empathic tools, such as "point of enunciation, point-of-view shots, close-ups, etc." and she elaborates:

> While clearly our own subject positions (male, female, gay, straight, etc.) influence how we respond to the cinematic images before us, there are specific filmic strategies [t]hat encourage the spectator to identify with a particular character. One such technique is the close-up: with the camera trained on another's face we are afforded intimate contact with the person's emotional life. *As her face registers pleasure or pain or humiliation or anger we cannot help but feel our own body respond in kind.*
>
> (2009: 224, *my emphasis*)

In this embodied spectatorship-informed articulation the possibility of critical detachment, of an intellectual engagement that is supposed to accompany the emotional affinity with the image is rejected: "we cannot help but feel". Even more startling, however, is the belief that the face in close-up functions as a gateway to the inner emotional life of a person. Signalled out as the most potent empathic tool, not only in the above passage but also in the analysis of *The Pianist* that follows on in Landsberg's essay, the face in close-up is endowed with the unique ability to offer access to the other, becoming a representational shorthand for the experience of empathy itself.

From a film theory perspective there are disturbing aspects in such conceptualisation. Despite a tokenistic nod to complexity, identification is used in a way that bypasses critiques of the apparatus theory, in effect throwing out the baby together with the bathwater. More importantly, in Landsberg's elevation of the close-up into the prime technique of empathy a key area of concern in film studies is completely ignored. Particularly significant in that respect is Mary Ann Doane's examination of the close-up in relation to face and scale (2003). Through a close scrutiny of the ways in which the close-up has been approached in film theory from Epstein to Deleuze, Doane notes the tendency to treat the close-up as separate and "stand-alone" and to privilege it as "the mark of cinematic difference and specificity", a discursive positioning that uncannily replicates the cinematic isolation of the close-up "from the scene, from the body, from the spatiotemporal coordinates of the narrative" (2003: 90–91). Doane's analysis of the close-up offers a systematic critique of its use and the theoretical assumptions surrounding it, providing particularly suggestive insights into the implications of its unqualified endorsement as an empathic tool.

Building on the linguistic divergence of the English term 'close-up' from the French '*gros plan*' she posits a second axis of signification, that of large/small, alongside that of proximity/ distance. In a screen filled with a face (the most typical object of the close-up according to

Doane), what is only a detail (of a character's body) assumes the status of wholeness and totality (the full screen and nothing beyond it). Given the affective significance bestowed in such shots, the face as detail is afforded autonomy and self-sufficiency, eclipsing in effect its cinematic or more broadly speaking historical, social and cultural context.

Moreover, as Doane argues, the ideological function of the close-up lies in its complete privileging of the imaginary over a profoundly concealed symbolic. The close-up, a detail that becomes a totality, relies on a surface, the face, which while only able to signify in relation to the rest of the film and its broader context, appears to be draped in an aura of self-sufficiency. But although the close-up denies depth (in its formal composition of narrative space) it offers the promise of access to the depths of the soul, the interiority of the other. In that way the close-up of the face, which is in reality "an image rather than a threshold onto a world" (Doane 2003: 91) becomes an imaginary gateway to the inner world of another subject.

The access to another's interiority that Landsberg assumes to be the most useful property of the close-up is an ideological trap for Doane. In the spectatorial engagement with the face in close-up its affective meaning is produced diachronically rather than synchronically and comes from the site/sight of the spectator and not from the space and place of the other. The close-up issues an invitation to read the other as a face privileging thus the illusion of access to interiority/subjectivity over the 'bigger picture' and isolating in effect the other from its broader context. In that way the dialectic of proximity/distance that should inform empathy is abandoned in a shot, the *gros plan*, in which closeness imposes totality. Doane's concluding remarks are particularly poignant if seen in the context of the political investment in the empathic potential of the close-up:

> As simultaneously microcosm and macrocosm, the miniature and the gigantic, the close-up acts as a nodal point linking the ideologies of intimacy and interiority to public space and the authority of the monumental. In the close-up the cinema plays simultaneously with the desire for totalization and its impossibility. The cinematic spectator clings to the fragment of a partial reality – a fragment that mimics the effect of a self-sufficient totality. The classical close-up assures us that we can indeed see and grasp the whole, in a moment rich with meaning and affect.
>
> *(2003: 109)*

Similarly in appropriations of the close-up as an empathic tool, an affectively charged moment brackets out historical, social and cultural particularity. Critical investigations of the history of *Einfühlung* (e.g. Nowak 2011; Brain 2012) identify in early conceptualisations of the term a similar exclusion of historical context and a tendency to lose the particular for the universal. Brain (2012: 337–8) connects a Hegelian suggestion that the aim of great art is to "strip the world of its inflexible foreignness" so that "man [sic] can enjoy in the shape of things an external realization of himself" with some early discussions of aesthetic empathy in Robert Vischer. The belief that identification, point-of-view and the close-up as empathic tools can allow the spectator to bridge the gap with the other harks back to that early, romantic and universalising definition of empathy. Significantly in Hegel and Vischer empathy as an abolition of foreignness originates in the self, any sense of difference dissolved in an all-enveloping sameness. If the critical usefulness of empathy is to be maintained a more reserved and qualified approach to the close-up is needed, backed up by formal analysis that takes into account the dialectics of proximity/distance.

Code Unknown: close-up didactics

There is no intention to engage with Michael Haneke's films in this chapter; there is now a considerable body of work on his films and any significant contribution to add to that literature is beyond the scope of the present argument. It is worth noting, however, the central position that the director occupies in considerations of ethics and politics in film (see e.g. Trifonova 2007; Stacey 2014) and, perhaps more importantly, the didactic nature of his work. Haneke's films force a consideration of our own spectatorial position and how we relate to others as citizens of the world and in the process they deliver lessons with political and ethical value.

While the close-up is not a key concern of *Code Unknown*, in fact it is only used in the conventional sense in only three scenes of the film, it is the object of a tangential but very evocative formal strand of the film. It is used twice in the main body of the film, in an encounter with Anne (Juliette Binoche) that is first presented as 'real', then recontextualised as 'performance' only to be repositioned as 'reality' later (Figure 16.1) and in a montage of photographic portraits of faces in close-up (Figure 16.2). In both instances the self-evident truth of the face in close-up is undermined, in the first case by shifting the referential frame, in the second by accompanying the collage of the portraits with a voice-over that bears no relation to the faces depicted. Another, non-conventional use of a close-up of a face in the film is as part of a mobile shot when a face appears close to the camera as part of a continuous movement, a shot that highlights the normative dependency of the close-up on stillness (Figure 16.3).

The film, however, is prefaced by a short (1′35″) scene sandwiched between two sets of opening credits which appear in white letters against a black backdrop with no soundtrack accompaniment. The scene consists of seventeen shots in total showing an anonymous girl who displays what might be an event or a feeling through a performance to a group of other children who then one at a time and in medium close-up offer personal interpretations of the meaning of the girl's performance. By the end of the scene the 'meaning' of the performance remains unknown, as no answer acceptable to the girl has been offered. All children appear not to be able to speak or hear and use sign language (promptly subtitled in the film) to communicate. While the girl's initial performance is in a long shot all the subsequent shots are medium close-ups.

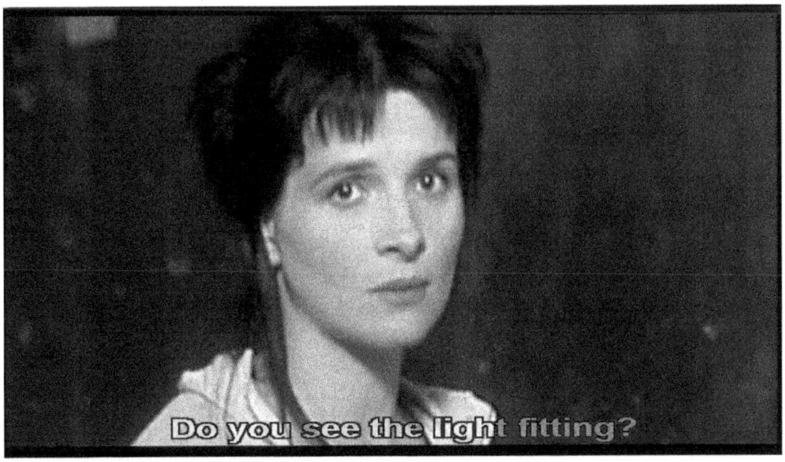

Figure 16.1 *Code Unknown*: medium close-up.

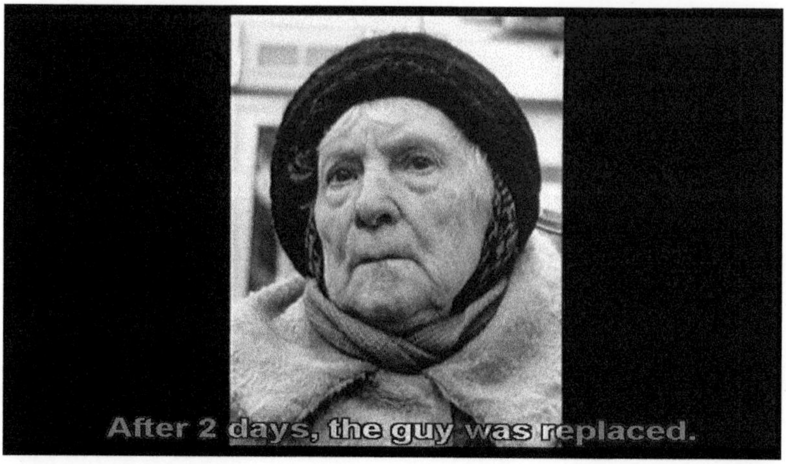

Figure 16.2 *Code Unknown*: photographic close-up.

Figure 16.3 *Code Unknown*: medium close-up in mobile shot.

The girl's performance is set against a white wall, possibly suggestive of a blank canvas on which the act is displayed (Figure 16.4). At 30 seconds this is by far the longest shot in the scene and it involves the girl moving away from the camera towards the wall and finally crouching in what might be seen as a foetal position (Figure 16.5). Its place and duration establish this shot as the key point of reference for the shots that follow, the children's faces in medium close-up, syntagmatically set up in response to this 'original' performance. There are ten shots of children, four of which can be loosely described as pure 'reaction' shots (e.g. Figure 16.6) with another six performing an interpretive sign (e.g. Figure 16.7). All of the latter are met with a medium close-up of the girl rejecting their suggestions with a shake of her head (Figure 16.8).

Several aspects of the scene are worth considering further. What does the girl feel when she nods negatively? Her 'no' rejects interpretations of the performance but also of the concepts performed by the other children (alone? hiding place? gangster? bad conscience? sad? imprisoned?).

Figure 16.4 Opening scene: beginning of opening shot.

Figure 16.5 Opening scene: end of opening shot.

Figure 16.6 Opening scene: reaction shot.

Figure 16.7 Opening scene: 'interpretation' shot.

Figure 16.8 Opening scene: back to the girl.

Is this lack of understanding a cause of sadness for her? Does the original performance refer to an event that has caused a sadness that is further aggravated by the difficulty in communicating it? As with so many aspects of this film the code required to answer these questions is unknown but the profound semantic ambiguity in this scene has didactic value especially in the way that the function of the 'face as gateway to the soul' is also brought into question. Not only the 'meaning' of the expressions performed is unknown but also the performance is in code, in sign language, which is itself translated into another code, subtitles. In the destabilising and ambiguity infusing proliferation of layers of signification the surface of the face loses its transparency, engulfed in an overwhelming semantic opacity.

The faces of the children in close-up invite but also express an act of reading, an attempt of interpretation, which nevertheless depends on the production of an expression that has a signifying function. All these shots are contextualised in a process of attempted but ultimately failed communication, and shift emphasis from the face as a transparent surface that lets out emotions or lets 'in' the spectator, to the face as an instrument of signification. In some of the shots the very act of expressing an emotion through the face is clearly marked as a performative act. Particularly striking in that respect is the shot of a girl that starts with a relatively immobile face (Figure 16.9) followed by the performance of the sign 'sad?', expressed as an intense movement of the hand in front of the face and an accompanying shriek (Figures 16.10 and 16.11), and a return to a smiling face at the end (Figure 16.12). In that way the beginning and the end of the shot frame and foreground the performance of a sign of emotion rather than simply displaying or registering an emotion, asserting in that way agency and intentionality in the production of affect. The face in close-up is explicitly acknowledged as both read and reading, interpreted and interpreting, produced and producing, drawing attention to the particular ideological configuration that constructs the face as the space of imaginary unity in the encounter between the spectator and the other, an ideological configuration that Deleuze calls the "affection-image", a "reflecting and reflected unity" (2005:89).

Figure 16.9 Opening scene: 'sad?' 1.

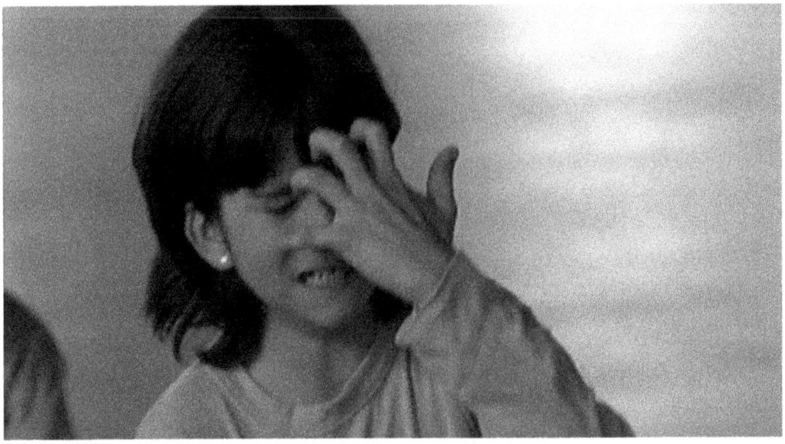

Figure 16.10 Opening scene: 'sad?' 2.

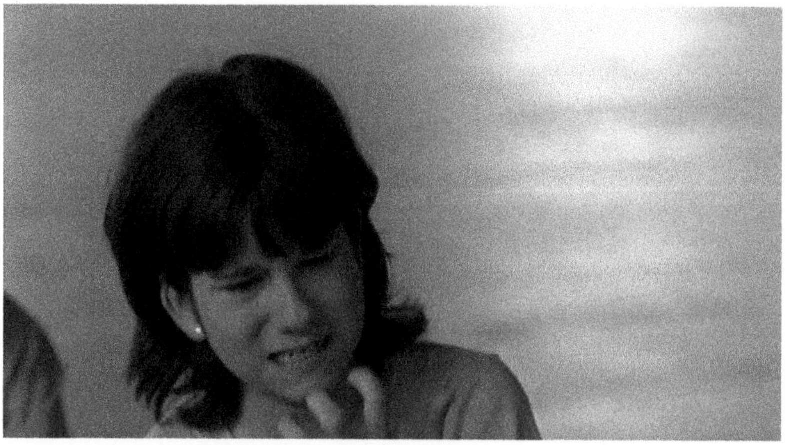

Figure 16.11 Opening scene: 'sad?' 3.

Figure 16.12 Opening scene: 'sad?' 4.

This short scene then is clearly didactic in its eloquent demonstration of some of the parameters that film theory and formal analysis should bear in mind in approaching the face in close-up. But to return to the key concern of this chapter, what is the spectator's engagement with these images and what if anything at all do they suggest in relation to empathy? In Landsberg's argument empathy seems to depend on a split between 'us', Western subjects whose memories are expanded, and 'others' whose experiences 'we' wish to share, a sharp division between those who experience and those who are the objects or 'vehicles' of the experience. In such formulation the face in close-up is indeed the transparent surface that allows access to the emotions of the other but also strips them of any agency or performativity. In the scene in *Code Unknown*, however, the spectator is also involved in the failed attempt to make meaning, to understand and feel the original performance properly, a spectatorial engagement that is failed but equitable in terms of a distribution of power.

The discourse of empathy almost exclusively revolves around instances of emotional closeness to the others' suffering, their personal or historical traumatic memories, a tendency that

Figure 16.13 Opening scene: amused reaction.

further augments the subject/object division and de facto constructs the experiences of others that are worth empathising with as negative. This is a tendency that is very eloquently confronted in the scene. There is no certainty that something traumatic or sad is being referred to in the 'original performance'. And if there is sadness in how we experience the unfolding of the scene overall this is relativised as only one possible affective interpretation in the prolific circuit of interpretations that we are caught up in. There are certainly performance signs indicating that sadness is not the only 'appropriate' reaction, the girl smiling with amusement at some of the suggestions (Figure 16.13). Thus the affective tone of the scene as well as the emotional significance of the faces in close-up is not self-evident but contested and relative.

The uncertainty that surrounds emotion and spectatorial position should not be understood in negative terms. The incompletion of meaning (an incompletion suggested by the subtitle of the French title of the film) signals the possibility of a desire to understand more, to feel properly, to learn the code. In the scene discussed here we are left desiring answers to pressing questions such as: What was the girl performing? Was it referring to a real experience or an imagined one? Is this part of a therapy group or possibly a training session? In order to understand and feel properly and appropriately we need to turn our look and attention away from the face of the other to the broader context; to understand what others feel you need a lot more than the face in a close-up. This exemplifies the dialectic of proximity/detachment that operates in the scene and points towards its application in analysing the affective implications of the use of the face in the close-up.

Haneke's didacticism forces a broader rethinking of the politics and ethics of cosmopolitanism in relation to film. Three key points arising from the analysis of the scene are particularly suggestive. First, that the self-sufficiency of the face as a signifier of another subjectivity must be challenged. *Code Unknown* points out that reading the face as a surface that reveals affect and emotion by and in itself only assimilates difference into sameness privileging a totalising understanding of others as existing beyond historical and cultural specificity. This implies that claims to 'prosthetic memory' via affective engagement with the face of the other, that assumes the wholeness of the partial, must also be treated with suspicion.[2] As Doane points out in relation to the close-up:

> [c]loseness is allied with possession, possessiveness, the desire to 'get hold of an object' by, somewhat ironically, making moot the question of ownership. [F]aced

> with an accelerating rationalization, specialization, and disintegration of the sense of a social totality, the subject clings to the hope of simulacra of wholeness. The close-up, with its contradictory status (as both detail of a larger scene and totality in its own right – a spectacle of scale with its own integrity) responds to this need.
>
> (2003: 92–3)

Then, agency in the production of affective images (in a close-up but also more generally) must be properly recognised. This should extend to both actors (or, at a time of a clear surge of the documentary as the form of choice in representing others, 'real' people) and to film-makers. The face of the other and its 'meaning' (affective or other) is always inflected by the performative agency of actor, film and filmmaker.

Finally, and partly as an extension of the previous two points, uncertainty about and frustration of easy accessibility of the 'meaning' of the face of the other must inform any ethics of spectatorial engagement. Furthermore, they can in themselves become valuable political and ethical tools by activating a desire for a better (but rarely ever complete) understanding of cosmopolitan difference.

Cosmopolitanism raises urgent ethical and political questions in relation to cinema, questions nevertheless that also have theoretical and analytical dimensions. While the move away from placing absolute critical value in detachment (what Bonitzer (1979) calls the 'intellectual eye') and towards a recognition of the political importance of affect is welcome, it seems to be spearheaded at the moment with an unqualified endorsement of empathy. The examination of the privilege afforded to the face in close-up in this chapter demonstrated that there are politically and theoretically disturbing assumptions underpinning some appropriations of empathy that seem to further entrench rather than alleviate global divisions in relation to position and power. Replicating a dialectic that underpins cosmopolitan discourse, film studies must inject the urgency of ethics and politics in analysis, scrutinising closely spectatorial positions and aesthetic dispositions from such perspectives, but also maintaining the critical edge that comes from attention to formal specificity.

Notes

1 'Mainstream' is here used in the manner that it was originally used in such discourses, as a general and sometimes confusing label that seems interchangeable with 'Hollywood', 'narrative' and 'dominant'; see Eleftheriotis (2001).

2 Importantly, Susan Sontag's consideration of the 'pain of others' discusses the destroyed faces of soldiers as appropriate signifiers of suffering (2003) – in effect repositioning the face as an empathic tool in its brutal destruction.

Bibliography

Althusser, L. (1969) *For Marx*, London: Alan Lane.

Anderson, A. (2001) *The Powers of Distance: Cosmopolitanism and the Cultivation of Detachment*, Princeton, NJ: Princeton University Press, 2001.

Baudry, J-L. (1999) "Ideological Effects of the Basic Cinematographic Apparatus" in Braudy, L. and Cohen, M. (eds) *Film Theory and Criticism: Introductory Readings*, New York and Oxford: Oxford University Press, pp. 345–355.

Beck, U. (2007) *The Cosmopolitan Vision*, Cambridge: Polity.

Bergfelder, T. (2011) "Love Beyond the Nation: Cosmopolitanism and Transnational Desire in Cinema" in Passerini, L., Labanyi, J. and Diehl, K. (eds) *Europe and Love in Cinema*. Bristol: Intellect Books, pp. 76–99.

Bonitzer, P. (1979) "Here: The Notion of the Shot and Subject in Cinema" in *Film Reader* 4, Evanston, IL: Film Division, Northwestern University, pp. 108–119.

Brain, R. M. (2012) "Self-Projection: Hugo Münsterberg on Empathy and Oscillation in Cinema Spectatorship" *Science in Context* 25.3, pp. 329–353.
Breckon, A. (2013) "The Erotic Politics of Disgust: *Pink Flamingos* as Queer Political Cinema" *Screen* 54.4, pp. 514–33.
de Lauretis, T. and Heath, S. (1980) (eds) *The Cinematic Apparatus*, London: Macmillan.
Deleuze, G. (2005) *Cinema 1: The Movement-Image*, London and New York: Continuum.
Doane, M. A. (2003) "The Close-Up: Scale and Detail in the Cinema" *Differences: A Journal of Feminist Cultural Studies* 14.3, pp. 89–111.
Eleftheriotis, D. (2001) *Popular Cinemas of Europe: Studies of Texts, Contexts and Frameworks*, London: Continuum.
Eleftheriotis, D. (2012) "The Foreignness of Jules Dassin: Notes on Cosmopolitan Authorship" *Screen* 53.4, pp. 339–358.
Friedberg, A. (1990) "A Denial of Difference: Theories of Cinematic Identification" in Kaplan, E. A. (ed.) *Psychoanalysis and Cinema*, New York and London: Routedge, pp. 36–45.
Gaut, B. (2010a) *A Philosophy of Cinematic Art*, Cambridge: Cambridge University Press.
Gaut, B. (2010b) "Empathy and Identification in Cinema" *Midwest Studies in Philosophy* 34, pp. 136–157.
Haney, K. M. (1994) "Empathy and Ethic" *Southwest Philosphy Review* 10, pp. 63–71.
Heath, S. (1981) *Questions of Cinema*, London and Basingstoke: Macmillan.
Landsberg, A. (2004) *Prosthetic Memory: The Transformation of American Remembrance in the Age of Mass Culture*, New York: Columbia University Press.
Landsberg, A. (2009) "Memory, Empathy, and the Politics of Identification" *International Journal of Politics, Culture, and Society* 22, pp. 221–229.
Loshitzky, Y. (2010) *Screening Strangers: Migration and Diaspora in Contemporary European Cinema*, Bloomington: Indiana University Press.
Marks, L. U. (2000) *The Skin of the Film: Intercultural Cinema, Embodiment and the Senses*, Durham, NC: Duke University Press.
Mellmann, K. (2010) "Objects of 'Empathy': Characters (and Other Such Things) as Psycho-poetic Effects" in Eder, J. (ed.) *Characters in Fictional Worlds. Understanding Imaginary Beings in Literature, Film, and Other Media*, Berlin and New York: De Gruyter, pp. 416–441.
Metz, C. (1983) *Psychoanalysis and Cinema: The Imaginary Signifier*, London and Basingstoke: Macmillan, 1983.
Mulvey, L. (1975) "Visual Pleasure and Narrative Cinema" *Screen* 16.3, pp. 6–18.
Naficy, H. (1996) "Phobic Spaces and Liminal Panics: Independent Transnational Film Genre" in Dissanayake, W. and Wilson, R. (eds) *Local/Global*, Durham, NC: Duke University Press, pp. 119–144.
Naficy, H. (2001) *An Accented Cinema: Exilic and Diasporic Filmmaking*, Princeton, NJ: Princeton University Press.
Nagib, L. (2011) *World Cinema and the Ethics of Realism*, London and New York: Continuum.
Nava, M. (2007) *Visceral Cosmopolitanism: Gender, Culture and the Normalisation of Difference*, Oxford: Berg.
Nowak, M. (2011) "The Complicated History of *Einfühlung*" *Argument* 1.2, pp. 301–332.
Ong, J. C. (2009) "The Cosmopolitan Continuum: Locating Cosmopolitanism in Media and Cultural Studies" *Media, Culture and Society* 31.3, pp. 449–466.
Said, E. W. (2001) *Reflections on Exile and Other Literary Essays*, London: Granta.
Schwartz, V. R. (2007) *It's So French: Hollywood, Paris, and the Making of Cosmopolitan Film Culture*, Chicago: University of Chicago Press.
Shaviro, S. (1993) *The Cinematic Body*, Minneapolis: University of Minnesota Press.
Silverman, K. (1996) *The Threshold of the Visible World*, New York: Routledge.
Simmel, G. (1964) "The Stranger" in Wolff, K. (ed.) *The Sociology of Georg Simmel*, New York: Free Press, pp. 402–408.
Sobchack, V. (1992) *The Address of the Eye: A Phenomenology of Film Experience*, Princeton, NJ: Princeton University Press.
Sontag, S. (2003) *Regarding the Pain of Others*, New York: Picador.
Stacey, J. (2014) "The Uneasy Cosmopolitans of *Code Unknown*" in Irving, A. and Glick Schiller, N. (eds) *Whose Cosmopolitanism? Critical Cosmopolitanism, Relationalities and Discontents*, New York: Berghahn, pp. 160–174.
Suner, A. (2006). "Outside in: 'Accented Cinema' at Large" *Inter-Asia Cultural Studies* 7.3, pp. 363–382.
Trifonova, T. (2007) "*Code Unknown*: European Identity in Cinema" *Scope* 8; http://www.nottingham.ac.uk/scope (accessed on 15 October 2013).

17

REGURGITATED BODIES

Presenting and representing trauma in *The Act of Killing*

Lúcia Nagib

Since its release in 2012, *The Act of Killing* has amassed a great number of fervent admirers and fierce detractors worldwide. Both sides would, however, agree that the film opens up uncharted territory on which to recast the tenets of documentary, world cinema and film-making in general. Evidence of this is a poll with critics and filmmakers conducted in 2014 by *Sight and Sound* magazine which enshrines *The Act of Killing* among the most important documentaries ever made. In every respect the film challenges and innovates, first of all through its focus on unrepentant murderers, involved in the massacre of more than a million so-called communists in Indonesia in the mid-1960s, who re-enact their most gruesome crimes in the style of their favourite Hollywood genres.

The labyrinthine controversies caused by this unusual documentary method have mainly centred on the crew's intimate dealings with the perpetrators during the eight years the film took to be completed.[1] Most of the reviews, however, fail to acknowledge the fact that the entire crew put their own lives at risk in the name of a project they hoped would change the way we experience cinema and reality with it. Ethical issues undoubtedly pervade the whole endeavour, given not only the unrevealed agreements between crew and cast that necessarily took place before such a film could be made, but also the obvious exploitation of its subjects, despicable though they might be. And it is indeed ethics which will be at the core of my approach, but one which I have elsewhere defined as an "ethics of realism" (Nagib 2011). I hold the view that *The Act of Killing*'s greatest political contribution is the rejection of simplistic dualisms which place criminals as radical others to human beings, positing instead filmmakers and film subjects as stakeholders in the same humanity capable of causing catastrophe as well as regeneration. In this, it resonates with Alain Badiou, when he claims in his book on ethics:

> In the context of a system of thought that is both a-religious and genuinely contemporary with the truths of our time, the whole ethical predication based upon recognition of the other should be purely and simply abandoned. For the real question – and it is an extraordinarily difficult one – is much more that of *recognizing the Same*.
>
> (2002: 25)

I argue furthermore that ethics in this film refers to the physical commitment on the part of crew and cast to the truth of the unpredictable events unfolding before the camera, an understanding which is tributary to André Bazin's (1967) realist formula that combines faithfulness to the profilmic phenomena with a belief in the inherent honesty of the film medium (Rancière 2006: 2). But an ethics of the real is also detectable in the film's allegiance to Brecht (1964: 91ff) and his championing of the unmasking of representational artifice as the only possible realist method. In what follows, I will examine how this ethical programme operates on three key cinematic arenas: genre, authorship and spectatorship.

As far as genre is concerned, the film's realist commitment emerges from where it is least expected, namely from Hollywood genres, such as the musical, the film noir and the western, which are used *as* documentary, that is to say, as a fantasy realm where perpetrators can confess to their crimes without restraints or fear of punishment, but which nonetheless retains the evidentiary weight of the audiovisual medium. Authorship, in turn, translates as Oppenheimer's unmistakable auteur signature through his role of self-confessed spy, or 'infiltrator', as he defines it, who disguises as a sympathiser of the criminals in order to gain first-hand access to the full picture of their acts. Authorship is felt precisely in Oppenheimer's authoritative recourse to ruse in order to conduct a clinical, even ruthless manipulation of his subjects. One of them, the protagonist Anwar Congo, is clearly affected by post-traumatic stress disorder, and his repetitive reliving of his killings is made to flare up in front of the camera so as to bring back the dead to the present time in their material reality, through his own body, including a harrowing scene of the actor's unpredictable and uncontrollable retching as he re-enacts the killing of his victims through strangulation. Finally, as the concluding section will aim to demonstrate, it is in the realm of spectatorship where oppositional binaries are radically abolished. The usual process of illusionistic identification on the part of the spectator is turned onto its head by means of disguising these criminals as amateur filmmakers, led to shoot, act within, and then watch their own film within the film so as to force them to experience beyond any illusion the suffering they had caused.

Addressing each of these concepts in turn, I will attempt to indicate ways in which scholarly thought on cinema can progress on the basis of the extraordinary political impact of this film.

Genre

What is *The Act of Killing*? It is, no doubt, in the first place, a film, but one uncomfortably sitting within the boundaries of the medium and permanently straddling other forms of discourse and also what I have elsewhere called 'non-cinema', or life itself (Nagib 2015). Let us see how. The film was primarily conceived as a core output from the AHRC-funded project 'Genocide and Genre', led by Joram ten Brink, a Professor of Film at the University of Westminster. The study of genre is hence at the very origin of the film, itself part and parcel of a wide-encompassing research project, including other outputs such as the anthology *Killer Images: Documentary Film, Memory and the Performance of Violence* (2012), edited by ten Brink and Oppenheimer himself. Oppenheimer's participation in the 'Genocide and Genre' project, in turn, fits naturally within an academic trajectory which started with his first degree in film at Harvard University, under the supervision of the radical Serbian filmmaker Dusan Makavejev, and continued with his practice-based PhD at Central Saint Martins College, University of the Arts, in London. This was followed by his relocation to Copenhagen, where, in 2002, with his collaborator Christine Cynn, he took up a project to film oil plantation workers in the outskirts of Medan, North Sumatra, Indonesia, as a pilot study on the effects of globalisation on agriculture worldwide. This resulted in *The Globalisation Tapes*, a collective film which brought the crew in contact with the victims and survivors of the 1965 genocide of over a million of so-called 'communists' in Indonesia. The film contains the germs of what was to become *The Act of Killing*, as it features Oppenheimer's encounter with Sharman Sinaga, one of the perpetrators of the 1965 massacre who boastfully describes to the camera his killing techniques. Having found a number of other perpetrators all-too eager to recount their deeds onscreen, the directors then decided to devote an entire feature-length film to such accounts.

This gives us an overall idea of the combined academic and practical developments through which the film came to existence, becoming the corollary of the research project 'Genocide and Genre'. How exactly these two terms combine in the film requires, however, further elaboration. In their introduction to the book *Killer Images*, ten Brink and Oppenheimer explain that their research project is not "a study of the history of screen violence or the genres of film violence", but rather an investigation of "cinema's engagement with the performance of violence" (2012: 4). Accordingly, *The Act of Killing* is structured upon the principle that murder and, in this case, genocide, are performative acts, reliant on social endorsement and empathetic spectatorship. Indeed the most astonishing aspect of *The Act of Killing* is to have found perpetrators who were willing to re-enact their murderous acts in the style of their favourite Hollywood genres, in particular the two protagonists, Anwar Congo, an executioner in the 1965 massacre, and Herman Koto, a gangster and paramilitary leader, as well as Anwar's sidekick. Benedict Anderson (2012), an authority on Indonesian twentieth-century history, has an interesting explanation for the phenomenon, arguing that the Medan gangsters, given their distance from the central power of Jakarta, probably felt "a lack of national-level recognition for their role in the massacres" of 1965 (281). Anderson continues:

> [Oppenheimer's] camera offers them the possibility of commemoration, and transcendence of age, routine and death [. . .] They have a commemorative idea about film, actually Hollywood films which they loved from their teens. The Lone Ranger, Batman, Patton, Shane, Samson, MacArthur and Rambo – all real or imaginary men – are figures of immortality for killers who are heroic patriots, not grand gangsters [. . .] Oppenheimer thus comes to them as a kind of providential 'Hollywood' ally. *(283)*

In the film, Anwar corroborates this hypothesis by stating, in a conversation with Herman, that "whether this ends up on the big screen or only on TV, it doesn't matter, we have to show that this is who we are, this is our story, so in the future people will remember". There is also the additional coincidence that Anwar and his accomplices used to work in the film exhibition sector and that, at the height of its power, the communist regime in Indonesia had demanded a ban on American films, badly affecting their business and giving them a further pretext to participate in the massacre of communists following their defeat by the Suharto army.

Does this, however, suffice to establish a direct connection between genocide and genre? Cinematic genres, like all genres, are a combination of repetition and variation that provides captive audiences with the reassuring recognition of a pattern whilst endowing each new product with a fresh attraction. Genre has also been seen in the light of the structure of the myth, that is, as a cultural ritual capable of ironing out differences and conflicts in a community (Stam 2000: 127), leading to general catharsis and reconciliation. Repetition and variation are equally discernible in genocide, which can by the same token be associated to forms of cultural rituals. But there is a fundamental barrier between the virtual realm in which any cinematic genre, including the documentary, takes place, and the real-life context of genocide. *The Act of Killing* seems intent on breaking this very separation, by forcing the conception of genre out of the safe haven of film and into the reality of life. The problem about this kind of procedure is, of course, that cinematic genres cannot be the subject of the same moral indictment applicable to genocide. Consequently, in proposing to equate the two, the film is either being excessive in its charge on cinema and genre, or too light with regard to genocide, and this apparent ambiguity has been the source of many of the ethical objections levelled against the film (see, for example, Fraser 2013).

The fact, however, is that neither genre nor genocide is the actual focus of the film, whose primary project is to document the mental and emotional processes of those who have seen death with their own eyes and caused it with their own hands. And its greatest achievement is, in my view, that the distorted, grotesque and horrifying imagery resulting from this process exudes a kind of realism that no cinematic genre, not even documentary, could ever produce. This is the reason why nothing we see in the film even remotely resembles a cinematic genre of any kind, despite all the genre paraphernalia deployed to convey the perpetrators' fantasies. An apt illustration of this effect can be found right at the beginning. The film opens with an image that has become emblematic and features in all its publicity: a giant rusty-coloured carcass, in the shape of a goldfish, against the backdrop of purple clouds, a blue lake and blue mountains, all obviously digitally enhanced. The sound is a mixture of wind, birds, cars passing, which are gradually taken over by incidental music, a mellow female choir over keyboard notes setting the pace for six female dancers who exit the giant fish's mouth one by one onto a suspended catwalk, holding the train of their strapless dresses. The music carries on to the next shot of a waterfall occupying the whole frame, whilst the camera slowly tilts down to capture the raised hands and then the full body of Anwar and Herman. The camera then recedes in order to include in the frame another group of female dancers, with tight shiny red tops, long white skirts and false feather headdresses swaying in front of the waterfall. By now the music has been replaced by an off-screen voice on a loudspeaker, urging the characters to convey joy, happiness and peace. Anwar, in a priestly cassock, smiles beatifically. Herman looks like a pregnant woman, with his huge stomach squeezed in a flashy blue dress (one of the many drag costumes he will sport throughout the film), a large-brim white hat with a blue lace and clownish make-up (Figure 17.1). The off-screen voice shouts 'cut' and helpers enter the scene to hand out towels to the cast drenched by the waterfall spray. The complete opacity and apparent absurdity of the whole sequence will be partially unravelled as the film evolves. However, thanks to

Figure 17.1 Herman in drag.

its implausibility as a realm of fantasy, this overture brings home to the viewer the all-too material and puzzling reality of the actors, the location and the cinematic apparatus.

Let me explain by resorting to Bertolt Brecht, whose epic theatre is usually described as promoting anti-realism insofar as it is aimed at disrupting narrative continuity and verisimilitude. This opening, and indeed *The Act of Killing* as a whole, is the living proof of the vital reality principle inherent in Brecht's anti-illusionistic method. Brechtian to the root, the film is entirely structured on the principle of systematically preventing the formation of a plausible fictional or narrative world in the name of the reality of the profilmic event. Peter Wollen defined as "narrative intransitivity" the Brechtian disruption of the fable as applied, for example, by Godard in his films (Wollen 1985: 501ff). In *The Act of Killing*, this and other procedures prescribed by Brecht, such as the disconnect between the scenes and the opacity of the characters who become "objects of enquiry" rather than "taken for granted" (Brecht 1964: 37), are followed to the letter in order to conjure up the material reality of the fiction-making apparatus, rather than the impression of reality of the fictional world. Thus the prelude with the goldfish and dancers, rather than enabling the recognition of a genre pattern, elicits estrangement for the real-life quality of the dirty, rusty carcass that prevails over the artificial colours around it, as well as that of the dancers who fall out of sync with each other revealing their life-like amateurism. The jump-cut to the waterfall scene further enhances the sense of realism, as it shows more clumsy dancers and amateur actors ill at ease in their roles, one of whom, the obese Herman, even spits to the side in the middle of his performance. As a result, the spectators are driven away from the "natural beauty" the voice in the loudspeaker refers to and instead presented with the unpalatable reality that inhabits it, even before they are told of the thousand people Anwar has killed with his own hands, assisted by the likes of Herman. This is how, in this film, disrupted fiction prevents the formation of cinematic genres, in this case, the musical, by means of the repulsive reality at its origin.

In the scenes that follow, other cinematic genres, such as the gangster film and the western, will be played out and equally deconstructed through the interference of the realism of the medium, which places the 1960s genocide as the constant and unavoidable backdrop to all performances. Making genre emerge from the spectre of death is not, however, a recognisable feature of the documentary genre, but the result of a strong authorial signature, that of Joshua Oppenheimer, which I will now address.

Authorship

As an intellectual straddling both filmmaking and film studies, Oppenheimer seems acutely aware of the place he wants to occupy in the auteur pantheon. His statements are strewn with references to directors devoted to documentarian activism focusing on crimes against humanity and human rights, such as Errol Morris, Jean Rouch, Rithy Pahn, Claude Lanzman, Werner Herzog and other filmmakers he aspires not only to compare with but even perhaps to surpass. In tune with this noble lineage of filmmakers, all of them celebrated for their risk-taking approach and fearless engagement with their subjects, Oppenheimer devised an "infiltrative method" which led him to penetrate right-wing militias, white-supremacist groups, UFO abductee groups, and cults as if he were one of them, a daring venture for a Jewish homosexual like him resulting in his two American films of the 1990s, *These Places We've Learned to Call Home* (1996) and *The Entire History of the Louisiana Purchase* (1997).

The Act of Killing also benefits from this kind of approach in a seemingly collaborative dynamics through which Oppenheimer gains intimacy with and the confidence of mass murderers to the point of having them re-enact their crimes onscreen in the manner of their Hollywood idols. A similar collaborative method had been employed, for example, by Jean Rouch, whose ideas of "shared anthropology" and "ethnodialogue" (Sayad 2013: 80ff) had been put to the test in films such as *Moi, un noir* (1958), in which Niger migrant workers in Abidjan tell their life stories under the guise of Hollywood and European stars such as Edward G. Robinson and Eddie Constantine, and here too a gruesome story of killings emerges through this seemingly playful method. Another of Oppenheimer's sources is said to have been the "Theatre of the Oppressed" (Lusztig 2013: 51), developed by Augusto Boal on the basis of his experience with deprived communities in different parts of the world. Key to Boal's method was the turning of passive spectators into active participants who directly intervene in the theatrical performance in order to change it into political action. In line with this kind of shared authorship and collaborative work, as practised by democratic ethnographers and politicised dramatists, in *The Act of Killing* parts of screen writing, directing, shooting and acting were also delegated to the film subjects, as explained in the initial titles:

> *In 1965 the Indonesian government was overthrown by the military. Anybody opposed to the military dictatorship could be accused of being a communist: union members, landless farmers, intellectuals and the ethnic Chinese. In less than a year and with the direct aid of western governments, over one million "communists" were murdered. The army used paramilitaries and gangsters to carry out the killings. These men have been in power – and have persecuted their opponents – ever since. When we met the killers, they proudly told us stories about what they did. To understand why, we asked them to create scenes about the killings in whatever ways they wished. This film follows that process and documents its consequences.*

Equally collaborative was the overall directorial work, shared between Oppenheimer, Christine Cynn and an Indonesian co-director who had to remain anonymous for security reasons. Oppenheimer's position at the helm of the decision-making process remains, however, abundantly apparent. His authorial voice and signature are clearly noticeable in every aspect of the film, providing a seamless continuation to the infiltrative work he had been consistently pursuing from the beginning of his filmmaking career. Indeed, *The Act of Killing* is Oppenheimer's most daring infiltrative film,[2] as it required him to stay for eight years in close contact with utterly dangerous and powerful criminals, including the Vice-President of Indonesia, Jusuf Kalla, himself a member of the Pancasila paramilitary militia who supported the killings and continues to crush opposing voices to this day.

Needless to stress the risk of such an enterprise given that the director is the exact opposite of the kind of providential "Hollywood ally" those criminals expected him to be, as suggested by Benedict Anderson. Every single shot of the film is aimed, not at fulfilling, but at undermining his subjects' hopes of gaining recognition and glorification for their acts. That his subjects have no say in the final product of the film becomes clear from the start. We know that the film was eight years in the making, and whichever version we are able to see today, be it the theatrical feature or the director's cut, is only a small and highly edited fraction of what was actually shot. In any case, this end product certainly does not correspond to any film the protagonists themselves had in mind, although several passages indicate that they were expecting their own edited version of it to be produced. There is, for example, a reasonably lengthy discussion between Anwar and Herman about whether a scene, in which the former is beheaded, should come at the beginning of the film and initiate a flash-back, or at the end.

The beheading scene, together with its replay on a TV set, is part of the finished version of *The Act of Killing*; however, we never see the film these two actors are talking about. The only possible conclusion from this procedure is that the film actors are being duped into believing they have any say on the final product.

Anwar, Herman and his friends seem to be dreaming of a film full of action, beautiful scenery and enjoyable music, but everything shown in *The Act of Killing* is visually and aurally revolting, as well as morally repugnant. Particularly disgusting is the appearance of the perpetrators themselves. Anwar is repeatedly captured in the act of removing his false teeth and then clicking them back in place (Figure 17.2a, b). Herman is not just overweight, but constantly exposing his gigantic belly, spitting and intimidating children and women (Figure 17.2c). Gangsters and Pancasila paramilitary refer to women in the most offensive terms, telling how much they enjoy raping 14-year-olds and similarly appalling stories. All these scenes and conversations are obviously shot and edited in under the director's direct command and surveillance, regardless of what his supposed actors and collaborators think of them.

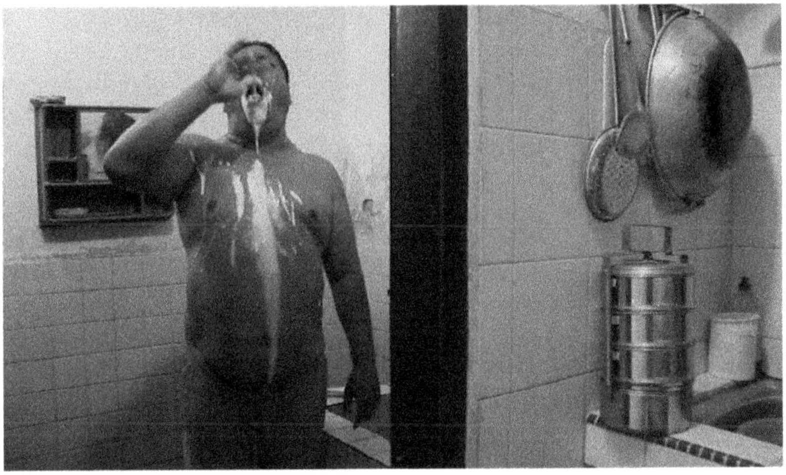

Figure 17.2a–c Revolting bodies: Herman and Anwar.

Oppenheimer might well be wary of the public's immediate perception of this betrayal, when he states, in the production notes:

> Anwar is the bravest and most honest character in *The Act of Killing*. He may or may not "like" the result, but I have tried to honour his courage and his openness by presenting him as honestly, and with as much compassion, as I could, while still deferring to the unspeakable acts that he committed.

As always, critics must be cautious when dealing with an artist's self-assessment, difficult though it is to resist Oppenheimer's compelling written and spoken prose. Rather than his personal statements, it is more enlightening to look at his authorial persona within the film itself in order to understand what is actually at stake. Oppenheimer's presence in *The Act of Killing* is subtle and camouflaged. He never appears on camera and his voice as an interviewer, in fluent Indonesian, is only occasionally heard, mostly when there are immediate ethical issues at play; for example, when Anwar calls his two pre-teen grandsons to watch footage of him re-enacting his strangulation methods and the director, off-screen, objects that the scenes are too violent for them – though the children end up watching the footage anyway. But a sense of the director's ubiquitous presence is rendered precisely for his absence, that is, for his refusal to help make sense of the chaotic spectacle those despicable criminals are trying to put together for the benefit of the camera. Because they are not professional actors and are entirely foreign to movie making, their "Hollywood" film within the main film turns them into grotesque and involuntary parodies of themselves and their acts. There is no attempt, on the part of the main film crew, at improving or polishing their imagined scenes, leaving the gangsters unmasked and exposed in their naïve enjoyment of their dreadful performances. Here again it is the reality of the medium that prevails, not just because the spectator is presented with all the discussions and preparations for the scenes, but because the theatrical performance fails to configure itself as such, leaving intact the deadly acts at their base as well as the authorial power of the non-intrusive director.

Alongside the infiltrative method, another clear authorial feature is the choice of Anwar Congo as the main protagonist. We are given no reasons for Anwar being singled out to monopolise the attention of the camera, but we soon realise that he is moved by a persistent obsession with death by the throat, through strangling, gagging or beheading. Despite the claim that he alone was responsible for a thousand deaths, no firearms or weapons of any kind other than primitive methods of compression or severing of the throat are suggested. This provides the film with the unifying imagery of the violated throat running through its entire length, determining its editing structure as well as visual and aural *mise-en-scène*. Variations of the motif of death by the throat multiply. In one of the most gruesome moments of the film, Anwar distributes hats to a handful of real gangsters, including Herman, in the style of his favourite Al Pacino gangster films and John Wayne westerns. He goes on to describe how he used to place the leg of a table on the neck of a victim and sit together with his accomplices on the table, who would shake their bodies to the rhythm of songs until their victim's throat was completely crushed; so all his fellow actor-gangsters sit with him on the table, singing "Hello, Bandung", to support him in the demonstration of this killing method.

The garrotte, made with a wire wound around the victim's neck and pulled with the help of a wooden handle, an idea which Anwar claims to have drawn from mafia movies, is played out as a leitmotiv. Anwar gives several demonstrations of the use of this weapon, whose main advantage he describes as being the little waste of blood. This is in fact the missing information which, towards the end of the film, completes the meaning of the opening musical sequence, in the form of a sequel. The waterfall scenario from the opening is replayed, now to the music track of the 1966 British film drama *Born Free* providing the backdrop to the swaying dancers, Anwar in his cassock and Herman in his drag costume. This time, however, two of Anwar's victims also appear, their faces smeared with white make-up to indicate their afterlife status. They ceremoniously remove from their neck the wire with which Anwar had strangled them. One of the victims then takes a ribbon with a medal out of his pocket and hangs it on Anwar's neck, declaring: "For executing me and sending me to heaven I thank you a thousand times" (Figure 17.3). Anwar seems elated when re-watching this scene on a TV set in his home, little realising his status as guinea pig in the hands of his psychoanalyst director, interested in tracking

Figure 17.3 Anwar feels elated with the pardon from his victim, little realising his status as guinea pig in the hands of his psychoanalyst director.

down to the very bottom his obsession with the garrotte. This goes as far as a shot of weird erotic overtones, in which Anwar, in one of his re-enactments, lies under a table, holding the ends of a wire wrapped around the neck of his victim on the table, and as he pulls the wire a sound emerges from his throat like an orgasm, following which he relaxes as his victim is now presumably dead.

Indeed, one little-explored aspect of *The Act of Killing* is its sexual symbolism, most blatant in the figure of Herman, who appears in extravagant drag characterisations throughout the film. Anderson (2012) seems to believe that, in so doing, Herman is trying to depict communists as homosexuals, and it is true that he tortures and kills in drag, his victim usually being played by Anwar, presumably to demonstrate the communists' cruelty and well-deserved punishment. However, the insistence on the drag characterisation goes far beyond the ridicule of the enemy, exposing instead some deep-seated desire or fantasy in its raw state, in tune with Anwar's sexually infused obsession with the garrotte and the neck. Ivone Margulies once described as the aim of re-enactment films to "conflate repetition with moral revision", providing a "symmetry between traumatic ordeal and social redemption" (2003: 217–18). By collaborating in the making of *The Act of Killing*, Anwar seems to be avidly seeking solace for his trauma through the re-enactment of his crimes. But the film firmly denies him such relief by exposing his and his comrades' ill-directed sexual drives and by piling up evidence to the enormity of their acts through their very re-enactments.

The extraordinary procedure Oppenheimer devised in order to achieve this effect was to resort to one of the symptoms of post-traumatic stress disorder (PTSD) from which Anwar is clearly suffering, which is presentification. Sufferers from this disease are haunted by the feeling that the traumatic event continues to happen in the present. This is obviously the case of Anwar, who reiterates, in the film, that he continues to be assailed by recurrent nightmares of the crimes he committed more than 50 years ago. Alongside the reliving of the traumatic events, other defining symptoms of PTSD are vivid flashbacks, intrusive memories and images, and physical sensations such as nausea, which is at the core of a key scene I will return to in the next section.

As Homay King reminds us a propos of *The Act of Killing* (2013: 31), Freud was the first to identify the symptoms of PTSD, which he described as "repetition compulsion" in patients suffering from traumatic neuroses, many of whom were war veterans. Moved by the aim of unveiling a horrific past, *The Act of Killing* attempts to bring back the dead from their graves and have them play a role in the present through the very trauma their death has caused. Anwar is nothing but an instrument to that end, stupendously devised by auteur Oppenheimer, who gives free rein to his own imagination in order to attach audiovisual figuration to Anwar's ghosts. These appear, for example, as a noisy swarm of nocturnal bats following a shot of Anwar sleeping, as if they had directly emerged from his nightmares. Or in the shape of a group of monkeys, who descend from the trees to feast on the red fruit used to represent blood in the re-enactment of the attack on a village, suggesting cannibalism as well as animal automatism, in a parable to the human murderous instinct.

In the process of presentification and documentation of traumatic symptoms lies the extreme originality of the re-enactment procedure utilised in this film, which rather than resorting to archive photos or footage, conflates the past with the present through the repetition of the act whose freshness and material reality is preserved in the traumatic symptoms and abject bodies of their perpetrators. Oppenheimer's auteurist role as an infiltrator and treacherous ally is that of removing the mask of his subjects as well as his own, in front and behind the camera, so as to attach the seal of material truth to the irreparable act of killing.

Spectatorship

The injection of realism into the realm of spectatorship is one of the film's central aims and greatest achievements. Anwar, Herman and other perpetrators, sometimes accompanied by members of their families, are made to watch the footage of their re-enactments, in scenes which are then interspersed with the re-enactments themselves. They react by suggesting here and there an improvement to their costumes or make-up. Mostly, however, they seem enthusiastic about what they see and convinced of the merit of their own stories, and this is clearly the reason why they continue to collaborate with Oppenheimer during the course of eight years. Anwar and Herman's spectatorial naivety could even be seen as providing credit to psychoanalytic theories that characterise the film spectator as passive and regressive, absorbed as they are in illusionistic voyeurism and ready for cathartic identification with themselves as actors.

It is not surprising that they should rejoice in recognising themselves in the skin of their imagined heroes, but it is positively baffling to see them incarnating, with apparent naturalness, both victims and perpetrators in their re-enactments, which results, for the spectators of Oppenheimer's film, in the experience of the unbearable reality of their illusion. In a particularly bizarre scene, both Anwar and Adi, his fellow executioner in 1965, play the role of interrogators but with their faces made up in lacerated flesh, as if they themselves had been tortured by the very interrogators they impersonate. It is as if the death mask described by Bazin as comparable to cinema's ontological link to the material world had become alive and were being applied to the faces of those pretending to be the killers, making the past re-emerge in the present in its *durée* (Figure 17.4).

Vivian Sobchack (2004: 59) called "interobjectivity" the process of "*subjective* realisation of our own *objectivity*, in the passion of our *own* material", and the film is undoubtedly pushing its subjects to experience themselves as objects. Viveiros de Castro, along similar lines, resorted to the concept of "perspectivism" to address an ethos among the anthropophagic Tupi-Guarani, which he defines as "the ability to look at oneself as the Other – a point of view from which one arguably obtains the ideal view of oneself" (2005: 5). It is not a coincidence that cannibalism is part of the horrors staged in *The Act of Killing*, in a carnivalesque sequence which, again, includes Herman in drag who forces a severed penis and a slice of liver into the mouth of the severed head of a victim, the latter being no other than Anwar

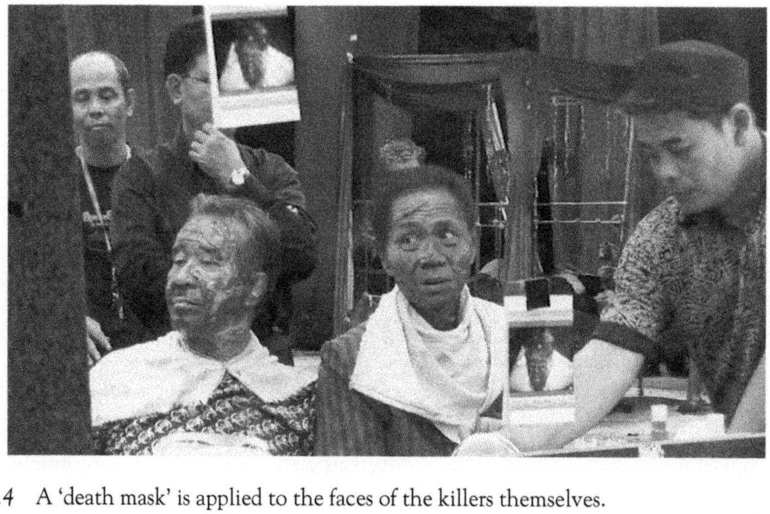

Figure 17.4 A 'death mask' is applied to the faces of the killers themselves.

himself. By blurring the boundaries between filmmakers and film spectators, through a psychoanalytic procedure that turns cathartic identification into the reality of acting, *The Act of Killing* renders palpable the agony of victims for those who were, at once, agents and privileged spectators of their killing.

In the hands of Oppenheimer, Anwar becomes the ideal ground for this radical experiment that turns narrative illusionism onto its head, that is, the reality of life. Two scenes placed at the beginning and the end of the film leave no doubt of the director's intention to force perpetrators into the skin of their victims so as to give them a physical sense of the plights they had caused. In the first one, Anwar, in a cheerful mood, visits a rooftop terrace that had been the site of many of his thousand murders, in order to demonstrate the use of the garrotte. In the second scene, Anwar revisits the same spot, but now, as the film leads us to believe, after having gone through various re-enactments of his crimes and sporting a more appropriate outfit for the occasion, a yellow suit instead of the white trousers and flowery shirt of the previous scene, and in a more sombre mood. As he attempts to convey the same description of the use of the garrotte, Anwar retches uncontrollably, as if he himself were being strangled and, at the same time, regurgitating, though alas only symbolically, the bodies of his victims. Adding a decisive difference to the second sequence from the first is the use of a single long take. Were it a cinema of montage, the retching could have been edited out, and Oppenheimer suggests that Anwar continued to perform, despite his sickness, probably in the hope that this would be the case. The decision to preserve the long take in its integrity is hence a political one, and simultaneously Oppenheimer's ultimate betrayal of his subject, negating cinema in order to let reality speak for itself.

Notes

1 For readers interested in gaining an insight into this literature, a good way to start is the special issue of *Film Quarterly*, Winter, Vol. 67, No. 2, devoted to the film.

2 The film Oppenheimer has directed thereafter, *The Look of Silence* (2014), changes the focus back onto the victims of the Indonesian genocide. For this reason, even though the risk for the crew and cast remains at a high level given that the criminals in focus continue to be protected by the current government, I would not classify this film as 'infiltrative'.

Bibliography

Anderson, B. (2012) "Impunity", in ten Brink, J. and Oppenheimer, J. (eds) *Killer Images: Documentary Film, Memory and the Performance of Violence*, New York/Chichester: Wallflower Press, pp. 268–286.

Badiou, A. (2002) *Ethics: An Essay on the Understanding of Evil*, London/New York: Verso.

Bazin, A. (1967) "The Ontology of the Photographic Image", in *What Is Cinema?* vol. 1, essays selected and translated by Hugh Gray. Berkeley/Los Angeles/London: University of California Press, pp. 9–16.

Brecht, B. (1964) *Brecht on Theatre: The Development of an Aesthetic*, edited and translated by John Willett. London: Methuen, pp. 91–99.

Fraser, N. (2013) "We Love Impunity: The Case of *The Act of Killing*", *Film Quarterly*, Winter, 67.2, pp. 21–24.

King, H. (2013) "Born Free? Repetition and Fantasy in *The Act of Killing*", *Film Quarterly*, 67.2, Winter, pp. 30–36.

Lusztig, I. (2013) "The Fever Dream of Documentary: A Conversation with Joshua Oppenheimer", *Film Quarterly*, 67.2, Winter, pp. 50–56.

Margulies, I. (2003) *Rites of Realism: Essays on Corporeal Cinema*, Durham, NC/London: Duke University Press.

Nagib, L. (2011) *World Cinema and the Ethics of Realism*, New York/London: Continuum.

Nagib, L. (2015) "Non-cinema, or the Location of Politics in Film", *Film-Philosophy* , 20.1, pp. 131–148, Available Online February 2016. DOI:http://dx.doi.org/10.3366/film.2016.0007

Rancière, J. (2006) *Film Fables*, Oxford/New York: Berg.

Sayad, C. (2013) *Performing Authorship: Self-Inscription and Corporeality in the Cinema*, London/New York: I.B. Tauris.
Sobchack, V. (2004) *Carnal Thoughts: Embodiment and Moving Image Culture*, Berkeley/Los Angeles: University of California Press.
Stam, R. (2000) *Film Theory: An Introduction*, Malden, MA: Blackwell.
ten Brink, J. and J. Oppenheimer (2012) *Killer Images: Documentary Film, Memory and the Performance of Violence*, New York/Chichester: Wallflower Press.
Viveiros de Castro, E. (2005) "A filosofia canibal"/ "Cannibal Philosophy", interview by Rafaello Cariello, Folha de S. Paulo, *Mais!*, 21 August, p. 5ff.
Wollen, P. (1985) "Godard and Counter Cinema: Vent D'Est", in Nichols, B. (ed.) *Movies and Methods, Vol. II*, Berkeley/Los Angeles: University of California Press, pp. 500–508.

18

AFTER DISPOSSESSION

Blackfella Films and the politics of radical hope

Felicity Collins

This chapter explores how a Sydney-based production company, Blackfella Films, has negotiated both the legacy of settler-colonial dispossession and the potential for a new relationship between Indigenous and settler Australia in a body of work that spans two decades (see Perkins n.d.). While sketching the political context in which Blackfella Films has produced award-winning documentaries, feature films and television series since 1993, the argument will focus on the archival documentary series *First Australians* (Perkins and Cole 2008). It proposes that *First Australians* marks a shift from a trauma cinema of dispossession to an ethical cinema of resilience by retrieving templates of radical hope from the settler colonial archives.

Drawing on a political and affective framework proposed by Bonnie Honig in her lecture series, *Thinking Out Loud* (2013a), this chapter is particularly concerned with how *First Australians* offers templates of radical hope. In an article based on the *Thinking Out Loud* lectures, Honig (2013b) explores the cost to democracy of neoliberal faith in privatisation, and strongly defends our attachment to 'public things' such as libraries, parks, Big Bird and public telephones. She draws on Jonathan Lear's concept of radical hope as an ethical response to the catastrophic decimations of settler colonialism, and applies Lear's argument to neoliberalism and its melancholic affect. Inspired by Honig's defence of public things and Lear's ethics of radical hope, this chapter departs from a body of work that approaches settler-colonial cinema in terms of memory, trauma, postcolonial poetics and decolonising ethics. This departure entails a shift in focus from settler revisions of the national story to Indigenous dialogue with the national archive. The value and significance of this dialogue has to be understood in the context of the erosion of public institutions by neoliberalism. Undermined by two decades of efficiency measures, the public institutions of national cinema and television broadcasting have pooled their diminishing resources to fund a range of initiatives that have placed the 'cinema of Aboriginality' at the heart of Australian screen culture. Public recognition of the Blak Wave (a critical mass of Indigenous film and television production over the last decade) can be understood, then, as not only an affective response to particular films, such as Palme d'Or winner, *Samson & Delilah* (Thornton, 2009), and box office hit, *The Sapphires* (Blair, 2012), but as an alignment with the politics of radical hope.

Dispossession

The production of the telemovie, *Mabo* (Blackfella Films, 2012), marked the twentieth anniversary of the High Court of Australia's historic *Mabo and others v. The State of Queensland (No. 2) (1992)* decision. This decision recognised the unjust dispossession of Aboriginal and Torres Strait Islanders by British colonialism from 1788 – a dispossession sustained, expanded and intensified by white Australia's nation-building policies from 1901. In its justification of the decision, the High Court specifically rejected the colonising myth of *terra nullius* and paved the way for legislation to recognise native title claims. Native title, while welcomed by many Australians, reignited the history wars – sparking a decade-long stand-off between 'black armband' and 'white blindfold' perspectives on the settler nation's origins in dispossession. The trenchant denial of any legacy of shame by vociferous right-wing commentators and think-tanks was encouraged by conservative governments from 1996 to 2007. In this context, a publicly funded Blak Wave of Indigenous films helped to create an alternative public sphere, addressing Indigenous and settler Australians committed to what Justice Gaudron saw as the need for "an acknowledgement of and a retreat from those past injustices" (quoted in *Mabo*, 2012). In 2000, the Sydney Harbour Bridge Walk, Sea of Hands and Sorry Books demonstrated the groundswell of public support for native title and an apology to the Stolen Generations, attesting to a paradigm shift in Indigenous–settler relations. This shift created the conditions, over the next decade, for the emergence of a reconciliatory, 'backtracking' settler cinema, and an unprecedented Blak Wave of Indigenous film and television production.

The 'backtracking' films, such as *Rabbit-Proof Fence* (Noyce, 2002) and *The Tracker* (de Heer, 2002), drew the cinema public into the history wars by going over old ground – contesting, retracting and revising colonial tropes such as the lost child and the black tracker (Collins and Davis 2006). The films of the Blak Wave, however, cut across the history wars by turning an Indigenous gaze on the colonial past and its afterlife in the present. The telling and retelling of the Mabo story is a case in point. In 1997, two documentary versions of the Mabo story were made by settler filmmakers. Trevor Graham's *Mabo – Life of an Island Man* is structured as an elegiac work of mourning, while John Hughes's collage film, *After Mabo*, focuses on the media coverage of fiercely contested native title legislation. In these documentaries, settler Australians seek to include Indigenous stories and perspectives in the public debate, at a turning point in the nation's identity.

But what happens when the story of Indigenous dispossession – culminating in settler recognition of the myth of *terra nullius* in the High Court's 1992 decision – is retold, not once but twice, by Indigenous filmmakers? Rachel Perkins's 2012 telemovie, *Mabo*, retells the story of Koiki 'Eddie' Mabo as a romance quest – chronicling Mabo's upbringing in traditional Meriam Law, his unjust banishment from his colonised homeland, his youthful struggles against a racist system in the state of Queensland, and his all-consuming quest to establish native title over his traditional land on Murray Island in the Torres Strait. While *Mabo* is a heritage film, creating a memory for future generations, it is also a biopic, a family melodrama and a stirring courtroom drama, produced, directed and largely performed by Indigenous Australians, including descendants of the plaintiffs in the *Mabo and others v. the State of Queensland* case. *Mabo* retells, in popular narrative form, the political events that constitute the closing episode of the epic, archival documentary series, *First Australians*. This award-winning, top-selling series was produced by Blackfella Films for the multicultural broadcaster, SBS Television. It documents and debates the dispossession of the Indigenous peoples of Australia from 1788 to 1992. Six years in the making, *First Australians* went to air a few months after Prime Minister Rudd's historic apology to the Stolen Generations in 2008. The series invites Australians to engage with what Justice Brennan described as the nation's "legacy of unutterable shame", but it does so in the spirit of Prime Minister Keating's 1992 recognition of the Mabo decision as "the basis of a new relationship between Indigenous and non-Aboriginal Australia" (both quoted in *Mabo*).

The politics of dispossession and belonging in settler-colonial nations differs markedly from the politics of displacement, diaspora and belonging in postcolonial Europe. The emergence of a transnational 'cinema of Aboriginality', or Fourth Cinema (Columpar 2010: 11–18), articulates a politics of survival and hope that has the potential to transform identity and belonging in the nation-states that derive from British colonialism. This politics was articulated for the Australian nation in December 1992, six months after the High Court's *Mabo* decision, when Prime Minister Keating (principal architect of neoliberal reform of the Australian economy by Labor governments from 1983–96) delivered the Redfern Park speech – an event overlooked at the time, but now enshrined in national history. In this speech, delivered live to an urban, Aboriginal gathering, Keating asked the nation "to see Australia through Aboriginal eyes" and "to see how much we owe indigenous Australians and how much we have lost by living so apart" (1992). Early in the speech, Keating made a statement that foreshadows both Marcia Langton's influential essay on Aboriginality as an intercultural subjectivity (1993), and Germaine Greer's essay (2003), exhorting settler Australians to recognize that we live in an Aboriginal country. Keating put it this way: "complex as our contemporary identity is, it cannot be separated from Aboriginal Australia"; Redfern, located just a mile or two from where the first European settlers landed in 1788, "is a good place to contemplate these things" (1992).

On the question of recognising the historic injustice of multiple forms of dispossession across generations, not everyone on the progressive side of politics lined up behind Prime Minister Keating and the High Court judges. In her influential book, *The Cunning of Recognition*, Elizabeth Povinelli claims that the politics of recognition calls upon "indigenous subjects … to perform an authentic difference in exchange for the good feeling of the nation and the reparative legislation of the state" (2002: 6). Moreover, Povinelli claims,

> this call does not simply produce good theater, rather it inspires impossible desires: *to be* this impossible object and to transport its ancient prenational meanings and practices to the present in *whatever* language and moral framework prevails *at the time of enunciation*.
>
> (*Ibid.*)

In a review essay responding to Povinelli, Stephen Muecke suggests that this mandatory performance of Aboriginality, in exchange for recognition, is for the "edification of the liberal multicultural cosmopolitans" (2007: 133–138). Such formulations, however, cast a pall over the success of the Blak Wave's highly acclaimed documentaries, feature films and television series, produced by companies such as Blackfella Films in collaboration with Screen Australia and the national television broadcasters. Looking closely at *First Australians*, then, I draw on the politics of radical hope as a counterpoint to Povinelli's critique of the 'cunning' of recognition. My premise is that *First Australians* addresses the paradox articulated by Indigenous scholar Phillip Morrissey: of Aboriginal "erasure as subjectivities and intelligences" while remaining highly visible as troubling, embodied beings (quoted in Healy 2008: 10).

Resilience

The provision of public places, such as Redfern Park where Prime Minister Keating asked the nation to contemplate such matters in 1992, is a key concern of Bonnie Honig's 2013 lectures, made freely available by two public institutions: ABC Radio National's *The Philosopher's Zone*, and University of Western Sydney's website, Philosophy@UWS. In a publication from these lectures, Honig proposes a democratic politics "rooted in common love for and contestation of public things" (Honig 2013b: 60). Drawing on object-relations theory, Honig argues that a democratic holding environment enables resilience when it recognises the generative power of public things and allows them to flourish (2013b: 59–63). For Honig, the damage to democracy posed by advanced capitalism and its catastrophic forms of exclusion – dispossession, assimilation, genocide – requires the creation of new public things around which to constellate. Arguably, the Blak Wave of film and television production in Australia is generating shared objects, or public things, around which settler and Indigenous peoples have begun to constellate.

The politics of dispossession, and the terms of survival after disaster, are the subject of Honig's concluding lecture. It begins by positing land as the basis of American democracy in the New World and goes on to discuss the resilience of the Crow People facing the settler-colonial destruction of their world. It concludes with contemporary responses to the neoliberal destruction of our world, played out by a range of characters in *Melancholia* (von Trier, 2011). Central to Honig's argument is Lear's concept of radical hope as a transitional affect that seeks to avoid the inauthenticity of assimilation. Lear's ethics of radical hope derives from his interpretation of the testimony of Crow leader, Plenty Coups, written down by a trapper in 1932. What captures Lear's attention in this testimony is Plenty Coups's statement that, after the Crow nation moved into an alliance with the United States against the Sioux nation, and moved onto a reservation, "nothing happened". Lear interprets this to mean that, although the Crow people succeeded in retaining part of their ancestral land, the Crow world lost its intelligibility and the Crow subject ceased to be (Lear 2006: 50–51). But this destruction of the Crow subject is not without hope of revival:

> What would be required [...] would be a new Crow poet: one who could take up the Crow past and – rather than use it for nostalgia or ersatz mimesis – project it into vibrant new ways for the Crow to live and to be. Here by "poet" I mean the broadest sense of a creative maker of meaningful space.
>
> *(51)*

In Lear's interpretation, Plenty Coups drew on tradition to face the reality of the coming devastation of Crow life – thus avoiding suicidal bravery or self-pitying despair. From the resource of the vision-quest, under the guidance of his elders, Plenty Coups was able to become "a creative maker of meaningful space" where the attentive capacities of the chickadee (to listen and learn) might turn out to be more helpful than the courage of the war eagle (Lear 2006: 90–1). For Lear, what makes Plenty Coups's "peculiar form of hopefulness" *radical* is "the hope for *revival*: for coming back to life in a form that is not yet intelligible" (original emphasis, 2006: 95). In this view,

> meager forms of survival do not constitute the full flower of Plenty Coups's hope ... yet, precisely because he is witness to the death of traditional Crow subjectivity, he is not in a position to say what the future form of Crow flourishing will be.
>
> *(Lear 2006: 96)*

Reading Lear, and listening to Honig, opens up an alternative to Povinelli's "impossible" Indigenous subject performing authenticity in exchange for settler recognition. In the remainder of this chapter, I want to explore, first, the ways in which the archival documentary series, *First Australians*, provides templates of radical hope from the colonial past, to enable Indigenous subjectivity to find future ways to flourish. Second, I want to make the argument that the 'cinema of Aboriginality', produced by Blackfella Films as part of the Blak Wave, is a 'public thing' that functions much like a transitional object for Indigenous and settler Australians – reviving the lost possibility of both subjectivities becoming 'minor' in the sense proposed by Healy in *Forgetting Aborigines* (2008: 192–3).

Stories of resilience in *First Australians*

Blackfella Films was established by Indigenous writer/director/producer, Rachel Perkins, in Sydney in 1992, coinciding with the Decade of Reconciliation – a decade galvanised by the politics of recognition of and apology to Aboriginal and Torres Strait Islander Australians who had been dispossessed of their land, language, culture and children by colonial violence and by the policies of a nation-state founded on the White Australia policy. Over the decade, Perkins took an activist role in film and television organisations and made two significant feature films, *Radiance* (1998) and *One Night the Moon* (2001), as well as producing the four-part documentary series *Blood Brothers* (1993) for SBS Television. In 2002, Darren Dale joined Blackfella Films in the role of producer, in 2010 Miranda Dear came on board as drama producer and in 2013 Jacob Hickey was appointed as head of factual. During its second decade, Blackfella Films developed a high profile within the industry, winning awards and critical acclaim for *First Australians* (2008), *The Tall Man* (Krawitz, 2011), *Mabo* (2012), *Redfern Now* (2012, 2013, 2015) and the reality TV series, *First Contact* (2014).

In 2002, when the multicultural broadcaster, SBS Television, commissioned Blackfella Films to make a documentary series that would give Aboriginal people back their history, Perkins felt that she had been "put on the planet to do this project"; what kept her going for six years was her desire to see the nation mature by taking on a "fuller version of the Australian story" (Perkins 2009). Going into the nation's archives Perkins found not only a "trail of horror" but also that:

> Indigenous people were there at every turning point of Australian history. We guided and saved explorers, we looked after and we also killed their sheep, we slept with them, we fenced their properties, we led them to gold, we worked on their ships; our wages financed their hospitals and roads, we lived in their houses, we fought against them, we fought side by side with them in the wars. Yet, we have been erased from the story of contemporary Australia and certainly from the building of Australia, as we know it today.
>
> (*Perkins 2006*)

Taking their cue from Ken Burns, director of *The Civil War* (American Documentaries Inc., 1990), Perkins and Beck Cole worked with writer, Louis Nowra, to recast the history of Australia with Aboriginal and Torres Strait Islander protagonists in the leading roles. A decision was made to focus on 'stories of resilience', narrated by Perkins with the support of Indigenous and settler voices from the archives. The pictorial record was intercut with interviews featuring settler historians (identified by their academic role) and Indigenous commentators (identified as belonging to one or more First Nations). While *First Australians* has become the top-selling, educational DVD series made in Australia, its makers acknowledge that one television series cannot do full justice to the history of dispossession that academic historians have documented and interpreted over several decades. What the series does do, however, is use the voices of Indigenous actors to bring the pictorial archive to life (Perkins, 2006). This is an act of *revival* in Lear's sense, but, more than that, each episode can be re-viewed, re-played, slowed down or fast-forwarded (on DVD or online), enabling viewers to get to know these stories intimately and to make them their own. This digital viewing practice allows the claim to be made that *First Australians* is not only a record of, but a resource for, radical hope.

Both Honig and Lear link radical hope to resilience. Yet they also cite characters (fictional and historical) who lack the resilience to survive cultural devastation, and they ask what makes resilience possible. The opening episode of *First Australians* chronicles four main responses to settler invasion and dispossession. Initial attempts "to come together and comprehend each other" are explored through four relationships: Bennelong's diplomatic relationship with Governor Phillip; warrior Pemulwuy's armed resistance to the colony's gamekeeper; the friendship between Windradyne, a Wiradjuri leader, and his neighbours, the Suttors; and the attempt to translate each other's culture by a young Eora woman, Patyegarang, and the colony's astronomer, William Dawes.

Bennelong's violent yet intimate relationship with Governor Phillip, including kidnapping, spearing and a voyage to England, can be understood as an attempt at cultural diplomacy, but one that separates Bennelong from his people for many years, leading to inauthenticity and despair before Bennelong finally turns his back on settler society and returns to his much depleted people. Pemulwuy's ill-fated attempt to wage war against the settler-invaders, in Lear's terms, is evidence of an excess of courage because it leads to an escalation of settler violence, and after 14 years, Pemulwuy's death and decapitation. Pemulwuy's fate contrasts with that of Windradyne who initially waged war against the settlers when, in the 1820s, the land grab moved over the mountains and into Wiradjuri country. One of these settlers, George Suttor instructs his 17-year-old son, William, to treat the Wiradjuri people with kindness and respect. William learns their language and this act of respect saves the Suttor family when Windradyne leads the counterattack to drive settlers away. But, as in the case of Pemulwuy, the violence of settler retaliation quickly threatens the very existence of the Wiradjuri. Faced with annihilation, Windradyne seeks peace, proudly leading 130 of his warriors on a 17-day walk into Parramatta where he is greatly admired by the crowd and receives a pardon. Like Plenty Coups, Windradyne's recognition that the settlers are here to stay, at any cost, saves his people. Unlike Pemulwuy, whose head was never returned from London, Windradyne lived out his life on Wiradjuri land, in friendship with the neighbouring Suttors, and was buried with full traditional rites.

On Lear's model of radical hope, the despair and isolation that ended Bennelong's diplomatic adventure, and the death and decapitation that ended Pemulwuy's heroic resistance to settler invasion, reveal the uncertainty and risks entailed in both recognising and failing to recognise the end of a known world. The devastating outcomes of these responses to the arrival of the First Fleet demonstrated the need for new, uncertain and risky forms of radical hope for future *revival* of Indigenous subjectivities and worlds. An alternative mode of neighbourly relations is briefly sketched in Episode One. It occurs between a young woman, Patyegarang, and the colony's first astronomer, Lieutenant William Dawes. Traces of their affectionate relationship survive in Dawes's notebooks where intimate exchanges, such as "you winked at me", reveal strangers listening to and learning the requirements and obligations of each other's culture and language (Gibson 2012). If Windradyne's peace offer is one form of radical hope – opting for maintenance of Wiradjuri land, language and culture in a devastating colonial context where the future is unknowable – then Patyegarang's friendship with Dawes, on her terms, counts as another. However, their extraordinary friendship ended abruptly when Dawes was sent back to England in late 1791, after refusing to join a second punitive expedition to avenge Pemulwuy's spearing of the colony's gamekeeper.

As Lear (2006: 92–100) points out, a politics of radical hope requires more than meagre survival, more than noble refusal, more than fatal rebellion, and something other than 'going through the motions' in a changed world that does away with the old meanings. Lear (2006: 63) and Honig (2013b: 70–71) draw on different strands of philosophy to speculate on what enables resilience, and what forms it might take in unprecedented situations of dispossession, destruction and loss. In the testimony of Plenty Coups, Lear finds that the traditional Crow virtue, of courage in battle, entails a degree of plasticity that allows Plenty Coups to 'thin' out and adapt a 'thick' virtue to circumstances as yet unknown (2006: 108). For Honig (2013a), Plenty Coups's response to conquest was a form of pragmatic realism, but "not without principle". It contrasted with three other responses to conquest, described by Lear: Sitting Bull's steadfast refusal to face reality; Wraps His Tail's brave but suicidal acts of rebellion which bring about his death by another Crow; and a Crow medicine woman violating a Crow ethical norm in a life she no longer understands.

Templates for living on after the end

How then does *First Australians* differentiate the responses of those who came after Bennelong and Governor Phillip, Pemulwuy and the gamekeeper, Windradyne and William Suttor, Patyegarang and Lieutenant Dawes? What forms of resilience and radical hope are to be found in the archival traces of those who 'lived on after the end' – after it had become clear that the strangers were here to stay? What forms of *revival* could be hoped for as settler colonialism reached into the traditional lands of the 250 First Nations of Australia? At the risk of being overly schematic, I want to propose that Episode One of *First Australians* sets up three dominant character templates for understanding Indigenous responses to two centuries of dispossession in Episodes Two to Seven. These templates entail a degree of plasticity in their respective modes of diplomacy (Bennelong), resistance (Pemulwuy) and hope for revival (Windradyne). I will return to the fourth template, of stranger relationality, below.

The first character template, and its mode of diplomatic acculturation, is that of Bennelong. Kidnapped and befriended by Governor Phillip to serve as a 'native informant', Bennelong quickly learns the language and culture of the new regime within which he becomes an emissary or diplomat – despite being misrecognised, during his visit to England, as a novelty and prize colonial exhibit. In Episode Two, 'Her Will to Survive', we see this template at work in the killing fields of Tasmania where Trugannini embarks on a diplomatic mission with George Augustus Robinson, the well-rewarded Protector of Aborigines whose job it is to end Aboriginal resistance to colonial dispossession by persuading those still alive on a brutal frontier to move to Flinders Island. Trugannini travels with Robinson, acting as an intermediary and guide, even saving Robinson's life on one occasion. But despite the evident closeness of their relationship, having achieved his goal, Robinson's star continues to rise while Trugannini ties her fate to that of the 'last' Tasmanian Aboriginal people who die on Flinders Island. Deprived of the proper burial rites, Trugannini's head is removed from her body, and like Pemulwuy's, becomes a trophy for colonial curiosity about 'the last Tasmanian'. What the colonial regime overlooked, however, were the Aboriginal women who refused 'protection' and survived by throwing in their lot with the disreputable and often cruel sealers.

Their descendants have lived to testify to the revival of Tasmanian Aboriginality in activism, scholarship and art.

The second character template takes its trajectory from Pemulwuy's spearing of the colony's gamekeeper in 1790. Pemulwuy's war against the settler colony took a new turn, a century later, in the stories of black trackers and their role in native policing in central and western Australia. Episode Five begins with the story of a Bunupa hero, Jandamarra, whose dilemma as a black tracker in the native police force in 1894 is resolved by heroic resistance. Born on a cattle station, at the age of 19 Jandamarra finds himself guarding prisoners from his own tribe, the Bunuba people of north-west Australia. After seven years in the native police, Jandamarra shoots his close friend and commanding officer, Constable Bill Richardson, and frees the Bunuba prisoners who are facing transportation to Rottnest Island for cattle-killing. Described as a charming person who 'enjoyed mastering another world and being recognised for it', Jandamarra had earlier broken the Bunuba marriage laws and been banished from his tribe. Fighting off a search party in the Napier ranges, the badly wounded Jandamarra forced the police to retreat and helped over 100 Bunuba men, women and children to escape. This heroic stand, however, unleashes 'murder by state action', the imprisonment of those who survive, and Jandamarra's death at the hands of a fellow black tracker. Suffering the same desecration after death as Pemulwuy and Truganinni, Jandamarra's body was decapitated and his head sent to England. Remembered by the Bunuba people as a hero and a freedom fighter, in Lear's terms, Jandamarra's rebellion was an excess of courage, without hope for the future.

Given the limitations of individual diplomacy (Bennelong and Truganinni) and heroic acts of war (Pemulwuy, Windradyne and Jandamarra), Episodes Three and Six focus on what it means to go on living in the shrinking spaces reserved for Aboriginal peoples in the colonies and, after 1901, in the nation-state. The warrior Windradyne provides the template for a viable response to this ethical problem. Like Plenty Coups, Windradyne's capacity to retain his traditional land and live a Wiradjuri life side-by-side with his settler neighbours, leaves a legacy, not of heroic defeat, but of hope for *revival.* By definition, this hope demands steadfast courage rather than heroic action: it is closest to the mode of response associated with the chickadee in Plenty Coups's vision-quest. The task set by the chickadee was to listen and learn from the successes and failures of the culture of the former enemy, now an (unreliable) ally, without giving up hope for cultural revival in future forms.

The Coranderrk story of 1860–90 in Episode Three, and the Cummeragunja story of 1937–67 in Episode Six, show how the radical hope of the past might flourish in future generations, in the face of entrenched racism and bureaucratic coercion. Through the stories of Simon Wonga and William Barak at Coranderrk, and William Cooper and Doug Nicholls at Cummeragunja, *First Australians* moves beyond the devastation of the frontier wars to discover what it takes to sustain radical hope in impossible circumstances. Here, revival literally means the coming back to life of Aboriginal intelligences and subjectivities, not in their traditional form but reshaped in response to nineteenth-century settler colonialism and twentieth-century nation-building. In the case of Wonga and his cousin Barak, the revival took the form of a successful farming enterprise, repeatedly undermined by the Aboriginal Protection Board in the colony of Victoria. The steadfast activism of Wonga and Barak against the colonial policy of 'smoothing the pillow of a dying race', was revived a century later in the walk-off from the intolerable conditions on the reserve at Cummeragunja. This action gave rise to a decades-long campaign for constitutional change, led by William Cooper and, later, his nephew Doug Nicholls who became not only a football star and a pastor, but the Governor of South Australia. What these two episodes make clear is that Aboriginal subjectivities and intelligences survived segregation and assimilation in new forms, providing a template for future generations who now remember these men as 'extraordinary human beings' and 'relentless campaigners', loved for their 'goodness' and their knowledge of traditions.

In the final episode of *First Australians*, the story of Koiki 'Eddie' Mabo picks up on the steadfast courage of these early activists to persist and endure against powerful opposition. Eddie Mabo's story also picks up on Bennelong (living away from his people and his traditional land for so long), and on Jandamarra – the sometime stockman, sheep-stealer and native police tracker who broke Bunuba and white laws, only to take a heroic stand against the colonial regime. And like Windradyne, Mabo is remembered posthumously for a great feat – recognition of native title after two centuries of dispossession, and (after desecration of his original tombstone) full burial rites on his traditional land. In Mabo's story, then, we can see traces of diplomacy, resistance and the revival of tradition in new forms. We also see the flourishing of Aboriginal subjectivity in ways that could not have been predicted by Pemulwuy or Windradyne, although Bennelong and Trugannini might well recognise their own intrepid hope for a productive alliance with the settlers in Mabo's alliance with the lawyers and supporters who helped take his case to the High Court of Australia.

Blackfella Films

What then of Patyegarang and Dawes who have figured so lightly in the templates of radical hope sketched so far? While linguists were the first to engage with the language notebooks of William Dawes when they were rediscovered in a London archive in 1972, it is only recently that Patyegarang and Dawes have begun to serve as a template for reimagining Indigenous–settler relations, most notably in Kate Grenville's novel, *The Lieutenant* (2008), Ross Gibson's *26 Views of the Starburst World* (2012), and Bangarra Dance Theatre's *Patyegarang* (2014). Through such revivals, Patyegarang and Dawes now serve as a template for new forms of stranger relationality, evident in public 'hunger' for the Blak Wave (Collins 2016).

While Lear offers Plenty Coups as an exemplar of radical hope, Honig, in her third lecture, turns to von Trier's *Melancholia* in order to argue that radical hope, in the context of neoliberalism, depends less on individuals than on the holding environment in which public things, such as cinema and public broadcasters, might flourish. Neoliberal attacks on policies that support such public things as a 'cinema of Aboriginality', a national cinema and a national broadcasting service, have been a constant feature of the political landscape in Australia since the 1990s. But though decimated, these public things find ways to flourish, and reanimate tradition, when they work as transitional objects supported by public-ness (Honig 2013b: 71–74). Public support and affection for Blackfella Films has only grown since the release of *First Australians*, evident in the awards accorded to *Redfern Now* – the first television drama series produced, written and directed by Indigenous Australians with Indigenous actors in all leading roles.

Blackfella Films has been a key player in the Blak Wave – a critical mass of screen production that had its origins in the independent filmmaking of the 1970s, as well as Aboriginal radio and television licences granted to remote Indigenous communities in the 1980s. The slow building of partnerships between national screen organisations and companies such as Blackfella Films to produce a 'cinema of Aboriginality' might find its character template, then, in the friendship between William Dawes and Patyegarang during the first years of colonisation. As the colony's astronomer, Dawes withdrew from the main settlement to a small hut overlooking Sydney Harbour, not far from where Blackfella Films produced *First Australians*. Drawing on Honig, this hut can be seen not so much as a retreat for Dawes but as a transitional space, a holding environment where intimacy, reciprocity, affection and cultural translation were able to flourish, not only between Dawes and Patyegarang but with their Eora visitors.

What happens, then, if we think of the tiny production house of Blackfella Films – located in and around Gadigal country on Sydney Harbour – as a contemporary iteration of Dawes's hut? Might we see in Blackfella Films's partnerships with public bodies, including Screen Australia, SBS and ABC Television, the *revival* of cultural translation as a viable form of stranger relationality (Warner 2002: 74–77), even though its first utterance was quashed so prematurely in 1791? In Dawes's regret at being coerced into joining the first reprisal party against Pemulwuy, and his steadfast refusal to join the second reprisal, we might see a character template for an anticolonial ethics where the roles of host and guest become interchangeable. In Patyegarang's generosity, intelligence and goodwill towards Dawes, and her commitment to their mutual enterprise of cultural translation, we might find a character template for neighbourly relations adopted by both Blackfella Films and, more broadly, the network of Indigenous filmmakers known as the Blak Wave. Like Patyegarang and Dawes, then, Blackfella Films and its public demonstrate "commitment to the idea that something good will emerge even if it outstrips my present limited capacity for understanding what that good is" (Lear 2006: 24).

When *First Australians* reached public screens in 2008, six years after the project began, producer/writer/director and founder of Blackfella Films, Rachel Perkins, remarked that, in the future, "our work will be looked back on as very ethnographic and politically incorrect" (Perkins 2009). At the same time, Perkins saw that the previous generation of Indigenous artists and activists "who fought for us to be in the position … to make these films … would also be satisfied that their work, or their dreams, had begun to be realized" (ibid.). This capacity to look back, to see the present as a momentary fulfilment of the radical hope of the past – while recognising that "our films will soon become old fashioned" – is a hard-won virtue. If, as Honig suggests, "the aim is to face reality with some authenticity" (2013a) then the political cinema epitomised by Blackfella Films might best be viewed as a public thing, a transitional object for both Indigenous and settler Australians. In the context of a dramatic shift from left-liberal policies of self-determination to neoliberal policies of individual responsibility, the 'public things' produced by Blackfella Films offer templates of resilience to all Australians, as an antidote to the ravages of intergenerational dispossession that continue to impact, so disproportionately, on Indigenous Australia.

Bibliography

Collins, F. (2016) "A Hungry Public: Stranger Relationality and the Blak Wave" in Marshall, P.D., D'Cruz, G., Macdonald, S. and Lee, K. (eds) *Contemporary Publics*, London: Palgrave Macmillan.

Collins, F. and T. Davis (2006) "Disputing History, Remembering Country in Australian Cinema", *Australian Historical Studies*, 37 (128), pp. 35–54.

Columpar, C. (2010) *Unsettling Sights: The Fourth World on Film*, Carbondale: Southern Illinois University Press.

Gibson, R. (2012) *26 Views of the Starburst World: William Dawes at Sydney Cove 1788–91*, Crawley WA: University of Western Australia Press.

Greer, G. (2003) "Whitefella Jump Up", *Quarterly Essay*, 11, pp. 1–78.

Grenville, K. (2008) *The Lieutenant*, Melbourne: Text Publishing.

Healy, C. (2008) *Forgetting Aborigines*, Sydney: University of New South Wales Press.

Honig, B. (2013a) "Public Things", *Thinking Out Loud*, Lectures 1–3, at http://www.uws.edu.au/philosophy/philosophy@uws/events/thinking_out_loud/2013 (accessed 9 October 2013).

Honig, B. (2013b) "The Politics of Public Things: Neoliberalism and the Routine of Privatization", *No Foundations* 10, at http://www.helsinki.fi/nofo/NoFo10HONIG.pdf (accessed 6 January 2015).

Keating, P. (1992) "Paul Keating's Redfern Park Speech [Part 1]", at http://www.youtube.com/watch?v=mKhmTLN3Ddo (accessed 1 October 2013).

Langton, M. (1993) *Well, I Heard it on the Radio and I Saw it on the Television*, Sydney: Australian Film Commission.

Lear, J. (2006) *Radical Hope: Ethics in the Face of Cultural Devastation*, Cambridge, MA: Harvard University Press.

Muecke, S. (2007) "Review of Deborah Bird Rose, *Reports From a Wild Country*", *PAN: Philosophy, Activism, Nature*, 4, pp. 133–138.

Perkins, R. (n.d.) "Rachel Perkins", Interview Transcript, Screen Australia, at http://aso.gov.au/people/Rachel_Perkins/interview/ (accessed 15 July 2013).

Perkins, R. (2006) *Keynote Address, 2006 ATSILIRN 2Deadly Conference*. http://aiatsis.gov.au/atsilirn/conferences/conf06/papers/Rachel Perkins [pdf download] (no longer accessible).

Perkins, R. (2009) "Interview with Rachel Perkins by ACMI", Blak Wave Collection, Australian Centre for the Moving Image, at http://generator.acmi.net.au/gallery/media/interview-rachel-perkins (accessed 15 July 2013).

Povinelli, E. (2002) *The Cunning of Recognition: Indigenous Alterities and the Making of Australian Multiculturalism*, Durham, NC: Duke University Press.

Warner, M. (2002) *Publics and Counterpublics*, New York: Zone Books.

19

THE HOLOCAUST DOCUMENTARY

Sense, meaning, and redemptive politics

Brad Prager

Shortly before the ending of *Schindler's List* (Spielberg, 1994), perhaps the most well-known feature film about the Holocaust, the Jews who had been under Oskar Schindler's protection are liberated by Germany's surrender and freed from servitude. A passing Soviet soldier, in response to being asked what they should now do, tells the former prisoners to go neither east nor west, because they are wanted in neither direction. He then points off-screen and proposes: "Isn't there a town over there?" The soldier's gesture is allegorical: it indicates the future represented by Palestine without actually naming it. At this point Spielberg cuts to a wide-angle shot of the survivors crossing a field, and, as an indication of the direction in which they are now meant to be walking, we hear the folk song "Jerusalem of Gold." Following a brief cutaway to a staging of Amon Goeth's hanging and then some words about Schindler's eventual fate, the film returns to the Jews. The image dissolves to color, moving the narrative out of the past and into the present. The actors are replaced by their older counterparts, and at the bottom of the screen the title appears: "The Schindler Jews today." This famous feature film thus concludes as a documentary. Spielberg ultimately cuts away to Schindler's grave marker, and one by one the still-living Holocaust survivors, in many cases accompanied by the actors and actresses who played them, reverently lay small stones on the protagonist's grave.

Spielberg's account of Schindler's activities – the main part of the film – is presented as true-to-life insofar as it exhibits the appearance of authenticity. It not only draws on fact-based source material, but is also rendered in black and white (or, rather, in shades of gray), which, many have asserted, makes the film seem closely connected to newsreel footage contemporary with the era it depicts (Ball 2008: 172–3). At the end of the film, however, Spielberg goes one step further, documenting his subjects' encounters with the actual gravesite of the film's true-life main character. If the film's status as having been based on a true story were not enough to impress viewers as authentic, real and close to its sources, the documentary ending is intended to seal the deal. The film at this point asserts that it is fact-based, and it projects all the gravitas of documentary realism.

Schindler List's conclusion drives home the reality of the storyline while also turning its attention to Palestine. Its narrative first brings all of its semi-fictionalized characters from Europe to the Middle East, and it then supplements that gesture with a documentary visit to Schindler's grave in Mount Zion Cemetery in Jerusalem. Omer Bartov describes this as a "Zionist/ideological closure" (1997: 45), and he directly addresses the fact that the film is meant to carry more weight because of its final nod to authenticity. Bartov adds, "the film's final Zionist twist" brings the matter "to a worthy conclusion, giving (retrospective) sense and meaning to an event which for its victims had neither" (1997: 48). The Holocaust, one might say, was senseless violence, and it seemed even more senseless for those who endured it. Presumably Bartov here is echoing a sentiment expressed by Holocaust survivor Ruth Klüger, who famously wrote that lessons learned from Auschwitz are typically "sentimental rubbish" and that they depend on "a false concept of suffering as a source of moral education" (2003: 52). Similarly, the Italian survivor Primo Levi elevated a description of the camps spoken to him by a guard at Auschwitz, "there is no 'why' here," to the level of a principle, and it became his own answer to those who sought an explanation for the causes of human evil (1996: 29). Although it is surely polemic to argue that there is nothing to learn from the Holocaust, Klüger and Levi positioned themselves against those who seek to reduce the event to either singular causes or redemptive consequences.

Bartov's critique of the "sense and meaning" implied by Spielberg's film appears in his discussion of its Zionism, and the type of closure he describes is common among Holocaust films, both documentaries and features. Israel was founded in May 1948, shortly after the Second World War, and its creation is irrefutably tied to atrocities committed against the Jews. However, linear arguments about that origin simplify history and potentially mislead. Zionism had been a movement long before the Biltmore Conference of 1942, dating back to the First Zionist Congress in Basel in 1897, if not long before, in a variety of antecedent forms. For many Jews who lived in Palestine before, during, and after the Holocaust, Israel was not perceived as having been founded on the basis of recent atrocities. The historian Dan Diner describes alternative narratives, and asserts that the direct connection to the Holocaust is based largely on the memories of Holocaust victims. Describing two strains of "internal historical interpretation and legitimation in Israeli self-identity," he designates them "*yishuv*-ist" and "*shoah*-centric," and these refer to differing tendencies that serve as points of orientation for collective memory (2000: 206–207).[1] Describing the changing conception of the Jewish people, Diner posits the formation of a "quasi-political notion" after the war, that was "intended to unite the Jews," but which failed "to do justice to the historical reality of the Jews in the diaspora prior to Auschwitz" (2000: 209). The proposition that Israel's founding was an immediate and logical postscript to the Holocaust is misleading, yet a number of Holocaust documentaries participate in the same narrative trajectory as *Schindler's List*: they conclude in Palestine or in contemporary Israel and, as in *Schindler's List*, they suggest that the birth of Israel provides redemptive closure to recent tragedies, thereby turning an event, which, from Klüger's and Levi's perspectives is irredeemable, into a story about the founding of a nation.

Claude Lanzmann, who directed the nine-and-one-half hour Holocaust documentary *Shoah* (1985), has notoriously spoken out against finding redemptive meaning in Holocaust atrocities, and his own film is calculated to offer hermeneutic resistance. It deliberately does not include any of the mostly black-and-white footage taken during that era, in part because most of those images were taken by perpetrators, but also because, as Henry Pickford notes, Lanzmann believes that the power of his film is located "precisely in its being composed entirely of speech and gestures surrounding the absence of the images it speaks about" (2013: 176). At its center is a conviction concerning unrepresentability; in Lanzmann's view no representation can approach the horrific depths of the event itself. If we accept the director's premise that *Shoah* relies on viewers confronting the ultimate ineffability of past atrocities, his film is not a documentary in the traditional sense at all; it avoids filmic and photographic depictions of what is supposedly its principal subject.

Owing to the success of the film, Lanzmann has become a leading French thinker on the topic of the Holocaust, and his assertion that there is an "obscenity in the very project of understanding" (1995: 204) the Holocaust is widely known. He explains that he had one principle when he made the film: "Not to understand was my iron law during all the eleven years of the production of *Shoah*. I clung to this refusal of understanding as the only possible ethical and at the same time the only possible operative attitude" (ibid.). In thinking about the causes of the Holocaust, Lanzmann says that the various explanations are "all true and all false." He summarizes that one cannot "engender" the Holocaust, and that:

> Between all these conditions – which were necessary conditions maybe, but they were not sufficient – between all these conditions and the gassing of three thousand persons, men, women, children, in a gas chamber, all together, there is an unbreachable discrepancy. It is simply not possible to engender one out of the other. There is no solution of continuity between the two; there is rather a gap, an abyss, and this abyss will never be bridged.
>
> *(1995: 206)*

Lanzmann is here speaking more about the obscenity of trying to reduce perpetration – the question of why the Germans and other perpetrators did what they did – to one cause, more than he is speaking about whether one can understand the victims' experience, which is a separate problem. It is, however, fair to ask whether *Shoah* steers clear of the pitfalls Lanzmann describes, or whether it is among those films that give, in Bartov's words, retrospective sense and meaning to the event. From Lanzmann's point of view such attempts are obscene, and it would seem that his film, with its more than nine hours of intense and extremely detailed interviews, makes no single, isolated argument. The Holocaust neither happened for any specific reason, nor is there one lesson that must be drawn from it.

Lanzmann's film was made in the years immediately following his *Pourquoi Israël* (1973), a 185-minute film about contemporary Israel, which he released at a time of particular turmoil: its US opening at the New York Film Festival coincided with the onset of the Yom Kippur War. Politicization was unavoidable. The *New York Times* reviewer concluded,

> as a French Jew [Lanzmann] loves Israel and is also highly critical of it. […] He's said that he didn't seek to make a political picture. Yet he knows that almost any aspect of life in Israel is hinged to politics.
>
> *(Sayre, 1973: 40)*

The film's first speaking subject is Gert Granach, a former member of the German Communist Youth, who sings for the camera a song about resistance to Hitler. Lanzmann then immediately cuts to a memorial to Holocaust victims at Yad Vashem in Jerusalem where the names of concentration and death camps are etched in the floor, surrounding an eternal flame. The words Auschwitz, Mauthausen, Jasenovac, and Bergen-Belsen appear on the screen in Hebrew and Roman letters. He then depicts a school group listening to a lecture: they are told that they should not forget the past. The film subsequently steers away from this theme, touching on it periodically during the course of the film. An Israeli policeman, for example, recounts how it hurts him when people call him a Nazi for merely doing his job, explaining that he himself is a Holocaust survivor, and Lanzmann's documentation of Israeli prison culture lingers on images of fences and watchtowers that resemble the camps. The film ultimately asks whether Israel can have laws, whether it can act as a government with police and prisons, while attempting to avoid reproducing repressive mechanisms of totalitarian states.

Pourquoi Israël is similar to *Shoah* in technique, but the central issue of the earlier film leans more toward a discussion of whether and how Israel functions as a multicultural, multilingual society, the pitfalls of occupation, and what kind of economic distribution would be best for the nation's people. Lanzmann reminds readers of his autobiography that there is no question mark in the film's title (2012: 410); *Pourquoi Israël* is, in other words, the answer to the question rather than the question itself. He also explains how his two documentary projects were connected: in 1973, his friend Alouph Hareven, director-general of the Israeli Ministry of Foreign Affairs, spoke to him, "with a gravity and solemnity" as never before. He congratulated him on *Pourquoi Israël* and then said:

> There is no film about the Shoah, no film that takes in what happened in all its magnitude, no film that shows it from our point of view, the viewpoint of the Jews. It's not a matter of making a film *about* the Shoah, but a film that *is* the Shoah. We believe that you are the only person who can make this film. [...] If you agree, we'll help you out as much as we can.
>
> (2012: 411)

Lanzmann summarizes: "So the idea for *Shoah* is not mine, I had not even thought about it: although the Shoah is central to *Pourquoi Israël*, I had never thought about tackling such a subject head on" (ibid.).

Seeing the films in connection with one another, a standpoint on Israel emerges: Lanzmann has made clear that Israel is absolutely necessary for Jewish self-defense, and Manuel Köppen connects *Shoah* with Lanzmann's later documentary *Tsahal* (1994), asserting that those two films, along with *Pourquoi Israël*, form a trilogy that narrates the story of the Jewish appropriation of power and force. *Tsahal* looks into the development of the Israeli Defense Forces (IDF), and Lanzmann, in his films, establishes a historical trajectory, one that links the massacres of innocents during the Holocaust to the heroism of Jewish soldiers in modern Israel. Köppen describes the uprising at Sobibor and the foundation of Israel as "reappropriations of power and force" (2007: 80). Lanzmann's assertion about the need for a state, and the logic, especially the progression from the uprising of prisoners at Sobibor (to which he also dedicated a film) to contemporary national defense could not be clearer. Although *Shoah* makes no singular meaning out of the Holocaust – it does not say that the answer to the Holocaust was the creation of Israel – it is linked to a number of other films where the story of violence against the Jews undergirds Israel's founding. It is part of the tale of the appropriation of Jewish military power, seen in acts of defiance in the Warsaw Ghetto and at Sobibor, each of which are stories of guerrilla resistance, and this three-part narrative concludes with *Tsahal*, a documentary about the IDF.

In his autobiography Lanzmann reflects on a speech he made in 1967 about the unconditional need for Israel, but he was careful to separate those claims from the idea that Israel only exists because of the Holocaust:

> Let me be clearly understood: I never considered Israel as the redemption for the Shoah, the idea that six million Jews gave their lives so that Israel might exist; such a teleological argument whether explicit or implicit is absurd and obscene. Political Zionism long pre-dates World War II.
>
> (2012: 388)

On this point he echoes that of the historian Dan Diner. He then voices his objections to the ending of *Schindler's List*, noting how it is distinct from the ending of *Shoah*:

> In contrast [with *Schindler's List*], the last scene of *Shoah* shows a goods train moving endlessly through the twilight of the Polish countryside. But there was no need to believe in any redemption or final salvation to be repelled by the prospect of a second bloodshed of the same people twenty-five years later. For it is also true that the state of Israel was born of the Shoah, that a causal relationship connects these two key events in the history of the twentieth century, and that a core of Israel's population is made up of survivors and refugees weary of suffering.
>
> (388–89)

Lanzmann begins *Pourquoi Israël* with the Holocaust, giving it central importance, even though political Zionism, as he well knows, "long pre-dates World War II." For his film to connect the Holocaust and the founding of Israel directly – to link them as straightforwardly as Spielberg had – would have been redemptive; it would have been anathema to his approach.

But Lanzmann is hardly the best interpreter of his own work, and viewers may disagree with him. Ferzina Banaji points out that Lanzmann's own idea about how *Shoah* ends does not tell the whole story, noting that the last words of the film actually belong to Simcha Rotem, one of the fighters in the Warsaw Ghetto Uprising, who, in narrating his return to the ghetto at the end of the uprising, describes the feeling that he was the last surviving Jew. Banaji observes that in *Shoah*'s penultimate sequence Rotem stands in the Ghetto Fighters' Kibbutz in Israel, and his placement underscores both that he was not the last Jew, and that he "eventually found his way to Israel, a state that commemorates this tragedy in the memorial from which he speaks." These final images thus expose a tension "between ruin and recovery," and, she adds, "the underlying assumption is that the Jew of Europe is not really safe until he or she discovers the safety offered by the state of Israel" (2012: 98–99). Lanzmann believes that his film does not share *Schindler's List*'s straightforward Zionist resolution, yet Banaji understands the film's ending in nationalist terms.

Until that point a good deal of French cinema about the Holocaust, especially Marcel Ophuls's *The Sorrow and the Pity* (1969), had concerned itself with French wartime experience and with the issue of collaboration. There had been exceptions such as Frédéric Rossif's *The Time of the Ghetto* (1961), which centered on Jewish suffering in the Warsaw Ghetto, but *Shoah*'s emphasis on the trans-European persecution of the Jews – Lanzmann's showcasing of German and Polish anti-Semitism and of the memories of survivors in Israel and the United States – was distinctive. Much postwar French thinking about the matter had been shaped by French involvement in Algeria and the Algerian War, which lasted from 1954 to 1962. On May 8, 1945 ("V-E Day"), when combat ended in Europe and German forces surrendered in France, hundreds of Algerian civilians were killed by French Army soldiers in what is known as the Sétif massacre, an event often cited as the true beginning of the Franco-Algerian conflict. It is therefore no wonder that the two wars were connected in French minds. In his autobiography Lanzmann states that Israel had disappeared from his thoughts "for a whole decade, between 1952, the year of [his] first trip there, and 1962, when the war in Algeria ended," then adding, "or at least it faded into the background" (2012: 376). He was more concerned with the role of the French in Algeria than with the embattled Jewish state, and in this regard his standpoint is similar to that of Alain Resnais, whose *Night and Fog* (1955) dealt with the Holocaust, even though he later averred that it really had been a statement about Algeria (Lichtner 2008: 29).

The dispute about *Night and Fog*'s true subject has been enabled by what is described as the film's "universalism." To be sure, Resnais's film does not directly refer to Algeria, but its ending is geared toward contemporary audiences and provokes them to consider their own potential culpability. Near its conclusion, as it is answering the question posed by the French poet Jean Cayrol, who wrote the film's screenplay, *Night and Fog* asks, "who is responsible?" The voice of the French actor Michel Bouquet explains that the faces of "new executioners" in the future will not be different from our own, and that somewhere among us there are still unknown kapos, officers, and informers. As the film's final shot depicts a crumbling crematorium, Cayrol's screenplay concludes:

> And there are those of us who sincerely look upon the ruins today, as if the old concentration camp monster were dead and buried beneath them. [...] Those of us who pretend to believe that all this happened only once, at a certain time and in a certain place, and those who refuse to see, who do not hear the cry to the end of time.

The ending is hardly redemptive. The ruined crematorium had been presaged by the film's emphasis on architectural space and on the apparatus of industrial murder; it would be difficult to connect this conclusion with a Zionist narrative insofar as Resnais and Cayrol do not explore in depth whether the destruction of crematoria or the rebellion at Auschwitz can be linked to a story of Jewish resistance, nor does the film spend time sanctifying Jewish fighters. Its argument is structural: the buildings in which all this violence was permitted now lie in pieces, and, these final images, when coupled with Cayrol's text, caution the viewer that this may only be a temporary condition. While these visions of ruins may suggest the fading of memory, and particularly the question of whether the icy waters nearby will overtake the site, erasing it, the allegorical remains also point toward another possibility. The act of completing the ruined structures in the imagination serves as a reminder that the horror could recur. It is, in this sense, not an image of renewal and hope, but rather one of renewal and fear. The fragments of buildings challenge viewers to envision the whole structures that once stood there and along with them the potential return of industrialized killing.

Night and Fog is considered iconic because, unlike *Shoah*, it draws from a visual archive of atrocity, relying on the most powerful footage its director could find. Some of its images were already widely known and others became so over time. Possibly because of his critical standpoint on perpetrator images, but perhaps more because of the compact nature of Resnais's film, Lanzmann forced a Parisian theater in 1987 to pull *Night and Fog*, when he discovered it was playing back-to-back with *Shoah* (Lowy 2001: 85–86). Most of the controversy that dogged *Night and Fog*, however, concerned its narrative content rather than its selection of iconic and powerful visual images: it is careless in failing to distinguish concentration camps from extermination camps; it does not provide some needed context (viewers may not know, for example, that British forces are driving the bulldozers that relocate the piles of corpses subsequent to the liberation); and it makes no direct reference to the victims' Judaism, apart from a single glancing mention of a Jewish student, a remark that remained for many years untranslated in the English subtitles. This dearth of references to Jews coupled with the universalism of its message led to criticism. Robert Michael, writing for the US journal *Cineaste* wrote, "*Night and Fog* omits the particularity of the Jewish Holocaust, and, in so doing, it emphasizes the universal at the expense of the particular. [...] The Jews vanish with hardly a trace" (1984: 36). Michael treats Erwin Leiser's less aesthetically pioneering documentary *Mein Kampf* (1960), released four years after Resnais's film, as far better in this regard. That film leaves no ambiguity: the Jewish community was the Nazis' main target. Ewout van der

Knaap summarizes that *Night and Fog* "was alleged to have 'unjewished' the Holocaust and not openly enough foregrounded the anti-Semitic goals of the Nazis" (2006: 18). Van der Knaap, however, points out that the French audience might well have known who the victims were, and that they did not need it said. He adds that Jews are visible throughout the film, and that viewers probably would have "recognized the names of places mentioned as being cities where Jews used to live" (ibid.).

The universal message of the film – its position against genocidal violence in general, rather than against anti-Semitism – was an issue for some Israelis, and there were calls for *Night and Fog*'s suppression. Nitzan Lebovic cites a review in March 1960 by a critic in the daily newspaper *Maariv* who viewed the exclusion of the Jews as deceitful and deliberate:

> Had Resnais not shown himself to be an intellectual and a great artist, I would have guessed that this 'small detail' had been forgotten, that the victims were merely Jews. But a person such as Resnais would not forget such a detail. Resnais set out to make us forget this fact. [...] the film makes an appeal for stricter morality, while presenting its own half-morality [...] It is painful enough to see the German 'Nuit et Brouillard' – we do not need Resnais's 'fog' as well – it's just too much.
>
> *(Quoted in Lebovic, 2006: 96)*

As *Shoah* was a documentary that seemed to exclude its principle object (the image of atrocity), *Night and Fog* was accused of excluding the suffering of Jewish victims. The films share in common an opposition to redemptive endings: whatever security there is, it may only be temporary, and genocide is an ever-threatening specter. Resnais's decisions were treated as having been political, and Israelis took umbrage. Given the instinct on the part of most institutionalized commemorative cultures to perceive the real estate of memory as limited, many did not feel there was room in *Night and Fog*'s reception for both its universalizing message, directed perhaps toward French imperialist policies, and a strong statement about Nazi violence against the Jews.

Only a year after this critical review was written, *Night and Fog* was screened at Adolf Eichmann's trial in Jerusalem. On June 8, 1961 the court watched films from the camps, and Eichmann, as he is captured in Leo Hurwitz's trial footage, barely seems to react. The Israeli journalist Haim Gouri describes the scene:

> The sound is not played ('so that the narration will not influence the court'). We are back in the age of the silent movies. And it is a good thing for us too, because it allows us to supply our own narration or to experience on a preverbal level what is being shown.
>
> *(2004: 133)*

This assertion is misleading when it comes to *Night and Fog*, which played for the court with its English language subtitles; viewers did not have to supply their own narration. Although the subtitles were imprecise, the film's argument was clear. And although some Israelis had objected to the perceived absence of the words "Jew" or "Jewish" in the film, it was deemed legitimate enough to be entered into evidence at the Jerusalem district court where the trial was being held.[2]

Eichmann's trial was a watershed. Even though much testimony had been collected in the period immediately after the war, this was the first time that many of these powerful accounts from the Nazis' Jewish victims in Israel had been publicly aired. In 1962 Gouri published his journal of the trial in Hebrew, and Lebovic contrasts the standpoint of Gouri's book with that of the film *Night and Fog*, noting that Gouri echoes "the heavily ideological language of description of the time." Gouri's praise for the prosecutor's arguments, Lebovic writes, opposes Resnais's emphasis. He notes that if Gouri's attention

> was directed here towards the present and its possible lessons for the future, Resnais's film seems embedded in the sadness of the catastrophic past, and the impossibility to carry anything out of its horrific fallout. If for Resnais the concentration camps illustrate the murky philosophical dead-end, for Gouri it seems more like a bright cathartic moment that shifts all eyes towards a new beginning.
>
> (2006: 94)

This constellation of positions had consequences for the trajectory of the Holocaust film insofar as Gouri went on to script the Israeli-made Holocaust documentary *The 81st Blow* (Bergman and Ehrlich, 1975). That film, as Golda Meir points out in a filmed introduction attached to most versions, was produced by people in the Ghetto Fighters' Kibbutz, among whose number were the last remaining survivors of the Warsaw Ghetto Uprising. Meir explains that the film is important because of the ongoing struggle against the influence of the propaganda connected with the invented Protocols of the Elders of Zion, propagated by anti-Semites. *The 81st Blow* is filled with archival material culled from many sources and spoken text drawn from evidence presented at the Eichmann trial. It concludes with an apology to those whose stories were not told, especially the partisans and Jewish soldiers who fought in the name of Israel under other banners. The Israeli documentary thus provides an answer to the universalism and lack of specificity Gouri might have seen in *Night and Fog*.

The trial itself changed Israel's orientation with respect to Holocaust memory; not only had Israel's Secret Service found and captured Eichmann, but the nation had prosecuted and punished him, and the proceedings were broadcast throughout the world. The trial was key both in terms of revelation and retribution, and these were the subjects of the Israeli filmmaker Eyal Sivan's Holocaust documentary *The Specialist* (2000). Sivan re-released 100 minutes of newly edited and digitally manipulated trial footage, which was intended to provoke a reckoning with the trial's theatricality, and it was also explicitly intended to serve as an adaptation of Hannah Arendt's 1963 *Eichmann in Jerusalem: A Report on the Banality of Evil*. Sivan's film emphasizes the extent to which Eichmann was a banal bureaucrat, as it underscores by showcasing his pencil pushing and his endless rearrangement of the small desk confined within his glass booth. Music and intermittent effects bring out the histrionic character of the Israeli prosecution. Arendt had been accused – by Gershom Scholem and many others – of being too harsh a critic of Israel, and the film, following her lead, holds the prosecution accountable for excessive stage management, highlighting the performative aspects of the prosecutor's speeches to the court (Buerkle 2008: 212; Sinclair 2013: 52).

The ending of *The Specialist* is curious: we are first presented with a familiar image of Eichmann in his glass booth, surrounded by guards. Gradually, the guards, the chairs, and Eichmann's booth are each digitally removed from the image and the screen is overtaken by Eichmann's desk, which is suddenly colorized and which consumes the image's bottom half, placing the unfeeling bureaucrat front-and-center. The manipulated image imposes Eichmann's banality on the viewer, as if to say that the menace endures as long as there are sneering middle managers. In these respects Sivan's film thinks with Arendt, as well as with *Night and Fog*, insofar as it is cautionary about the persistent presence of murderers among us, and it is also directed against Gouri: the prosecution was far from perfect, and the true hazards have outlived the verdict. Darcy Buerkle points out that this irredemptive stance is taken still further in the film's lack of a clear endpoint: close-ups of Eichmann's face accompany the rolling end credits, and the repetitive strains of Tom Waits's "Russian Dance" insistently play, reaching a near climax and then, one time after the next, starting over again. Buerkle writes, "the film is not over until the point at which it literally stops rolling," which she views as an extension of Arendt's claim that, "it could happen again and that, in fact, it would not be that difficult to accomplish since Auschwitz did not require the unimaginable. The horror, thus, has also not fully come to an end" (2008: 229).

Sivan's earlier film *Izkor: Slaves of Memory* (1991) tackles related issues, and provides important background for understanding *The Specialist*. That documentary was shot in April 1990 during the single month in which Israel commemorates Passover, the Day of Holocaust Commemoration, the Day of Commemoration of Israeli soldiers, and Israeli Independence Day. In that film Sivan examines how Israel suffers beneath the weight of its surfeit of memory. The documentary moves through the holidays, centering specifically on school children and arguing that acts of remembrance share ground with indoctrination. The camera surveys places such as the dimly lit Children's Memorial at Yad Vashem and the Warsaw Ghetto Fighters memorial, and we watch children prepare for a commemorative pageant, knowing neither how to pronounce the words Bialystok or Theresienstadt, nor what those names signify. Teachers explain to students that Israel is built upon the ruins of the Shoah, and Sivan depicts a number of disaffected teenagers learning about the Biltmore conference, that is, that Israel was founded in answer to the Holocaust. The teacher dictates and the students write down that it was necessary to implement the Biltmore Program after the war because the lesson of the Shoah was clear: "we must have an independent state." Sivan is unambiguously critical of this overabundance of memory. Even if Yeshayahu Leibowitz, an outspoken critic of Israeli policy, were not articulating these positions throughout the film, it would be evident that Sivan believes these young people are being made to vocalize a history they do not understand.

Even American Holocaust documentaries frequently treat Israel as a point of orientation. *Forgiving Dr. Mengele* (2005), an independent documentary by Bob Hercules and Cheri Pugh focuses on Eva Kor, a Romanian Holocaust survivor who places herself at the center of a controversy: she openly and insistently proclaims her forgiveness for Josef Mengele and other Nazis. The documentary, which follows her from place to place, was shot mainly between 2001 and 2004, and its present – its 'here and now' – is contemporary Terre Haute, Indiana. Kor works there as a real-estate agent, who sometimes wears a red, white, and blue American flag silk scarf around her neck. She is sympathetic in her desire to convince others that forgiveness is a worthwhile project, even (and perhaps especially) if you are forgiving people for the worst imaginable crimes. Although her position aggravates her fellow survivors – particularly those who, like herself, are twin siblings, on whom Mengele performed his worst experiments – she is a source of great inspiration for school children and others.

The film eventually turns its attention to the Arab-Israeli conflict. Near to its conclusion Hercules and Pugh bring Kor to Israel's West Bank in 2003 during the second intifada. There, she has an awkward dialogue with Palestinian teachers and an Israeli peace activist. She meets with a professor, who, along with other Palestinians, tells stories of his victimization at the hands of the Israeli secret service. In these situations Kor becomes uncomfortable and resists engaging in productive exchange. She rationalizes the difference – the fact that she can forgive Nazis but is unwilling to warm up to Palestinians – by claiming that, "the idea of forgiveness cannot really happen while people are fighting for their lives." It is an interesting analogy for the film to pursue, especially because the filmmakers choose not to make the terms explicit. The sequence does not really say who is meant to forgive whom and for what, and this may be its strength. As a documentary about redemption, it resists redemption. The trip to Israel depicts Kor as having a history she cannot get beyond. There are, it seems to suggest, limits on her ability to forgive.

Whether such films are French, Israeli, or American, they generally find points of contact between their representations of the Holocaust and the founding of Israel. There is no denying that the two are connected. What becomes difficult to imagine, however, is a Holocaust documentary that would avoid somehow becoming ensnared in narratives about the nation's founding. Political hazards are endemic to the Holocaust documentary where expectations of realism, relevance, and authenticity creep in, compelling the filmmakers to make claims concerning Israel's past legitimacy and future accountability. It is no surprise that the conclusions – the final sequences of the films in question – are frequently the places where these perspectives are expressed; it often becomes the endpoint of the argument where the Holocaust is concerned.

Notes

1 The term *yishuv* refers to the Jewish people of Palestine prior to the establishment of the State of Israel. *Shoah* is a Hebrew word for "catastrophe" that has come to mean "Holocaust."

2 The version of the film screened at the trial did not subtitle the word "Jewish," as did some later versions.

Bibliography

Ball, K. (2008) "For and Against the *Bilderverbot*: The Rhetoric of 'Unrepresentability' and Remediated 'Authenticity' in the German Reception of Steven Spielberg's *Schindler's List*" in Bathtick, D., Prager, B. and Richardson, M. D. (eds) *Visualizing the Holocaust: Documents-Aesthetics-Memory*, Rochester, NY: Camden House, pp. 138–61.

Banaji, F. (2012) *France, Film and the Holocaust: From* le génocide *to* la shoah, New York: Palgrave Macmillan.

Bartov, O. (1997) "Spielberg's Oskar: Hollywood Tries Evil" in Loshitzky, Y. (ed.) *Spielberg's Holocaust: Critical Perspectives on* Schindler's List, Bloomington: Indiana University Press, pp. 41–60.

Buerkle, D. C. (2008) "Affect in the Archive: Arendt, Eichmann and *The Specialist*" in Bathtick, D., Prager, B. and Richardson, M. D. (eds) *Visualizing the Holocaust: Documents-Aesthetics-Memory*, Rochester, NY: Camden House, pp. 211–38.

Diner, D. (2000) *Beyond the Conceivable: Studies on Germany, Nazism, and the Holocaust*, Berkeley: University of California Press.

Gouri, H. (2004) *Facing the Glass Booth: The Jerusalem Trial of Adolf Eichmann*. 1962. Trans. Michael Swirsky. Detroit, MI: Wayne State University Press, 2004.

Klüger, R. (2003) *Still Alive: A Holocaust Girlhood Remembered*, New York: Feminist Press at CUNY.

Köppen, M. (2007) "Erinnerungslandschaften. Claude Lanzmanns *Sobibor* (2001) und Romuald Karmakars *Land der Vernichtung* (2004)" in Stephan, I. and Tacke, A. (eds) *NachBilder des Holocaust*, Cologne: Böhlau Verlag, pp. 77–90.

Lanzmann, C. (1995) "The Obscenity of Understanding: An Evening with Claude Lanzmann" in Caruth, C. (ed.) *Trauma: Explorations in Memory*, Baltimore, MD: Johns Hopkins University Press, pp. 200–20.

Lanzmann, C. (2012) *The Patagonian Hare: A Memoir*. Trans. Frank Wynne. New York: Farrar, Straus and Giroux.

Lebovic, N. (2006) "An Absence with Traces: The Reception of *Nuit et Brouillard* in Israel," in van der Knaap, E. (ed.) *Uncovering the Holocaust: The International Reception of* Night and Fog, London: Wallflower Press, pp. 86–105.

Levi, P. (1996) *Survival in Auschwitz*. 1947. Trans. Stuart Woolf. New York: Simon and Schuster.

Lichtner, G. (2008) *Film and the Shoah in France and Italy*, London and Portland, OR: Vallentine Mitchell.

Lowy, V. (2001) *L'histoire infilmable. Les camps d'extermination Nazis à l'écran*, Paris: L'Harmattan.
Michael, R. (1984) "A Second Look: *Night & Fog*," *Cineaste* 13.4, pp. 35–7.
Pickford, H. W. (2013) *The Sense of Semblance: Philosophical Analyses of Holocaust Art*, New York: Fordham University Press.
Sayre, N. (1973) "Film Fete: 'Israel Why'. Lanzmann's Documentary Captures a Country Seething with Complexity," *New York Times*, 8 October, p. 40.
Sinclair, P. (2013) "Drama and Narrative in Hannah Arendt's Eichmann in Jerusalem," *Journal of Narrative Theory* 43.1, pp. 41–63.
Van der Knaap, E. (2006) "The Construction of Memory in Nuit and Brouillard" in Van der Knaap, E. (ed.) *Uncovering the Holocaust: The International Reception of* Night and Fog, London: Wallflower Press, pp. 7–33.

20

A BRIDGE OVER TROUBLED WATER?

Loving Jews and Muslims in two recent Mediterranean films

Yosefa Loshitzky

One of the dominant themes in contemporary European films about migration and diaspora is the trope of 'forbidden love', "the cross-racial love story or union which very often is presented as the 'solution' (or allegory) to the 'immigration problem'" (Loshitzky 2010: 78). The films discussed in this chapter, *Seres queridos/Only Human* (Harari and Pelegri, 2004) and *Mauvaise foi/Bad Faith* (Zem, 2006), respectively 'representing' two major Mediterranean countries, Spain and France, involve a narrative of interfaith love affair between a Jewish woman and a Muslim man. Like many other films of this emerging genre in European cinema *Only Human* and *Bad Faith* convey the escalating dominant discourse of Europe's anxiety regarding its new migrants and others within. Yet, what is particularly interesting in the love stories portrayed in these films is that religion crossing, and not 'race' constitute the act of 'transgression' and 'miscegenation'. Consequently, this chapter suggests that *Only Human* and *Bad Faith* both confront and renegotiate the symbolic political space that the new cultural racism occupies in the growing debate on 'the immigration question' in Europe. This debate has 'racialized' religion (particularly Islam) because 'race', in its former 'biological' and pseudo-scientific guise, is not only a taboo but also, a legally sanctioned concept in post-Holocaust Europe.

Following the tradition of cultural studies and its interest in popular, low-brow cultural products through the deconstruction of the interweaving domains of culture, power and politics, I argue in this chapter that the emergence of these two relatively popular films at this particular juncture of time also needs to be addressed in relation to the wider, global context and particularly to the ongoing discourse on 'the war on terror' and the escalation of Islamophobia in Europe, and the West at large, as well as the growing impact of the Israeli-Palestinian conflict on these attitudes and trends.

The, predominantly Catholic, countries, Spain and France 'represented' by the two films, have traditionally been perceived (along with Italy) as epitomizing the so-called Mediterranean civilization "shared among the French, the Spaniards and the Italians, present both on their native shores and in their colonial possessions in North Africa and the Middle East" (Abulafia 2013: xxvi). Furthermore, these countries bear complex relationships with both the 'Muslim question' as well as with the 'Jewish question'. Hence this chapter aims to show how the films negotiate the issue of migration against the memory and the presence of Islam and Judaism in these countries. My analysis focuses specifically on the relationships between the 'Muslim Question' and the 'Jewish question' as sometimes hidden, or even taboo histories of Jewish and Muslim presence in Europe and asks how they project on present-day Europe, still defined as Christian and white, particularly in relation to contemporary European attitudes towards migration and integration.

Only human: humanism, Spanish style

Of the two Mediterranean countries, Spain is the most notable one due to the long historical presence of Islam on its land. Muslim Spain is still a living presence in contemporary Spain and the architectural influence of the Moors, from the monumental Alhambra palace in Granada to the Mezquita de Cordoba, is a recognizable legacy and one of the country's major attractions. Currently, there is a growing Muslim minority in Spain constituted mostly of migrants from Morocco but also new converts to Islam mostly in Granada, the last Muslim emirate in Spain (Rogozen-Sotlar 2012: 611–23). Spain also has a legacy of troubled history with the Jews who were expelled from the country by the Catholic monarchs in 1492, following the fall of the Emirate of Granada. In 2013, Spain gave the opportunity to claim citizenship rights to Sephardic Jews to redeem this expulsion. No such offer was given to Muslims, the *Moriscos*, whose brutal expulsion from Spain continued until 1614 (the decree of expulsion was issued in August 1609).

Only Human, written by Teresa de Pelegrí and Dominic Harari, needs to be read and interpreted against this complex historical backdrop, despite the fact that it was made before the recent announcement of the Spanish government to offer plans to fast-track the naturalization of Sephardic Jews, whose ancestors were expelled five centuries ago from Spain. The film evolves the story of Leni (Marian Aguilera), a television reporter who introduces her Palestinian fiancé Rafi (Guillermo Toledo) to her Jewish family in Madrid, Spain. The encounter is shocking for the apparently prejudiced Jewish family composed of Leni's neurotic and sexually frustrated mother, Gloria (Norma Aleandro), her mostly absent father Ernesto (Mario Martin), her born again Jewish brother David (Fernando Ramallo) and her senile grandfather Dudu (Max Berliner). The only family member who is not scandalized by Leni's 'transgression' is her belly dance-student sister Tania (María Botto), who tries to seduce Rafi. After Rafi accidentally drops a block of frozen soup, hitting a man on the head who might just be Leni's father, the plot gets entangled with many comic turns and surprises and the film finally ends with a happy reunion of this crazy, semi-hysterical family and the Jewish-Palestinian couple.

Israeli new historian, Ilan Pappe, claimed that

> most Israeli filmmakers...feel the need to use the sexual and romantic bridge as a way to understand the other side. Most of the films that courageously deal with Arab-Jewish relationships choose the medium of a love story, which is usually tragic ....

According to Pappe, this need is

> a way to avoid and evade rational recognition of the arguments and feelings of the other side. Nevertheless, these films reflect impressive progress relative to the films made before 1967, in which collaboration with Arabs was possible only given unconditional support of the Zionist project.
>
> (*Pappe* 1998: 108)

Pappe, however, did not forget to mention that there is one salient difference between the attitude of Israeli cinema and the new Israeli historiography towards the topic of friendship and cooperation: "Whereas the historians draw optimistic conclusions from these attempts at collaboration, Israeli cinema, by contrast, chooses the model of Greek tragedy in order to convey a pessimistic message about the impossibility of overcoming the mutual hatred" (1998: 110). In response to Pape's observation, I have argued elsewhere that the shifting of the Israeli-Palestinian conflict into the terrain of forbidden love

> is used in Israeli cinema as a distanciation device. Ultimately the tautological logic of these cinematic tales is that the end of the forbidden love story, and by implication of the conflict, is a chronicle of a death well foretold.
>
> *(Loshitzky 2001: 113–4)*

What is interesting about *Only Human* is that it chose comedy, and not tragedy, to deal with the issue, perhaps because as a Spanish film it maintains some distance from the so-called Israeli-Palestinian conflict, thus allowing it to treat it comically. The choice of comedy to discuss what may look to many Spanish viewers as a faraway conflict is further enhanced by some of the peculiar choices and strategies employed by the film. The Jewish family, which is at the narrative centre of the film, is from an Eastern European background, some of its members have a strong Argentinean accent and it is introduced through a background *Kleismer* music. The otherness of the family and their Eastern European Ashkenazi (rather than Sephardic) origin is enhanced comically by their hair colour. All the family members have ginger hair with the exception of Leni's dark-haired sister who studies belly dancing. Both her appearance as well as her love of belly dancing position her closer to Arab/Muslim culture and it is, therefore, no surprise that she tries to seduce Rafi through an erotic dance. The most ginger of all the family members is the observant brother, who, as the writers explain in the extras commentary to the commercial English DVD release, is naturally blond. David is a born again Jew with fundamentalist, yet according to the *Hallacha* (the Jewish religious law) incorrect and ignorant views.

The otherness of the 'crazy' Jewish family is viewed, within the liberal perspective adopted by the film, in the context of the emerging multicultural Spain resulting from new migration from Africa and Asia. There is a black prostitute in the film and in the end a Chinese girl (who brings the father back on her scooter) with whom, presumably, the born-again David will lose his virginity. The embracing of multicultural Spain is testified by the writers who, ironically, comment in the extras to the commercial English DVD, that here there is another cross love affair and this will be a sequel to the cross love story between a Jew and a Palestinian.

The Palestinian character is, in the words of the writers, very academic: "He is not the stereotypical Palestinian you see on the screen". Rafi is an educated man, a professor of Arabic literature and as one of the writers, correctly, points out, "you identify mostly with Rafi. I think that he is the most sane character". And indeed the film to a large extent is viewed from his point of view, that of the stranger who intrudes into the intimacy of this crazy family and, involuntarily, discovers its dark secrets and paranoias. Yet, despite the characterization of the Palestinian as a 'normal' highly educated individual, the relationships to terrorism, so dominant in mainstream media and Hollywood cinema in particular, are at the centre of this comedy of errors. The identification and association of Palestinians and Muslims with terrorism constitute the comic turn of the film. As the writers in their commentary explain, the filming started before the Madrid bombing. But it happened while shooting the film so the audience is expected to identify with David's 'white paranoia' (Sharma and Sharma 2003: 301–18).

To a certain extent the film subverts the logic of paranoia and violence, which are perpetrated by Jews only, either by the observant son or by the senile grandfather. The political positioning of the film is conveyed in the central scene in which for the first time the lovers quarrel. In a rapid accusatory exchange of the usual cliché type positions of the respective two sides, the Palestinian and the Israeli, they blame each other for the collapse of their relationships. Each of them raises the standard position associated with his/her respective ethno-national-religious group. The verbal exchange of mutual accusations equalizes the two sides and shows them both as 'crazy', forever locked in their eternal conflict. This climactic scene is obviously oblivious to the imbalance between the two conflicting parties. The film essentializes the two sides to the clash, and indeed the writers, in the extras to the commercial English DVD release, openly exposed their position, explaining that the big scene when the couple explodes and throws everything at each other "is a scene when they are both right. Rafi and Leni feel apart because they think apart". This is the reason that the film ends with the essentialist exclamation by the couple that "we'll never think alike".

The question to be asked with regard to the film's depiction of the two minorities, Jews and Muslims, which are intimately connected to the history of Spain, is why did they choose the so called Israeli-Palestinian conflict as the major topic and the immediate political backdrop? Is it an indirect way to discuss this 'hidden' history, these repressed memories of Jews and Muslims? Is it a way to come to terms with the past, the expulsion and forced conversion of Jews and Muslims? And why did the filmmakers choose an Ashkenazi family? Furthermore, the film condenses all the clichés, icons and ideas prevalent in the post-Holocaust European popular imagination of 'the Jew' into the film. The grandfather is a Holocaust survivor and he fought for the 'independence' of the Jewish state built on the forced expulsion and destruction of its indigenous Arab Palestinian population (the *Nakba*).

The choice of the Israeli-Palestinian conflict is not only a way to talk about Jews, Muslims and Christians in Spain but also demonstrates how the ongoing Israeli-Palestinian conflict projects on and affects European attitudes towards Muslim presence in Europe and, consequently, towards migration to Europe. The film's ideology as such, reflects present-day debates on the representations of history subordinated to Eurocentric Zionist historiography, centred, in the words of Ella Shohat, on a "homogenous, static Jewish history of relentless persecution" (1992: 27). Essentializing the conflict and turning it into a conflict between Jew and Arab, Jew and Muslim, ultimately subsume the film, despite its liberal and progressive façade, into the Zionist narrative, which constructs the Arab as the enemy. The film conflates 'the Jew' with the Israeli Jew, hence equating both Judaism and 'Jewishness' with Zionism, thus not allowing a space for other independent Jewish voices be they non-Zionists, post-Zionists or anti-Zionists.

Bad faith: challenging the humanism of the French Republic

Whereas in Spain there is today a visible and sizeable Muslim minority and an almost invisible tiny Jewish presence, France has the largest Muslim and Jewish communities in Europe. There are approximately five million Muslims and 500,000 Jews, half of them from North Africa.[1] The complexity of France's relationships with its Jewish and Muslim minorities (mostly of Maghrebi origin) needs to be addressed, among others, against the historical background of French colonialism, the Dreyfus Affair, Nazi (and Vichy France) anti-Semitism, the foundation of the state of Israel, decolonization of the Maghrebi countries, as well as current events in the Middle East, and particularly the ongoing escalation of the Israeli-Palestinian conflict.

Yet the presence of Islam in France has an even longer history and needs also to be examined against the long history of relationships between France and Muslim populations which include battles against Moorish invasions from Spain, the leadership of the Franks in the Crusades, the history of Napoleonic conquests and massacres in Egypt and Palestine, nineteenth century French colonialism in North Africa, France's imperial designs in the Levant, in Syria, Lebanon and Palestine before, during and after World War I, as well as the participation of France in the 1956 Suez Operation. It is important to mention, even in passing, this history because the tendency today is to focus mainly on the colonization of the Maghreb due to the visible presence of Maghrebi communities in France. Yet, the relationships, as I briefly sketched here, go earlier and deeper. At the expense of making a sweeping generalization it would be not too far-fetched to argue that whereas in the European popular imagination Spain has been 'contaminated' by Muslim blood, France on the other hand, has been seen as the major bastion against the spread of Islam to Western Europe and beyond achieved through its victory in the battle of Poitiers in October 732.

The fact that France is the home of the largest Jewish and Muslim communities in Europe has created its own dynamic of interfaith relationships between these two minorities. In her book *Muslims and Jews in France: History of a Conflict* (2014), Maud S. Mandel challenges what she views as a reductionist narrative of Muslim-Jewish hostility in France, arguing that the conflict between the two minorities has emerged from processes internal to French society itself and not from the ongoing Israeli-Palestinian conflict. Although I agree with Mandel's groundbreaking and scrupulous study, it should be noted that the period that her research covers ends in 2000, before the outbreak of the *Al Aqsa* Intifada in October 2000 and the consequent 9/11 events which have seen the significant escalation of the conflict between the two communities. Since then Muslims have become Europe's new Jews and "Israeli policy has aspired to globalize the Palestinian-Israeli conflict so as to include it in the larger ideological and political frame of the so-called 'war on terror'" (Loshitzky 2006: 331).

Roschdy Zem's first feature *Bad Faith* was released in 2006, the year when the troubled relationships between Muslims and Jews in France reached one of their most tragic peaks with the kidnapping, torture and murder, by a group of young Muslims, of Ilan Halimi, a mobile phone salesman from a Jewish-Moroccan background, in a Paris *banlieue* (Bagneux). *Bad Faith* that was co-written by Zem, a French Muslim from a Moroccan origin (whose own partner is Jewish) with his Jewish co-star Pascal Elbe, is a conscious intervention in this explosive political scene. The narrative centres on a mixed couple, the Jewish Clara (Cecile de France) and the Muslim Maghrebi Ismael (Rochdy Zem) whose relationship starts to deteriorate after Clara discovers that she is pregnant. The objection of Clara's, upper middle class, Ashkenazi family to their union increases the tensions within the couple and triggers a religious-cultural war between them, leading to Clara's decision to abort the unborn child. The film, however, leaves the ending ambiguous and it is not clear whether the pregnancy was terminated or not.

Like Rafi in *Only Human*, Ismael is the antithesis of the media-based stereotype of the Muslim. He is highly educated and articulate. Furthermore he is a musician and a conservatory piano (an icon of the so-called western civilization) teacher. The film not only exposes prejudices of French Jews and French Muslims against each other but also exposes internal Jewish racism existing between the Sephardic and Ashkenazi communities within French Jewry. In a conversation between Clara and her mother, prior to Ismael's first visit to Clara's family home, the mother asks her daughter "Is he one of us?". "'No he is not", Clara responds and the mother, still unaware of the shock awaiting her and pretending to be progressive, responds "We like Sepharadim too".

The film starts with Ismael and his mother watching television clips of Israeli soldiers in a checkpoint preventing Palestinians from crossing. This sets the tone of the forthcoming personal conflict between the lovers and implicitly suggests that the Israeli Palestinian conflict plays a big role in the deteriorating relationships between Jews and Muslims in France. The film, thus, shows the role that news and images from the outside world play in the public sphere and how they affect the most intimate space of the lovers, deeply and disturbingly intruding into their most private sphere. As an antidote to these news images which show the Arab Muslim (embodied by the Palestinian) and the Jew as enemies, at a certain stage in the film, they also watch a TV programme on *Neve Shalom* (the name in Hebrew means literally an oasis of peace), a bi-national cooperative village near Jerusalem (within the boundaries of the green line) where Jews and Palestinians live together, consciously trying to build a common community based on shared life and education and mutual respect. *Neve Shalom*, thus, which not only challenges the politics of 'us' and 'them' but also offers a utopian vision of convivial co-existence between Israeli Jews and Palestinians, Jews and Arabs, Jews and Muslims, becomes the film's organizing utopian vision.

The tension between Jews and Muslims is investigated in the film within the framework of French Republicanism and its supposedly colour/religion/ethnicity blindness. The mother asks the daughter whether her son will be Jewish or Muslim. "French", Clara says, thus stating her loyalty to this ideology based on universalism and secularism (*laicite*). But as soon as Clara violates these very ideals by installing the *Mezuzah* and literally marking the flat as Jewish ("but we said no religion here", Ismael responds), the conflict between the lovers escalates and each resorts to the exhibition of ostentatious religious signifiers associated with his or her 'community' of origin (communitarianism is obviously a very problematic notion in the French context). Ismael begins to fast for the Ramadan, and Clara starts to investigate what is Judaism, or what does it mean to be a Jew in contemporary France. They start as a secular French couple but once the pregnancy (the future) arrives the conflicts start.

The film shows how the Israeli-Palestinian conflict escalates 'Islamism' and contributes to the so-called radicalization of young disenfranchised Muslims and their growing hatred of the French state. The film also subtly raises the French debate and legislation with regard to the veil controversy (*Affaire du foulard*) when in a scene where Ismael and his friends meet at a Ramadan meal in a neighbours' flat he does not recognize Brigitte, a young woman who came back from a visit in Morocco covered with a veil. The growing 'differences' between Clara and Ismael, and their respective growing attachment to practices, rituals and symbols associated with their 'communities' reach their climax in a big row which is very similar to the key quarrel scene in *Only Human*. All the usual accusations identified with each camp are voiced leading to what they view as incompatible routes. Thus, the attempt to save the life of the baby, to prevent an abortion at the last moment is an attempt to salvage the fragile co-existence of Jews and Muslims in France/Europe. It is the attempt to give a rebirth to the Arab Jew and to dissolve the binarism of the Jew and the Muslim in Christian Europe hiding behind the façade of secularism and humanism. Viewed from this perspective the closing scene of the film, depicting a 'normal' professional middle class French couple leaving their apartment in the morning at the start of a busy day and 'disposing' their two little children to the loving and caring arms of their two mothers in law, one an upper class Ashkenazi woman from a Polish background, and one a Muslim Meghrabi woman from the *banlieue*, can be seen as a utopian vision of a convivial cosmopolitan existence in the French capital. The fact that this scene appears as a cinematic and narrative rupture, an extreme temporal (but also ideological) jump cut from the previous scene in the hospital when Clara, lying on a stretch, fixes what can be interpreted only as an accusatory gaze at the devastated Ismael, is a testimony to the utopianism of this cinematic vision of a happy, multi-faith, hybrid family.

Love or hate: Jewish and Muslim identities in the New Europe

Only Human and *Bad Faith* show how European society is struggling to come to terms with its new 'others', particularly Muslims, and demonstrate how the Israeli-Palestinian conflict projects on the relationships between Jews and Muslims (particularly in France) as well as shapes the attitudes of Europe to its Muslim communities and consequently to migration from outside Europe. *Only Human* is a crazy comedy/farce where the screening time almost overlaps with the narrative time. In one-and-a-half hours the problems between Jews and Palestinian Muslims are both exposed and comically resolved. In *Bad Faith*, on the other hand, the ending can be read simultaneously as utopian and realistic. To a large extent *Bad Faith* follows the classical tradition of French cinema psychological realism, leaving it open whether or not Clara had an abortion, whether or not a normal half-Jewish, half-Muslim family is feasible in the contemporary French republic where a chant in colloquial Arabic: "*Ina'al abouk la France*" – "Fuck France" – in riots in mostly Muslim-populated *banileues* is quite common, and where Muslims associate Israel's oppression of the Palestinians with Anti-Muslim Western Imperialism is pervasive. Israel, in the words of Alain Badiou, Eric Hazan and Ivan Segre, is identified "as an advance outpost of the West. It is 'more one of us than we are ourselves', out there on the front line" (Badiou *et al.* 2013: 29). Such a point of view, in fact, reminds us that it was indeed the original vision of the founder of political Zionism, Theodor Herzl, who, as Shlomo Sand observes, was a proponent of Western Orientalism and "saw the future Jewish state vis-à-vis Asia as 'the advance post of civilization against barbarism'" (Sand 2014: 44).

In both *Only Human* and *Bad Faith* the pregnancy of the fair-skinned Jewish woman is impregnate with utopian hopes for transcending the schism of 'the Jew' and 'the Muslim' as well as with realistic (though sometimes comic) difficulties. The hope for *Convivencia* (in Spanish: the co-existence of Jews, Muslims and Christians in Muslim Spain) is a driving force in the two films despite the difference in the political, social and cultural contexts in which they operate. The French film works within the ideology of the French Republic asking what is the meaning of being a Jew or a Muslim in a racist postcolonial society hiding behind the big universalist slogans of *liberte*, *fraternite*, *egalite*. The Spanish film, on the other hand, is attempting to face the 'challenge' of increasingly multicultural Spain, a country still in denial of its Muslim legacy. Within Spain, as Simon R. Doubleday argues, the combined effects of 9/11, the March 11, 2004 attacks in Madrid, the 'war on terror' and North African immigration, have led to

> new exchanges on the 'Oriental question' – Spain's relationship with the Islamic world (and by extension, with Europe) – not least because anxieties in relation to the return of the Muslim 'colonizer' coincide with the concern to present Spain as a fully European nation.
>
> *(2008: 10)*

Daniela Flesler argues that "Spaniards' difficulties with Moroccan immigrants, and their perception of them as 'Moors', becomes a symptom of the slippage between the present and past they produce, and the unsolved historical trauma they awake" (2008: 117). The most obvious example of the slippage of past and present produced by Moroccan immigrants is, according to her, in the way Spaniards name them, and thus recognize them, as *Moros* (Moors). The term is used very loosely in Spain, she explains, "to signify any Arab or Muslim, and carries with it considerable negative connotations" (118). The 'invasion' trope, a very common image to speak of immigration in many different national contexts, has in Spain, she emphasizes, "very specific historical referents, awakening very local affects (ibid.). The return of the past is seen, she argues, in analogy to past 'invasions' and constitutes one of the most contentious issues in the present relationship between Spaniards and Moroccans. Moroccans are imagined not as guests but as hosts who have come to reclaim their territory. What is 'dangerous' about the contemporary return of the 'Moor', she explains, is that "it awakens these fears, encapsulated in the French aphorism 'Africa begins at the Pyrenees', precisely at a moment when Spain seems to have finally achieved truly 'European' status" (121).

Nelly in *Only Human* is a fair-skinned woman with red flaming ginger hair, so unusual in Spain and yet so contrasting with the dark (yet Spanish-looking) Rafi. Clara in *Bad Faith* is blond and European-looking. Her whiteness contrasts with the dark brown Ismael. The look of the two Jewish women epitomizes Europeanness perceived as whiteness. Both could easily pass as 'non-Jewish-looking' young European women. The attempt, in both films, to save the life of the expected baby and to prevent an abortion is, as I argued earlier, an attempt to save the possibility of co-existence of Jews and Muslims in Europe. In both films the Muslim men feel ambivalent about the pregnancy and the prospect of having a child in a racist society. It is the women who try to protect the pregnancy and ensure the birth of the child. As a comedy, *Only Human*, seems to introduce an optimistic tone into the possibility of Jewish-Muslim co-existence. Yet, the film's very generic choice only proves and perpetuates the idea that this co-existence is impossible. The happy ending of the French film, the two grandmothers playing together with their mixed – *metisage* – grandchildren, is also presented as a visualization of a fantasy, a utopian vision more than a realistic portrayal. Yet, the fact that the film leaves it open whether or not the final scene is utopian or not still leaves some space for hope.

Only Human and *Bad Faith* question the compatibility of Muslims with Europe while that of the Jew is unquestioned. In both films the Jewish families pass as European with their white masks (though in the Spanish film they are too red-headed to look Spanish) and assimilation into European middle class culture. The irony is that in both films the Muslim man is highly educated and involved with very prestigious, typically western, professions. Rafi is a university professor and Ismael is a music teacher. In both films the Jewish mother is the most hostile to the idea of marriage, thus acting as the self-appointed custodian of the 'ethnic blood-group' and the 'religious-national womb'. On the other hand, in *Bad Faith* the Muslim mother is very welcoming and glad to hear that she would be a grandmother soon; however, she warns her daughter (with whom she is in constant conflict) to marry only a Muslim man, hence affirming the role of women as the guarantors of the purity of the 'blood group'. In both films the confrontation with the family is the blood test. It exposes the limits of liberalism and open-mindlessness by resorting to culturally constructed symbols and myths of belonging. Yet, both films take pains to establish an imagined contact zone in which cohabitation between Europeans (epitomized by 'the Jew') is deemed to have been possible or not. The idea of *convevienca* is worked through by the films' use of popular genre formats to introduce a utopian solution to the Jew and the Muslim conflict. This is particularly true for the more progressive *Bad Faith*, which laments the growing hostility between Jews and Muslims in France (due mainly, as the film implicitly suggests, to the growing prominence of the Israeli-Palestinian conflict) and yet is prepared to offer what now looks like a utopia of co-existence.

In the supranational context of the European Union, from the vantage point of a supranational Europe, Matti Bunzl argues, "Jews no longer figure as the principal Other but as the veritable embodiment of the postnational order" (2005: 502). As president of the European Commission, Romano Prodi has invoked Europe's Jews in exactly these terms: "in many ways they [the Jews] are the first, the oldest Europeans" (ibid.). Prodi's words, I would argue, interestingly echo Hannah Arendt's who in *The Origins of Totalitarianism* (2009) claims that the

Jews were the first Europeans. The Jew in contemporary post-Holocaust Europe is no longer a pariah. To the contrary, he has become the bearer of Europeanness. Whereas, until the end of World War II it was common to see 'the Jew' as a foreign body, or even, in more virulent forms of Anti-Semitism, as a virus planted in the European body, an alien and dark element contaminating the white body of Europe, contemporary Europe perceives him as the quintessential European.

The normalization of the Jewish presence in Europe, however, is associated with or is coming at the price of delegitimizing Muslim presence in Europe. In contrast to the elevation of 'the Jew' to 'the European', Europeans question whether Muslims can be good Europeans. Islamophobia, in other words, as Matti Bunzl suggests, "functions less in the interest of national purification than as means of fortifying Europe (ibid.)". The European Union "has coupled a nominal commitment to integration with efforts at centralization broadly intended to curb migratory movements, particularly, although not exclusively, from the Arab and Islamic world (504–5)". Moreover, Jews are increasingly constructed as allies in the struggle over Fortress Europe. Europe is no longer threatened by Jews but by 'more dangerous', 'darker' communities, as Muslim Africans and Asians become targets for surveillance and exclusion. The real danger to Europe now, according to this Islamophobic position, is coming not from the other within, 'the Jew' (whose newly acquired white mask is making him 'one of us') but from the other from without, from the influx of mostly Muslim migrants from North Africa and the Middle East. This dynamic is manifested through the growing post-Holocaust rhetoric on the Judeo-Christian heritage of Europe with the expulsion of the Muslim component from this ideologically constructed 'legacy'.

The Palestinian-Israeli conflict also affects the relationships between Jews and Muslims within Europe, particularly in France as *Bad Faith* suggests. The Jewish French scholar Esther Benbassa explains that the attendance of French politicians in the annual dinners of the Representative Council of Jews of France (CRIF) reinforces the view of Arab-Muslims and Blacks of the Jews as insiders, "while they remain *outsiders*" (2007: 80). She argues that because of the ongoing Israeli-Palestinian conflict, Arab-Muslims tend to identify with the plight of Palestinians in the Occupied Territories "assimilating the injustices which they face in Europe with the victimization of their 'brothers' under the Israeli occupation. The next step of conflating all Jews with Israelis is one easily taken" (81). The majority of French Jews called *les sepharades*, Benbassa explains, are North African Jews who "were forced to flee from their lands because of their association with the colonial conditions and among them, one finds the most hardened anti-Arab racists …" (83). Furthermore, she expands, many of them, as is evident in *Bad Faith*, live in the same *banlieues* and even in the same buildings as Arab Muslims. Since the recent aggravation of the Israeli-Palestinian conflict, France's anti-Arab Muslim tendency has found support among Jews, "who espouse this position in hopes of defending Israel. In this respect, the French colonial heritage of discrimination against Arab-Muslims endures among French Jews as well" (ibid.). According to Benbassa, following the invitation of the leader of the far right Phillipe de Villiers, to the funeral of Ilan Halimi "Islamophobia, and especially anti-Arabism, thus serves to unite the Jewish leadership and the Far Right at this particular historical conjuncture" (84). She also blames the Jewish leadership in Europe which has deployed anti-Semitism in order to defend Israel. In France, she elaborates, the Jewish leadership has similarly deployed anti-Semitism and moreover "has used it to provoke a wave of emigration to Israel that has been greatly coveted by Israeli authorities who see France as having the largest supply of Jews in Europe" (84), a claim also made by Badiou *et al.* (2013). Benbassa concludes that in today's world "the expansion of the European Union, unfettered globalization, and economic neo-liberalism have resulted in the hardening of identities and the growth of nationalisms. This time the Other is the Muslim Arab, who replaces the Jew of yesteryear" (ibid.).

The role of the Arab-Israeli conflict in the formation of European identity and its impact on European attitudes towards migration and integration deserves more analysis. This cultural, historical and political background explains, to a certain extent, the reason why I attribute so much historical importance to two films, overloading them with meaning. It is my understanding of them as emblematic films on and of the new Europe, or rather 'fortress Europe'.[2] As films about the experience of migration, they not only signify the emergence of Europe's new strangers and others, but also the shift from the 'Jew' as the classical other of old Europe to the principal 'darker' other of the new Europe, 'the Muslim'. *Only Human* and *Bad Faith* are significant as narratives of identity and sites of struggles over what it means to be a Muslim in contemporary Europe, which as I attempted to demonstrate, is inseparable from what it means to be a Jew in contemporary Europe (or in the European imaginary). In their own peculiar way the two films search for, to use Haun Saussy's words said in a different context, an "ethical solidarity supported by the Mediterranean, a fluid connection among East and West and the three Abrahamic religions" (2013: 5).

Notes

1 The figures have been obtained from the Pew Research Center (www.pewresearch.org – accessed on 16 July 2015).

2 See *Third Text*, vol. 20, no. 6, 2006. This is a special issue on 'Fortress Europe: Migration, Culture and Representation', guest editor, Yosefa Loshitzky.

Bibliography

Abulafia, D. (2013) *The Great Sea: A Human History of the Mediterranean*, London and New York: Penguin Books.

Badiou, A., Hazan, E. and Segre, I. (2013) *Reflections on Anti-Semitism* (trans. David Fernbach), London and New York: Verso.

Benbassa, E. (2007) "Xenophobia, Anti-Semitism, and Racism: Europe's Recurring Evils?" in Bunzl, M. (ed.) *Anti-Semitism and Islamophobia: Hatreds Old and New in Europe*, Chicago: Prickly Paradigm Press, pp. 77–89.

Bunzl, M. (2005) "Between Anti-Semitism and Islamophobia: Some Thoughts on the New Europe", *American Ethnologist*, 32(4), pp. 499–508.

Doubleday, S.R. (2008) "Introduction: 'Criminal Non-Intervention': Hispanism, Medievalism, and the Pursuit of Neutrality" in Doubleday, S.R and Coleman, D. (eds) *In the Light of Medieval Spain*, Basingstoke: Palgrave, pp. 1–32.

Flesler, D. (2008) "Contemporary Moroccan Immigration and Its Ghosts" in Doubleday, S.R. and Coleman, D. (eds) *In the Light of Medieval Spain*, Basingstoke: Palgrave, pp. 115–32.

Loshitzky, Y. (2001) *Identity Politics on the Israeli Screen*, Austin, TX: University of Texas Press.

Loshitzky, Y. (2006) "Pathologising Memory: From the Holocaust to the *Intifada*", *Third Text*, 20(3–4), pp. 327–35.

Loshitzky, Y. (2010) *Screening Strangers: Migration and Diaspora in Contemporary European Cinema*, Bloomington and Indianapolis: Indiana University Press.

Mandel, M. S. (2014) *Muslims and Jews in France: History of a Conflict*, Princeton, NJ: Princeton University Press.

Pappe, I. (1998) "*Mada v'Alila bSherut Haleumiyout: Historiographia v'Kolnoa BSichsuch HaAravi-Yisraeli*" / "Science and Plot in the Service of Nationalism: Historiography and Film in the Arab-Israeli Conflict" in Gertz, N., Lubin, O. and Ne'eman, J. (eds) *Mabatim Fictiviyim: Al Kolnoa Yisraeli/ Fictive Looks: On Israeli Cinema*, Tel Aviv: The Open University Press 1998, pp. 92–119.

Rogozen-Soltar, M. (2012) "Managing Muslim Visibility: Conversion, Immigration, and Spanish Imaginaries of Islam", *American Anthropologist*, 114(4), pp. 611–23.

Sand, S. (2014) *How I Stopped Being a Jew* (trans. David Fernbach), London and New York: Verso.
Saussy, H. (2013) "The Refugee Speaks of Parvenus and Their Beautiful Illusions: A Rediscovered 1934 Text by Hannah Arendt", *Critical Inquiry* 40(1), pp. 1–14.
Sharma, A. and Sharma, S. (2003) "White Paranoia: Orientalism in the Age of Empire", *Fashion Theory Journal*, 7(3–4), pp. 301–18.
Shohat, E. (1992) "Rethinking Jews and Muslims: Quincentennial Reflections", *Middle East Report*, 178, pp. 25–29.

PART V

Political Hollywood

INTRODUCTION

Brian Neve

No study of the relationship between contemporary film and politics can avoid separate and distinct treatment of the role of Hollywood. The mainstream American film industry in many ways anticipated contemporary globalisation, and despite the passing of the Cold War and the 'American century' the forms and concerns of cinema in the United States are still rich sources for understanding dominant and recurring representations of its politics. Politicians, like filmmakers, return to an established well of myth and genre, even as they struggle to enact the legends of American global leadership. Contemporary Hollywood needs to reference a variety of public anxieties and the country's internal 'cultural wars', but its treatment of politics in the new century often returns to the shock and trauma of 9/11, and to a 'war' on terror that plays more easily as rhetoric than coherent narrative.

While George Bush's presidency ended in domestic crisis and foreign policy failure, Obama's quieter 'realism' has invoked limited enthusiasm at home, while only partially redressing international scepticism. Hollywood, while still attracted by notions of heroic and patriotic mission, has often embedded them in dystopian stories of science fiction or apocalypse. The chapters in this part explore these and other developments, from the trend towards spectacle as the key attraction, to the depiction of visceral and numbing battleground experience and the retreat from coherent plotting, perhaps especially in long-form 'small screen' drama. There are few easy answers for those in authority in Washington, and it is perhaps not surprising that the cinema turns to scenarios of crisis, catastrophe and global threat to engage or exorcise their public's anxiety.

The writers discuss these trends and explore various sources of political dramaturgy, including contemporary fears of disaster and social crisis, American foreign policy represented in action cinema terms, the doomed heroism of 9/11, and constructions of a wished for (at least by some) forthright presidential response. The final chapter sees the present as part of longer-term developments originating with the revivalist, conservative entertainment of the Reagan era.

Douglas Kellner first reviews contemporary American cinema in terms of its treatment or construction of key notions of social catastrophe and potential apocalypse. He finds a generally pessimistic mix of ideological motifs, from anxieties about corporate conspiracy and an out-of-control biotechnology, to the consequences of a world in turmoil. Allegories drawing on the horror and science fiction genres provide only strained opportunities for positive narrative resolution and traditionally heroic agency. To Kellner, reading film diagnostically as a form of historical testimony, the transition from the George Bush era to the Obama years has seen rather limited change, given perceptions of the impotence of the American state in an age of potential disaster and collapse.

For Geoff King the focus is on a sample of cases dealing with the 2003 Iraq war and its aftermath – films that both question and reassert the status of a central heroic protagonist. King also tracks the way they reference Vietnam War motifs and tropes from the nation's traditional mythology, notably the 'frontiersman'. By concentrating on specialists, mavericks or individuals distinct from the main conflict, the films can combine elements of a broader critique with an intense identification and empathy with the protagonist 'on the ground'. This vicarious experience, achieved with frequent use of an 'unsteady-cam aesthetic', is seen as central to the cinematic impact and appeal.

Ian Scott approaches the topic by examining conflicts between narrative and spectacle in contemporary Hollywood action movies dealing with politics. He traces a tradition beginning with *Star Wars* (1977) through to the super-hero franchises and (using Tom Gunning's phrase) the 'cinema of attractions'. Scott refers to relevant conceptual approaches while also, like King, exploring a small sample of cases. For all their 'inauthentic preposterousness' he finds in two 2013 films (both drawing generally on the terrorism agenda) a forceful projection of a survival struggle with existential meaning for the nation. His key examples bypass precise ideologies but cast a political spell by virtue of the emotional response encoded in the reception experience.

The experience and memory of September 11, 2001 casts a powerful shadow on the twenty-first century treatment of American politics. Eleftheria Thanouli examines the two Hollywood films that directly represent the drama and trauma of that day: *United* 93 and *World Trade Center*. She finds in both an emphasis on ordinary people taking heroic action, and offers revisionist readings that stress their similar process of preparation (consulting the real participants), a complex, fragmented narrative and a sense of the necessary failure of individual (and collective) agency. The author elaborates on this sense of purposeful failure, and the pathos of doomed action. Hollywood's traditional belief in human initiative is countered by overwhelming material constraints, and the films are seen as a significant departure from the classical Hollywood tradition.

Finally in this part, Gary Needham explores 'Reaganite' film, opening and closing his analysis with a discussion of two revealing examples of such cinematic politics of the eighties. He sees the conservative consolidation of American film, between 1976 and 1989, as relevant today, while accepting the greater mix of ideological influences in contemporary Hollywood filmmaking. Needham places this era, with its comfortable place for the film spectator compared to that of the sixties and early seventies, in historical context. Patriarchy and the military were both restored, and the film itself became defined more as a commodity. The writer discusses the long-term effects of this cinema of feeling (rather than thinking), relating it to changing industrial practice, including the emergence of a music-film cross promotion and MTV style.

Together these grounded discussions suggest some key Hollywood responses to a political terrain of Western frustration and vulnerability. There is wish-fulfilment, and a shift to attractions based on spectacle and the direct experience of military engagement. There may be room for critical discourses, but realist treatments of a decisive American mission in the world are difficult to imagine, for politicians and filmmakers alike.

21

SOCIAL APOCALYPSE IN CONTEMPORARY HOLLYWOOD FILM

Douglas Kellner

Introduction

Hollywood films have often provided scenarios of catastrophe, with natural disasters, wars, alien invasions and other natural and fictional forces wreaking catastrophic destruction.[1] In the 2000s, a series of Hollywood films have portrayed apocalyptic catastrophe ranging from environmental disasters to socio-political cataclysms in the forms of genre entertainment and popular films. Global warming, climate change, an unrestrained corporate globalization and neoliberalism that put profit and the marketplace above all other issues, escalating political conflicts and wars, and growing inequality between the 1 percent and 99 percent of global population, have arguably endangered the fate of the earth and the socio-political order. Contemporary Hollywood social apocalypse films have thus addressed a wide range of environmental and socio-political issues concerning threats to the survival of humanity, nature, and civilization.

In general, Hollywood films in the contemporary era put on display historically specific fears, hopes, conflicts, and political ideologies within the contested terrain of 2000s US society. In the 2000s, a cycle of social apocalypse films appeared across traditional Hollywood genres, in which one can distinguish between social apocalypse films that portray social chaos as a product of existing society and technology, those that present forces of nature as perpetrators of catastrophe, and those that present supernatural or alien forces as the agents of apocalypse. One can also differentiate between social apocalypse films that portray potential or unfolding social apocalypse, and films that portray post-apocalyptic conditions, both of which are evident in Hollywood cinema of the 2000s.

In this chapter, I shall suggest how social apocalypse films represent existing political fears and discourses and are grounded in historically specific socio-political contexts. In particular, I shall suggest how a cycle of Hollywood films from the early 2000s through 2008 ground their fears in anxieties over the Bush–Cheney administration and offer specific critique of how their policies could lead to catastrophe.[2] I argue that contemporary Hollywood films transcode fears of apocalyptic crisis and collapse in areas ranging from the environment to the political, economic, and societal order. I deploy a method of diagnostic critique which uses cinema to gain critical historical knowledge of the past and present, constructing readings that tell us what films indicate about the historical period they represent and the period in which they are produced and distributed.[3] From my diagnostic perspective, films provide important insights into the psychological, socio-political, and ideological make-up of a society and culture at a given point in history. Reading film diagnostically allows one to gain insights into social problems and conflicts and to appraise the dominant socio-political problems and crises, fears and hopes, and ideological and political conflicts of the contemporary moment.[4] This approach involves a dialectic of text and context, using texts to read social realities and context to help situate and interpret key films of the epoch. Accordingly, I will engage Hollywood films that contain allegories of catastrophe within the context of the Bush–Cheney era.

The cinema of crisis and apocalypse in the Bush–Cheney era

The Bush–Cheney years were arguably an epoch of unparalleled social and economic crisis. It was a time of crisis in the real estate industry, financial industry, and job market where millions of people lost their homes, savings, jobs, and family, culminating in the economic crisis of 2008 which had global dimensions. The administration pursued wars in Afghanistan and Iraq, declaring a war on terror that has not ceased. Their policies of deregulation privileged oil, gas, energy, weapons and related industries that pose a serious threat to environment, while rolling back environmental protections and policies put in place by previous administrations. Media and popular culture promoted images of violence, social chaos, terrorism, and war that arguably heightened social anxiety, a claim that I shall argue in this chapter is evident in Hollywood films of the era.[5]

Since proliferating catastrophes of everyday life are difficult to face in the mode of realist cinematic representations, many of these extreme experiences of crisis and environmental and societal collapse were represented allegorically in contemporary Hollywood cinema in horror, fantasy, and science fiction genres. Roland Emmerich's *The Day After Tomorrow* (2004) uses the conventions of the disaster film to dramatize the dangers of climate change and global warming, ignored by the Bush–Cheney administration, providing a vision of ecological catastrophe mutating into social apocalypse.[6] In an eco-disaster extravaganza featuring tornados devastating Los Angeles, a massive tidal surge sweeping through Manhattan, and the freezing of the northern hemisphere, Emmerich takes the disaster film to new extremes. The film opens in Antarctica where Professor Jack Hall (Dennis Quaid) and other scientists confront a polar ice shelf cracking. At a New Delhi environmental conference, Hall warns that a change in the Gulf Stream caused by global warming could bring about a dramatic decrease in temperature. The Dick Cheney look-alike Vice President (Kenneth Walsh) is skeptical and notes adverse effects of the Kyoto accord – an international treaty that sets binding obligations on industrialized countries to reduce emissions of greenhouse gases – on the economy. Yet a Scottish scientist (Ian Holm) tells Hall that his studies of plummeting ocean temperatures in the North Atlantic support the hypothesis that sudden climate change could produce another Ice Age.

Highlighting the global nature of ecological crisis, *The Day After Tomorrow* portrays extreme weather events in India, giant hailstones hitting in Japan, and a tsunami inundating New York, followed by a hard freeze of the entire northern hemisphere, with international astronauts viewing the murderous storm systems wreaking havoc in their wake. In an ironic reversal, the film shows people from the northern hemisphere desperately trying to cross the border into Mexico, with Mexican police trying to turn them away.

Climatologist Jack Hall warns the US government that: "in seven to ten days, we'll be in a new Ice Age." When the clueless President (Perry King) in a baseball hat is confronted with the magnitude of the cataclysm, he asks his now-chastened Vice President, "What do you think we should do?" Furthermore, when the disaster hits the cowardly President flees, reversing images of strong Presidents in previous disaster and catastrophe films.[7] Such images transcode popular perceptions of Bush as incompetent and disengaged, of Cheney running the presidency, and highlight the dangers of having an administration which ignores serious problems like global warming and climate change.

The Day After Tomorrow puts on display the potentially devastating effects of failing to take ecological crisis seriously and not having plans to deal with environmental problems. Resonant images of a wall of water crashing down on Fifth Avenue in New York, the Empire State Building and New York skyscrapers cracking apart, the Statue of Liberty half-buried in a frozen ice block, and tornadoes ripping the letters off of the Hollywood sign produce an imagination of disaster that provides cautionary warnings that current problems like climate change, if not addressed, could bring environmental breakdown. While the disaster films of the 1970s presented specific disasters in airplanes, high-rise towers, tour ships, or other sites of modern transportation and life, the social apocalypse films often present the specter of global catastrophe, including apocalyptic scenarios that would end human life on earth.

The Day After Tomorrow can be seen as a socially critical film in that it puts climate change and environmental devastation in a political context related to dangerous effects of human beings on the environment and incompetent political regimes.[8] On the other hand, a catastrophe film like Danny Boyle's *Sunshine* (2007) is politically ambiguous, as in its science fiction scenario, a "Q-ball" that entered the sun's sphere of gravitation caused a cooling of the sun, requiring a dangerous mission to re-ignite it, with a crew flying close to the sun and launching a super-bomb. This scenario calls attention to the fragility of the galaxy and need to take care of the earth, but it does not focus on human practices that cause environmental catastrophe and proposes destructive nuclear technology as the solution to the problem.

Indie auteur Larry Fessenden's *The Last Winter* (2006) provides a cautionary eco-horror/disaster film about the consequences of global warming. Set in the high Arctic circle, the film opens with a PR documentary discussing how a corporation (North Industries) just received a government contract to begin Arctic National Wildlife Refuge (ANWR) exploration in an area previously denominated a wildlife preserve geared to discover new oil supplies to make the US more energy independent. The microcosm of oil explorers and scientists already stationed in the wilderness is beginning to suffer stress, with one young worker Maxwell (Zach Gilford) taken to roaming the empty tundra on his own at night and mumbling about what he sees out there. Project manager Ed Pollack (Ron Perlman) returns to discover that Hoffman (James LeGros), an environmental activist who has been hired to monitor the project, has become convinced that the ANWR ecosystem is melting down and that with winter temperatures well above normal, the permafrost is melting, making the building of "ice roads" needed to bring in heavy equipment for the project impossible. Further, Hoffman is sleeping with Abby (Connie Britton), Pollack's second in command and previous lover, leading to conflicts between the corporate oil officials that want to "drill, baby, drill," to cite Sarah Palin's famous solution to the energy problem, and the ecologists in the film who are worried about effects on the environment.

As it quickly turns out, Maxwell is getting weirder, mumbling about the revenge of nature against human meddling and exploitation, and that oil, which consists of dead fossils and animals, is emanating strange phenomena after centuries of resting undisturbed. Indeed, the cracking ice and wind are emitting mysterious sounds and a "sour gas" may be, one scientist theorizes, driving Maxwell crazy (while a Native employee mentions Wendigo, or native spirits in the area). After Maxwell's death from freezing and increasingly bizarre sights, the macho Pollock and the ecologist Hoffman leave for help after a plane that has flown into rescue them inexplicably crashes into their station. The ending is not a cheerful one and the film closes with chirpy and brightly lit newscasts reporting strange weather occurrences throughout the earth, thus suggesting that climate change and global warming could be producing extreme weather events that could plague the earth for decades to come, leading to cycles of eco-catastrophe and perhaps collapse.

In addition to eco-disaster films, Hollywood has many other genre films portraying social apocalypse in the 2000s.

Social apocalypse in horror and fantasy film

Crises of the 1960s and 1970s were often represented allegorically in horror, fantasy, disaster, and other popular genre films (Kellner and Ryan 1988). Social crises and horrors of the Bush–Cheney regime were represented as well in a cycle of horror and fantasy genre films which help generate a social apocalypse genre of the era, as the horrors often suggest societal crisis and potential collapse. One of the first of the horror/social apocalypse films in the 2000s, *Resident Evil* (2002), was based on a popular Japanese video game and inspired a cycle of succeeding films. Directed by Paul W.S. Anderson, *Resident Evil* has a strong corporate conspiracy subtext and opens with a detailed description of how a mega-corporation has taken over the US:

> At the beginning of the 21st century, the Umbrella Corporation had become the largest commercial entity in the United States. Nine out of every ten homes contain its products. Its political and financial influence is felt everywhere. In public, it is the world's leading supplier of computer technology, medical products, and healthcare. Unknown, even to its own employees, its massive profits are generated by military technology, genetic experimentation and viral weaponry.

Resident Evil opens with the release of a deadly gas in a secret underground corporate research facility called "The Hive," which turns the staff into murderous zombies who release mutated Lab "Animals" that they were studying, setting off a biohazard warning. An elite crew is sent to contain the infestation, but as it gets out of control the Red Queen computer that manages the underground facility orders a shutdown so that the crew must struggle against zombies, infected animals, corporate henchmen, and a malevolent computer to escape. The crew, led by two super-empowered women, Alice (Milla Jovovich) and Rain (Michelle Rodriguez), appear to shut down the Queen, but countless zombies escape, giving rise to sequels in the franchise.

Resident Evil articulates fears of evil corporations and biotechnology getting out of control, as well as technology coming to dominate human beings and outbreaks of deadly biochemical plagues, a fear inflamed in the aftermath of the anthrax attacks, never explained, following the 9/11 terror attacks whose representation and impact on Hollywood cinema and US culture was a major force of the era (see Kellner 2010; Faludi 2007).

At the end of *Resident Evil*, the main character, who we will learn in sequels is Alice, survives, but observes that the city above the underground research facility has been overrun by zombies, and she faces a desperate future. While the first *Resident Evil* film took place largely underground in a claustrophobic environment, where new evils and challenges appeared around every corner, *Resident Evil: Apocalypse* (Witt, 2004) takes place in a situation of urban apocalypse in which Alice, endowed with genetic superpowers, fights zombies, monsters, and corporate thugs, teaming up with some other survivors, including two strong women, to escape before the quarantined city is nuked by the evil corporation. Alice and a couple of her companions make it out for the sequel, but *Apocalypse* ends with the nuclear attack covered over by the Umbrella corporation as the malfunction of a nuclear power plant, playing on fears of out of control nuclear technology and government cover-ups. Further, news reports claimed that earlier stories of corporate malfeasance were false and that the people should be grateful to the Umbrella Corporation for preserving their way of life, a barely disguised allegory of lying by corporations and the state during the Bush–Cheney era.

In *Resident Evil: Extinction* (2007), urban life has been destroyed globally and Alice and a small band of survivors try to survive amidst the zombie hordes in a mostly desert environment. Directed by Australian Russell Mulcahy, this zombie gore film shamelessly rips off *Mad Max* (Miller, 1979) and Mad Max 2: *The Road Warrior* (Miller, 1981) with endless battle scenes, highlighted by an attack by a flock of virally infected birds, who make Hitchcock's flock tame and harmless by comparison. Superpower-endowed Alice kills scores of birds, and hooks up with Claire Redford and her band of uninfected survivors, who are falling fast to the zombies who are taking over the world. Las Vegas is in ruins and the only hope for the group is to make it to Alaska where they hear reports that there are survivors.

The ultra-violent and nihilistic *Resident Evil: Extinction* can be read as a rightwing survivalist fantasy where after the collapse of civilization only the most violent can survive in a dog-eat-dog and zombie-eat-the-few-humans universe. Cumulatively, the *Resident Evil* films fall into subgenre cycles of a rebirth of zombie films, all derivative of George Romero's *Night of the Living Dead* cycle (1968, 1978, 1985), who returns, as we shall shortly see, to pastiche himself and resume his *Living Dead* cycle in the 2000s.

A series of other mutant vampire and zombie films focuses on the dangers of science and technology careening out of control and producing catastrophic consequences. Danny Boyle's *28 Days Later* (2003) opens in a research lab in which monkeys have been injected with a pure aggression virus to study violence and its control. Animal rights activists inadvertently 'liberate' the monkeys who begin a murderous rampage, infecting the entire population with a rage virus that turns people into murderous zombie-like killers. Produced during 2000–2001 at a time when hoof-and-mouth disease in England was causing epidemics in the countryside, forcing the slaughter of hordes of cattle, and the anthrax attacks after September 11, 2001 were creating anxiety, the film appeared during the year of the outbreak of the SARS epidemic in 2003, hence the pandemic shown in the film had all too real resonance in the real world.

The DVD commentary and a documentary *The Making of 28 Days Later* dramatizes the dangers of global pandemics that have emerged as an anxiety of the present moment. Yet fear of an out-of-control military is another subtext of the film as a small group of survivors of the aggression virus outbreak flee to a military camp in the north of England, responding to a broadcast message that survivors associated with the military are seeking a cure to the virus. The small group finds the military encampment, but the survivors include a young black woman (Naomie Harris) and a teenage girl (Megan Burns), and it is soon evident that the military running the camp seek to make the two females sex slaves in a scheme to repopulate the earth (and satisfy their sexual desires), thus positioning the audience against male predatory militarism.

A sequel, *28 Weeks Later* (2007), directed by Spanish filmmaker Juan Carlos Fresnadillo, articulates specific fears of the US military as out of control. A continuation of the previous story, with new characters, the film envisages a US-led NATO occupation of England to deal with the dangers of another outbreak of the aggression virus after the initial hosts appeared to have all died. Predictably the virus and monster rampage reappears and US-led troops, some of whom were complaining about the lack of 'action,' begin shooting the zombies, with some troops exulting in the kills. In the context of the US occupation of Iraq, the 'Code Red' order to exterminate survivors of the first virus wave, along with the newly infected, and the protracted slaughter and eventual fire-bombing of a rehabilitation camp, produces resonances with real-world horrors.

Both films have a survivalist and Darwinian subtext, but also express fears of societal breakdown and resultant unrestrained aggression. The hand-held jittering camera and quick editing in the action sequences of, especially, *28 Weeks Later*, creates a sense of existence careening out of control, of being thrown into an unbearable chaos, vividly evoking fears of catastrophe and social collapse. A refrain through both films expresses the ultimate anxiety, 'it's all fucked,' suggesting that everything is so fucked up there is not fuck all to do to improve things or provide any hope for the future.

Yet it is perhaps Alfonso Cuaron's *Children of Men* (2006) that is the most complex and thought-provoking meditation on the breakdown of the contemporary political system in its allegory of a world careening into apocalyptic collapse and Orwellian fascism. In its science fiction premise, based on a novel by P.D. James, the story presents a world fallen into terror and hopelessness when global infertility (mysteriously) erupts after a flu pandemic in 2009. Set in 2027 London, the truly frightening scenario shows political tendencies of the present leading to chaos and collapse. Cutting from long shots to close-ups and medium takes, Cuaron's camera forces the viewer to explore an environment that looks very much like present-day reality, only more drab, dangerous, and frightening. Opening television images present a montage of a world in collapse where "only Britain soldiers on":

> [*Newsreader:*] Day 1,000 of the Siege of Seattle.
>
> [*Newsreader:*] The Muslim community demands an end to the Army's occupation of mosques.
>
> [*Newsreader:*] The Homeland Security bill is ratified. After eight years, British borders will remain closed. The deportation of illegal immigrants will continue. Good morning. Our lead story.

Since the economy and social order have disintegrated everywhere except England, streams of refugees flood into the country, where they are welcomed with internment and concentration camps. A revolutionary group, the Fishes, fights for immigrant rights and the end of the police state and plans a violent uprising. All hope has been drained from a world without children and a future after the death of the world's youngest human, 'Baby Diego,' throws the world in despair. A government bureaucrat Theo (Clive Owen) leaves a café that is bombed by terrorists and is kidnapped by them. His ex-wife Julian (Julianne Moore) is a member of the group and she helps persuade him to get exit visas for a refugee pregnant woman Kee (Clare-Hope Ashitey) to take her to the Human Project, where attempts are being made to regenerate human life. Observing the horrors of state repression, Theo becomes an active participant in the quest to smuggle Kee and her baby out of the country, and this plot-line provides the occasion for a stunning montage of a police state, terrorism, refugee internment camps, and accelerating social disintegration, intensifying tendencies of the present moment and providing a cautionary warning tale that if things are not dramatically changed we are sliding into social apocalypse and the collapse of civilization.

While Alfonso Cuaron's *Children of Men* calls attention to tendencies toward growing fascism and the collapse of democracy and civilization in the present age, it has a conservative subtext. The disintegration of civilization makes one yearn for the good old days and it celebrates childbirth as the key to humanity. The revolutionaries are shown to be brutal terrorists, who gratuitously shoot Theo's lovable friend Jasper (Michael Caine) and who plan a quixotic "Uprising" that appears to be leading to more destruction and the rebels' probable extinction.

While the film valorizes political activism and charts Theo's transformation from a depressed cynic into a committed activist, hope is projected onto a nebulous Human Project and the birth of a lone child who becomes an object of religious adoration. Throughout *Children of Men* there are media images of Islamic terrorism, and one long scene near the end, where Theo and Kee seek to escape and deliver the child to a boat that will take it to the Human Project, features a menacing demonstration of what appears to be an Islamic radical group, thus reproducing tendencies to fear Jihadist Islamists in the contemporary moment, replicating a dominant trope of rightwing and media discourse. Yet on many levels, the film provides prescient critical visions of the present era, evoking the horrors of militarism and a fascist police state. The images of social decay and faded and saturated colors in *Children of Men* provide a gloomy vision of where contemporary trends may be leading if action is not taken and change embraced.

Another allegory of apocalypse, Francis Lawrence's *I am Legend* (2007), is also highly politically ambiguous, as in its sci-fi scenario a vaccination seeking to cure cancer mutates into a virus that kills scores of humans and creates monstrous murderous killers, encompassing humans and animals. Based on Richard Matheson's 1954 novel of the title, the story features a surviving scientist Robert Neville (Will Smith) immune from the virus staying in a New York deserted by humans, searching for a cure, and battling the vampirish/zombiesque mutants in his forages out of his apartment for food. He eventually finds a cure for the virus, but must sacrifice his life to battle the mutants so that a young woman who found her way to his abode can take the cure to a colony of survivors in Vermont and presumably eliminate the scourge. Since the film presents science as causing the problem and producing the cure, it is ambiguous in targeting the cause of the evil.

Another category of more socially critical horror films, however, sees monstrosity as a product of the existing society. Films like the 2006 and 2007 remakes of *The Hills Have Eyes* and *The Hills Have Eyes 2* presented genetic mutations resulting from nuclear testing as producing a monster family, as previous horror films featured nuclear fall-out creating monsters like The *Creature from the Black Lagoon* (Arnold, 1954), *Godzilla* (Honda, 1954, remade in 1998 and 2014), and a large number of low-budget films including *Night of the Lepus* (Claxton, 1972), *Frogs* (McCowan, 1972), or *Day of the Animals* (Girdler, 1977). While Wes Craven's 1977 version of *The Hills Have Eyes* was valorized as providing radical critique of the bourgeois family,[9] the 2006 remake, produced by Craven and directed by Alexandre Aja, highlighted the theme of the mutant monsters emerging from genetic mutations caused by US nuclear testing in the desert. An opening montage mixes images of nuclear bomb tests with a spectacle of radioactive sand blasts, explosions, dropping of Agent Orange in Vietnam, and quick flashes of the mutants in the earlier *Hills Have Eyes*, exposed to nuclear radiation.

The 2006 *Hills Have Eyes* highlights the theme of the dangers of nuclear radiation as a middle-class family discovers itself stranded in the desert, and learns that the area was the site of nuclear tests, and that the families who lived in the surrounding desert, now mutant cannibals who prey on tourists, were exposed to radiation and suffered genetic mutations. In one encounter with the monsters, a mutant tells the family that "You made us what we are, Boom! Booom! Boooom!" While the middle-class family is initially portrayed as petty and bickering, under assault from the mutants they become savage killers themselves, deconstructing the line between civilization and barbarism, and showing that a society that produces extreme violence engenders reactive violence as a response. The extremely gory and ultra-violent spectacle of rape, cannibalism, and brutal murder thus puts on display behavior that a violent society engenders when those under assault fight for their survival.

A quickie sequel, *The Hills Have Eyes 2* (2007), written and produced by Jonathan and Wes Craven and directed by Martin Weisz, depicts National Guard troops undergoing training for deployment in Afghanistan in the desert, when they learn that scientists and a military team have sent distress signals and have gone missing in the surrounding desert. The mutants then go to war with the young National Guard unit, with the narrative coding the mutants as terrorists, as they live underground in caves and emerge to kill the young troops in grisly fashion. The extreme gore, torture scenes, and deadly violence of the film evoke the horrors of Terror War in Afghanistan and Iraq, creating a troubling view of apocalyptic horror returning from these wars to the US itself.

Hence, while conservative social apocalypse films show evil coming from sources external to the existing system, or more supernatural sources, a socially critical tradition, exhibited in some of the 2000s social apocalypse films under discussion here, shows evil and monstrosity emerging from out of control aspects of the existing society. Master horror film impresario George Romero's *Land of the Dead* (2005), *Diary of the Dead* (2007), and *Survival of the Dead* (2009) provide updated constructions of his zombies-returning-to-life series that provide critical allegories on the present moment. If the zombies in Romero's *Night of the Living Dead* (1968) could be read as the silent majorities threatening a young counterculture in the 1960s, and *Dawn of the Dead* (1978) could be read as an allegory of how consumerism makes zombies out of people, then *Day of the Dead* (1985) could be seen as a satire on the greed and violence of the Reagan era, and *Land of the Dead* can stand as an allegory of the deterioration of life in the Bush–Cheney era.

In *Land of the Dead*, after years of zombie attacks on one of the few urban sites of safety, society is divided in Romero's critical vision between those living in a high-rise luxury apartment, a fitting figure for gated communities, while the lower classes live in squalor in deteriorating urban conditions, and a small cadre of police try to protect them from the zombies and to scavenge supplies from the countryside. The class division represents the growing discrepancy between rich and poor during the Bush–Cheney years, which by 2011 was defined by the Occupy movement as a chasm in the US between the 1 percent and the 99 percent (see Kellner 2012).

The zombies in *Land of the Dead* initially appear as working-class types who have had the life sucked out of them and are distracted by firework displays which keep them entertained. In Romero's vision, however, the zombies are becoming more intelligent, learning to communicate, use weapons, and organize their forces to assault the city of the living. The high-rise city is ruled by Kaufman (Dennis Hopper), an impervious dictator who is resonant of Donald Trump and Donald Rumsfeld (in a DVD video accompanying the film, Hopper said he intended to play the character like Rumsfeld). In a scene where a rogue policeman (played over-the-top by John Leguizamo) threatens to use stolen weapons against the compound, Kaufman snaps "We don't negotiate with terrorists," an obvious jab at the Bush–Cheney administration, which popularized such discourse.

Led by an African American zombie called Big Daddy (Eugene Clark), who has learned to use weapons, the zombies attack the gated high-rise, an image of revolutionary insurrection against the ruling elites. A fireworks display fails to distract the rampaging zombies, a symbol of growing revolutionary class consciousness, and the zombies continue to systematically assault the ruling-class refuge in Romero's fantasy of class revenge.

Romero's *Diary of the Dead* goes back to the beginnings of his "Dead" mythology to show the emergence of the Living Dead zombies. In the film's narrative conceit, a student filmmaking crew from the University of Pittsburgh are filming a horror film in the woods when media reports of a strange eruption of people returning from the dead to feast on the living occur. When the students observe the phenomenon themselves, a young filmmaker Jason resolves to capture the horrors on video, to produce a document of the event in which 'everything changed.' The cineastes get media footage from Internet video and discern that the government is lying, covering up the enormity of the horror, and the young crew resolves to shoot footage of what is really happening and upload it on the video. This sequence points to an era of new media and sources of news and information, in which 'viral video' can be shot across the world and used to critique existing media and society.

Of course, the theme of a lying media evokes US corporate media in the run-up to the 2003 Iraq war and during large stretches of the Bush–Cheney administration. *Diary of the Dead* is full of such topical commentary, as when a radio talk show speaker announces that "the real immigration problem" is now about people crossing the line between life and death, a dig at conservative commentators who hystericize immigration problems. In a larger sense, in the current environment, the very notion of Dead returning to life points to the cycle of death and vengeance, endemic for centuries in the Middle East and other parts of the world that the US has stirred up with the Pandora's Box of its Afghanistan and Iraq intervention and drone wars during the Obama era. Compared to real life horrors, Romero's zombie films seem relatively tame and subdued.

Conclusion

As this study indicates, the number of post-apocalyptic films in the Bush–Cheney years dramatically proliferated, as conditions of life worsened for many and crises intensified. Yet the cycle of post-apocalypse films continued during the Obama years including 9 (Acker, 2009), *The Road* (Hillcoat, 2009), *2012* (Emmerich, 2009), *Knowing* (Proyas, 2009), *Zombieland* (Fleischer, 2009), *The Book of Eli* (Albert and Allen Hughes, 2010), *Oblivion* (Kosinski, 2013), *Pacific Rim* (del Toro, 2013), *Elysium* (Blomkamp, 2013), *Godzilla* (Edwards, 2014), and *World War Z* (Forster, 2013), among many others.

Questions arise as to why at this point in history Hollywood is churning out so many social and eco-apocalypse films, in several genres and in the form of both marginal horror and sci-fi films and big-budget blockbusters. Obviously, post-9/11, there was an imagination of disaster as images of terror bombings and violent destruction were nightly appearances on television news and other media. Further, as the ongoing Terror War, rooted in two wars in Iraq and Afghanistan, and continuing in violent conflicts in the Middle East and elsewhere, provided nightly images of horror, punctuated by frequent incidents of terrorism all over the world, audiences could feel that the familiar world around them was collapsing. Perhaps fears of social apocalypse and collapse were intensified by the 2008 global financial and mortgage crisis, in which millions lost, and continue to lose, homes and jobs. With the Gulf deep-water BP oil blowout in the summer of 2010, dread concerning eco-catastrophe is all too real, and different religious sects were seeing all these disasters as signifying the End of Days.

In fact, surveys and scholarly analysis have indicated growing belief in religious versions of apocalypse (Stroup and Shuck 2007), which have perhaps contributed to Hollywood creating a seemingly proliferating cycle of apocalypse films in the 2000s. I have argued that a cycle of contemporary Hollywood social apocalypse films discussed in this chapter offer allegories of social crisis and catastrophe, dystopias that provide cautionary warnings that trends of the present age can spiral out of control and produce catastrophic disaster on a grand scale. While on one hand, allegories of social apocalypse may reproduce the politics of fear exploited by rightwing politicians, they also provide warnings that an era of conservative politics may produce catastrophe, providing representations of social crisis and catastrophe suggesting subliminally that the Bush–Cheney era of war and militarism, social Darwinism, growing inequality, and the politics of fear may produce the sort of societal collapse evident in *Land of the Dead*, *28 Days Later*, *Children of Men*, and other films discussed in this chapter. These films can also be read as allegories of the disintegration of the social infrastructure and the emergence of a Darwinian nightmare under a conservative regime where the struggle for mere survival occurs in a Hobbesian world where life is nasty, brutish, and short. In this register, the zombies and monsters in the cycle of horror films of the era represent not only conservative nightmares, but visions of where the ultra-right Bush–Cheney regime took the US and put on display the nightmares it has produced and from which we have not yet awakened, as evidenced by the continuation of apocalypse films in the Obama era.

Notes

1 See my discussion of social apocalypse films in *Cinema Wars* (2010), Chapter 1, pp. 80ff, upon which this chapter draws and expands.
2 The cycle of catastrophe and social apocalypse films continue during the Obama administration, and my forthcoming book, tentatively titled *Cinema Wars 2: Hollywood Film in the Age of Obama*, will critically engage social apocalypse films appearing during the Obama era.
3 On films transcoding social discourses and diagnostic critique, see Kellner and Ryan (1988); Kellner (1995, 2010).
4 See Kellner (1995, pp. 116–117).
5 On the Bush–Cheney era, see my trilogy of books (Kellner 2001, 2003, 2005).
6 On the disaster film, see Kellner and Ryan (1988). *The Day After Tomorrow* grossed an astonishing $544,272,402 worldwide (see *http://www.boxofficemojo.com/movies/?id=dayaftertomorrow.htm*; accessed January 2, 2009).
7 In an article on the evolution of the US president's image in the cinema of apocalypse from Bill Clinton to Barack Obama, Araceli Rodríguez Mateos and Antonio Sánchez-Escalonilla (2014) document changes in representations of US Presidents from 1990s to 2000s social apocalypse films from positive representations during the Clinton years to strongly negative or absent Presidents during the Bush administration, reflecting increasing disaffection and anger with their policies.
8 For alternative readings of *The Day after Tomorrow* see Murray and Heumann (2009).
9 Critic Robin Wood (2003) and other associates at the journal *Movie* and later *Cine-Action* valorized the radical potential of the horror genre in the 1970s and 1980s (see also Murray and Heumann 2009). Generally, for much of the post-1980s, the horror genre has not taken progressive directions and engaged in social critique, but as I attempt to show in this chapter, horror, fantasy and other popular film genres articulate fears of the present moment concerning the state and the military, technology, corporations and the economy, ecological and social crisis, and other phenomena, and can thus provide critical images and provide experiences that raise questions about the existing society.

Bibliography

Faludi, S. (2007) *The Terror Dream: Fear and Fantasy in Post-9/11 America*, New York: Metropolitan Books.
Kellner, D. (1995) *Media Culture: Cultural Studies, Identity and Politics between the Modern and the Postmodern*, London and New York: Routledge.
Kellner, D. (2001) *Grand Theft 2000: Media Spectacle and a Stolen Election*, Lanham, MD: Rowman and Littlefield.
Kellner, D. (2003) *From September 11 to Terror War: The Dangers of the Bush Legacy*, Lanham, MD: Rowman and Littlefield.
Kellner, D. (2005) *Media Spectacle and the Crisis of Democracy*, Boulder, CO: Paradigm Press.
Kellner, D. (2010) *Cinema Wars: Hollywood Film and Politics in the Bush-Cheney Era*, Malden, MA: Blackwell.
Kellner, D. (2012) *Media Spectacle and Insurrection, 2011: From the Arab Uprisings to Occupy Everywhere*, London and New York: Continuum/Bloomsbury.
Kellner, D. and Ryan, M. (1988) *Camera Politica: The Politics and Ideology of Contemporary Hollywood Film*, Bloomington: Indiana University Press.
Mateos, A. R. and Sánchez-Escalonilla, A. (2014) "The Depiction of the US President in Apocalyptic Cinema" *Literature Interpretation Theory*, 25(3), 334–358.
Murray, R. L. and Heumannn, J. K. (2009) *Ecology and Popular Film: Cinema on the Edge*, Albany, NY: SUNY Press.
Stroup, J. and Shuck, G. (2007) *Escape into the Future: Cultural Pessimism and Its Religious Dimension in Contemporary American Popular Culture*, Waco, TX: Baylor University Press.
Wood, R. (2003) *Hollywood from Vietnam to Reagan ... and Beyond*, New York: Columbia University Press.

22

REASSERTIONS OF HOLLYWOOD HEROIC AGENCY IN THE IRAQ WAR FILM

Geoff King

Hollywood features that are in some respects critical of the United States, either generally or in some particular dimensions, often do so at least partly through a questioning or undermining of the status of the central heroic protagonist, a key feature in the history of studio production and a major vehicle for the projection of dominant/prevailing ideology. This is the case in some of the most prominent treatments of the 1991 American invasion of Iraq, even if the questioning involved is often provisional or limited in its extent. *Courage Under Fire* (Zwick, 1996), for example, is structured around two such points of doubt: an investigation by an army officer into the actions of a female helicopter pilot, to determine the merits of the proposed award of a posthumous Medal of Honor, accompanied by the officer's own feelings of guilt about the cover up of a 'friendly fire' incident in which he was involved. Heroism is eventually reaffirmed in general in both cases, although the impression of doubt is one that strongly shapes the bulk of the piece.

A later example, *Jarhead* (Mendes, 2005), offers a scenario that seems to capture some broader dynamics of the 1991 conflict, an encounter that was waged primarily through massive air bombardment on the part of US forces. The central character, Swofford (Jake Gyllenhaal), is given the kind of 'special' role that often typifies sources of Hollywood heroic agency in the war film – a topic to which we return below – in this case that of a Marine scout sniper, whose operations are separate from those of the main troop body. Much of the film offers a reflection of the situation of most of the ground forces involved in the invasion, their time being spent waiting for an opportunity for action that never comes to fruition. Towards the end, Swofford seems about to get his chance to put his particular skills to work – to perform his individual agency, if not in a particularly heroic manner – by shooting from a distance two high-ranking Iraqi officers at an airfield. At the last second, however, an air-strike is called in instead, displacing any such individual on-the-ground activity in a manner that seems representative of the dynamics of the conflict as a whole.

Some treatments of the subsequent invasion of 2003 are more openly critical of the activities of individual soldiers, a number focusing on atrocities committed by American troops, although representation of these varies and tends to be most critical in productions of more marginal industrial status (for example, the independently produced and released *Redacted*

[De Palma, 2007]). Divisions tend to be made in such films between individual troops who are more or less to blame for the commitment of war crimes, while such figures are also sometimes represented as victims of the conflict themselves (see, for example, *In the Valley of Elah* ([Haggis, 2007]). The general tenor of many of the first wave of films to reflect aspects of the 2003 invasion is largely critical of the enterprise, if not always of the individuals involved, presenting downbeat portraits that might be associated with their lack of commercial success (for more on this, see Barker 2011). Such criticism continues to be present in some subsequent treatments of the conflict and its aftermath in Iraq, but a number of these combine material of this kind with a notable reassertion of a greater dimension of individual heroic agency, with all the ideological baggage that this entails. This is the focus of this chapter, through an analysis of three examples: *Body of Lies* (R. Scott, 2008), *The Hurt Locker* (Bigelow, 2008) and *Green Zone* (Greengrass, 2010). In each case, we find not just a reassertion of individual heroics but a tendency to draw on structuring oppositions that offer broader resonances with long-established American myth/ideology, including articulations associated with notions of the 'frontier' or the 'frontiersman', as a grounding for such activity. This is accompanied, and to a significant extent driven, by a reassertion of a particular kind of cinematic action-thrills, through which such activity is foregrounded, celebrated and offered in vicarious form to the viewer. In focusing on these two different dimensions, this chapter mixes two analytical approaches: a reading at the level of mythical/ideological structure combined with examination of formal qualities that are rooted in particular industrial regimes of contemporary Hollywood action cinema.

In drawing on such material, particularly in relation to the mythic/ideological resonances of certain forms of individual action, these films demonstrate a strong vein of continuity with Hollywood treatments of war and related activity (for more on this, see King 2000). The employment of such tropes, in relation to a conflict that was or had become a source of increasing controversy in American society, repeats a dynamic that lies at the heart of many Hollywood representations of the war in Vietnam. Figures bearing clear resemblance to the tradition of the frontiersman are found at the heart of prominent titles as different in other respects as, for example, *The Deerhunter* (Cimino, 1978), *Rambo: First Blood Part II* (Cosmatos, 1985) and *Platoon* (Stone, 1986) (King 2000: 132–138). The Iraq theatre does not lend itself so well to some of the explicit frontier trappings found in these examples – particularly, the jungle/wilderness landscape or the tendency for some key figures to dress themselves in 'Indian' style fashion, such as long hair and bandanas – but a number of similar underlying and structuring dynamics can be found in each case. The fact that an important source of continuity can be identified across such films is significant in itself, to our understanding of the potential function of Hollywood films as purveyors of myth and ideology. More specifically, though, it also serves to question the simplistic claims made by some commentators – whether academic or otherwise – that very much changed in Hollywood in the post-9/11 era (see for example the hyberbolic claims made in, and some sources cited by, Pollard 2011). In essential underlying dynamics, I argue, very little if anything changed; just the same as, in essential underlying dynamics, very little changed in American or other 'Western' foreign policy itself (for a convincing demonstration of continuity at this level, see Gregory 2004).

From 'wild man' to almost going native: figuring heroic agency and its opposites

A key dimension of each of the three examples considered here is the particular manner in which a version of individual heroic agency is constructed. Each of the central protagonists is given a 'special' role in which he is extracted from what might be taken to be the more routine norm of 'ordinary' military activity. In *The Hurt Locker*, Will James (Jeremy Renner) is not just a member of a bomb disposal team – a specialist 'on the edge' kind of role – but one with a particular addiction to the thrills involved. Roger Ferris (Leonardo DiCaprio) in *Body of Lies* is an ardent on-the-ground CIA agent working in Iraq and Jordan. Roy Miller (Matt Damon) in *Green Zone* is an army chief warrant officer leading a team in the search for supposed Weapons of Mass Destruction (WMD) in Iraq, a relatively specialist task that becomes more so as his role changes during the course of events. These are the kinds of activities typically assigned to the heroic protagonists of recent or contemporary Hollywood films set in war or immediately post-war scenarios such as these, for reasons that seem to relate to both implicit political-ideological resonances and the devising of situations that lend themselves to particular regimes of cinematic action-entertainment.

In each case, the particular figuration of heroic agency associated with the protagonist is sharpened through contrast with opposing forces of one kind or another; again, a very familiar component of the dynamic. A key structuring opposition is between notions of proximity and distance, particularly when the latter involves technological and/or bureaucratic mediation. The most explicit example of this is found in *Body of Lies*, where the work of Ferris on the ground, with what is presented as a commitment to the specific realities of the Middle Eastern theatre, is juxtaposed with the interventions-from-a distance of his mendacious CIA superior, Ed Hoffman (Russell Crowe). While Ferris risks the life of himself and others in direct engagements with enemies, allies and those located somewhere in between, Hoffman seeks to manipulate events from afar, typically monitoring the activities of Ferris via sources such as the panoptic overhead images provided by drone aircraft (Figure 22.1). Ferris is on one occasion assisted by air support called in with the help of the view from on high, but it is notably absent when most needed, in a climactic mission during which a dust cloud is generated by a fleet of enemy vehicles, to prevent the observers from above knowing into which of them he has been taken; the vehicles head off in opposing directions, leaving Ferris without any CIA backup. Ferris is presented in some respects in the classic mould of the frontiersman, the Middle Eastern equivalent of 'the man who knows Indians', a figure able to mediate between two worlds through his real commitment to an understanding of the 'Other', as manifested

Figure 22.1 Duplicitous interventions from a distance: the overhead view from CIA headquarters in *Body of Lies*.

here by his mastery of Arabic and his preparedness to respect at least some of the social conventions of the foreign terrain on which he is an expert operator.

A more localized version of the proximity/technological-mediation opposition is found in *The Hurt Locker*. The film opens with a sequence in which a bomb disposal team is tackling a device with the help of a remotely controlled robotic vehicle. Part of the vehicle fails and a member of the team dons his protective suit and helmet and sets out to do the job more directly himself, subsequently being killed when the device is activated. Cue the arrival of James as his replacement, who promptly refuses the use of the 'bot' when confronted with a similar scenario. He is immediately labelled 'reckless' by fellow team member Sanborn (Anthony Mackie), and subsequently described as a 'wild man' by an admiring officer, establishing a 'maverick' character that provides another very familiar ingredient in the typical make-up of the Hollywood hero. James is, in fact, in some respects an almost carbon copy of the 'Dirty Harry' persona enacted in numerous features by Clint Eastwood, a figure whose *modus operandi* is to stride decisively into difficult situations and to take direct action in disregard for established procedural conventions. When a taxi drives aggressively into the street involved in this sequence, for example, James confronts it head-on, standing and pointing a pistol at the vehicle, and subsequently to the head of its driver after shooting out its windscreen – after which the driver, suitably cowed, it seems, by such bravado, backs away.

If the Ferris of *Body of Lies* is sometimes plagued by communications-at-a-distance from Hoffman, James' assertion of maverick individuality includes a refusal of such contact. After the first incident, he is berated by Sanborn for failing to talk to him on his radio, to keep the latter informed of what is happening (he also lets off a smoke grenade that obscures himself from view, a self-inflicted version of the masking by the dust cloud experienced by Ferris). In the second defusing incident dramatized by the film, a case involving a suspicious car parked outside a UN-occupied building, James removes his radio headset and throws it to the ground, preferring again, it seems, to engage in a manner characterized as more direct, individual and unmediated. He also removes his protective suit and helmet, commenting that if he is going to die, 'I'm going to die comfortable', another gesture that emphasizes a state of unmediated engagement (Figure 22.2).

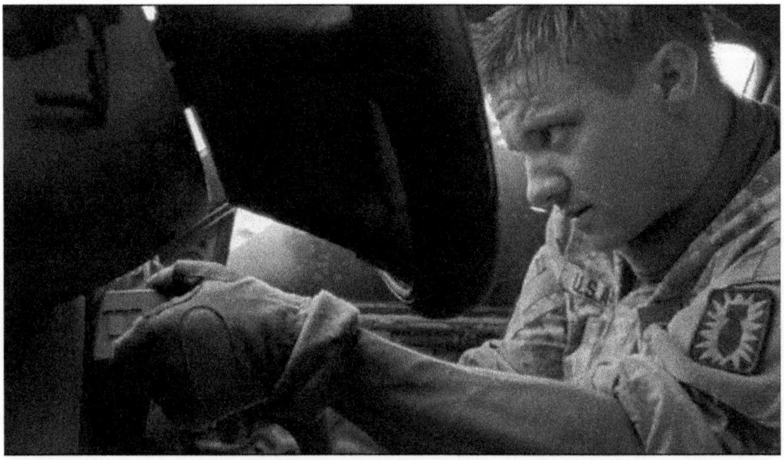

Figure 22.2 Stripped back on the ground: James (Jeremy Renner) after removing his protective clothing and radio headset to defuse a car bomb in *The Hurt Locker*.

Oppositions between the figure of the 'man on the ground' and those who operate at a distance, in various ways including via politico-bureaucratic and technological mediation, also figure centrally in *Green Zone*. Miller is characterized as a relatively more 'ordinary' or 'everyman' figure than James or Ferris; more a case of a 'decent' soldier whose direct experience on the ground convinces him to question the veracity of intelligence on the basis of which he is sent out to investigate a number of supposed WMD sites – again, at direct personal risk to himself and others. Working with supportive CIA agent Martin Brown (Brendan Gleeson) and a reporter who has been duped into running false stories, he eventually manages to expose the truth: that forces in the American administration, represented here by smooth Pentagon suit Clark Poundstone (Greg Kinnear), have faked the intelligence to justify the invasion of Iraq. The articulation of individual heroism is provided here, then, at least partly in the service of making a strongly critical political point with powerful resonance in real-world understandings of the war.

The extent to which any such criticism is offered varies among these three films. It is strongest and most explicit in *Green Zone*. This dimension is less specific and pushed more into the background in *Body of Lies*, highlighted particularly in an outburst from Ferris to Hoffman that underlines the distance theme ("You're a million fucking miles away. I'm here, Ed, and I see the unnecessary travesties of this war that the rest of you backstabbing fucking political bureaucrats only look at pictures of") and dramatized in the killing or other ill-treatment of a number of marginal characters (the term 'unnecessary' seems to imply, however, that the war could have been pursued in an acceptable manner). Nothing specific is articulated in *The Hurt Locker*, which relies on the more common Hollywood expedient of restricting its focus to the immediate experiences of the protagonist in order to avoid engaging in anything much more than a 'war is hell' truism (or, in this case, 'the hell of war suits some maverick individuals') that avoids any consideration of specific context.

Where criticism is offered in these films, this is achieved through another familiar ideological manoeuvre: that in which the American presence is divided into 'good' and 'bad' components, a process that enables one half to be separated out (lies, politics, bureaucracy, manipulation from a distance) while that represented by the heroic protagonists can be celebrated. The impression that results is that the latter is the 'true' representation of the essence of the American – ardent, honest, well-intentioned, if not always entirely successful – while the former represents a betrayal of its core values (an opposition that depends on an appeal to very longstanding, and still widely prevalent, sedimentation of American myth and ideology). This is developed in *Green Zone* to the extent that, by the end of the film, Miller is actually being hunted down by military forces from his own side, at the behest of the scheming Poundstone. If technologically mediated vision from above represents constant interference-at-a-distance by Hoffman in *Body of Lies*, data from airborne monitor screens is used towards the climax of *Green Zone* to identify Miller, along with more obvious enemy figures, as a potential target for termination. A notable shift of roles is found on this occasion, the military figure established as his nemesis being the leader of a special forces unit of the kind more often located on the positive side of such mythic-ideological divides. The special forces team is associated with helicopter-based operations, again occupying a position that is marked as disconnected from the realities on the ground (first introduced swooping in to take a prisoner from Miller, one of a number of occasions on which the film suggests that certain Iraqis could have been sources of cooperation that might have helped to avert prolonged instability in the country, if not for the imposition from on high of the politically motivated agenda of the US administration).

Another customary dimension of the heroic protagonists of *The Hurt Locker* and *Body of Lies* that fits them into longer traditions, including those of the frontiersman, is their lack of any real attachment to the home or the domestic arena. The status of James seems somewhat unclear when he informs a colleague that he is divorced but that his former wife still lives with him. Sanborn, meanwhile, explains that he has a girl he likes but is resistant to her desire to have children. By the end of their period of rotation, Sanborn has been changed by his experiences, one close shave in particular, and says he wants a son. His desire, that is, is to establish a settled life back in the 'civilized' world that constitutes the opposite pole, in long-established cultural schemas, to the world of frontiers of direct and dangerous action (for the classic expression of such oppositions in relation to the western genre, see Kitses 2007). We see James return home but he is not capable of such commitment, as might be expected. A few brief scenes depict his discomfort in the world of everyday domesticity – particularly a sequence in a supermarket, where a Muzak-tinged aisle full of myriad varieties of breakfast cereal seems, very conventionally, to symbolize a state of suburban/domesticated banality – before we see him returning for another tour.

Ferris is also in the process of becoming divorced; during one operation, the source of distraction from afar is a phone call from his lawyer. Offered a break after being injured during one operation, he declines, experiencing no pull from the world of domesticity or home. At the end, Hoffman offers him a desk job – more money, 'a fancy title' and a corner office, just down the hall from Hoffman's own. It goes almost without saying, given the structure of the opposition between the two, that this is not an attractive option. Ferris declines again, expressing an intention to remain in Jordan (where this phase of the plot is located). For Ferris, the prospect exists of a sustained life in this part of the world, if not quite that of settling down with the nurse, Aisha (Golshifteh Farahani), with whom he has begun a relationship (we see him watching her through a window close to the end but he turns and walks away, as if not wanting further to embroil her in the risks of his profession after a previous incident in which she was kidnapped). If Ferris has not entirely 'gone native', he appears to have travelled some distance in this direction. 'You are a secret Arab', quips the head of Jordanian intelligence, Hani (Mark Strong), with whom he works. He speaks the language sufficiently well to be able to identify Aisha's Iranian accent and is able to 'pass' as a local when suitably dressed (helped by a wispily bearded chin). If James remains a figure only capable of operating 'on the edge' of the frontier, as it were, at the point of most intense adrenaline-rush engagement, Ferris is presented as an individual who might be able to live in a sustained manner on the other side. *Green Zone* is notable for not engaging in these dynamics at all, in its figuration of its central protagonist in significantly less exceptional terms, no mention being made of Miller's status in relation to the domestic/home sphere.

If these films set up classically familiar oppositions such as direct hands-on action vs. remote manipulation or frontier-style world of action/engagement vs. domesticity, they can also be seen to offer some of the mythic reconciliations often associated with this way of interpreting popular texts (for classic accounts of this process in Hollywood, see Schatz 1981; Ray 1984). While Ferris is presented as knowing and respecting the world of the Middle East, he certainly does not 'go native' to the extent of in any way supporting or even providing an objective understanding of the 'terrorists' he remains committed to apprehending, whose location in this schema remains customarily that of the 'savage' situated beyond the pale of 'civilization.' When confronted eventually with the sheik behind a series of attacks, for example, he launches into angry tirade of criticism, just to make clear that he remains on what is still established as the side of the 'good guys', whatever reservations are expressed about some of their methods; that he could entirely 'go native' and join them would be beyond the bounds of what could remotely be contemplated in a Hollywood production. It is notable also that, in a classic instance of the kind of having-the-best-of-both-worlds associated with these dynamics, it is through his idea for a technologically based scam that a way of tracing the sheik is devised (a plot that involves the electronic manipulation of various email and bank accounts, with the aid of a CIA computer expert, as well as the staging of a fake bombing). Ferris is thus able to embrace both direct physical action and a world of remote manipulations of his own (he is also manipulated himself, in the end, by Hani, who succeeds in capturing the sheik for his own side rather than for the Americans).

Similarly, if James in *The Hurt Locker* is figured as a non-domesticated hero, he is also able to offer a significant degree of more human-centred nurturance to the frail member of his team, Eldridge (Brian Geraghty), and to work closely with Sanborn (both cemented under the heightened duress of an attack by enemy snipers). James also establishes the beginnings of a relationship with a young Iraqi boy he knows as Beckham (Christopher Sayegh), a development the narrative/action consequences of which are considered below. Hoffman, too, is situated in something of a middle position, although this is less positively coded on both sides. He is clearly established as a man with a family, often communicating with Ferris while performing child-care duties, but he seems equally distanced from each: physically from the one but also distracted by the pull of his work from the other.

'Adjusting coverage. Boost image factor': staging and plotting heroic action-thrills

What are the driving factors behind the production of films of this kind? From a broadly socio-cultural, political/ideological perspective, we can view them as offering some kind of reflection; not so much of the reality of American engagement in Iraq but of the manner in which dominant/prevailing myths and ideologies are able to frame such encounters. The three examples examined here offer some material that seems grounded in certain of the realities of the situation – most obviously, perhaps, the exposure of blatant lies that were used to justify the invasion of 2003, as suggested in *Green Zone*. But this is closely mixed with heavy doses of mythology and the application of very familiar fictional tropes. It is a usual process for Hollywood features that deal with such issues to mobilize tropes of these kinds, to fall back on familiar routines, as was also the case with many examples set in Vietnam. The effect of so doing might be highly political – and usually conservatively so – but no overtly political motivation on the part of the filmmakers needs to be demonstrated for this to be understood.

If we proceed to examine more closely some of the specifically cinematic dimensions of the films – what *kinds* of films they are, in what manner the dynamics sketched above are mobilized on screen, audio-visually and at the level of the plotting of certain events – we find some parallels with the thematic dimension outlined above but also some points of disjunction. Each of these films adopts certain formal approaches that make claims to the status of realism or verisimilitude, most strongly to the fore in *Green Zone* and *The Hurt Locker*. This creates a texture that might be considered to be at odds with the deployment of highly familiar fictional tropes; or, alternatively, it might be seen as seeking to ground the fanciful in something that claims the status of greater immediacy. Such an approach also has the effect of offering the viewer a vicarious impression of sharing something of the intense individual experiences of the protagonists, an impression of embodied exhilaration that might include a perceptual mimicry of the fictional action (for more on this process, see Purse 2011). Their actions might seem to be motivated less by their mythic-ideological resonances than as a source of particular kinds of specifically *cinematic* thrills: heroic escapades that translate into the stuff of action cinema as a generic component of the work, one that leans closer to what is likely to be of broadly mainstream commercial appeal than some of the more critical (and, therefore, potentially controversial) dimensions found, particularly, in *Green Zone* and *Body of Lies*. A conjunction can be suggested, then, between readings of these films from a political-ideological perspective and as products of a particular industrial regime, although the two are far from always or entirely aligned.

The most obvious potential source of disjunction between some of these different components is found in *Green Zone*. As was commonly noted on the release of the film, it offers an in some ways incongruous mixture of earnest political message – that the war was based on a fabricated premise – with a visual style and star presence strongly associated not just with hurly-burly action cinema in general but the specifics of a single franchise, that of the first three Bourne films (2002, 2004, 2007), also starring Matt Damon, the second and third instalments of which were from the same director, Paul Greengrass. The direct-action-on-the-ground in which the protagonists of all three films engage is, of course, the primary source of the vicarious action-cinema excitement offered to the enjoyment of the viewer: tension, the intensity and suspense of violent engagements, the spectacle of firefights and explosions, etc. This is another potential source of contradiction that also has resonance with the thematic oppositions sketched above. Much of the cinematography employed in these instances is unsteady, hand-held and designed to create an impression of documentary-like provisionality – an effect particularly strong in *Green Zone* and *The Hurt Locker*. The effect can be to make the viewer feel intimately involved in the action, sharing to some degree – clearly, greatly attenuated – in the intensity of the experience undergone by the protagonists (Figure 22.3). At the same time, ironically, the viewer is, in reality, located in a position closer to that of a distant observer such as Hoffman, if not able to manipulate events in the same manner. The overhead view from the drone is often presented to us directly, but also seen on numerous occasions as, specifically, a wide-screen spectacle being viewed from Langley by Hoffman and its operators.

If these films invest, formally, in the creation of substantial impressions of verisimilitude, they also push the bounds of credibility in some of their plotting, not just in the deployment of familiar tropes but in some of the extended actions in which their heroes engage. The act of putting the individual heroic protagonist constantly at the centre – and providing sufficient direct action to maintain a certain kind of cinematic action-excitement – risks a straining of plausibility. The conventions in play here, and likely to be accepted as part of

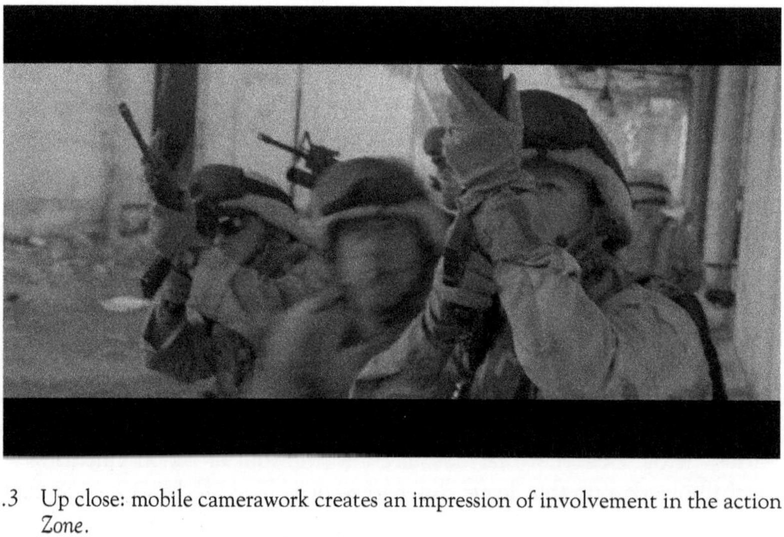

Figure 22.3 Up close: mobile camerawork creates an impression of involvement in the action in *Green Zone*.

the standard recipe by many viewers, are those of 'typical Hollywood confection', rather than anything specific to the realm of the mythical oppositions that are also being enacted. The 'Jason Bourne-ness' of some of Miller's actions, particularly as heightened through the aesthetic of the unsteady-cam and abrupt editing, provide clear examples of this phenomenon. From the more plausible domain of being part of a team searching for weapons, Miller is cast into an action-heroics role via a subsequent attachment to the CIA operations of Brown. A typically Hollywood/mainstream convenience ensures that it is our hero who happens to be working in the general vicinity of a high-level meeting of Iraqis and thus who gets a tip-off that sets the main plot mechanism in motion. He abandons what is marked as a clearly pointless search at another alleged WMD site, declaring: "I want to get something done". Miller is subsequently deployed on a number of missions well beyond his normal/plausible domain, culminating in the frantic hunt/chase sequences in which he seeks to make a key intervention in the developing political situation, while also being pursued by US special forces. From a specific military role, that is, his activity ends up cutting, highly implausibly but in typically Hollywood style, to the heart of the entire broader situation regarding the putative future of the country, including a face-to-face engagement with a senior Saddam-era general located within the film as a pivotal figure. Having earlier been declared to be operating "off reservation" (an apt and loaded term, used separately by both Brown and Poundstone), Miller's transfer to the CIA is revoked, leaving his operation entirely in the realm of maverick individual action, without any official sanction.

A similar stretching of the bounds of credibility is found in *The Hurt Locker*, although accompanied by some questioning of certain escapades within the diegesis. The film is not limited to a series of dramatizations of the tensions involved in the defusing of bombs. It starts with two of these, but a whole movie's worth of this material might become tedious – or, rather, less appropriate to the mainstream ground on which the film seeks primarily to move. Hence the addition of a number of other action sequences, spurred by the movement of James, like Miller, beyond his usual realm of operations. One, mentioned above, comes when James' team happens upon a British squad whose vehicle has become immobilized, an eventuality that leads into a lengthy sequence as they come under sniper fire and a number of the Brits are killed. James takes a leadership role here and in two later sequences that seem to extend further beyond the likely activities of such a figure.

The first of these follows his discovery of a 'body bomb' that James assumes – wrongly, as it turns out – to be the corpse of Beckham. Driven by his maverick genes, we are led to assume, and the relative bond he had established with the boy, James embarks on an ill-thought-out solo mission outside the fortified army camp. Seeking to find the home of the boy and, presumably, some kind of vengeance, he ends at the house of what appears to be a kindly Iraqi professor, retreating sheepishly after being berated by the professor's wife. Later, while investigating the aftermath of the bombing of a petrol tanker, James is sufficiently driven to persuade his team, against their will, to go off on their own after those responsible. It is made clear to him that this is a mission well beyond their brief (the notion that figures responsible for one part of a specialist task might also get involved in the 'action' further down the line is a fictional convenience familiar from other examples such as the various *CSI: Crime Scene Investigation* television series [2000–]). The result is the temporary kidnapping of Eldridge, who is rescued but at the cost of a serious leg wound and who berates James afterwards for risking their lives in order to achieve his adrenalin fix. It is notable that these two excursions come in for criticism – implicitly or explicitly – within the diegesis. That they are essentially foolish actions, as judged from within the fictional world, adds an extra dimension to the narrative, but does not seem to detract from their ability to offer significant doses of action-thrills to the viewer – our equivalent, again vicariously and much attenuated – of the adrenaline rush sought out by the protagonist.

Much of the visual style of *The Hurt Locker* and *Green Zone* relies on the creation of an impression of often intense, generically 'thrilling', proximity to the action, through the use of some of the devices cited above. A general employment of unsteady, hand-held camerawork is heightened further through the use of sudden, awkward zooms and whip-pans, and abrupt editing, the impact of the latter often increased through cutting across shots in which the camera is already in motion; and a general tendency to favour closer perspectives in which any such instability is magnified (a style broadly in keeping with some of the norms of what David Bordwell terms 'intensified continuity': Bordwell 2006). The viewer is often given the impression of going along with the characters on their missions, the camera situated *among* the participants and sharing in some of their responses. A fully subjective camera is deployed at times, although this remains a minority tendency. The decoupage generally offers a heightened variety of a more widespread and traditional Hollywood shift between positions of quasi-subjective location – *close to* but not actually point-of-view – and somewhat more objectively located, but still often relatively proximate, perspectives. This blend – intimate but without being all-engulfingly close – is employed widely in both films, including during the two more implausible escapades in *The Hurt Locker* detailed above, offering a familiar brand of tension/intensity/excitement thrills to the viewer.

The unsteady-cam aesthetic is used consistently throughout *The Hurt Locker* and *Green Zone*. Heightened versions are employed during sequences of high intensity, often evoking an impression of jumpy, nervous, claustrophobic anxiety during unstable encounters in and around the streets of Baghdad: in, for example, the opening mission of *Green Zone*, when Miller takes his crew into a supposed WMD site against the advice of others and before it has been stabilized, or the early bomb disposal sequences of *The Hurt Locker*. A toned-down variant is found more widely, though, even in scenes in which the protagonists are sedentary (for example, an early 'briefing' session in *Green Zone*, in which the camera wavers distinctly from side to side when capturing an exchange between a seated Miller and an officer who is standing still).

Body of Lies makes far less use of such techniques, reserving the 'boosting of the image factor' (the quotation used in the heading for this section is from one of the operators of the drone-based camera) for occasional heightened sequences such as the impact of a bomb detonated in the UK at the start of the film, in chase sequences, or when Ferris is involved in an intense close-quarters struggle with an antagonist and a pack of wild dogs (on the latter occasion, the camera is highly unstable, coupled with rapid cuts and pans that create a distinct strobing effect). A slight impression of 'edginess' is created elsewhere in the film through peripheral movement of the camera as well as regular panning and reframing, but not in so overtly noticeable a manner. Rather than the rhetoric of the intense, up-close action film, that of *Body of Lies* pitches for a more 'classy', more smoothly 'classical' status. The film also makes quite frequent use of sweeping aerial shots: bold overhead perspectives that couple with the drone view in lifting the viewer out of the immediate zone of action. These are used, for example, to accompany the helicopters called in to help Ferris in one early mission and in a sequence in which he is again taken out into the desert at the start of the climactic stage of the film. While creating its own form of visual spectacle, the use of this technique seems not unconnected with the employment of the distance/proximity trope at the thematic level.

Green Zone makes occasional use of sweeping shots from on high, as transitional devices leading from one sequence to another – a standard-enough motivation – but in contexts that provide scope for similar thematic interpretation. The first two of these lead directly into sequences in which the emphasis is on the world of dubious political manoeuvring. This is another perspective that accompanies a flight of helicopters, bringing us to the airport at which a group of long-absent Iraqis are returning to be welcomed by Poundstone as the American-chosen hopes (or, less charitably, stooges) to form a new government. This sequence is followed later by a sweeping view over rooftops that introduces us to the former Saddam palace in which the 'coalition' has its headquarters and where Poundstone is based. A third occasion in which such a perspective is deployed takes us again to the palace. This time, the resonances of the transition are more positive, as we are following a phone call from Miller to Brown, but the destination remains the zone of disconnection from the on-the-ground realities outside. It seems notable that when Miller actually enters the Green Zone himself, we are given the impression of being taken inside *with him*, at ground level in his vehicle, with the more familiar shaky-cam visuals, to the unreality of the world of pool-side luxury that awaits within.

If the intensity of action, and action-thrills, on the ground mirrors the heroic positioning of the likes of Miller, Ferris and James, the cinematic view from on high seems quite consistently to be associated with the world of manipulation and deception (although, from the perspective of this time of writing, it is notable that the principal threat posted by the drone-view in *Body of Lies* is to the activity of the Hollywood hero, rather than any equivalent of the numerous real-world victims of extra-legal assassinations perpetrated through the use of drones during the Obama era). There are some exceptions to, or complications of, this dynamic, however. Sweeping overhead perspectives and the drone-view from above are themselves offered as pleasurable vistas, giving the viewer a share in the mastery of space that they imply, even if this is diegetically associated with sources we are encouraged to distrust. At the para-textual level, *Body of Lies* seems positively to fetishize the panoptic grids of overhead perception, which feature in somewhat spectacularly stylized manner at the start of the closing credits and as a central part of the texture of the DVD menu. *The Hurt Locker* does not participate in this part of the dynamic at all, either in its visuals – which eschew any such perspectives – or in the manner in which its thematic oppositions are deployed.

Not all of the dimensions considered above line up so neatly in all of the three films examined in this chapter. But the consistency of some central threads is striking, nonetheless, as is the conjunction that can be identified between the thematic dimension, in which a particular form of heroic individual action is reasserted and juxtaposed with other negatively coded qualities, and the modes of engagement offered to the viewer as part of the wider realm of contemporary Hollywood action cinema. These films can be interpreted as distinctly conservative interventions, in their mobilization of such familiar, and generally regressive, thematic tropes, in relation to the geopolitical contexts within which they are imposed. But their enactment also permits some space – varying in degree and extent – for more critical discourses. This remains the case, potentially at least, even within a process in which the sources of any blame take the form of familiar kinds of scapegoats from which the viewer is encouraged to be distanced through both thematic and formal strategies.

Bibliography

Barker, M. (2011) A '*Toxic Genre*': *The Iraq War Films*, London: Pluto Press.

Bordwell, D. (2006) *The Way Hollywood Tells It: Story and Style in Modern Movies*, Berkeley: University of California Press.

Gregory, D. (2004) *The Colonial Present*, Oxford: Blackwell.
King, G. (2000) *Spectacular Narratives: Hollywood in the Age of the Blockbuster*, London: I.B. Tauris.
Kitses, J. (2007) *Horizon's West: The Western from John Ford to Clint Eastwood*, London: BFI.
Pollard, T. (2011) *Hollywood 9/11: Superheroes, Supervillains, and Super Disasters*, Boulder, CO: Paradigm Publishers.
Purse, L. (2011) *Contemporary Action Cinema*, Edinburgh: Edinburgh University Press.
Ray, R. (1984) *A Certain Tendency of the Hollywood Cinema, 1930–1980*, Princeton, NJ: Princeton University Press.
Schatz, T. (1981) *Hollywood Genres*, Austin: University of Texas Press.

23
SPECTACLE VS. NARRATIVE
Action political movies in the new millennium

Ian Scott

Spectacle is hardly a new concept in Hollywood film studies. Having been part and parcel of the commercial, artistic and academic approach to the industry from its inception, by the 1970s it was, as Scott Bukatman reminds us, the reinvention of the science fiction genre with *Star Wars* (Lucas, 1977) that paved the way for the summer blockbuster routine that has subsequently become a staple of the Hollywood calendar. George Lucas's film was important for a number of reasons: "With that first shot [*Star Wars*] redefined space, displaced narrative, and moved cinema into the revived realm of spectacular excess," confirms Bukatman (1998: 248).

In Bukatman's telling description, *Star Wars* "exploded the frame of narrative cinema" referencing the medium's early epics while pointing towards the technological revolution in on-screen pyrotechnics as well as future home-viewing wizardry (ibid.). In short it "re-legitimated the spectacular" as Barry Langford would have it, after a period of reflexive reconsideration during the so-called New Hollywood renaissance of the early 1970s (2010: 248). Nevertheless, Bukatman is keen to emphasise that the film did not forsake narrative entirely; merely reproduced it in a comforting formula for a new generation that could appreciate its age-old good vs. evil scenario on a whole new level. What *Star Wars* achieved with its camerawork therefore, became the template for sci-fi to explore space, planets, cities and alien craft in a blaze of wonderment *and* traditional story-telling: from *Star Trek: The Motion Picture* (Wise, 1979) to *Stargate* (Emmerich, 1994), from *Close Encounters of the Third Kind* (Spielberg, 1977) to *Blade Runner* (Scott, 1982) (Bukatman 1998: 252).

Still, whatever these films – and this genre – achieved by way of productive narrative ingenuity, the argument stuck that the blockbuster spectacle was here to stay and narrative was starting to be devoured at its expense. Geoff King contends that spectacle had an important economic retort to confront too. That the challenges from beyond the movies such as TV and consumer culture more widely, pushed Hollywood to create ever more lavish sci-fi, disaster, and 'sword-and-sandal' epics, all reimagining the studio routine in ever greater, larger-than-life situations. As if to remind us that the industry likes reinvention, twenty-first century incarnates such as *Gladiator* (R. Scott, 2000), *Alexander* (Stone, 2004) and *Troy* (Petersen, 2004) not only served to cast the latter sub-genre's historical epic tradition in a new light, with the latest special effects on display, but also served, King states, as a "reminder of the extent to which little has changed in nearly a half century of New Hollywood tradition" (King 2002: 178). Recurrent tropes in the action spectacle have also been accompanied by key scholarly interventions in aspects of capitalism, history – as above – and masculinity, a trait David Bordwell describes as one of the longest running 'crises' in film studies, let alone blockbuster action movies (2006: 104).

Nevertheless, despite such interventions, the central conceit remained. "Some suggest that spectacle has become the dominant tendency of contemporary blockbuster production. Narrative is usually identified as the victim", King surmised in the early 2000s (2002: 179). A generation on from Bukatman's examples, spectacle had reached well beyond the confines of blockbuster science fiction, crisscrossing genres with creatures of all kinds in *Alien* (R. Scott, 1979) and *Predator* (McTiernan, 1987) as well as the dinosaurs of *Jurassic Park* (Spielberg, 1993) and the submerging *Titanic* (Cameron, 1997). Indeed the trajectory that Bukatman and King describe might be seen to have its apotheosis in the current, powerful age of spectacle epitomised by the *Dark Knight* (2005–), *Iron Man* (2008–), *Avengers* (2012–), *X-Men* (2000–), *Thor* (2011–) and *Captain America* (2011–) franchises. Hollywood film has reaffirmed itself as a "cinema of attractions" to use Tom Gunning's famous phrase (quoted in Bukatman 1998: 254).

Graphically plotting the change in structure of films over time also seems to confirm the trend for visual display. An evolutionary line rising to a crescendo of action at the climax of movies of the earlier period has now been transformed into a contemporary rollercoaster ride where the spectacle film today is interrupted by periodic, and concentrated, bursts of excitement, maintaining an audience's emotional but also thrill-seeking involvement throughout the duration of the movie (King, 2002: 185–193).[1]

Despite this plotting, King, like Bukatman, is right to speculate as to whether narrative has truly been superseded, not least working on the premise that, as hinted at, spectacle has in fact *always* been an endemic part of Hollywood's cinematic construction, and narrative *continues* to remain prevalent within current spectacle-induced fantasies like those above as well as the *Twilight* (2009–12) and *The Hunger Games* (2012–) series, to name but two more variants. More than that, as the likes of David Bordwell (1985), Richard Maltby (1995), Elizabeth Cowie (1997) and others have pointed out, narrative has hardly been a stable construction on its own terms either, and whatever "classical narrative form" there is in Hollywood works within a multitude of different strains adaptable to these and other blockbuster behemoths. "Narrative and spectacle aren't mutually exclusive concepts," charges Bordwell. "Every action scene, however 'spectacular' is a narrative event" (2006: 104). Indeed, where this argument logically ends up is accepting, if not purposefully arguing for blockbusters adopting their own ranking according to quite discreet and sophisticated spectacle and narrative conceits *combined*. To achieve both while at the same time maintaining a critical and commercial trajectory, is the sign of blockbuster spectacle heaven, or, as King puts it, "something akin to the sublime" (King 2006: 334).

At the head of this construction in modern Hollywood is a director such as Christopher Nolan. At once a blockbuster franchise luminary, exemplified by the rebooted *Batman* series, while also an auteurist visionary capable of engaging his audience with stand-alone spectacle in the form of *Inception* (2010) and *Interstellar* (2014), Nolan has become the spectacle-auteur *par excellence* in the early twenty-first century. Of crucial concern here, though, is that his films have also offered something of the 'political' in their fixations on corporations, establishment forces and institutional characters and representatives. Furthermore, the penchant for comic book adaptation derived from Marvel and D.C. Publications especially, has seen dystopian science-fiction mix action and adventure with fantasy and even horror as the archetypal templates of such franchises. Despite Nolan's presence, however, the 'political', where it does intervene, largely remains a 'lower-case' idea, rather more than it is an 'upper-case' precept. It is true that his *Dark Knight* trilogy has reimagined Batman's Gotham milieu as a site of political allegory in the global terror age; and a series like *X-Men* has provoked critical responses in its attention to historical political settings – the Cuban Missile Crisis, the assassination of President Kennedy, etc. – as well as constructed diegetic political actors within the confines of the stories' world view. But these films have been very different texts in comparison to 1990s movies such as *Independence Day* (Emmerich, 1996) and *Air Force One* (Petersen, 1997) where overt political actors appear in largely recognisable situational form – though the former does of course involve alien invasion! – whilst being wedded to blockbuster aesthetics.

In 2013 then, in the face of the overwhelming dominance of the blockbuster/comic book adaptation juggernaut, it was with some surprise that two 'politically' charged spectacle movies *did* appear staking a claim for a newly energised role in a crowded summer movie marketplace. *Olympus Has Fallen* (*Olympus*) directed by Antoine Fuqua and 'blockbuster veteran' Roland Emmerich's *White House Down (WHD)* were curious entities in a number of ways. For one, their premise – of the White House being attacked and taken over by rogue/foreign/mercenaries – appeared nearly identical to each other. In *Olympus*, ex-communicated presidential protection agent Mike Banning (Gerard Butler) launches a one-man rescue mission to rid the White House of invading North Korean terrorists, while *WHD* features Channing Tatum's aspiring Washington DC cop who wants to work on the presidential detail and yet finds himself on nothing more than a White House tour with his daughter when a selection of mercenaries led by retiring Head of Detail, Martin Walker (James Woods), bomb the Capitol and take over the Oval Office.

Second, with the so-called 'war on terror' of the Bush era well over a decade old and American forces removed and/or retreating from Iraq and Afghanistan, the films' forceful reactionary nature towards the politics of terror seemed – on the surface at least – somewhat at odds with Obama-era positivism; though the events in the Middle East at the time of release as well as the films' prototypical national nemeses, Iran and North Korea, chimed with the fecundity of fear about events taking place in those regions. Within a year, indeed, the rise of Islamic State (IS) across large swathes of Syria and Iraq brought fears of further instability and global threat so the films might be accused of being not far short of the foreign policy mark retrospectively. Third, while the two films – presidents once again in peril and called upon to save the day – had clear antecedents in the form of the aforementioned 1990s pictures – one of which Emmerich directed – their socio-cultural agendas and political rationale were anything but straightforward and gung-ho, even if the two paved the way for obviously redemptive ideological and political endings.

The sudden re-emergence of the spectacle political movie confirmed their paucity in the Hollywood stable. The spy thriller, foreign policy movie and war-on-terror age had produced notable franchises in the early 2000s, not least the *Bourne* series of films (2002–) where security and military services linked directly and indirectly to political affiliates. And the minor franchise *National Treasure* was an unexpected hit with an original in 2004 grossing over $370 million worldwide and a 2007 sequel (an even more impressive $457 million worldwide take), both of which toyed with the idea of conspiracies and secrets related to America's founding fathers and the nation's political past.[2]

The 'war on terror' in its military guise received plenty of attention too (*Rendition* [Hood, 2007], *Lions for Lambs* [Redford, 2007], *Redacted* [De Palma, 2007]), not least the twin assault by director Kathryn Bigelow on the dangers of foreign policy incision and occupation

(*The Hurt Locker* [2008]) and the belated identification and elimination of Osama bin Laden (*Zero Dark Thirty* [2012]). And on television, the runaway success of Fox TV's *24* over eight seasons from 2001 (with *24: Live Another Day* rebooting the show in 2014), as well as *Homeland* (2011–) and *Hostages* (2013–), saw successive political figures – predominantly presidents – caught in the web of terrorist cabals and repetitive threats to office and country.

And yet while Fuqua's and Emmerich's films had lineage to these previous productions, their films were respectively at odds with this collection and they were anything but obvious rejoinders to a youth market coached in the manner of modern Marvel/D.C. pedagogy where, thanks to almost limitless technological CGI, space, time and possibilities for conflict and destruction on an epic scale seemed endless. Indeed, surrounding *Olympus* and *WHD* during 2013 were examples – *Iron Man 3* (Black, 2013), *Avengers Assemble* (Whedon, 2012), *Star Trek: Into Darkness* (Abrams, 2013), *Man of Steel* (Snyder, 2013) – whose spectacle and conflagration appeared to visually throw the White House assaults into anachronistic relief. The sub-texts of these sci-fi/superhero movies also offered the appearance of deliberative and philosophical engagement with America's actual diplomatic world view, captured in a sci-fi vortex of 'unknown others', institutional secrecy, and conflictual world-policeman status.

And yet *Olympus*, on a budget of $70 million, recouped just short of $100 million by the spring of 2013 in the US alone. Its worldwide gross turned out to be $161 million placing the movie forty-third on the 2013 list of highest box-office takes. *White House Down* had a production budget that was more than double its rival but still managed to take a very respectable $205 million worldwide in 2013, putting it thirty-seventh on the year-end list. These were hardly record-breaking returns but they were anything but commercial flops either.

Olympus has Fallen and *WHD* lacked substantial critical appeal as well. Both were objected to on a number of levels, the principal one being their preposterousness. Both films lacked what Terry Christensen and Peter Hass would describe as the ability to "mimic and/or re-create reality" or, put simply, to be convincingly authentic (Christensen and Hass 2005: 6–7). The look, aesthetics, construction and generic form of political movies are what give meaning and understanding to their mimicking of the actual political establishment around them, argue Christensen and Hass. By their model, *Olympus* and *WHD* failed spectacularly in this regard.

From the latter's opening sweep across the Capitol with the Marine One helicopter making any number of illegal manoeuvres, to the gapingly lax security inside the Capitol Building that gets blown to smithereens early in Emmerich's film, *WHD*'s action film pretensions literally overwhelm the political settings from the very first moments, to little effect for some. As critic Peter Bradshaw observed: "[t]he basic silliness of all those CGI effects and all the digitally fabricated action mean that real thrills – dependent on real, believable jeopardy – are not on offer: just cheerfully absurd spectacle and a little bit of humour" (Bradshaw, 2013).

Olympus, on the other hand, begins with the president (Aaron Eckhart) engaged in an unlikely boxing scene, sparring with Banning, his personal protection detail, and joking that he's not supposed to be hit in the face, a signal of his resilient fighting ability later in the picture. The audience are subsequently confronted with a Korean diplomatic mission sprouting into an all-out assault force who proceed to take over the White House inside and out without any thought to security and background checks having ever been entertained. Trapped inside while the carnage rages outside, Banning and the president's young son display an alarmingly good knowledge of every nook and cranny of the White House almost as if their inside information had been waiting for just such a crisis to emerge.

Yet inauthenticity like this actually helps explain some of the appeal of the two films. Preposterousness alone may not act as a guiding principle for the critical or commercial acceptance of action spectacle political movies or indeed their relevance and import beyond the confines of today's multiplex culture. But inauthentic preposterousness has actually been quite a significant factor in political drama and, I want to suggest in this chapter, has in fact encompassed a political discourse over the last decade that has some ideological force and resonance. Using Thomas Elsaesser's arguments concerning narrative, realism in cinema can have a "purposive" reading to it on the part of the audience who are willing to suspend disbelief for the benefit of some wider goal. "Such an interpretation could account for the fact that one can tolerate a good deal of improbability in the characters [and] lack of plausibility in the situations," says Elsaesser. As long as there are "sufficient elements which allow for the possibility of 'consistent reading' on another level of articulation," the film can have meaning and import for its audience (2012: 99). In political spectacle movies, this import may not be along the lines of an ideological left and right built out of aesthetic signifiers, a conservative and liberal binary contesting policy and philosophy if you will. But it does operate figuratively, in a more deeply embedded psychological arena where politics now resides in the inauthentic space between culture, meaning and discourse. Examining that space offers some profitable analysis to contend with.

Spectacle as political agency

Debating the merits of whether spectacle has displaced narrative or whether narrative has always been subject to translation and reformulation, is a useful exercise in building up seams of inquiry in the post-Classical era then. Spectacle is, as King restates, the "interruption", the "intrusive presence" (2002: 179) that forces us to gasp, or behold, the visual repertoire before our eyes. Narrative remains the traditional trajectory of a film; and today it has become increasingly idealised as theoretical/conceptual shorthand for character-driven, thoughtful, intensive, maybe even cerebral fare. In other words, narrative films belong for some in a particular mode of filmmaking while in the blockbuster world at least, spectacle has more or less triumphed as an object of narrative momentum in and of itself. Narrative is thus the stuff of drama, be it historical, social and/or political.

Spectacles, on the other hand, maintain central components that are energetic and confrontational on an epic scale, increasingly concerning the fate of the planets/universe. While films such as *The Dark Knight Rises* (Nolan, 2012), *Prometheus* (R. Scott, 2012) and *Iron Man 3* have garnered some praise for their complex inner-workings within a spectacle-fuelled milieu, the intended rush of adrenalin accompanying action-driven films like the *Fast and Furious* series (2001–), the Marvel/DC adaptations led by *Avengers Assemble*, and the eye-popping scale of *Oblivion* (Kosinski, 2013), *After Earth* (Shyamalan, 2013) and *Pacific Rim* (del Toro, 2013) leaves one in no doubt as to spectacle's force, driven on by ever-increasing technological capability.

It would be amiss, however, not to recognise the "coercive dimension" of spectacular *mise en scènes* too, as Barry Langford's description would have it. Quoting Robert Kolker – a critic of Steven Spielberg's blockbuster mentality – Langford sees spectacular films like *Close Encounters of the Third Kind* as a potential sublimation of free-will predicated on such an overwhelming confrontation with spectacle form, that the viewer has no choice but to succumb to the will of the visual meta-narrative. For Kolker, this tactic has a "fascist aesthetic" to it that he believes closely ingratiates Spielberg's work, for example, with outright propagandists, even extreme ones, like Leni Riefenstahl (Langford 2010: 249; see also Kolker 2010). For Langford and Kolker, as for others then, the political force of what appear on the surface as very unpolitical texts emanates out of a bridge joining spectacle to ideological construct or fascism as art, as German political thinker Carl Schmitt's writings have sometimes been translated as, within a film context.[3]

But what then of the spectacle/narrative debate translated into overt political spaces like the White House with specific political characters attached? As the likes of *Escape from New York* (Carpenter, 1981), *Deep Impact* (Leder, 1998), *Independence Day* and *The Day After Tomorrow* (Emmerich, 2004) demonstrate, it is not like political actors and/or settings have not been purposefully engaged with in a series of spectacle movies before; but rarely have any of these types of film been analysed for their political content or inference, and even more rare has been their analysis pitted against more 'traditional' political films; political films where 'narrative' in its various guises seems to rule the day, lauded upon classic exponents of the genre like *Mr. Smith Goes to Washington* (Capra, 1939), *The Manchurian Candidate* (Frankenheimer, 1962) and *All the President's Men* (Pakula, 1976) that are especially pre-disposed to classical Hollywood narrative concepts rather more than post-classical conceits. However, if we accept Philip Giannos's maxim that "politics and movies inform each other .... Both tell about the society from which they came," and ally this to Elsaesser's "purposive" reading, one might begin to gauge the greater unidentified impact of spectacle political movies, as well as considering their merits in the light of 'classic' political texts such as the examples above (Giannos, quoted in Christensen and Hass 2005: 4).

In the first instance, it helps to discover where narrative and spectacle political cinema first drew the battle lines. Douglas Kellner's *Cinema Wars* (2010) locates the dimensions of a cultural battle for supremacy in political cinema dating back to the 1960s with the counterculture, the end of the studio era, and political hot-button issues that raged throughout society and in the name of right- or left-wing agendas. More recently, though, for Kellner, everything in American society since the 2000 election and the post 9/11 Bush era has been a political contest, not least film, and hence a reason why he thinks certain forms of genre, the social engagement of particular actors, directors and producers and subject matter itself, all compete for the ideological oxygen and influence around them. American film, he asserts – encompassing more than just Hollywood – is a "highly contested terrain" exhibiting a "wide range of styles and aesthetics" (2010: 3). And the historical narrative established from this political battle forged in different artistic formulations is also clear for Kellner: "[O]ver the 2000s, a hegemonic right-wing conservatism was defeated by a social liberalism represented by the Obama [2008] campaign and that battle was played out in Hollywood film of the era" (ibid.). He goes on to reason that representing a political era, intentionally or obliquely, is done by what he calls "transcoding", or how the likes of Reaganism, liberalism and, more recently, Tea Party conservatism are translated or encoded into media texts (2010: 2).

Film is not just a social barometer of the times by this argument then, so much as it is a contestable political space where ideology and critique can be engaged and deliberately provoked in the service of particular agendas. In Kellner's eyes at least, a variety of movies came and went in the early 2000s that entertained just such a crucial battleground – and a picture like *The Passion of the Christ* (Gibson, 2004), he argues, provides important evidence for this – and the rise, influence and cross-over of TV and film working in cahoots with each other, adds even more piquancy to this theory (2010: 3–4). Kellner's social influence, for instance, is to equate movies like the *Saw* horror franchise (2004–10) as well as *The Dark Knight* with causal, metaphoric pastiches of the Bush–Cheney "nightmare" era as he unapologetically describes it (2010: 1). They are codes, in other words, for the state of society around them and the ideological and philosophical conflicts that so infused the first decade of the new millennium. If the thesis is quantitatively difficult to prove, you nevertheless know what Kellner means when trying to portion off mere influence and allegorical interpretation, from immersive political contestation.

The question is, does such a theory hold true; and even if it does, is this any different from other Hollywood eras? Are the violently sociopathic and nihilist characters of the films above shorthand signifiers for American or even western society in the grip of fundamentalist and/or extreme thought that challenges every staple of institutional and cultural life around it? The proliferation of horror may seem an obvious rejoinder for a society steeped in random violence, but there are all sorts of other connotations to do with its recent renaissance, not least the freeing of censorious restriction as well as developing cinematic technology, accounted for above. It is nevertheless prevalent to Kellner's argumentative treatise to recognise that a government which is unequivocal about violence cannot expect society to be any less so. Horror had popularity in 1930s Hollywood too, in another era of social and economic dislocation, but Kellner's sense that it is a genre loosened of any prevailing moral and restorative foundations is certainly persuasive.

The contemporary crop of films also exemplifies Hollywood's ability to pick up on social fears/norms/perceptions as a manifestation of the zeitgeist in some way. The Cold War

Figure 23.1 Landmark monument destruction in (a) *White House Down* and (b) *Olympus Has Fallen*.

nuclear texts of the 1960s for instance, led by *The Manchurian Candidate*, *Dr. Strangelove* (Kubrick, 1962), *Fail Safe* (Lumet, 1964) and crossover British/American texts like *The Spy Who Came in from the Cold* (Ritt, 1965), *Funeral in Berlin* (Hamilton, 1966) and of course James Bond, all preyed upon the fear of nuclear and bipolar rivalry. The 1970s paranoia pictures, including *The Parallax View* (Pakula, 1974), *Three Days of the Condor* (Pollack, 1975) and *All the President's Men*, laid into fears about government secrecy and unaccountability in the backdrop to Watergate. The 1990s comedic revival of screwball terms and conditions set in train by *Dave* (Reitman, 1994), *The American President* (Reiner, 1995) and *My Fellow Americans* (Segal, 1996) rang out as a nostalgic revisitation upon a kinder, gentler age, suddenly becalmed in the period immediately after the Cold War. So *Olympus* and *WHD* are no different in that respect in picking up on the scent of terrorist cabals, prominent monuments and buildings subject to attack, and government undermined, all part of the decade-long fear of collusion and infiltration brought on by the 'war on terror' (see Figure 23.1).

If this potted history of the political film makes sense and tells us that a wide array of movies provide a rich vein of institutional and ideological engagement with wider issues, where do we begin to theorise out the separation between narrative-driven texts above from the spectacle-induced politics of *Olympus* and *WHD* in particular; and why might these latter movies have as much if not more political capital immersed within them as the better known, seemingly more resonant movies above? One answer is to consider that link to television for a moment.

Imagine a story where a White House communications director relinquishes her role only to go into private business where she 'fixes' things for clients in all sorts of trouble, from an office in the capital that nobody but the Washington DA it seems, knows exists. Only she seems to have trouble of her own kind, principally for having been formally the mistress of the President of the United States, for whom she now works on occasion, and to whom she appears to have virtually unending access both around and within the White House, whenever she likes. Giving new meaning to the preposterous and inauthentic, the resume is for ABC's leading TV drama, *Scandal* (2012–) starring Kerry Washington as fixer Olivia Pope.

Shows as outlandish and yet as compulsive as *Scandal*, the aforementioned *24* and even the more serious and acclaimed *Homeland* have found viewers and plaudits on the small screen, while the likes of *Olympus*, *WHD* and lesser action fare such as *Shooter* (Fuqua, 2007), *The Sentinel* (Johnson, 2006) and *Vantage Point* (Travis, 2008) have consistently been denigrated as implausible, histrionic, cartoonish and preposterous. Why? Well, as the viewing figures testify to, *Scandal*, *Homeland* and the rest are successful and compulsive because, not in spite of, being over-the-top, wholly unreconstructed, removed-from-reality, inauthenticised texts. It also helps that multiple episodes and several seasons allow time for characters to develop, plots – however ludicrous – to unfold and tension to ripen.

It is true too that these series have had competition for their political settings among shows that place a far greater emphasis on 're-creative realism'. The continued prevalence of the award-winning *The West Wing* (1999–2006) in the early 2000s, and more recently the popularity of series like *The Good Wife* (2009–) and *House of Cards* (2013–) give pause for thought about the way the iconic and ideological work in tandem with the authentic. But even these shows knowingly add humour, bathos and outlandish Machiavellian plotting to their substantive political milieus. They thus demand a "purposive reading" of their storylines that condition audiences to the practice and discourse of political elites working at the margins of any institutional accountability, let alone logic.

If TV in the 2000s has seemingly been able to work politics into any form it liked, could the extension of preposterous inauthenticity as a theory hold true for the Hollywood spectacle film? And if the relative success of *Olympus Has Fallen* and *White House Down* has any meaning to it, might we suggest that these films subliminally and discursively set an agenda for political discourse that is now more freely and actively reflective of wider opinion? Certainly more freely accepted and encoded than a host of pedagogic texts in the 2000s, like the above-mentioned *Rendition*, *Lions for Lambs* and *Redacted*, conjoined with worthy but also commercially poor-performing movies such as *In the Valley of Elah* (Haggis, 2007), *Battle for Haditha* (Broomfield, 2007) and *Green Zone* (Greengrass, 2010). Moreover, does the emergence of these two films also suggest two strands of political filmmaking that have reached a very distinguishable impasse? If the former is more important than the latter, if *Olympus* and *WHD* are likely to elicit ideological responses from the demographic they are both aimed at, what does this suggest about political filmmaking overall in the twenty-first century?

Conclusion

In conclusion, I want to suggest that *Olympus has Fallen* and *White House Down* are but two examples of a persistent and formidable force in contemporary Hollywood political films. They are utilising what Michael Shapiro interprets as, drawing on Jacques Rancière's work on Sergei Eisenstein, "aesthetic treatments" of their subjects. In other words they are political texts in a critical sense, rather than an ideological one. They are concerned with being "about what we see", as Rancière noted of Eisenstein's films (Shapiro 2009: 4). This goes to the heart of not only a popular cultural consensus about what political movies might be doing as pedagogic and ideological tools, but it also hints at the issues of scholarly interrogation too. In his book, *Cinematic Geopolitics*, Shapiro happily confesses to the scepticism of certain audiences to which he has relayed his work. Where is the empiricism, is film not just a mediated practice that conjoins a certain fictional narrative with some immediate reference points and no more? It is just about movies isn't it, they all cried? In short, says Shapiro, "many academics tend to dismiss the epistemic significance of cinema" (Shapiro 2009: 5). If that under-appreciation of cognition is true of films with a pervasive social and political critique to hand, then one might question how spectacle films like *Olympus* and *WHD* could ever really achieve such an impact upon wider philosophical attitudes and general public opinion.

Shapiro's answer is to allude to what Elsaesser conceives of as the "phatic aspect of communication" heightened by recognition that contributes towards an emotional response at the heart of going to the movies. This emotion is then translated into an "intellectual" calculation that does not need "real" or actual emotion/recognition/cognition to inform it on the screen, but merely "typical drive patterns" that prompt responses and trigger mechanisms of acceptance, understanding and ideological coherence (Elsaesser 2012: 102–3).

This assertion moves on from Christensen and Hass's interpretation of already grounded political texts having aesthetic rights imbued within them that add meta-textual dimensions. It also advances further than Kolker's formulation through Langford of the blockbuster text being injected with ideological venom that catches the unsuspecting viewer unawares. Here, the spectacle-induced political text connotes what we might term obviousness. In short, the kidnapping of the President, the destruction of the Washington monument, the blowing up of the Capitol Building and the White House, are not encoded with anything other than American democracy's battle for preservation, and that is the strongest political/critical/ideological statement there is in the US polity. Does that automatically mean that the movies can only be gung-ho, protectionist, patriotic and conservative? Possibly, but *Olympus* and *WHD* have a female vice-president and an African American president, not characters one would affiliate with the right-wing automatically. Political allegiance for these highly politicised figures is often mediated out of such texts to the point of abstraction, but even so are they meant to be Republicans necessarily? With Aaron Eckhart as Benjamin Asher in Fuqua's film, and especially Jamie Foxx as James Sawyer in Emmerich's, the assumption is far from clear. Indeed, the premise upon which the attacks are made is that these presidents and their administrations have somehow been too lenient, progressive and liberal in their past dealings with foreign powers and rivals.

And while identifying a clear-cut political manifesto in these constructed political figures is testing in itself, a wider examination of ideology also adds to the confusion. Daniel Franklin, for one, mentions political values and beliefs in his book *Politics and Film* (2006) that add up to a checklist of democratic criteria permeating movies. Franklin privileges Lockean liberalism as a recurrent value in films thrusting forward capitalism, individualism, natural rights and even the immigrant experience as quintessential factors in the politicising of Hollywood (2006: 20–22). They are key ideological staging posts in iconic landmark films as diverse as *Mr. Smith Goes to Washington*, *Young Mr. Lincoln* (Ford, 1939) , *JFK* (Stone, 1991) and *All the President's Men*. However, what none of these films has that *Olympus* and *WHD* deal in is the political mandate to survive: as a nation, as a superpower and perhaps as the world's policeman.

The survival of the American democratic experiment therefore resides in these two pictures; an ideological precept that crosses political, social and ideological boundaries regardless of the debate as to whether Asher and Sawyer are Republicans or Democrats, and which readily connects with Elsaesser's emotional and intellectual compact. Survival of a nation not only deeply divided along ethnic, religious and social lines, but divided from a world that increasingly sees no redemption for the US; no outlet from its self-appointed role as protector and purveyor of the world's cultural and political norms. As James Woods's rogue Chief of Staff informs the president in *White House Down*'s climatic sequence as he presses for nuclear annihilation of America's enemies: "The Middle East will be our last war. It will either be us or them." The end game of the nation's world role can only be ultimate triumph or catastrophic failure, therefore; no other route is explainable by a decade-long crusade to shape hearts and minds in the world's most traumatised regions. Walker meanwhile, inspired to take over the White House as a result of the loss of his son in combat, justifies avenging this death with ultimate American might as an act of patriotic redemption. Patriotism as momentum for continued military endeavour in perpetuity is the reasoning, and Republican or Democrat, left or right, neo-conservative or liberal can have no differentiation in this war to the end. As the politics of the war-on-terror age have demonstrated, avoiding America's recurrent military and diplomatic destiny, whether you are George W. Bush or Barack Obama, is a tricky and unavoidable pursuit.

If this one unifying treatise is the real ideological "phatic connection," as Elsaesser has it, for audiences attuned to blockbuster aesthetics, then the subtleties and nuances of narrative political films like *The Ides of March* (Clooney, 2010), *Lincoln* (Spielberg, 2012) and television series like *House of Cards* are not the route to understanding American institutional ideas and philosophy. Political spectacle movies like *Olympus Has Fallen* and *White House Down* are the real purveyors of America's twenty-first century cultural politics and discourse on screen.

Notes

1 King, using Pfeil, plots this out on a series of graphs with the later blockbuster structure starting to emerge in the late 1990s in films like *Die Hard with a Vengeance* (McTiernan, 1995), *Speed* (de Bont, 1994) and *Armageddon* (Bay, 1998).

2 All figures were taken from *Box Office Mojo* (www.boxofficemojo.com), accessed 9 January 2014.
3 Richard Wolin identifies a direct link within Schmitt's writings between political ideas and aesthetic representation. Wolin uses Schmitt as an inversion of the bourgeois depoliticisation of art so as to fashion an idea of the self-sustaining fascist state, "the state is a work of art" (Wolin 1992: 443).

Bibliography

Bordwell, D. (1985) *Narration in the Fiction Film*, New York: Routledge.
Bordwell, D. (2006) *The Way Hollywood Tells It: Story and Style in Modern Movies*, London: University of California Press.
Bradshaw, P. (2013) "*White House Down* Review", in *The Guardian*, 23 September, 2013.
Bukatman, S. (1998) "Zooming Out: The End of Off-Screen Space", in Lewis, J. (ed.) *The New American Cinema*, Durham, NC: Duke University Press, pp. 248–272.
Christensen, T. and Hass, P.J. (2005) *Projecting Politics: Political Messages in American Films*, London: M.E. Sharpe.
Cowie, E. (1997) *Representing the Woman: Psychoanalysis and Cinema*, Minneapolis: University of Minnesota Press.
Elsaesser, T. (2012) *The Persistence of Hollywood*, Abingdon: Routledge.
Franklin, D.P. (2006) *Politics and Film: The Political Culture of Film in the United States*, Oxford: Rowman & Littlefield.
Kellner, D. (2010) *Cinema Wars: Hollywood Film and Politics in the Bush-Cheney Era*, Oxford: Wiley-Blackwell.
King, G. (2002) *New Hollywood Cinema: An Introduction*, London: I.B. Tauris.
King, G. (2006) "Spectacle and Narrative in the Contemporary Blockbuster", in L.R. Williams and M. Hammond (eds) *Contemporary Hollywood Cinema*, London: McGraw-Hill, pp. 334–352.
Kolker, R. (2010) *A Cinema of Loneliness: Penn, Stone, Kubrick, Scorsese, Spielberg, Altman*, 3rd edition, Oxford: Oxford University Press.
Langford, B. (2010) *Post-Classical Hollywood: Film Industry, Style and Ideology since 1945*, Edinburgh: Edinburgh University Press.
Maltby, R. (1995) *Hollywood Cinema*, 2nd edition, Oxford, Blackwell.
Shapiro, M. (2009) *Cinematic Geopolitics*, London: Routledge.
Wolin, R. (1992) "Carl Schmitt: The Conservative Revolutionary Habitus and the Aesthetics of Horror", in *Political Theory* 20(3), pp. 424–447.

24

REPRESENTING 9/11 IN HOLLYWOOD CINEMA

Eleftheria Thanouli

The representation of the terrorist attacks on September 11, 2001, in the United States has not attracted the interest of the Hollywood film industry as much as one would expect, given the spectacular nature of the events and the extensive media coverage that followed minutes after the first explosion in the North Tower of the World Trade Center (WTC) in New York. To this date, only two Hollywood feature films have attempted to reconstruct aspects of the 9/11 attacks, namely Paul Greengrass' *United 93* (2006) and Oliver Stone's *World Trade Center* (2006). The former depicts a chain of events that stretch over a few hours on the morning of September 11, starting with the takeoff of United 93, the plane that was hijacked by Muslim terrorists and crashed into the ground in a field in Pennsylvania. The latter is set in New York and focuses on the rescue attempts of two police officers trapped in the rubble of the WTC. The fact that both films were released a few months apart and pioneered a direct fictional recounting of the traumatic events in question led numerous scholars and critics to engage in long and detailed comparisons of the two filmic narratives (Burgoyne 2008; Kendrick 2008; Prince 2009; Redfield 2009; Giglio 2010; Kellner 2010; Rommel-Ruiz 2011; Morris 2012; Hoberman 2012). Weighing the similarities and differences between the films, these accounts often result in contradictory conclusions in regard to specific elements, such as, for instance, the matter of 'comprehensiveness' of their stories (Rommel-Ruiz 2011: 241; Prince 2009: 107). What binds them together, however, is the overall tendency to consider them markedly different. In Rommel-Ruiz's words, "similarities aside, the two films differ in meaningful ways" (2011: 241).

Two of the most notable readings of the films are found in Robert Burgoyne's and Douglas Kellner's work, each focusing on a different side of the 9/11 reconstruction, namely its resonance for history and politics, respectively. Burgoyne's (2008) chapter entitled "The topical historical film: *United* 93 and *World Trade Center*" examines how these two narratives focus on a narrow slice of history and discusses whether they contribute or not to coping with the historical trauma caused by the attacks. Drawing on concepts of trauma theory from Cathy Caruth and Dominick LaCapra's writings, Burgoyne ventures a tentative parallel between 9/11 and the Holocaust, as two traumatic events of a different scale but with similar barriers to the politics and aesthetics of representation. Despite this admittedly broad theoretical backdrop, Burgoyne crafts a quite nuanced portrait of the films' thematic and stylistic properties, aptly embedding them in their cinematic history. For instance, he notes the "nervous, verité visual style of *United 93*" (151) and the Eisensteinian montage that simultaneously advances the multiple threads of the story (156). On the other hand, *World Trade Center* prefers "a minimalist, nearly abstract visual approach" (151). Particularly the scenes under the ruins, according to Burgoyne, resemble "compositions in black, gray, and white, as if they were drawings in charcoal" while the lack of movement "at times seems like something out of the avant-garde plays of Samuel Beckett, where forms of emptiness, nothingness, and the utter absence of event express the profound isolation of the characters" (151). Thematically, however, the two narratives equally strive to emphasize human agency and collective heroic action. They feature stories where individuals take matters in their own hands while they fight to survive an overwhelming disaster. Yet, such portrait of affirmative action is framed differently in each film, leading to a strikingly different message. Whereas *United 93* concludes with a sudden blackout, the characters in *World Trade Center* emerge into light to signify hope. As Burgoyne writes:

> *World Trade Center* draws on the discourses of commemoration. However, in its defamiliarization of daily life, its surrealistic juxtapositions, and in its palpable sense of loss and missed connections, an essential melancholy comes through. The past "possesses" the film despite its attempt to stop time and inhibit forgetting. *United 93*, by contrast, attempts to break down the defenses of the audience in order to prevent the traumatic events of 9/11 from being relegated to memory.
>
> (167)

With *World Trade Center* visioning a more hopeful future grounded on collective memories of death and rebirth and *United 93* trapped in the present moment, each narrative offers a different response to the traumatic events of 9/11.

The emphasis on difference also characterizes Kellner's (2010) comparison of the two films drawn with even starker demarcating lines. In an openly evaluating tone, Kellner considers *United 93* to be a better film, mostly because it shies away from a number of traditional Hollywood formulas. As he succinctly puts it, "*United 93* presented no Hollywoodesque individualized heroes in its ultra-realistic, low-key, and understated portrayal of the events leading to the crash" (101). The emphasis on ordinary people taking heroic action is welcomed as a deviation from the classical norms and so is the portrayal of the government and military agencies, which fail to handle the crisis in a professional and competent manner. The problems of communication and coordination of the various institutional forces that take up so much of *United 93*'s story space are interpreted by Kellner as a political message that "US citizens cannot trust their government for national security or to protect them from terrorists" and that "groups of people must decide to protect themselves and organize to fight for their own survival" (104). On the other hand, Oliver Stone's film takes an opposite turn. According to Kellner, "*World Trade Center* is the ultimate un-Oliver Stone film: restrained, understated, often slow and somber, and conservative" (104). Surprisingly enough, the signs of restraint, understatement and somberness are overly neglected, as Kellner swiftly moves on to characterize the film as "shamelessly sentimental" and melodramatic (104). His overall judgment of the film is fairly negative; Stone's politics are deeply conservative because his film "extols the humanity and courage of ordinary Americans, but fails to explore the reasons for the attack" (106). The paradox of this statement cannot go unheeded. Whereas the focus on everyday life and ordinary people was deemed a strong asset of Greengrass' film, it is now considered neutral at best. At the same time, the fact that neither film explores the reasons behind the attacks is not weighed equally against both filmmakers. It is only Stone who is held accountable for not shedding light on the roots of the 9/11 events.

Reading *United 93* and *World Trade Center* against each other and not 'next to each other' has often resulted in conflicting views regarding their historical significance and their political orientation. In the rest of this chapter I will attempt to reverse the prevalent rationale and dig up a number of remarkable similarities between Greengrass' and Stone's approach to 9/11. Yet, this is not merely planned as a rhetorical exercise. By outlining three principal affinities in the representations in question, I would like to argue that these two cases offer a more nuanced approach to historical tragedy, one that helps us come to grips with the complexities, the retro-active causalities and the contingencies involved in any large-scale national trauma.

Complex narratives, anti-spectacle, and the performance of failure

Without any disregard for some noticeable stylistic differences between *United 93* and *World Trade Center*, which mostly amount to differences in shot composition, cutting rate and editing style, I would like to group their similarities in three sections: their plot construction, their preference for anti-spectacular or oblique framing of the action and, most importantly, their depiction of 'agents in crisis' or what Thomas Elsaesser (2013) would call 'the performance of failure,' a term I will explicate below.

Starting with the narrative analysis of the two films, it is important to highlight the equally episodic plot in both films. In *United 93* the episodic structure becomes more obvious thanks to the relentless crosscutting, which swiftly and often abruptly takes us from one place to another. Contrary to what most plot summaries may suggest, *United 93* is not merely about the eponymous flight that crashed in Pennsylvania. That story amounts only to one section of the plot, while the rest depicts the national tragedy from the perspective of various air traffic control centers, including those in Herndon, Boston, and Newark. The opening sets a misleading focus on the Muslim characters getting prepared to board the plane but that focus soon fades into the background as the narrative begins to sketch the reaction of the air traffic control and the national air defense systems to a series of confirmed and suspected hijack reports followed by a series of strikes on the Twin Towers and the Pentagon. The disjointed editing style works on a par with the fragmented story trajectory that aims to encompass a wide variety of characters and actions and emulate the sense of confusion and disorientation that dominated that day on all levels, from the personal to the operational and the political. There does not seem to be any consistency in anybody's actions – not even the kidnappers' to some extent – or any planned or well-prepared reaction to the breaking disaster. The chronicle of the events on the morning of September 11 found in Greengrass' film is deliberately fragmented, while the tragic fate of the passengers on United 93 merely works as a provisional narrative locus around which an abundance of activities, such as the other planes, the attacks, the air traffic controls, and the military commands, may be loosely organized.

Similarly, the rescue of the two trapped officers under the Towers in *World Trade Center* is merely one episode, albeit a significant one, among a series of other important events that took place that day and are connected in a piecemeal or even random manner. In fact, Oliver Stone plots his 9/11 movie in an episodic fashion with multiple characters and various potential narrative paths, loosening significantly the classical goal-oriented Hollywood formula. In this sense, I disagree with the emphasis on the film's classicism reflected in Kellner's aforementioned characterization (the 'ultimate Un-Oliver Stone film') or in other reviewers' comments about *World Trade Center* being "a Ron Howard film" or a "disaster movie" (Kendrick 2008: 521; Randell 2010: 142). The focus on the plight of the two police officers functions as a compass in the greater disaster hitting the people and the city of New York and not the other way around; unlike most classical historical dramas who deployed traumatic historical events, such as World War II, merely as a backdrop for a personal adventure, the rescue of the two protagonists is a key narrative hub for a larger chain of incidents that took place on September 11 in New York. Thus, the film opens with officer John McLoughlin's alarm clock going off and soon switches to the awaking of the city, featuring the emblematic characteristics of New York, such as landmark monuments, transportation means and, finally, the Twin Towers. A series of other characters are introduced in an indirect fashion, mostly through the names on their lockers, and we begin to glimpse moments of the everyday routine of Port Authority Police. As soon as the first Tower is hit, the film sets a provisional goal for McLoughlin and his team to evacuate the building as a precaution but the situation already seems out of control. For the first twenty-five minutes the plot portrays a series of fragmented moments, including explosions and dust, ordinary people being terrified or confused, depending on their point-of-view, and policemen in disarray.

The collapse of the Towers and the entrapment of the protagonists open a new chapter in the narrative and give Stone the opportunity to focus on a series of aspects of that tragedy, such as the rescue attempts on the site, the response of the families waiting at home or in hospitals, the response of ordinary civilians in other parts of America and the volunteers, such as Marine David Karnes. Even though his editing style is not as abrupt as Greengrass' in *United 93*, Stone maintains an equally comprehensive scope on 9/11, crosscutting between different spaces and different speaking positions on what happened that day. Indicative of his loose construction of the plot is the two-minute scene in the hospital when McLoughlin's wife talks to the mother of another missing person and feel each other's pain. Even though the focus is on McLoughlin's survival, the film is populated with small incidents and details of that day that regularly address the tremendous human loss caused by the strikes. The narrative complexity of both *World Trade Center* and *United 93* is impressive for mainstream Hollywood productions and it should not be understated due to the filmmakers' reputations or political convictions. Both Stone and Greengrass worked extremely closely with the families of the people involved in this national tragedy and they both explicitly strived to stay true to the facts and the testimonies they received (Halbfinger 2006; Timmons 2006). The plethora of statements, photos, videos and memories available from this traumatic event broadcast live across the world combined with the popularity of complex storytelling over the last couple of decades (Buckland 2009) could possibly account for the narrative choices evidenced in these two 9/11 films.

The ubiquity of the images of the planes crushing into the WTC might also account for another representational strategy embraced in both films, namely the avoidance of any sensationalistic or spectacular rendering of the attacks (Žižek 2009: 154). Contrary to the CNN images that endlessly replayed on every TV set around the world, focusing on the moments that the planes hit the glass buildings, the explosions, the dust clouds and, finally, the collapse of tons of steel and concrete, *United 93* and *World Trade Center* opt for a restricted narration that frames the event in manners that are partial, fragmentary, random, and, sometimes, inaccessible to the public eye. Starting with Greengrass' approach, the attacks on the World Trade Center pertain to a significant part of the plot, as the air traffic control centers and the military struggle to figure out the course of the hijacked planes. Yet, the adherence to the point-of-view of their staff members limits the representational and communicative possibilities of the film. For instance, the crucial information about the multiple hijacks under way is presented to the viewers as hearsay from a flight attendant and the confirmation is only possible when they find and replay the cockpit tapes. Furthermore, the trajectories of the planes are constantly presented through their indexical traces on the controllers' monitors as blips on the radar.

Those blips build a rather opaque view of the situation, blocking the characters and the viewers from immediately realizing the tremendous impact of those actions in reality. Particularly when American Airlines Flight 11 approaches the North Tower, the characters merely witness the image of a blip disappearing; no noise, no rubble, no death, only a sign suddenly switching off a board. The second attack is portrayed more realistically but it is still anchored to the characters' direct or mediated experience through windowpanes and assorted screens. The air traffic controllers at Newark have an immediate eye contact with the plane flying low over the Hudson River and stunningly watch it crush into the South Tower. At the same time, the military commanders watch it on one of their big screens tuned to the CNN live reports. The few seconds that the film actually shows real footage from the towers are followed by fragmented and shaking shots of people's reaction of bewilderment. Once again, the focus of the narration explicitly lingers not on the catastrophic event of 9/11 but on the various repercussions caused on a personal and operational level in its immediate aftermath.

In the same vein, *World Trade Center* does not reconstruct a cinematic version of the spectacle shown on TV. The first attack is also represented by means of an indexical sign, namely the shadow of the plane reflected on a skyscraper near Port Authority Police where officer Will Jimeno is patrolling. Once again, the use of restricted narration confines the visual information that the film can convey, while it alters the scale of the disaster "to the extent that it becomes an offscreen event," as Stephen Prince notes (2009: 102–3). Unlike Prince, however, I would not consider the limitations of restricted narration as an injustice to the size of the tragedy but as a potential strength intrinsic to the cinematic language. Compared to other means and modes of representation and documentation, the ability of the lens to zoom-in on the individual perspective of 9/11, or any other historical event of that size, is a remarkable and possibly unique feat. This emphasis on the subjective experience, which is ipso facto partial and probably random, is further demonstrated in the scenes of entrapment under tons of debris. McLoughlin and his team experience the collapse of the buildings from below the ground, reversing entirely the widespread top-down view of the event disseminated in the media. The long dark sequences underground, so beautifully described by Burgoyne above, reconstruct for the viewer an unreachable perspective; no images from those spaces could ever be taken. Stone's choice of this impossible narrative space is not unlike Greengrass' control rooms. Both filmmakers opted for a less spectacular rendition of the 9/11 events, exploring those circumstances that did not or could not be covered on an average television report or documentary. This distinctive penchant for the individual perspective and the resistance towards the spectacular side of 9/11 is also related to the third common denominator in the two narratives in question, namely an unclassical approach to agency and the role of individuals in shaping the course of history.

One of the pillars of the classical Hollywood film was the character-centered causality built on the male hero as a goal-oriented personality who undertakes and often accomplishes a mission (Bordwell *et al.* 1985). The success of the mission was predominantly dependent on the protagonist's personal initiative and resolve, while all other factors, including technology, chance or natural and historical forces, were portrayed as secondary to the course of action. In the case of *United 93* and *World Trade Center* this classical premise is abundantly challenged on two grounds: first, the depiction of material forces and technology and second, the agency of the key characters vis-à-vis the unprecedented attacks. Starting with the former in Greengrass' film, one is easily struck by the equal emphasis of the plot on the objects and the humans inhabiting the story world. For instance, the images of the passengers in the waiting room of the airport in the opening minutes are crosscut to the engines, the fuel tanks, and the equipment necessary for the take-off. The scenes in the various air traffic control rooms throughout the United States stress the important role of technologically advanced devices while picturing humans as entirely reliant on the screens, the radars, and other monitoring systems. Similarly, the role of telephones and credit cards is instrumental in the passengers' portrayed revolt on the plane, as they provide access to information and determine their decision to take matters in their own hands. Throughout the film, the characters and the technology form an integrated network of agents that strive rather unsuccessfully, as I will argue shortly, to withstand the overwhelming circumstances of the terrorist attacks.

Along the same lines *World Trade Center* accentuates the power of material objects on numerous occasions. On the family front, either at home or at the hospitals around the city, the TV sets are not merely a part of the décor. The characters are literally hooked on them, waiting anxiously for the latest news update and hoping that they will get a glimpse of their loved ones somewhere amidst the chaos. On the action front, the protagonists are unable to 'take action' without their gear. It is almost uncanny to watch officer McLoughlin and his men slowly assemble the necessary equipment before attempting to rescue anyone in the towers. The explosions and the dust hinder their pace to such an extent that they never, in fact, manage to embark on their mission. The collapse of the buildings comes unexpectedly, for the characters and the viewers alike, to stress the utter smallness of human life compared to tons of concrete. As our screen switches to black and then reframes the leading protagonists in their new immobile status, the overwhelming presence of the material conditions takes reigns of the cinematic frame. Along with the two powerful steel structures collapse the efforts of the police officers to perform their duty.

Even before this definitive moment, the mission assigned to the key characters was far from clear. As McLoughlin told his partners, "there is no plan. Not for something this size." After the hit of the first tower, the authorities and their technical support system seemed unready to handle the crisis. The ensuing confusion regarding the damage in the WTC and the difficulty with which people exchanged reliable information rendered any chance for purposeful action moot. *World Trade Center*, for the most part, focuses on characters that cannot really act. The narrative establishes the premise of a 'mission' by sending the police officers on site only to thwart it moments later by trapping them in the most incapacitating situation. Similarly, people at home are also cancelled out. The families of those missing can do nothing but wait and pray. Only the rescue teams and a few volunteers, like Karnes, struggle against time to accomplice their mission, saving McLoughlin and Jimeno's lives but failing to trace so many others under the rubble.

The death toll of 9/11 and the crisis of individual agency is also manifest in *United* 93. There, everything breaks down too. In Greengrass' words (2006), "a broken system is what this movie is about." Every episode of the plot, from the air traffic control centers to the military headquarters and the hijacked flight, exposes the shortcomings and weaknesses of human agency when faced with a catastrophe of that scale. The air traffic controllers are caught entirely by surprise and appear incapable of tracking the hijacked planes in time. The military forces are equally incapable of taking any preventive action, while the passengers on United 93 confront serious dilemmas about 'what taking action' means and to what end. First, we watch the terrorists hesitate and dither. When they decide to move forward with their plan, it is too late. The Twin Towers have been hit and the news reaches the passengers who manage to piece together the information and realize the doomed fate awaiting them. At that point, the film depicts moments of purposeful action to the extent that the passengers as a group struggle to seize control of the plane. Their mission fails and succeeds at the same time. They fail to save their lives by landing the plane safely but succeed in saving many others by crashing the plane to the ground and not on the terrorist target. The ambivalence of that outcome reflects entirely on the overall frame of agency portrayed in *United 93* and *World Trade Center*. In other words, the classical trope of the mission in Hollywood filmmaking is severely challenged, allowing for failure to come into play. Historically, of course, this would not be the first time that Hollywood films question the character-centered causality and rational agency as a narrative choice with hidden ideological underpinnings. A string of films in the late 1960s and 1970s made by a young generation of American filmmakers, such as Robert Altman, Arthur Penn, and Sam Peckinpah, had expressed what Elsaesser dubbed the 'pathos of failure', creating characters who lacked motivation and eventually came face to face with total failure (Elsaesser 1975).

This is not the type of failure, however, that we come across in the two 9/11 narratives. The characters here manifest a type of agency that resembles Elsaesser's more recent concept, that of 'parapraxis' (Elsaesser 2013). Parapraxis is the English translation of *Fehlleistung*, a term initially coined by Sigmund Freud to describe an error in speech, memory, or action, which is more widely known as a 'Freudian slip'. Elsaesser takes the concept's literal meaning merely as a starting point for constructing around parapraxis a nexus of qualities, which are particularly apt for describing cinema's approach to historical traumatic events. Specifically, he expands on the meaning of *Fehlleistung* ('*Fehl*' means failure and '*Leistung*' is performance), noting how its compound nature allows us to consider it both as a 'failed performance' and a 'performance of failure,' serving possibly as a solution to the unrepresentability of trauma or to the paradox of Samuel Beckett's paraphrased dictum 'it can't be represented, it must be represented' (Elsaesser 2013: 11). In Elsaesser's account, parapraxis is presented as a double-sided and self-divided concept which plays around certain key antitheses, such as active/passive, language/embodiment, intention/contingency, past/present, and other/self and opens us to multiple interpretations at varying historical junctures. A parapractic film chooses to tackle the impossibility of representation and the excess of information or emotion in ways that resist closure, symmetry, or balance, bringing forward poetic elements that suggest miscommunications, reversals, causal gaps, unanticipated consequences, and deferred action. The notion of failure ingrained in *Fehlleistung* is often instantiated through the suspension of the normal codes or conventions of representation or the deployment of figurative tropes, such as *catachresis* or *zeugma*, to indicate a double purpose (Elsaesser 2013: 104–06). When it comes to the issue of agency, which is my focus here, it is interesting how the idea of failure allows us to re-evaluate a hero's purposeful action, identifying potential gaps in his intentional/rational actions. According to Elsaesser:

> [I]nsofar as parapraxis is a form of agency, but one manifesting the gaps between intentionality and rationality, while also pointing to the different temporalities or 'timing' of an action, the term also wants to engage with notions of active and passive, voluntary agency and involuntary memory. By defining parapraxis not as the 'slip of the tongue', or the lapse in attention, I focus on it as a kind of effort, persistence, even a tragic-comic heroic 'insistence': usually one with unexpected or unintended results, including typical reversals of cause and effect.
>
> *(107)*

In this light, parapractic heroes are not simply individuals lacking motivation, wandering aimlessly and exchanging purposeful action with the 'pathos of failure' but, rather, individuals who know they cannot act and yet they must act. The development of parapraxis as a hermeneutic tool for analyzing the representation of trauma in the cinema could help us read the trajectories of the protagonists in *United 93* and *World Trade Center* in a way that identifies the simultaneous presence of affirmative action and its cancellation. In this light, the missions taken up in both films are better understood as 'performances of failure' under incommensurable circumstances that challenge any notion of linear chronology and cause-and-effect logic. One of the recurring motifs in the depiction of trauma is the feeling of bad timing, the sense of being too late; *United 93* is rife with moments when the characters are always lagging a step behind, always unable to keep track with the unfolding disaster. All that energy and all those people mobilized in the effort to take hold of the situation turns into a well-orchestrated performance of failure that would require a repeated return to that day in order to understand what went wrong.

Similarly, Stone's crosscutting between past and present and the long regretful conversations under the rubble serve to indicate how the characters were out of step with the surrounding reality both at home and at work. Even their accidental rescue is portrayed in a way not meant to emphasize healing and closure but rather an open wound both literally and metaphorically. When McLoughlin's wife is informed that her husband has been rescued, she drives to the police station expecting to see him alive and well. Her expectations are crushed, as she finds out that there has been a mistake and that he is still trapped and seriously injured. The gaps in communication and the lack of reliable information are further emphasized in the scenes at the hospital where Stone gets a chance to dwell on the fact that McLoughlin's rescue was the exception and not the norm. And even that rescue came with a heavy toll. According to the closing titles, McLoughlin was put into a medically induced coma for six weeks to allow for 27 surgeries. By bracketing the success of McLoughlin and Jimeno's rescue not only with the medical complications of their survival but, above all, with the fact that they were merely two survivors against the 2,749 people who lost their lives, *World Trade Center* seeks to do justice to the devastating loss for the people in New York on September 11, struggling to represent what cannot be represented and, thus, resigning itself to another failed performance.

Overall, the extensive debates about trauma and memory that have been rehearsed in the academic and cinematic discourse over the last few decades (Elsaesser 1996: 146–150; Rosenstone 2006: 134–153) seem to have instilled a certain knowingness in contemporary filmmakers about the difficulties with which one approaches the vanishing past, especially when it comes to large-scale catastrophic events. Greengrass and Stone do not abandon the idea of heroic action or the need to craft a portrait of bravery for the people involved in such circumstances, but the faith in human initiative is posed against a wider context of material constraints and contingent parameters. In this light, the human 'praxis' is always already bound to other parapraxes, which allow a level of ambiguity and complexity that was uncommon in the classical Hollywood tradition.

Conclusion

> Nowhere in *United 93* or *World Trade Center* are the compound contexts, the traumatic cultural and social effects, the devastating losses, or the profound alterations of national life that characterize 9/11 registered; instead, linear narrative patterning and classical limitations of character, place and time impose a rigorous and singular structure. The dramatic organization of both works suggests a kind of fixation or obsession, a determined refusal to acknowledge the radical alteration of national life wrought by 9/11.
>
> *(Burgoyne 2008: 149)*

My analysis of the two films in the preceding pages has attempted to reach the opposite end of Burgoyne's statement. He is right in aligning the two works – at least, in this passage – but his conclusion does not do justice to level of complexity and sophistication evidenced in both films in the ways they seek to cope with a national tragedy. In this limited space I have tried to demonstrate that the two narratives are characterized by a wealth of information regarding the 9/11 events that stemmed from Greengrass' and Stone's avowed intention of the getting the facts right and using as many testimonies as possible. This meticulous attention to accuracy and detail coming from the exhaustive discussions with survivors or the families of the missing people resulted in a restricted narration that privileged the subjective experience of that day in American history. By framing the 9/11 attacks from a very personal perspective, Greengrass and Stone transformed creatively the limitations of the point-of-view into a powerful suggestive tool. The expectation for a film to behave as a historical treatise that spells out the deeper socio-politico-economic factors leading up to a national tragedy is bound to be failed. Cinema does not work like that, especially when it comes to the dramatic feature. Leveling such accusations at historical fiction films has been a standard strategy by most critics but a grossly misguided one, too (Rosenstone 2006: 34).

In terms of the films' classicism, I have tried to indicate a number of significant departures from the classical Hollywood tradition, such as the multiple and fragmented plotlines, the loosening of the goal-oriented progression of the story, the oblique ways of portraying the otherwise spectacular and overexposed hits on the WTC and, above all, the modified take on heroic action in this enormously unexpected and paralyzing situation. Despite the occasional melodramatic moments in both cases, which predominantly involved the family scenes and the exchanges of love messages or farewells, the overtone in *United 93* and *World Trade Center* is not one of classical balance and closure but one of parapraxis. Both films are filled with gaps, deferred actions, reversed causalities, and random occurrences that do not exactly aim to comfort the audience and offer an easy 'working through' solution. In this sense, contrary to Burgoyne's claim, these first two 9/11 Hollywood narratives do register a meaningful difference in America's national imaginary after the attacks. What is still difficult to determine, though, is the clout of this difference for the broader historical imagination in American cinema. To this date, 9/11 remains a traumatic event so sensitive and controversial for the American public that the Hollywood industry finds it hard to exploit on either economic or ideological grounds. Even more so than Vietnam a few decades ago, 9/11 remains, fifteen years later, too major a risk for mainstream feature filmmaking (Prince 2009: 122). No matter how one chooses to approach *United 93* and *World Trade Center*, as similar or different, as classical or groundbreaking, it is unequivocal that they constitute a milestone in the representation of 9/11 in American cinema.

Bibliography

Bordwell, D., Staiger, J. and Thompson, K. (1985) *The Classical Hollywood Cinema: Film Style and Mode of Production to 1960*, New York: Routledge.

Buckland, W. (2009) *Puzzle Films: Complex Storytelling in Contemporary Cinema*, Oxford: Wiley-Blackwell.

Burgoyne, R. (2008) *The Hollywood Historical Film*, Oxford: Wiley-Blackwell.

Elsaesser, T. (1975) "The pathos of failure. American Films in the 70s: Notes on the Unmotivated Hero," *Monogram*, 6, pp. 13–19.

Elsaesser, T. (1996) "Subject Positions, Speaking Positions: From *Holocaust*, *Our Hitler*, and *Heimat* to *Shoah* and *Schindler's List*" in V. Sobchack (ed.) *The Persistence of History: Cinema, Television and the Modern Event*, New York: Routledge, pp. 145–183.

Elsaesser, T. (2013) *German Cinema: Terror and Trauma: Cultural Memory since 1945*, New York: Routledge.

Giglio, E. (2010) *Here's Looking at You: Hollywood, Film and Politics*, New York: Peter Lang.

Greengrass, P. (2006) "Director's Commentary," *United 93* [DVD], United States: Universal Pictures.

Halbfinger, D. (2006) "Oliver Stone's 'World Trade Center' Seeks Truth in the Rubble," *The New York Times*, July 2, http://www.nytimes.com/2006/07/02/movies/02halb.html?pagewanted=all&_r=0. Accessed February 10, 2014.

Hoberman, J. (2012) *Film after Film (Or, What Became of 21st Century Cinema?)*, Brooklyn, NY: Verso.

Kellner, D. (2010) *Cinema Wars: Hollywood Film and Politics in the Bush-Cheney Era*, Malden, MA: Blackwell.

Kendrick, J. (2008) "Representing the Unrepresentable: The Violence of 9/11 in Oliver Stone's *World Trade Center* and Paul Greengrass' *United 93*" in P. C. Rollins and J. E. O'Connor (eds) *Why We Fought: America's Wars in Film and History*, Lexington: University Press of Kentucky, pp. 511–528.

Morris, N. (2012) "2006: Movies and Crisis" in T. Corrigan (ed.) *American Cinema of the 2000s: Themes and Variations. Screen Decades: American Culture/ American Cinema*, New Brunswick, NJ: Rutgers University Press, pp. 147–171.

Prince, S. (2009) *Firestorm: American Film in the Age of Terrorism*, New York: Columbia University Press.

Randell, K. (2010) "'It Was like a Movie': The Impossibility of Representation in Oliver Stone's *World Trade Center* (2006)" in J. Birkenstein, A. Froula and K. Randell (eds) *Reframing 9/11: Film, Popular Culture and the "War on Terror,"* New York: Bloomsbury, pp. 141–152.

Redfield, M. (2009) *The Rhetoric of Terror: Reflections on 9/11 and the War on Terror*, New York: Fordham University Press.

Rommel-Ruiz, W. B. (2011) *American History Goes to the Movies: Hollywood and the American Experience*, New York: Routledge.

Rosenstone, R. (2006) *History on Film/ Film on History*, Edinburgh Gate: Pearson.

Timmons, H. (2006) "Four Years On, a Cabin's-Eye View of 9/11," *The New York Times*, January 1, http://www.nytimes.com/2006/01/01/movies/01timm.html?ex=1293771600&en=f5a28a31bbbc6611&ei=5090&partner=rssuserland&emc=rss. Accessed August 24, 2008.

Žižek, S. (2009) *Violence: Six Sideways Reflections*, London: Profile Books.

25

REAGANITE CINEMA

What a feeling!

Gary Needham

In a revolutionary and political turn in *Cahiers du Cinema* at the end of the 1960s, published shortly thereafter in *Screen*, Jean-Luc Comolli and Paul Narboni's "Cinema/Ideology/Criticism" asserted the need for the political and ideological to be examined in relation to cinema, stating that "every film is political, inasmuch as it is determined by the ideology which produces it" (1971: 30). Flash-forward a number of years to 1986, with a Memorial Day weekend release and a tagline that reads "crime is a disease, meet the cure" and "strong arm of the law," *Cobra* (Cosmatos), a film starring and written by Sylvester Stallone, appears to be a typical example of a 1980s film absolutely "determined by the ideology that produces it." *Cobra* appears definitive in its mutual entanglement with the political rhetoric and assumed public sentiments of Ronald Reagan's Republican America. The film, or rather Stallone, ostentatiously gestures towards such presidential connections in displaying a giant portrait of Reagan in his character Marion 'Cobra' Cobretti's office; this is the man I serve, it implicitly proclaims.

Cobra is just one of a number of films that respond to the notion that America has gone soft and needs a 'strong arm' or better a strong body (Jeffords 1993), here in the shape of Stallone's detective, to bring America back in check after decades of waywardness. In *Cobra* the threat to national security is domestic rather than foreign with a group of Darwinian terrorists called New World Order going on a relentless killing spree in order to refashion social order through the extermination of the weak and, by extension, the survival of the strongest, which, as I will argue below, conveys Reaganite logic *par excellence*. *Cobra* seems to condemn these right-wing terrorists, yet their ideology and the pleasures of the film itself are not that far removed from the policies and practices of the New Right that *Cobra*, in its character's response to crime and violence, seems to be of equal reaction. As a right-wing text, *Cobra* revels in eschewing proper judicial and legal practice in the fight against crime. Instead, this film privileges the muscular male action hero, a man of few words, with a body and actions that speak for him and his power, and the use of more violence as the only way to deal with home-grown 'terrorists' in this home-front war. *Cobra*'s fantasy is meant to accord with Reagan's domestic policy in which the nation and the family, one and the same thing in Reagan's America, are under serious threat, both real and imagined. The female lead in *Cobra* is fashion model Ingrid (Brigitte Nielsen), then Stallone's real wife, correspondingly reduced to a pre-feminist passive spectacle and obligatory soundtrack-selling montage sequence, in which we are positioned to consume her body and the music as a 'package.' She will soon be adding 'damsel in distress' to her Reaganite film resume.

The film's 'position' is quite clearly mapped out in the opening and closing scenes as Reaganite films are neatly organized by their opening thematic distillations: here's the problem; and a firm closure: here's how we fixed it. Thus, *Cobra* begins with Stallone's voice-over narrating a series of crime statistics: "In America there's a burglary every eleven seconds, an armed robbery every sixty-five seconds … and two-hundred and fifty rapes a day," while the barrel of a gun is turned to point directly at the audience and fires a slow-motion bullet that explodes into the film's title. We, the audience, America, are quite literally under attack. The credits are then intercut with a silhouette of an unspecified menace on his motorbike and the rallying together of the axe-wielding New World Order gang he represents, the members of which all share the same skull and crossbones tattoo we see in close-up. The gang member parks his bike outside a supermarket, walks inside, and begins gunning down the shoppers in cold blood. Even worse, this is all happening in the Christmas period reinforced by having someone blasted by the maniac's shotgun, in visually impacting slow motion, towards a Christmas tree in the decoration isle. The premise of this opening scene is one of total threat reinforced with the gun pointing directly at the spectator followed by the gun fired at the seasonal shopper. Even the symbolism of children's toys, Christmas, and the Pepsi stand (integrated marketing even during heightened violence, see Figure 25.1) being obliterated is surely not lost on the audience as America itself is under attack. The 'Cobra' arrives in his vintage car (the number plate reads 'Awsom 50'), all reflective shades and chewing on a matchstick; he's just what we need, of course! He enters the supermarket, finds time to open a can of Coors beer (another product placement) and then shoots the 'domestic terrorist' dead. Following the event a journalist dares to question Cobra's actions as 'both judge and jury' only to be quickly grabbed and pushed aside; a clear and forceful silencing of the liberal voice.

The ending of *Cobra* is similarly brutal in its ideological transparency and confidence. Following the defeat of the gang and its leader, nicknamed the Night Slasher, Cobra gets on his bike with recently rescued Ingrid and a montage of them hitting the road is accompanied by a soft rock track titled "Voice of American Sons." The closure of *Cobra* suggests this character

Figure 25.1 Marketing and violence hand in hand in *Cobra*.

knows exactly where he is going and the woman is certainly willing to follow (and should be grateful for having been rescued anyway). The music is overtly masculine in its genre conventions and patriotic in its lyrics, and on the whole the last few minutes present a form of closure which is absolute in terms of confidence, motivation, and direction. Narrative resolution here functions as a form of political assertion, but more than that, if one is to understand these films as a response to a previous form of American cinema, *Cobra*'s triumphant closure could be seen as a provocative reversal, even erasure, of *Easy Rider*'s narrative resolution (Hopper, 1969). Both films are about 'the search for America,' both conclude on motorbikes, but the quest brings each protagonist to a very different ending, with the two easy riders, Captain American and Billy the Kid, shot and killed by American South hillbillies. In other words, *Cobra* is an implicit response to the nihilistic, directionless, incoherent, experimental questioning of American in the previous two decades of American cinema by a host of films broadly associated with the Hollywood Renaissance. The seeds of this sentiment and desire for coherence, simplicity, momentum, and aggressive reassurance were sown well before Reagan's election in a revealing statement by George Lucas in which he describes his film *Star Wars* (1977) as "an intergalactic story of heroism. Total fantasy for today's kids who don't have the opportunity to grow up watching *Flash Gordon* and have to sit through movies of insecurity instead" (Lucas, 1978). Lucas probably means films like *Five Easy Pieces* (Rafelson, 1970), *Klute* (Pakula, 1971), *The Last Detail* (Ashby, 1973), or *The Parallax View* (Pakula, 1974), and of course *Easy Rider*.

Despite *Cobra*'s obviousness as a reactionary and right-wing text, film culture, film reception, and the film industry are more complex than Comolli and Narboni perhaps assume, in addition to what such easy ideological readings at first suggest. Indeed, *Cobra* is not just a prop in popular culture's support for the moral conservatism and domestic policy of the New Right. The film also had the highest opening weekend box office of that year with $15.6 million and "opened in 2,131 theaters in the United States and Canada, breaking the movie industry's all-time record for bookings" (Scott, 1986). Yet, despite the box-office success, which can translate into the idea that there is a public demand and desire for these macho action films, *Cobra*'s production and reception recount several layers of unease, as I will discuss below. These layers suggest that affording these films such a monolithic status as "Reaganite Entertainment" (Britton, 1986) in our writing and perception of American film history, that is, the idea that film, politics, and public sentiment in this particular period are unquestionably reinforcing one another, is far from the straight-forward complicity that the term 'Reaganite' perhaps suggests. Nonetheless, one cannot think of another period in American film history in which such a concerted appeal to see film and presidential and political rhetoric so ruefully interconnected, further exacerbated by the continued evocation of film dialogue and references in the speeches and national addresses made by Reagan himself.

Back to the layers of unease, *Cobra* had a difficult time at the Motion Picture Association of America (MPAA), which gave the first cut of the film an X rating, resulting in a situation in which the film could not have been advertised in newspapers and on network television, and therefore not deemed acceptable for mainstream consumption, despite Stallone's headlining status. Produced independently by Cannon Films and distributed by Warner Bros., *Cobra* suffered extensive re-editing to remove excessive violence and a bloated running time in order to secure both an R rating (a moral concern) and, importantly, to increase the number of possible daily screenings (an economic concern). What is interesting then is that this openly right-wing wish-fulfillment story about a muscular hero who gets the job done at the edge of the law (as Cobra says: 'this is where the law stops and I begin') and for which there was a significant audience at the time is also at odds with the moral conservatism driving American film censorship in the 1980s.

The film was also a critical failure and, despite a great opening weekend, was subject to excoriating reviews. For instance, *New York Times* critic Nina Darnton writes that it "is a disturbing movie from many points of view: disturbing for the violence it portrays, the ideas it represents and the large number of people who will undoubtedly go to see it and cheer on its dangerous hero" (1986). She also goes on to state that *Cobra* "shows such contempt for the most basic American values embodied in the concept of a fair trial that Mr. Stallone no longer, even nominally, represents an ideology that is recognizably American" (ibid.) Therefore, *Cobra*'s critical failure is that it is a dumb, violent movie with an ideology that is completely out of step with 'core American values.'

The reason for opening this chapter with this substantial examination of a lesser, now all but forgotten, 1980s film, which nonetheless *is* typical of Reaganite Entertainment, is that contradiction is a defining feature of *Cobra*; it is equally supported and rejected by its own culture as a film, and it believes in the same ideological principles that its hero fights with a vengeance. In the final part of this chapter, I will return to another 1980s film, *Flashdance* (Lyne, 1983) to discuss its own contradictions, but before that it is necessary to revisit the political landscape and ideological sentiments of the decade and examine the ways in which they have seemingly shaped an entire decade through the conceptual terms 'Reaganite Cinema' and 'Reaganite Entertainment.'

American cinema/American politics

Every period in American cinema, whether decade long, longer, or even shorter, is of course inseparable from its political, social, and cultural contexts, whether it challenges, supports, or renders ambiguous the ideological and hegemonic relations of the 'feeling' of the majority and of those who represent governmental power. All American films seemingly enable readings whether implicit or explicit in either supporting or rejecting the policies and sentiments adopted by alternating Republican and Democratic presidencies and administrations. Much has already been written of Hollywood's response to Roosevelt's New Deal in the 1930s, (Muscio 1997; Giovacchini 2001), the effect of the McCarthy witch-hunts of the 1950s (Prime 2013; Smith 2014), the grappling with counter-culture in the late 1960s (James 1989), the wave of ideological disintegration in the 1970s (Wood 1986; Elsaesser and King 2005), and so on. Despite these 'moments' of historical circumstance and political reification in American cinema, film scholarship has tended to recognize them as complex and often contradictory, especially compared to the monolithic status and neatness that is often afforded to 1980s Hollywood cinema.

However, while those earlier examples are by definition historical, the long-term effects of the consolidation of American cinema between 1976 and 1989 are still being felt today, through ways in which Reaganite films and their defining features and structures of feeling are evident in contemporary Hollywood. An index of the enduring appeal of *Star Wars*, *Grease* (Kleiser, 1978), *Ghostbusters* (Reitman, 1984), *Raiders of the Lost Ark* (Spielberg, 1981), *ET: The Extra Terrestrial* (Spielberg, 1982), *Dirty Dancing* (Ardolino, 1987), and *The Terminator* (Cameron, 1984), the list goes on, with audiences too young to have seen them the first time around, signals their canonical status in popular culture but also their existence beyond Reagan's two terms in office. So profound were the political and industrial shifts in American cinema in those years, the aesthetic and formal consequences of how the films looked and, arguably more important, how they were experienced by audiences, that culture has seemingly not yet recovered from the 'interminable solipsism' (Britton, 1986) that defined Reaganite cinema as one of pure, unadulterated entertainment and which goes a long way to explain the recent remakes of classic 1980s films such as *The Karate Kid* (Zwart, 2010), *Footloose* (Brewer, 2012), *The Thing* (Van Heijningen Jr., 2011), *Conan the Barbarian* (Nispel, 2011), and several others.

Superman (Donner, 1978) was perhaps an early gesture that American cinema was changing in the late 1970s since the most fervent cycle of films with no sign of abating is the contemporaneous super hero juggernaut, with productions planned by Marvel Studios and its ilk well up to 2019 and beyond (Graser, 2014). It would seem therefore that Reaganite Cinema was both an historical moment and a founding template of contemporary Hollywood. What Reaganite Cinema and the contemporary Hollywood films share is a foregrounding of the 'experience' of cinema as an immediate and affective one; the triumphant endings of both *Star Wars* and *Cobra* attest to this over-investment in heavy affect, as do many latter-day examples such as *National Treasure* (Turteltaub, 2004) and *War of the Worlds* (Spielberg, 2005). However, and this is a key difference between the 1980s and now, the power of contemporary Hollywood cinema is not always, evidently, concertedly, tied to left or right, Republican or Democrat, especially when films like *The Dark Knight* (Nolan, 2008) are canny to exploit and negotiate both positions. Of course, not all films are that ambiguous or open to possibility, with *Taken* (Morel, 2008), for instance, unabashedly updating the right-wing vigilante trope, thus providing a strong example of a reactionary film in the late 2000s. As the most commercially successful film of all time, *Avatar* (Cameron, 2009), seemingly of Reaganite fashion (let us not forget the military jingoism of Cameron's *Aliens* (1986)), privileges the spectator and his or her propensity for pleasure and awe, all the while providing positions that both celebrate military and scientific supremacy (the right position), while valuing environmentalism and condemning the genocide of an ersatz Native American race of blue aliens (the left position). How we have arrived at this current formation of American cinema is a direct consequence of the Reaganite Cinema of the 1980s and its legacy that cinematic value lies in pleasure rather than politics.

1980s: political and cultural context

While Ronald Regan's first term in office was not until 1981 there was already a cultural and political shift underway in the latter half of the 1970s that was indicative of how the New Right came to power with a landslide victory. The 1979 'Disco Sucks' riot in Chicago was a symbolic event that speaks of an idea that the long party and the fun of the 1970s were over. Baseball fans gathered to blow-up disco records during a baseball match half-time that became a riot chanting 'disco sucks' that quite explicitly targeted two groups seen to have been over-privileged in the preceding decades, namely, women and gay men since the slogan of 'disco sucks' itself is hardly veiled in its attack to be read simply as 'cocksuckers like disco.' Republicans characterized the 1960s and 1970s as wayward decades, unruly and hedonistic, insecure and paranoid, leading the US towards moral and economic decline, distrust in the government, and a weakened international image. Despite the associations with the uplift of disco and a hit soundtrack, one should remember that *Saturday Night Fever* (Badham, 1978) is actually an anti-disco movie that also de-gays and de-blacks the music phenomenon and instead, almost as a prediction, asserts a hegemonic white masculinity. It would seem natural then that Sylvester Stallone would helm the film's sequel *Staying Alive* (1983) and that John Travolta's slender disco body would be transformed by hard muscle to such an extent that it might appear that Rambo had instead taken to the dance floor.

The blame on the wayward decade was directed towards a disorganized Left, the Carter administration, poor fiscal mismanagement, feminism, gay rights, civil rights, as if they were all conspiring to take the US into a state of decline. In this sense, the eventual success of the Right, to the extent that they also controlled The Senate for the first time since 1956, was connected quite explicitly to both the perceived and the actual failures of the Left. Reagan counselled a return to *Father Knows Best* (CBS/NBC 1954–60) sitcom politics of 1950s, the decade in which he was also a Hollywood film star and conservatism and containment culture were at their peak, while one should also note that when he was president of the Screen Actors Guild in that decade Reagan provided testimony in support of the communist witch-hunts (Rogin 1988: 28–32). In this respect, it is no surprise that that 1950s operate as a halcyon decade in 1980s Republican discourse, rewritten as the time before it all went wrong in the 1960s and 1970s. The 1950s also became a popular setting for a number of 1980s films, including the appropriately titled *Back to the Future* (Zemeckis, 1985) alongside *Peggy Sue Got Married* (Coppola, 1986), *Diner* (Levinson, 1982), *Grease 2* (Birch, 1982), *Stand By Me* (Reiner, 1986), and *Streets of Fire* (Hill, 1984).

The return to 1950s values is a return to family values, that is to say, a return to patriarchal values, and the political battles of the Reagan era were often couched in familial and moral terms evocative of the 1950s. Robin Wood (1986: 162–4) refers to the 1980s as an era of 'reassurance' and 'reaction' and one might add a range of alliterating terms to capture the breadth of sentiments and situations of Reagan's America: restoration of the family; recuperation of the military image; renewal of right-wing policy; regression of intellect and left-wing thinking; return of patriarchy; revenge on minorities who made significant progress in the two preceding decades; retaliation against foreign powers after a series of humiliating defeats and military interventions; renaissance in moral conservatism and religion; rejection of Equal Rights Amendment; repeal of Roe v. Wade. Furthermore, this brutal neo-conservatism emphasized a new faith in technology, consumerism, capitalism, and the service economy, all to be delivered by newly deregulated private sector companies. The consequence of this is where the world currently is, namely, Neoliberalism.

Reaganite film culture

Cinema did not immediately shift to the right all of a sudden in 1981 as Reagan took root in The White House. Seeds of conservative reassurance appeared by the latter half of the 1970s, and even the 1980s did not overwhelmingly embody all the sentiments of the New Right. On reflection, there are numerous films released around 1980, interestingly all commercial failures, such as *Cruising* (Friedkin, 1980), *All That Jazz* (Fosse, 1979), and *Thief* (Mann, 1981) that belong to the cinema of the 1970s, 'incoherent texts' (Wood, 1986), existentialist and concerted in their refusal to make it 'easy' for the spectator. *9 to 5* (Higgins, 1980) continues to explore some tenets of second-wave feminism in the workplace, the horror in *Day of the Dead* (Romero, 1985) is not the zombies but what happens when a macho military is in total control of everything, while *They Live* (Carpenter, 1988) is an exercise aiming to reveal how ideology works to keep us all in check. But the majority of films, especially blockbusters like *Superman* (which saw three sequels in the 1980s), exerted a simplified narrative structure, were loaded with spectacle and acts of heroism, and provided a more comfortable and reassuring place for the film spectator than earlier films such as the *The King of Marvin Gardens* (Rafelson, 1972) that typified a bleak nihilism while also being formally challenging.

Robin Wood (1986) and Andrew Britton (1986) both outline a series of dominant tendencies or characteristics that articulate the Reaganite ideology on several levels including form, genre, predictability, and experience. Chief among those ideological tendencies or goals are the above-mentioned restoration of patriarchy and recuperation of the military (*The Great Santini* (Carlino, 1979), *An Officer and a Gentleman* (Hackford, 1982)), alongside the alleviation of nuclear anxieties (*War Games* (Badham, 1983), *Ghostbusters*) and the regression of the audience to a state of infantile wonder (*ET: The Extra Terrestrial*, *Short Circuit* (Badham, 1986)). It is the latter affect of regression that supports the former ideological project, a sort of renewed faith in the power of the apparatus (Baudry, 1986), in that one is supposed to self-consciously make sense of 1980s film as quite simply harmless entertainment, in Britton's terms: a cinema defined by "interminable solipsism" (1986: 3) and entertainment "defined as a commodity to be consumed rather than a text to be read" (1986: 4). "Keep repeating 'it's only a movie'" used to be the tagline for the most cruel and disturbing horror movies of the 1960s and 1970s like *Mark of the Devil* (Armstrong, 1970) and the shocking *Last House on the Left* (Craven, 1972) but by the 1980s the same phrase became the solipsistic mantra associated with not taking the movies seriously and thus not seeing them as having any political agency and efficacy in relation to highly persuasive ideologies, lest one be accused of spoiling all the fun of the apparatus. In apparently constructing the adult spectator as a child, socially and psychically, there is no place to think when confronted by awe and wonder. During the exhilarating mine cart sequence in *Indiana Jones and the Temple of Doom* (Spielberg, 1984) one is caught up in the suspense and energy of a good old-fashioned chase reconfigured as an ersatz rollercoaster ride for the spectator so that we forget, regress, or not even notice that the film is one of the most outrageously racist films of the decade; a nadir of neo-colonial fantasy in which the 'savages' are an immoral bunch of Asians who include child slavery, human sacrifice of white women, and a gluttony for eyeball soup and cold monkey brains, among their many bizarre and heinous practices.

The key theme of the restoration of patriarchy is often complemented by meting out punishment against women for their, mostly, sexual transgressions outside the family. The backlash against feminism (Faludi 1991; Modleski 1991) and, put even more simply, women's economic and familial independence are repeatedly recoded through themes and images of frequently violent punishment and male moral superiority, which, at one end, includes a vicious trial by jury and expulsion of the mother from the family (*Kramer versus Kramer* (Benton, 1979)) and, at the other, in the most extreme versions includes homicidal misogyny (*Maniac* (Lustig, 1980), with a tagline 'I told you not to go out tonight'). *Dressed to Kill* (De Palma, 1980), *Terms of Endearment* (Brooks, 1983), and *Fatal Attraction*

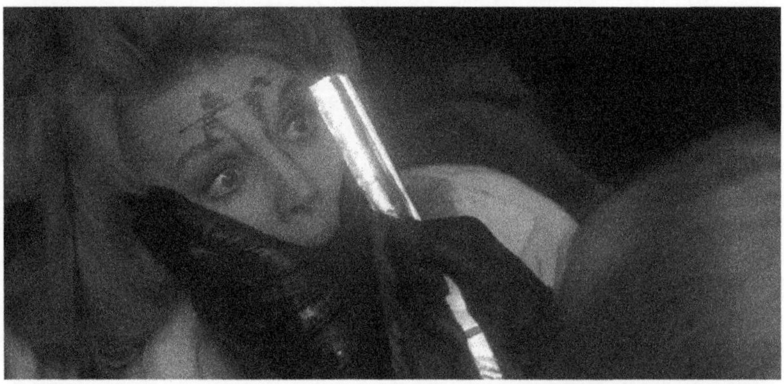

Figure 25.2 Stylized murder in *Dressed to Kill*.

(Lyne, 1987) are all exemplary of Reaganism in this respect. In *Dressed to Kill*, Angie Dickinson's extramarital pick-up in an art gallery, a dialogue-free ten-minute cinematic tour de force of steadicam ingenuity and film scoring, results in her contracting a sexually transmitted infection. Upon discovery of a medical note and after she flees her one-night-stand's apartment, she is greeted in the elevator by a transvestite killer who slashes her to death with an open razor (see Figure 25.2). The 'problem' with *Dressed to Kill* is that it is such a beautifully edited, shot, and scored film, playful in its Hitchcockian allusions, but it just so happens that its formal qualities are used to show the explicit murder of woman by a queer killer; a punishment for female sexual transgression meted out by another pervert. So much care has gone in to those shots in terms of framing and their relationship to each other that unflinchingly depict a straight razor slashing upwards towards a woman's genitals and across her cheek that we are meant to think about form, suspense, and shock rather than politics, message, and meaning.

The message here is that she deserves it! Like the mine cart sequence in *Indiana Jones*, we are meant to focus on the immediacy and sensation of the scene, which in *Dressed to Kill* is all about surprise and shock, rather than what it actually means in the context of a political climate in which women's agency is being compromised, feminism undone, misogyny plainly accepted, and the fantasy played out is one of deadly punishment for an anti-familial transgression. Gender and the family are but one area among many that get 'worked over' by Reaganite ideology and one could also draw links between Reagan's increase of defense spending and militaristic fantasy and macho heroics (*Firefox* (Eastwood, 1982), *Blue Thunder* (Badham, 1983) *Invasion U.S.A.* (Zito, 1985), *Iron Eagle* (Furie, 1986), and *Top Gun* (T. Scott, 1986, perfectly encapsulated in the title of the main song from the film "Take My Breath Away!")) which equally dominate the decade and have been mapped out in details by others (Ryan and Kellner 1990; Jeffords 1993). However, I would like to use the space here to conclude with a discussion of dance-musical *Flashdance* as a model example of Reaganite filmmaking. Despite the fact that, on first sight, it does not seem to be an obvious choice for a discussion of a political film in the 1980s, as I will argue, *Flashdance* speaks both of industrial transformations in Hollywood, a decade also characterized by transitions in industry practice and structure (Prince, 2000), and provides secure ideological consent through solipsistic pleasures that are created by its textual structures.

The politics of *Flashdance*

Flashdance is the story of Alex (Jennifer Beals) who works as a welder by day and an erotic dancer by night. Her life gets complicated when she falls in love with Nick Hurley, the owner of the steel mill in which Alex works, while hoping to apply to the Pittsburgh Conservatory of Dance and Repertory. Alex aspires to be a ballerina and transcend her current conditions but she lacks the confidence and formal education to do so. After a series of relationship ups and downs, Alex secures an audition at the Conservatory thanks to Nick's connections. Following a successful audition in which both the audition panel and film audience are blown away by her dancing she runs outside in to the arms of Nick who was waiting with a bunch of roses. The film ends on a freeze-frame of Alex and Nick as the triumphant music from the dance studio continues uninterrupted: narrative closure, romance, success, achievement …'what a feeling,' indeed!

Flashdance is illustrative of the industrial transformation of Hollywood cinema in the 1980s, in part a result of the processes of mergers and acquisitions, deregulation and increased market competition, all of which were exacerbated by the Reagan administration's economic policies. The 'big business' mindedness of 'Reaganomics' brought about an overt integration of the film and music industry as well as diversification of the Hollywood majors into a range of ancillary markets. The conspicuous interdependency of the music and film industry in the 1980s becomes key to the success and appeal in a number of films that make heavy use of popular music and songs, including: *Desperately Seeking Susan* (Seidelman, 1985), *Footloose* (Ross, 1984), *Top Gun*, and *Dirty Dancing*, although the model and benchmark for this kind of cross-promotion was set in the previous decade by *Saturday Night Fever* (see Smith 1998). In *Flashdance*, the synergistic cross-promotion between two industries resulted in two hit singles: the film's pre-release single that generated 'buzz' for the film, Irene Cara's "Flashdance .... What a Feeling," and a further single, Michael Sembello's "Maniac," released during the film's theatrical run. The *Flashdance* album, released in conjunction with the film in 1983, sold well over six million units in the US alone (RIAA). Deriving from this industrial cross-promotion of music and film was the development of a new, montage-driven audio-visual aesthetic, also marked by the introduction of MTV in the early 1980s.

Montage sequences in 1980s films are cynically used not so much to capture the film's theme or manage temporal relations as in earlier films, like *The Graduate*, (Nichols, 1967) but are instead promotional tools, adverts for the soundtrack of the films. For this reason, in films like *Flashdance*, *Xanadu* (Kelly, 1980), and many others, there is an over-driven music track that frequently competes with image and narrative for structural dominance. In other words, the look and the sound of *Flashdance* signifies an integration of marketing and industrial synergy, and the text becomes merely an advertisement for other products and a 'component' in a larger capitalist-entertainment-business system of "commercial intertextuality" (Maltby 1998: 26) and "high-concept" (Wyatt 1994). The impact of music video promotion and advertising codes, often called "the MTV aesthetic" (Dickinson 2003), upon the spatial and temporal construction of *Flashdance* cannot be understated. For example, both the first Mawby's bar sequence ("He's a Dream") (see Figure 25.3) and the gym sequence ("I Love Rock and Roll") are able to stand alone as self-contained music videos or 'modules' (Wyatt 1994: 17) whether in *Flashdance* or on MTV.

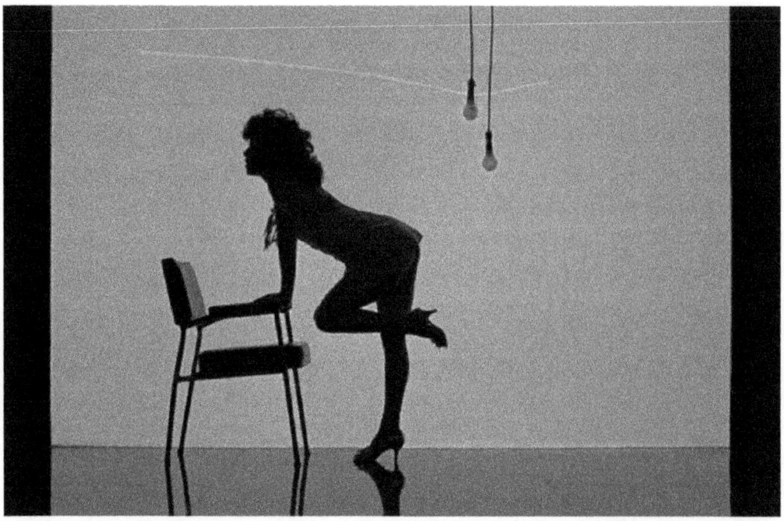

Figure 25.3 MTV aesthetics in *Flashdance*.

Flashdance's Reaganomic business practices seem to be matched by the regeneration of the musical in the 1980s as an ideological genre project concomitant with conservative politics. In *Flashdance*, as in *Dirty Dancing*, both music and dance play key roles in securing the ideological consent through solipsism and film form in which a woman's place is determined through patriarchal relations: men lead and women follow. *Flashdance* uses the pleasure of music and dance to position its female protagonist Alex as far away as possible from both her financial independence and 'masculine' job as a welder, at the beginning of the film, into the more traditional trajectory of a career in both ballet and romance, by the end of the film. Like *Cobra*, *Flashdance* poses a problem in the opening scenes of the film (Alex is too independent and masculine) and resolves it by the end (she is in a relationship and ready to start studying ballet). The position that she finally takes up at the end of the film, captured in a freeze-frame and echoed in the lyrics "What a Feeling" secures her a place in a traditional, appropriately feminine, patriarchal system.

Flashdance achieves its ideological consent not through overt politic means but rather through the use of narrative closure and genre motivated spectacle. The 'true' ending of *Flashdance* is the point at which we realize Alex has won over the audition panel with her energetic performance to "What a Feeling." The music at this point is established as diegetic, since Alex brings along the record and we see her play it as part of her audition. Her dancing is impressive, combining elements of both ballet and street dance (at one point she leaps in the air and descends in a tumble, with the same spectacular shot repeated three times in succession). The gradual acceleration and momentum of this scene in terms of performance, music and editing and the fact that it does not even have to be spoken that she has won over the conservatory make for a truly uplifting moment that takes the audience to the giddy highs of plenitude. This, however, is not where *Flashdance* actually ends. In a single cut we see Alex run out from the Conservatory and in to the waiting arms of Nick and only then does the film end on a freeze-frame of the embracing couple and the credits begin. It is in that single cut from interior to exterior, from audition to romance, from the loss of an independent life to one of coupledom and financial dependence where *Flashdance* does make its politics known. The power of this shift and the ideological sentiments that it secures are achieved by having the pleasures of the dance audition (the generic element) mapped on to the romance and loss of independence (the ideological element). Everything that we feel about Alex's success as a dancer through her performance and the music is hijacked at the point the music shifts from diegetic to non-diegetic so that our 'feeling' about success, performance, and dance is conflated with romance, surrender, and the loss of independence. The 'trick' of *Flashdance*'s ending is to confuse two endings, to exploit the feelings generated from within the genre (the music and the dancing) so that those pleasurable generic elements are experienced in the service of ideology; that is how the Reaganite cinema secures is ideological consent.

Criticizing *Flashdance*'s gender politics would of course be taking away the fun, just as it would if we started talking about race in *Indiana Jones and the Temple of Doom*. It is an ideal situation in which the pleasure of triumphant, celebratory, and uplifting moments obscures the ways in which ideology works to maintain a social status quo based on inequality. *Flashdance* provides what Jameson calls "imaginary resolutions" (Jameson 1992: 26) to real-world contradictions (women's rights and agency, gender equality) that, in context, relate to the film's place in the neoconservative gender politics and the backlash against feminism in the Reagan era. The sleight of hand in Reaganite cinema is those canny textual strategies, also emerging from shifts in industrial practice, that transform politics into pleasures, a cinema that has exchanged thinking for feeling and is seemingly here to stay.

Bibliography

Baudry, J. L. (1986) "Ideological Effects of the Basic Cinematographic Apparatus" in P. Rosen (ed.) *Narrative, Apparatus, Ideology*, New York: Columbia University Press, pp. 286–298.
Britton, A. (1986) "Blissing Out: The Politics of Reaganite Entertainment," *Movie*, No. 31, pp. 1–42.
Comolli, J. L. and Narboni, P. (1971) "Cinema/Ideology/Criticism," *Screen* 12 (1), pp. 27–38.
Darnton, N. (1986) "*Cobra*," *New York Times*, May 24, 1986. http://www.nytimes.com/movie/review?res=9A0DE5DF103AF937A15756C0A960948260 (accessed August 26, 2014).
Dickinson, K. (2003) "Pop, Speed, Teenagers, and the "MTV Aesthetic", in K. Dickinson (ed.) *Movie Music: The Film Reader*, London: Routledge, pp.143–151.
Elsaesser, T. and King, N. (eds) (2005) *The Last Great American Picture Show: New Hollywood Cinema in the 1970s*, Amsterdam: Amsterdam University Press.
Faludi, S. (1991) *Backlash: The Undeclared War Against Women*, New York: Crown Publishing.
Giovacchini, S. (2001) *Hollywood Modernism: Film and Politics in the Age of the New Deal*, Philadelphia: Temple University Press.
Graser, M. (2014) "Marvel Announces New Wave of Superhero Movies," *Variety*, October 28. http://variety.com/2014/film/news/black-panther-inhumans-captain-marvel-marvel-announces-new-wave-of-superhero-movies-1201341076/ (accessed February 13, 2015).
James, D. E. (1989) *Allegories of Cinema: American Film in the Sixties*, Princeton, NJ: Princeton University Press.
Jameson, F. (1992) *Signatures of the Visible*, New York: Routledge, pp. 9–34.
Jeffords, S. (1993) *Hard Bodies: Hollywood Masculinity in the Reagan Era*, New Brunswick, NJ: Rutgers University Press.
Lucas, G. (1978) "*Star Wars* advertisement" *Sight and Sound*, 48 (1), Summer, pp. 27–28.
Maltby, R. (1998) "'Nobody Knows Everything': Post-Classical Historiographies and Consolidated Entertainment" in S. Neale and M. Smith (eds) *Contemporary Hollywood Cinema*, London: Routledge, pp. 21–43.
Modleski, T. (1991) *Feminism Without Women*, London and New York: Routledge.
Muscio, G. (1997) *Hollywood's New Deal*, Philadelphia: Temple University Press.
Prime, R. (2013) *Hollywood Exiles in Europe: The Blacklist and Cold War Film Culture*, New Brunswick, NJ: Rutgers University Press.
Prince, S. (2000) *A New Pot of Gold: Hollywood Under the Electronic Rainbow, 1980–1989*, Berkeley: University of California Press.
RIAA (Recording Industry Association of America) "*Flashdance*," http://www.riaa.com/goldandplatinum data.php?artist=%20Flashdance (accessed February 13, 2015).
Rogin, M. (1988) *Ronald Reagan, the Movie: and Other Episodes in Demonology*, Berkeley: University of California Press.
Ryan, M. and Kellner, D. (1990) *Camera Politica: the Politics and Ideology of Contemporary Hollywood Film*, Bloomington: Indiana University Press.
Scott, V. (1986) "*Cobra* Biggest Draw for Box Office Bucks," *Sun Sentinel*, May 26, 1986. http://articles.sun-sentinel.com/1986-05-29/features/8602010901_1_poltergeist-ii-top-gun-short-circuit (accessed August 26, 2014).
Smith, J. (1998) *The Sounds of Commerce*, New York: Columbia University Press.
Smith, J. (2014) *Film Criticism, the Cold War, and the Blacklist*, Berkeley: University of California Press.
Wood, R. (1986) *Hollywood from Vietnam to Reagan*, New York: Columbia University Press.
Wyatt, J. (1994) *High Concept: Movies and Marketing in Hollywood*, Austin: University of Texas Press.

PART VI

Alternative and independent film and politics

INTRODUCTION

Yannis Tzioumakis

Ever since there has been a concentrated, industrially organised basis that assumed (often problematically) the label 'mainstream film production' there has always been unorganised, semi- or fully organised film production that has been considered 'independent' or 'alternative', that is, different in a number of ways from the films of 'the mainstream'. This can be seen within individual countries and national film industries whereby once a particular mode of filmmaking becomes dominant (and is deemed to support the dominant power structures and the ideologies that hold them together) then other, alternative or independent, forms of filmmaking emerge with many of them providing the diversity of representation and plurality of viewpoint that are perceived to be missing from the films of the mainstream. Taking the United States as an example, one can see a huge range of independent film production practised at the margins of Hollywood cinema as this became crystallised into the films of a handful of major film studios that have dominated American film production since the late 1910s. Of course, not all of this independent film production has supported alternative ideologies or has been openly political or oppositional to the mainstream. Nonetheless, a large number of filmmakers have used film production at the margins or even away from the centre of a film industry and its dominant players to make often strongly political pictures that challenged established power structures, went against national narratives and attacked dominant ideological positions.

Independent and alternative film politics, however, are not only enacted within individual countries and national film industries but also on a global arena, especially as Hollywood cinema has dominated the theatres of most countries and has been widely perceived as a global mainstream, the conduit for a sustained cultural imperialist project designed to promote American ideas, values and products. With mainstream film production in many countries often modelling itself on Hollywood cinema in an effort to produce commercial films that would be able to compete against Hollywood productions for audience attention (and more recently for finance), filmmakers around the world and throughout the history of cinema have tried consciously to curb Hollywood's charge. Alternative and independent film movements, have fought on a double front, against the homogenising juggernaut of Hollywood cinema and its mirror image as this has shaped mainstream film production in specific countries and larger geographical regions. Nowhere has this been seen more clearly than in the emergence of the New Latin American Cinema of the 1960s which targeted both the cultural imperialism of

Hollywood and the anodyne Hollywood imitation genre films that had been dominating the theatres of Latin American countries till that time.

What complicates matters, however, is that independence and alternative expression do not only take place outside the dominant system. Especially if commercially successful, independent and alternative approaches to film and culture at large have time and again attracted the attention of dominant players which try to co-opt and depoliticise certain openly critical or oppositional aspects of such expression with a view to exploit them for commercial purposes. Such processes, however, do not necessarily strip films completely from their political aspirations, and a very substantial literature on American 'indie' film in recent years has demonstrated clearly the potential of such films for expressing often strongly political positions while also benefiting from being part of a commercial production and distribution environment and from using stylistic, narrative, generic and thematic elements that bring them often close to the films of the mainstream. Similarly, all national cinemas have dealt at one point or another with filmmakers that have managed to find ways to integrate themselves in the system only to dismantle it with their work from within, that is, by managing to make films that retain their subversive and openly political qualities. In this respect, openly political, even radical, filmmaking is still possible to take place within the structures of mainstream film production when particular circumstances allow it.

This part explores a number of ways through which alternative and independent film practices have been articulated: from the staunchly independent practices of filmmakers who have resisted the mainstream completely to auteurs who have managed to find spaces in the system and consistently tried to dismantle it from within; from US filmmakers who have tried to marry openly political subjects with more commercial filmic elements such as love stories to Israeli films that try to reimagine history with films that do offer the possibility of understanding the 'other'; from film festivals and their role as sites where alternatives to mainstream cinema are celebrated and marginal voices can be heard to American 'indie' cinema and the often substantial spaces it allows for political critique, despite its increasing convergence with Hollywood. Whether in dialogue with the mainstream or completely removed from it, alternative and independent film practices have the potential to put forward political positions and viewpoints that are often radical and that can be endorsed by audiences that are often substantial in size.

Marijke deValck starts this part with an examination of film festivals and how they mediate mainstream and marginal voices. Many key film festivals, she argues, openly appropriated characteristics associated with Hollywood cinema to establish themselves as part of a cosmopolitan film culture, while the rise of global media economy has helped erase many differences between what has been considered mainstream and what independent or alternative. Still, what is clear is that film festivals continue to be destinations for low-budget films which often deal with openly political concerns, though these tend to co-exist increasingly with more popular film productions in a globalised and popularised media arena.

The co-existence of the popular with the openly political is also at the core of my own chapter. Taking as a starting point the increasing popularisation and commercialisation of American independent cinema during the early 1990s, I examine how 'difficult' political matters, in this case US hegemony in global geopolitics, can still be tackled. While popular Hollywood cinema films tend to make core political matters a background against which genre-driven narratives take priority, indie film, I argue, does allow for more complex representations, as is the case with the film *Barcelona* (1994) where genre and politics are married in much more complex ways than in Hollywood political dramas or action films.

Jacqui Miller continues the thread that examines the often complex relationship between Hollywood cinema and alternative politics by looking at one of the most celebrated anti-establishment filmmakers, who nonetheless worked for large parts of his career within the system making unconventional films, Robert Altman. Through an examination of some of his early and lesser-known films that were made for the Hollywood studios, Miller demonstrates how Altman has managed to find ways to critique the system and weaken the ideological force that normally sustains genre film production within Hollywood cinema.

The notion of the critique of the system through films that seek to provide alternative political positions compared to what has been on offer by dominant cinematic traditions is also explored by Nurith Gertz through an examination of a group of recent Israeli films that have interrupted what she calls a 'historical continuum' built on representations of trauma and inability to understand the 'other'. Rather than adhering to such dominant narratives, several recent Israeli films have sought to provide alternative representations that offer the possibility of hope for the future. Utilising the conventions of the multi-plot film together with European art cinema aesthetics, these films are reinventing and reimagining history, shaping it in alternative ways.

This part closes with an examination of the film practices of a US filmmaker who has consistently resisted any links with the mainstream and has followed a staunchly independent path throughout his career, Rob Nilsson. Often credited as one of the main filmmakers to kickstart the American independent cinema movement of the late 1970s/early 1980s with his critically acclaimed *Northern Lights* (co-directed with John Hanson), Nilsson developed a distinct filmmaking approach, "the way of seeming", which was further crystallised with the Tenderloin yGroup Manifesto signed by Nilsson and eighteen other workshop members in 1998. Authoring the chapter himself, Nilsson explains how this approach to filmmaking was developed and discusses its potential for political and social critique. Together these five chapters demonstrate the often extremely broad range that alternative and independent film practices can take when it comes to them being used for political purposes.

26

FILM FESTIVALS

Mediating the mainstream and marginal voices

Marijke de Valck

Early publications on film festivals explained how film festivals acted as nodes in an alternative network for the circulation of non-mainstream film (de Valck 2007; Elsaesser 2005). Although the adjective 'alternative' was accompanied with plenty of disclaimers, it is worthwhile to ask if the characterization of the film festival network as committed to 'alternative' cinemas might not be misguiding our understanding of contemporary film festivals, in particular with regard to the different hierarchies that exist between them today, and in relation to the variety of cinemas that these festivals showcase. While film festivals are part of the spaces and opportunities for alternative forms of filmmaking that have always existed – spaces where marginal voices could be heard and counter discourses were created and sustained – they also foster relations with the mainstream and produce new power relations of their own.

Clearly, when described as alternative, film festivals are foremost regarded in relation to Hollywood. This chapter therefore starts by revisiting the theorization of festivals vis-à-vis Hollywood, briefly discussing key studies that demonstrate the extent of the Cannes Film Festival's engagement with Hollywood (Schwartz 2007; Jungen 2009). From the specific – and norm-setting – circumstances of the world's premier film festival in Cannes, the chapter moves to consider relations and differences *between* festivals. Today's international film festival circuit is a vastly proliferated phenomenon, comprising many singular events that are hard to reduce to one common denominator. Moreover, globalization has radically transformed the production of both 'mainstream' and 'alternative' cinemas. Distinctions between centre and peripheries become increasingly blurred and lead to aesthetic hybridity and economic collaborations. The chapter therefore also considers the specific role film festivals play in the rise of a global economy for art cinema. Finally, it briefly addresses the increasing influence of film festivals in Asia and their relation with industries and the regional mainstream. Film festivals are proliferating on the Asian continent as the region is undergoing rapid economic growth, and this trend in particular challenges the Eurocentric tendency in Film Festival Studies that considers festivals primarily in relation to Hollywood.

Hollywood, festivals and cosmopolitanism

In my earlier work, scrutinizing the founding histories of European film festivals (de Valck 2007), I have described festivals as an alternative network that maintains complex interrelations between the mainstream and its alternatives, explaining how Hollywood acts both as festivals' main antagonist and as key player in the 'alternative' exhibition network that was formed around festivals as nodal points. The alternative dimension of this network refers to its commitment to screen films that fall outside regular distribution channels, which are typically dominated by Hollywood fare and in some countries, like China and India, also popular national cinemas. Unlike regular cinema theatres, film festivals show films from a wide range of countries. And where the mainstream distribution circuit has a commercial prerogative, film festivals typically boast the ideological agenda of celebrating cinema as art form. However, Hollywood is not absent on the festival stage, and the presence of well-known Hollywood stars was, and continues to be, one of the major attractions of film festivals in their capacity of media event (cf. Beauchamp and Béhar 1992).

Vanessa Schwartz (2007) and Christian Jungen (2009) have studied the specific interrelations between Hollywood and the Cannes Film Festival with an eye for historic detail. Where Schwartz focuses on the period up to the 1960s, Jungen spans the festival's history until 2008. As part of a book that explores the constructive relations between Hollywood and French film culture, Schwartz makes a strong and well-received argument about the international aspirations driving the founding of the Cannes Film Festival: "The Festival organizers sought to establish and direct world cinema from the beaches of the Mediterranean and readily envisioned France as the perfect place because of its association with both internationalism and a commitment to excellence in culture" (2007: 65–66).

To achieve such high international ambitions the festival turned to Hollywood. The choice of location, a beachside town with pleasant climate, mirrored California. Moreover, American stars were courted to visit the festival and add glamour to the event. Pictures of stars posing on the red carpet and relaxing on the beach played a crucial role in promoting Cannes, putting it on the map as a city of cinema, and introducing the format of festivals as media events. Less well known but no less relevant is Schwartz's historical work on the ways in which Cannes collaborated with American film professionals to "get films" for its programmes.[1] In particular, films that featured a French connection were actively acquired (2007: 92). By including films like *An American in Paris* (Minnelli, 1951), which featured in the Cannes competition of 1952, Hollywood was strategically made part of the festival's vision of a cosmopolitan film culture, and Cannes was able to seize its influential position in the world of cinema.

Importantly, in the cosmopolitan exchange that enfolded between the Cannes Film Festival and Hollywood distinguished roles were reserved for either side of the Atlantic. Andrew Sarris put it strikingly into words when he referred to Cannes as "Hollywood's licentious mistress" (1982: 29). The festival on the French Riviera did not restrict itself to mimicking the Californian atmosphere and adopting Hollywood's successful celebrity system, rather it presented its own naughty version of the American model, with scantily clad girls on the beach that were reminiscent of the French tradition of the Folies Bergère (ibid.). Thus, while Hollywood until the mid-1960s applied strict Catholic morality norms in a gesture of self-censorship of its film production, precluding interventions by industry censors (Black 1994), an open attitude that was particularly progressive towards sexuality was embraced on the European continent. Countering Hollywood's conservatism, Cannes confirmed the classic idea that sex sells. Where American studios were bound by the Hays Code and the moral conservatism of mainstream American audiences in general, Cannes enjoyed more freedom both in programming and staging thanks to its festival identity – constituting an out-of-the-ordinary event (Falassi 1987) – also benefiting from the looser ethical regulation of the French. Hollywood clearly thrived under the arrangements; boosting the attraction of its stars by parading them in the suggestive setting of European festival extravaganza, without violating any ethical boundaries on the home turf.

If the relation between Hollywood as mainstream and Cannes as alternative had a distinctly moral dimension up to the mid-1960s, other facets were brought to the fore in later periods. The study by Jungen reveals how relationships between Hollywood and the Cannes Film Festival developed in conjunction with larger historical transformations: for instance, Hollywood has sometimes seemingly withdrawn its efforts on the Riviera – notably in a period during the 1980s when the majors were reluctant to participate in the competition and turned to out-of-competition screenings to avoid critical press – while at other times it has found inspiration and legitimization in French film culture. Two pertinent examples of Hollywood–Cannes cross-fertilization were the embracement of auteur theory in Hollywood and the success of New Hollywood at the Cannes Film Festival, beginning with *Easy Rider* (Hopper, 1969) as the American competition entry, and subsequently giving way to a series of festival awards for films produced by the major studios in the period up to 1979 (Jungen 2009: 186–187).[2] Jungen's study, moreover, points out the extent to which the interactions between Cannes and Hollywood have been defined by economic motives, a point to which we will return later.

The arrival of New Hollywood in America coincided with anti-Vietnam demonstrations, worldwide social unsettling and a formative moment in festival history: the upheavals at European festivals – Cannes 1968, Venice 1968, Berlin, 1970 – that led to new programming strategies (de Valck 2012). If before, festivals functioned mainly as showcases of national cinemas, the idea that festivals ought to exert curatorial control over their programmes found widespread resonance in the late 1960s and 1970s when countercultural movements swept across the United States and Europe, and New Hollywood and New Waves were gaining momentum. Although the dissatisfaction with festivals had been brewing for a couple of years, it was not until Francois Truffaut, Jean Luc Goddard and their followers travelled to the Cannes Film Festival of 1968 to express solidarity with French strikers and ended up disrupting the event that a proper start towards rethinking the festival format was undertaken. Many felt festivals had become vehicles for the industry, and too preoccupied with stars, glamour and parties, moreover. In the 1968 call for change the emphasis was put instead on festivals' unique position to nurture film as art, and utilize film for activist agendas. With the more pronounced turn to artistic selection criteria and political ideals, major international film festivals like Cannes, Berlin and Venice were to be redefined as safe havens for art cinema and as platforms for films with political messages, such as films supporting liberation movements, addressing social issues, or breaking cultural taboos. It is in this period that film festivals fully manifest themselves as spaces for voices that are marginalized in the mainstream, screening 'other' films and supporting emancipatory discourses.

The alternative that was promoted in this way through the festival circuit, I would like to suggest, is best considered aligned with the ideologies of the (new) social movements that took place in the United States and Europe from the 1960s onwards. In this period collective action was mobilized against authority; conservative ideas about sexuality, women's role in society, race and class inequalities were challenged, and new concerns for the environment and peace articulated. The movements were not only about expanding national rights, but had a distinct cosmopolitan character, and collective action would also be taken to support, for example, democratization struggles or the fight for women's rights in, what were then called, Third World countries. The international platform of the film festival offered a perfect stage to advocate such cosmopolitan political agendas, as they had been used for the celebration of cosmopolitan film culture since the 1950s. One might argue that festivals were positioned on the Left wing of the political spectrum in this period. The commitment to screen films that have political relevance and/or serve an (explicit) activist cause continues today, and is most clearly visible in the sub-circuits of themed social-concern festivals that emerged after festivals proliferated in the 1980s.

Festivals and the logics of proliferation

While trends at large so-called A-list festivals like Cannes, Berlin and Venice are certainly norm setting, they cannot be considered representative for film festivals in general. Film festivals come in many forms and shapes, and their relations to what we so far have considered as mainstream are by no means uniform. Film festivals have proliferated, especially since the 1980s, when the festival phenomenon spread globally (de Valck 2007: 20). Every day of the year one or more film festivals take place somewhere in the world. In the first book-length study on film festivals, veteran film critic Kenneth Turan writes that estimates of total numbers of festivals vary from just over 400 to an "outlandish-sounding" figure of more than 1,000 festivals (Turan 2002: 2). More than a decade later we know that the sources in Turan's book in fact heavily underestimated the proliferation of festivals. Today's online directories range from 1,651 (British Film Council 2014) and 2,582 (Festival Focus n.d.) to more than 5,000 (Withoutabox n.d.) film festivals organized annually. These large numbers give an indication of the wide variety among film festival events. Everybody knows about the Cannes Film Festival, cosmopolitan film aficionados will also be familiar with Sundance and Locarno, and the general film-loving audience is likely to take their local 'big international' festival as a template for the global phenomenon. But this is just the tip of the iceberg.

Since festivals boomed in the 1960s there has also been a steep increase in *types* of festival events. There are identity-based festivals (e.g. LGBT/queer, women's or Jewish film festivals), genre festivals (e.g. horror, fantasy, documentary, archive or children's film festivals), social-concern festivals (e.g. human rights, disability or environmental film festivals), festivals that focus on a certain region (e.g. Latin-American, Japanese or French film festivals) and also festivals for short films, some of which are organized online. Apart from variety in the types of films being screened or the audiences that are served, festivals differ in other ways as well. Some festivals operate on a shoe-string budget, drawing mainly on a large pool of (activist) volunteers, while others can count on (substantial) subsidy from national and local governments and yet others have professional fundraising departments that work year round to close the corporate sponsorship deals needed to stage their elaborated events. There are festivals that are renowned for their cutting-edge artistic programming, but also events whose main purpose is to contribute to the cultural image of its host city or to support a city or region as tourist destination.

Clearly we cannot measure all festivals by the same standards; and when assuming festivals are by default part of one homogenous 'alternative' media landscape, one fails to acknowledge what James English has called 'the logic of proliferation' in his study on cultural awards (2005: 50–68). Film festivals are subjected to a similar dynamic, in particular since the global spread of the festival phenomenon in the 1980s, which led to competition between festivals and a hierarchy of events. English reminds us that prizes are instrumental in the arts to affirm the autonomy of the cultural domain, and explains how "new prizes would emerge to compete with established ones, to try to tarnish them or at least to steal some of their luster" (2005: 53–54). He continues in Bourdieuan tradition "that all prizes would struggle to defend or improve their positions on the field of cultural production as a whole" (ibid.). Similarly, new festivals that were founded did not simply emulate existing events, but competed for attention. Film and film festival scholar Julian Stringer has rightfully described festivals' strategies for competition as double-sided. "Film festivals market both conceptual similarity and cultural difference" (Stringer 2001: 139). He argues that, due to globalization, festivals need to both be similar to each other, conforming to expectations and playing by the rules of competition over titles, audiences and press, while also highlighting unique characteristics, for example local culture or tourist attractions, that might garner special interest and work to differentiate the event from the confounding supply.

The logic of proliferation at film festivals then involves two specific mechanisms of distinction: increasing specialization, and counter-events. The first is a result of the inevitable criticism that established festivals fail to consider, or do justice to, the full scope of film production. This led to the founding of themed festivals, dedicated for example to children's films, or African cinema, because the new festival organizers deemed these films to be marginalized in the general international events. Many of the newly founded regular international film festivals moreover also complied with this logic and tended to profile a more specific image, such as the International Film Festival Rotterdam (Netherlands, 1972) that over time has chosen to focus on first or second feature filmmakers for its flagship Tiger Award, and the International Istanbul Film Festival (Turkey, 1984), which has a thematic competition, presenting cinema that "brings the world of arts and artists together with the seventh art, or reflect literary works to the silver screen" (International Istanbul Film Festival 2009). New events in their turn again fail to be sufficiently inclusive in the eyes of others and give way to further specialized festivals, such as Images Santé/the International Health Film Festival (Belgium, 1994), a documentary film festival that is dedicated to improving knowledge of health and health care, or the Queer Women of Color Film Festival (2000), organized in San Francisco, hometown of the renowned Frameline Festival (1977), one of the first LGBT festivals, and similarly Outfest Fusion (Los Angeles), that is certainly part of the Outfest organization, but staged separately as a festival about queer people of colour (cf. Rastegar 2009).

The second mechanism of proliferation comprises the logic of counter-events. Here, a new festival opposes the dominant programming choices of one or more existing events, and offers an alternative set-up. In this vein the International Documentary Film Festival (Amsterdam, 1982) that is known for favoring politically engaged films gave occasion to a counter-event, called Shadow Festival, in which artistic criteria were prioritized (cf. de Valck and Soeteman 2010). Another interesting example is the Udine Far East Film Festival (Italy, 1998) that focuses on popular Asian cinemas, and thereby embraces a counter-programming strategy against the elitist taste for art and author cinema that is prevalent on the 'mainstream' festival circuit (Lee and Stringer 2012). The point I want to make here is that both mechanisms generate a myriad of possible connections within the festival network, with several sets of mainstream–alternatives/center–peripheries relations at work at the same time. Dina Iordanova has rightfully argued there is no such thing as one coherent nor "orchestrated" festival circuit, and one should rather think of the festival world as existing of parallel circuits (for global art cinema, documentary, LGBT/Queer etc.), a world that is not essentially networked (Iordanova 2009: 26). In addition to the ranking of such circuits in relation to one another – with the A-list festivals and their taste for global art cinema firmly located in the centre – individual circuits are hierarchically constituted as well. The relation of these separate circuits to mainstream cinema and/or commercial film industries, moreover, can differ significantly. LGBT festivals, as Skadi Loist and Ger Zielinski write, have a distinct history as grassroots and activist identity-oriented events (2012: 50) that originally sat uneasily with cinema's corporate dimensions, while children's festivals seem to have developed a more collaborative attitude towards the film and television industries from the start.

Globalization, niche marketing and marginal voices

> The cinematic periphery is a constantly shifting constituent in a dynamically evolving relationship. It is elusive and intangible, as the center to which it relates keeps redefining itself.
>
> (*Iordanova* et al. *2010: 6)*

If we return to the question of how to understand festivals' relation to Hollywood, and by extension to commercial media industries and popular cinema in general, we should first acknowledge that the cultural field is in a constant process of transformation. Some of the most influential trends of recent times include the economization of film culture (de Valck 2014), the rise of Asian film industries and festivals on the circuit (Stringer 2016) and the makeover of Hollywood as part of global entertainment conglomerates (Grainge 2008). Jungen makes two important observations on Hollywood that are particularly relevant for contemporary festival transformations. The first is that Hollywood's international revenues have surpassed the national US box office. "From Hollywood to Hollyworld," Jungen calls this (2009: 300). It is a titanic shift that redefines Hollywood as part of a global film economy, and an important shift also, for our initial framing of festivals as the alternative and Hollywood as the mainstream. As America turns from a home to world market the playing field of centre and peripheries fundamentally changes. The hypothesis that festivals have become intrinsically less alternative at a time when international audiences are the default market, though, demands further scrutiny. How is globalization visible on the festival circuit? What does it mean for production, and what is the effect on aesthetics?

Clearly the festival circuit has been 'global' in certain senses from the onset, offering a platform for different national cinemas and fostering cosmopolitan culture. But if we follow the most common definition of globalization, the one that refers to the development towards an increasingly integrated global economy with free trade and free flow of capital than globalization has not become truly visible on the festival circuit until the late 1980s and particularly the 1990s. This is when a world market for niche films emerged that had led to a new generation of film companies specialized in the art cinema niche. With *sex, lies, and videotape* (Soderbergh, 1989) as a well-studied turning point (see Perren 2001; Tzioumakis 2013), niche marketing takes centre stage in the new independent scene that can be argued to mimic Hollywood strategies on a smaller scale, aiming for indie blockbuster success or festival hits. Festival prizes then have become preferred promotional tools for the brand of 'quality' cinema that emerged. Today posters used for theatrical releases of indie, independent and art films feature almost without exception a series of festival logos and make mention of the prestigious competitions for which the film was selected and the awards it has won. It is the brand name of the festival that serves as a hallmark of quality; something familiar, trustworthy and established that makes it easier for moviegoers to decide to see a small film by a new director, with unknown actors, and/or from an unfamiliar culture. This 'quality film' model has been so successful, in fact, that a significant part of the projects being launched on the festival circuit transcends the small film category proper, and is realized on a decent size budget, and has established names attached to it. Lars von Trier, for example, premiered in Cannes with *Antichrist* (2009) made for $11 million, and *Melancholia* (2011), made for $7.4 million, and screened *Nymphomaniac I & II* out of competition in Berlin and Venice (2013), realized on a budget of $4.7 million. Of these films, only *Antichrist* resulted in a loss, bringing in a mere $791,867 in revenues, while *Melancholia* and *Nymphomaniac* performed well with $15.9 and $11.4 million, respectively.[3] The parallel with Hollywood strategies can be found in the use of well-known actors and actresses – Von Trier's films feature Charlotte Gainsbourg, Kirsten Dunst, Willem Dafoe, Kiefer Sutherland, Shia LaBeouf, Christian Slater and Uma Thurman – and the careful consideration of potential media hooks for promotion – revolving in the case of Von Trier around controversial portrayals of sex that hark back to interest in breaking cultural taboos that emerged in festival programming in the late 1960s and 1970s. Other examples of auteur-directors making films in the $5–20 million budget range include Wong Kar-Wai, Michael Haneke and, after long commitment to small-budget films, Abbas Kiarostami with *Certified Copy* in 2010.

What is shared by such film projects and pertains to the work of most filmmakers mentioned above is the dependence on co-production, another clear symptom of globalization tendencies. Typically, there are several production companies from different countries that contribute to the production of these quality films. Because both small- and medium-budget quality films are produced with international audiences in mind, different countries are not simply involved to spread the risk of film funding; having an international production team also facilitates tailoring projects to the global market. Film festivals responded to this development in international film production by organizing markets, aimed at lubricating the interactions between filmmakers and industry representatives. In the case of co-production markets, a limited number of projects is selected by the festival market and matched with potential financiers. Again, it is the name of the festival that connotes prestige and attracts attention from the industry. Especially in recent years, relations between festivals and industries have tightened considerably.

In an influential piece in film festival studies, Mark Peranson notes the world's most powerful festivals are the ones for which industry partners (in particular distributors, buyers and sales agents) constitute the most important interest group, while filmmakers and film critics are bringing up the rear of the ranking for what he calls business festivals (Peranson 2008). Since then several others have observed how festivals themselves are expanding their activities to include services that foster the *making* of art cinema, such as the organization of the previously mentioned (co-production) markets, but also funds and training events (Campos 2012; Falicov 2010; Ostrowska 2010; Ross 2011). While acknowledging the positive role such initiatives may play in supporting filmmakers, there is also widespread concern that festival involvement in the pre-production phase has far-reaching consequences for the ways in which cinemas are shaped and understood. Writing about festival funds Falicov, for example, warns that:

> in the realm of European sponsorship of global South filmmaking, one could argue that transnationally funded films are shaped to be more universally understood … [and] … such sponsorship can help reinforce assumptions that Northern audiences might historically have about the South.
>
> (2010: 7)

In other words, there is a fear that cosmopolitan tastes come to dominate world cinema production, and paradoxically – for the aim of these festival funds is to foster cultural diversity – shall lead to less space for the true marginal voices and real counter discourses of our time. For Falicov the roots of contemporary dominant film festival aesthetics ought to be located in the Art Cinema genre, defined by Steve Neale as relying heavily on universal values, and thriving on the international prestige distributed by festivals (quoted in Falicov 2010: 5). The issue that is raised here of course is if this is not a particular European conception of universalism that is promoted.

It brings me to Jungen's second point. He calls attention to the efforts of some countries, in particular France, to apply a cultural exception for cinema in the trade negotiations for this globalizing economy (2009: 302). Cinema, the argument goes in short, should not be subjected to the general trade agreements, because it is an art form that allows people to express and sustain authentic cultural identities and this is something that ought to be protected from market interference; every people has a right to its culture. In this sense we see a continuation of the rhetoric of film festivals as spaces for the alternative, namely in their commitment to cinema as art and cinema as important form of cultural expression that is under the threat of media imperialism. These two elements come together in a quite particular mix in the work of festival funds like the Hubert Bals Fund (Rotterdam) and World Cinema Fund (Berlin). On the one hand, these funds aim to support films from countries where production money is not readily available. More specifically, the ideological motivation for spending this money is to support people in their rights for cultural expression. On the other hand, the work of the fund is legitimized by its commitment to art cinema, and the film projects that receive support follow a particular, universal (European) aesthetics, which may not resonate very well with local audiences. A philosophical question that is raised by the work of these funds, then, concerns the compatibility between marginality and marketing. Can the cause of supporting peripheral cinemas go hand in hand with the demands of (niche) marketing for global audiences, or is something inevitably lost when marginal voices do not exert full control over their own images and narratives?

New hierarchies, new cosmopolitism

At the same time, it is interesting to note that while these festival funds favour a certain brand of world cinema – typically low-budget productions, adhering to cosmopolitan aesthetic standards, sometimes explicitly dealing with socially relevant concerns – general festival programming, and here I refer to programming at big international film festivals, seems to have become *less* exclusively focused on art cinema. In addition to the ubiquitous festival film, festivals screen plenty of films with cross-over appeal, and there is also a growing interest in what we can tentatively refer to as popular world cinema; e.g. Korean blockbusters, Japanese martial arts and Chinese costume epics. The old label 'alternative' seems particularly unapt for these films, because in the former case the distinction between art and popular culture does not uphold, and in the latter – though not belonging to *mainstream Western* cinema – many of these films ought to be considered popular locally; produced commercially, with lavish budgets, and attracting large domestic audiences in the regional territories.

Globalization, we may conclude, has spurred a wide range of developments that may thwart existing hierarchies and turn categories upside down, while creating new ones. The rise of Asian film festivals is a case in point. In the wake of East Asia's ascendency on the world economic ladder, East Asian cinemas boomed, and so did film festivals in the region (Iordanova 2011: 2). Ruby Cheung points out how the development of East Asian festivals and festival markets enfolds as a geopolitical clustering, "challenging the omnipresence of the U.S. in Asia and moving towards becoming the voice of the region" (Cheung 2011: 43). Even if it proves extremely difficult to challenge the major global industry players and rival Western A-list festivals (see Mark Nornes 2011), Asia's strategy of regionalization is paying off. Hollywood is steadily losing market share to domestic and regional productions. As the *Hollywood Reporter* conveyed in the summer of 2013: "The box-office revenue of domestic movies in China has overtaken that of foreign films in the first half of 2013, which will have given a major boost of confidence to the Chinese movie industry". At the same time, Hollywood is heavily emulated and courted in the bid for global cinema prestige and power. American stars are considered indispensable on the red carpets of major film festivals and award ceremonies. In its turn, Asia, and East Asia in particular, have gained attention on the Western festival circuit. Although it is much too early to make bold statements, we can discern a tentative development taking place at festivals that involves complementing Hollywood as festivals' main antagonist, towards East Asian media companies.

The growing awareness on the festival circuit of the weight and relevance of these East Asian cinemas might be compared to festivals' relation to Hollywood in the 1940s and 1950s when Cannes had a special eye for American films with a French connection, like Minnelli's *An American in Paris*. Likewise, today's international film festivals are eager to present instances of the budding collaboration between China and Hollywood, and the big premier events readily screen Chinese blockbusters featuring American stars like Zhang Yimou's *Flowers of War* (China/Hong Kong, 2011) with Christian Bale (Berlin premiere) and *Back to 1942* (Xiaogang Feng, 2012) starring Tim Robbins and Adrien Brody (Rome premiere). By cultivating relations with rising film powers, Western festivals preserve their claim to internationalism, and thus their claim to matter in the world of cinema. In the quest for cultural cinematic diversity, and the celebration of peripheral films, relations with the mainstream still need to be fostered, and a new version of cosmopolitanism promoted.

Notes

1 It is important to underline that the Cannes Film Festival lobbied with the American film industry, and not with the government, as was the case for other nations.

2 In 1979 Francis Ford Coppola won the Golden Palm for *Apocalypse Now*, which was screened as work in progress. The film was initially supported by United Artists, but ultimately completed under the umbrella of Coppola's own Zoetrope Studios, which marked the beginning of a period of lesser artistic freedom for filmmakers under the Hollywood majors.

3 All figures were retrieved from Box Office Mojo (www.boxofficemojo.com) (accessed on 19 February 2015).

Bibliography

Beauchamp, C. and Béhar, H. (1992) *Hollywood on the Riviera: The Inside Story of the Cannes Film Festival*, New York: William Morrow and Company.

Black, G. D. (1994) *Hollywood Censored: Morality Codes, Catholics and the Movies*, Cambridge: Cambridge University Press.

British Film Council (2014) "Festivals Directory", http://film.britishcouncil.org/festivals-directory (accessed on 3 November 2014).

Campos, M. (2012) "El Circuito de Financiación de los Cines Latinoamericanos/Le circuit de Financement des Cinémas Latino-Americains", *Cinémas d'Amérique Latine* 20, pp. 172–180.

Cheung, R. (2011) "East Asian Film Festivals: Markets", in Iordanova, D. and Cheung, R. (eds) *The Film Festival Yearbook 3: Film Festivals and East Asia*, St. Andrews: St. Andrews Film Studies, pp. 40–61.

Coonan, G. (2013) "China Box Office: 'Pacific Rim' Still Rules as Domestic Film Push Starts", *The Hollywood Reporter*, August 13, http://www.hollywoodreporter.com/news/chinabox-office-pacific-rim-604860 (accessed on 3 November 2014).

de Valck, M. (2007) *Film Festivals: From European Geopolitics to Global Cinephilia*, Amsterdam: Amsterdam University Press.

de Valck, M. (2012) "Finding Audiences for Films: Programming in Historical Perspective", in Ruoff, J. (ed) *Coming Soon to a Festival Near You: Programming Film Festivals*, St. Andrews: St Andrews Film Books, pp. 25–40.

de Valck, M. (2014) "Film Festivals, Bourdieu and the Economization of Culture", *Canadian Journal of Film Studies*, 23(1): 74–89.

de Valck, M. and Soeteman, M. (2010) "'And the Winner is…': What Happens Behind the Scenes of Film Festival Competitions", *International Journal of Cultural Studies* 13(3), pp. 290–307.

Elsaesser, T. (2005) *European Cinema: Face to Face with Hollywood*, Amsterdam: Amsterdam University Press.
English, J. (2005) *The Economy of Prestige: Prizes, Awards, and the Circulation of Culural Value*, Cambridge, London: Harvard University Press.
Falassi, A. (1987) *Time Out of Time: Essays on the Festival*, Albuquerque: University of New Mexico Press.
Falicov, T. (2010) "Migrating From South to North: The Role of Film Festivals in Funding and Shaping Global South Film and Video", in Elmer, G., Davis, C.H., Marchessault, J. and McCullough, J. (eds) *Locating Migrating Media*, Lanham, MD: Lexington Books, pp. 3–21.
Festival Focus (n.d.) "Film Festivals Database", http://www.festivalfocus.org/ (accessed on 3 November 2014).
Grainge, P. (2008) *Brand Hollywood: Selling Entertainment in a Global Media Age*, New York: Routledge.
International Istanbul Film Festival (2009) "28th International Istanbul Film Festival, April 4-April 19, 2009", http://ftp.filmneweurope.com/events-festivals/festivals/2469-28th-international-istanbul-film-festival-april-4-april-19-2009/menu-id-127 (accessed on 18 February 2015).
Iordanova, D. (2009) "The Film Festival Circuit" in Iordanova, D. with Rhyne, R. (eds) *Film Festival Yearbook 1: The Festival Circuit*, St. Andrews: St. Andrews Film Studies, pp. 23–39.
Iordanova, D. (2011) "East Asia and Film Festivals; Transnational Clusters for Creativity and Commerce", in Iordanova, D. and Cheung, R. (eds) *The Film Festival Yearbook 3: Film Festivals and East Asia*, St. Andrews: St. Andrews Film Studies, pp. 1–26.
Iordanova, D., Martin-Jones, D. and Vidal, B. (eds) (2010) *Cinema at the Periphery*, Detroit, MI: Wayne State University Press.
Jungen, C. (2009) *Hollywood in Canne$: Die Geschichte einer Hassliebe, 1939–2008*, Marburg: Schüren.
Lee, N.J.Y. and Stringer, J. (2012) "Counter-programming and the Udine Far East Film Festival", *Screen* 53(3), pp. 301–309.
Loist, S. and Zielinski, G. (2012) "On the Development of Queer Film Festivals and Their Media Activism", in Iordanova, D. and Torchin, L. (eds) *Film Festival Yearbook 4: Film Festivals and Activism*, St. Andrews: St. Andrews Film Studies, pp. 49–62.
Nornes, A. M. (2011) "Asian Film Festivals, Translation and the International Film Festival Short Circuit", in Iordanova, D. and Cheung, R. (eds) *The Film Festival Yearbook 3: Film Festivals and East Asia*, St. Andrews: St. Andrews Film Studies, pp. 37–39.
Ostrowska, D. (2010) "International Film Festivals as Producers of World Cinema", *International Film Studies Journal* 10 (14–15), pp. 145–150.
Peranson, M. (2008) "First You Get the Power, Then You Get the Money: Two Models of Film Festivals", *Cineaste* 33, pp. 37–43.
Perren, A. (2001) "Sex, Lies and Marketing: Miramax and the Development of the Quality Indie Blockbuster", *Film Quarterly* 55(2), pp. 30–39.
Rastegar, R. (2009) "The De-Fusion of Good Intentions: Outfest's Fusion Film Festival", *GLQ: A Journal of Lesbian and Gay Studies* 15(3), pp. 481–497.
Ross, M. (2011) "The Film Festival as Producer: Latin American films and Rotterdam's Hubert Bals Fund", *Screen* 52 (2), pp. 261–267.
Sarris, A. (1982) "The Last Word on Cannes", *American Film*, 8(7), pp. 26, 29–30.
Schwartz, V. (2007) *It's So French! Hollywood, Paris and the Making of Cosmopolitan Film Culture*, Chicago/London: University of Chicago Press.
Stringer, J. (2001) "Global Cities and International Film Festival Economy", in Shiel, M. and Fitzmaurice, T. (eds) *Cinema and the City: Film and Urban Societies in a Global Context*, Oxford: Blackwell, pp. 134–144.
Stringer, J. (2016) "Film Festivals in Asia: Notes on History, Geography, and Power from a Distance", in de Valck, M., Kredell, B. and Loist, S. (eds) *Film Festivals: History, Theory, Method, Practice*, London and New York: Routledge, pp. 34–48.
Turan, K. (2002) *From Sundance to Sarajevo: Film Festivals and the World They Make*, Berkeley: University of California Press.
Tzioumakis, Y. (2013) "'Independent', 'Indie' and 'Indiewood': Towards a Periodisation of Contemporary (Post-1980s) American Independent Cinema", in King, G., Molloy, C. and Tzioumakis, Y. (eds) *American Independent Cinema: Indie, Indiewood and Beyond*, London: Routledge, pp. 28–40.
Withoutabox (n.d.) "Withoutabox: The World's Largest Independent Film Community", https://www.withoutabox.com/index.php?cmd=public.index (accessed 3 November 2014).

27

POLITICS, 'INDIE-STYLE'

Political filmmaking and contemporary US independent cinema

Yannis Tzioumakis

In a recent critical symposium organised by film journal *Cineaste* under the title "The Prospects for Political Cinema Today", John Sayles, one of the most-well established American independent filmmakers of the last 35 years, and occasional screenwriter and screen doctor for Hollywood films, such as *Apollo 13* (Howard, 1995) and *The Spiderwick Chronicles* (Waters, 2008), commented on his experience in doing the latter job:

> As a screenwriter for Hollywood movies, my job is often to take out factors which get in the way of a smooth flow of story or the perceived enjoyment of a mass audience, and these are often the political and economic realities of whatever era the movie is set in. In the case of my own movies, the closer to the present situation the film is dealing with, the more complaints from critics (and sometimes audience) we get that the film has 'an agenda' – as if this is in some way breaking a covenant with them or betraying what 'the movies' is supposed to be about.
>
> (*Sayles, quoted in Hill 2011: 15*)

Such an account, of course, does not necessarily suggest that all Hollywood films are devoid of political substance or that they refuse to deal with political and economic issues in sophisticated and even controversial ways (and Sayles himself admits that films coming from the Hollywood studios occasionally delve into difficult and complex political and economic matters). It does beg the question, however, of the extent to which American films originating outside of the major Hollywood studios are subject to such pressures and whether 'independent' filmmakers are able to have a political agenda without necessarily compromising the entertainment value and the commercial appeal of their films. For Sayles, this question has an easy answer. In the independent film sector in the US, a filmmaker is freer to be "politically conscious", that is to question or challenge "the reigning orthodoxy of thought about present or past realities" than in Hollywood films (ibid.).

More than any other filmmaker in contemporary American independent cinema, Sayles' name is synonymous with uncompromising politically conscious filmmaking. However, the majority of independent filmmakers, especially after the 1990s, have traded a strongly articulated political consciousness for a much more 'commercial' outlook that quickly found a name, and arguably an identity, under the label 'indie' cinema. Whether it was the increasingly slick production values, the presence of often famous stars, the more prominent role that genres played in the construction of stories, the more easily accessible narratives or indeed many films' lack of interest in politics, it seems that the politically conscious filmmaking that had largely defined the emergence of what was labelled the "independent feature movement" (Collective Editorial 1981: 57) of the late 1970s/early 1980s in the US eventually gave way to a new type of independent film, the 'indie' film.

Not surprisingly, even filmmakers who continued to make politically conscious films had to reposition themselves in a constantly evolving marketplace and find new ways to articulate openly political ideas in their films. With production and marketing budgets increasing substantially in the 1990s (compared to the often extremely low costs associated with independent film in the 1980s), and with audiences starting to demand commercial elements in indie film productions (Vachon, quoted in Biskind 2005: 164–5), it was clear that politics and its representation had to renegotiate its place in indie film narratives. This was especially true for the representation of political subjects that dealt with national and international economic and political institutions and processes, and the actors involved in them or what Michael Coyne has called "US politics per se" (2008: 8) as opposed to "identity politics" (ibid.), which remained if not the defining characteristic, certainly a key staple of a large part of indie cinema. This renegotiation did not mean that the presence of such politics disappeared from indie film or that it started functioning as mere background against which generic formulas and fully motivated narrative trajectories were played out, as is the case in the political dramas, thrillers and even action films that come from Hollywood studios. As this chapter will demonstrate, although the number of indie films that dealt with such political issues decreased substantially in the 1990s compared to the previous decade, there are certainly examples of films that continued to tackle key areas of US politics and policies and their impact on people's lives, often with significant box office success. The difference is that they did this through interweaving such core political issues with identity politics.

This chapter then will examine the shift from 'independent' to 'indie' cinema, and what this meant for politically conscious filmmaking in the United States. As a case study, it will use Whit Stillman's *Barcelona* (1994), an example of an indie film where politics (in the shape of geopolitical concerns about the hegemonic role of the US in Europe and beyond) and commerce (in the form of strong generic registers, stardom, spectacle, appeal to young demographics, a marketable auteur filmmaker, and others) have managed to co-exist without affecting the commercial performance of the film and, significantly, without compromising its political agenda. Produced by a number of production outfits, including Castle Rock Entertainment, and distributed by New Line Cinema's specialty film division Fine Line Features, *Barcelona* was a solid commercial success grossing $7.2 million at the North American theatrical box office and receiving theatrical distribution in a number of countries, especially in Europe (IMDb). As I will argue, the film succeeds in expertly interweaving a number of complex positions about the place of the US in the international political arena with a narrative about expatriate Americans looking for love in Spain during the last decade of the Cold War. As a result, *Barcelona* fulfils both its generic – romantic comedy – objective and provides extensive and often surprisingly rich political commentary on international political relations.

Independent film politics vs indie film politics

Despite the production and release of numerous quality independent films before the 1970s, for most critics, contemporary American independent cinema commences in the 1978–81 period, when a significant number of feature-length narrative films and documentaries produced by and large away from the Hollywood industry found commercial distribution and limited box office success, including *Northern Lights* (Hanson and Nilsson, 1978), *Gal Young 'Un* (Nunez, 1979), *Heartland* (Pearce, 1980), *Return of the Secaucus Seven* (Sayles, 1980), *The Life and Times of Rosie the Riveter* (Field, 1980), *The War at Home* (Silber and Brown, 1980) and several others. "Where before there had been a trickle of poorly funded documentaries, supplemented by the occasional underfinanced grainy picture," Peter Biskind wrote, "there was now a comparative flood of slick, reasonably well-produced films ..." (2005: 17).

This "flood" prompted a number of contemporaneous critics, like Annette Insdorf, to pronounce the arrival of a new era in independent filmmaking. Writing as early as 1981 and as part of an *American Film* editorial dedicated to independent cinema in the United States, Insdorf noted that what distinguished these films from fare produced and distributed by the Hollywood studios were:

> casting, pace, cinematic style and social and moral vision. Countering big stars with fresh faces, big deals with intimate canvasses and big studios with regional authenticity, these filmmakers treat inherently American concerns with a primarily European style. [. . .] Geographically rooted directors resist[ed] Hollywood's priorities and potential absorption.
>
> *(1981: 58)*

These films, Insdorf continued, were also separate from other independent film productions, which mobilised conventions and characteristics that are associated with Hollywood practices. For instance, despite also having been produced and distributed by companies other than the majors, films by directors such as George Romero, John Carpenter, Tobe Hooper and David Cronenberg demonstrated a propensity for what Insdorf calls "Grand Guignol, violence and sex" which put them in a place in the market where they could (and did) attract "commercial money" (1981: 58), with Hooper already showing 'absorption' from Hollywood, as by the time of the publication of Insdorf's article he had already secured a project at Universal.

With exploitation, genre and other key components of 'commercial' independent filmmaking excised from the critical canon from the start, it is clear that the dominant discourse in terms of independent filmmaking in the US during that time lay with a very particular type of "low-budget, low-key quality film," which, as I discussed elsewhere, "mostly dealt with mature themes targeting specifically an adult, educated audience" (Tzioumakis 2012a: 32). Part of the reason why this was the case for this dominant expression of independent filmmaking in the US was because a substantial number of these films were produced and distributed outside the studios and received often extensive financial support from organisations such as the National Endowment for the Arts (NEA), the National Endowment for the Humanities (NEH) and from the US public service broadcaster PBS as part of its American Playhouse series (Cornwell 1981: 62). In this respect and given the remit of these institutions, the independent filmmakers of the early 1980s often had to tackle topics with a strong social register, if not openly political subject matter, in order to qualify for grants and other forms of assistance. These topics were not limited to US politics institutions, actors and processes but extended to wider political issues, including race, ethnicity, gender identity, and others. For instance, the NEH provided substantial funding as part of its Public Media (Hidden Histories) programme to *Heartland*, a film that dealt with pioneering women in the frontier (Smith 1978), while a film like *Northern Lights* that deals with the establishment of the Non Partisan League in the state of North Dakota was "the first feature-length dramatic film to be produced [...] with substantial funding from a state-based Humanities Committee, the North Dakota Committee for the Humanities and Public Issues" (Hanson 1978).

A related reason for the way in which American independent cinema was being shaped in this particular fashion at that particular time had to do with a general perception on the side of independent filmmakers in terms of what this kind of cinema should be about and how it should be organised. Following a major conference in New York City in 1979 that provided the springboard for the emergence of the Independent Feature Project as one of the main associations for independent filmmakers in the US, American independent cinema was initially conceptualised as completely separate from Hollywood and as much closer to models of post-World War 2 European national cinemas that enjoyed heavy subsidies from their countries' governments in order, among other things, to mount competition to Hollywood films (Tzioumakis 2016: forthcoming). Although such conceptualisation quickly proved impossible to materialise for a number of reasons that are beyond the scope of this chapter, it nonetheless demonstrates that the origins of the American independent film movement of the late 1970s and early 1980s lay outside the profit-driven Hollywood cinema. And if industrially, independent film's position away from the Hollywood studios and in the various regions that comprise the vast United States of America was an obvious enough signifier about its separation from Hollywood cinema (with early critics often conflating independent cinema with "regional cinema" [Lev 1986: 60]), another such signifier was its ability to tackle issues that Hollywood studio films would not, especially ones related to traditionally political topics such as unionisation, civic corruption, migration, and others. It is within this context that some of the more successful independent (and politically conscious) films released later in the decade, including *El Norte* (Nava, 1983); *Stranger than Paradise* (Jarmusch, 1984); *Kiss of the Spider Woman* (Babenko, 1985) and *She's Gotta Have It* (Lee, 1986), were produced.

However, the late 1980s and early 1990s witnessed a paradigm shift in American independent filmmaking, marking the beginning of what Michael Z. Newman has called "The Sundance-Miramax era" (2011: 1), itself part of larger developments that saw what Thomas Schatz has called the consolidation of "Conglomerate Hollywood" (2012). According to Schatz, the merger-and-acquisition wave that engulfed Hollywood in the late 1980s and resulted into a "cadre of global media giants" such as Time Warner, News Corp. and Sony also extended to the independent film sector that started seeing investment by "mainstream Hollywood – ie., the studios and their new parent companies" (2012: 127). Film historians and independent film critics have focused on the success of *sex, lies, and videotape* (Soderbergh) in 1989 and the meteoric rise of Miramax Films, the film's distributor, which only four years later was taken over by Disney, as some of the key indicators about the increasing popularisation of American independent cinema at the time (Pierson 1995: 126–7; Merritt 2000: 351). But perhaps it is more insightful to focus on the emergence of Fine Line Features, the first specialty film division of a large film company, New Line Cinema, to be set up after the short-lived experiment of the studios' classics divisions in the early 1980s that were established to distribute non-US art-house films and occasionally a small number of locally produced independent titles.

Established in 1990 under the direction of Ira Deutchman, Fine Line was not interested in art-house cinema. As its parent company was moving increasingly towards expensive mainstream productions, Fine Line focused on independent filmmaking, primarily produced in the US but also in other English-speaking countries such as Britain and Australia. But rather than being involved with the type of cinema that dominated the discourse of "low-key, low-budget" quality American independent film for most of the 1980s, Fine Line concentrated on "getting to the next level of slightly more commercially oriented movies, but films that were not big-audience types of films" (Deutchman 2011). With independent film companies such as Miramax Films and

October Films moving to a similar direction and therefore in need of access to substantial levels of finance, it did not take too long for them to agree to become parts of Hollywood conglomerates, with Disney taking over Miramax in 1993 and Universal becoming a major stakeholder and investor in October in 1997 (Tzioumakis 2012b: 180). With Sony also establishing Sony Pictures Classics in 1992, it is clear that mainstream Hollywood was quickly moving to "the annexation of key factions of the indie movement," as Schatz has argued (2012: 127).

With the major entertainment conglomerates moving gradually to the independent sector, and with the standalone companies upping their game to remain competitive, what becomes evident in this 'indie' phase of American independent cinema (between the late 1980s and the mid-1990s) is the emergence of a particular type of independent film that often had only a few points of contact with the films of the 1980s. Indeed, while Miramax, Fine Line and a number of other distributors (and producer-distributors) continued to release "low-key, low-budget quality films", which often had difficult subject matter or which utilised unusual formal codes in the first half of the 1990s, they also ensured that a lot of these titles were also equipped with a number of commercial elements that could be exploited by these companies' marketing departments. As I discussed elsewhere (2012b: 8), these elements included: the presence of recognisable stars, even if stardom was meaningful only within narrow demographic constituencies (for instance, former teen film stars found themselves often as leading men and women in independent films of the early 1990s, such as River Phoenix in *My Own Private Idaho* [Van Sant, 1992] and Diane Lane in *My New Gun* [Cochran, 1992]); the use of much stronger generic frameworks than the films of 1980s, which also allowed the films' distributors to sell them as genre pictures (for instance, the heist movie in *Reservoir Dogs* [Tarantino, 1992], the con-artist film in *The Grifters* [Frears, 1990]); a pronounced focus on servicing a well-defined niche demographic (most of the 'hood films of the early 1990s were independent productions appealing primarily to black audiences); the presence of auteurs behind the camera and the deployment of their perceived authorship as a major marketing tool, once several filmmakers started gaining critical and audience recognition (which endowed particular films with more commercial potential and attracted increasingly large investment in films by particular filmmakers than in the past).

Arguably more controversially, the main point of departure for the post-1989 independent film was the inclusion of the themes of sex and violence, often gratuitous and explicit, suspenseful plots and all sorts of other commercial 'content' elements that were mostly absent from the low-key, low-budget quality independent film canon as this was shaped in the previous years. If, as Rosen and Hamilton noted in a study co-sponsored by the Sundance Institute and the Independent Feature Project, independent films in the 1980s broadly shared a "common humanism" and steered clear of being racist, sexist and exploitative (1990: xvii), an increasing number of indie films in the early and mid-1990s trod a thin line in these aspects with titles such as *Reservoir Dogs*, *Bad Lieutenant* (Ferrara 1992), *Boxing Helena* (Lynch, 1993), *Kids* (Clark, 1995) and many others attracting huge controversy. At the same time, a whole cycle of 'hood films, many of which produced and distributed by independent film companies, including *Straight Out of Brooklyn* (Rich, 1991), *Menace II Society* (Hughes and Hughes, 1993) and *Fresh* (Yakin, 1994) also attracted criticism for their representation of sex and violence. However, such a shift in American independent cinema did not necessarily mean a convergence with or adoption of the low-budget aesthetics of the cinema of Romero, Carpenter or Cronenberg. Instead, this expansive independent cinema was repackaged as a hip, filmmaker-driven, quality cinema upon which the industry, the press and the film-going public almost immediately agreed to impress the label "indie," the "hip offspring" of independence, as Alisa Perren put it (2002: 37).

Within this new institutional environment for American independent cinema, which came part and parcel with increasingly large production and marketing costs for independent films, it became progressively difficult for politically conscious filmmaking to take place, especially films that dealt directly with the complexity of US politics and policies. In his comprehensive account of American independent cinema, Emanuel Levy questioned the absence of political films, calling it "one of the anomalies of contemporary indie cinema", and labelling it a cinema that does not represent "an 'engaged' art form" (1999: 284), as one might have expected, given its stated emphasis on difference from Hollywood; while for Peter Biskind, it is this kind of rhetoric, the "us versus them" attitude towards the studios and other dominant American institutions, that made indie cinema seem much more progressive when, Biskind argues, "indie films were not programmatically left wing or even political except in the most attenuated fashion" (2005: 20). Geoff King, on the other hand, placed the problem of the relative lack of successful political and politically conscious films on "the problem of what sells and to whom", noting that this was particularly important for "filmmakers inspired by strong social, political and or ideological agendas." As he put it:

> Independent features offering alternative social perspectives are often dependent on the existence of niche audiences, rooted in particular social groups, capable of sustaining a particular level of production. But … there is no guarantee that audiences defined in terms of one specific attribute according to which they are denied adequate representation in the mainstream (such as race or sexual orientation) are likely to have radical or alternative tastes in other respects.
>
> *(2005: 200)*

Although some of the issues identified by Levy, Biskind and King can also be found in many films during the more 'independent' 1980s decade,[1] they became much more pronounced in the 'indie' cinema of the 1990s. Because of these problems, the gradual introduction of commercial elements, and the increasing pressures that higher budgets and marketing costs brought in, openly political subject matter had to renegotiate its place in the indie films of the 1990s, while the filmmakers' handling of it had to be such that it would not hurt their films' chances for box office success. While there is a number of films from the period that could be discussed as key examples of this trend, including *Bob Roberts* (Robbins, 1992) or John Sayles' *City of Hope* (1991), I focus on Whit Stillman's *Barcelona* (expanding on work I did on the film in Tzioumakis 2012b: 104–5). This is because despite a very obvious and very strong generic status as a 'light' romantic comedy that focuses on the problems of young adults' cross-cultural romances, the film also presents an equally strong political register in the form of intensely debated questions about US foreign policy and how this can impact young people's lives, which is rather unexpected in a romantic comedy. In this respect, *Barcelona* is both a film that delves into 'US politics per se' and an example of 'politically conscious' filmmaking interested in how politics impacts people's lives.

Barcelona: romance vs politics

Barcelona was writer-director Whit Stillman's second feature film. His debut film, *Metropolitan* (1990), a low-budget film about the upper-class debutante scene in Manhattan, was both a critical and commercial success, and led its distributor, New Line Cinema, to establish Fine Line Features in order to handle similar types of film (Deutchman 2011). With *Barcelona* substantially higher-budgeted than *Metropolitan* and with a number of commercial elements, including location shooting in the Catalan capital, a story firmly anchored in the romantic comedy genre, the presence of a host of young, attractive actors (some of whom were known to the indie film scene from previous indie films) and a young filmmaker at the helm whose previous film had already entered the US independent cinema canon, it was clear that it was an indie film with substantial commercial aspirations. In this respect, it fitted perfectly the remit of a specialty film division such as Fine Line Features that was interested in films that had the potential to cross over and record significant box office success.

The film's narrative revolves around the experiences of two American cousins in the Spanish city of Barcelona in the 1980s, during the last years of the Cold War and a time when anti-American sentiment was at its peak, especially in Southern European countries like Spain, Italy and Greece. These experiences are recounted through an endless series of parties, dates and talks with young local women, who provide ample romantic interest for the two protagonists. However, while a substantial part of the narrative deals with the formation, dissolution and re-formation of cross-cultural couplehood, an equally large part of the story deals with the political climate of the time, often in startlingly rich detail. As a result, all romantic entanglements are intricately linked to opinions and ideas about geopolitical concerns and questions of US hegemony, with the American protagonists' actions often represented and debated as Spanish perceptions of US cultural imperialism at work.

The tone of the film is registered right from the beginning. The film opens with a black screen and an intertitle providing the location of the film, the Spanish city of Barcelona. This is immediately followed by a second intertitle that locates the action in "the last decade of the Cold War," giving it a concrete political context. Upbeat music and two establishing shots of Barcelona follow before the third shot shows the city's American Library. Another intertitle names that location followed quickly by an explosion coming from the building. In the next shot, a Spanish man looks at a young woman putting make up on in front of a mirror and registering his admiration of her beauty with the word "perfecto" (Figure 27.1).

Figure 27.1 A 'perfecto' young woman's face.

Figure 27.2 Ted turns around to admire local women.

This is followed by the shot of man throwing what looks like a self-made bomb at IBM's offices in the city, causing another explosion, while immediately after we see the film's protagonist, Ted Boynton, a young professional in a suit walking on a street and turning around to admire young local women dressed in a striking red and black two-piece suit, the trademark costume worn by young Spanish women working in Barcelona's major trade fair (Figure 27.2).

This brief montage sequence clearly demonstrates the film's major organising principle, that is, romantic relationships between young people take place in and are inextricably linked with the political climate of the time, characterised by a strong anti-American sentiment, with terrorist attacks to American institutions and corporations being part of everyday life. The film's first dialogue sequence that comes after this montage confirms this fully. Fred Boynton, a young US naval officer arrives unannounced at his cousin Ted Boynton's house. The two men go immediately out to a cafe where they discuss Ted's disappointment with his romantic encounters. In the following scene, as they walk to their car, a group of locals sees Fred in his military uniform, calls him *facha* (fascist) and shouts *Yanqi fora* (Yankee out). Shaken from this expression of hostility, Fred and Ted continue their evening with a drive through Barcelona's famous sights. Ted explains that there is a lot of anti-NATO feeling in Spain, which leaves Fred incredulous. However, at that point Fred reveals that he has come to Barcelona as "an advance man for the Sixth Fleet" as the Fleet's last visit in Spain was not received positively and it is his job to "smooth things out" before the next visit. The next scene sees the cousins continue their talk about Ted's romantic experiences in another café, which is followed by a scene in which Fred sees graffiti on a wall that says "*OTAN – No! Bases fuera! Cerdos Yanqis go Hoem*!" (No to NATO! Out with the military bases! Yankee pigs go home!). Fred tries to add and change some of the letters in an effort to lessen the negative connotations of the slogan, amending *Cerdos* to *Ciervos* (*ciervos* means deer).

Given the light-hearted and often humorous register in Fred's response to the expressions of political climate he encounters but also the equally strong presence of discussions about romance and love that keep interrupting the scenes about politics, one could be tempted to think that this particular political context is a narrative distraction that adds 'local colour' to the film and an interesting background against which one or more cross-cultural love stories will take place. In some ways this is true. Fred's main stated objective to smooth things out in advance of Sixth Fleet's next visit is quickly forgotten. There are no official meetings where the visit's details are discussed, while instead a new narrative strand develops which sees Fred suspected of being a CIA agent and shot by local extremists (Figures 27.3–27.5). This storyline too, however, develops as an outcome of Fred's involvement in the local young people's scene and his conversations at parties and picnics rather than his involvement with politicians and military personnel.

Although such a strategy seems to make light the film's contribution to any political debates about geopolitics and imperialism, what surprises is both the frequency of such contribution as this materialises in the everyday conversations among all the characters in the film and especially the detail in which some of these conversations engage. One of the most memorable such examples takes place roughly in the middle of the film. With the background of a spectacular Night of San Juan and after attending a party where Spanish journalist and womaniser Ramon was briefly heard talking about the CIA's involvement in other countries' politics, Marta, one of the local girls and Fred's romantic interest, recounts Ramon's version of particular political events by talking about how "after WW2 representatives of the American Labor Union, the AFL-CIA were sent to Europe to crush progressive unionism" equipped "with sacks of money and the anti-communist tactics of senator Joseph McCarthy". Fred questions the name of the union but Marta is quick to label it "America's largest union, terribly right wing and *facha*", in line with dominant perceptions of all American involvement in Southern Europe at the time. The scene ends there but in the next one, which takes place at

Figure 27.3 Fred is accused of being a CIA agent.

Figure 27.4 Fred notices that someone is ready to shoot him.

Figure 27.5 Fred is shot.

another party on the same night, Ted picks up the issue again with a view to respond, though his audience is not Marta, but Montserrat, another local young woman and his own romantic interest: "There is no such thing as the 'AFL-CIA'. It's the AFL-CIO, actually AF of L-CIO; it was formed when the American Federation of Labor merged with the more militant CIO".

Prompted by Montserrat to explain how he knows so much about such a topic, Ted cites the time he spent in Chicago, "the capital of twentieth century American trade unionism", before moving to bring examples such as Jay Lovestone as key "American labor leaders who came to Europe". Somewhat confused, Montserrat now believes that Ramon's version of events is "partly true" and questions if what she heard was AFL-CIA or AFL-CIO.

The level of detail here (and in certain other scenes) with which political issues are discussed is very unusual and brings with it an educational value that is certainly rare in a film that on the surface is a romantic comedy. Equally unusual is the transition to the next scene which shows people dancing at the party before Ted and Montserrat start talking about moving in together, with the political conversation that preceded it seemingly forgotten, before, that is, it is picked up again two scenes later when at the same party Ramon supports that some of the recent bombings of US targets in Spain had been carried out by Americans themselves in order to remain closely involved in the politics of his country.

This rare mix of geopolitics and cross-cultural romance provides the film with a very distinct texture. Rather than functioning as background for the romantic entanglements among young people and the anxieties these generate, politics and the characters' views about political matters are an integral part of the discourse that characterises the lives of all these people. No matter the time, the place or the situation, political discussions are always part of the mix in the exchanges between the film's characters and, not surprisingly, politics becomes one of the key reasons why Montserrat and Marta at some point in the narrative end their romantic relationship with the two American protagonists.

Despite this unusual emphasis on the articulation of political arguments and positions about global geopolitics from both sides, what is particularly interesting is that none of the film's characters is represented as a stereotype of the political or politicised young person. No character is seen taking place in protests, being members of political organisations, or even making political statements through dress code, appearance and personal styling. On the contrary, when we first meet Aurora and Marta, two of the key female Spanish characters in the film, they are dressed in elaborate ballroom gowns and are on the way to the disco on a theme night (Figure 27.6). This creates no suspicion whatsoever that they might be knowledgeable in political matters. In this respect, the film manages to make political debate part of everyday life without having to resort to conventional political iconography and stereotypes of any kind.

As it becomes clear then, in trying to construct cross-cultural heterosexual couples and comment on the politics of this kind of romance, the filmmaker opts to alternate the emphasis from gender and sexual politics (which is the norm in more heavily genre-imbued romantic comedies) to geopolitics and cultural politics. Dates, picnics, evenings at cafes and bars, dancing, rides in a car and other courtship rituals that normally become the battleground for the expression of gender and sexual politics in Barcelona *also* become the terrain where geopolitics and cultural politics are being played out. This is repeated throughout the film and constitutes its main structural axis, as the opening montage sequence also demonstrated. In this respect, Stillman succeeds in making a romantic comedy that is 'political' in the full meaning of the term.

The filmmaker's weapon of choice in the construction of such an unusual film is editing. The use of long scenes and takes where the characters have the space to explore fully ideas on love, romance and politics is rare. Instead, the film consists of a large number of shorter scenes that allows for the quick alteration from one focal point to another. The brief scenes and quick editing allow the characters to 'dip' in and out of conversations, shifting focus from scene to scene and sometimes from shot to shot. As a result, the characters' perspectives on both romance and politics are presented in a fragmented, incomplete but also extremely immediate way. Such perspectives also clearly suggest that there is no 'complete' or 'right' version of how

Figure 27.6 Despite the ballroom costume the young women can debate international politics.

international political events were played out in the Cold War era (and afterwards), and that the writing of history is always open to debate. To this view, the American Consul in Barcelona (played by the director himself in a cameo appearance) adds also the role that media around the world have played in shaping people's views against America, suggesting that politics, like everything else, acquires particular meaning when it becomes the subject of representation.

Conclusion

As the example of *Barcelona* has demonstrated, openly political subjects could still find a place in the increasingly popularised indie cinema of the early/mid-1990s, and in this case in a quite prominent position in the narrative, provided they were handled *appropriately* by filmmakers. Despite the constant interruption of romance by discussions of political matters

Figure 27.7 Spectacular Barcelona.

and the often obscure references to US political organisations and events, *Barcelona* manages to maintain a delicate balance between politics and genre, not allowing either to dominate the mood of the film, offering entertainment deeply rooted in political debate and finding success at the box office. This balancing act was also perfectly encapsulated in the marketing materials that accompanied the theatrical release of the film, with the tagline in the film's poster reading: "Americans, anti-Americans in Love".

Although certainly removed from the more openly political films of the 1980s, *Barcelona* fits well the remit of the more hip 'indie cinema' of the time, managing successfully to package its often difficult political subject matter together with a number of elements that kept it 'in check' for the duration of the film: spectacular shots of a major metropolitan city (Figure 27.7), young and attractive people in search of love and relationships, a clear genre framework, fast pace, a nostalgic look to the recent past, a hip filmmaker (who also appears in the film) and absence of political film stereotypes. At the same time though, the detail with which politics is debated and the frequency with which it appears in everyday conversations, ensures that it transcends the background status it normally occupies in US films. This makes *Barcelona* not just a film that deals with a political subject matter but also a politically conscious film that manages to show how history and politics influence every aspect of life, including romance.

Note

1 Critics and scholars have used the term "independent" and "indie" in very different ways and often interchangeably. When Biskind, Levy and King discuss indie cinema they tend to also include what here is discussed as "independent" cinema associated primarily with the films of the 1980s as well as what I distinguish as "indie" cinema.

Bibliography

Biskind, P. (2005) *Down and Dirty Pictures: Miramax, Sundance and the Rise of Independent Film*, London: Simon & Schuster Paperbacks.

Collective Editorial (1981) "The Independent Feature Movement: Changing the Rules of the Game" in *American Film*, 6 (10), September, p. 57.

Cornwell, R. (1981) "Cents and Sensibility or Funding Without Tears" in *American Film*, 6 (10), September, pp. 63, 64 and 80.

Coyne, M. (2008) *Hollywood Goes to Washington: American Politics on Screen*, New York: Reaktion Books.

Deutchman, I. (2011) Phone interview with the author, 2 June, 1 hour and 15 minutes.

Hanson, J. (1978) "Partial Financing of Features through State Humanities Committees" in *The Independent Feature Project Conference Papers*, Independent Feature Project File, Margaret Herrick Library, pp. 1–2.

Hill, J. (2011) (ed.) "The Prospects for Political Cinema today: A Critical Symposium" in *Cineaste*, 37 (1), pp. 6–17.

Insdorff A. (1981) "Ordinary People, European Style: How to Spot an Independent Feature" in *American Film*, 6 (10), September, pp. 57–60.

King, G. (2005) *American Independent Cinema*, London: I.B. Tauris.

Lev, P. (1986) "Regional Cinema and the Films of Texas" in *Journal of Film and Video*, 38 (1), pp. 60–66.

Levy, E. (1999) *Cinema of Outsiders: The Rise of American Independent Film*, New York: New York University Press.

Merritt, G. (2000) *Celluloid Mavericks: A History of American Independent Film*, New York: Thunder's Mouth Press.

Newman, M. Z. (2011) *Indie: An American Film Culture*, New York: Columbia University Press.

Perren, A. (2002) "Sex, Lies and Marketing: Miramax and the Development of the Quality Indie Blockbuster" in *Film Quarterly*, 55 (2), pp. 30–39.

Pierson, J. (1995) *Spike Mike Slackers and Dykes: A Guided Tour Across a Decade of American Independent Cinema*, New York: Hyperion/Miramax Books.

Rosen, D. with Hamilton, P. (1990) *Off-Hollywood: The Making and Marketing of Independent Films*, New York: Grove Weidenfeld (originally published in 1987).

Schatz, T. (2012) "Conglomerate Hollywood and American Independent Cinema" in King, G., Molloy, C. and Tzioumakis, Y. (eds) *American Independent Cinema: Indie, Indiewood and beyond*, London: Routledge, pp. 127–139.

Smith, A. (1978) "'*Heartland*': Financing a Feature with N.E.H." in *The Independent Feature Project Conference Papers*, Independent Feature Project File, Margaret Herrick Library, pp. 1–3.

Tzioumakis, Y. (2012a) "'Independent', 'Indie' and 'Indiewood': Towards a Periodisation of Contemporary (post-1980) American Independent Cinema" in King, G., Molloy, C. and Tzioumakis, Y. (eds) *American Independent Cinema: Indie, Indiewood and beyond*, London: Routledge, pp. 28–40.

Tzioumakis, Y. (2012b) *Hollywood's Indies: Classics Divisions, Specialty Labels and the American Film Market*, Edinburgh: Edinburgh University Press.

Tzioumakis, Y. (2016) "From Independent to Indie: The Independent Feature Project and the Complex Relationship between American Independent Cinema and Hollywood in the 1980s" in King, G. (ed.) *The Blackwell Companion to American Independent Cinema*, Cambridge: Wiley.

28

DISMANTLING THE SYSTEM FROM WITHIN

The early films of Robert Altman and the politics of anti-establishment

Jacqui Miller

Robert Altman and his work seem to embody challenges to cinematic convention captured in David Thomson's description of Altman as "[t]hat rarity in American cinema: a problem director, a true object of controversy, and a man whose films alter or shift at different viewings like shot silk" (Thomson 2002: 13). If Altman was a 'problem' director, this was because his altering and shifting cinema encompassed political challenge in so many ways that his work was thoroughly anti-establishment. His 'major' filmmaking career began in the 'first phase' of the New Hollywood, that uniquely innovative time in American filmmaking, running roughly from 1967 to 1980, with *M*A*S*H** (1970), perhaps the most multi-pronged attack upon American norms in the history of Hollywood cinema. This chapter will mainly explore the political nuances of Altman's early films, *The Delinquents* (1957), *The James Dean Story* (1957), *Countdown* (1968) and *That Cold Day in the Park* (1969), arguing that their cumulative gradations present him as an anti-establishment figure, even, or perhaps particularly, because he mainly worked within mainstream Hollywood, and lay clear foundations for what will follow in the New Hollywood and beyond.

Discussion of what 'counts' as political crystallised in film criticism with the publication of Jean-Louis Comolli and Jean Narboni's "Cinema/Ideology/Criticism" in *Cahiers du Cinema* (translated into English in 1971). Written in the aftermath of the civil upheavals across France in May through June 1968, their editorial interrogated film's relationship with dominant ideology, and defined several categories of film which either directly or indirectly constructed challenges to the ideological status quo. This might be through category (b), those which "deal directly with a political subject" whilst also subverting traditional depictions of reality through innovative and challenging cinematic technique. Category (c) might present subject-matter which is not expressly political but becomes so by the spectator's re-reading across the grain of its surface meaning. Category (e) refers most specifically to Hollywood products and their "dismantling the system from within'" by apparently endorsing mainstream ideology whilst being ambiguous, presenting "a noticeable gap, a dislocation, between the starting point and the finished product" (Comolli and Narboni 1976: 26–27). Altman's cinema, across his oeuvre, and within individual films, captured the range of these categories, serving to undermine the ideology of the establishment.

Altman's work engaged directly with explicit political themes, most obviously in *Nashville* (1975), which has as its backdrop a political rally for a presidential candidate. His work often engaged with countercultural themes, from the anti-authoritarianism of *M*A*S*H**, to the exploration of the sub-cultures of criminal outsiders in films such as *Thieves Like Us* (1974) as well as acknowledging the alienation increasingly experienced by such outsiders. His films consistently addressed the politics of cultural identity for the marginalised, including gender (for example, sensitive exploration of women's and transgendered lives in *Three Women* [1977] and *Come Back to the Five and Dime, Jimmy Dean, Jimmy Dean* [1982]) and race (for example, beginning with *The Delinquents*, his incidental inclusion of African-Americans, a demographic often strangely absent from New Hollywood productions). Although not expressly Marxist, Altman's work considered the dialectical process of history, and the ways the media has worked to effect mystification for the powerless, for example in his critique of American mythology and the construction of the 'West', in *Buffalo Bill and the Indians, or Sitting Bull's History Lesson* (1976). His cinema was also 'political' in that, he was regarded as "a director who has consistently challenged the traditions of American cinema" (Hacker and Price 1991: 127), "distinguished by innovations of technique as well as structure" (O'Neill 1996: 470) and has specifically taken advantage of developments in film technology (Allen and Gomery 1985: 113), pioneering visual and aural techniques that overturned normative methods of viewing Hollywood pictures, most specifically the disorienting use of overlapping sound, and his distinctive hovering zoom lens. This device, in particular, became uniquely his own, developing an "aesthetic of voyeuristic irony [that] was entirely new and established Altman as the most distinctive stylist in America" (Cousins 2004: 337).

Altman's work also serves as an exemplar of challenges to prior conventions of genre, stardom and the role of the director. Altman worked within genres, but is best known as the master of genre revision, revoking and re-inscribing almost every established type: the war film – *M*A*S*H**; the Western – *McCabe and Mrs Miller* (1970); the private eye/noir – *The Long Goodbye* (1973); the list is literally as long as Altman's filmography. Whatever subject matter he addressed, Altman maintained his political vision of debunking establishment structures. Thus the superficialities of haute couture fashion are mocked in the title alone – in *Prêt-à-Porter* (1994), the machinations of Hollywood itself in *The Player* (1992), and the British (and American) class system in *Gosford Park* (2001).

This chapter then will examine the often complex and multi-layered ways in which Altman has mounted on his anti-establishment critique by focusing on the much less known feature films he made before he found fame and critical appreciation within the discourses of New Hollywood in the 1970s. In doing this, the chapter will demonstrate how dominant or hegemonic ideas and positions within America cinema have been undermined through creative uses of narrative, style and genre, providing spectators with positions through which they could see these ideas and positions as unstable and therefore open to critique. It will also argue for a more expansive approach to determining Altman's authorial signature, an approach that does take into consideration his work before the 1970s in more firm ways, thus contributing to the substantial existing scholarship on Altman.

The early work

Altman's pre-New Hollywood work was varied. Before *Countdown*, he tended to take production jobs where he could. What is striking, however, is how threads of his anti-establishment signature, whether making contact with those who would be important players within the New Hollywood or addressing themes and styles that would be developed, are apparent from the outset.

The Delinquents' self-explanatory title was an archetype of the teenage exploitation pictures that proliferated in the 1950s. Although usually containing a few sensational scenes, they rarely sustained artistic merit over their full running time, but as a phenomenon they are of interest in two related ways. They were an undoubted strand of influence on the New Hollywood, and it can be argued that few New Hollywood films do not have an exploitation/teenpic precursor, whether they share the same historical source, such as *The Bonnie Parker Story* (Whitney, 1958)/*Bonnie and Clyde* (Penn, 1967), a common youth phenomenon, such as *Motorcycle Gang* (Edward L. Cahn, 1957)/*Easy Rider* (Dennis Hopper, 1969), or a genre relationship, for example *The Creature From the Black Lagoon* (Jack Arnold, 1954)/*Jaws* (Steven Spielberg, 1975). The exploitation films were also a training ground for many whose careers would flourish in the New Hollywood, most notably actors including Dennis Hopper and Jack Nicholson, but also production personnel. In fact, *The Delinquents* would presage the New Hollywood career of Tom Laughlin, who would later write, produce, direct and star as the titular Billy Jack in the cult countercultural 1971 film.

Despite the sensationalism of 1950s exploitation films, they usually probed genuine social issues, and *The Delinquents* brought together themes explored in bigger budget productions such as the major independent film, *The Wild One* (Benedek, 1953), and the studio picture, *Rebel Without a Cause* (Ray, 1955). Credence was also added by the casting in *The Delinquents* of Peter Miller who had also had a significant role in *The Blackboard Jungle*, one of the most influential studio films that tackled the issue of juvenile delinquency. Perhaps the most notable aspect of *The Delinquents* with reference to Altman's nascent challenges to convention was the prominence of the soundtrack, but most specifically the opening live number by an African-American jazz singer, Julie Lee, and her backing band, the Bill Nolan Quintet Minus Two, which set an early indicator of his use of cinema to overturn racial inequality (Thompson (ed.) 2006: 177).

The Delinquents formed a thematic segue to Altman's first directing work in California, the documentary, *The James Dean Story* as the screenplay was by *Rebel Without a Cause* writer, Stewart Stern. Altman was now finding his creative feet. It was during this film that he first took advantage of the recent technological development of the zoom lens (O'Brien 1995: 20), and it was also the first time that Altman worked on a feature with Lou Lombardo who would become one of the leading New Hollywood editors, cutting, for example *McCabe and Mrs Miller* as well as *The Wild Bunch* (1969) for Sam Peckinpah (Zuckoff 2009: 83). *James Dean* explores the cult of celebrity and its dangers, both to the idol and their followers, that would run through many Altman films, most notably *Nashville*. It also anticipates popular culture's prolonged fascination with James Dean, such as the scene in *Badlands* (Malick, 1974) when an adoring cop somewhat homoerotically tells Kit (Martin Sheen) to "Kiss my ass if you don't look like James Dean". Altman also explores the role of the media in constructing and transmitting meaning, and in inserting its presence into everyday life, creating cultural homogeneity rather than supporting individualised existence. The close-up of media apparatus, seen later in ubiquitous domestic television sets in *Countdown* and *That Cold Day in the Park*, the camp megaphone of *M*A*S*H**, and the radio of *Thieves Like Us* is first presented by Altman through the public speaker system used by Dean to commentate on a motorcycle race in his home town. Later, when Dean is pursuing an acting career in Hollywood, the documentary's narrator warns him to beware "the probing eye and the listening ear". This may be advice to guard his privacy, but if the 'probing eye' represents the hovering zoom lens, and the 'listening ear' is the complex overlapping soundtrack, and the spectator's relationship in decoding its layers, this phrase prophetically anticipates Altman's at once voyeuristic, but in its creativity, liberating cinematic style.

Countdown

Countdown, Altman's first feature for a major studio, may be interpreted as a highly political film, taking as its subject matter the space race with Russia which John F. Kennedy had cited as a cornerstone of his presidency when he "won support for an accelerated space program with the goal of landing on the moon before the end of the decade" (Tindall and Shi 1996: 1401). In a way this theme picks up the atmosphere of *The Delinquents*, which has been described as using gang culture as a means of examining 1950s paranoia (Armstrong 2011: 101). Nowhere had Cold War paranoia remained more marked by 1968 than in governmental and other discourses on outer space which had entered the American mindset as the last bastion of colonial conquest. This notion proliferated throughout popular culture from *Star Trek*'s 'final frontier' which underscored the mythological conception of space by its conflation with the original westward expansion of North America, to the countercultural philosophising of *2001 A Space Odyssey* (Kubrick, 1968). *Countdown* may share its year of production with Kubrick's film, but it is very different in style and perspective. Although produced at Warner Bros., which had recently blazed a trail with *Bonnie and Clyde*, and was to gain the reputation of having a New Hollywood renaissance that matched the studio's confrontational "social conscience" ethos of the 1930s (Biskind 1998: 84), *Countdown* came out of their low-budget division, and was not intended, by the studio, at least, to rock any boats (O'Brien 1995: 26).

At first glance (and listen) it is possible to see why it is usually excised from Altman's oeuvre or at least described as "atypical" (O'Brien 1995: 8). Filmed in a hyper-real saturated Technicolor, and peopled by the conventionally groomed, it has the look of a late 1950s/early 1960s melodrama in its domestic scenes, and a World War II 'preparedness' propaganda piece in its space station locations. The music score is also un-Altman-like in its conventions: portentous for the base/space scenes and jaunty to enhance domesticity.[1] The contrast in lighting between high key for domestic scenes and low key to convey the uncertainties and tensions of space exploration also mirrors this sense that the world and its experiences may be neatly categorised. However, it is worth closer examination to detect an encroaching Altman imprint in terms of style and political commentary. Altman hungered after a Hollywood career, but learned to apparently remain within its letter whilst subverting its spirit. As he put it, "I was making films under a system and trying to sneak my own personal message through all that veneer [...] I learned how to say things without saying them directly" (quoted in Keyssar 1991: 52).

Countdown features two actors, Robert Duvall and James Caan, who would have prolific New Hollywood careers. Altman, although no respecter of stars per se – having once said "It was more exciting to work with an unknown cast than it was to do a picture with whomever the reigning stars were at that time. Because then you're just taking orders" (Biskind 1998: 95), nonetheless built constructive relationships with his actors, many of whom worked with him on multiple films. This nurturing style was evident on *Countdown*. While making the film, Michael Murphy, whose conventional good looks were in keeping with the casting overall, received an anodyne Hollywood offer because he "had a look that they used". That career path changed for him when Altman advised: "You'll make some money if you do that kind of stuff. But if you use your head and make good choices, you'll do interesting work". Murphy reflected on Altman's mentoring: "He was probably the biggest influence in my life [...] I [...] didn't know much about politics [...] And he just led me" (Zuckoff 2009: 145–6). Altman's improvisational style was developing, even within the confines of a studio's 'B' unit. Duvall recalled that in contrast to directors "who want to control it. [...] It was always a very relaxed scene with Bob", echoing his method on *The Delinquents* of encouraging actors to bring their own ideas (Zuckoff 2009: 145).

Countdown saw Altman's first use of his trademark overlapping dialogue. In the first training session the viewer can simultaneously hear the voices of the crew and mission control. This challenges convention in that the audience is given no clue as to which conversation has pre-eminence, disturbing hierarchies of authority; it also sets up the recurring theme of oppositions – America v. Russia, PR and politics v. the space programme as scientific endeavour, conformity v. individuality – in this case between the astronauts who want to continue and ground control which wants to abort the test. The studio head, Jack Warner, took exception to this technique, and removed Altman after principal photography was completed, but before editing took place (Thompson (ed.) 2006: 38), which clearly demonstrates the studio's lack of tolerance to strong challenges to convention.

Countdown was Altman's first film using Cinemascope's successor, ultra-wide Panavision (O'Brien 1995: 10). On the one hand, the vast space lab buildings and launch pad machinery are a show-window for American technology and prowess, heightened by the stars and stripes prominently sewn into the men's space suits. This is undercut by the spatial sense that the astronauts are literally and figuratively dwarfed; they are merely cogs in an establishment machine. There is a sense that everyone must be compliant for the good of the programme, but individuality is excised by conformity. A doctor who expresses fears for the safety of the astronaut going into space is told not to open his mouth for anything but eating, and that the best way to avoid worrying about a friend is not to make friends. This sense of individuality suppressed by hegemonic control is reinforced by media devices. Television sets are not just ordinarily present in domestic environments, but fitted within items of furniture so as to be absolutely integral to life. Public relations is seemingly a more necessary part of the space programme than scientific research, and the astronauts and their wives' images are manicured for best effect. Again, this parallels the media circus surrounding politicians, exposed in such films as *The Candidate* (Ritchie, 1972) and anticipates the melding of celebrity and politics in *Nashville*.

In Washington, a vast exterior establishing shot of the White House and an interior shot catching sight of a portrait of Abraham Lincoln also work to establish hegemonic political ideology, but this is once more undercut. The American decision to launch to the moon has been prematurely catalysed by the unexpected news that Russia is days away from a moon flight. Tension is further heightened because the original choice for the solo voyage, Chiz (Robert Duvall) is deemed unsuitable because he holds military office. In the Cold War context this would presumably make America seem aggressive given that the three Russian cosmonauts are all civilians, the leader being a geologist. Although Chiz has been in training for years, he is passed over for a civilian, Lee (James Caan). Consequently, not only is America stripped of its global supremacy as one of the space team asks "Who really calls the shots, the White House or the Russians", but the space programme itself is, by implication, sullied as an exercise in PR rather than an aspiration to truly extend the parameters of human achievement and scientific endeavour. This notion that the 'race' was all important and 'space' as a means of extending knowledge was not only secondary but expendable is underscored as the question is raised as to whether the mission should be abandoned entirely if the Russians will unquestionably arrive first. As Michael Murphy said "you've got to remember, we were in the middle of the Cold War at this point – and Bob [Altman] was already talking about the futility of it all" (Zuckoff 2009: 145). This sense of futility is made more ironic by the programme's title; as an adjunct to Apollo, it is Pilgrim, implying "a transcendental journey full of adversity made at great risk into a new realm, in a context of spiritual values" (Kagan 1982: 2). Just as the space programme is demeaned by its need to kow-tow to PR spin, its possibilities and failures regarding human achievement were paralleled by the course of the original Pilgrim Fathers. Their aim might have been to seek a new land in which to practice religious freedom and democracy, but this was corrupted by the persecution of the native population, and importation of slavery.

Countdown engages with direct, if conflicting political commentary. The opening credits are in a lurid red, recalling the metaphorical, McCarthy-haunted space films of the 1950s such as *Red Planet Mars* (Horner, 1952), which implied Russia, rather than space invaders, as the thinly veiled threat to America. The source novel, *The Pilgrim Project*, too, was "all about 'beating the Russians'" (Thompson (ed.) 2006: 38). In Altman's original ending, upon landing, Lee finds the Russians dead, but places the American flag beneath Russia's, and the film fades as he walks in the direction away from where the audience can see the shelter. The ending imposed by the studio after Altman was removed has triumphal implications. Lee has landed on the moon, but has defied mission control; he was only to land if he had identified the shelter that would be his base for a year. In fact he lands without seeing the shelter but finds that the three Russians had arrived first but are all dead. He superimposes the American over the Russian flag, and with only moments before his oxygen will expire, locates the shelter by following the direction of a toy mouse brought as a keepsake from his young son. Even this sentimental ending has some ambivalence. We see Lee go towards the shelter but not arrive. Throughout the film, and in his original ending, Altman shifts the politics away from binary oppositions to an exploration of the human condition, in its seeming futility, anticipating New Hollywood productions such as *Five Easy Pieces* (Rafelson, 1970), and even hints at the counterculture that was all around in 1968 by references to the military's LSD research programme, and a joking aside about the Pilgrim astronaut spending his year on the moon 'stoned'.

Kagan sees *Countdown* as Altman's first genre revision – of science fiction (1982: 1). Although the film is fictionalised, it is much more about current affairs than the futuristic realms of sci-fi. Indeed, once homage has been paid to American technological supremacy at Cape Kennedy, the film becomes existential rather than technological and from the outset is "ambivalent towards the 'heroics' of space flight" (O'Brien 1995: 8). Altman's intention was "to show astronauts as human beings with problems" (Thompson (ed.) 2006: 38). Once Lee is in flight to the moon, we do not see exterior, crowd-pleasing shots of space; the camera remains focused on Lee and his isolation – even during a training session, ground control refused to give guidance when he was running out of oxygen because "Who'll be there to help him on the moon? Not a soul". It is only in this context of removal from normative society and its conventions that Lee can take control of his actions, and make the choice to land knowing he does not have the shelter in sight; he has passed beyond the binaries of the 'space race' and the individual has become subordinate to the possibility that this time 'pilgrim' may mean purity of endeavour. Despite Lee's retrieval of his individuality, the 'futility' referred to by Murphy is apparent in the modern context. Jack Warner saw this ending as 'a Communist plot', but the still ambiguous revisions could not excise Altman's commentary on the human condition.

Countdown is also thought-provoking for its explorations of women's lives. The astronauts' wives may apparently be there simply to support their husbands, but they are not just well-groomed accessories. Although they are structured to be supportive at all times, their stress is implied by their constant intake of alcohol, which makes for an even more striking point because it is never commented on, just accepted. As Murphy noted:

> What Bob did that was interesting was he focused a lot on the wives. They all drink too much. [...] He shifted it off the action of the space shot into the sociological thing of being married to one of those guys. What it does to your soul to live on one of those bases.
>
> *(Zuckoff 2009: 145)*

Countdown enabled Altman for the first time to demonstrate in a studio feature his aforementioned self-defined ability to make films under a system whilst subverting that system's veneer. A film which Warner Bros. devised as a triumphalism of space conquest, the 'final frontier' of American geographical and ideological colonialism, under Altman's direction, becomes full of ambiguities and contradictions that necessarily undermine its conservative political force.

That Cold Day in the Park

The puzzle of modern existence with particular reference to women was continued in *That Cold Day in the Park*. This was an independent production for a small Canadian company and gave him full directorial control. *That Cold Day* fits so many archetypes of the New Hollywood that it is hard to see why Altman's career is stereotypically seen to have 'really' begun with *M*A*S*H*. It also took further steps to build Altman's regular team, including art director, Leon Ericksen, who had already gained New Hollywood credentials working on Francis Ford Coppola's *The Rain People* (1969) and would build the mining town in *McCabe and Mrs Miller*. The cinematography was by Laszlo Kovacks, in the same vein, especially in the use of lens flare, as his work on *Easy Rider* (Hopper, 1969) a few months earlier. *That Cold Day* also presents the countercultural milieu and is challenging in its presentation of nudity and drug-taking.

That Cold Day studies the obsession and its consequences of Frances Austen (Sandy Dennis), a wealthy 'straight' young woman, with a 'hippy' boy (Michael Burns). She asks him into her lavish but emotionally chilly home, ostensibly so he may take shelter from the cold, but she locks him in his bedroom at night and tries to bar all exits when she leaves the building. Eventually her jealousy and sexual fixation will explode when she kills the sex worker she has hired for him.

Partly this film is making an issue about class and money; Frances seems to believe that the boy, much like a Victorian child being plucked at whim from the streets, is an object that may be 'bought' by material comfort, his free will playing no part in the equation. It is also clear that Frances extends this objectification to his sexuality, and unlike other films made around the same time addressing economic and sexual possession, such as *The Collector* (Wyler, 1965), the woman is the dominator. For her, the young male character remains the nameless, depersonalised, 'boy' throughout. This sense of possession and objectification also recalls *Vertigo* (Hitchcock, 1958), especially when Frances goes shopping alone to buy the boy clothes and then delights in dressing him. Altman may be an acknowledged genre revisionist, but in *That Cold Day* he is not so much revising the structure of the psychological thriller as its gendered allocations. Frances further seeks to express her sexuality, taking the then courageous step for a single woman of seeking birth control pills, for which she has to flout the prudish norms which require her to assume impending marriage. At the clinic, women chatter bawdily about men, and in what has been identified as a running gag through Altman's films, one of them undermines male prowess by reference to small penis size (Self 2007: 151).

Altman's 'aesthetic of voyeuristic irony' was carefully crafted in *That Cold Day*, the interior set designed to enable a camera to move into every crevice, but the 'irony' here is that the voyeurism is mainly Frances'. Six years before Laura Mulvey would define "woman as image" and "man as bearer of the look" (Mulvey 1975: 4), it is 'the boy' who connotes "to-be-looked-at-ness" from Frances' gazing at him through her window, to the erotic and tantalising dance he performs, deliberately for her spectatorship, to her gramophone records. He even continues to be an object of erotic scrutiny for the audience in Frances' absence. When she leaves the apartment, we see him bathing, the hastily grabbed items covering full frontal nudity serve to tease in a continuation of the striptease performed for Frances.

Central to constructing this representation is the zoom lens, the distinctive use of which Altman develops in this film. As Susan Hayward has noted: "A zoom-in picks out and isolates a person or object, a zoom-out places that person or object in a wider context. A zoom shot can be seen, therefore, as voyeurism at its most desirably perfect" (Hayward 2013: 500). Frances first sees the boy, but pays him no immediate attention, when she walks past him in the park facing her apartment as she returns from shopping for lunch-party food. Once home, Frances' study in voyeurism begins with repeated zoom-ins on him from her point of view. He is further objectified, both in the sense of being a sexual commodity, and as a lower-class plaything to be exploited, by the zoom-ins being intercut with interior shots of plump game birds being put in the oven then served and devoured, emphasising both the beauty and desirability of his own slightly puppy-fatted body. Thus, in *That Cold Day*, the zoom is used at least partly to signify and explore the shifting relationships between class, sexuality and gender.

From the outset *That Cold Day in the Park* addresses a theme that had been apparent in *Countdown*; the solitude of the human condition. Following Lee's isolation in space, and presaging McCabe's lonely journey to Presbyterian Church across lashing rain, we first see Frances walking alone through the park. Visual motifs present literal barriers that connote emotional isolation and a sense that meaningful human connection can never be made. Frances initially looks out at the boy through a series of visual impediments – Venetian blinds, blurring soft focus – and when she invites him in, they speak through the park's towering perimeter wire fence. Once in the apartment they see each other in mirrored reflections and through clear glass bricks rather than direct exchanges of looks.

It is unusual for cinema of this era to recognise specifically that women may find life alienating. Whereas New Hollywood films such as *Five Easy Pieces* often explored male angst, women were mainly presented as emotional satellites. Frances' isolation is heightened subliminally in the opening sequence by the musical score in its use of solo instruments.[2] She is isolated not necessarily because she has no companions; she has daily 'help', numerous relatives, and is romantically pursued by a doctor, but they are all much older than she is. This is poignantly emphasised in the contrast between Frances' youth and her companions' age at her lunch party and at a crown-green bowling tournament, the latter a particularly incongruous activity for a young woman. Frances' isolation is generational, in this case she is isolated from her generation. 1968 might be stereotyped as the maelstrom of the counterculture, but not all young people were living countercultural lives. Frances' demeanour may make her appear far older than 'the boy' but she is probably close to his age. She has a pitiful sense of wanting to belong to a milieu of which she has little understanding. One of her first questions for the boy is "Are you a student, do you go to school" presumably because she has seen student protests on TV news, and when she later buys him an approximation of up-market hippy garb, she is embarrassed when he does not put on the socks she has bought with his sneakers; clearly she does not understand the nuances of countercultural dress codes. Thus Altman posits sympathy for a true youth 'outsider'; not those standing outside the establishment like Billy or Wyatt of *Easy Rider*, but one of the many cut off, perhaps ironically by their status and privilege, from the excitements happening elsewhere.

These 'excitements', the *raison d'etre* of contemporary films such as *Easy Rider* and *Alice's Restaurant* (Penn, 1969) are glimpsed in *That Cold Day*. 'The boy' has a beautiful sister, and on one of his nocturnal escapes out of his bedroom window, he visits her at the riverboat she shares with her Vietnam War draft-dodging boyfriend. The three smoke joints and – the boy speaks normally with his sister despite being mute when he is with Frances – we find he was sitting in the park waiting for the other two who had gone on a drugs run to Seattle. He later returns to Frances' apartment with hash brownies which she eats unwittingly. This unrealised entree into the countercultural world releases Frances from inhibitions perhaps for the first time. The scene is anti-establishment both in its aesthetic challenges to prevailing Hollywood style, and its marking Frances' movement to independent action. Unlike merely witnessing the drug-taking in the riverboat scene, the audience shares the effect through Kovacs' employment of the lens flare he also used on *Easy Rider*. Frances' new-found mental liberation, along with her confusion at its prospect, is evoked by her distorted self-images glimpsed in the glass bricks. She revises the repressions of her former life by blind-folding the boy with her school tie and teasing him as to her location by playing snatches of Beatles tunes on her school harmonica. Her hair symbolically falls from its tight coils, and her unzipped housecoat resembles a kaftan. Although unconsummated, it is an erotically charged scene that cuts directly to Frances seeking contraception.

However, Altman does not fall into the trap of romanticising the counterculture; some of its denizens are as facile and corrupt as Frances' rapacious elderly relatives. When the boy arrives at his sister's houseboat, she and her boyfriend are having sex. Although she shrieks at her brother to get out, knowing he is waiting outside, she becomes highly vocal in her sexual response, turning the audience, but more importantly, her brother into voyeuristic eavesdroppers. The act complete, she calls him onto the boat and teasingly slips on a sweater, the process of dressing only emphasising that she has recently been naked, and the reason for her nakedness. A few days later, when Frances is out, she appears at the apartment, and demands to take a bath. Afterwards, she rolls seductively on the bed, and tells the boy she wishes he was not her brother, asking him if he didn't likewise wish that she wasn't his sister. In his review, Charles Champlin (1969) felt that Altman included this scene for titillation, but the boy has no erotic interest in his sister. Rather, Altman, as Luchino Visconti was to do in his non-judgemental study of pederastic desire in *Death in Venice* (1971), was using the new cinematic freedoms of the late 1960s to openly explore subjects that had not only been previously taboo on film, but forcing audiences to confront issues about which they remain squeamish today.

That Cold Day in the Park took further cinematic projects begun in *Countdown*, for example the loneliness of the human condition. However, whereas *Countdown* only incidentally addressed existential problems of modern women, the theme was central from the outset of *That Cold Day*, unusually for a masculinist period of cinema, and anticipating by several years pictures considered trailblazing in the field, such as *Klute* (Pakula, 1971) and *Alice Doesn't Live Here Anymore* (Scorsese, 1974). Although not directly exploring a topic as explicitly political as the space race, it is immersed in a countercultural milieu of anti-establishment, anti-authoritarianism that is only hinted at in *Countdown*, and is all the more impactful because its central protagonist transitions from a highly repressed to a transgressive young woman.

Conclusion

This chapter set out to demonstrate not only that Robert Altman's cinema was anti-establishment in its form and content, but also that those traits were discernible from his earliest work. When Robert Altman died in 2006, one of his press biographies described him as an "anti-establishment success story" (Butler 2006). This apparent oxymoron in fact captures the nature of Altman's method and his work. Like a psychedelic liquid light show, or Thompson's 'shot silk', Altman's cinema was liminal in its challenges to fixed establishment norms. His work might be anti-establishment through direct attacks on the industrial-military complex, through revealing the media's role in normalising hegemonic ideology, through revising gender, racial, and sexual stereotyping, through genre revisions, and by using cinematic technique as a political tool that led audiences to rethink their relationship to cinema and thus to society. Although a countercultural figure who embraced an alternative lifestyle, Altman understood that his films would be most impactful if seen by a wide audience and so sought and achieved Hollywood success, 'dismantling from within' or as he put it himself, knowing when to sneak in his personal message. Although the work for which these various facets are best known date from 1970, as this chapter has demonstrated, every anti-establishment strand was in place before he began work on *M*A*S*H*. Altman scholarship, despite his exceptionally long and consistently successful career, has focused too exclusively on his films from the height of the New Hollywood, specifically from *M*A*S*H* to *Nashville*. I have shown that Altman's work should be studied in full and that the elements of his pictures erroneously considered unique to the New Hollywood – the subversions of *M*A*S*H*, the political satire of *Nashville* – are explicit from the outset of his career.

Notes

1 Richard R. Ness points out that "Altman has not worked consistently with one composer to develop what could be called an 'Altman sound'". However, "there is a consistency of approach in Altman's efforts to foreground music [. . .] and the use of music to subvert dominant ideology or patriarchal authority" (Ness 2011: 39). This will be apparent in every Altman film subsequent to *Countdown*.

2 The music was scored by Johnny Mandel who would go on to compose the soundtrack for *M*A*S*H*.

Bibliography

Allen, R. C. and Gomery, D. (1985) *Film History: Theory and Practice*, New York: McGraw-Hill.

Andrew, J. D. (1976) *The Major Film Theories*, Oxford: Oxford University Press.

Armstrong, R. (2011) "*Brewster McCloud*'s 1960s Hangover" in Armstrong, R. (ed.) *Robert Altman: Critical Essays*, Jefferson, NC: McFarland, pp. 100–119.

Biskind, P. (1998) *Easy Riders Raging Bulls: How the Sex'N'Drugs'N'Rock'N'Roll Generation Saved Hollywood*, London: Bloomsbury.

Butler, R. W. (2006) "Robert Altman 1925–2006: An Anti-Establishment Success Story" in *Sun Journal*, 21 November.

Champlin, C. (1969) "A Sick Character Gets Sicker" in *Los Angeles Times*, 26 June.

Comolli, J-L. and Narboni, J. (1976) "Cinema/Ideology/Criticism" in Nichols, B. (ed.) *Movies and Methods: Volume I*, Oakland: University of California Press, pp. 22–30.

Cousins, M. (2004) *The Story of Film*, London: Pavilion.

Gilbey, R. (2004) *It Don't Bother Me: Nashville, Jaws, Star Wars and Beyond*, London: Faber & Faber.

Hacker, J. and Price, D. (1991) *Take 10: Contemporary British Film Directors*, Oxford: Oxford University Press.

Hayward, S. (2013) *Cinema Studies: The Key Concepts*, 4th edition, London: Routledge.

Kagan, N. (1982) *American Skeptic: Robert Altman's Genre-Commentary Films*, Ann Arbor, MI: The Pierian Press.

Keyssar, H. (1991) *Robert Altman's America*, Oxford: Oxford University Press.

Mulvey, L. (1975) "Visual Pleasure and Narrative Cinema" in *Screen* 16 (3) (Autumn), pp. 6–18.

Ness, R. R. (2011) "'Doing Some Replacin': Gender, Genre and the Subversion of Dominant Ideology in the Music Scores" in Armstrong, R. (ed.) *Robert Altman: Critical Essays*, Jefferson, NC: McFarland, pp. 38–58.

O'Brien, D. (1995) *Robert Altman: Hollywood Survivor*, London: Batsford.

O'Neill, E. R. (1996) "Robert Altman" in Nowell-Smith, G. (ed.) *The Oxford History of World Cinema*, Oxford: Oxford University Press, pp. 470–471.

Searls, H. (1964) *The Pilgrim Project*, New York: McGraw-Hill.

Self, R. T. (2007) *Robert Altman's McCabe & Mrs. Miller: Reframing the American West*, Lawrence, KS: University Press of Kansas.

Thomson, D. (2002) *The New Biographical Dictionary of Film*, 4th edition, London: Little, Brown.

Thompson, D. (ed.) (2006) *Altman on Altman*, London: Faber and Faber.

Tindall, G. B. and Shi, D. E. (1996) *America*, 4th edition, New York: W. W. Norton.

Zuckoff, M. (2009) *Robert Altman: The Oral Biography*, New York: Alfred A. Knopf.

29

ETHICAL TIME, ETHICAL HISTORY

Recent Israeli films

Nurith Gertz

Introduction

At a period when societal and national polarity, xenophobia, intolerance of minority opinions, and lack of compassion are intensifying in Israeli society, some works of literature and film created in Israel are seeking possibilities for a different discourse, based on understanding of the other. The need to discuss and analyze those works becomes vital, particularly now, in light of the extremism, hate, and polarity during the recent war in Gaza (also known as Operation Protective Edge) and due to the constantly exacerbating tendency to silence any discourse that diverges from the national, ethnocentric one.

The films discussed in this chapter in fact encapsulate the quests for an alternative history that have taken place in Israeli culture over the years. Such quests have focused on finding: a substitute for the cultural memory of historical traumas; a replacement for multicultural ideologies that promised to create a dialectic of historical memories of minorities, but instead of generating a stratified multicultural society created an assortment of groups constantly at loggerheads with each other; a replacement for the utopian time of nascent Zionism that promised to create a new society and provide justice and equality for all, but failed to keep and fulfill those promises; an alternative to the historical amnesia, desperation and void left behind by those collapsed ideologies. (For a discussion of traumatic narrative in Israeli cinema, see Neeman and Munk 2011; Morag 2013; Duvdevani 2010; Zanger 2005. See also Gertz and Hermoni 2008, 2011a, 2011b, 2013.)

Walter Benjamin (1969a, 1969b) maintains that until a way is found to connect the past to the future, the past is transmitted aesthetically; it is the work of art which ensures that the accumulated culture will endure. In the specific case of Israeli films, disconnecting the historical continuum – breaking away from the former dominant ideologies – impels the films to seek an alternative tradition in cinema.

Several recently made Israeli films (among them, *Meduzot/Jellyfish* [Geffen and Keret, 2006], *Shnat Effes/Year Zero* [Pitchhadze, 2004] and *Nuzhat al-Fuad* [Ne'eman, 2006]) reflect that search by connecting up to different cinematic aesthetics: that of contemporary American films, and that of European art cinema and its roots in the great works of the mid-twentieth century, such as those by Federico Fellini, Michelangelo Antonioni, Jean-Luc Godard, Ingmar Bergman and others (for a discussion of recent Israeli cinema as a whole, see Utin 2008; Friedman 2005; Meiri 2008; Zanger 2011, 2012). That blend of different aesthetics has economic and commercial functions, as it helps Israeli films reach different populations in a global world, film festivals as well as other networks of circulation for world cinema (Elsaesser 2009). In this chapter, my focus is on the way this blend of different aesthetics creates an ethical, perhaps even utopian time, that leads from the narrow time of the individual towards a broader, transcendental time, in Emmanuel Levinas' phrase: "the time of the other" (Levinas 2006 [1972]). The transition to the time of the other, according to Levinas, enables going "beyond the horizon of my time," towards "a time that would be without me … a time after my time" (Levinas 2006 [1972]: 27).

This transcendental time that, according to Levinas, prevails beyond the life and death of the individual, is diachronic time, founded on separation, differentiation and difference as the antithesis of synchronic time, which creates unity and identity. This time is created by subjects who do not consider themselves to be the center of creation and do not view others as identical to them: they are capable of opening up "beyond" themselves, "beyond the basin of the consciousness – to powerful otherness that we encounter long before we award it a place within ourselves" (Kenaan 2008: 52; author's translation). Those subjects turn to the other as 'an other,' who will never be wholly understood. Relationships with the other are shown in certain works as prevailing between any individual and any other, while elsewhere the relationships are conducted between different national groups – Arabs and Jews, Israelis and Palestinians. This chapter deals with examples of both types of works.

Between two aesthetics

The films discussed here are structured according to the mosaic film (also known as the multi-plot film) genre, which has become common in the past few years, especially in American cinema: they present a polyphony of protagonists, plots, and stories unfolding in diverse settings, apparently without a unifying center (Montoliu 2009). While those films flourished against the backdrop of multicultural perspectives that acknowledge ethnic, racial, national, and gendered differences, they also often presented the failure of these perspectives that led to unending strife between races, genders, nationalities, and ethnicities with no shared basis for dialogue.

Like *Magnolia* (Anderson, 1999), *Babel* (González Iñárritu, 2006), *21 Grams* (González Iñárritu, 2003), *Crash* (Haggis, 2004) and their precursor *Short Cuts* (Altman, 1993), these Israeli films are built along differing plot-lines and on disconnected spaces. What occasionally unites them is only human indifference, violence, hate, and racism. Like other films in this genre, they also form a kind of polyphony that makes it impossible to grasp the knowledge they produce and channel it in a single direction. Though they are dispersed over different times and feature diverse protagonists living in a variety of spaces, they are concentrated into a series of moments in the present, which block any exit to the past or the future. However, out of the trauma of severance and loss, these Israeli films are trying to find a new place and time – a new human connection, a new ethics, shaped by the European film aesthetics of the mid-twentieth century.

In his book, *Cinema 2: The Time-Image* ([1985] 1989), Gilles Deleuze describes the disintegration of the plot action (the sensory motor-action scheme) and its replacement by images of sights and sounds (pure optical and sound situations – time images). The plot and the action halt and are interrupted, while the images that were meant to lead to them are delayed via sequence-shots, a static camera, panning movements and other techniques.

These images, Deleuze maintains, require the spectators to observe rather than be swept away by the plot, making it possible, among other things, to reflect on the ruptured duration of time and the rupture between human beings that was instigated by the fall of the great narratives. Spectators can reclaim their lost ability to create continuity with past and future and between 'fellowmen,' or, in Anton Kaes' words: "the autonomy of filmic time ... draws the gaze away from narration toward the images themselves," forcing "audiences to change their viewing habits" (2011: 95–96).

The European films of the mid-twentieth century process those experiences through silent spaces that separate people, long takes that keep them apart from each other, long-shots of the protagonists swallowed up in space, moving away from each other and the camera, hidden by objects, disappearing behind bars, walls, smoke, and other barriers. And yet at certain points in these films, the aesthetics of space creates an illusion of wholeness, which, following Jameson (1991), we can call utopian time. It is discerned through the beach and the magnificent music in *Il Deserto Rosso/Red Desert* (Antonioni, 1964) – the absolute contrast with the gray industrial city; through Fritz Lang's gods in *Le Mépris/Contempt* (Godard, 1963) – the total opposition to the protagonists' commodified lives; through the scene of the innocent young girl on the other bank of the river in *La Dolce Vita* (Fellini, 1960) – a luminous contrast to the indulgent life in which the film wallows until that point; and through the blocked memory of the past in *Hiroshima, Mon Amour* (Resnais, 1959) and *L'année dernière à Marienbad/Last Year in Marienbad* (Resnais, 1961). It is also the primal landscape of the desert in Herzog's *Fata Morgana* (1971) – an attempt, according to Kaes, to create the world anew in cinematic terms (2011: 95–96).

The new Israeli films use the European art cinema aesthetic in two ways: on the one hand, instead of signifying a break in the duration of time as well as human alienation, they use this aesthetic in order to present human relationships that do not attempt to take control of the other, and enable a mutual understanding that does not efface the presence of the abyss that separates the self from the other. On the other hand, like their predecessors, they use those images to create a utopian transcendental time – in this context what can be called the ethical utopia.

In his book *Otherwise than Being, or, Beyond Essence* (1991 [1974]), Levinas distinguishes between the 'Said' (*le dit*) and the 'Saying' (*le dire*). *Le dire*, Levinas maintains, like the face, is the rustle beyond the voice that precedes the delivery of the semantic content (Kenaan 2008). It is a residue, as Levinas terms it, that does not permit the revealed content to be essentialized and reduced to its logical meaning (1991 [1974]). One can describe Levinas' attitude to the term mise-en-scène similarly – as an encounter of countless semantic streams. Like the human face, mise-en-scène prevents us, Levinas maintains, from reducing and rendering identical the other, the different; it requires us to accept them without negating the dimension of their otherness. Despite Levinas' unequivocal stance against the cinematic image, which he defines as flat, we can describe the aesthetic on which the new Israeli films draw as a sort of mise-en-scène: it is intended to hear echoes that lie beyond the plots and actions, within the time image, along the vast spaces, through the face of the protagonists. It makes it possible to touch the other without taking control of them. Such relationships preserve the difference of the other, do not efface them, do not make them resemble us, and do not allow us to put down roots or assimilate within them (Levinas 1991 [1974]). This attitude towards the other broadens the constricted time of the self through the lives and deaths of others.

The Israeli films discussed in this chapter try to shape such a transcendental utopian time by integrating the aesthetics of European and American films. We can thus say that, instead of turning to the historical past of Israeli society and culture, contemporary Israeli cinema turns to the European and American cinematic past in order to generate a new picture of its own historical past and future. It does not adopt the cinematic past as it exists, but corrects, amends and modifies it according to new ethical perceptions.

Shnat Effes/Year Zero

The film *Year Zero* – like *Jellyfish, The Band's Visit/Bikur Ha'Tizmoret* (Kolirin, 2007), *Nuzhat al-Fuad*, and other recent Israeli films – deals with the marginalized and the disenfranchised: a woman who has lost her job is tossed onto the streets and forced to resort to prostitution; an Israeli arms-dealer chased by the mafia; a blind man who, in an accident, lost his seeing-eye dog, the only friend he ever had; an old man abandoned by his kibbutz; a radio technician worn down by a violent consumer culture. All of them exist within a cruel, merciless society, which feeds off their suffering and does not need them – not even in order to use them, not even as victims. According to Giorgio Agamben (1998 [1995]), these people live bare lives, being defined as '*Homo Sacer*,' while in the words of Thomas Elssaser we could also call them "out of service" (2010: 117). However, it is here of all places, on society's margins, where foundations are laid down for a new kind of relationship between fellow humans. It is in this estrangement and distance that the film finds compassion, empathy, and human responsibility. It finds it by combining the mosaic film genre with the European art film aesthetics.

Michal finds out that she is pregnant, tells her husband Reuven, and incites his rage. He does not want children, and an argument breaks out. The film cuts from this argument to Anna, who meets her son after school and hugs him. One plot's refusal to bring children into the world is met in the second plot with the great love of a mother for her son, and at the same time the impossibility of that love – the mother, thrown out on the street, cannot take proper care of her son. The relationship between the two plots changes by the end of the film, when Anna dies tragically and her boy is orphaned, while in the other plot, Reuven has accepted responsibility for raising his own son. While life is cut short in one plot, the hero of the other one shows willingness to broaden his life by taking responsibility for his soon-to-be-born son. The two plotlines are not parallel, but rather continue each other in winding ways: when one plot is stuck at a dead end, the other plot shows the possibility of a way out. Thus, by its unique shaping of the multi-plot genre, the film succeeds in broadening the time of the protagonists and their plots onto the time of the other.

The different protagonists and the disconnected plots are also linked in *Year Zero* by the way the time images highlight composition, light, color, form, and texture in the same way that mid-twentieth-century European film and some later works would convey meaning, though the Israeli film uses them and instills them with meanings that would not have been found in its predecessors. Indeed, the European art film aesthetic brings to *Year Zero* everything that is not directly articulated, neither in speech nor in action; everything that prevents turning the other, the different, into the identical (identical to me, to my group). This means that such an aesthetic is used as a tool to transfer meanings from one plot to another, and thus to tie together the ruptures caused by the film's mosaic structure.

Michal enters a dark apartment, following a painful separation from her husband, who has refused to accept her pregnancy. The apartment is empty. A black wall in the foreground blocks our view. Confounded by the darkness, she phones her husband, who has stayed behind in his office. In the office, it is dark as well. He is not planning on coming home. She sits down. Then a light source shines in the darkness, and she can be seen in it. The camera zooms in, and now, as well as the beam of light that shines in the darkness, music is heard. The camera cuts to Eddie, the blind man who is practicing Tai-Chi: the same strip of light, the same music, and the same darkness surround him. It is as if we have stayed with the same image, while the protagonists have swapped places. Now the camera zooms out, and the light slowly brightens until it floods the room, the walls, the furniture, and the blind man in his dazzling white clothes. The light and the music are the statement without which both plots would remain meaningless: she has lost her husband and possibly her son; he has lost his dog, which was a substitute for a son. They are both alone in the dark, each in their own house, each in their own plot, but as the light intensifies, a connection is formed between them – there is something that transcends and links them together, even if they are unaware of it.

In European cinema, the disconnection between people is often represented by shots of vast empty spaces in which the protagonists are lost, vanish, and recede from each other. For instance, in Godard's film *Contempt*, two protagonists, a man and a woman, are sitting in a spacious apartment, a wall separating them. The woman stands up, walks to the window, while the man remains at a distance. He is on one side of the large living-room, she is at the other end. She walks through a partition, out of the frame, returns to the frame, to the now empty living-room and sits down on the couch, alone in the room. Around her are windows, walls, and a tremendous emptiness. The two people are separated by partitions, walls, and an empty space. In the commodified world that the film portrays, a world built on profit and loss, investments and budgets, people move like nomads through space, unconnected, not touching. In *Year Zero*, on the other hand, those spaces and distances do not affect adversely the possibility for the protagonists to be completely comprehensible to each other. Instead, the distances between them enable a mutual understanding that does not efface the presence of the abyss separating them from each other.

In *Year Zero* we again see two people divided by a partition. Anna, the protagonist, is staring through the bars of a fence separating her from her son: she is on one side of the fence, he is on the other. This time though, the two protagonists, mother and son, do not give up. Through the partition separating them, they look at and touch each other, then walk to the place where the fence ends, where they meet and embrace. She has just been evicted from her apartment and is about to lose her job, and yet they have each other. The impassable barriers of the older films now paradoxically signify the distance necessary as a foundation of and condition for human relationships.

In another scene in *Contempt*, screenwriter Paul Javal is alone, pacing through a smooth, empty space, the roof of a villa in Capri, and calls out to his wife Camille. He turns, searches the foreground of the frame, then the background, and walks away, leaving the empty space. Camille enters it now, searching, taking the same route to the background, then to the foreground. There is no one around. She walks away as well, and the space remains empty.

Empty spaces fill *Year Zero* as well, though the characters are not left alone and abandoned in them – there is always somebody somewhere at the edge of the frame, off in the distance. Anna and her son are filmed in an empty space, a sort of playground on the shore. A fence separates the two: she is in the foreground and he is deep in the background. She removes a scarf from her neck. The scarf flutters in the wind, and the camera follows, gliding, going off into the empty space. Now the fence is between her and the scarf. The same participants and the same elements reappear toward the end of the film, after Anna has lost her home and her job. Once again, she is at the beach with her son, in the same empty playground. She looks at the sea from a distance, seen from beyond the fence, and once again the scarf flutters. The camera follows it, closing the distance at a slow pace, but this time at the end we see a man standing. He catches the scarf, hands it to her, and a bond is formed.

The fences that separated Anna from her son and from the spectator do not collapse in the course of *Year Zero*. The distances that separate her from her future lover have not decreased, and the abyss that divided the protagonists in European cinema separates the protagonists here too. But while in European cinema all these elements signified alienation, now paradoxically they signify the possibility of closeness, of discovering the other beyond the fence, beyond the distance, beyond the abyss. A wall keeps people apart in both cinematic periods, but in *Year Zero* – beyond the wall – an encounter is created.

The Band's Visit and *Nuzhat al-Fuad*

In certain films, the wall that separates people is the 'Separation Barrier' that keeps apart Jews and Arabs, Palestinians and Israelis. In the *The Band's Visit*, that wall stands in the desert and collapses there. The same desolate arid realm that features in films by Antonioni, Wenders, Angelopoulos, and Herzog also appears in that film and is shot similarly. Here though, like in *Year Zero*, the silent wasteland does not create alienation, but again provides a backdrop for a human encounter. In the film's final sequence, an Egyptian man who is a musician is depicted singing a song. He is alone in an empty space – a gritty town square, with gray buildings in the background and the desert surrounding it all. The camera moves towards him, and gradually reveals that in fact he is not alone. Two other musicians are also there, in the same exposed place and, at some distance from him, their music joins his voice. What appeared to be a solo voice in the wasteland is revealed to be an orchestra.

In the next scene, Dina, the Israeli protagonist, parts from the Egyptian band's members, who spent the night in her forsaken township. They stand before her, as if ready for a photo-call, they wave goodbye to her, she waves back, and when the camera passes in front of her to the town square, the band is already receding, no one remains. In the next shot, the band members have already left the township. The desert landscape is stark and empty, power lines leading away towards the horizon, like in films by Antonioni and Angelopoulos. Only the desert sands surround it. And then, in overlap from the next shot, the sound of music enters that silent desolation – the band's performance in the small town Petach Tikvah's concert hall. The music's vivid beauty pours into the desert emptiness, imbuing it with aesthetic depth and engendering a world of art and legend – a fantastic utopia where human connections are possible.

In early Zionist cinema, the national utopia is located in the desert after the wells were excavated, the first furrow ploughed, water soaked and fertilized the arid earth, with a soundtrack of singing men, women and children who performed a stormy *hora* dance. In films made in the 1980s, the utopia of national revival while making the desert bloom is replaced by a utopia of different peoples – Jews and Arabs – uniting. For instance, in a renowned scene from *Avanti Popolo* (Bukai, 1986) the desert provides a magnificent aesthetic backdrop to the revolutionary anthem "Avanti Popolo," sung by Egyptian and Israeli soldiers, who have joined forces and march like shadows towards the evening sun as it drops to the horizon. The meeting occurs at the end of the Six-Day War, while two Egyptian soldiers are trying to go back home, and encounter, on their way, a group of Israeli soldiers. Despite the tension prevailing between the two peoples, brotherhood and friendship grow between them. As they march along, the revolutionary anthem, that an Egyptian soldier starts to sing and is then joined by Israeli soldiers, becomes an immense (extra-diegetic) chorus that sets the pace of the marching men. At first sight *Avanti Popolo*, like other films with multinational protagonists in Israeli cinema of the 1980s, tried to throw off its protagonists' trappings and to reveal people, citizens of the world, who can talk to and meet each other. As Zanger describes it, the desert is a fine place to throw away all national costumes, all cultural heritages, because here there is nothing, this is where the beginning begins (2012: 7). Looking more closely, however, the national costume does not disappear in *Avanti Popolo*, since the Israeli soldiers accept the Egyptian soldier and permit him to drink water only after he recites Shylock's speech, drives a Jeep to the sound of the march that opens Israeli army radio broadcasts and marches with the Israeli soldiers to the sound of the anthem of Israeli youth movements. In other words, he is accepted by the Israelis when he throws off Arab national dress and enfolds himself in the "dress of a Jew."

In the film *The Band's Visit*, the setting is again a desert, and once more Egyptians encounter Israelis, but this time the national traits or signs are blurred. The Egyptians are members of the Alexandria Police Band, who took a wrong turn on their travels and ended up in a godforsaken Israeli development town in the desert, where the Israelis host them. The encounter unfolds not as a meeting of two peoples, but between individuals. Frictions, struggles, and reconciliations do not cross the borders dividing the Egyptians from the Israelis, or Jews from Arabs; they take place among the Jews themselves, among the Arabs themselves, and between the two groups. Throughout the film, grudges and incomprehension are attendant on every kind of human connection. However, in the midst of suspicions and grudges, human ties are formed through imagination, fantasy, and legends.

The colorful fantastic utopia of *Avanti Popolo*, in which Arabs and Jews mingle with each other in the desert, is replaced in *The Band's Visit* by an ostensibly more meager moment, when the aesthetics of sound and picture illuminates people and generates reciprocal connections. Two people, the Egyptian guest and his Israeli host, are sitting in a small room, with a baby cot between them. During the family dinner they have just eaten, the meager and miserable world in which they live out their lives was disclosed. The Egyptian has never completed the concerto he dreams of composing; the Israeli is unemployed, at loggerheads with his wife but accepting her complaints in silence. The two men are sitting in an arid room, recalling the desert that surrounds the town. However, when the Israeli gets up to leave the room, he stops momentarily, saying:

> You know, maybe that's how your concerto ends, I mean, not a huge ending with trumpets and violins [...] perhaps that's the end. Just like that, suddenly, not sad, not happy, just a little room, a light-bulb, a sleeping child and tons of loneliness.

The Egyptian remains alone in the room, and in a few static shots the camera observes a white, empty wall, the cot railings, the Egyptian's face, and a mobile toy suspended over the bed. Now the cot mobile emits a sound, and the unwritten concerto erupts from it, initially a kind of inner voice emanating from the musician's head, and later, as in *Avanti Popolo*, like an extra-diegetic orchestra that accompanies the camera as it exits the little room, out into the township, into the desert.

The utopian experience illuminated by such a cinematic aesthetic does not reflect an experience of international merging in this case, but rather that of a handful of protagonists, who cannot find shelter in groups or social and national constructs. Through an aesthetic of music and picture, they are able to establish a reciprocal connection in that emptiness and mute isolation. A connection of that kind, which links the inter-personal theme with the international one, happens also in *Nuzhat al-Fuad*. Like in *Year Zero*, this film is also structured in discrete episodes, but here the inter-personal connection between peoples and religions emerges from the links between real plots and imaginary ones.

The film begins with parallel plots that intersect. Odelia is a film-director and Tamara acts in her films. Both are links in a broken family dynasty and live without parents or children. Odelia's mother committed suicide, and she is in a state of conflict with her father who does not recognize her talent and work. Tamara's father is absent from the film, and her mother is distant from her. The two women undergo abortions, and throughout the film they quarrel with the men they live with, and with each other. However, they find substitutes and build different kinds of relationships within the realm of imagination and fantasy. At a certain stage and after a spontaneous abortion, Odelia becomes depressed and starts writing a story in which people close to her – her father and girlfriend – are imaginary characters. From the film's fictional setting, the plot now enters a fantasy within a fantasy. In this fantasy, the film opens up towards different national and religious spaces: Arabs, Palestinians, Christians. In her story Odelia creates an imagined distance from the people close to her, changes their lives and identities, leads them towards death and away from it – towards rebirth. Tamara is now suffering from cancer; she chooses not to undergo treatment and to spend her final months in a hospice located in a convent in Jaffa. There she meets a Palestinian who is also close to death and a relationship of love and understanding grows between the two. The man is played by Mohammed Bakri, the same Arab actor who played her father. The man who was the father, a Jewish-Iraqi writer, now becomes a different character, an Arab artist, and both characters are played by an Arab actor, in a case where the personal becomes the national.

The distance that Odelia, the author, creates from the main figures in her life is built from several such transitions that indirectly introduce the national story into her personal narrative. There is a transition from the Jewish city of Tel Aviv in the present, to the Arab city of Jaffa and its buildings which are saturated with the Arab past; from a Jewish Israeli experience to a Christian convent in an Arab setting; from Wagner's opera music and blues to *a cappella* liturgical music, and to a blend of Western and Oriental music, consisting among others of motifs from Scheherazade, played by Arab musicians and sung by an Arab woman vocalist. The way to the past, blocked by the narrative of the women and the parents, opens up and unfolds within the music and the space. It is the road towards the other, the other's landscapes and voices. The otherness of the national, religious, and cultural scenes furnishes a backdrop to the private and personal plot: Odelia is incapable of understanding her father and his Iraqi heritage – his attitude to her mother, to her, to women in general. She cannot build a relationship with Tamara, while Tamara constantly quarrels with Odelia, her partner, and her mother. In the plot that Odelia writes, she distances herself from those figures, transforms them into others, strangers, trying to understand them from afar – through the possibility of their death. Levinas (1991 [1974]) talks about the incomprehensibility of the death of the other, which is not identical with 'my death.' The finite, he claims, cannot produce the infinite from itself, it requires taking responsibility for the other. In the story she conjures up, Odelia undermines the similarity between her and Tamara, and what is common to herself and her father. She unrolls transcendental time that leads from life to the edge of death, the death of her father and girlfriend, and in the process constructs from a distance the possibility of genuine relations with them, the possibility of love. The bridge built over the distance is not only a bridge between people but also a bridge between nations, religions, cities, life, and death. It is composed of links of imagination constructed by the European cinematic aesthetic.

The European cinematic aesthetic of the mid-twentieth century that bridges the gaps between people creates also a distance between past and present to form a sequential time that heals – even if only a cinematic healing – historical time that was shattered by individual and collective quarrels, wars, and traumas. In the convent in Jaffa, an argument breaks out between Tamara and her mother. Tamara is in the Christian hospice in Jaffa, close to death; her mother tries to convince her to undergo treatment and return to life. The acrimonious conversation ends with renewed connection and understanding that is tracked by long, slow camera movements resembling those of Angelopoulos, Antonioni, Herzog, and others – from the two women embracing, to the steeple of the church beyond the walls and the mosque minaret in the distance. In those spaces of cultures and religions, the two women meet each other.

Nuzhat al-Fuad, like *Year Zero* and *The Band's Visit*, and like many films and books authored recently in Israel, searches for a different place where a human bond can be formed. These texts signify a metaphysical yearning for "a country we were not born in ... which was not our motherland, and we shall never relocate there" (Levinas 1991 [1974]: 16). It is the country of the other that the protagonists arrive at by keeping a distance that prevents resemblance, assimilation, and domination.

Seeking an alternative past, these films have found it in the European cinematic aesthetic and linked it to bleak portrayals of contemporary global society as these can be found in American mosaic films. At that intersection of cinematic times, they introduce ethical perceptions that open a door to an alternative way of shaping history. It is the way to the other, that Israeli history has not yet managed to find.

Bibliography

Agamben, G. (1998 [1995]) *Homo Sacer: Sovereign Power and Bare Life*, Stanford, CA: Stanford University Press.

Benjamin, W. (1969a) "On Some Motifs in Baudelaire" in Arendt, H. (ed.) *Illuminations*, New York: Schocken Books, pp. 155–200.

Benjamin, W. (1969b) "Unpacking My Library – A Talk about Book Collecting" in Arendt, H. (ed.) *Illuminations*, New York: Schocken Books, pp. 59–68.

Deleuze, G. (1989 [1985]) *Cinema 2: The Time-Image*, Minneapolis: University of Minnesota Press.

Duvdevani, S. (2010) *First Person Camera*, Jerusalem: Keter [in Hebrew].

Elsaesser, T. (2009) "Ingmar Bergman in the Museum? Thresholds, Limits, Conditions of Possibility," *Journal of Aesthetics & Culture*. 1. Online, http://www.aestheticsandculture.net/index.php/jac/article/view/2123 [accessed 16 August 2015]

Elsaesser, T. (2010) Hitting Bottom: Aki Kaurismaki and the Abject Subject, *Journal of Scandinavian Cinema* 1(1), pp. 105–122.

Friedman, M. R. (2005) "Witnessing for the Witness: *Choice and Destiny* by Tsipi Reibenbach," *Shofar: An Interdisciplinary Journal of Jewish Studies* 24(1), pp. 81–93.

Gertz, N. and Hermoni, G. (2008) "History's Broken Wings: 'Narrative Paralysis' as Resistance to History in Amos Gitai's Film *Kedma*," *Framework: The Journal of Cinema and Media*, 49(1), pp. 134–143.

Gertz, N. and Hermoni, G. (2011a) "Smashing up the Face of History: Trauma and Subversion in *Kedma* and *Atash*" in Talmon-Bohm, M. and Peleg, Y. (eds) *Israeli Cinema: Identities in Motion*, Austin: University of Texas Press, pp. 294–310.

Gertz, N. and Hermoni, G. (2011b) "The Muddy Path Between *Lebanon* and *Khirbet Khizeh*: Trauma, Ethics, and Redemption in Israeli Film and Literature" in Hagin, B., Meiri, S., Yosef, R. and Zanger, A. (eds) *Just Images: Ethics and the Cinematic*, Newcastle upon Tyne: Cambridge Scholars Publishing, pp. 35–58.

Gertz, N. and Hermoni, G. (2013) "History of Violence: From the Trauma of Expulsion to the Holocaust in Israeli Cinema" in Yosef, R. and Hagin, B. (eds) *Deeper than Oblivion: Anthology on Trauma and Memory in Israeli Cinema*, New York: Bloomsbury, pp. 223–261.

Jameson, F. (1991) *Postmodernism Or, The Cultural Logic Of Late Capitalism*, Durham, NC: Duke University Press.

Kaes, A. (2011) "Requiem for a Lost Planet: Notes on Werner Herzog's *Fata Morgana*" in Hagin, B., Meiri, S., Yosef, R. and Zanger, A. (eds) *Just Images: Ethics and the Cinematic*, Newcastle upon Tyne: Cambridge Scholars Publishing, pp. 94–104.

Kenaan, H. (2008) *Emmanuel Levinas: Ethics as an Optics*, Tel Aviv: Hakibbutz Hameuchad [in Hebrew].

Levinas, E. (1991 [1974]) *Otherwise Than Being, or, Beyond Essence*, Dordrecht: Kluwer Academic Publishers.

Levinas, E. (2006 [1972]) *Humanism of the Other*, Champaign, IL: University of Illinois Press.

Meiri, S. (2008) "History, Trauma and Ethics in Judd Ne'eman's Cinematic Oeuvre," *Israel: Studies in Zionism and the State of Israel, History, Society, Culture* 14, pp. 35–69 [in Hebrew].
Montoliu, M. M. A. (2009) "A Time to Love and a Time to Die: Desire and Narrative Structure in *21 Grams*," *Atlantis* 31(2), pp. 111–123.
Morag, R. (2013) *Waltzing with Bashir: Perpetrator Trauma and Cinema*, London and New York: I.B. Tauris.
Neeman, J. and Munk, Y. (2011) "*Avanti Popolo*: Battle Cry of the Fallen," in Gugler, J. (ed.) *Film in the Middle East and North Africa: Creative Dissidence*, Austin: University of Texas Press, pp. 177–186.
Utin, P. (2008) *The New Israeli Cinema – Conversations with Filmmakers*, Tel Aviv: Resling [in Hebrew].
Zanger, A. (2005) "Blind Spaces: Roadblock Movies in Contemporary Israeli Film," *Shofar: An Interdisciplinary Journal of Jewish Studies, Special Issue: Israeli Cinema* 24(1), pp 4–37.
Zanger, A. (2011) "*Beaufort* and *My Father, My Lord*: Traces of the Binding Myth and the Mother's Voice" in Talmon-Bohm, M. and Peleg, Y. (eds) *Israeli Cinema: Identities in Motion*, Austin: University of Texas Press, pp. 225–239.
Zanger, A. (2012) *Place and Memory in Contemporary Israeli Cinema*, London: Valentine Mitchell.

30
THE WAY OF SEEMING

Rob Nilsson

yGroup Manifesto [Figure 30.1]

The needed revitalization of the American cinema begins with the human heart, the nervous system alive to tender and passionate human encounter. There can be no cinema outside the artist's inner life . . . galvanized by intelligence, intuition and energy, glowing with memory, inspired by the desire to live fuller, richer, deeper.

The collaboration of artists . . . writers, directors, actors, cinematographers and craft people of all kinds is given shape and energy by the kinetic release of the inner fountain. No art is interesting without reference to the internal sources where our tragedies, comedies, low farces and ecstatic epiphanies are formed.

Whereas the pale and anemic truth that "all Art is political" has spawned legions of nodding heads in the exclusive pews of race, gender and class . . . the living truth is that there can be no art without vision, no vision without emotional awakening, no emotional awakening without an umbilical to nature energy, no nature energy without high flying in the slipstream of spiritual intuition.

Originating in Shamanic practice, in the "wild surmises" of poets and sages who learned languages beyond the cosmic silence, this insight into our fears, agonies and misgivings is the reason and justification for Art.

There are many entertainers and their job is to help us forget, for a time, the conundrums of a universe without a kindly God, with no assurances of redemption, and no other visible destination than extinction of the personality and decay of the body.

But the Artist's job is to look this Gordian knot in the face... and in the cauldrons of imagination and shape fashioning... to hammer out resistance to fate, acceptance of contradiction and to produce in the face of no hope . . . joy, the Barbaric Yawp, the on-going quest for courage at any cost.

The yGroup artist pledges to be alive in body and mind and to manifest the energies which bind us to universal force. We pledge ourselves as individuals to the communal circle of risk and protection where we reveal our secrets, power up our energy, open flesh and intuitive mind to received vision. We pledge to sing the songs of discovery handed down to us by ancestors who taught us above all . . . to live with passion and to sing at the top of our lungs.

(Written 1985; signed August 12, 1998)

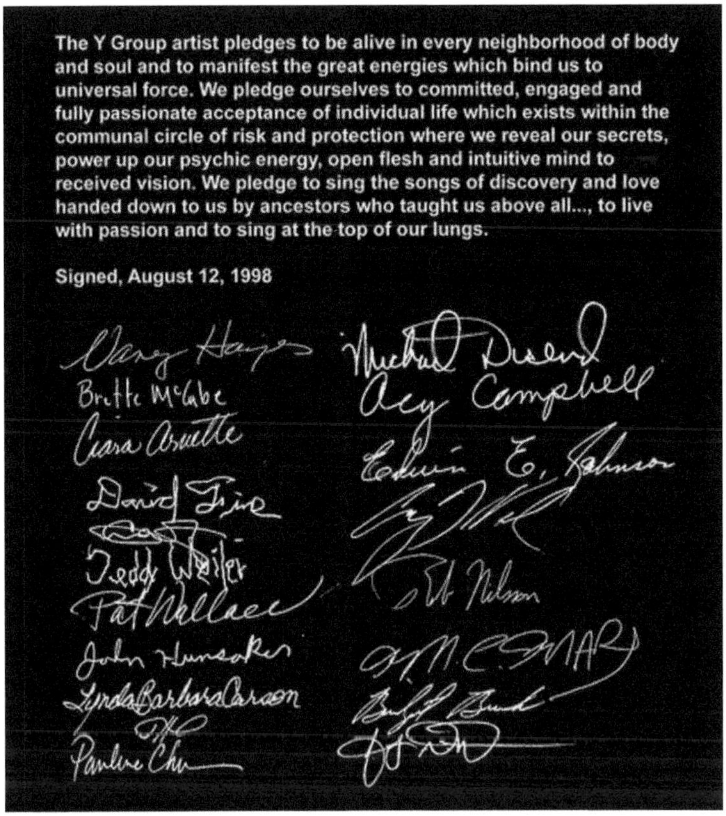
The Y Group artist pledges to be alive in every neighborhood of body and soul and to manifest the great energies which bind us to universal force. We pledge ourselves to committed, engaged and fully passionate acceptance of individual life which exists within the communal circle of risk and protection where we reveal our secrets, power up our psychic energy, open flesh and intuitive mind to received vision. We pledge to sing the songs of discovery and love handed down to us by ancestors who taught us above all..., to live with passion and to sing at the top of our lungs.

Signed, August 12, 1998

Figure 30.1 The yGroup Manifesto.

I've never been able to take Hollywood seriously. So much money, so many mansions, Beamers and better, so many flacks touting talent which has decided, like Osceola, to come in out of the terrifying and contradiction-ridden Okefenokees of personal art making and surrender to THE MOVIES made, as we used to say, "for the Man." And I'm serious when I say 'talent.' They are smart down there, feral smart for sure, but also book smart, in many cases, well-read, aware of high art, even collecting it with the cash they make, and often liberal in politics, and charming of personality. They are generally kind down there (although the connection between killing and kindness has been noted) and they don't ask you to sell out. They redefine the terms and over time, so that before you really notice it, you are different. You're political where once you were passionate. You're tolerant where once you insisted. You're a team player where once you were a team leader. It's been fully discussed in novels by Bud Schulberg, F. Scott Fitzgerald, Nelson Algren, etc. and documented in movies Hollywood made about itself, such as the classic *Sunset Boulevard* (Wilder, 1950), the less than classic *Bob and Carol and Ted and Alice* (Mazursky, 1969), and the one I like best, albeit about musical theater, *All that Jazz* (Fosse, 1979). It's all been said a million times before. And I say some of it in my new book *Wild Surmise: A Dissident View* (2013). The Power and the Glory, Amen.

I started following the impulses to make things which nagged at me to be made, the inner urge and the outer thrill of dropping into a slipstream which dragged me into their force fields demanding to be known ... with poetry. And then, when I went to sea in 1960, leaving school and working on Swedish ships, one of which, the MS *Iberia,* took me to the port cities down the east coast of South America and a one month sojourn in Buenos Aires and then another, the MS *Frederika,* headed north to Hamburg and the better part of a year living in Paris and hitchhiking through Europe … when I started painting.

Filmmaking began for me while teaching in up-country Nigeria four years later when I made a one-hour dramatic spoof on neo-colonialism with friends and the tools at hand. Our used 8-mm camera, a Bell and Howell Sun Dial 220, which could fit in the palm of your hand, sits on my book shelf to this day. It had a way of frequently jamming, and Chuck, the smallest of our band of fellow thespian school teachers, would be jammed into the bottom drawer of a huge wooden armoire at my house, the only completely dark place for miles, where he would reset the single sprocket 8-mm film, and shooting would resume.

The film had to be purchased in London and shipped to me in Okeagbe, Akoko via Ikare, Western Region, and I edited on a wooden board with brads hammered in to hold the sprockets. There was no sound but it was narrated by a teacher writing subtitles on a blackboard teaching *The Lesson* to a group of Yoruba children. We had a World Premiere at the Automatic Cafeteria in Lagos, one of two screenings before the only copy was stolen, along with all my film equipment, from my apartment back in Boston. I'm sure it's still decomposing in a landfill somewhere.

So that's how I started out. No economic expectations. I had written my college thesis on the poet Conrad Aiken, who eked out a living with his novels and articles and never made much from poetry. So I took on the job of being a recorder of thoughts, feelings, and observations as a personal mission. I've never wavered from the thought that this was what a creator should do. The work is personal. You might change a line or a color at prompting from a mentor or a talented friend. But you are following the mysterious dictates generated by … what? Voices from the regions of kinetic languages, wild surmises, flashes of neural lightning. What happens if you violate the trust and sanctity of this land of received messages and blithely beguiling elixirs? Entertainment? Work in the film industry?

I drove a night cab in Boston so I could paint during the day. While there I made my next dramatic film, *The Country Mouse* (1968) and a documentary, *Bag* (1968), a film I shot while on the streets and cab stands. Later, in the early 1970s I helped form Cine Manifest, a leftist filmmaking collective in San Francisco which operated on a "from each according to his ability to each according to his need" (Marx 1875) economic basis which freed all of us to combine art and politics with a form of communal collaboration. Then John Hanson and I made *Northern Lights* (1978), which won the Camera d'Or at Cannes; I turned my attentions to full-time filmmaking, even though I continued to write and paint, and in 2007 self-published my poetry book *From A Refugee of Tristan da Cunha.*

I bring up these early signposts to make a point. If you want to be yourself in your work and follow out the skein of listening, as a dedicated schizophrenic might, to the inner voices, and express them in their full and unimpeded form (not excluding the demands of your brutal editor self), you have to find means you can control and collaborators willing to concede you final cut. You want to know who to blame, at the end, and who to praise. Few directors get that chance out in the real world. And so you have to create your own world with respect for the talents of those you work with and determination to follow the best idea in the room, with a rather Draconian insistence on your judgment as final arbiter. You can wish for an Ezra Pound to be the 'miglior fabbro' of your Wasteland, but he might never show up. And so you're stuck with yourself.

Some of the ways I do it

The 9 @ Night Film Cycle (1996–2008) is the bell cow on this round-up of ideas, techniques, and things I experienced in the night streets and alleys of the San Francisco Tenderloin, and the windy days in homeless encampments we built along the Berkeley railroad tracks, and the hobo ruins we expropriated for our use out on the Albany Bulb. That's where I learned the value of techniques, taken from an experience here or something I read there, and came to call the result Direct Action. You can read more about it in my book *Wild Surmise: A Dissident View* but the short version is that it's a way to prepare players to produce dramatic feature films using back story and production improvisation.

After working with a combination of professional actors and the farmers of North Dakota in *Northern Lights*, and with San Francisco cab drivers in *Signal 7* (1986), I developed a lot of faith in the miracles of the ordinary and the performances of everyday people, when prepared with certain basic techniques. This led to the formation of the Tenderloin Action Group, and later the Tenderloin yGroup which met at the Faithful Fools Street Ministry in the San Francisco Tenderloin. Between 1992 and 2007 I ran free workshops for homeless, street populations, inner city residents, and all-comers, during which time we made 10 feature films featuring our workshop members, including *Chalk* (1996), produced by Rand Crook and Ethan Sing. Robert Viharo performed in several 9 @ Night Film Cycle Productions and Ron Perlman also did a turn with us in the 9 @ Night feature *Stroke* (2000).

Everybody's expressive. But some people are more expressive than others. And some would say that even fewer are interesting when expressive. But I disagree. I think the most interesting thing to do is watch expressive people, even boring ones. Because if you arrange their performance in your film to include the idea of their being boring, that's interesting. But what I don't like is dishonesty. The worst kind of person is the 'come on' partygoer who buttonholes you, babbles on with a lot of baloney, and won't let up. But if you capture that honestly, using the babbler as a player in a movie scene, you've done a service to humanity. And you've provided the babblers the honesty they didn't have, and maybe they've learned something as well.

Here's a list of 10 common notions I employ in conducting Direct Action Movies, which are largely improvised, but always working for surprise, inspiration seemingly discovered on the hoof, raw as tarmac road rash:

1 There are no scenes. Junk that notion. You're ongoing. You do, you say, you sulk and refuse to play. You're rude. You're tender and considerate. Joy, rage, despair and whatever intimate connection is. That's what you're doing. No scenes. Circumstances and the force of character(s).
2 Silence is best. Anyone can guess what's up and why. And they do. Eyes go to the silent player. What is he/she thinking? This and that. Everything at once. The fact that it all happens at once is what makes language possible. And fascinating cinema.
3 Don't pimp for the play. I don't want to be pleased. I want to be challenged. Hide on me. This is not *High Noon* (Zinnemann, 1952) where we march down the street towards each other and draw. Make a left and meander through the neighborhoods. There's plenty of time for gunplay later.
4 Don't jump on the first cliché. It will be wrong. Check out the second. Probably too easy. Move on until the apt word, the exact unexpected line occurs. Now you can talk. I can cut out all the rest.

5 Don't be nice. Try on a suit two sizes too big. Yell and curse. Be selfish. Everyone wants to be. No one thinks it's ok. But that's the only way to break the mold. The best actor is selfish and expects you to be too. No grudges. Constant warfare. Save your empathy and human kindness for real life.
6 Know what the through line is. Then start somewhere else. The non-sequitur is a blessing. Ride backwards, inside out. Gap out. Forget what you're saying. The scene will come in its time. Almost no one forgets the scene. And if they do, what's a director for?
7 Talk to the players while you're shooting. All the skein of both sense and energy is destroyed by the word 'Cut'. Keep going and try to find a way to jump in between words, say something simple, non-complicated and SHORT. Then back out and let the scene do what it's doing.
8 The unexpected. Trust it. We're hungry for it. Not novelty. The unexpected.
9 Beauty is beautiful. Power is power. Neither is illusory. Embrace beauty and power. Different you say, with every person? Beware the kind of person who thinks so.
10 Tears are beautiful. Rage is like the thunder and lightning. Ravishing. Tenderness, sensitivity, empathy. Please love them, allow them, embrace them. Be joyous. If you can bear intimacy, show it, show us.
10A Keep your crews as small as possible. Work with friends, and if you don't have any, make some. Tell them what you want to do. If they want to, you have a crew. If not, remember, you can make a film with yourself. Even a dramatic feature requires no one but you. Dream the possible dream and you'll figure it out.

I guess you can see from this that my system, developed with comrades and collaborators in the alleys and warehouses of the San Francisco Tenderloin, is a sort of anti-system, my cinema anti-cinema, my outlook eclectic, measured second by second, shot by shot in the peculiarities of the moment. I call what I do Direct Action and I see myself as a sort of infiltrator, a spy on reality as well as a sapper seeking to limpet a mine on the hull of what is expected and to let it free-fall into the abyss. Maybe the mine is a depth charge which will go off at a certain point in the free-fall of an idea. Maybe a suggestion will trigger an unruly emotion which gives off smoke, or a violent fiery harangue which nobody wanted or expected, but which might provide an experience like that of the arrival of the Eskimo in the old Synanon game, someone you didn't know you needed until they appeared.

I think of jazz music, the small combos that started up in New York City in the late 1940s when cabaret licenses were too expensive but you could have live music in small clubs as long as no one was dancing; $300 fees which suddenly became $3,000 gave birth to Charlie Parker, Miles Davis, John Coltrane, Dizzy Gillespie and the high wire quartets and quintets and even sextets of musical wizards whose improvisational trances made them the Sufis and shamanic seekers of their time.

During the shooting of *The Steppes* (2011), a film I recently made featuring Irit Levi (Rest in Peace, Irit) I learned that the bar we were shooting in (once the 222 club, the 3 Deuces, San Francisco version) back in 1957 connected with the Blackhawk, a famous jazz club next door (today a parking lot). I was told that cables went through the adjoining wall to recording equipment making records of live performances including "Friday Night, Miles Davis in Person at the Blackhawk" (1961). I was there in 1958 as a kid just out of high school, sitting behind the chicken wire where minors could sit and take in the scene. That night I saw the Miles Davis sextet which had both John Coltrane and Cannonball Adderley, and I believe, Bill Evans on piano. Miles turned his back on the audience and refused to play. Now maybe that was rude, but it was drama. It didn't help the music that night, but it was a scene from a Direct Action movie I wish I had made.

Small-combo jazz (bebop, hard bop, and its various off-shoots) starts with virtuoso players. My view is that in cinema acting, virtuosity is a personal talent. We are all soloists in our own lives and if, as players, we can conquer fear, relax, open up the emotional taps, and spelunk into nether regions of our characters and personalities, we can all play dynamic characters similar to ourselves. Yes, we can be dynamic in our own desuetude, our baggy-kneed selves. No we can't do Shakespeare. That's another kind of music. Nor can we be John Gielgud, Laurence Olivier, or Gary Oldman or be a member of the great brother/sisterhood of chameleon actors, able to do either Hal or Falstaff, or Ophelia or Lady Macbeth on different nights after months of preparation.

But we can play the obvious characteristics as well as the difficult mysteries of ourselves in extended improvisational sessions if we learn and practice some simple rules: silence, patience, listening, limiting talk and emphasizing action, avoiding the obvious "High Noon" confrontations, and seeking instead the unexpected outburst, the unthinking rude attack, the timid demur, the sudden burst of automatic speaking sometimes available and waiting to live out the ways in which we are uncertain handlers, somewhat bumbling practitioners of speaking and behaving the way humans do, half bright and half muted, half talkative and argumentative, half appeasers, kissing up to somebody for personal gain, and half honest practitioners trying to discover the most cogent way of seeming.

We need to 'gap out' as we do in our lives, forgetting what we were saying and going off on apposite tangents and mixed modalities of impatience, self-aggrandizement, false (or true) empathy, tenderness, skepticism, joy, rage, despair, intimate connection ... anyone can do all of these with practice. And if we are able to have our language at the ready even during the incandescent moments of rising emotion, and not get too flustered (except in an interesting way) by the neural fireworks going on inside of us, and if we can avoid pimping for the play, narrating, rather than experiencing the dramatic context, avoiding the rescue operation the first cliché seems to offer, and waiting instead for the off-center, telling remark which has just enough sense in it to avoid sounding precious and calculating, well, we can do the drama of our emerging selves with quite a bit of talent, even genius, and with cinema's magic last line of offense, editing, we can do a certain kind of film, the Direct Action film, as well as, and better than, a Viggo Mortensen or Willem Dafoe working from a script, with table readings, rigid set blocking, and hitting our light as the tears begin to flow. This is the insight I found down in the Tenderloin. Maybe it started that night behind the chicken wire when Miles refused to play, leaving Cannonball and Trane alone on the stage to pick up all the pieces and come out triumphant, inventing from Miles' absence, a presence even more unique for all that it lacked.

One thing I've learned to value over the years is the power of contradiction and paradox. Many might think that I'm advocating a sort of hippie anarchism, but what we do is structured with what I call a script scenario which lays out a tentative scene order and dramatic objectives. As with jazz players, we have to have chops (self-knowledge, awareness of the ensemble, a foundation of language and even literacy), and, wherever available, the imponderable: talent, genius, an ability to risk and to accept the results. "My Favorite Things" was just a silly Broadway tune until Coltrane got hold of it. We too have a starting point, and as soon as we can, we look for the miracles of the ordinary in character and circumstance.

Whenever I hear myself proclaiming the 'truth' of something I hear the opposing distinct ring. 'True ... but.' Which is why I can't use the word 'truth.' It seems to end the discussion, but all there is is the on-going discussion. Bergman once said a couple of things I remember this way. The human face is the one great subject of cinema and the actor can only play one mood or mode on that face at a time. But the great actor plays one after the other in a masterful sequence which seems so simple and is yet highly pyrotechnic. Something like that. The great player, the great director lives in the closest possible approximation of saying one thing and its opposite at the same time. Light can be both a particle and a wave at the same time. Why should we think that we are put on earth to take sides?

Why do politics seem to require that we honor the one thing that we all know for sure doesn't work: the hushed declaration of the dubious shibboleth, the feet of clay beneath the perfect candidate, the Big Idea, the 'ism' which says it all when, in our best moments we know that nothing works that way. 'For sure' is for imposters and bag men, con artists, and three-card monte specialists, all of whom know that they are basically fakers anyway. All art participates in a realm where the tangible presence of languages and techniques comes up against the intangible nature of reality, and therefore to a lamentable but very real place, where 'on the one hand and on the other hand … and then on those other hands, and even a few feet thrown in'… uncertainty rules. The unknown rules, no matter how we struggle against it and eventually we come to the realization that all we really have is something I call "The Way of Seeming," our personal collection of opinions which vies with everybody else's personal opinions on the way things seem to be.

Last thoughts on what I do

Filmmakers. We're all so important and mysterious about what we do. Most films begin in a rarefied military atmosphere. We gather in Albania to train for our campaign. But by the time we begin shooting, Albania is more like Albany. We have transformed it with our unwieldy crew with all its trucks, all those lights and dollies and grip equipment and smoke machines. We've lulled our actors into a stultified trance, driven off the local ecology and substituted 'serious business' for 'miraculous play' and so… we're not shooting Albania, we're shooting what our bucks have built from it … where big budgets and worried money types need the reassurance of a script, a budget, memorized dialogue, shooting diagrams, paid shepherds to herd paid sheep, and feed bags … lots of them.

I can think of movies I love which have been done that way. *Come and See* (1985) by Elem Klimov, *Last Tango in Paris* (Bertolucci, 1972), Oshima's *In the Realm of the Senses* (1976), many others, in fact, but precious few considering the billions spent to make them. Why spend so much money on films which are so much less interesting than life? Life is the teacher and it is all around us. Only the sounds of grip trucks and screaming ADs can scare it away.

What's the easiest way to lie? I'd say it was with words. Change facts and figures and cook reality … describe things differently from how you know them to be. Harder to do with emotion, with the interweave of behaviors, reactions, annoyances, hesitations, mind changes, twisted thoughts, and broken ideas which constitute the reality of a given day in the life. Hard enough to know the truth there, let alone a lie. But that's where we live everyday, in the eye of the present which is always the high wire act of not knowing anything exactly … what we think, where we are, what comes next, what went before. In response to knowing little, I like feeling, I like the little cataclysms of electricity, the mixed joy, rage and despair, the catalogue of smaller states … annoyance, impatience, momentary satisfaction mixed with worry and levels of anxiety.

I hate lying, all forms of equivocating, disguising, concealing, including the lie of the over-designed screenplay which pretends to be lifelike, the attitude-ridden youth genre picture with its simpleton view of life, the marketing argument disguised as a film … Hollywood's stock in trade. But lying is good … if the result is that the lying is observed. Exposed. A lie stripped of its disguise … that's drama. And sometimes we can depict that in a film. But most of the time it's really more confusing and foggy than that. Because in the soup of what we do each day, there's fibbing, exaggeration, and misconception, but not much outright lying. And the truth seems to be in seeing the brilliant mosaic of the undefined … and being fascinated by it. This idea is important to our films. When we look 'over there' and the film emerges, it feels like what I just described.

So 'looking over there.' The first step. I start to see things in various workshop members. The proverbial light bulb goes on and characters start coming to light. We talk about them, a scenario begins to form, maybe written down, maybe improvised, often experienced differently than conceived and seed moves toward seedling. A Direct Action film begins … the day it begins. But we have been filming the lives of these people way before that.

We create back-story lives … by living them. On camera, in locations … we rehearse our characters' life experiences, the ones we choose amidst the potential thousands. Start at the beginning. The birth experience. We have improvised it with results which varied from groaning skepticism, to visionary epiphany and places in between. Primary experiences at different ages. Important events. The first date. The first meeting between characters. The arguments, misunderstandings, attractions and repulsions, the making love and the unmaking of it, the mud of what we do building up the bricks of who we think we are.

Instead of just talking about it, we do it and try to live it out in front of our rehearsal cameras, getting pregnant with circumstances, until one day the camera becomes the production instrument and now we're living into our film.

Workshop exercises on expressivity and emotional availability are also included in this process and in *Wild Surmise* I have given examples of some of them and how they contribute to the work. Although back stories can only cover high points of a character's former life, one of its values is that it provides experiences rather than ideas, fictional (but actual) moments rather than character descriptions a player can only 'know.' Writing out a character description is like looking at a map rather than traveling a road. Neither will produce a character with total self-knowledge, but, I quote Walt Whitman (1856):

> Allons! Whoever you are come travel with me!
> Traveling with me you find what never tires.

I think this an honest way to begin a film: experiencing as much as possible, thinking analytically as little as possible, and moving into the unknown with an open heart and a freedom to go wherever whim, desire, and design will lead. There is endless cant about story in the film business, but most of it is second rate. All the stories have been told and now they're being used to sell us products. Let's forget about stories for a while and think about starting points and possible areas of travel, about likes and dislikes, passions and aversions, places … milieus of mind and action, desire, curiosity, and where it might lead. Cinema is the one art where searching within these places brings us magically not to a story … but to a film. And a film begins when we 'look over there,' and follow our fascination. In the end, our film need not be much more than a record of how it became itself but if our gaze has been avid and alive … that is the film I want to see.

Dependent filmmaking

I'm tired of all those Independents out there. Hollywood is where most of them live and they're so independent they need a minimum of $5–20 million to show how close to the ground they travel, and how deep their roots sink into the muck. But muck is not really the soil where good work sticks its innocent head out of the earth and cautions us not to see filmmaking as a business. Still, the paradox (and in my view when we get to contradiction and paradox we're nearing 'the way things seem to be') is that the best of American film still comes out of that Moloch of a town. However, maybe once or twice a year, tops. Maybe that's why I live in the San Francisco Bay area and am a Dependent filmmaker: dependent on my wits, my friends and collaborators, on the brilliance of the everyday man and woman, and only marginally independent when I actually have the necessary money to do what I always do without it.

Re: the good Hollywood does. I'm talking about Paul Haggis with *Crash* (2005) and with *Third Person* (2013), a film with many faults but with the major virtue of sailing far over the heads of the Critical Majority which panned it. I'm saying that the best American filmmakers are English: Mike Figgis with *Leaving Las Vegas* (1995) and, most of all, *Time Code* (2000), a film I desperately wish I had been smart enough to make.

And they are Mexican. Alejandro Iñárritu made *Amores Perros* (2000) with Altavista Films in Mexico and *Babel* (2006) with Paramount Pictures in tinsel town. It takes a very smart, a very talented man to do that. And Alfonso Cuarón made *Y Tu Mamá También* (2001) with Anhelo Producciones in Mexico and *Children of Men* (2006) with Hollywood industry techniques and Universal Pictures. He also made *Gravity* (2013) which in 3D, leaving aside scuba diving, gave me the closest experience of the other-worldly in this very worldly world, of any I've ever had.

I recently went to see Iñárritu's latest film *Birdman* (2014). I e-mailed the young directors I value and asked them to come and see it again, and discuss it with me. I don't know if they're coming or not but I want to say that the film pushed all my buttons. It was mostly brilliant but, to me, kind of ruined at the end. But I hope it wins all the awards it's up for. I hope that everyone goes to see it. Because this film is more about dead-end and pretend America than almost anything I've seen since *Babel*. Why is it that it's made by a Mexican? Once this chapter is published we will all know how it turned out at the box office and at the Oscars but we won't know the answer to my question.

But just to underline the contradictions and paradoxes of anything you want to say about film, or art, or about Hollywood or American politics, the film had at least three distinct endings, and the least interesting was the one they ended with. The second one would have been brilliant but this is, after all, tinsel town. I'd be happy to hear from anyone who thinks they know the ending I'm talking about. The ending they used felt like the result of the cliché studio executive's dictum to append some kind of a positive ending to a comedy which had already ended with a tragic stroke of brilliance. That's why I never wanted to work in that town. If I had been misguided enough to end a good film that badly, I would have preferred to blame myself.

Bibliography

Marx, K. (1875) *Critique of the Gotha Programme*, https://www.marxists.org/archive/marx/works/1875/gotha/ch01.htm (accessed on 20 February 2015).

Nilsson, R. (2007) *From A Refugee of Tristan da Cunha*, Bloomington, IN: Authorhouse.

Nilsson, R. (2013) *Wild Surmise: A Dissident View*, Bloomington, IN: Authorhouse.

Whitman, W. (1856) "Song of the Open Road" in *Leaves of Grass*, http://www.poetryfoundation.org/poem/178711 (accessed on 20 February 2015).

PART VII

The politics of cine-geographies

INTRODUCTION

Ewa Mazierska

According to such prominent authors as Michel Foucault, Henri Lefebrve, David Harvey and Edward Soja, we live in an area when space conquered time. Human geography is pronounced as the most important branch of the social science, heavily impacting on other disciplines, including film studies. Yet, the relationship between spaces and places and the moving images tends to be scrutinized when the researcher deals with the periphery, rather than the centre. In line with this approach, this part comprises five cases of marginality, ranging from African to Welsh cinema. However, rather than taking marginality for granted, their authors examine its circumstances, which have to do with the legacy of colonialism and the hegemony of neoliberal ideology. The effect of neoliberalism on cinema consists of privileging profit over non-monetary values it produces and the opening and deregulation of national markets, so that a film produced in one country potentially has to compete with films coming from all corners of the world. The more that neoliberal economy dominates over its alternatives, especially socialism, the more difficult it is for cinema produced in the periphery to preserve its distinctiveness and the more it needs institutional protection to thrive. The authors also point to the contradictory effect of the development of technology on the position of the cinema. On the one hand, new technologies, many of them summarised by the term 'digital shift', democratise the process of film production, due to its low cost and accessibility. On the other hand, they strengthen the existing hierarchies, most importantly the hegemonic position of high-budget films in the world market, the bulk of which is produced in the United States.

In the first chapter, Kenneth W. Harrow offers a comparison between 'New Nollywood' video films, dominating the African scene in the last quarter of century with 'celluloid films', made by prominent African directors of the earlier period. These two types of films are very different in their production modes, textual characteristics and distribution. The 'celluloid filmmakers', in part thanks to subsidies coming from the countries which were their colonial oppressors, created cinema that did not pander to popular taste and served an important place in the creation of African postcolonial culture. The Nollywood filmmakers, by contrast, working under conditions of neoliberalism, do not enjoy the privileges of their predecessors and are geared towards quick profit. Hence, they embrace genre conventions and lack a clear approach to the colonial past. Nevertheless, Harrow observes that irrespective of their politics African films in all periods struggled with attracting African audiences, hence were marginal even within its own borders.

Unlike African cinema, Bollywood is seen as a commercial success story amongst its primary audience of Indian people and enjoys a growing popularity outside the borders of India. According to Peter C. Pugsley, their success owes to its accessible form, and the way it uses location, both foreign and domestic. Bollywood directors adopt the strategies used by tourist guides, including selection, beautification and homogenisation, focusing on what is seen as most attractive from the perspective of a potential visitor, while hiding anything which might be seen as off-putting. Pugsley examines the reasons and effects of using foreign and local locations, arguing that the recently observed return to the homeland, apart from reflecting the weakening of the Indian currency, points to new nationalistic tendencies in India, with filmmakers being keen to promote the nation's urban gentrification and recognition of the natural environment as a tourist drawcard.

Armida de la Garza discusses the case of Latin America, where the idea of Third Cinema, understood as a cinema advocating the plight of colonised nations and other oppressed groups was born. She considers the films made by/on/for indigenous peoples as a form of continuation of the political ideals of Third Cinema. De la Garza uses the categories of 'domestication' and 'foreignisation', borrowed from translation studies, to argue that the filmmakers whom she considers employ 'foreignisation' as a means of resistance to the dominant politics and aesthetics. She also draws attention to the role of digital cinema in facilitating the process of self-representation by oppressed groups.

European cinema does not come across as an obvious candidate to present the plight of the margins, given the fact that cinema in Europe is subsidized by national governments and pan-European institutions. Nevertheless, in commercial terms, it cannot compete with Hollywood. Petar Mitric and Katharine Sarikakis take a closer look at the history of creating postwar European cinema through the introduction of specific policies as a means to forge a united Europe and creating a different paradigm from that offered in Hollywood – what used to be described as 'Second Cinema'. In common with Harris, they also draw attention to the effect of neoliberal hegemony, which demands that films are profitable and by the same token embrace values identified with Hollywood rather than modernist European cinema, based on the concepts of auteurism and quality.

Finally, Ruth McErloy investigates the case of Welsh cinema, using as her tool the idea of 'small cinema' and 'minor cinema'. This is because the (cinematic) voice of Wales can be compared to that of Kafka, a Jew living in Prague and writing in German. She draws attention to the similarities and differences between the representations of Wales offered by Hollywood and London-based directors on the one hand and those offered by Welsh filmmakers on the other. McErloy considers the role of directors, policy-makers and actors in developing the 'voice of Wales' and, in common with the other authors of this part, draws attention to the tension between the demands of profitability, and a requirement to preserve and develop a specific cultural identity.

The cine-geographic approach adopted in this part is revealed not only by the content of the chapters but also by the terms used and elucidated by the authors, such as 'global cinema', 'world cinema', 'transnational cinema', 'small-nation cinema' and 'Third Cinema'. The last term, which prevailed in the discussions about marginal cinema in the 1970s, is clearly on the wane, while 'global' and 'world cinema' dominate. This does not mean, however, that the difference between the power of the centres and margins disappeared, but rather that films produced at the margins stopped being seen as a separate political and aesthetic proposition.

31

AFRICAN CINEMA IN THE AGE OF POSTCOLONIALISM AND GLOBALIZATION

Kenneth W. Harrow

African cinema has changed significantly in the past twenty-odd years since Nollywood's 'video films' came on the scene. Two of the key parameters that mark this change are the recently developed technology of digital filmmaking that Nigerian, Ghanaian, and others have used to transform the ways African films are directed, produced, distributed, and exhibited. New spaces have been opened up for popular genres and for inexpensive productions, radically changing the landscape in which African film can be seen. We are now at the point where a second generation, dubbed New Nollywood, has emerged, again shifting the parameters of what we consider African film. At the same time, outside of Nollywood, African filmmakers are not only drawing upon funding from a wide range of diverse sources and are no longer dependent on such single European entities as the French Ministry of Cooperation. The filmmakers identified with independent filmmaking or global filmmaking are living abroad more and more, creating a cultural body of works that reaches 'inside' and 'outside' the continent. These two developments, Nollywood film and 'serious,' world cinema, are the result of developments with long roots in African culture and in film history.

African Global South cinema in an age of globalization and transnational cinema has often been divided along the lines of a binary: "Nollywood" vs. FESPACO [Festival panafricain du cinéma et de la télévision de Ouagadougou] films; video films vs. auteur or Independent filmmaking. Even when the lines of the binary are fissured, as into world cinema as regional, transnational, local, or global cinema, the terms remain vexed. How can we negotiate around such loaded terms when approaching African cinemas? By defining them as Global South we are already putting a geographical frame around the question. But geography is malleable, and we can reframe the South in terms of space, approach, and address that respect the local or regional conditions of production and distribution.

This chapter will attempt to distinguish between African films that employ an address that conveys immediacy to a local audience and those that are more generally categorized as destined for the world cinema circuit. Spatial distinctions between distance and closeness enable us to situate African cinema along the global–local divide, while placing the binary under erasure. To do this I will turn to the work of Carmela Garritano (2013), Mette Hjort (2010), and Bhaskar Sarkar (2010) who enable us to think of the relationship between space and broader generic differences that characterize these categories of cinema. Sarkar's warning that the turn to transnationalisms as categories that define contemporary world cinema risks reinscribing the same old position of dominance to Hollywood, or 'Western' cinema, bears repeating:

> Just as multiculturalism within one nation-state recognizes differences, parades minorities and promises a politics of identity, all the while maintaining the naturalized dominance of one ethnic position, similarly *a transnational multiculturalism would seem to institute a hierarchical global order in which a few ethnically and culturally similar nations retain a locus of primacy and privilege. Global multiculturalism would appear to provide the cultural basis of neocolonialism, arranging various local cultures in a global hierarchy, exhibiting them to a cosmopolitan audience as a global menagerie, and fostering exceptionalist nativism and civilizationalism.*
>
> (2010: 42, *my emphasis*)

In response to this warning, Sarkar proposes an approach that was developed powerfully in Garritano's study of Ghanaian film and especially its relationship to Nollywood. She calls it a minor cinema of a minor cinema.[1] In that regard, Sarkar's words, referencing Chinese martial arts cinemas in India, as part of the body of Asian cinema, are particularly apt:

> The global, in the true sense of the word, should designate a situation in which each local is shot through with other locals; thus a translocal approach must work to transcend every local, challenging any extant inter-local hierarchy. Second, the instances of transnational cultural exchange I bring up are neither fully outside the purview of, nor completely inscribed by, the nation-state or global capital; rather, they operate at the level of the translocal-popular – the level which, while largely complicit with hegemonic apparatuses, continues to hold as-yet-unrealized promises of democratic imaginations and interventions. By examining this translocal-popular exchange, *we can avoid slipping into the problems of exceptionalism, exoticism and containment associated with the multiculturalist paradigm.*
>
> (2010: 49, *my emphasis*)

Garritano focuses her work on the Ghanaian film industry, where she has constructed a portrait of the globalized local centered in Accra and Kumasi, as well as in locations where Ghanaians are living abroad. She establishes a baseline of what Ghanaian audiences and filmmakers understand as 'professional' cinema – those we might otherwise define as commercial film, mainstream, or Hollywood cinemas – in contrast to the variants of the local or minor cinemas in Ghana, often marked by melodramatic or magical indices. Broadly the distinction can be made between African 'video films' that address the local audience within a close space, with a narrow horizon of familiarity, and those that stretch the sense of distance and transnational appurtenances, films at times dubbed New Nollywood or New Wave African cinema (Diawara 2010).

African celluloid cinema – before the video film boom in the late 1990s and their phenomenal growth thereafter, and before the terms 'global cinema' or 'world cinema' had acquired any caché – always struggled to acquire an African audience. The reasons for this are complex. Analyses that assume that African audiences preferred Hollywood action films, Bollywood, and Kung Fu films ignore the impact of a tightly controlled distribution system that impeded showings of African films (Diawara 1993). One often hears the claim that the polemical didacticism alienated audiences seeking entertainment. However, this cannot be substantiated on the face of it since almost all of the films being made by African directors from the

1960 to the 1990s could not be considered esoteric auteur cinema. The only exception might be Djibril Diop Mambéty's *Touki Bouki* (1973), which differs in this regard from his subsequent films. Most of the films made by major African directors like Sembène or Cissé or Idrissa Ouédraogo were narrative realist films, often marked by humor and emotion, accessible to the ordinary African spectator. The main difficulty in achieving popularity was that there was almost no way for most Africans to see their films. And that remains the case.

Nollywood films, on the other hand, were born at a time when the conventional venues for seeing film, originally large downtown theaters and quartier cinemas, were coming undone, not only in Nigeria but throughout the continent. Again there were many factors responsible for the decline. It was expensive to maintain thirty-five millimeter projectors, and when any of the celluloid film projectors became outmoded, they scratched the prints. Eventually this could be taken as a metaphor for the collapse of the entire viewing experience: the downtowns became increasingly unpleasant for evening outings, the audience was moving further and further away from the downtowns, the quartier theaters were frequented by local thugs, in some areas making it too unpleasant for any women to attend (Larkin 2008). Eventually, more and more African countries followed the pattern detailed by Mahamat-Saleh Haroun in Chad, in *Bye Bye Africa* (1999), in which the audiences were bidding their adieux to the last of the cinemas.

At the same time, the digital revolution made it possible for audiences to purchase inexpensive videos, and later VCDs, which they could watch at home, without the costs or inconveniences of attending a theater performance. Only recently has the trend started to be reversed as new multiplex centers are being built (Lagos, Dakar, Nairobi). Ironically, in my latest experience of attending such a center in Lagos in the summer of 2013, all but one of the films were foreign, i.e., Hollywood, the one exception being a Nollywood film. In addition to this shift, Nollywood films are currently being continually broadcast, continent-wide on South African TV stations (MNET's AfricaMagic), including another one in Nigeria, and web platforms (e.g.TvNolly, IROKOtv) and apps (Afrinolly). There they represent a viewing experience that might be seen as halfway between that of a theatrical film release and a television telenovela. The conditions of digital film production – quick, cheap – are enormously different from those that marked most earlier celluloid African films in almost every way: Nollywood films might be shot in a week or less;[2] might have one week of post-production; and are distributed by a network of marketers who focus on local venues, like the giant markets, or video shops, in urban centers. They are also highly vulnerable to piracy. Classic African celluloid films, on the other hand, had their post-production in Europe; Francophone films often in Atria, in Paris, with French Cultural Ministry support, and with sophisticated, highly trained editors, like Andrée Davanture. The costs, sources of funding, training of personnel, length of time taken to create the films, and distribution networks all contributed to the creation of two vastly different forms of cinema.

The films ultimately might be said to have served different purposes. The goals of the video films were intensely shaped by commercial needs, and the video filmmakers financed their own films through private money. The celluloid directors, on the other hand, sought outside funding, sometimes with their own government agencies, usually with European funds (like the French Ministry of Cooperation or Culture, the British Film Institute, Canal Plus, Fonds Sud Cinema; UNESCO; the European Union), and after the projects were funded, their success was not entirely measured in profits. The celluloid and the video films served different worlds of culture; circulated in different global flows; addressed different audiences. Although Nollywood directors came to acquire their own professional competencies, their initial training and expectations of what kind of film they were making were not tied to concepts of professional filmmaking and world cinema that were at odds with the makeshift, entrepreneurial approach of Nollywood. The celluloid filmmakers created a body of films that served an important place in the creation of African culture, of postcolonial culture; the Nollywood filmmakers created an industry when neoliberal capitalism determined the patterns of globalization. World cinema never became a proper home for either side: African celluloid filmmaker addressed questions of burning importance to Africans, although their principal venues increasingly were foreign film festivals, foreign art house audiences, and foreign university students. Nollywood films were primarily intended for local audiences, but included many in the African diaspora.

As Nollywood films came to be made in the hundreds, and then the thousands, they posed an enormous challenge both to African celluloid filmmakers, who felt their training and expertise to be slighted, and to critics of Third World Cinema or what had been known as African film. For the critics, terms like political engagement, Third Cinema, revolution, national liberation, progress, Africanity, etc., denoted specific values to which real African films ought to and largely did aspire. Third Worldists and celluloid-trained filmmakers felt Nollywood films betrayed those ideals, and detracted from the unspoken admiration filmmakers and critics had for the thoughtful, brilliantly crafted films, such as those of Abderrahmane Sissako or Mahamat Saleh Haroun, or the more feminist-oriented work of Safi Faye or Fanta Nacro. Important social and political issues and talented filmmaking were scanted, victims of a commercial system in which many artist-creators, like Kwah Ansah felt the insult to the point of abandoning the attempts to make films. Simultaneously the number of Nollywood filmmakers multiplied to the point where it was becoming almost impossible to make a profit, or to escape the predations of piracy. The flip side of the commercial industrial boom was the cliff edge of bust, which drove out of business those who could not consistently raise the needed funds. The radical shifts in critical approaches that marked the ascension of global cinema and world cinemas as concepts became imperatives for African cinema as well.

In his introduction to *Nigerian Video Films* (2000), Jonathan Haynes delineated the ways in which Nollywood called for new critical approaches that would change the ways in which African film had been mediated to European or American audiences. Nollywood decidedly did not lend itself to the familiar ideological readings that had marked African film criticism from the outset. For Haynes, the crucial differences resulted from the fact that Nollywood was not created through the use of French or other European funding, with their own approaches or agendas and was not marked by European post-production, or by the exigencies of distribution networks that welcomed African cultural products. "Nigerian video production exists almost entirely outside the pan-African institutions and international circuits that have shaped most of African cinema" – circuits that shaped most western cinemas as well (2000: 5). Haynes turned to questions of globalization, the economic and social factors that accounted for Nollywood's production and entertainment values, and sought in studies of modernism, of genre (particularly melodrama), and cultural anthropology, approaches that would make more sense in analyzing the phenomenon of Nollywood and its new approach to African film.

Haynes made the question of where postcolonial studies were situated central to his demand that different questions be put to this body of films, and to the context in which it appeared. His call was heeded, and classic film studies analyses, which had been heavily inflected by questions of desire, the gaze, subjectivity, and performativity, were generally not deployed. The cultural and ideological framings of critics like Garritano and McCall (2007) were necessary and invaluable, but inevitably left cinema critics with the question of how to reconcile such approaches with those marked by poststructuralism or psychoanalysis. This question became all the more fraught as the ascension of 'world cinema,' within the context of globalization studies, has heightened the emphasis on economic markers and their influence on "mediascapes" and global cultural flows (Appadurai 1996). With the focus on new, popular entertainment genres, with their broad transnational appeals, it became increasingly dated to seek an account for agency and subjectivity, the two motors that drove a cinema of commitment and of individual identity.

These two variant perspectives, with the study of subjectivity on the one hand, and global economies with their stagings of world literature and world cinema on the other, seemed to be incompatible. And yet they remain at the core of the essential approaches facing contemporary African film production. With the explosion of the numbers of Nollywood films since Haynes's call for change in the 1990s, the number of different genres has expanded considerably beyond early narratives that turned on evil ways of acquiring wealth and love, and the employment of magical means. The need to highlight luxurious surroundings, with interior shots conveying signs of wealth, originally led to the occlusion of visual signs of urban impoverishment – creating a Lagos in which, as Haynes put it, the camera vaulted over the streets and gutters in poor neighborhood:

> [T]he commodity fetishism extends to luxurious walled mansions, cell phones, exercise equipment, fancy hotels and restaurants, and establishing shots across Lagos Lagoon or Five Cowries Creek that, overlooking the squalor and chose of this most unnerving of West African cities, makes Lagos look like any other international capital.
>
> (*Haynes 2000: 3*)

In the years since Haynes penned this claim, Nollywood has expanded its repertoire of genres, and it is no longer uncommon to see the holes in the social fabric as well as the trash in the mise-en-scène.

Nollywood films, like the earlier celluloid African cinema, worked on a binary logic, shifting the notions of good and evil from political to moral and spiritual sources. If the police or ruling classes are corrupt, it is now not explained as due to the fact that they embody the essentially exploitative nature of capitalism, but rather because the devil has seized their souls. The solution is not revolution but exorcism; the punishment is not geared to restore an authentic or just African community, but to purify the spirit of those tempted by satanic forces. If the anxiety over the neoliberal period's excesses, over the seemingly magical acquisition of wealth by the ruling class, drives the narrative, the solution is to counter the magic with the Holy Spirit (Meyer 1999). Films that emphasize the outsized emotions surrounding acquisition of money or love, loss and despair, revenge and murder, all violate the earliest codes of Ferid Boughedir and Teshome Gabriel, in which the distractions of Hollywood were set at the opposite end of the spectrum of the goals of early African or Third World cinemas.

Third Cinema vs. global mass culture

'Third Cinema vs. global mass culture' expresses something of this split between an African cinema of the postcolonial period and the New African cinema of the global period, the former 'Third Cinema' designation having now been replaced by the slot allocated for Africa in World Cinema classificatory systems. Situating African culture within World Cultures, or now within Global Cultures, has always been problematic since the act of situating has been framed in terms that either marginalize African culture, or worse, that defer to a token African contribution. Just as Area Studies as a discipline belonged to the period of Third Worldism, so too does African culture today, even in its local configurations, occupy a location in the global market that is determined by the global impact and power of the publishers or distributors – a location often legitimized by the allocation of awards in notable film festivals. If 'worldliness' designates the conditions of cultural interactions where borders no longer function as barriers, the old-school borders have been replaced by the armature of the fortress when global economics are at play. Thus Nuttall and Mbembe's definition of worldliness must be taken as relative:

> Worldliness has to do not only with the capacity to generate one's own cultural forms, institutions, and lifeways, but also with the ability to foreground, translate, fragment, and disrupt realities and imaginaries originating elsewhere, and in the process place these forms and processes in the service of one's own making.
>
> *(2008: 1)*

The mechanisms for this entry into the spaces of worldliness mark Nollywood cinema, African popular culture, as conditions and limits:

> [Nollywood films'] appeal is linked to their enormous capacity to recontextualize and localize forms and styles associated with global mass culture, and much as in the African urban environments in which video movies circulate, it is the meeting of the local and the global that generates the energies and uncertainties that drive their production and consumption. As modern African cultural articulations, they participate in the "worlding" of Africa (Simone 2001) and the "indigenizing" (McCall 2002) of global technologies, styles, desires and discourses.
>
> *(Garritano 2013: 15)*

Here it is the technologies of the local production that disturb Appadurai's overly optimistic assessment of what the global flows can accomplish. Garritano relativizes the African cinematic form as the global vernacular: "As global vernacular forms, they trouble generalizations about an African or national identity because they emerge from, are shaped by, and reshape 'a mass-mediated imaginary that frequently transcends national space' [Appadurai 1996: 6]" (Garritano 2013: 77).

How does the mass-mediated imaginary that reaches to the transnational space of a global cinema correlate with the conditions of production under which African cinema has labored? Before the digital revolution, funding came very largely from European governmental ministries or European NGOs intended to support culture in the 'South' – versions of French aid to the francophone African countries – or entities like the BFI or Canal+. With the digital revolution, the need for Nollywood directors to find local funds, typically without a government attachment, meant that a two-tier system was set in place. The former aspired to create the film worthy of a world cinema denomination; the latter aspired to make a profit from local distribution channels. The former adhered to standards of production that required outside funding, and that were created by an industry dominated by European and American standards; the latter emulated the standards of the telenovela or the Yoruba Traveling Theatre, could best be described as local, and was largely viewed as amateurish. Although 'amateurish' is no longer applicable for an industry that has grown into a vast, multi-tentacled enterprise, the conditions that characterize much African local production in other areas obtain for cinema as well. As Garritano states:

> Their very low budget and amateur production values create another, complementary layer [to their aesthetic]. The cheaply and rather haphazardly made video

> features reenact and render immediate the dire economic situations of their creators and patrons, erasing the distance between the audience and the video narrative.
> (*Ibid.*)

She explains how the early productions were shot with rented VHS cameras, and were made as quickly and cheaply as possible. The actors were amateurs, drawn from family members or acquaintances; production crews were small: "perhaps one person to hold one boom microphone, and another to operate the camera, although many directors also doubled as camera operators. … The camera was rarely steady and shots often arbitrarily or badly composed" (ibid.).

She concludes that these videos looked more like home videos than feature films, as could be seen in their "abrupt shifts in time and location, rapid camera movements, jump cuts, and illogical shifts in perspective and point of view" (ibid.). Not having two cameras meant that the shot–reverse-shot pattern, typically employed in scenes with intimate conversations, lost the eye-line match, and created disjunctures in the images, and disoriented the spectator.

For video film audiences in Nigeria and Ghana the ideal represented by commercial cinemas was identified with the polish and spectacle of Hollywood. As Garritano writes, these were the attributes of films they dubbed 'professional,' and as such were marked by qualities to which the local, cheap, amateurish productions ought to aspire. A new division thus arose between the qualities of professionalism and those of the typical Nollywood (or Ghannywood) film. Nowhere was to be found the aesthetic promoted by Sembène, his "mégotage," meaning getting by with little,[3] but intellectually grounding the narrative in issues of political importance. Instead, the globally dominant cinemas imposed a dominant aesthetic whose moniker of 'professional' conveyed its commercial status. When Ghanaian or Nigerian directors had the means to emulate those standards, they generally sought to do so.

Thus, for instance, the films of Veronica Quarshie that sought to reach an international audience pursued "a clean, generic global look and feel by concealing the gritty reality of the historical present and so making visible an African landscape and African characters similar to those found in any global media form" (Garritano 2013: 102–3). That look signified "professional," not "African shooting back," as Melissa Thackway (2003) described celluloid Francophone cinema. The new digital 'global' director Quarshie distanced herself from the conventions of witchcraft or ghost movies "because they did not meet the global, Hollywood standards the company sought to maintain" (Garritano 2013: 102). A professional movie was "more suitable to a global audience," as one director put it, because "it transcended its local context" (ibid.). As classical Hollywood narratives sutured the audience into the diegetic space by such techniques as "linear narration, parallel and continuity editing, compositional unity, and closer framing" (Garitano 2013: 103) that required no affiliation with local, familiar settings or contexts, viewers were solicited to enter into a space in which they would substitute identification with the characters on screen for an awareness of themselves as spectators. The local productions, on the other hand, could not replicate these qualities very easily with limited means, and compensated for that lack with emotional accents that befitted melodrama, the very genre whose excesses the professional directors eschewed (ibid.). The local became the site for excess, be it in luxury, desire, or emotion that gestured toward the deficiencies in the everyday life of the spectator; the professional film aspired to convey a reality unto itself with which every viewer could identify, regardless of their status or location. The local was expressive to the limits of the image; the professional sought to contain expressivity within the horizon of the narrative.

Transnationalism and the global auteur

That these distinctions became fundamental to what is largely contemporary African cinema means that any notion of transnationality might be more aspirational than actually realized. The successful Nollywood films could not shed entirely the techniques and conditions of production that made them local; but they could reconfigure their address to the spectator so as to flatten out the visible markers of the local, and contain the excesses that made the local characteristic of the popular and vernacular. Thus, when Teco Benson sought to create an action hero in his drama about love and government corruption, he chose Hanks Anuku who speaks with an American accent, and whose name as the protagonist in *Formidable Force* (2002) is Bill. It is appropriate that the leading lady playing opposite Anuku in *Formidable Force* is the Nollywood megastar Genevieve Nnaji, whose character's name in the film conveys an equally global item: she is called Nike!

The qualities that would mark a transnational film as either strong or weak, according to Hjort, are those that convey the traits of the 'professional' film within the new digital dispensation in African cinema. "A given cinematic case would qualify as strongly transnational, rather than only weakly so, if it could be shown to involve a number of transnational elements related to levels of production, distribution, reception, and the cinematic works themselves" (2010: 13). By this measure most African celluloid films, despite their creators' desire to create something culturally specific and appropriate for African people, would qualify as transnational as almost all the elements related to production, distribution, and exhibition were constituted by institutions and people from different nations and cultures. The films themselves, in a sense, fought against this flattening effect of the international dispensation with their determined projects and ideals. Ironically, the designation of "weakly transnational" that Hjort's standards would identify with Nollywood films fails to take into account the broad international circulation of those very local, non-professional films, which are now shown on several television chains across all of Africa, and which are widely distributed along the paths of the African diaspora in Europe, the United States, and Latin American countries like Brazil.

'Transnational,' like 'global,' is a term that harmonizes with the overcoming of distance. Unlike 'international,' which had always echoed the great distances involved with travel overseas, across continents, transnational and global are terms Appardurai has famously associated with a motion as smooth and natural as the movement of water currents, 'flows'; or as the vistas spread out before one's gaze, 'scapes.' Bridging the gap depends upon the sense of closeness or distance that the spectator experiences in reaction to the film's address. The intimate spaces of chamber room romances ask little of the spectator, especially as the international language of English, genres like romance, and heightened emotions like love and despair, are engineered into the narrative and discourse of the characters.

In contrast, 'world cinema' auteurs like Mahamat-Saleh Haroun and Abderrahmane Sissako construct narratives whose global span resonates with the full reach of Diaspora, with exile and return motifs joined to philosophical and subjective introspection that are incommensurate with the surface noises of excess. This notion is figured into Haroun's title "Un homme qui crie," and Sissako's refrain, citing Césaire, in *La Vie sur terre* (1999), that man is not a dancing bear whose misery is displayed for the entertainment of the crude audience: "Un homme qui crie n'est pas un ours qui danse" [a man who screams is not a dancing bear].

The contemporary shift measured in Nollywood is so "noisy" (Larkin 2008) that the silence of such sensitive films as Idrissou Mora Kpai's *Si Gueriki* (2003) or the subtleties of *Heremakono* (2002) by Sissako might be drowned out. The modernist turn in post Third Worldist culture emerges in ironic, playful, at times postmodern auteurism, as seen in Bekolo's films, and Teno's brilliant film essays. For an example of what might be termed global auteurism we will take a careful look at Abderrahmane Sissako's *La Vie sur terre* (1999), one of the most aesthetically appealing films from Africa.

Sissako's vision of African beauty contrasts greatly with that embodied in the retinues of wealthy and corrupt women in Nollywood, or in the travelogues generated for the tourist vision in Hollywood. To understand his perspective, we begin with the role played in the film by Césaire's famous poem *Cahier d'un retour au pays natal* (1939), where the return home is marked by nostalgia. Sissako takes the spectator on a voyage from the north to the south, beginning in the Global North with the appropriate site for wealth and commodity consumption, the Parisian supermarket. There we see the protagonist Dramane shopping for presents to bring on his return home to Sokolo, Mali. The camera captures him looking over row after row of delicious, rich French butter, an endless display of camembert and chèvre. As the well-dressed African man, he wears a somewhat outsized fedora and overcoat and is seen carrying a silly-looking white teddy.

We glimpse Dramane through the interstices of the supermarket shelves filled with toy ducks, hats, and endless goods to delight the family back home. As he is quietly presented to our gaze we hear the background sounds of the disembodied supermarket voice addressing its customers. When he takes the escalator we see him looking upward, as if attending to another sound. The vibrating resonance of the ngoni, an African stringed instrument, is heard for 25 seconds as Dramane ascends. Sissako makes the passage with a transitional jump cut, transporting us from ordinary life in Paris to home in Mali. The fade from the supermarket opens onto the sight of a majestic savannah tree with its complicated interplay of branches – a symbol of the endless multiplicity of lineage ties that are united in the earth and that exfoliate outward in their reach toward the skies. For a full minute Sissako carries us on the emotional journey into Africa with the music and the camera's zoom in on the tree. The resonances of the notion of distance are captured in this opening shot that moves us from Europe to Africa.

In his majestic epic poem *Cahier d'un retour au pays natal* Césaire creates a Negritude manifesto on returning home, to self and to race. Like Césaire, after a long sejour in Paris, Dramane begins the return voyage to his father and fatherland in time to celebrate the New Year and the passage of the new millennium. While we see his father reading a letter from Dramane, the voiceover of Dramane is heard announcing his intention to come home, echoing Césaire's words when the poet took the ocean liner back to Martinique to revisit the world of poverty from which he had emerged. "Partir," he writes to his father, to leave – the desire to leave Europe and return home, his voice sustained with the sound of the ngoni again, and a setting sun posed against the outline of the savannah. Dramane has learned what he needed in Europe, but asks, was it worth it, since the price he paid was to forget about home.

The story of the return mimics the Nollywood travel film whose genre Garritano analyzes as having a double movement, here and there, in Africa and abroad, that "inserts Ghana, and the Ghanaian spectator watching the movie, into the time of the global modern" (Garritano 2013: 138). In the process it "constructs a relationship of proximity between Ghana" and the world at large (Garritano 2013: 138–9). In a contrary movement Dramane's return, like Césaire's, negates the proximity between the metropole and its former colony. We are continually reminded of this by the recurrent, fragmentary gestures of global media reaching across the space. The radio broadcasts convey the immediacy of the conditions in Sokolo, the weather and birds threatening the crops as, simultaneously, we hear of the festivities commemorating the new millennium being celebrated across the world, especially through the excited words of the broadcaster in Paris for whom the little town of Sokolo in Mali could only be at an extreme distance. For Paris, Sokolo is a place where time stands still, a place that is far away. In contrast, the local radio in Sokolo focuses us on the reflections of another voice, another time. Again it is Césaire whose humanism matches the quiet display of beloved images of home, with the branches of the tree reaching upward, with the movements of people and animals marking some other calendar's rhythm. Ultimately one is left with an immense sense of nostalgia and quiet loss that is evocated in the minor notes of an occasional piece – appropriate for what one might call this minor transnational cinema, in the Deleuzean sense of a minor literature.[4]

In his major works, including *La Vie sur terre* and *Bamako* (2006), Sissako reaches for an African cinema that is not defined in terms of the global capitalist order. He returns us to a familiar African cinematic space where a certain voice, a certain master of the word, a certain singer and his voice give us the place where we want to center ourselves when asking the question, "which Africa"?

The travel film in Nollywood moves the spectator along a trajectory that catches her up, tracking over space like money transfers from shoddy financial agencies that strip the diaspora immigrant of a significant portion of his earnings in the transaction of sending money home. The momentousness of the journeys of Césaire, Sissako, Mambéty, or Sembène across the oceans no longer exists in the same forms in the postcolonial moment. Instead, the fortress and its armed borders are evoked on all levels. The global counterpart of today's 'African' voyage is evoked in scenes from travelogues of open beaches waiting for European tourists to visit, without need of visa.

In conclusion, we can see that like Nollywood, Sissako rewrites the earlier notions of political engagement and African subjectivity. For the former, the transfer of capital, the images and affects driven by the representations of luxury, sin, or crime, seek to engage the spectator in a 'New Africa' where the proximity to global modernity is shaped by desire and anxiety. When the former prevails, we imagine pleasure without guilt; when the latter prevails, loss overcomes the protagonist, leaving us quaking with negative recriminations. Sissako's modernity, on the other hand, combines both global sophistication and a sense of rightness about the gifts of African sensibilities and their fragility. His subject is positioned against a European hegemony that threatens to engulf all that Sissako embraces, and that he conveys in the musicality of African voices and instruments, and in the portraits that adorn the walls of African homes, self-portraits for the family. The 'New African' cinemas, from the violence of *Viva Riva*'s (Djo Munga 2010) mad sexuality to *Timbuktu*'s (Sissako 2014) tender offering of love mark the considerable distance from the strictures of Third Worldism. Yet we are still able to discern the continuities with those beginnings in the framing of the films' narratives and images as something the African spectator would want to mark as 'her own.'

Notes

1 Following Lionnet and Shih, Garritano describes collaborations between global north producers and smaller, global south industries as major–minor, in contrast to the relationship between Ghana and Nigeria where

> movies coproduced or made collaboratively by commercial videomakers in Ghana and Nigeria represent an instance of what might be called minor-to-minor transnational collaboration; these minor transnational practices operate independent of partnership with a former colonial power or reliance on international multiplex distribution.
>
> *(2013: 166)*

2 According to anecdotal sources, in some recent (2013) film production there is a goal of two-to-three days of shooting, given the dire economic conditions now obtaining.

3 Sugnet (2010) writes:

> Sembene invented the term 'mégotage' (building with cigarette butts) instead of 'montage' to describe what African directors were forced to do. He sometimes had to mortgage the house he had built with his own hands to start the financing for a new film.

4 The term "minor transnational practice" is employed by Adejunmobi (2007) in describing Nollywood filmmaking. Here I am reversing the usage, as it were, in applying it to the 'worldly' filmmaking practice of Sissako that aims at a non-commercial space of exhibition and audience.

Bibliography

Adejunmobi, M. (2007) "Nigerian Video Film as Minor Transnational Practice" in *Postcolonial Text* 3(2), pp. 1–16.

Appadurai, A. (1996) *Modernity at Large: Cultural Dimensions of Globalization*, Minneapolis: University of Minnesota Press.

Césaire, A. (1939) *Cahier D'un Retour Au Pays Natal*, Paris: Volontés.

Diawara, M. (1993) *Black African Cinema*, New York: Routledge.

Diawara, M. (2010) *African Film: New Forms of Aesthetics and Politics*, Munich: Prestel.

Garritano, C. (2013) *African Video Movies and Global Desires: A Ghanaian History*, Athens, OH: Ohio University Press.

Haynes, J. (2000) "Introduction" in Haynes, J. (ed.) *Nigerian Video Films*, Athens, OH: Ohio University Press, pp. 1–36.

Hjort, M. (2010) "On the Plurality of Cinema Transnationalisms" in Durovicova, N. and Newman, K. (eds) *World Cinemas, Transnational Perspectives*, New York: Routledge, pp. 12–33.

Larkin, B. (2008) *Signal and Noise: Media, Infrastructure, and Urban Culture in Nigeria*, Durham, NC: Duke University Press.

McCall, J. (2007) "The Panafricanism We Have: Nollywood's Invention of Africa" in *Film International* 5.4 (28), pp. 92–97.

Meyer, B. (1999) "Popular Ghanaian Cinema and 'African Heritage'" in *Africa Today* 46(2), (Spring), pp. 93–114.

Nuttall, S. and Mbembe, A. (2008) "Introduction: Afropolis" in Nuttall, S. and Mbembe, A. (eds) *Johannesburg: The Elusive Metropolis*, Durham, NC: Duke University Press, pp. 1–33.

Sarkar, B. (2010) "Tracking 'Global Media' in the Outposts of Globalization" in Durovicova, N. and Newman, K. (eds) *World Cinemas, Transnational Perspectives*, New York: Routledge, pp. 34–58.

Sugnet, C. (2010) "Ousmane Sembene: A Silenced Continent Speaks" in Crosscuts, http://blogs.walkerart.org/filmvideo/2010/10/06/ousmane-sembene-a-silenced-continent-speaks/ (accessed on 21 September 2014).

Thackway, M. (2003) *Africa Shoots Back: Alternative Perspectives in Sub-SaharanFrancophone African Film*, Bloomington: Indiana University Press.

32

NATIONALIST GEOPOLITICS AND FILM TOURISM IN INDIA'S HINDI CINEMA

Peter C. Pugsley

The vast array of national cinemas across Asia employ a number of cine-geographic approaches that fulfil ongoing geopolitical and development agendas. Disparities exist though, as the more economically developed Japan and South Korea deal with different imperatives than those of nations such as Malaysia or Vietnam, or perhaps more significantly given their respective populations and increasing roles as global powers, China and India. It is India that is the focus of this chapter as its most commercially successful cinema industry, the Hindi-based films of Bollywood, present highly nationalistic images based around the geographic importance of India. Unlike many of the cinema industries in the region, Bollywood enjoys almost complete autonomy as it is studio-based and not under the direct political or economic control of the state. The geopolitical images it presents therefore serve as an unofficial political project that works in tandem with state aims to present a united India.

Over several decades Indian cinema has increasingly presented India as part of the global community through the use of foreign locations, not just for its musical items, but often as the entire setting for films. As an example of Asian cinema, India's Bollywood films have tended to highlight the transitory, mobile nature of its citizens (a familiar story to many Asian nations such as China, Malaysia and Singapore). Indian films have been presenting a cine-geography based on foreign landscapes (and cityscapes) that offer a visual escape from the realities of urban and rural poverty in India. But a *Times of India* article in 2013 (Singh and Vohra) suggested that the weakening of the rupee was prompting a return to productions based solely in India. This chapter suggests that financial considerations are only part of the story, and that a return to the homeland location is part of a larger geopolitical project indicative of a new pride in the Indian nation. Several recent films will be drawn upon to show that the state has been able to mobilise the geopolitical aspects of film by encouraging India's filmmakers to promote the nation's urban gentrification and recognition of the natural and rural environments as tourist drawcards. Thus, a newly politicised and highly nationalist cine-geography has emerged alongside the earlier desire for all things foreign.

Singh and Vohra's article drew from a report by The Associated Chambers of Commerce and Industry of India (ASSOCHAM) in 2013 that noted the falling value of the rupee meant a rise of some 25 30 percent in international travel costs, and a corresponding drop of "up to 35% of Bollywood movies being shot in exotic foreign locales" (*Deccan Herald* 2013). In this chapter, I explore the importance of location and the way that cine-geographies arise as political acts that guide the meaning-making properties of India's regional and national cinemas. Eshun and Gray's definition of cine-geography as a form of cinema that "designates situated cinecultural practices in an expanded sense, and the connections – individual, institutional, aesthetic and political – that link them transnationally to other situations of urgent struggle" (2011: 1) is instructive, particularly in their context which extends notions of Third Cinema and its resultant militant agendas. However, this term is also useful in a less militant sense to capture the political, economic and social imperatives that, to a nation like India, are no less of an "urgent struggle". Consolidating the economy and providing a more stable sense of national pride are key factors in India's on-going development as a power bloc as it deals and competes with other regional and global powers, most notably China and the European Union. India's film industries offer a site for reinforcing parochial notions of identity and the homeland through films that present a cine-geography of landscapes and cityscapes readily identifiable to Indian audiences, and ensuring that film investment and tourist dollars remain in India.

Defining Bollywood

Bollywood exists as a form of cinema recognised for its high melodrama interspersed with song-and-dance numbers. Mostly produced in the studios of Mumbai (Bombay), Bollywood is a force to be reckoned with in global cinema, with its stars household names to over a billion people and a highly productive industry that contributes many billions of dollars to the Indian economy. Bollywood differs significantly from its US industry counterpart, Hollywood, in a variety of ways that are "not just cosmetic, but structural [...] grounded in a civilizational difference, expressed as an aesthetic alterity" (Paranjape 2012: 30). Its place in the day-to-day lives of the populace is unparalleled as Bollywood is seen as "a cinema of feelings, moods, emotions, and sympathy" (30), founded upon recognition of a 'filmi' society that has emerged from a "long and shared relationship between viewer and film, with a knowledge and familiarity on the part of the former of its codes and conventions" (31). The onscreen recognition of urban, suburban and rural India is a key factor in the success of the Bollywood cinema.

As the most well known of India's cinemas, Bollywood therefore serves as more than mere entertainment. Mehta points to the idea of the 'Return of the Nation' and that "Nation, despite not having gone away anywhere, has come back with a vengeance in globalized India" (2010: 2). The role of the media is paramount in such a reinvention of Indian nationalism, not only through the still highly influential traditional print press, and the ever-present broadcast services, but film, perhaps far more so than in other nations, has an enormous impact on the public psyche, with Hindi cinema leading the charge. Its importance reaches far beyond that of an occasional form of amusement, as it is found to operate as an "unofficial ideological apparatus" (Mehta 2010: 2). This view reiterates Chakravarty's observation that sees Indian cinema as a site for discussion of

> the question of national identity, the production of films in numerous Indian languages as an assertion of regional identities, and the highly taboo subject of the representation of communal discord and violence as a threat to the nation's fragile sense of unity.
> *(2000: 228)*

The 'fragility' of the nation is often addressed in the geographical representations of India's techno-urban spaces and unblemished natural environment that take on a central role in film as representative of the nation. In India's case, Goa's beaches or Mumbai's clean and technologically sophisticated business districts speak for the entire nation, not just specific regions.

Temporal factors play a large part in the cine-geographic imaginings of a national India. The 1990s saw major social and economic changes take place across India, when the emergence of a "new class of workers, better-paid than ever, flourished in renewed realms of consumption, carrying the bourgeois consumerist ambition to new levels" (Mehta 2010: 4). This was also an important time for Bollywood cinema as it saw what Mehta refers to as the "naturalizing" of the "free-floating Non-resident Indian as an essentialist cultural signifier" (4–5). The created representations of a new nationalism based around the cine-geography of India as a physically and spiritually grounded 'centre', an ontological base for one's 'Indian-ness' to develop, reflect Bose's claim that Hindi cinema has produced "an extremely canny grasp of what the Great Indian Dream may be constituted of, and has then been able to make a great song and dance about its disparate, constituent parts" (2011: 45). In speaking directly to its mass audience (both home and abroad) it is India's mainstream and fixedly commercial cinema that "embodies the dream landscapes of the Indian middle class and, in regional cinema as well as in the more trans-national Hindi feature films, breathes life into its many desires" (46). For many years, these desires were encompassed in the need for exposure to foreign countries and the mobilities afforded by the economic, linguistic, and cultural means that could enable travel to these countries.

The allure of the foreign

The first major Bollywood film to capitalise on foreign locations (excluding those that used geographically similar neighbouring locations like Kashmir or Pakistan) was said to be Raj Kapoor's *Sangam* [*Confluence*] in 1964, which made use of the dramatic landscapes of Switzerland (Shah 2012). However, it was renowned director and producer, the late Yash Chopra who is most associated with the regular use of foreign locales in his films, firstly as backdrops to musical items, and then increasingly as settings for narrative structures based on global mobility through migration, study or travel scenarios. Amongst his many films to use foreign locations, Chopra shot in The Netherlands in 1981, Switzerland in 1989 (a country that was to become a favourite location for him) and Germany in 1997. His use of Switzerland as a backdrop capitalised on the cine-geography of snow-covered peaks and endless meadows. Seeing the value in such international promotion, Swiss tourism authorities welcomed the attention of Bollywood's filmmakers, and as of 2010 over 200 Bollywood films had featured scenes shot in Switzerland (Shah 2012). In 2006, only two of Bollywood's major box office hits were shot entirely in India, while at least six others relied on overseas locations including the USA, Poland, Singapore and Brazil (Ramnath 2007).

By the early twenty-first century, India's major filmmakers seemed all but convinced that foreign locations were a necessary ingredient for a film to gain strong box office takings, as it became apparent that "Overseas shoots enhance a movie's glamour quotient, allow audiences to become armchair tourists and, when the plot demands it, allow for an exploration of the encounters between Eastern and Western cultures" (Ramnath 2007). But foreign locations have not always been accessible to India's independent filmmakers or those from the less affluent studios, beyond the reach of Hindi-based, Mumbai producers. Financial restrictions led to a situation where "[u]ntil the mid-1990s, the quest for spectacle often took Indian filmmakers to diverse sites of regional and national tourism, such as the lakes and forests of Kashmir" (Pandian 2011: 59). Indeed, the 1990s were a pivotal time for India's filmmaking to enter the global arena as one of Bollywood's biggest ever box-office successes emerged in 1995.

Capitalising on long-nurtured personal relations and networking opportunities with an increasingly strong diaspora, *Dilwale Dulhania Le Jayenge* (often referred to as simply *DDLJ*) (produced by Yash Chopra and directed by his son, Aditya) became a career-launching platform for actors Shah Rukh Khan (SRK) and Kajol by exploiting its UK (and other European) locations to provide local and diasporic audiences with a feast of exotically romanticised images of foreign lands. The diasporic audiences lapped up the use of recognisable locations, and were keen to have the opportunity to be close to a piece of Bollywood action when a film crew came to their part of the world. Andrew Hassam (2012) notes, for instance, the excitement among fans in Melbourne, Australia at the call for extras for another SRK film, *Chak De! India*. This type of spectatorship and self-recognition offers both ontological and nationalist comforts as it "plays to a parochialism that looks for similarity rather than difference, particularly among audiences more used to seeing Mumbai or Delhi on-screen than their hometown" (Hassam 2012, 274).

DDLJ shifted the representation of the Non-Resident Indian (NRI) from "the marginal outsider with affected speech and behaviour" and validated him as "not just a possible Indian national subject, but possibly one of the best" (Mehta 2010: 1). Through SRK's portrayal of Raj, and Kajol's as Simran, the dilemmas of migration and its dichotomous modes of tradition versus modernity are explored, but by the film's conclusion we see the "newly-weds returning to England, as Indians [sic] as they ever were" (Mehta 2010: 1). What stood *DDLJ* apart from previous Bollywood films was that:

> it was openly vocal about Indian values and customs, in spite of the fact that the major protagonists lived their lives in England. Moreover, the NRI was not required to return to India and stay there – and that was the twist that made it for DDLJ – the NRI could remain NR and be the 'I,' that is, Indian.
>
> (*Mehta 2010: 2*)

The films of renowned Bollywood director Karan Johar (often abbreviated as KJo) most famously use foreign locations such as Scotland in *Kuch Kuch Hota Hai* [KKHH] (1998), England in *Kabhi Khushi Kabhie Gham* [K3G] (2000), and the US and Canada in *Kabhie Alvida Naa Kenha* [KANK] (2006). The incredible success of these films (each of them huge box office hits both at home and with the global diasporic audience) is because of their ability to build on the melodrama of 1970s Bollywood and to romanticise the values and attractions of India as the desired homeland.

The use of foreign landscapes and cityscapes is neatly encompassed in films such as *Delhi 6* (Mehra, 2009) with its portrayal of Roshan's (Abishek Bachchan) dual life as an American and an Indian returning home to Delhi. During the musical item "Dil Gira Dafatan" the action cuts between old Delhi and an imaginary New York bristling with Indian people and a mass confusion of Yellow Cabs and Indian rickshaws. For Rashmi Sawhney this allows the city (if, as seems apparent, Roshan is still in Delhi seeing as he has just walked from his bed through the gates of a nearby laneway) to mimic "the encounter between the first and third worlds, in ways that allow for revising and reframing the idea that modernity walks down a one-way street, from West to East" (2012: 396). Therefore, the audience accepts Roshan's dream-like merging of Delhi and New York as symbolic of India's transformation into modernity.

As "Dil Gira Dafatan" closes, director Mehra cleverly keeps up the ruse (India or the USA?) by cutting to what looks to be an iconic 1950s American convertible as it blows out a tyre. The car pulls onto the shoulder of the road against a desert-like landscape that could be anywhere in the mid-West of the USA. It is Roshan's car though, and as he climbs out and changes the tyre, quick glimpses of a woman in a saree, a roadside stall and the high-pitched tone of the horn of a passing truck quickly reassert that this is India. Again, the inference is one of a simple transference of the character from one geographic setting to another, albeit one marked by a series of cultural signifiers.

The allure of the romanticized West not only pertains to these Hindi-based Bollywood films but across many of India's regionally based cinemas. Anand Pandian writes of the 2007 Tamil film *Malaikottai* (B. Pandian) where Anbu (played by Vishal), a young man, infatuated with a girl, Malar (played by Priyamani), stands beneath her balcony, is splashed by droplets of water from Malar's sari being washed by her grandmother. As Pandian notes of the lead in to the song "Uyire Uyire", "Anbu closes his eyes as the droplets hit his face, and the film cuts to a wide-angle panning shot of verdant green slopes and snow-clad peaks" of Switzerland (Pandian provides a fascinating insight into the filming of these scenes), taking Anbu far from the arid, noisy streets of the South Indian town where the encounter takes place (2011: 50). Because this is the fantastical world of Indian cinema, the geographical shift to the Swiss Alps does not have to be written into the narrative as an element of realism, it just *is* – it becomes an example of the power of affect by providing "a totally foreign landscape of immersive expression" (2011: 51) in which Anbu, at that moment, is engulfed.

For India's filmmakers *Malaikottai*'s grand imagery is also available locally in the mountainous regions of India's north and the rolling hills of the south, a fact that is not lost on a government keen to gain political capital from highlighting the nation's own geographical attributes and the many filmmakers looking to be more frugal in their location spending. Pandian's case study exemplifies the "protracted discussions, negotiations, and unexpected deviations" that can all but subsume foreign film shoots, especially in the final weeks of a production shoot (2011: 60). Shooting closer to home can alleviate such difficulties as well as those encountered through difficulties with language, currency exchange and local regulations.

The return home

While India's filmmakers have long been aware of the cost benefits of shooting at home, these have become more apparent in the wake of the weakened rupee, diverting filmmakers from preoccupations with foreign vistas, to search for stories that require local content. *Chennai Express*, for instance is a film that dwells on South Indian difference, in terms of geography, climate and culture, in comparison to the "normality" of its urban-based Mumbai lead (SRK). For SRK's character, Rahul, who finds himself heading to Tamil Nadu instead of his intended Goa, a parochial loyalty to India remains central, but his sense of longing for 'home' remains with the now geographically distant Mumbai.

The urban expanse of Mumbai houses the major Bollywood studios giving them ready access to a range of locations that highlight the modern built environment of the city. Set in the high-end corporate advertising sector, Sidhir Mishra's 2013 sexual-harassment drama *Inkaar* was shot entirely in Mumbai, including extensive location shoots in the offices of global advertising companies. The imagery of the clean, sophisticated world of advertising executives reflects a global cosmopolitan view of India, and mirrors Bose's claim that the Indian metropole is constructed onscreen as both "a confrontational as well as contemplative space that signifies 'modernity' and its concurrent promise as well as ills in relation to the 'traditional' ethics of a very old culture" (2011: 45). *Inkaar*'s portrayal of the unbridled greed and questions around the place of women in corporate culture reflect how Mumbai is caught between a world of such "promise" and the "ills" that challenge the nation's ethical traditions.

Mumbai also features in Subhash Ghai's *Kaanchi: The Unbreakable* (2014) as a wealthy, cosmopolitan site for provincial thieves and conmen to move to once they have exploited and corrupted their home village. It is a place of danger and vice. Ghai is a renowned filmmaker perhaps best known for *Pardes* (1997), another SRK 'starrer' that explores the diasporic challenges faced by an American-born Indian. With *Kaanchi*, Ghai returns home to present a local story that shifts from rural India to Mumbai. As a geographical site Mumbai is significant in the rise of Indian cinema as "from its very beginnings Bombay has attracted labour, capital and enterprise and has embodied the diversity, anxiety and thrill of modern cosmopolitanism" (Sawhney 2012: 400). The Mumbai presented in *Kaanchi* contains panoramic views of the city's modern, twenty-first century skyline, its waterways and the striking contemporary architecture of its many bridges. Even when the eponymous Kaanchi (Indrani Chakraborty aka Mishti) recalls the brief time spent with her fiancé back home in Koshampa, before tragedy struck, her thoughts are interspersed with lingering images of the beauty found in the natural environment around her home village, before she returns to deep contemplation alongside Mumbai's waterfront.

These onscreen representations of Mumbai play a key role in India's on-going development where Bose sees "the cinematic text itself as a cultural, sociological and intellectual intervention in this process of the making, breaking and shifting of metropolitan identities in post-independence India" (2011: 45). By creating a firm link between the cinematic hero and their geographical position, filmmakers reinforce the complexities of the multi-state India. It is not just the cultural and linguistic differences that confront characters such as SRK's Rahul in *Chennai Express*, but the geographical changes encountered in the hills and lush tropicality of southern India.

The unexpected voyage in *Chennai Express* into India's natural rural environment contrasts considerably with the urban landscape that is symbolically important in constructing modernity, suggesting that an understanding of the "Euro-American idea of modernity" (Sawhney 2012: 397) is needed in order to better conceptualise the intersection of film and modernity. Chief amongst the factors in this conception of modernity was the quasi-geographical sense that

> The processing of knowledge was topographically linked to the clustering involved in the creation of modern cities and, in as much as cities were a result of industrialisation and urban migration, the modern rational individual was a creation of the city
>
> *(Sawhney 2012: 397)*

Thus, the portrayal of Mumbai, or indeed, the Mumbai-bred and educated protagonists, global-savvy and economically secure, played by enduring stars such as SRK or Amitabh Bachchan, becomes emblematic of India and its modernisation.

Rural and natural environments

Although *Kaanchi* features scenes of urban Mumbai, the first half of the film is focused on rural India through its location shots of the Himalayan foothills around the (fictitious) village of Koshampa. The title sequence features sweeping aerial views of lush green mountains. Ghai uses intense colour saturation to highlight the contrast between Mumbai and the utopian, verdant world of rural India. The air is clean and a villager fetches a glass of crystal-clear water from a stream, a pointed illustration of the natural beauty of the region. The early parts of the film reflect a return to India's roots, with only the bad guys using digital technologies and the villagers portrayed as honest rural dwellers, riding pushbikes and making small attempts to combat corruption. The landscape is an important feature, with the repeated use of multiple wideshots and aerial views, including sweeping shots circling an Indian flag mounted high upon a hill and song lyrics proclaiming "Everyone's tri-colour flag", and "Heaven on Earth, Koshampa".

It is not just the mountainous north that symbolises the benefits of India beyond Mumbai. One of India's box office hits of 2014 was *2 States* (Verman), a film that utilizes the new mobility within India where a university graduate can move quite effortlessly between states. Beginning in Ahmedabad in the state of Gujarat where he is studying for an MBA, Delhi boy Krish (Arjun Kapoor) meets southerner Ananya (Alia Bhatt), a native of Chennai in Tamil Nadu, and a romance ensues. After graduation, and some visible friction between the parents of the new couple, Krish and Ananya return to their hometowns. Their relationship continues across the two states, but unable to stay apart, a large part of the action takes place in the modern, urban Chennai where Krish works hard to integrate himself into his new family, highlighting regional cultural, linguistic and religious differences. With Ananya's family now onside, the couple returns to Delhi to convince Krish's parents. After a temporary truce, the families fall out again, and all looks doomed for the couple but, in true Bollywood style, it is ultimately love and a sense of national unity that brings them together again. The sense of ongoing transit also plays out in numerous airport scenes, an opportunity to showcase the technological sophistication of new public infrastructure throughout India. The final wedding scene takes place with sweeping panoramic shots of a stunning hillside temple, reiterating a return to the physical importance of India's cultural traditions.

Similar imagery is found in *Chennai Express* when Rahul (Shah Rukh Khan) carries Meena (Deepika Padukone) up some 300 steps to reach a temple as part of a village tradition to show his devotion to his (pretend) bride-to-be. The logistics of such location shooting, even on home soil, can be fraught with difficulties:

> The *Chennai Express* team had only limited access to the temple, and had to film additional scenes on a set in Mumbai. But the key scenes were able to be filmed at the site. Temple authorities explained, "Usually, permission is not given to conduct shooting in temples. The reason is that the movie crew litter the place where shooting is conducted. This hurts the sentiments of devotees. Devotees protest against conducting of shooting. Also, other temples in Tamil Nadu do not allow movie shootings."
>
> *(Dooley 2013)*

Other films take a more realist look at the landscape, especially those dealing with rural areas. For instance *Gulaab Gang* (Sen, 2014) is set in the (fictional) north central Indian village of Madhopur offering a glimpse of the harsh dusty landscape and the corruption and patriarchal abuse found in provincial India, far from the modern urban centres. Basic facilities like electricity and water supplies dominate the day-to-day realities of the people. The creation of a women's *ashram* (commune) across the lake from the village serves to highlight the spatial and social distance of women unable to accept the burdens imposed on them by some of the men (and women) who wield power in the village.

Gulaab Gang operates a narrative that is clearly familiar to Bollywood audiences. Anuradha Ghosh notes that since the 1970s, Bollywood's cinematic narratives were

> the subject of discourses that [were] charted through stories that deal with a plethora of genres like romance, action films, crime thrillers, film noir, war films, films with explicit sociopolitical overtones, religious cycles – all dealing either directly or obliquely with the dystopic-utopic bind in a symbolic portrayal of the predicament of the post-colonial nation.
>
> *(2012: 101–2)*

Of course this built on feelings that had existed from around the time of Independence in 1947 when the concept of Indian nationalism "often needed a Hindi versus the other(s) in terms of a cultural opposition of the national and the regional where the butts of ridicule were often south Indians" (2012: 107). In other words, geocultural divisions existed and were promoted *within* the nation, let alone beyond the nation. These divisions are clearly addressed in *Gulaab Gang* with its decidedly feminist overtones as the women struggle in the barren rural environment and seek retribution for the ills of their society.

There is also a more pragmatic reason for shooting beyond the studio-based sound stage, and this has been enabled with the increasing portability of the technologies for producing a film: the cameras, lighting rigs and sound recording facilities. The move toward a more authentic realism also fed into the move out of the studio, and the use of landscape and location shooting began in the midst of a

> decline of integrated studio shooting in Chennai in the 1970s, [when] Tamil filmmakers broached two everyday environments as filmmaking bases: the urban middle-class households and neighborhoods of Chennai, and the rural villages and landscapes of the western and southern Tamil countryside.
>
> *(Pandian 2011: 54)*

The use of local settings proved successful, and what followed was that "many contemporary Tamil filmmakers made their reputations by depicting on-screen their own native neighbourhoods and villages, showing their own social classes, castes, and local communities and their own spatial trajectories from countryside to metropole" (Pandian 2011: 58).

The use of location shooting opened up the on-screen image from the closed studio approximations of 'reality' where "[a]s marked spaces of fantasy, imagination, and desire, song sequences have especially come to express the more dispersed horizons of emergent middle-class aspirations" (Pandian 2011: 58). As India's middle-class grows, their economic rise is coupled with increases in leisure time and the mobility to travel beyond their home city, and for many, this affords the opportunity to see places that have previously only been viewed onscreen.

Film tourism

The cine-geographic images that promote tourism are a valuable by-product of the cinema industry. A national push to increase tourism includes a clear recognition of the benefits of film tourism, with India's Minister of Tourism keen to pursue a national approach by writing to all of India's state and Union Territories to urge them to "recognise the potential of film tourism and constitute special bodies/cells to facilitate filming in their States/UTs" (*The Hindu* 2013a). Films offer the audience a travel experience that may be beyond their economic or physical means, instead offering a sense of performativity mimetic of "the multi-sensual practices and experiences of everyday life that includes both representational and the non-representational" (Diekmann and Hannam 2012: 1318). In the cine-geographic landscapes of new Bollywood cinema the emphasis is on the visual landscapes and nostalgic reimaginings found across the nation's vast array of locations, all as possible tourist destinations.

Tourism is often seen as an activity based upon the desire to capture "various hedonistic bodily experiences, from sunbathing to dancing and drinking" (Diekmann and Hannam 2012: 1318), factors often found in foreign-based films. These experiences are exemplified in films such as *Salaam Namaste* (Anand, 2005), filmed exclusively in Australia, and *Blue* (D'souza, 2009), the film noted as the most expensive Bollywood film ever produced (as of 2009) because of its extensive location shoot in the Bahamas. Increasingly this hedonistic behaviour can be found in films that utilise India's own tourist playgrounds, most notably that of Goa. Since 2008 a number of films have made use of Goa's tropical beaches, seascapes and holiday atmosphere, including the two sequels in Rohit Shetty's 'Golmaal' films – *Golmaal Returns* (2008) and *Golmaal 3* (2010) and his 2011 action drama *Singham* [*Lion*], Rohan Sippy's *Dum Maaro Dum* (2011), Vivek Sharma's ghost comedy *Bhoothnath* (2008), starring both Amitabh Bachchan and SRK, Sanjay Leela Bhansali's controversial *Guzaarish* (2010, starring Hrithik Roshan and Aishwarya Rai) and even the Tamil blockbuster of 2010, *Enthiran* (*The Robot*) that teamed Tamil superstar Rajinikanth with Bollywood's Aishwarya Rai. As noted, in *Chennai Express* Goa is spoken of as an extremely desirable destination, a playground for drinking and partying. However, because Rahul does not make it to Goa, his long train ride to the south allows for grand sweeping views of rural landscapes, dramatic waterfalls, quaint railway stations and majestic rivers as the train traverses the nation.

Director Mani Ratnam also called upon rural locations in the south-western state of Kerala when filming *Dil Se* (1998, starring SRK). The use of such locations is supported by national and local state governments. Nationally, this fits with the broader remit of the Ministry of Tourism to develop 'rural tourism' by capitalising on "the growing interest in heritage and culture and improved accessibility, and environmental consciousness" across India (Ministry of Tourism 2014a). The benefits arising from increased tourism are seen as a positive for "the local community economically and socially as well as enabling interaction between the tourists and the locals for a more enriching tourism experience" (Ministry of Tourism 2014b). At the state level, Kerala Tourism pro-actively seeks filmmakers to utilise its locations, making the bold claim on its website "More art per shot" (Kerala Tourism 2013). A number of films have used Kerala as a shooting destination, including Ratnam's *Dil Se* and *Bombay* (1995), Ram Gopal Varma's *Nishabdh* (2007) and even Paul Mayeda Berges and Gurinda Chadha's US-produced *The Mistress of Spices* (2005). These films have drawn upon Kerala's "beaches and backwaters, hill stations and forests" (Kerala Tourism 2013) to provide a geographical setting that is recognisably Indian.

In an international context, David Martin-Jones (2006) once pointed out the benefits to the Scottish economy by having Bollywood films utilising Scottish locations. For Martin-Jones there were three main benefits: the location spend; box office from both diasporic Indians and other locals keen to see their home on the screen; and ongoing tourism from fans. It is the first of these that is most pertinent here, the fact that many thousands of dollars (he quotes an estimated figure of £85,000 spent just on the Scottish portion of the shoot for *Kuch Kuch Hota Hai*) can remain in India in the provision of local crews, catering, accommodation and transport, rather than being outsourced to a foreign location. Martin-Jones contends that recognisable foreign locations provide "geographical specificity" (2006: 54) for audiences that may be well aware of foreign (iconic) settings through their earlier viewing of Western films. The arrival of Bollywood stars in these sites "reaffirms" both the global mobility of the Indian people, and the "impression of attainability" of reaching the desired destination (Martin-Jones 2006: 54). At a local level, India's state attempts to capitalize on film tourism are designed to complement its global 'Incredible India' campaign "through the medium of cinema, [and to] develop synergy between [the] tourism and film industry and provide a platform for enabling partnerships between the Indian and global film industry" (*The Hindu* 2013b).

Conclusion

Will this mean the end of Bollywood's extravagant overseas explorations? It is doubtful. India's rise as a global power and its continued integration into world communities through migration (temporary and permanent), will see the continuation of complex relationships brought to the screen. The tensions of cultural difference provide strong fodder for scriptwriters as their protagonists struggle between the values and customs of "home" and the invasion of foreign behaviours. However, it is the politically expedient visions of home on the big screen that reinforce the cine-geographies and provide a sense of ontological security, a strong, heartfelt grip on the sense of Indianness that permeates its films and film industries.

Across Asia, global deals are being struck that provide production and distribution deals for the cinemas of the region. Trans-Asian cooperation is increasing, with actors, directors and studios all keen to work together. Strange bedfellows exist in the cooperation of China with Japan, Singapore with Hong Kong, or even India with Pakistan. The rise of co-production tax and investment incentives with Hollywood, the UK and countries such as France and Australia will continue to tempt filmmakers to look beyond their borders for new sites, new locations and new possibilities for their stories to play out on cinema screens across the globe. The cine-geographies that will emerge allow for texts that fulfil the geopolitical project of illuminating foreign audiences and showcasing the splendour (or otherwise) of each individual nation.

Bibliography

ASSOCHAM (Associated Chambers of Commerce and Industry of India) (2013) "Weak Rupee Dampen Spirits of Bollywood Film-makers in Foreign Location", *ASSOCHAM*, http://www.assocham.org/prels/shownews-archive.php?id=4156 [accessed on 13 June 2014].

Bose, B. (2011) "Cities, Sexualities and Modernities: A Reading of Indian Cinema", *Thesis Eleven* 105:1, pp. 44–52.

Chakravarty, S. S. (2000) "Fragmenting the Nation: Images of Terrorism in Indian Popular Cinema" in Hjort, M. and MacKenzie, S. (eds) *Cinema and Nation*, London: Routledge, pp. 222–237.

Deccan Herald (2013) "Weak Rupee Scuttles Bollywood's Shooting in Alien Lands", *Deccan Herald*, 2 September, http://www.deccanherald.com/content/354817/weak-rupee-scuttles-bollywood039s-shooting.html [accessed on 17 July 2014].

Diekmann, A. and Hannam, K. (2012) "Touristic Mobilities in India's Slum Spaces", *Annals of Tourism Research* 39:3, pp. 1315–1336.

Dooley, L. L. (2013) "Filming India: Chennai Express 'Temple Scene' at Vattamalai Murugan Temple, Tamil Nadu", *Falling in Love with Bollywood*, 23 October, http://dooleyonline.typepad.com/bollywood/2013/10/filming-india-chennai-express-the-temple-scene-vattamalai-murugan-temple-tamil-nadu.html#sthash.lVQbsPBN.dpuf [accessed on 22 July 2014].

Eshun, K. and Gray, R. (2011) "The Militant Image: A Cine-Geography", *Third Text* 25:1, pp. 1–12.

Ghosh, A. (2012) "Bollywood, Tollywood, Dollywood: Re-visiting Cross-border Flows and the Beat of the 1970s in the Context of Globalisation" in Roy, A. G. and Huat, C. B. (eds) *Travels of Bollywood Cinema: From Bombay to LA*, London: Oxford University Press, pp. 98–119.

Hassam, A. (2012) "'It Was Filmed in My Home Town': Diasporic Audiences and Foreign Locations in Indian Popular Cinema" in Roy, A. G. and Huat, C. B. (eds) *Travels of Bollywood Cinema: From Bombay to LA*, London: Oxford University Press, pp. 260–278.

Kerala Tourism (2013) "Shooting Locations", *Keralatourism.org*, https://www.keralatourism.org/shooting locations [accessed on 14 May 2014].

Martin-Jones, D. (2006) "Kabhi India Kabhie Scotland: Recent Indian Films Shot on Location in Scotland", *South Asian Popular Culture* 4:1, pp. 49–60.

Mehta, R. B. (2010) "Bollywood, Nation, Globalization: An Incomplete Introduction" in Mehta, R. B. and Pandharipande, R. V. (eds) *Bollywood and Globalization: Indian Popular Cinema, Nation, and Diaspora*, London: Anthem Press, pp. 1–14.

Ministry of Tourism (2014a) "Scheme of Rural Tourism", *Government of India*, http://www.tourism.gov.in/TourismDivision/AboutScheme.aspx?Name=Tourism InfrastructureDevelopment&CID=66&INO=5 [accessed on 14 May 2014].
Ministry of Tourism (2014b) "Film Tourism", *Government of India*, Available at: http://www.tourism.gov.in/writereaddata/CMSPagePicture/file/Press Release/film tourism.pdf [accessed on 14 May 2014].
Pandian, A. (2011) "Landscapes of Expression: Affective Encounters in South Indian Cinema", *Cinema Journal* 51: 1, pp. 50–74.
Paranjape, M. (2012) "Cultural Flows, Travelling Shows" in Roy, A. G. and Huat, C. B. (eds) *Travels of Bollywood Cinema: From Bombay to LA*, London: Oxford University Press, pp. 19–34.
Ramnath, N. (2007) "Production – International Locations – The Travel Bug", *Screen Daily*, 23 February, http://www.screendaily.com/production-international-locations-the-travel-bug/4031181.article [accessed on 4 May 2014].
Sawhney, R. (2012) "The Virtual Reality of Indian Cinema: Spectatorship as Enactment of 'Becoming Modern", *Interventions: International Journal of Postcolonial Studies* 14: 3, pp. 395–409.
Shah, G. R. (2012) "The Man Who Sparked Bollywood's Love of Foreign Locales", *The New York Times*. 23 October, http://india.blogs.nytimes.com/2012/10/23/the-man-who-sparked-bollywoods-love-of-exotic-locales/?_php=true&_type=blogs&_r=0 [accessed on 31 March 2014].
Singh, R. and Vohra, M. (2013) "Will B'wood Ditch Foreign Destinations?" *Times of India*, 4 September, http://timesofindia.indiatimes.com/entertainment/hindi/bollywood/news-interviews/Will-Bwood-ditch-foreign-destinations/articleshow/22281203.cms [accessed on 16 April 2014].
The Hindu (2013a) "Film Tourism to Be Promoted as Niche Product: Chiranjeeri", *The Hindu*, 31 January.
The Hindu (2013b) "Film Tourism", *The Hindu*, 30 June.

33

POLITICAL CINEMA IN LATIN AMERICA

From nation-building to cultural translation

Armida de la Garza

Historically, film and politics in Latin America have been closely related. Indeed, "for the modernist tradition, the cinema was the art form and mass medium specific to the twentieth century that could provide the formal frame within which key issues of radical aesthetics could find expression" (Mulvey 2003: 263), and as Laura Mulvey notes this was especially so in Latin America. It has been widely held, however, that under the 'postmodern condition' of the twenty-first century, utopian ideas of social progress were abandoned, and the belief in the transformative power of art and the media in general, and cinema and particular, was put into question. A number of insightful and sophisticated theories seeking to reconceptualize politics in altogether less grand, more provisional terms have been put forward. One of these has been to recast the political as the means whereby individuals cope with the anomie, precariousness and atomization of postmodernity, from social into personal terms (Bauman 2007; Berlant 2011). Even those who see the 'new', digital media as delivering utopias of activism and participation cast these in terms of individuals or life-style communities, rather than in terms of citizenship. Another way is to conceive of the political as a way of finding the means to disrupt the fit whereby each one of us is "socially plugged" into the system by culture, a capacity to create "a dissociation between the work of the arms and the activity of the gaze [… a disruption of] the way in which bodies fit their functions and destinations" (Rancière 2009: 70–72). But these subversive acts are temporary only.

In the paragraphs that follow, I first provide a brief overview of the relation between cinema and politics in Latin America during the twentieth century, before contesting the view that the postmodern has meant abandonment of aspirations to social justice in the region, or indeed a decline of the nation-state as widely held. I will then look at the role of indigenous peoples on film and argue that cinema, in its digital and transnational incarnation, continues to play an important role in redefining multicultural national identities.

Cinema and politics: nation-building and the public sphere

It could be argued that cinema was used politically in Latin America from its inception. During the twentieth century, cinema became a privileged site where the political goals of the leaders that started the wars for independence in the subcontinent a century earlier eventually took shape and were, to variable extents, achieved (de la Garza 2012). These goals included the overturning of hierarchies of European domination; broadening citizenship so as to include mestizos, indigenous and black people, and, later in the century, women; and last, to unify what had been the Spanish empire into a single Latin American nation, *la patria grande*. There were various ways in which cinema was central here. First, building on Benedict Anderson's arguments on the role of the printed media bringing about national public spheres (Anderson 1991), it has been argued that cinema helped broaden citizenship by quickly becoming a leisure activity that cut across class and gender cleavages, as it was affordable, did not require literacy, and it was considered a 'respectable' public place for women – especially if compared to its predecessors, theatre and vaudeville (Hansen 2002). Although this account of cinema was initially developed in relation to the United States and Western Europe, research on Latin America has found this was the case there too (see, for instance, Noble 2005). Second, from the 1930s, Hollywood genres were frequently adapted, transformed to suit local tastes or used as forms for local content, as Latin American literature and history were the inspiration of early historical films, including foundational national narratives and adaptations (Hart 2004: 5). See for instance *La Guerra Gaucha* (Demare, 1942, Argentina), *La Virgen que forjó una patria* (Bracho, 1942, Mexico) and *Macunaíma* (de Andrade, 1969, Brazil) among others. These narratives sometimes put forward representations of a national 'we' that included indigenous and black people, albeit within a framework of assimilation rather than multiculturalism. While initially derided as derivative, inauthentic and poor copies of the 'original' Hollywood genres, more recent criticism (Shaw and Dennison 2007; García and Maciel 2001) that places value on both hybridity and popular culture has acknowledged their progressive potential, exerting agency even if the narratives themselves were sometimes conservative.

Throughout the century, documentary filmmaking contributed to the desired overturning of hierarchies of domination. In Mexico, from the early 1900s, the Alva brothers, Jesús H. Abitia, and Salvador Toscano, among others, started recording the military battles of the Mexican revolution. In the 1960s and 1970s, Fernando Solanas and Octavio Getino's *La Hora de los Hornos* (1968) in Argentina, and in Chile, Patricio Guzmán's *La Batalla de Chile* (1972) were instrumental in the struggle against Latin American dictatorships, and foundational of the Third Cinema movement. Last, cinema also provided the grounds for an imagined Latin American community. A large part of what is labelled 'Mexican' cinema – the most prolific in the region at the time – often included actors, crews, music and plots from Cuba and Argentina, and the films from Mexico and Argentina also often circulated across the subcontinent and indeed, even among the Latin American diasporas in the United States, a fact that has allowed Marvin D'Lugo to trace "the beginnings of an aural bonding of a Hispanic transnational community" in the tango film and the *comedia ranchera* during the first half of the twentieth century (D'Lugo 2010: 163). Latin American art cinema – such as the 'imperfect cinema' movement in Cuba, and Cinema nôvo in Brazil – was also political in that it aimed to raise consciousness in viewers, and ultimately, to achieve social justice. In Latin America in the 1960s, "belief in the cinema merge[d] with belief in radical political change [...] so, a commitment to social transformation [...] and a commitment to the cinema's place in enabling that transformation [...] work[ed] together" (Mulvey 2003: 263).

The 'multiplex': privatization and commodification

As for the role that cinema has played in the politics of the subcontinent in twenty-first century, this remains contested. One account maintains this role changed with the rise of neoliberal economic policies, the onset of postmodernity and the "death of metanarratives" (Lyotard, 1984), including the narrative of social progress. With the retreat of the state from all sectors of the economy, not least from the film industries of Mexico, Brazil and Argentina, and the large-scale privatization that followed, these industries declined in the 1980s and 1990s. The lowest point was reached in 1992 and 1993 when only 11 films were made in Mexico, and 10 in Argentina (Falicov 2007: 81). Moreover, this was initially viewed as the end of the Latin American national cinemas proper, with most critics seeing the scant production as almost exclusively devoted to commercial, light comedies (for instance, Alfonso Cuarón's Opera Prima, *Sólo con tu Pareja* (1991) and Antonio Serrano's *Sexo, Pudor y Lágrmas/ Sex, Shame and Tears* (1999)) narrowly appealing to the middle classes – the main audience of the then new, and expensive, multiplex cinemas – or soft porn. The larger, properly 'national' or mass audiences for cinema became fragmented.

Other accounts, however, contest this narrative, and see political engagement in recent Latin American cinema, despite its 'commercial' label. Laura Podalsky's reading of recent Cuban, Mexican, Brazilian and Argentine cinema as political, grounded on a Deleuzan understanding of affect in which the films are valued for their capacity to elicit "qualities of experience" and to "help name, codify or channel lived intensities" (2011: 12–13), holds that genre and other types of middle brow cultural production can "encourage an embodied recognition of loss" or "invite spectators to feel as a means of questioning their knowledge of recent history" (2011: 20). *Madagascar* (Pérez, 1993), *Amores Perros/Love's a Bitch* (González Iñárritu, 2000) and *O Que É Isso, Companheiro/Four Days in September* (Barreto, 1997) are some of the films from Cuba, Mexico and Brazil, respectively, that she analyses through this framework. Luisela Alvaray and Joana Page too maintain that some of the Latin American cinema that is derided as commercial and apolitical, notably genres such as horror, have in fact become ways of engaging deeply traumatic history, for instance, the legacy of dictatorship in Argentina (Alvaray 2013), and also an equally traumatic recent past, as regards the economic crisis (1999–2002) (Page 2009). Primary instances here are *El túnel de los huesos/ Tunnel of Bones* (Garassino, 2011) and *Nueve Reinas/Nine Queens* (Bielinski, 2000).

I would like to argue, however, that although some contemporary Latin American cinema is certainly apolitical, and although there is a case that the political can now be cast in terms of the personal or reimagined within the narrow terms of the commodified as described above, there is also a strand of Latin American cinema that remains political in the former utopian sense, namely concerned with broad social transformation, dealing with issues of citizenship and the nation-state. Here I will refer to the cinema that is about or made by Latin American indigenous people, a field of film production, and film studies, that has been growing increasingly. To this end, I shall draw from theorists such as Walter Mignolo (2010) and Arturo Escobar (2004), who contest the view of the present as apolitical, to focus instead on the many counter-hegemonic movements that have emerged in opposition to globalization, movements in which indigenous peoples, and importantly their cinema, have been crucial. In a sharp contrast to the influential account of modernity as the progressive diffusion of European enlightenment famously espoused by Anthony Giddens and others, with its processes of urbanization and industrialization that flow from Europe to the rest of the world, Mignolo and Escobar see it rather as constitutive of colonialism. Not only because the European 'progress' in this narrative could not have taken place without the control, domination and exploitation of the Americas, starting with the Spanish and Portuguese conquest in the sixteenth century and disguised in the language of salvation, but also because indigenous people became the Other, savage, uncivilized and objectified, against which Europeans could emerge as the subjects of history. They also contest whether this 'stage' has ended at all, arguing instead for its continuation in the neoliberalist policies adopted today by most states. I further follow Robert Stam, Richard Porton and Leo Goldsmith's contention that:

> Against the grain of the assumption that political modernism is the only path to subversive aesthetics, we argue that the old and the archaic can be mobilized in favour of the new and the radical [...] Alternative aesthetics deeply rooted in millennial traditions, such as oral epic, Menippean satire, and carnivalesque inversion [...] bear perennial relevance; they remain always already available for renewal
>
> (*Stam* et al. *2015: forthcoming)*

This is indeed the case with indigenous cinema in the subcontinent. It is inherently political, I would argue, first, in that the national identities of the Latin American states were from the start constituted in relation to the 'Indian', whether "as the enemy to be massacred and displaced, or as the recuperated symbol of national difference from Europe" (Stam *et al.* 2015: forthcoming). The status of indigenous peoples vis-à-vis the nation-state on its own presents an ongoing political challenge. Second, while the dispossession and injustice that indigenous peoples suffer is not only social and economic, but also epistemological, since imperialism has led to the disparaging of alternative knowledges (Santos 2005), contemporary communication technologies, including digital cinema, have enabled indigenous worldviews and knowledge to be put forward and circulated, facilitating resistance. These worldviews are centred on community and participation, especially shared forms of ownership of land and resources that go beyond the concept of property. Land and resources are instead viewed as organically related to the community, perennial and sacred. Indigenous societies are based on intergenerational commitment, and stand in sharp contrast to the advanced warfare, urban congestion and environmental degradation that have come with modernization. Being able to express and circulate these worldviews through the many options afforded by digital cinema makes it a possibility not only that alternative modernizations may emerge, but in fact that "alternatives to modernization" (Escobar 2004) might become viable.

Importantly, both Escobar and Boaventura de Sousa Santos have acknowledged the need for translation processes that make cross-cultural understanding possible. Here the potential of cinema is obviously paramount. In a similar vein, Mignolo speaks of contact zones where "Western knowledge and subjectivity, control of land and labor, of authority, and ways of living [...] have been 'contacting' other languages, memories, principles of knowledge and belief, forms of government and economic organization since 1500" (Mignolo 2010: 351). It is in these contact zones, he argues, that the epistemic colonization, that is, the violent suppression of alternative forms of knowledge that has been taking place can be subverted. Cinema can be conceptualized as such a contact zone as well, and therefore becomes a significant locus for acts of subversion as I will demonstrate in the following sections.

The transnational: repoliticizing Latin American cinema

Here I shall take the metaphor of translation further, to discuss the ways in which two transnational films from Latin America, *Eréndira Ikikunari* (Mora, 2006) and *También la Lluvia/ Even the Rain* (Bollaín, 2010),[1] translate, as it were, indigenous worldviews to non-indigenous audiences.

Translation is about engagement with the Other, and issues of power are at stake.[2] It is never simply a hermeneutic task, about rendering the foreign intelligible. For as Mona Baker has pointed out, although often overlooked, there is agency in the translator (Baker 2006).

Choices are made as to the lexicon, grammatical structures, and particularly framing strategies, that render a translation 'fluent', that is, that create the illusion of transparency. And

> [...] most publishers, reviewers and readers regard a translation as acceptable when the absence of any linguistic or stylistic peculiarities makes it seem transparent, giving the appearance that it reflects the foreign writer's personality or intention or the essential meaning of the foreign text – the appearance, in other words, that the translation is not in fact a translation, but the 'original'.
>
> *(Venuti [1995] 2008: 1)*

However, this kind of translation actually both performs and hides "an ethnocentric reduction of the foreign text to target-language cultural values" (Venuti [1995] 2008: 20) leaving, so to speak, the reader 'in peace', while moving the author towards her. This is why Lawrence Venuti has called this strategy 'domestication' of the source text, pointing out that its widespread use in translations to English has engendered parochialism, as all cultures are made to sound like contemporary fluent English. He has proposed instead a strategy of 'foreignization' in which the translation registers difference, as a strategy of resistance (Venuti [1995] 2008: 305–6). Some of the strategies that have been advocated to jar the reader with a heterogeneous discourse include adhering as closely as possible to the source text structure and syntax, the use of calques, the use of archaic structures and even of British English when translating for American audiences. When foreignizing a translation, the translator leaves the writer in peace, moving the reader towards the writer, thus 'sending the reader abroad' (Robinson 1997: 1).

Extending the concepts of foreignization and domestication to the analysis of films on or by indigenous people as cultural translations, I use them here to analyse *Eréndira Ikikunari* and *Even the Rain* as these films are clear instances of each strategy, which many others inevitably follow. I argue with Venuti for foreignization as the more ethical choice and the one that further advances the film's political agenda.

Eréndira Ikikunari

Indigenous peoples have featured frequently in the national productions of Latin America (Franco 1993), but as mentioned above, this was mostly in narratives of assimilation that upheld the nation-state. In the 1990s, however, a revisionist project started that aimed to put forward an indigenous point of view, or "an attempt at the rewriting of history" (Haddu 2007: 157). Salvador Carrasco's *La Otra Conquista/The Other Conquest* (1998) is seminal in this respect. It tells the story of the conquest in what may be called a bilingual and bicultural way, presenting, for every alleged Indian 'atrocity', such as human sacrifice, the many Spanish-perpetrated massacres,[3] and pointing to the way an equivalence was historically forged between the Aztec goddess Tonantzin (our mother) and the Virgin Mary that eventually led to the syncretism that facilitated the conquest, and later the formation of the nation-state in what is Mexico today. Further, the film highlights the role of the visual image in the process of documenting alternative versions of the conquest, as its protagonist, a scribe called Topilzin, is frequently shown recording scenes of the battles and destruction by means of painting (Figure 33.1).

For all its merits, however, the film is still told through a Western aesthetic, realism, frequently drawing from the Bible for dialogues, even if spoken in Náhuatl, and casting Topilzin in a role of self-sacrifice similar to that of Jesus Christ. For instance, when contemplating the scale of the destruction Topilzin is recording on the Codex he is working on, it is "My God, my God, why have you forsaken us?" that he cries.

Figure 33.1 Battles and destruction are recorded through painting in *La Otra Conquista*.

The Western perspective is also frequently conveyed visually through the mise-en-scène. For instance, when Topilzin is first introduced to Cortés, the scene, shot with the camera taking the point of view of a statue of the Virgin Mary (Figure 33.2), resembles a game of chess, with the white King (Cortés) and the white Knight (his Lieutenant) clearly placed on the board, while the role of the Queen is ambiguously taken by Marina/Malinzin, the indigenous princess who used to be accused for siding with the Spaniards, even though she has recently been portrayed as more of a victim (Cypress 1991). The film nonetheless redeems her as she seeks to save Topilzin's life by convincing Cortés that he is not a pawn in the struggle, but a son of the late Emperor, Moctezuma. Notably, as a fluent speaker of both Náhuatl and Spanish, Malinzin is herself most valuable to all characters as a translator, and she frequently uses this role to further the indigenous cause.

While the film's intervention bringing alternative versions of the 'discovery' of the Americas is thus welcome, as is its suggestion that the contact zone had an impact both ways, it ends up being less heteroglossic than it might have seemed. From Venuti's point of view, *La Otra Conquista* has more of a domesticating role in both its form and content, focusing as it does on the central role of religion, both among indigenous peoples and Spain in the sixteenth century, and in much of Latin America up to this day.

On the other hand, Juan Mora's *Eréndira Ikikunari* does take a step forward. It is based on an Indigenous (Purépecha) legend, of a young girl who, in the words of the director, "became an icon of bravery during the destruction of her world by the Spanish conquistadors when she captured and learned to ride one of the Spaniards' horses, which must have seemed as terrifying creatures to the natives" (Mora, quoted in Caballero 2007). Eréndira thus became a symbol of resistance, female agency, and the preservation of indigenous cultures. Indigenous actors were cast, often acting for the first time, and although the film is nominally bilingual, Spanish characters have minimal dialogues, so that it is nearly all in what seems to most viewers a foreign language. Without being didactic, the film gives equal attention to conveying what is known today about indigenous ways of governance and social organization, the plot of Eréndira's preparation for her achievement, and the eventual defeat of her people.

Figure 33.2 A Western perspective privileging mise-en-scène in *La Otra Conquista.*

It highlights internal divisions amongst the indigenous cultures, and sometimes even within the same culture, as a major reason why the Conquest became possible.

Significantly, in a major departure from the films made during the twentieth Century, realism has been rejected in favour of a more surrealistic rendition of the story. One of the strategies to aesthetically put forward an indigenous point of view was to have the Spanish characters wear masks for the first part of the film (Figure 33.3), until one of them is killed and bleeds. At that point, the Indians realize that the Spaniards are human rather than gods, and the actor's face is shown for the first time. From then on, masks disappear and Spanish actors' faces become visible.

The masks that were chosen for these scenes are used in indigenous traditional dances from the region (Figure 33.3). And in a further attempt to draw from indigenous practices of visual representation, various scenes are introduced via juxtaposition with an animated version of the painted Codex of the legend that guided the mise-en-scène, the animation then

Figure 33.3 The indigenous perspective is served through the use of masks in *Eréndira Ikikunari.*

Figure 33.4 The Codex becomes the source of the story in *Eréndira Ikikunari*.

gradually fading and giving way to actors (Figure 33.4). At other times, actors and settings fully interact with the Codex animations, as when Eréndira remembers there was once a brave woman warrior that she seeks to emulate. This gives the film a very haptic feeling. This is important because in some accounts on the origins of cinema, film is understood as inherently imperialistic in that it continues the efforts to represent a three-dimensional space on a bi-dimensional surface from the point of view of the individual subject of the Renaissance, a highly ideological project that sought to make of human vision the rule of representation (Aumont 1992). Counter to this approach is haptic visuality, an approach to pictorial representation typical of non-Western cultures who "prefer to process representations as if they were independent objects that exist out there, all by themselves, regardless of any producing or receiving agency" (Dalle Vacche 2003: 5), outside of the perspectival regime of the West. To Laura U. Marks, haptic cinema "tends to move over the surface of its object rather than to plunge into illusionistic depth, not to distinguish form so much as to discern texture" and can be described "like an act of touching through visual perception" (Marks 2000: 162). Thus *Eréndira*'s haptic aesthetics eschew a Western tradition of representation that has been regarded as imperialistic in nature, in that it seeks mastery over the depicted world, firmly aligning it with the tradition of the indigenous culture it seeks to represent.

Unlike *La Otra Conquista*, which also quotes images from Codex by first presenting shots of the 'reality' being painted by Topilzin (see Figure 33.1), then showing how he is capturing this in his paintings, *Eréndira* proceeds the other way round. The Codex, massive and occupying half the screen, is the source, it is its story that we see unfolding (Figure 33.4). And unlike the chessboard of *La Otra Conquista*, *Eréndira* begins the story quoting the square or quadrilineal universe, which indigenous people from these regions believed in (Figure 33.4), where cardinal directions were represented by a deity and her/his corresponding colour and number as cosmological cycle. These most effective foreignization strategies powerfully succeed in representing an indigenous worldview based on community and with a close relationship with nature in which women had agency, potentially encouraging activism.[4] And as Mora puts it, it was digital cinema that allowed him to shoot such a poetic, visually hunting epic with a budget of merely 14 million MXN (around £658,900).

También la Lluvia/Even the Rain

También la Lluvia/Even the Rain is perhaps the quintessential transnational film, a Mexico–Spain–France co-production, starring Gael García Bernal and Luis Tosar, written by Paul

Laverty. It tells the story of a group of Spanish actors and crew, who are making a film on the 'discovery' of the Americas in Bolivia – the city of Cochabamba standing for the Hispaniola, the Caribbean island on the territory of present day Haiti and Dominican Republic, where Columbus first encountered indigenous American people – when the fighting started that led to the nationalization of water and eventually to the rise of Evo Morales to the presidency of that country, a movement now called 'the Water Wars', in 2000. In this way, the film is able to set parallels between the European colonization of the land in the 1500s, driven by a search for gold, and the contemporary attempts at colonization by transnational corporations, driven by a search to control natural resources such as oil and water.

Prior to being co-opted by advertising, reflexivity in film was long held to be inherently progressive. Calling attention to the fiction's mode of construction, and to its status as fiction, were regarded as tools that would enable Brechtian distanciation and the awakening of conscience, facilitating engagement, in-depth understanding of the mechanisms of social oppression, and critique. The film-within-the-film device has often played this role, rendering the apparent transparency and immediacy of its visual representations a problematic construct. By their very nature these films focus on performance, since their plots rely on problems or situations actors face or encounter. In *También la Lluvia/Even the Rain* the film that the actors are working on carefully documents the many injustices suffered by the indigenous peoples at the hands of the conquistadors, including enslavement, torture and genocide, as well as the (often timid) efforts of a divided Catholic Church at playing the role of a moral compass. The film on their tribulations making the film tells the story of the present-day injustices the indigenous peoples continue to suffer at the hands of the present-day conquistadors, with the filmmakers themselves seemingly taking over the role claimed for the Church before. Introducing a further layer of reflexivity, some scenes present an assistant camera woman recording interviews and general footage for what will be 'the making of' the film, all of these in black and white, in contrast to the previous two stories, which are in colour, thus drawing a further equivalence between them. Dialogues often quote original texts from the letters Columbus and other conquistadors sent the Queen and King of Spain, speeches given by the Fathers of the Church and the missionaries who defended the Indians, highlighting their high moral ground as precursors of the doctrine of human rights, and arguments made by the present-day high-priests of neoliberalism, here the Washington-supported Bolivian president at the time, Hugo Banzer (and later Gonzalo Sánchez de Lozada). In a Socratic fashion, the viewer sees the debate unfolding as positions for and against the privatization of water are played out between government representatives and the film actors and crew. But the story takes a turn from the social to the personal as the Indian main actor, Daniel, becomes involved leading the demonstrations against the privatization of water, getting beaten and even sent to prison, endangering the completion of the film. The plot thus advances through narrating director and producer's efforts to ensure Daniel's participation, and this brings about character change, as Costa, the producer, moves from his initial cynicism to ethical responsibility and care.

The film's focus on the plight of the indigenous peoples of Latin America, on long-standing injustice and on the specific present-day threat posed to the whole of humanity by the scarcity of resources such as water, along with the present-day incarnation of exploitation as transnational capital, certainly resonates with the aims and objectives of the counter-hegemonic movements regarded by Mignolo, Escobar and others as the real sources of radicalism today. From this point of view, it certainly is a prime example of the kind of committed filmmaking intending to raise awareness and possibly elicit action. However, as the plot unfolds, the film continuously undermines its own progressive agenda.

From the beginning, the establishing shot of a Bolivian shantytown where would-be extras are queuing waiting for casting is seen from the perspective of the Spanish actors arriving in a van. This European perspective is maintained throughout, as the film ends up telling the story of *their* awakening, and as they increasingly become protagonists, when the film turns from the social concerns of demonstrations and police violence to the personal realm of Daniel and his daughter, whom the Spanish producer saves from death. The very choice of a young daughter for the indigenous character already renders him vulnerable. Had he had a teenage son instead of a young daughter, the need of the European hero to come to the rescue would not have seemed as pressing. Thus, in *También la Lluvia/Even the Rain* the indigenous people, who were in fact the protagonists of the water wars and won this struggle – although we never get to see them victorious on the screen – are turned into secondary characters, again objects and not subjects of history, made into eternal victims and in need of the aid and protection of the West, in the past as well as the present.

También la Lluvia/Even the Rain also fails to take advantage of the epistemological potential of performance. "From the Platonic point of view, the stage, which is simultaneously a locus of public activity and the exhibition-space for 'fantasies', disturbs the clear partition of identities, activities and spaces" (Rancière 2004: 13). Not so for the Spanish actors, who seem condemned to repeating the roles of their ancestors, as do the Indians. The constructed nature of power, and the ability of indigenous and marginalized knowledge to question and challenge it, is not highlighted. Crucially, the film also misses the opportunity to become a contact zone by incorporating either an indigenous point of view or presenting alternative approaches to ownership of the water and land, or indeed the profound indigenous challenges to the nation-state in general. In sum, despite its excellent choice of frame for its translation strategy, it is too much of a domestication that fails to do justice to the very important concerns that lie at its heart.

Conclusion

As should be evident from the discussion above, cinema and politics have long been closely related in Latin America, and this continues to be the case despite the present context in which the role of the state is much reduced, citizenship has become commodified and the boundaries between the public and the private have become blurred. One of the ways in which this engagement continues to take place is through the participation of Latin American indigenous people in the various manifestations of visual culture in the region, increasingly as subjects rather than objects. Their worldviews pose both challenges and alternatives to the status quo that cinema, especially in its digital incarnation, can now represent and circulate, contributing in this way to that important process of cross-cultural translation that the Latin American theorists, academics and activists have long been calling for. And while 'domesticated' cultural translations can have their merits, as I have argued elsewhere (de la Garza 2010), especially in contexts when forging consensus is a priority or when they can lead to revising received versions of history, the value of registering difference as a strategy of resistance in its own right cannot be overlooked.

Notes

1 Despite the fact that *Eréndira* has been widely marketed and received as a Mexican film, I here categorize it as transnational rather than national cinema in that "the global language for claiming indigenous status" has allowed tribal communities to emerge "as global subjects and not as national citizens" (Chakrabarty 2006: 239, 241). This is in fact one of the reasons that indigenous cinema is inherently political.

2 At the level of language, Alfonso Arau has recently launched an initiative, entitled Cidilux Project, to translate Mexican cinema, including his famous *Como Agua para Chocolate/Like Water for Chocolate* (1992), into indigenous languages and show the films in purpose-built theatres in various indigenous communities. The first two have opened in the states of Chihuahua and Oaxaca, and he expects that 5,000 such theatres will be operating within 5 years (Arau 2012).

3 The population of the Americas went from 25 million inhabitants in 1490 prior to the arrival of the Europeans to 700,000 by 1623. Only 3 per cent of the indigenous people survived.

4 *Eréndira* was shot with indigenous actors, who had the opportunity to tell a story of their community by means of cinema for the first time, generating a sense of empowerment, and providing training with digital media that can be used to continue furthering local agendas. Further, at the indigenous communities in Michoacán where it was first screened *Eréndira* generated debate about both received accounts of history, and the indigenous communities present situation of internal division (Caballero 2007).

Bibliography

Alvaray, L. (2013) "Hybridity and Genre in Transnational Latin American Cinemas" in de la Garza, A., Shaw, D. and Doughty, R. (eds) *Transnational Cinemas*, 4 (1), pp. 67–87.

Anderson, B. (1991) *Imagined Communities: Reflections on the Origins and Spread of Nationalism*, London: Verso.

Arau, A. (2012) *Traducirán Cine Mexicano a Lenguas Indígenas*, http://moreliafilmfest.com/traduciran-cine-mexicano-a-lenguas-indigenas/ (accessed 30 September 2013).

Aumont, J. (1992) *Aesthetics of Film*, Austin: University of Texas Press.

Baker, M. (2006) *Translation and Conflict: A Narrative Account*, London and New York: Routledge.

Bauman, Z. (2007) *Liquid Times: Living in an Age of Uncertainty*, Cambridge: Polity.

Berlant, L. (2011) *Cruel Optimism*, Durham, NC and London: Duke University Press.

Caballero, J. (2007) "*Eréndira Ikikunari*, la Conquista desde la visión de los indígenas,"/ "*Erendira Ikikunari*, the Conquest as Seen by the Indigenous Peoples", *La Jornada*, np.

Chakrabarty, D. (2006) "Politics Unlimited: the Global Adivasi and the Debate about the Political" in Karlsson, B. and Subba, T. (eds) *Indigeneity in India*, London: Kegan Paul.

Cypress, S. (1991) *La Malinche in Mexican Literature: From History to Myth*, Austin: University of Texas Press.

Dalle Vacche, A. (2003) *The Visual Turn: Classical Film Theory and Art History*, New Brunswick, NJ: Rutgers.

de la Garza, A. (2010) "Diversity, Difference and Nation: Indigenous Peoples on Screen in Mexico" in *National Identities*, 12 (4), pp. 413–424.

de la Garza, A. (2012) "The Digital Option: Interpreting Independence in Latin American Cinema Today" in Richardson, W. and Kelly, L. (eds) *Power, Place and Representation: Contested Sites of Dependence and Independence in Latin America*, London: Peter Lang, pp. 173–184.

D'Lugo, M. (2010) "Aural Identity and Hispanic Transnationality" in Durovicová, N. and Newman, K. (eds) *World Cinemas, Transnational Perspectives*, London: Routledge, pp. 160–185.

Escobar, A. (2004) "Beyond the Third World: Imperial Globality, Global Coloniality and Anti-globalization Social Movements," *Third World Quarterly*, 25 (1), pp. 207–230.

Falicov, T. (2007) *The Cinematic Tango*, New York: Columbia University Press.

Franco, J. (1993) "High-tech Primitivism: the Representation of Tribal Societies in Feature Films" in King, J., Lopez, A. and Alvarado, M. (eds) *Mediating Two Worlds: Cinematic Encounters in the Americas*, London: British Film Institute, pp. 81–94.

García, G. and Maciel, D. R. (2001) *El cine mexicano a través de la crítica*, Mexico D.F.: UNAM/IMCINE.

Haddu, M. (2007) "The Power of Looking: Politics and the Gaze in Salvador Carrasco's 'La Otra Conquista'" in Shaw, D. (ed.) *Contemporary Latin American Cinema: Breaking into the Global Market*, Lanham: Rowman and Littlefield, pp. 153–172.

Hansen, M. (2002) "Chameleon and Catalyst: the Cinema as an Alternative Public Sphere" in Turner, G. (ed.) *The Film Cultures Reader*, London: Routledge, pp. 390–419.

Hart, S. M. (2004) *Introduction to Latin American Film*, Rochester: Tamesis.

Lyotard, J. (1984) *The Postmodern Condition: A Report on Knowledge*, Manchester: Manchester University Press.

Marks, L. U. (2000) *The Skin of the Film: Intercultural Cinema, Embodiment and the Senses*, Durham, NC: Duke University Press.

Mignolo, W. (2010) "Delinking: The Rhetoric of Modernity, the Logic of Coloniality and the Grammar of De-coloniality" in Mignolo, W. and Escobar, A. (eds) *Globalization and the De-colonial Option*, Abingdon: Routledge, pp. 303–368.

Mulvey, L. (2003) "Then and Now, Cinema as History" in Nagib, L. (ed.) *The New Brazilian Cinema*, London: I. B. Tauris, pp. 261–269.

Noble, A. (2005) *Mexican National Cinema*, London: Routledge.

Page, J. (2009) *Crisis and Capitalism in Contemporary Argentine Cinema*, Durham, NC and London: Duke University Press.

Podalsky, L. (2011) *The Politics of Affect and Emotion in Contemporary Latin American Cinema*, London: Palgrave.

Rancière, J. (2004) *The Politics of Aesthetics* (translated G. Rockhill), London: Continuum.

Rancière, J. (2009) *The Emancipated Spectator*, London: Verso.

Robinson, D. (1997) *Translation and Empire: Postcolonial Theories Explained*, London and New York: Routledge.

Santos, B. (2005) "The Future of the World Social Forum: The Work of Translation," *Development*, 48 (2), pp. 15–22.

Shaw, L. and Dennison, S. (2007) *Brazilian National Cinema*, London and New York: Routledge.

Stam, R., Porton, R. and Goldsmith, L. (2015) *Keywords in Subversive Film/Media Aesthetics*, Oxford: Wiley Blackwell.

Venuti, L. ([1995] 2008) *The Translator's Invisibility: A History of Translation*, London and New York: Routledge.

34

EUROPEAN CINEMA

Spectator- or spect-actor-driven policies

Petar Mitric and Katharine Sarikakis

Introduction

With the project of European integration, the European Single Market signaled a new phase of international politics and trade, whose focus on cultural goods was among the major aims of its core economic policy. Without borders, double taxation or duties, complex administrative hurdles, and conflicting legislation of national markets and territories, films produced in the EU or entering the EU would be circulated at much lower costs. This means that together with broadcasts crossing borders, the conditions for the circulation of films and audiovisual services became easier and less costly in a 'borderless' internal market than in one with multiple administrations and borders. European filmmakers and politicians raised the issue that, given the global integrationist tendencies of the market, the position of the European audiovisual industries required strengthening if they were to compete in an increasingly globalized market. Furthermore, as Europe aimed at furthering its political integration, cultural services and goods, and especially cultural content, was thought to be an important asset, both financially and politically, that could not be left to the forces of 'free' market alone.

As a result, a set of film and audiovisual policies and instruments was developed, deriving from and reflecting conflicting, albeit occasionally intersecting, motivations. On the one hand, the aim has been to protect European cinema industries against neoliberal tendencies of commodification of audiovisual products. The political aim has been to ensure that in the integration process, the stories of cultures and nations in Europe would be told in authentic ways. On the other hand, the protection of European film industry was based on the aim to strengthen an industry vis-à-vis the US global majors. Although these two motivations are not necessarily exclusive, they prioritize different aims and require different tools to achieve those. As we are discussing in this chapter, these differences often result in clear divisions of support for film and audiovisual content more generally.

Specifically, we explore the ways in which, under the pressure of the current economic crisis, film policy in Europe is disrupted, while the traditional notion of *quality* inherent to what has been mainstreamed as 'autonomous auteur European cinema' is being redefined. In pursuing this objective, we will evoke some of the main discourses on European cinema from the field of media and film studies – from the ones that see cinema primarily as part of job-creating cultural industries and 'new economy' to the Marxian discourse of European cinema as a stronghold of European social-democratic values. We will also demonstrate the presence of certain neoliberal tendencies within the film sector, especially as these are explored through attention to quantitative *quality evaluation methods* suggested by the European film policies, and we will finish by putting these in the context of the dichotomous *spectator/spect-actor* concepts as these were developed by Augusto Boal and Thomas Gutierrez Alea. As we will argue, despite the proclamations of film being one of the core ways of authentic European 'story-telling' as an antipode to commercialized, prescription-based stories, European regulation and practice have positioned such film-making increasingly at the margins of a policy framework that prioritizes marketability.

The two philosophies of European cinema

The major policy principles governing European cinema are the exemption of audiovisual goods from free-trade agreements, as in the case of the World Trade Organization (WTO), inclusion of cultural 'Europeanness' in the constitutional laws of the EU, and the ratification of the European Convention on Cinematographic Co-production and Audiovisual Services Directive. Their joint goal has been primarily to address the domination of Hollywood production in European markets through developing mechanisms of support for European films and through this way to strengthen the sense of European identity by safeguarding its cultural diversity (Pauwels, De Vinck and Van Rompuy 2007; De Vinck 2009; de Smaele 2007; Sarikakis 2004; Wayne 2002; Finney 1996; Rivi 2007). A symbolic act in this regard was the establishment of the European Film Awards in 1988, which was based on the idea of celebrating the uniqueness of European filmmaking and common European identity in the unifying post-Cold War Europe. At the first Award ceremony held in Berlin in 1988, Polish filmmaker Krzysztof Kieslowski won the Best European Film Award for his *Short Film about Killing* (1988) produced in – at the time still – socialist Poland. The award was also accompanied by the public appeal of the most renowned European film auteurs of the time from both sides of the iron curtain,[1] whereby they alarmingly warned of the danger of "cultural homogeneity, a downfall in artistic taste and a pollution of intellectual and spiritual values – all of which would gradually suppress national identity, native tongues, [their] inborn desire for the natural beauty of 'otherness'."[2]

Nowadays, more than 25 years later, while Europe is struggling with the effects of the global financial crisis, socioeconomic divisions between the rich North and the 'peripheral' South become increasingly brazen "leading to the construction and reinforcement of a selective Europeanness" (Sarikakis 2014: 65–66). When the vision of a united post-1989 Europe paradoxically resulted in division (Western and Eastern Europe) or even the tri-vision (East, West and the Balkans) of Europe (Ellmeier and Rasky 2006: 13), the idea of preservation of the authentic European cinema driven by autonomous authors in an ever-unifying Europe necessitates a revisit.

The historical Hollywood–Europe antagonism, a burning issue in the public agenda for the policy-makers in the 1990s, has given way to new issues, such as questions of governing digital content, copyright or privacy. However, the issue of digital content and protection of culture remains a terrain of tensions. Despite state support, the European film industry fails to attract audiences for its films as envisioned but also defies the prevalent neoliberal logic "that if something is not popular, then it is not necessary – or, in other words, consumers determine the market" (Lodge and Sarikakis 2013: 168). Hence, the rich European countries invest in national film-making with the aim to attract audiences – often at any price – thereby improving annual statistical data the public film agencies are obliged to present to the tax-payers and politicians. As a consequence, in an attempt to ensure more audience for, and visibility of, their films, European national cinemas increasingly sacrifice their long-standing emphasis on auteurism and autonomy in favor of more 'predictable' commercial successes. Accordingly, they reconfigure their initial film policy goals and the type of communication they used to maintain with their audiences, the basis of which was primarily the art film. As it is clear then, the problem does not only come from Hollywood anymore, but also from within Europe, from the national and supranational policies that remain neither liberal enough to pursue large audiences and profit by commercial films (despite many such recent tendencies) nor reforming enough to open up for the social and political risks and experiments film-making in Europe used to be famous for.

If we evoke the notion of auteurism in European cinema from Francois Truffaut's concept of *politique des auteurs* (1954) via the *auteur theory* (1962) by Andrew Sarris, to theoretically less constrained concepts that do not reduce authorship to directors but define it as synergy of different creative agencies (Finney 1996), it is the idea of autonomy and recognizable 'stamp' (discursive and intellectual as much as visual and aesthetic) in the film content that have traditionally characterized the art cinema in Europe.

The idea of auteur cinema emerged in the 1950s when a group of film critics, known as the *Cahiers* group, dismissed the traditional French cinema for being "script-led, redolent with safe psychology, lacking in social realism and of being produced by the same old scriptwriters and filmmakers" (Hayward 1996: 32). They assigned the central role in the film to the director/auteur as "sole producer of meaning" (ibid). In the decades to come, the auteur concept would evolve. It was influenced by structuralism in the 1960s when the auteur ceased to be the only source that produces meaning since other structures (linguistic, social and institutional) emerged along with the significance of the auteur's relation to them. In the 1970s, under the influence of post-structuralism, feminism and deconstruction, the notion of ideology and its relationship to viewers was introduced. What became designated as the producer of meaning in the European auteur cinema was the "interplay between double articulation of discourses and non-discourses (that is the said and the not said)," 'auteurial intertextuality,' and film-spectator relationship (Hayward 1996: 32–38).

From the 1950s through 1970s, auteur cinema became the representative cinema of individual European countries from both sides of the Iron Curtain, and of Europe as a whole, taking over the primacy from popular/commercial and propagandist cinemas. Its prominence grew, however, not because of its market share or big audience, but thanks to its visual and philosophical qualities. It can be said that auteur cinema reflected the "social-national, supranational and micro/individual contexts of identity formation and representation" (Sarikakis 2014: 59). Therefore, many films of Italian Neorealism, French New Wave or East European film styles provided new post-World War II national identities based on the "common experience of resistance and liberation" (Rivi 2007: 45) and breaking away from anachronistic canons. Their supranational dimension reflected in the fact that most of them were set up as co-productions or meant to tell local stories using a universal language and, on the top, they provided new aesthetic experiences with their often revolutionary and innovative visual styles. In her book, *European Cinema after 1989: Cultural Identity and Transnational Production*, Luisa Rivi shows that the important status of the auteur cinema was already visible with Italian Neorealism. Namely, only 10 per cent of the Italian production in the first post-World War II decade was neorealist, and very few of the neorealist films were acclaimed, but they managed to rehabilitate the Italian nation and give it a new identity and international visibility (Rivi 2007: 44–46). The neorealist movement and, later on, the French New Wave defied the dominant mainstream cinema and the hegemonic values it mediated in its respective country, providing the freedom for a diversity of voices to speak up. At the same time, auteurism showed a distinct Europeanization potential since it spread throughout both sides of Iron Curtain, contesting the concept of 'the Other Europe' and creating a cultural Europeanness. The influence of Italian Neorealism can be seen in Poland as early as in the 1950s.[3] The French New Wave inspired the internationally acclaimed Czech New Wave and the Yugoslav Black Wave, whereas the rise of the so-called Polish School and the cinema of moral anxiety in Poland inspired Western cineastes like Peter Greenaway and Lindsay Anderson to visit the film school in Lodz.

The development of the auteur cinema, however, was not immediately followed by the extensive policy measures and institutionalization that would emphasize a supranational European identity. Cross-national collaboration in the form of bilateral co-production treaties among the European states became part of the international film industry in the 1950s, after France and Italy signed the first agreement of the sort to rebuild their national film industries in the aftermath of the World War II. The phenomenon grew stronger after the Treaty of Rome instituted the European Economic Community in 1957. Indeed, the results of this collaboration left imprints on film budgets, access to film locations as well as cast and crew from other European countries enabling auteur cinema to become more competitive with Hollywood. However, the idea of official co-production treaties signed between government representatives was still rather pragmatic than cultural. It was primarily about intergovernmental policies that did not "translate into a supranational dimension but operated rather as the autonomous acts of national governments that had formed a privileged and circumscribed sphere of action" (Rivi 2007: 42).

The advent of European co-productions was both criticized and praised. On one hand, it gave birth to so-called 'Euro-puddings' – co-productions that by combining too many elements of different nations in order to attract more financing and bigger audiences eventually create the opposite effect, "appealing only to the lowest common denominator of cultured interest with little hope for broad social or political resonance" (quoted in Morawetz *et al.* 2007: 428). Co-productions were also designated as a "murky area" or "thorn problems" (Hayward 1993: 37) and disastrous and forced "swerving away from national tradition" (Betz 2001:8; Liehm 1984: 183). Perhaps more important, co-productions also tended to be perceived as a new chance for the Hollywood majors to penetrate into the European cinema and 'corrupt' the European auteurs with their financial investments and distribution arrangements (Guback 1969).

On the other hand, co-produced films certainly offered a starting point for an inquiry into the first policy moves toward the establishment of a 'European' cinema. Already by the 1960s co-productions became "a necessity for countries with a modest film industry and a small market potential" (Jaeckel 2001: 155). France signed bilateral co-production treaties with countries from 'the Other Europe' (Bulgaria, Czechoslovakia, Hungary, Poland, USSR, and Yugoslavia) in the late 1960s and early 1970s.[4] Germany and Italy followed the same example. Although the policy of bilateral co-production treaties led to many so-called "marriages of convenience" (industry driven co-productions) among the European states, it also resulted in a number of so-called "true loves" ('natural' co-productions) (Morawetz *et al.* 2007: 426) that Europeans could identify with.[5]

In terms of content, ideology, and audience, European auteur films tried to establish a balance between national and international points of view. Peter Lev, however, argues that the European "art film does not only aim at the international audience but is *intended* for an international audience with shared class and cultural backgrounds or pretensions" (quoted in Betz 2001: 15). As a result, the term 'European auteur film' has been "employed to indicate separate movements across time, 'major' directors or auteurs, and a canon of supposedly 'great' works, while it has often been identified with an elitist and denationalized idea of art cinema" (Rivi 2007: 39). Indeed, Albert Moran posits the idea of European art cinema in the context of a cultural imperialist discourse that he discards as anachronistic and a "rerun of the mass culture/high culture debate," arguing that proponents of this discourse only showcase their personal aesthetic taste (in particular against Hollywood films) (Moran 1996: 10).

Despite the fact that the idea of pan-European cinema and identity remains strongly highlighted in the policy field, in the past two decades, the European auteur cinema has tended to be described as "audience failure" since it "never lived up to the expectations aroused for audiences by the often exaggerated claims of the critics" (Finney 1996: 56). Some producers and policy-makers have criticized the European subsidy structures for emphasizing "creation of art over an industrial product," and for "doing away with the producer" (Finney 1996: 116). In order to make the European cinema more inclusive and blur the high-/low-culture line, some new film policies have been set to support films that will gain more audience through hybridization of its commercial/popular, artistic and, whenever possible, political value, and through prioritizing widely appealing classical narratives. The funding guidelines of national film funds thus introduce separate market schemes that favor large-audience films whose cultural aspect is narrowed down to the mere use of the local language or dealing with a popular historical topic.

> The change from a 'protect the national culture' paradigm that had permeated most film support policies in Europe in the past, to a 'build the local industry' strategy is also to be seen against the background of the film industry becoming increasingly viewed as a shining example of the 'new economy.'
>
> (*Morawetz* et al. *2007: 428)*

A variety of new neoliberal financial incentives such as tax credits/rebates/shelters/breaks have been introduced to bring additional investment into the film industry and raise the number of mid- and high-budget films to the detriment of small and low-budget projects.

It is clear then that such a status of the European audiovisual industry symbolically reflects two conflicting philosophies in European film industry and policy. On the one hand, there is still a determination on part of the national European governments to sustain the tradition of social democracy through willingness to intervene in cultural market outcomes to protect the European audiovisual industry (and the individual national industries that constitute it). On the other hand, the second tradition is the 'neo-liberal' philosophy whose keystone is doing away with as many social (cultural) and political commitments as possible (Wayne 2002: 10; Lodge and Sarikakis 2013: 176).

Current film policy framework in Europe

In the end of 2013, after long negotiations with and interventions from the film industry professionals, the European Commission passed the 2013 Cinema Communication on state aid for films and other audiovisual works which updated aid and incentives that had been introduced by earlier policies (European Commission 2013). It welcomed approval of the Creative Europe Programme by the European Parliament, while the Council of Europe's co-production film fund Eurimages had launched already in 2012 the initiative for the revision of the European Convention on Cinematographic Co-production in order to foster co-production activity in Europe. However, certain neglected processes in Europe, such as national state aid and funding, support for distribution, training and educational support, as well as a wider economic malaise that has pushed to poverty levels more than one-third of the population in Greece and over 60 percent of unemployment among youth in Spain stemming from the current economic crisis, threaten further implementation of policies of support in general (Trading Economics 2015). Indeed, if policy approaches do not adjust to the crisis-struck Europe, we may soon witness new forms of 'Othering' due to the intensified North–South division, internal political and cultural hegemonies within the EU, and, finally, the absence of diverse voices of autonomous auteurs.

The hegemonic position of powerful and rich countries represents an imbalanced information flow between North and South. "Rich and dominant countries fail to account for processes of hybridity, evolution and dialogue among cultures" (Sarikakis 2005: 81). In the 1990s, cultural imperialism and cultural hegemony were linked to the domination of global entertainment conglomerates supported by Hollywood production whose invasion threatened the cinemas of Europe. The main goals of the film policies then emphasized freedom of expression, cultural diversity, and development of co-productions. In post-2008 Europe, it seems that the Hollywood cultural hegemony has been superseded by similar practices of *internal cultural domination* (Sarikakis 2007: 95–112), currently most visible at the expense of the crisis-hit Europeans, especially, the South European countries, the Baltic countries and even the UK. Protectionist film cultural policies thus become controlled by and beneficial only for the economically stable nation states. The absence of solidarity among the states, on the other hand, threatens to distance the large and weaker European audiovisual industries, whereas the voices from the crisis countries are getting weaker and their access to the pan-European funds scarcer.

Film professionals in many European countries are severely struck by the economic crisis and consequent saving measures imposed by their respective governments. Public film funds in Greece, Portugal, and Spain, to mention a few, were drastically cut down. The Hungarian National Film Fund was entirely restructured in 2011 to suit primarily production of profitable, commercial Hungarian films, which provoked vociferous protests among the European film auteurs (Hertlik 2010). The Brussels administration stays mostly supportive of these public spending cuts since they are all in compliance with the principle of subsidiarity in the cultural field. This principle states that the central organs of the Community should only be concerned with the most essential areas of policy, leaving everything else to sovereign national governments (Rivi 2007: 28; Kaufmann and Raunig 2003: 21). Instead, the European Commission is engaged primarily in communicating positive messages about European governance in "an anodyne, nonprescriptive, nonpartisan a-political way" (Lodge and Sarikakis 2013: 176).

The pan-European film fund Eurimages, established in 1989 with the objective to safeguard European cultural diversity, freedom of expression, and development of democracy, is facing the lack of financial sources to help out the European national cinemas in financial crisis. The annual budget of Eurimages never exceeds 25 million euros. The fund supports up to 70–80 co-productions per year from its 36 member states, and at no more than 15 percent of the total budget of a film. The fact that up to 500 co-productions are annually produced in Europe (EAO 2010), and that the public film funds in rich European countries have budgets two to three times higher than Eurimages (MEDICI 2012) demonstrates that Eurimages' support gives only a quality label to a supported project. Its mission, in fact, completely depends on the status of the public film funds in the member countries. Namely, the basic Eurimages criterion is that the project applying for the Eurimages support already secured at least 50 percent of its financing (Eurimages 2012). On the other hand, film production in European countries, especially the crisis-stricken ones, relies exclusively on the public funding that in the time of economic crisis gets cut down as part of governments' rationalizations of the public spend. Consequently, the producers of arthouse films in such countries face difficulties to secure money from what are often the only major sources available – public film funds. Without their support they could not seek for co-producers or apply to Eurimages. In such a situation, Eurimages runs the risk of turning into a fund only for co-productions among the rich European countries that can afford to subsidize national cinema.

In order to diminish this problem, Eurimages launched the initiative for revision of the European Convention on Cinematographic Co-production in 2012 with the intention to decrease the minimal participation of minority co-producers from 10 percent (as it is now) to 5 percent (Olsberg 2012), and therefore express support for the smaller film cultures. Whether this is going to produce better results than in the past for the most crisis-affected European film industries remains to be seen.

Another problem is that such limited financing resources in the European countries with small production capacity become available mostly to members of the highest cultural elite – renowned filmmakers whose commercial and festival success is predictable. Therefore, young directors or filmmakers with innovative projects are often prevented from securing enough financing to enter co-production deals and releasing their films outside the home country. Facing the lack of financing, they are doomed to shoot films with micro budgets and cheap technology, which, more often than not, neither helps them to qualify for any major film festivals nor makes their films appealing to sales agents. As a consequence, their voices remain unheard. The auteurs' freedom within the scope of the representative cinema production becomes restricted, and filmmakers are increasingly compelled to seek for alternative forms of film production outside the state subsidy structures in order to ensure higher creative freedom.

The second pan-European film fund, MEDIA program of the European Union (which has been merged into the Creative Europe scheme), was set up to support so-called "harmless areas" (Kaufmann and Raunig 2003: 12) of the European film industry (development, distribution, and training), unlike Eurimages that mainly supports the core segment in the film value chain – production. MEDIA has a higher budget than Eurimages; its beneficiaries include mostly experienced companies (never individuals) and big distributors whose turnover is often significantly realized through distribution of Hollywood blockbusters. In addition, the development schemes of MEDIA do not include separate calls for young and first-time filmmakers, although there are incentives in the form of extra points for the MEDIA-member countries with small audiovisual industries. Some critics of MEDIA took issue with the abandonment of smaller, individual creative people in favor of large companies and industries already with the second MEDIA cycle in the mid-1990s. They accused the MEDIA program of "doing little more than support Europe's largest countries and advantaged companies" (Finney: 1996: 135). Hence, a project, say, by a first-time Greek director would compete against major filmmakers such as Lars von Trier or Ken Loach and therefore is unlikely to receive funding.

Furthermore, MEDIA co-sponsored training programs for students or young filmmakers usually include high fees that make such programs financially inaccessible to applicants from the poor European countries in particular. The new cycle of MEDIA program, merged together with Culture program under Creative Europe, unfortunately did not take into consideration any of these challenges, although it launched three new schemes in 2014: a support scheme for international co-production funds, a scheme for video game development, and an action dedicated to audience development (Petti 2013), which might start redressing the balance. However, the question of two conflicted European philosophies comes up again. Will Creative Europe additionally support economy and large companies to the detriment of independent and autonomous artistic expression and talent across Europe?

Audience building as a cultural policy? An outlook

When the auteur cinema was defined in the late 1950s with the advent of the French New Wave, the dictum to provide aesthetic pleasure just as to be "strong, honest, intelligent and provocative," and to "speak about politics but not to be political" (de Beacque 1998: 84, 106) prevailed. Films about personal topics, produced mostly at low cost, reflected and contemplated society. Although they often appealed to significant audiences (both national and European/international), their main purpose was to 'free' viewers from the hegemony of the mainstream dominant cinema coming from both Hollywood and Europe. 'Audience-building,' one of the 'buzz-words' of the current European cultural policies, seems to have revolved around the building of what theatrical practitioner Augusto Boal calls *spect-actors*. According to Boal, *spect-actors* "liberate themselves, they think and act for themselves instead of delegating their power to any ruling structure that solely portraits their ideals and makes the audience passive spectators and the victims of the dominant ideology" (quoted in Frances, 2004: 75).

Film theorist Tomas Gutierrez Alea applied the same spectator/spect-actor dichotomy to cinema in his seminal book *The Viewer's Dialectic* (1988). He differentiates between the *passive-contemplative* and *active* spectators. The former contemplate film as a mere object. By watching a movie the spectator satisfies "their need for enjoyment and aesthetic pleasure, but their activity does not go beyond the cultural plane." As he put it, "here cultural plane is offered to people as a simple consumer object and any reference to the social reality that conditions it is reduced to the affirmation of its values or, in other cases, to a complacent critique" (1988: 38). On the other hand, an *active spectator* engages himself or herself in a consequent participation that implies people's concrete reaction to social reality they live in. Just as Augusto Boal, Gutierrez Alea refers here to Berthold Brecht's *estrangement effect (Verfremdungseffekte)* in order to emphasize that in cinema, as much as in theater, spectators should not communicate with a film only at the emotional level through identification with the characters and catharsis. "The estrangement effect must replace any emotion with the specific emotion of discovering something, of finding a truth which has previously been obscured by accommodation to daily life" (Gutierrez Alea 1988: 45; Leslie 2005: 47–52). According to this view, the ultimate goal of a filmmaker should be to estrange or alienate the spectators from the reality they live in, because only by distancing themselves from that reality emotionally, they can understand it rationally and objectively, and act accordingly.

In the past decade, the dominant policy goal of the European cinema has been an amalgamation of artistic and commercial quality where quality is measured quantitatively (box office, numbers of territories with theatrical release, admissions, number of festival awards, etc.). What triggered such a policy were the significant economic potential of film as part of creative industries and the fact that poor circulation of European films became a serious argument of the neo-liberal lobbyists against public film funding in Europe.

What occasionally increases the market share of the European films, though, are high-budget UK–US co-productions (for example, the Harry Potter films, the James Bond franchise, or high-profile films such as *The King's Speech* (Hooper, 2010)). In many countries such films generate multiple times higher box-office than the rest of the theatrically released non-domestic European films altogether. They are mostly made for the European audiences that frequent the commercial multiplex cinema theatres merely as consumers and not as active citizens, whose participation, to use Gutierrez Alea's words, is *illusory* not *real* and whose response could be elicited during a film but never *vis-à-vis reality* (1988: 39–40).

The other instrument for increasing the market share of domestic cinema is the favoring of renowned authors whose films predictably attract attention, and improve quantitative performance of domestic production, at least short-term. Therefore, European countries tend to give generous grants to a single project of a celebrated filmmaker. A recent example is the 8 million euro *Amour* (2012) by Michael Haneke, a film that was shot in a few locations only but which was predicted to have a big audience and make annual statistical reports show an increase in market share, neglecting the fact that this has happened thanks to a single film.[6] As a consequence, we can hear news about a successful year of Dutch, Austrian, or Lithuanian cinema thanks to one or two films only, but the market share most often drops again next year.

Due to this economy/art dichotomy, the ideal European film for the European public financiers has increasingly become one that is visually and aesthetically striking, opens up grand controversial topics (wars, racism, xenophobia) but by the end is reduced to a warm human story of the main hero, isolated from the European social totality. Such a trajectory distracts spectators, preventing them from any critical examination of their reality and invisible hegemonic ideological apparatuses. Instead, it makes them only identify or empathize with problem-solving heroes that, instead of improving their society, normalize it as it is, through conflict and resolution. In the words of Gutierrez Alea again: "we leave the theatre with the sensation that all is [eventually] well, that we do not need to change anything" (1988: 38).

The ideological and political neutrality of the majority of European filmmakers makes the essential challenging of axiomatic truths an absence. The 'European' ways of seeing are found in 'creative' documentaries, by well-funded directors from wealthy European countries who embark on costly trips to 'exotic' destinations like North Korea, Afghanistan, Kosovo or Colombia and present those countries' tragedies as disturbing but exotic stories of uncivilized 'Others'. These films disturb Western audiences for a moment, make them feel engaged and shaken for a while, but eventually tranquilize them with the feeling that they were lucky to be born *In a Better World* (2010) as the Oscar-winning film by Suzanne Bier's suggests by its title. Showing the violence of the openly repressive world regimes on screen, they only incite cheap repulsion of the audience towards easily recognizable and predictable violence in North Korea, Sudan or elsewhere – the type of violence that is visible, albeit in more stylized ways, in an average Hollywood thriller. At the same time, European cinema starts lacking films that would create a discerning audience, capable of tracing hidden, symbolic violence that is not apparent and explicit (Milovic 2006: 243–257).

Conclusion

The European film policies are increasingly taking a market-prioritizing turn. The quality of European films is measured through quantitative data (box office, admissions, number of awards, etc.), while their socio-political relevance is neglected. Audience-building, as one of the major activities dictated by the most recent European film policies, is perceived as an ideal marketing tool for proving that even subsidized films can make money. However, while collecting and counting spectators is a skill, creating socially disobedient *spect-actors* remains a difficult art. In the crisis-hit Europe, when quality keeps being measured through the number of consumers, an essential task of creating socially and politically aware citizens seems quixotic. Hence, in addition to providing an overview of the film policy field in Europe, we want to mention here that there are still filmmakers in Europe who keep up the paradigm of a European cinema marked by social disobedience, subversion, and other supranational unifying drives. Sometimes such filmmakers exist because they live in rich European countries whose governments, despite neoliberal policies, still maintain arthouse support schemes (for instance, the work of the acclaimed Dardenne brothers from Belgium or by young Swedish director Lisa Langseth). In 'poor countries' these filmmakers increasingly operate underground, guerilla-style, because their governments are dismantling subsidy structures, thus segregating the local scenes from any kind of a common European cinematic landscape. A non- homogenous, but authentic, cinematic 'voice' seems to occupy almost a fetishist status in European film policies and practices, depending on structural and ideological pre/dispositions: while wealthy countries may use arthouse productions as proof of their 'commitment' to domestic political demands for supporting the Arts and towards European-wide proclamations of protection of European culture, others under the discourse of austerity, crisis, and scarcity of resources ensure that subsidies dry in this direction. In either case, policy scripts are not innocent bystanders of national idiosyncrasies, but rather actors in shaping the European cinematic landscape.

Notes

1 The list includes Theo Angelopoulos, Ingmar Bergman, Dusan Makavejev, Istvan Szabo, Wim Wenders, Federico Fellini, to mention a few.
2 The full letter available at: http://www.europeanfilmacademy.org/Appeal-from-European-Film-Directors.187.0.html (retrieved as of 25/09/2013).
3 For example, *The Five from Barska Street* (1953) by Polish director Alexander Ford that won the special mention at the Cannes Film Festival in 1954 shows a clear neorealist influence in describing the post-World War II drab Polish reality.
4 For the full list of co-production treaties signed by France see: *Centre national du cinema et de l image animee*, http://www.cnc.fr/web/en/co-production-agreement (accessed on 15 January 2014).
5 *Blow-Up* (1960) and *La Notte* (1961), both directed by Michelangelo Antonioni, *Canterbery Tales* (*I racconti di Canterbury*) (1974) by Pier Paolo Pasolini, and later on, *Paris, Texas* (1984) by Wim Venders or *Europa* (1991) by Lars von Trier are largely considered to be "marriages of love." On the other hand, film such as *I am Dina* (2001) by Ole Bornedal (Norway/Sweden/France/Germany/ Denmark) and *The Disappearance of Finbar* (1996) by Sue Clayton (Ireland/Sweden/UK) have been cited as "marriages of convenience/europudding," as case studies of forced and compromising co-productions (see Neumann and Appelgren 2007; Wayne 2002).
6 Indeed, *Amour* was successful, commercially grossing $20 million worldwide (www.imdb.com).

Bibliography

Betz, M. (2001) "The Name above the (Sub)title: Internationalism, Coproduction, and Polyglot European Art Cinema," *Camera Obscura*, 16(1), pp. 1–44.

de Baecque, A. (1998) *La Nouvelle Vague: Portrait d'une jeunesse*, Paris: Flammarion.

De Smaele, H. (2007) "More Europe: More Unity, More Diversity? The Enlargement of the European Audiovisual Space," *European Studies: A Journal of European Culture, History and Politics*, 24(1), pp. 113–134.

De Vinck, S. (2009) "Europudding or Europaradise? A Performance Evaluation of the Eurimages Co-Production Film Fund, Twenty Years after its Inception," *Communications*, 34(3), pp. 257–285.

EAO (European Audiovisual Observatory) (2010) *Focus 2010. World Film Market Trends/Tendances du marche´ mondial du film*, Strasbourg: European Audiovisual Observatory.

Ellmeier, A. and Rasky, B. (2006) *Differing Diversities: Eastern European Perspectives. Transversal Study on the Theme of Cultural Policy and Cultural Diversity*, Strasbourg: Council of Europe Publishing.

Eurimages (2012) *Regulations Concerning the Co-Production Support for Full Length Feature Films, Animation and Documentaries*, Strasbourg: Eurimages.

European Commission (2013) Communication from the Commission Concerning the State Aid Assessment Criteria of the Commission Communication on Certain Legal Aspects Relating to Cinematographic and other Audiovisual Works (Cinema Communication) of 14 November 2013 (2013/C 332/01). *Official Journal of the European Union*, 15. 11. 2009, C332/1.

Finney, A. (1996) *The State of European Cinema: A New Dose of Reality*, London: Cassell.

Frances, B. (2004) *Augusto Boal*, London: Routledge.
Guback, T.H. (1969) *The International Movie Industry: Western Europe and America since 1945*, Bloomington: Indiana University Press.
Gutierrez Alea, T. (1988) *The Viewer's Dialectic*, Havana: Jose Marti Publishing House.
Hayward, S. (1993) *French National Cinema*, London: Routledge.
Hayward, S. (1996) *Cinema Studies: The Key Concepts*, London and New York: Routledge.
Hertlik, B. (2010) "Letter from Balázs Hertlik (Received 23 December 2010)," *Studies in Eastern European Cinema*, 2(1), pp. 133–135.
Iordanova, D. (2002) "Feature Filmmaking within the New Europe: Moving Funds and Images across the East-West Divide," *Media Culture Society*, 24(4), pp. 517–536.
Jaeckel, A. (2001) "The Search for the National in Canadian Multilateral Cinematographic Co-Productions," *National Identities*, 3(2), pp. 155–167.
Kaufmann, T. and Raunig, G. (2003) "Anticipating European Cultural Policies," http://eipcp.net/policies/aecp/kaufmannraunig/en (accessed on 19 February 2015).
Leslie, E. (2005) "Adorno, Benjamin, Brecht and Film" in Wayne, M. (ed) *Understanding Film: Marxist Perspectives*, London/Ann Arbor, MI: Pluto Press, pp. 34–58.
Liehm, M. (1984) *Passion and Defiance: Film in Italy from 1942 to the Present*, Berkeley: University of California Press.
Lodge, J. and Sarikakis, K. (2013) "Citizens in 'An Ever-Closer Union'? The Long Path to a Public Sphere in the EU," *International Journal of Media and Cultural Politics*, 9(2), pp. 165–181.
MEDICI (2012) First Workshop Report, 25–27 April, Sigtuna (Sweden), http://www.focal.ch/medici-training/reports/docs/Funds_budgets_def.pdf (accessed on 19 February 2015).
Milovic, N. (2006) "Burdijeova koncepcija simbolickog nasilja u filmovima savremene evropske kinematografije"/ "Pierre Bourdieu's Conception of Symbolic Violence in Modern European Cinema" in Nenadic, M. and Spasic, I. (eds) *Nasledje Pjera Burdijea /Pierre Bourdieu's Legacy*, Belgrade: Institut za filozofiju i drustvenu teoriju – Zavod za proucavanje kulturnog razvitka, pp. 243–259.
Moran, A. (1996) *Film Policy: International, National and Regional Perspectives*, London: Routledge.
Morawetz, N., Hardy, J., Haslam, C., and Randle, K. (2007) "Finance, Policy and Industrial Dynamics: The Rise of Co-productions in the Film Industry," *Industry and Innovation*, 14(4), pp. 421–443.
Neumann, P. and Appelgren, C. (2007) *The Fine Art of Co-Producing*, Copenhagen: NeumannPublishing.
Olsberg, S.P.I. (2012): Evaluation and Proposed Revisions of the European Convention on Cinematographic Co-production. A Report Prepared for the Council of Europe, http://www.coe.int/t/dg4/cultureheritage/culture/film/COE Report_print_final.pdf (Accessed on 19 February 2015).
Pauwels, C., De Vinck, S., and Van Rompuy, B. (2007) "Can State Aid in the Film Sector Stand the Proof of EU and WTO Liberalisation Efforts?," *European Studies: A Journal of European Culture, History and Politics*, 24(1), pp. 23–43.
Petti, S. (2013) "The European Parliament adopts Creative Europe" in *Cineuropa*, 20 November, http://cineuropa.org/nw.aspx?t=newsdetail&l=en&did=248049 (accessed on 19 February 2015).
Rivi, L. (2007) *European Cinema after 1989: Cultural Identity and Transnational Production*, New York: Palgrave Macmillan.
Sarikakis, K. (2004) *Powers in Media Policy*, Oxford: Peter Lang.
Sarikakis, K. (2005) "Legitimating Domination: Notes on the Changing Faces of Cultural Imperialism" in Hamm, B. and Smandych, R. (eds) *Cultural Imperialism: Essays in the Political Economy of Cultural Domination*, Peterborough, Ontario: Broadview Press, pp. 80–92.
Sarikakis, K. (2007) "Regulating the Consciousness Industry in the European Union: Legitimacy, Identity, and the Changing State" in Chakravartty, P. and Zhao, Y. (eds) *Global Communications: Toward a Transcultural Political Economy*, Lanham, MD: Rowman and Littlefield, pp. 95–112.
Sarikakis, K. (2014) "Identity and Diversity in European Media Policy: Crisis Changes Everything(?)" in Donders, K., Pauwels, C., and Loise, J. (eds) *The Palgrave Handbook of European Media Policy*, London: Palgrave Macmillan, pp. 54–69.
Sarris, A. (1962) "Notes on the Auteur Theory in 1962," http://alexwinter.com/media/pdfs/andrew_sarris_notes_on_the-auteur_theory_in_1962.pdf (accessed on 19 February 2015).
Trading Economics (2015) "Youth Unemployment 1998–2015" in http://www.tradingeconomics.com/greece/youth-unemployment-rate (accessed on 2 March 2015).
Truffaut, F. (1954) "Une certaine tendance du cinema français," *Cahiers du cinema*, 31, January, pp. 15–29.
Wayne, M. (2002) *The Politics of Contemporary European Cinema: Histories, Borders, Diasporas*, Bristol: Intellect Books.

35

MINOR CINEMA

The case of Wales

Ruth McElroy

The opening illustration in Film Agency Wales' 2011–12 annual report is a DVD library of films produced with financial support from the agency. They include *The Gospel of Us* (McKean, 2012), *Hunky Dory* (Evans, 2011) *Resistance* (Gupta, 2011), *The British Guide to Showing Off* (Benstock, 2011), *Submarine* (Ayoadae, 2011), *Seperado* (Goch and Rhys, 2010), *Patagonia* (Evans, 2010), *Third Star* (Dalton, 2010), *Mugabe and the White African* (Bailey and Thompson, 2009), and *Sleep Furiously* (Koppel, 2009) – a list which evidences significant and diverse film production in and from Wales. Whether all these films could be regarded as examples of a Welsh national cinema or indeed of a minor cinema is another matter. Whilst some of these films such as *Patagonia* and *Resistance* have a recognisably Welsh identity stemming from a substantial combination of subject matter, language, directors, actors, writers, producers and crew, others – such as the documentaries *The British Guide to Showing Off* and *Mugabe and the White African* – might be less easily identified as Welsh films per se, though they both have Welsh co-producers (Sue Jeffries and Lizzie Morgan Hemlock, respectively) whose involvement was the principal rationale for Film Agency Wales support. The question of national definition is not unique to Welsh film nor, in my view, is it always the most rewarding approach to take to the assessment of any individual film. However, because film critics, scholars, policy-makers, funders and, let us not forget, viewers, *do* still attach meaning to the idea of nation in their appreciation of film as both a cultural and an economic entity, it is vital that any exploration of film and politics examine how aspects of nationhood and minority status operates in contemporary cinema. The cinema of small nations, some of which might be understood as constituting minor cinema, and all of which is now produced in global as well as local contexts, is necessarily a political entity whose very frame of reference troubles film studies' earlier reliance on 'national cinema' as a category with a self-explanatory force. This chapter therefore sits alongside those in this volume with both a regional (including continental) frame for understanding the cultural geography of film and those with a critical, transnational approach to cinema beyond Hollywood.

What's in a name? Small nations, minor and global cinema

Even as globalisation is seen to be dissolving the force of nations, our world continues to be shaped by the distinctly modern notion of the 'nation' and by the power structures in which nations and nation-building are embedded. The arts and culture are integral to these processes *both* because of their representational and philosophical potential, *and* because they are themselves embedded within the wider neo-liberal marketisation that is a vital, but not uncontested, element in marking contemporary globalisation as a distinct historical phenomenon. Faced with this paradox, film scholars have adopted a diverse range of critical frameworks in their attempts to construct a productive analytic model for understanding cinema's relationship to national elements within increasingly transnational industries and cultures. This section explores some of these different frameworks. It acknowledges both their different starting points and their different possibilities for film scholars and aims to examine how the adoption of these different frameworks can both reveal and obscure some of what is happening in contemporary film cultures.

Published in 2007, Mette Hjort and Duncan Petrie's edited collection *The Cinema of Small Nations* made an ambitious intervention in the field of film studies both by arguing for the analysis of small national cinemas and by providing a dozen detailed case studies of such cinema in countries as diverse as Scotland, Singapore and Tunisia. Although the book's dust-jacket introduces the reader to "what we might term minor or small nations cinema", the volume overall uses small nations not minor as its principal conceptual frame. In doing so, it echoes Hjort's (2005) earlier claim to the importance of the notion of small nations as an analytic tool; one which does not have quite the same implicit evaluation of significance that minor perhaps carries. Nonetheless, the concept of a small nation is, as Hjort and Petrie point out, a necessarily relational one; a small nation is defined in its relation to larger ones. For the most part, this relation is not just one of quantity – of size or scope – but of power. Small nations may be small due to their geographical size, their relatively small population, the size of their GNP and internal market, or their relative political size when compared to larger nations (as in the case of domination by former colonial powers). Small nations may not be self-explanatory but they are numerous and increasing in number, thanks both to processes of decolonisation and the reconfiguration of states after the Cold War. For example, using population as their measure (with 1.5 million being the rather arbitrary upper threshold), Bray and Packer note that over "half the sovereign states have populations below five million, and 54 have populations below 1.5 million", hence, they argue, "the world is a world of small states" (Bray and Packer cited in Hjort and Petrie 2007: 4). Increasingly then, size has come to matter to both political and social science analyses of nations as evidenced, for example, by Alberto Alesina and Enrico Spolalore's (2003) *The Size of Nations* and Josep M. Colomer's (2007) *Great Empires, Small Nations*, two very different volumes which nonetheless share a concern with how the size of nations shapes both their economic and democratic potential. Whilst larger nations may be better placed in relation to international markets, smaller ones may be more democratic and responsive to their populations from which they are less detached or distanced.

This geopolitical reality begs questions of cultural critics and challenges scholars to reflect critically upon which relations and which processes shape cultural production and consumption. For example, how is film made in small nations? How do small nations regard the idea of a national cinema? What problems and answers do small internal markets pose for cultural labour in small nations? How does small nationhood inflect itself in the thematic elements of film? Does small nationhood entail a particular mode of address and relation between film-maker, film text and cinema audiences? These are diverse questions and the answers will necessarily be different depending on the specific nation in question. Some small nations such as Denmark make a large number of films (22 Danish fiction film releases in 2010, for example, with four of the Top 20 films that year being Danish releases (see DFI 2011) and their cinema, including the distinct aesthetic sensibility of the films of Lars von Trier, is well-known and highly regarded within international film cultures. However, other small nations such as Bulgaria are small in the size of their cinema, producing today relatively few films and having sold off much of its former state film infrastructure, including film studios, in the aftermath of communism (see Iordanova 2007). Despite such diverse realities, though, the questions listed above reveal how a small nations framework, when applied to cinema, can productively denaturalise the concept of a national cinema and, simultaneously, can probe the myriad historical and contemporary relationships that shape film production and consumption outside the globe's dominant powers.

Moreover, a comparative perspective between the cinemas of small nations can reveal those characteristics that are common challenges faced by many such cinemas. These include the limited size of their domestic markets, the precariousness of their minority and regional languages, the relative position cinema and film institutions play in nation-building, the particular power of American and other large or mega-nation cinema which, one might argue, has been consolidated under the neo-liberal conditions of modern globalisation, and the reconfigured realities of what Toby Miller *et al.* have characterised as the "new international division of cultural labour" (Miller *et al.* 2005) whereby governments' creative industries policies drive nations to compete with each other to attract inward investment for film production from Hollywood. In turn, such challenges are met with some shared responses and may also be countered by some common benefits. These include: the relative proximity of filmmakers to their own audiences (social distance being less common in small nations), shared commitment to the value of indigenous cultural production between cultural actors (including policy-makers) and the potential of what Hjort (2011) terms "affinitive transnationalism", that is, co-operation and interaction between small nations emerging from shared ideals and common aspirations, as in the case, for example, of the Scotland and Denmark Advance Party initiative, or the Celtic Media Festival, which aims to promote the languages and cultures of the Celtic countries (Cornwall, Brittany, Ireland, Scotland and Wales) on screen.

On the other hand, many countries are today asserting their rights as nations exemplified in 2014 by the independence referenda in Catalonia and Scotland. Nationhood is being renegotiated within existing states such as the United Kingdom, Spain and Belgium, and transnational structures of governance such as the European Union. We might argue that what we are seeing currently is a process of becoming – of becoming a nation in a simultaneously post-national and transnational world.

It is here that the minor cinema framework comes into its own, for its starting point is precisely the relationship between cinema and the process of a people's becoming as theorised by Gilles Deleuze in his *Cinema 1* (orig. 1983) and *Cinema 2* (orig. 1985) and, with Félix Guattari, in *Kafka: Toward a Minor Literature* (orig.1975). As David Rodowick explains:

> Rather than being based on a unified or unifying discourse, minor cinema must produce collective utterances (*énoncés collectifs*) whose paradoxical property is to address a people who do not yet exist and, in so doing, urge them toward becoming.
>
> *(1997:154)*.

So conceived, minor cinema is both the product and aspiration of a consciousness that refuses the existing régime of national representation (including the misrepresentations of colonial powers of its 'others') and which is sensitive to a different collectivity which, even as it does not yet exist, can be enunciated, for example, through the characters in minor cinema. As David Martin-Jones explains:

> [A] work of minor cinema attempts to break free of the dominant discourse's representation of the native population. In this respect, minor cinema functions with a different conception of 'the people' from the classical cinemas of directors such as Eisenstein, Riefenstahl and Capra. Here, the people are thought of as an already existing whole awaiting manipulation in accordance with the film's ideological positioning. In minor cinema, by contrast, the people are something yet to be created.
>
> (*Martin-Jones 2004: 229*)

Perhaps because Deleuze approaches minor cinema through the literary work of Franz Kafka, he is especially sensitive to language and to the notes it strikes, both literally and through its metaphorical power. As a Czech Jew writing in German, Kafka is understood to be wresting a major voice to make it speak in a minor way, "to make it stutter or stammer" (Deleuze in Martin-Jones 2004: 229). Minor cinema is composed of such interruptive enunciations. In the case of a film like Peter Mullan's *Orphans* (1998), this can be heard in the way in which the characters' working-class Glaswegian dialect challenges the British tone of much English-language UK film. Here, the tone of national politics lives on the tongue of Scots still coming to terms with devolution and what it might mean for them in the process of becoming a people:

> It is in order to counter these London-based views of a unified Britain – an essentially English vision – that a distinctive Scottish regionality is evoked in *Orphans*, through its distinctive setting and Glaswegian dialect. It is this international, 'first cinema' aim of British cinema which Mullan causes to stutter through his focus on the difference between the specifically local and the stereotypically 'international' view of Scottish identity after Britain.
>
> (*Martin-Jones 2004: 236*)

Where minor cinema is precisely concerned with the alterity of a new subject, a people in the process of becoming, the global cinema approach advocated by Martin-Jones (2010) in his *Scotland: Global Cinema* casts the net far wider, seeking to reinsert the analysis of popular genres in the analysis of filmmaking in small nations. Here the focus is not a national or minor cinema per se, but rather the whole range of filmmaking in a country, thus "it does not focus solely on films made by Scots, about Scots, for Scots" (2010:1). Changing the frame in this way means that indigenous films sit alongside both "coproductions Scotland has been involved in . . . and the location shoots of a number of British, French, US and Indian films in Scotland" (ibid.). This approach has the merit of recognising that a great deal of filmmaking in small nations is undertaken by producers from outside the nation. Furthermore, by broadening the scope from art cinema to popular genres, the interaction between popular film and existing myths of the nation can be revealed. The effect of putting place at the centre of the frame is that *all* film activities in that location become subject to analysis. This has the potential to reveal some relatively neglected areas including, for example, the increasing importance of television drama production to the industrial and representational ecology of small nations. Martin-Jones' avowedly global cinema approach therefore shares with the small-nations framework advocated by Hjort and others a concern with film politics in the arenas of policy, production and representation. It is to these key areas that this chapter now turns in its exploration of Wales and cinema.

Wales on film: national representations

It is because screen stories hold such imaginative power in their everyday circulation that attention to how Wales has been represented on film matters so greatly to film and cultural critics. Writing in 1979, the year of the first (and unsuccessful) referendum for Welsh devolution, the Welsh-language filmmaker Wil Aaron argued that:

> Film was never made to feel very welcome in Wales. As a two or three year old infant, stinking slightly of gin and the sweat of the fairground, it ran slap up against Evan Roberts and the [religious] Revival of 1904–5 and was severely mauled. It survives – but remains retarded to this day.
>
> *(Aaron, quoted in Woodward 2006: 49)*

For Aaron, the Protestant ideology of chapel-going Wales was a key reason why film, then the most modern form of visual culture, was rejected. It is worth noting such a filmmaker's criticism of the nation itself precisely because it puts into perspective many of the established and important criticisms made of how Wales has been represented on screen by filmmakers from outside Wales. In the dominant screen language of British and Hollywood cinema of the 1940s and 1950s, Wales was populated by salt-of-the-earth labourers (principally coal miners) living in close-knit communities who combined sentimentality with song and cunning. Overwhelmingly the image was one of intimate working-class life framed as an amusing, if rather moving, 'other'. This alterity, framed perhaps by the nostalgic longings of a self-depicting middle class of modern filmmakers, was the dominant frame for representing Wales; indeed, it is impossible to disaggregate the representation of working-class life and values from the representation of Wales in the cinema of the period. The mythology of the nation is also the mythology of an industrial, semi-rural working class.

Despite this, rather than being seen as either a critique or subversion of the dominant ideologies of the period, films such as Irving Rapper's *The Corn is Green* (1945) starring Bette Davis, and Pen Tennyson's *The Proud Valley* (1940) which starred Paul Robeson, have tended to be read as anti-communist, anti-socialist and anti-trade union. Even if the dominant message of these texts is conservative, they demonstrate how melodrama is used in representing Wales as a place of different values which, in the case of Robeson's performance, forges connections well beyond England to the African-American experience in the USA. Robeson plays David Goliath, a migrant labourer from the American South who has sailed to Cardiff (one of the UK's oldest multi-ethnic cities) and arrives at the coal-mining village of Blaendy. Music and religion draw him to the men of the village as he hears them singing in a male voice choir rehearsing for an Eisteddfod, a traditional Welsh arts competition. Robeson's deep solo voice makes him the perfect candidate to perform at the Eisteddfod and thus begins a relationship that yields one of the most memorable lines of cinema in Wales when the choirmaster angrily responds to one of the men's racially motivated criticisms of Goliath getting a job in the pit by exclaiming, "Damn and blast it man! Aren't we all black down that pit?" Problematic though such discourse may seem today, the articulation of cross-racial solidarity in labour, even in this sentimental form, was surely radical in its day. Moreover, Robeson's own relationship to industrial Wales was one which inflected the film's sentimental narrative with a different subtextual voice. In 1928, whilst on the West End stage, he met with a miners' delegation who had walked to London to protest their poor pay conditions and he frequently visited Wales during the 1930s in support of miners' causes. Visiting Wales in 1958, he proclaimed, "You have shaped my life – I have learnt a lot from you. I am part of the working class. Of all the films I have made the one I will preserve is *The Proud Valley*" (Robeson, quoted in Morris 2012).

The kind of representations found in this film and in the Irish-American director, John Ford's Oscar-winning *How Green Was My Valley* (1941), present a very masculine Wales, one in which women's principal role is to mother. The actress who made the role of the Welsh mam her own was Rachel Thomas who, as Michelle Ryan has argued,

> modelled her 'Mam' characters on her mother and grandmother and the many women she grew up with. She merely distilled those qualities into one character [...] these women might not have had much say in the world of politics, work and public life, but they were the absolute bedrock of family, community, and chapel life.
>
> (*Ryan 2000: 39*)

Ryan herself sought to do justice to this history in her film work in the 1980s as part of Red Flannel, a Channel 4 women's film workshop, which worked with working-class women in the South Wales valleys, providing them with training in video skills. Their first film, *Mam* (Red Flannel, 1988), documented the role played by women in the very kind of mining communities which Rachel Thomas sought to depict fictionally. Thomas appeared in numerous feature films including Jill Craigie's *Blue Scar* (1949), Gilbert Gunn's *Valley of Song* (1953) and, alongside Richard Burton and Elizabeth Taylor, in a film adaptation of Dylan Thomas' play, *Under Milk Wood* (Sinclair, 1972).

Thomas' film career was one of the main ways in which Wales was mediated nationally and internationally and her screen presence in both British and Hollywood films is evidence of how important actors have been to Wales' cinematic representation. For Wales as a small nation, the overwhelmingly dominant force of England and of Britishness means that films that might be considered Welsh are actually more likely to be named internationally as British. These are not necessarily antithetical terms – a significant proportion of the population of Wales might accept being named as both Welsh and British – but neither are they identical. For many, the distinction between these two terms is at the heart of Welsh identity. Indeed, Wales, it might be argued, is commonly an invisible nation in cinema even when it is the location, the narrative setting, and homeland of film characters. For example, J. Lee Thompson's 1959 film, *Tiger Bay*, set in Cardiff's docks area, is listed on the BFI's Screenonline website without a single mention of having been made in Wales (or indeed of Rachel Thomas who appears in the film alongside Hayley Mills). It is perhaps unsurprising in this context that if asked to name a cinematic figure from Wales, the average non-film critic is more likely to mention Richard Burton, Rachel Roberts, Rhys Ifans, Catherine Zeta Jones, Iwan Gruffudd and/or Matthew Rhys than any director, script-writer or producer. Actors and acting are an under-researched yet culturally significant way in which small-nations cinema gains visibility and audience awareness both within and beyond the borders of its own territory (see Murray 2007). Chris Williams' (2013) edited diaries of Richard Burton begins this work from an important historical perspective, but more critical attention needs to be paid to the careers and presentation of actors from small nations if we are better to understand their contribution to the myriad ways in which national elements are mediated in contemporary film culture.

Rhys Ifans' career offers a good example of how Welsh actors negotiate working in both Welsh cinema and Hollywood. One of his earliest films was *Twin Town* (Allen, 1997), a darkly comic satire set in Swansea. It was released in the same year as New Labour won a landslide victory in the UK government election and in which the second devolution referendum was won in Wales, leading in 1999, to the establishment of the Welsh Assembly Government. Ifans plays Jeremy Lewis, a delinquent drug addict whose quest for revenge structures the film's narrative and provides an opportunity to play with national mythologies, as the film's trailer announces:

> Rugby. Tom Jones. Male Voice Choirs. Shirley Bassey. Llanfairpwllgyngyllgogerychwyndrobwllllantisiliogogogoch. Snowdonia. Prince of Wales. Anthony Hopkins. Daffodils. Sheep. Sheep Lovers. Coal. Slate quarries. The Blaenau Ffestiniog Dinkey-Doo Miniature Railway. Now if that's your idea of thousands of years of Welsh culture, you can't blame us for trying to liven the place up a little can you?

As Daryl Perrins (2000) has argued, the film's irreverent tone was ill-received by most domestic critics who perhaps felt that the film's send up of national discourse was out of kilter with what was then being termed Cool Cymru, an era of Welsh popular music success populated by bands such as Catatonia, Super Furry Animals and the Manic Street Preachers which became linked discursively to Cool Britannia, itself a New Labour discourse aiming to rebrand the UK as the home of revived creative industries. However, as Kate Woodward argues, the film's carnivalesque atmosphere "emphasizes that its subjects form a close-knit community of individuals" even as it traces the murderous outcome of the brother's revenge narrative. Music and singing, so central to earlier cinematic representations of south Welsh families, endures here but with a heavily ironic twist as "Myfanwy" (a staple of the choral repertoire) is sung at the pier head whilst Jeremy and his twin, Julian (played by Ifans' own brother, Llyr), bury their father at sea in "a bittersweet victory over the corrupt local police force" (Woodward 2006: 60). The film's mode of address to the audience is one of a knowing guile; it assumes a shared familiarity with a host of national representations both old – as in the Hollywood movies of the post-war era – and new to the nationalist tone of Wales in the late 1990s. Yet Ifans' skill in delivering this laddish 'nod and a wink' also earned him a place in one of the biggest romantic comedy hits of the decade, *Notting Hill* (Mitchell, 1999). Ifans' character, Spike, is in many ways a reprise of earlier representations of the Welsh in London – comic, hapless, innocent in the big city but whose heart is in the right place. The mobility and flexibility of a career such as Ifans' suggest that Welsh actors have been successfully negotiating what it means to be Welsh in both small-nations and dominant large-nation/Hollywood cinema.

Ifans (a Welsh-speaker) gained some of his earliest parts on S4C television programmes, and S4C has certainly been important to film in Wales. A prime example is the Oscar-nominated *Hedd Wyn* (Turner, 1992), a First World War drama based on the real life and death of the young Welsh poet, Ellis Evans, in which the military ideology of Britishness, articulated through the medium of English, is repeatedly undercut by a pacifist Welsh-speaking voice including that of the poet himself who cries, "Saeson diawl!" ("Bloody English") when he sees the army on preparatory manouveres back in his Welsh homeland. The power of both language and landscape to establish a critical voice of alterity is an important feature in those Welsh films that directly address Welsh identity and its tense relation to Britain and its dominant English-language culture. Indeed this is a central theme of Karl Francis' film for S4C, *Milwr Bychan* (*Boy Soldier*) (1986), which places a young Welsh solider in Northern Ireland so as to explore the tremendous tensions faced by the boy as he fights his Celtic cousins on behalf of the British army. Francis' avowedly left-wing filmmaking here delves into the strains of personal identity as it is lived in the midst of international and, arguably, colonial conflict. In industrial terms, moreover, his own career exemplifies these very strains. In 1993, he threatened to take Channel 4 (the UK broadcaster established to serve minority audience interest) to the race relations board for failing to treat Welsh-originated material fairly and equally, whilst on his own website he writes, "Someone wrote about me in TIME OUT – Karl Francis is one of Britain's best filmmakers and the least known probably because he is Welsh" (Francis). Such a statement eloquently testifies to the challenges of working in small-nations cinema.

Wales and film: strategies, policies and production

One of the most productive elements of the small-nations approach to cinema is its emphasis on understanding the particular challenges that filmmakers experience and the extent to which they can be both peculiar and shared with other small nations. This has the potential to offer both film scholars and practitioners (i.e. filmmakers, policy-makers, distributors and educators) a refreshingly international horizon for problems that are commonly negotiated at local level. With this in mind, I want now to focus on some particular structural characteristics of film in Wales in order to explore how the configuration of film agencies and policies in this small nation exemplify wider political, economic and ideological processes that are shaping film production. In particular, I want to consider the role of Wales Screen Commission (est. 2002) and Film Agency Wales (est. 2006) so as to tease out some of the approaches and opportunities each body has taken to film in this small nation. In doing so a particular dynamic will be considered between, on the one hand, advocacy for filmmaking in small nations via location support for external producers, and on the other, support for filmmakers in Wales to expand their creative output and its reach both within and beyond Wales.

The Wales Screen Commission is part of the devolved Welsh Government's Creative Sector team led by the Department of Business, Enterprise, Technology and Science. The emergence of such a body needs to be understood within the context of several distinct, though often entwined, processes. While there is not space to discuss each in detail here, they include the globalisation (or, perhaps more accurately, the Hollywoodisation) of the film and television industries; the rise of a broad set of neo-liberal policies by numerous governments since the 1990s which have favoured the values of the market over the values of the public good; and the emergence of the concept of the creative industries as a salve to a host of economic ills facing post-industrial societies. The Wales Screen Commission aims to support international and local productions to use Welsh locations, crew and facilities. As its website states, it "markets Wales as a location and assists both inward investment and indigenous productions on a practical basis ensuring that their spend within the Welsh economy is maximised" (Wales Screen Commission). Clearly, the Commission's *raison d'etre* is economic; its aim is to support growth both directly in terms of jobs in the film industry and indirectly via jobs in related service sectors. The Commission has been successful, working with numerous high-profile international feature films such as *Harry Potter and the Deathly Hallows* (Yates, 2010), *Wrath of the Titans* (Liebesman, 2012), *Robin Hood* (R. Scott, 2010), *The Edge of Love* (Maybury, 2008) and *Pride* (Warchus, 2014). As a screen rather than a film commission, it has also worked with several television productions, including BBC Wales' *Doctor Who* (2005–), *Torchwood* (2006–11), and *Merlin* (2008–12) as well as international productions such as *Da Vinci's Demons* (2013–).

This strategic goal – growing creative industry jobs as a response to the post-industrial economic problems facing many Western small nations whilst simultaneously raising their international profile through selling their particular landscapes and skills ecology to external investors via branding their specific landscapes and production skills – is not unique to Wales. Björn Nordfjörd, for example, has explored how in Iceland "increased emphasis has been put on attracting foreign film crews" with publicity materials being developed that promote "the country's filmmaking potential with heterogenous landscape pictures, many taken from actual films or work on location" (2007: 51). In a similar vein, Northern Ireland Screen has promoted its "strong crew base, stunning locations, studio facilities and financial incentives" and now claims that "Northern Ireland is becoming one of the most sought-after filming locations for both film and television productions" (Northern Ireland Screen). Even as the rhetoric used by these agencies seems to celebrate success in putting Wales or Northern Ireland on the map, it is striking how often they exemplify success through recourse to Hollywood and US television shoots. In other words, whilst place – often instantiated in these agencies' websites by aerial view shots of 'stunning' natural landscapes – is a hallmark of each nation's distinctive offering to the camera, the power to make place valuable is instantiated by external producers such as HBO (a division of Time Warner) from much larger nations. For example:

> Since 2007, when the region pulled in its first high-profile US studio project from Tom Hanks' production outfit (*City of Ember*), inward investment in the industry has shown significant growth. Followed by another US studio, Universal Pictures, who brought feature film *Your Highness* to Northern Ireland, HBO arrived in 2009 to film a pilot of *Game of Thrones*, has subsequently returned to shoot 4 series and is currently filming Season 5 there.
>
> (*Northern Ireland Studios*)

Even such a cursory focus on the strategic goals of these small nations' agencies is revealing. First, it makes evident how hard and fast distinctions between cinema and television filming are now inappropriate when delivering a specifically 'jobs and growth' agenda as part of a creative industries economic strategy. Small-nation cinema scholars may need to undertake comparative studies with peers in television studies to examine how the ecology of moving-image production is shaped by relations with *both* these global industries on the ground. Second, whilst the driver behind such agencies is economic, in undertaking their role they also become ambassadors for these nations, advocating to the wider world the appeal and value of the places they represent. Consequently, they enjoy a privileged, and potentially highly productive, position in representing the small nation internationally. This tiny cadre of film workers are significant cultural intermediaries who mediate between the small nation and the international professional audiences they aim to engage and importantly, whose cultural (mis)perceptions they may challenge. Third, the workings of an agency like Wales Screen Commission exemplifies how neo-liberal tendencies to marketise cultural value operate within small nations' film industries and may do so productively in ways that counter cultural misrepresentation, even though they cannot reasonably be understood as counter-cultural in the sense that minor cinema aims ideologically to speak otherwise.

In contrast with the Commission, Film Agency Wales (FAW) has a broader remit "to ensure that the economic, cultural and educational aspects of film are effectively represented in Wales, the UK and the world". It aims "to facilitate a viable and sustainable Welsh film sector infrastructure and to promote access to a vibrant and dynamic film culture" (Film Agency Wales 2011). Its chief executive, Pauline Burt, made a point of noting in its first annual report that the Agency has "clearly demonstrated our talent rather than location spend focus, with a particular emphasis on the talented writers, directors and producers in and from Wales" (Burt, quoted in Film Agency Wales 2007). FAW realises its support for film in Wales through a range of means, many of which are characterised by a collaborative, multi-agency approach and responsiveness to diverse Government policies. For example, in 2010–11, the Agency "worked with and funded 14 independent venues across Wales with a particular focus on broadening provision in rural, Community First (a programme that supports the Welsh Government's Tackling Poverty agenda) and under-served areas" (Film Agency Wales 2011). Working in 2011–12 with the UK charity FILMCLUB it has also supported 42 clubs in Welsh-language schools (Film Agency Wales 2012), an important address to the bilingual educational needs of younger Welsh film audiences. Most importantly perhaps, FAW has also sought to act as an advocate for the specifically *cultural* value of Welsh cinema.

Conclusion

Both small-nations and minor-cinema approaches begin from the premise that cinematic representation entails questions of power. These may be understood in terms of relative global size and scale, their relationship to dominant global cinemas and the economic apparatus that underscores their hegemony, and in terms of the cultural, linguistic and tonal alterity that minor or small-nations cinema provides. In many parts of the post-industrial world, the increased prominence of creative industries policies has meant that an economic agenda has loomed large in the governmental evaluation of how mediated art forms such as cinema can provide jobs, support economic growth and lever both national and international private finance. However, small-nations cinema should never be reduced solely to the financial benefits it brings. A nation's cinema contributes to a people's imagination, their intellectual horizons, and a sense of themselves. As FAW's former chairman, Peter Edwards, put it, without a modern Welsh cinema "we would be poorer in every sense and the meaning of our lives would be further starved of intellectual and cultural sustenance, international status and aspirational confidence of and for the Welsh people" (quoted in Film Agency Wales 2011).

Note

This chapter represents research on film policy in Wales up to 2014 when it was submitted for publication in this volume. Film policy initiatives that were developed after that year have not been taken into consideration.

Bibliography

Alesina, A. and Spolalore, E. (2003) *The Size of Nations*, Cambridge, MA: MIT Press.

BFI Screenonline (n.d.) "Tiger Bay: 1959", available at http://www.screenonline.org.uk/film/id/492613/ (accessed on 18 February 2015).

Burt, P. (2007) "Introduction: Chief Executive and Chairman" in *Film Agency Wales Annual Report 2007–8*.

Colomer, J.M. (2007) *Great Empires, Small Nations: The Uncertain Future of the Sovereign State*, New York: Routledge.

Danish Film Institute (2011) "Facts and Figures 2011: Production and Exhibition Figures for 2010", available at http://www.dfi.dk/Service/English/News-and-publications/News/May-2011/Facts-og-Figures-2011.aspx (accessed on 18 February 2015).

Deleuze, G. (1983/1986) *Cinema 1: The Movement-Image* (trans. by Hugh Tomlinson and Barbara Habberjam), Minneapolis: University of Minnesota Press.

Deleuze, G. (1985/1989) *Cinema 2: The Time-Image* (trans. by Hugh Tomlinson and Robert Galeta), Minneapolis: University of Minnesota Press.

Deleuze, G. and Guattari, F. (1975/1986) *Kafka: Toward a Minor Literature* (trans. by Dana Polan), Minneapolis: University of Minnesota Press.

Film Agency Wales/Asiantiaeth Ffilm Cymru (2007) *Annual Report* 2006–7.

Film Agency Wales/Asiantiaeth Ffilm Cymru (2011) *Annual Report* 2010–11.

Film Agency Wales/Asiantiaeth Ffilm Cymru (2012) Annual Report 2011–12, available at http://www.ffilmcymruwales.com/index.php/en/company-details-and-contact/annual-reports (accessed on 18 February 2015).

Francis, K. (n.d.) "My Life", available at http://www.karlfrancis.com/mylife.html (accessed on 18 February 2015).

Hjort, M. (2005) *Small Nation, Global Cinema: The New Danish Cinema*, Minneapolis: University of Minnesota Press.

Hjort, M. (2011) "Small Cinemas: How They Thrive and Why They Matter", *Mediascape*, available at http://www.tft.ucla.edu/mediascape/Winter2011_SmallCinemas.html (accessed on 18 February 2015).

Hjort, M. and Petrie, D. (eds) (2007) *The Cinema of Small Nations*, Edinburgh: Edinburgh University Press.

Iordanova, D. (2007) "Bulgaria" in Hjort, M. and Petrie, D. (eds) *The Cinema of Small Nations*, Edinburgh: Edinburgh University Press, pp. 93–110.
Martin-Jones, D. (2004) "*Orphans*: A Work of Minor Cinema from Post-Devolutionary Scotland", *Journal of British Cinema and Television*, 1(2): 226–241.
Martin-Jones, D. (2010) *Scotland: Global Cinema*, Edinburgh: Edinburgh University Press.
Miller, T., Govil, N., McMurria, J., Maxwell, R. and Wang, T. (2005) *Global Hollywood 2*, London: British Film Institute.
Morris, P. (2012) "Wales on Film: *The Proud Valley* 1940" in *Wales Arts Review*, 7, available at http://www.walesartsreview.org/wales-on-film-the-proud-valley-1940/ (accessed on 18 February 2015).
Murray, J. (2007) "Scotland" in Hjort, M. and Petrie, D. (eds) *The Cinema of Small Nations*, Edinburgh: Edinburgh University Press, pp. 76–92.
Nordfjörd, B. (2007) "Iceland" in Hjort, M. and Petrie, D. (eds) *The Cinema of Small Nations*, Edinburgh: Edinburgh University Press, pp. 43–59.
Northern Ireland Screen (n.d.) "Northern Ireland Film and Television Studios", available at http://www.northernirelandscreen.co.uk/sections/10/film-and-television-studios.aspx (accessed on 18 February 2015).
Perrins, D. (2000) "This Town Ain't Big Enough for the Both of Us" in Blandford, S. (ed.) *Wales on Screen*, Bridgend: Seren, pp. 152–167.
Rodowick, D. N. (1997) *Gilles Deleuze's Time Machine*, London: Duke University Press.
Ryan, M. (2000) "A Woman's Place: Women and Film in Wales" in Blandford, S. (ed.) *Wales on Screen*, Bridgend: Seren, pp. 38–49.
Wales Screen Commission (n.d.) "Welcome", available at http://walesscreen.com/welcome (accessed on 18 February 2015).
Williams, C. (ed.) (2013) *The Richard Burton Diaries*, London: Yale University Press.
Woodward, K. (2006) "Traditions and Transformations: Film in Wales during the 1990s", *North American Journal of Welsh Studies*, 6(1): 48–64.

PART VIII

The politics of documentary

INTRODUCTION

John Corner

Documentary is often regarded as a generic area with an *unavoidably* political character, one given to it by its very attempt variously to connect 'directly' with social reality in however naïve or sophisticated a combination of ways. Its use of an array of modes, including archive, actuality footage, testimony, observation and exposition, in pursuit of this goal connects with historical and social space in ways which carry political implications even if these are not recognised or even denied by the film-makers. Such a sense of documentary's inherent politicality is a productive idea and one to be kept in mind in all documentary analysis. However, it should not be allowed to block our perception of the distinctive project which some documentaries set themselves, of a self-conscious engagement with those core economic and political structures which regulate the social order and exert a framing influence on social consciousness. This way of being 'political' (indeed of making films which can be described as 'political documentaries') presents special challenges. Among these are the handling of political ideas in relation to political events and circumstances, a handling which often involves both analysis and suggested ways forward, and the placing of 'politicians' as a group of distinctive actors. In both cases, viewers are frequently addressed, explicitly or otherwise, as kinds of political actor themselves, albeit one placed in a spectatorial role by the film. Their own political subjectivity, both in its affective and cognitive dimensions, is a key element of the viewing positions offered. The film-makers have to work with a sense of what viewers might know already, what the likely range of their existing beliefs and values (including prejudices) might be. With some projects for some audiences, this is not so demanding a requirement; with others, however, especially those involving a broader potential audience, it will take strategic care and perhaps some compromises.

The chapters collected here engage with questions about the documentary representation of 'core politics' using varied material. Four of the five are organised around work with a strongly national character in terms both of the themes addressed and the infrastructures through which documentary material can be produced and distributed.

Betsy A. McLane reviews a range of documentary approaches to politics within the USA, noting how different versions of the 'betrayal of the American Dream' have been dominant. Recognising the importance of the work of Michael Moore, particularly in terms of popular accessibility, she places him in the broader context of other critical film-making, often taking very different approaches. How to go about analysing a political system and its deficiencies within the space of an hour or so and how to position and use politicians themselves are among the questions raised. Her account includes the important issue of how the 'Right' not just the 'Left' can use documentary as a political tool.

Luke Robinson explores the changing profile of documentary production in China, examining how technological change in combination with social and cultural shifts has produced a more expansive documentary engagement, one in which versions of 'observationalism' are no longer so pronounced. What ways of showing and telling can be used in a situation where open criticism is dangerous? He notes the continuing precariousness of the infrastructure for Chinese documentary production, particularly for that on politically sensitive themes, but sees emerging notions of 'the public' as a reference point of promise for the future.

Lydia Papadimitriou tightens the focus in her examination of four films about the political and economic crisis in Greece. How was this specific, ongoing set of political events and circumstances portrayed by documentary film-makers? What repertoire of forms was used to record events and testimony? To what extent were critical judgements offered to viewers or was there a genuine invitation for them to make up their own minds? Her comparisons, illuminating about the particularities of the Greek case, also bring out the broader possibilities and limitations within which political documentary works, including those affecting distribution.

The question of possibilities and limitations is the main theme of Michael Chanan and Lee Salter's account of their own experience in making the film *Secret City*, about the political and economic dominance of the City of London Corporation. This is an account of political documentary very much from within, discussing both the new options which social media allow across various kinds of network and the continuing marginality of the critical voice in the overall media pattern. In addition, as academic film-makers, they note the challenges presented by an academic culture in which performance is increasingly measured in terms of metrically based 'impact'.

Finally, James Lyons reviews the current state of the 'interactive' documentary, as it rapidly develops across diverse models, looking at a number of examples to raise questions about organisation and structure and different kinds of participatory involvement. The continuities and the disjunctions with conventional documentary film-making are examined along with the play-offs between forms of cohesion and modes of openness that the interactive approach brings. Raising issues that are central to the whole idea of documentary politics, Lyons asks how might viewers' involvement in constructing documentary meanings variously relate to possible civic and political involvement beyond the textual borders.

All of the pieces, to different degrees, bring out the way in which critical attention to what is often an international economic order is increasingly a requirement for documentary's political address. I have looked at some responses to this situation myself (Corner 2015) believing, like the writers here, that representing the working of a complex system which mostly defies direct portrayal will be a key challenge for the future.

Bibliography

Corner, J. (2015) "System Down: Three Documentary Accounts of Crisis" in Murdock, G. and Gripsrud, J. (eds) *Money Talks*, Bristol: Intellect Publishing, pp 169–185.

36

TWENTY-FIRST CENTURY POLITICAL DOCUMENTARY IN THE UNITED STATES

Betsy A. McLane

Introduction

Some herald the early twenty-first century as a "Golden Age" of political and social-issue feature length documentaries, citing films such as Michael Moore's *Bowling for Columbine* (2002) and *Fahrenheit 9/11* (2004) and Errol Morris' *The Fog of War* (2003). Many, although by no means all, notable political documentaries are made in the United States of America and deal with subjects specific to that country's concerns. This essay is a cumulative examination of specific trends in cultural norms, problems, political affairs, and experiences as represented in major documentary films that originated in the US from 2000 through 2014. The subjects of the films under consideration are also US centric, although American filmmakers have investigated and continue to explore countless international topics, and makers from dozens of countries are responsible for the worldwide documentary explosion.[1] Two other concerns also define this essay: timeframe and subject matter. Especially significant earlier films are referenced too, since documentarians working in the early 2000s are obviously influenced by earlier films and filmmakers. Films of the 1970s, 1980s, and 1990s set the popularity of documentary features as a voice of dissent. These created precedents for the twenty-first century when over 100 feature political documentaries received critical and public attention. Films considered here are defined as being in some way directly concerned with government and politics. All social issue films include politics, whether personal or governmental, but documentaries concerned chiefly with topics such as health, sexual orientation and abuses, natural resources, discrimination, animal rights, immigration, self-portraiture, and to some extent earth's environment are not the primary focuses. This distinction does not diminish the importance of such films and the abilities of their makers. Decisions about which films are included or excluded are the author's own, based partly on personal judgment about their influences on American democratic processes.

Amidst the exciting exponential growth of diverse approaches to documentary making around the globe, the US retains hegemony on much of the world's media form and content. The fact is that long-established Hollywood film styles largely remain dominant 120 years after the beginning of cinema. Some documentarians continue to challenge those forms with innovations in both style and content, but even documentary has deep roots in white male Anglo/European/American norms. The field is thankfully diversifying in the twenty-first century, but the US and its narrative-based traditions continue to blanket world media.[2] The same is true of the economic, military and diplomatic powers that the US wields; a fact that makes American documentaries uniquely influential. This chapter considers the ways in which technologies, economic factors and artistic choices reveal how a representative group of American documentarians sees their country, question its past and present, and look to its future.

Common among many twenty-first century documentaries is a cynicism and a sense of apocalypse that is more intense than that of twentieth century films. Government, finance, industry, the media and the people who control these institutions are seen as corrupt and uncaring, operating for short-term gain without regard for the well-being of humanity. Solutions to problems often seem unreachable and the optimism for creating a better world that characterized earlier documentaries has dimmed. Exceptions exist. Some makers express beliefs in the future, but the films that get the greatest exposure tend to be those that reveal the betrayal of the American Dream. Perhaps the film-going public senses something similar and is turning in some very small measure, to the more interesting "truths" of documentaries.

Stage set – curtain up

Undoubtedly, kudos are due to the ubiquitous presence of Michael Moore for making political documentary a part America's popular cultural landscape. Moore makes clear that sensationalism and humor used in a non-fiction film can repeatedly capture and perhaps politicize a large crowd. Fans make his books bestsellers and his films box-office record breakers. Ironically, this is the direct result of the marketing departments of some of the very conglomerates that he attacks as being the root of America's troubles. His 2001 book *Stupid White Men . . . And Other Sorry Excuses for the State of the Nation!* was published by Harper Collins Regan Books (owned, along with Twentieth Century-Fox, by Rupert Murdoch), and remained on the *New York Times* bestseller list more than 14 weeks – without ever being reviewed in the *Times*. *Dude, Where's My Country?* was published in 2004 by AOL/Time Warner; Warner Brothers released Moore's first film *Roger & Me* in 1989.

Roger & Me, Moore's personally charged manifesto against the economic havoc created by the demise of the auto industry in his home town of Flint, Michigan, was a game changer in terms of marketing and audience size. The distribution of *Fahrenheit 9/11*, about unholy business ties between the Bush and Osama bin Laden families, became one of Moore's more splashy publicity moves when hue and cry was raised about the Disney studios' unsurprising refusal to release the picture through its subsidiary Miramax. The media buzz surrounding this film created a moment in documentary history, pushing the form to the forefront of popular Western culture. Whereas the popularity of *Roger & Me*, despite the extent of Warners' advertising clout, was a surprise, the selling of *Fahrenheit 9/11* brought highly organized attention to Moore as he and his film were featured by many news outlets. Individuals and organizations rallied to both support and decry Moore's anti-Bush expose of the war on terrorism and the war in Iraq. The film won the Palme d'Or at the 2004 Cannes festival. This astonishing feat reflected – aside from the merits of the film – the anti-American sentiment of Cannes-attending elites at the time. In its opening weekend, in the United States it grossed $23,920,637 from 868 screens and £1,304,115 in the UK from 132 screens.[3] The film's intent was to mobilize the American public to vote President George Bush out of office. In this, *Fahrenheit* failed, but it takes the personal ideas of a political documentarian to its logical democratic conclusion.

Moore's notoriety is fitting for the celebrity-driven times. His muckraking Joe-Average persona (complete with baseball cap and unfashionable girth) strikes a responsive chord in a public grown cynical about its own institutions. Moore's films also raise innumerable questions about documentary ethics, but there is no denying that they present serious issues in an unusual and effective form: that of serio-comic entertainment. He crosses documentary's ethical line most egregiously in *Bowling for Columbine*, a film that takes its name from the fact that Columbine, Colorado school killers, Eric Harris and Dylan Klebold, went bowling the morning that they committed the massacre. The main thrust of the film is an attack on the lack of sufficient gun control laws in the US. The film is replete with Moore's standard "everyman" persona, hectoring institutions and their representatives with mock naiveté. Documentary ethics evaporates when Moore goes to the home of long time National Rifle Association pro-gun spokesperson, Charlton Heston. Moore, a gun owner himself, uses that fact to obtain an interview with Heston. The aged and frail actor is harangued in his own home by a filmmaker who uses false pretenses to gain access. This reprehensible sequence almost negates the film's message and shows up the callous self-absorption that makes Moore a questionable documentarian. He did receive a Best Feature Documentary Academy Award for this film in 2003, signaling Moore's long-sought acceptance by Hollywood.

Secrets, squealers, and spies

Made earlier than Moore's semi-comical assertions are the personality infused films of Danny Schechter, a long-time left-wing media activist. Schechter has monitored wars since the American War in Vietnam, steadily making films in the 1980s 1990s, and 2000s. He thus provides a transition, even stronger than Moore does, between the two centuries. Although much of his early work covers international concerns, the films of the 2000s deal more with the domestic scene. Schechter is a self-identified left-wing 'news dissector' rather than a traditional documentarian, and his films offer pointed perspectives on American media. His journalistic background begets films that emphasize content over cinematic technique and production values. His stance is that of a (circa 1968) American New Left agitator. Among his work are two documentaries that probe the reasons for America's financial disaster, *In Debt We Trust: America before the Bubble Bursts* (2006) and *Plunder: The Crime of Our Time* (2009). His best-known film, however, is *WMD: Weapons of Mass Deception* (2004). Somewhat like *Fahrenheit 9/11* it is an investigation into the many falsehoods that duped the American public into believing that Saddam Hussein harbored WMDs and was directly responsible for the 9/11 attack on America. As does Moore, Schechter appears on camera and is the narrator, calling himself a "self-embedded" (mostly from a desk chair) journalist of the media war. The compilation of stills and clips he edited together with various songs, along with Schechter's commentary, create a scattershot effect that targets the administration's plan to control access to information through a sales and public relations plan formulated prior to the war. Numerous leading journalists from US and international organizations are interviewed on camera, relaying their stories and opinions about how the American media allowed itself to be manipulated. Similar subjects have been investigated by other filmmakers with greater depth and subtlety, but Schechter is a muckraking journalist of the old school who jumps on topics as they happen.

Robert Greenwald is also representative of a similar grassroots tradition but came to it through background in mainstream filmmaking. Greenwald is a product of the heightened emotions of 1960s and 1970s counter-culture; he too uses a somewhat scattershot approach. In 2002 Greenwald was the Executive Producer of *Unprecedented: The 2000 Presidential Election* (Perez and Sekler) and in 2004 he directed both *Uncovered: The War on Iraq* and the widely seen *Outfoxed: Rupert Murdoch's War on Journalism*. Because of its direct attack on the powerful television organization, the latter was among the most discussed films of the year. Like Schechter,

Greenwald uses clips taken from Fox News edited in such a way that the organization damns itself. Key among his points is how Fox employees are treated and ordered to report stories in certain ways, ways that ally with Rupert Murdoch's points of view. Their testimonies are as repugnant as are the reprisals, which include immediate dismissals for any deviation from policy.

The Fox employees' emotional personal stories of coercion increase the appeal of *Outfoxed*, but both Schechter's and Greenwald's films suffer from their non-mainstream approach. *WMD* and *Outfoxed* had limited theatrical releases, and are usually shown through grassroots distribution networks to those already inclined toward the makers' views. Cinema Libre, a Canadian company whose name describes its goals, distributed both theatrically, and they are currently two of its top three theatrical releases, with *Outfoxed* grossing $461,572 and *WMD* $238,924,[4] amounts that are miniscule in relationship to Hollywood fiction films but significant for theatrical documentaries. Neither work has the visual or aural quality meant for theaters; it is content that drives their popularity. Schechter and Greenwald continue to produce works that are purposefully crude, but provide jumping-off points for more thorough political critiques.

A highly complex film that deals with government secrets and the way that information is disseminated and distorted is *We Steal Secrets: The Story of Wikileaks* (2013), produced by Marc Shmuger, produced and directed by Alex Gibney. At this point in their respective careers, both men have had numerous theatrical successes. Shmuger was at one time the chairperson of Universal Pictures and prior to that was a Senior Vice President for Columbia Pictures Advertising. Having secured an independent production deal with Universal, Shmuger is able to fund projects like *We Steal Secrets* with budgets significantly larger than typical of grassroots advocacy productions. Gibney is a highly respected Oscar-winning documentarian who, after decades of work in the field, is able to choose which projects to produce and/or direct. His many notable credits date from 1980 and in the twenty-first century include: *Mea Maxima Culpa: Silence in the House of God* (2012), *Client 9: The Rise and Fall of Eliot Spitzer* (2010), *Casino Jack and the United States of Money* (2010), *Enron: The Smartest Guys in the Room* (2005), and *The Trials of Henry Kissinger* (2002). Each of these films investigates stories that contain implied or direct political content. *Taxi to the Dark Side* (2007), for which he won an Academy Award, is the most brutal visually and in terms of its subject, and interestingly, is the most personal of his works; its coda directly references his father's experiences in World War II.

Investigation is a key word in describing Gibney's oeuvre. His extensively researched films are carefully written and demonstrate a deep and thoughtful approach to their subjects. They move at a steady pace, using traditional invisible Hollywood editing that allows viewers to follow the often-complex circumstances and facts surrounding their subjects. Gibney is the unseen interviewer and narrator, a role that emphasizes rather than exploits the subject. This is investigative documentary-making at the highest level of disciplined double-checked journalism. Technically and artistically well crafted, these films look and sound good on the big screen. Forgoing haranguing and any hint of levity, Gibney builds both cinematic and artistic tensions that draw viewers into what are essentially mystery stories. *We Steal Secrets* is no exception. As *The Guardian* wrote:

> In *We Steal Secrets* he [Gibney] is at his forensic best in fairly and lucidly telling the story of how the infinitely devious Julian Assange became the world's most famous whistleblower through his revelation on Wikileaks of American state secrets, and of how one of his most significant sources, Private First Class Bradley Manning, a lonely, idealistic, cross-dressing military intelligence analyst, had his identity revealed to the CIA by the young bisexual, possibly autistic hacker Adrian Lamo
>
> (French 2013)

Assange' s mission to publish secret documents is a reminder of that of Daniel Ellsberg, the Lyndon Johnson administration insider who leaked the "Pentagon Papers" to the *New York Times* in 1971. Officially entitled *United States – Vietnam Relations, 1945–1967: A Study Prepared by the Department of Defense*, the documents revealed, among other facts, that the US secretly bombed Cambodia and Laos and, more damningly, that four administrations – from Truman through Johnson – had repeatedly lied to the public about the US role in Southeast Asia. *The Most Dangerous Man in America: Daniel Ellsberg and the Pentagon Papers* (Ehrich and Goldsmith, 2009) explores why and how Ellsberg leaked the Papers. This film and *We Steal Secrets* present somewhat similar scenarios in that Ellsberg and Manning were both intent on breaking walls of secrecy around what they perceived as unjust wars, although Manning was a soldier serving during an ongoing war and Ellsberg was dealing with an historical report. Forty years of changes in media technologies and the relationship of the public to news sources are dramatically evident. The recreations in *The Most Dangerous Man in America* of Ellsberg sneaking into a dark office to photocopy tens of thousands of sheets of paper and then handing them to the venerable *New York Times* represent an antiquated contrast to the instantaneous and emotionally driven computer sharing of secrets from Manning to Lamo to Assange, to billions of individuals. Traditional journalistic considerations about the reliability and the right to secrecy of sources are raised, but even then, the press responds with garbled punditry.

America's wars

Secrecy and surprise are critical in every nation's wars, as is home-front propaganda. Battlefield heroes are manufactured from versions of truth to rally support in the military and among the public. American icons Sergeant York and Audie Murphy, from World Wars I and II, respectively, are twentieth century examples. War's elusive truth became deeply personal and wrenchingly emotional in *The Tillman Story* (bar-Lev, 2010). Although Pat Tillman did not consider himself a hero, he did think of himself as patriot. It was news when he left a successful and lucrative career as an NFL football player to join the US Army Rangers in 2002, and bigger news when Tillman died in Afghanistan in 2004. Officially, he was a 'hero' who sacrificed his life for others when enemy forces shot him during an ambush. The film explains how Army commanders and the Bush administration covered up the truth of what had happened.

The heroine of *The Tillman Story* is Pat's mother Mary, who refuses to accept the official version of her son's death. bar-Lev conveys her dedication, passion for justice, and sheer love for her son as she tells the story of years of searching thousands of pages of records and begging authorities for facts. Her doggedness pays off, as she proves the truth about her son's death: he died from friendly fire. Ironically, it is a letter signed by her attorney husband that finally gets the Army to acknowledge the circumstances of a dreadfully botched Army mission. The scene of the attack is detailed convincingly by bar-Lev. General Stanley McChrystal was the commander of special operations in Afghanistan when Tillman died in April 2004. Soon after, McChrystal wrote his commanders a memo stating, "It is highly possible that Corporal Tillman was killed by friendly fire." McChrystal then wrote to his superiors to make sure they knew the truth in order to "preclude any … public embarrassment if the circumstances of Corporal Tillman's death become public." According to the Tillman family, at the same time McChrystal was part of the propaganda effort pushing a false narrative about Tillman's death.

Errol Morris is one of the two most innovative documentarians working in America, the other being Werner Herzog. Morris' *The Fog of War: Eleven Lessons from the Life of Robert S. McNamara* (2003) is a starkly beautiful revelation of the political and personal machinations that drove this Former Secretary of State. Aided by Philip Glass' score, *The Fog of War* won the Oscar for Best Feature Documentary. As Secretary of Defense under John F. Kennedy and Lyndon B. Johnson, McNamara is best known for his role in leading the US into its war in Vietnam, a series of acts the moral consequences of which haunted him. Twenty hours of interviews, using the Interrotron, a two-way optical device devised by Morris to allow subjects to look directly into the camera lens, became 95 minutes of mesmerizing narrative. Interrotron is a hybrid of "interview" and "terror." Despite the appellation, Morris believes the machine makes interviewees feel at ease; it works with the highly guarded McNamara. Almost without emotion, strategies formed at the highest level of government are revealed as McNamara examines his own decisions. Beginning with his first memory of the victory celebration for World War I at age 2, the film presents major events of the twentieth century as seen by an essential behind-the-scenes part of the military/industrial engine. The eleven "lessons" Morris extracts become a list of maxims about war and human error with, as Stephen Holden wrote in *The New York Times*, "a cumulative message suggesting that in wartime nobody in power really knows anything" (Holden 2003). Another way of saying this is that reason has its limits, a belief demonstrated in other political films that take war as their subject, such as Eugene Jarecki's decades-spanning analysis of the US 'Military Industrial Complex' *Why We Fight* (2005).

Politics as usual

Many documentaries directly address campaigns and elections in the first part of the twenty-first century. This growing trend was in part the natural result of several factors: numerous accusations of election fraud, the presence of Hillary Clinton as the first viable female Presidential candidate, and by the nationally divisive election of President Barack Obama, an event that caused America's centuries-long conflicts over race to erupt. One film that addressed race on a local political level is *Street Fight* (2005), a breakthrough work by first-time feature filmmaker Marshall Curry. The documentary reveals a seldom-explored aspect of race relations in America, black vs. black, as it chronicles the mayoral competition between incumbent Sharpe James and activist city council member Corey Booker. Curry literally takes to the streets in classic cinema verité style, almost innocently picking up his camera and gradually coming into direct conflict with James' old-time political machine, which threatens Curry and shuts down filming. Booker has the opposite response to the camera, realizing that he needs every advantage available to end James' 14 years of power. He also possesses powerful charisma that the film highlights, and this documentary became significant in Booker's rising career. Although he lost this 2002 Newark, New Jersey race, James did not run in 2006 and Booker scored a 75 percent majority that elected him Mayor in 2006. *Street Fight* clearly demonstrates how old-fashioned door-to-door campaigning, money, and personal slurs are part of the fiber of American elections. The divides among the African American population is perhaps the most interesting aspect of the film. James accuses Booker of not being "black enough." Interestingly, when shown to young Israelis in 2011, *Street Fight* evoked responses of surprise and recognition. This audience did not know that blacks in America held widely different points of view and the Israelis recognized the similar situation between the many factions of Jewish citizens in their country (White 2009).

Presidential campaigns are natural documentary subjects, with important examples ranging from Humphrey vs. Kennedy during the Wisconsin primary in Robert Drew's *Primary* (1960) to James Carville leading the Bill Clinton charge in D.A. Pennebaker and Chris Hegedus' *The War Room* (1993). Documentaries are better than the traditional news media in explaining the complexities of the "hanging chads" debacle in Florida as well as other alleged and proven voter frauds, especially in Ohio and Florida, that took place during both the 2000 Bush–Gore and the 2004 Bush–Kerry elections. Danny Schechter's *Recount Democracy* (2002), and *Uncounted: The New Math of American Elections* made by David Earnhardt in 2008 cover this ground. The most reasoned and convincing is *Stealing America: Vote by Vote* (2008) directed by Dorothy Fadiman, a documentarian who has made social issue documentaries for over 30 years. *Stealing America* probes the extent of election manipulation in the United States by focusing on proven cases of voter disfranchisement, the use of rigged electronic voting machines and anomalies such as uncounted ballots, inaccurate final vote tallies, and vote-switching. Thousands of facts assembled by Fadiman over a five-year period were rigorously vetted. Testimony from one technician explains how he personally rigged voting machines on orders from the regional government, another impartial election monitor describes how he was prevented from counting votes, and the hours of waiting designed to block poor and minority individuals from voting are detailed with chilling precision. *Stealing America* uses archival news footage intercut with numerous talking heads and is narrated by actor/activist Peter Coyote. It received substantial theatrical release in about 80 theaters, a feat made possible by private donations, and like many activist films it is available for free download. The power of this film, the complexities of economic censorship in America, and the threat *Stealing America* posed to the Bush administration is made clear by its Executive Producer Mitchell Block, who offered the film to the chief executive of documentary for a major cable network and was told, "I love your film, I could buy it, promote it, air it and it would do well. Then I would be fired" (Block 2012).

The term "social change" is itself neutral, but in modern American usage, it has acquired a connotation of Leftist activism. All types of documentarians of every race, age, and gender make social change documentaries, but white men make most of the directly political films that receive wide attention. Fadiman's *Stealing America* is an exception. Annie Sundberg's and Ricki Stern's *The End of America* (2008) based on a book of the same name by Naomi Wolf is an historical morality tale. It draws parallels between current events in the US and the historical rise of dictators and fascism in once-free societies. The film cites ten steps a society goes through as it becomes Fascistic and notes how those ten steps exist today using examples such as the rise of paramilitary groups, secret prisons and selective suspension of the rule of law. *The End of America* is political in the contemporary sense, and is historical. Historical re-examination is also the context for Shola Lynch's 2004 documentary *Chisholm '72: Unbought & Unbossed*, which examines the 1972 presidential campaign by the late Congresswoman Shirley Chisholm, the first African-American credible run for the office, and her *Free Angela Davis and all Political Prisoners* (2013), about the activist icon's notorious 1971 trial on charges of conspiracy, kidnapping, and murder. Lynch, the only woman-of-color documentarian discussed in this essay, is one of the few filmmakers working in the twenty-first century to examine the political experiences of African Americans. Her work is also chiefly archival compilation, as is that of Stanley Nelson, the director/producer/writer of the historical film *Freedom Riders* (2010), the first feature documentary about civil rights activists, both black and white, who challenged segregation in interstate transport in the American South during the spring and summer of 1961. The attention the movement generated caused the federal government to take down Jim Crow signs of "whites only" and "colored only," allowing every American to travel freely.

A lighter take on electioneering, made by a woman, is Aaron Lubarsky and Alexandra Pelosi's 2002 *Journeys with George*. Pelosi, the daughter of US Congresswoman from California, Nancy Pelosi, was at the time an NBC television producer. She creates a video diary of her year and a half on the press bus campaigning with George W. Bush. Self-described by Pelosi as a "home movie" that "does more than just document the drama behind the scenes of a political campaign," the promotional ads claim: "This is W. unplugged, the baloney and

Cheetos-eating matchmaker you didn't see on tv." Pelosi appears on camera, getting some special recognition by Bush as the daughter of the then House Minority Whip. He is seen as chummy with supporters around the country. Whatever one thinks of Bush, he charms the people in this film. Pelosi's other political subjects are not so fortunate. In *Fall to Grace* (2013), she covers New Jersey Governor Jim McGreevy's departure from politics when it is revealed that he is gay and had an extramarital affair. She engages in a type of sneak attack documentary as a junior/female Michael Moore and she states, "It's better to beg for forgiveness than to ask for permission .... I don't ask for permission. I think anytime you have to ask for permission your project is doomed" (quoted in Gavin 2013). No one who needs to "beg for forgiveness for their film" should be called a documentarian.

The rights of the Right

One criticism of contemporary American political documentaries is that they usually are made from a left-leaning perspective, an assumption that dates back to the earliest cinema and key examples of the genre by Soviet filmmakers such as Dziga Vertov, Alexander Dovshenko, Esther Shub, and others. In this respect, politically conservative documentaries have not tended to attract significant attention or feature in major film festivals (Morfoot, 2014).

One conservative film that did get a large amount of attention is *2016: Obama's America* (D'Souza and Sullivan) which grossed approximately $33,499,86.00 since its release in July 2012, a date timed to influence the 2012 Mitt Romney–Barack Obama Presidential campaign. This figure makes it the fourth-highest-grossing theatrical documentary of the twenty-first century.[5] Produced by Gerald L. Molen, it postulates a grim scenario of what life would be like under Barack Obama's second term as President. "Love Him, Hate Him: You Don't Know Him" is its tag line, and the filmmakers obviously subscribed to the latter view. D'Souza emigrated from India, then went on to success as a policy analyst in Ronald Reagan's administration and later became a respected conservative intellectual. The film is based on his 2010 book *The Roots of Obama's Rage*. The premise of both book and film is that Obama's personal background leads him to believe "that America's sins of colonialism be set right and that America be downsized" (quoted in *2016: Obama's America* trailer). It uses recreations, interviews, Obama's own words, archival footage, and the unlikely presence of Obama's half-brother, George Obama, to create an anti-Barack Obama message. Like many other contemporary documentaries, it takes cues from Michael Moore with its seemingly guileless searching-the-world-for-answers approach. Filmed in Washington, Hawaii, Mumbai, Oklahoma, Kenya, and other locations, *2016* was funded by a Utah-based limited-liability corporation, named "Obama's America Foundation."

Supporters of *2016* created a small ruckus when the film was not included in the Academy of Motion Picture Arts and Sciences (AMPAS) short list for documentary nominees in 2012. The film's producer, Gerald L. Molen, who in a career spanning over 30 years in Hollywood also co-produced *Schindler's List* (Spielberg, 1993) among other films, wrote to the Academy protesting the exclusion with charges that his film was not considered because of its conservative point of view. Molen (an AMPAS member himself) also cited the fact that Michael Moore was at that time an AMPAS Documentary Branch Governor as reason for its exclusion. Governors actually have no particular power in selecting Oscar nominees, as Molen probably well knew, while this protest seems ironic given the outcry from Leftist filmmakers over the same Academy's supposed snub of *Roger & Me* in 1990 and the more decried lack of recognition in 2005 for Moore's *Fahrenheit 9/11*. D'Souza in fact credits Michael Moore's approach to selling *Fahrenheit 9/11* as the inspiration for *2016*'s timing and marketing campaign (White 2012). Both films benefitted in terms of recognition, and probably in box office receipts from the publicity generated by not receiving nominations. As for the funders of *2016*, D'Souza raised about $2.5 million from a wide range of conservative contacts under the for-profit Obama's America Foundation (White 2012; Bond 2012). Molen does not publically mention that he is a member of the Church of Latter Day Saints (Mormon) as is Romney, whose Mormon faith, along with the church's campaign contributions, became contentious points in the election.

Other documentary exceptions to the Left perspective exist, particularly related to the rise of the Christian Right and the Tea Party movement. One example, The Moving Picture Institute, whose motto is "Promoting Freedom through Films," lists a catalogue of 22 titles that range across a spectrum of topical subjects. The online descriptions are relatively balanced. 2012's *U.N. Me* (playing off the title of Morgan Spurlock's *Supersize Me*, 2004) by Ami Horowitz and Matthew Groff uses a Moore/Spurlock-esque approach, traveling to expose the alleged incompetence of the United Nations. More telling is *The Rubber Room* (2010) by Jeremy Garrett, described on the site as

> a gripping revelation of the abominable waste and corruption in New York City's public schools, *The Rubber Room* exposes a system in which hundreds of teachers are banned from their classrooms and reporting to 'rubber rooms,' where they are not allowed to work but continue to collect their full salaries.
>
> (*Moving Picture Institute*)

Conclusions

Were the first 15 years of the twenty-first century the American political documentary's Golden Age? This period did give us a multitude of forceful and meaningful nonfiction voices, more than ever before, but the era must be viewed within the context of all film history. Looking at documentary making as a 120-year process, there are several periods when the form was at the fore of cultural life. Many of the very earliest films just around the turn of the nineteenth into the twentieth century were nonfiction actualities. Despite a few exceptions, principally *Nanook of the North* (Flaherty, 1922), documentary of almost any kind was not obviously prominent in the teens and twenties. In the 1930s in the UK, Germany, and the US, documentaries and the often-conservative newsreels were very much a part of the film world. World War II was filled with documentary political statements, although, while the early years of television produced good news coverage, documentaries were not especially prominent. The 1960s changed that, and American TV networks produced many fine stand-alone and series documentaries that reached millions of people, although the vast majority did not focus on politics. By the late 1960s a new generation of 16-mm filmmakers were creating theatrical documentaries that played on college campuses, in art houses, and in repertory theaters; most of these were highly political, loudly championing the causes of civil rights, the student movement, anti-war and anti-nuclear activities, the second wave of feminism, etc. The numbers and breadth of distribution of these films became even stronger in the 1970s and continued to morph through the 1980s with stronger environmental themes, personal stories of liberation and critiques of government agencies. These films possessed optimism: the war could be stopped, nuclear weapons would be eliminated, people would legally vote for change.

The point is that given the total numbers of all types of independent films that emerged in these previous periods, the percentage of important political documentaries made and seen was smaller than that of foreign language and independent fiction films. Relatively, the overall ratio of documentary to specialized fiction seems about the same today. Technological morphing has not resulted in a greater percentage of documentaries, despite the ease with which people can capture events. Still, as technology becomes simpler and less costly to use, more and more people make more and more films of every stripe. As distribution networks clog screens around the world, more and more people see more and more work of every kind. Worldwide, documentary making is increasing and the form often is a large percentage of the film output of many developing countries. The traditional US global filmmaking domination makes its case different. Yes, America now popularizes some documentarian 'superstars,' but such celebrities are manufactured throughout every sector of society in endless numbers now. The broad public recognizes Michael Moore, Ken Burns, and now maybe Morgan Spurlock in ways that previous documentary makers never experienced. The public also knows about Quentin Tarrantino, Michael Bay, John Waters, and James Cameron in ways that were foreign for earlier decades of directors. D.W. Griffith and Charlie Chaplin each made a stir, but the public knew little or nothing of silent filmmakers. During much of the "Golden Age" of the Hollywood studios, filmmakers were also generally unsung. The movie-going public knew a Cecil B. DeMille or Alfred Hitchcock film, but almost no one at the time went to see a movie directed by John Ford or Raoul Walsh. They went to see a Western, or a Humphrey Bogart picture.

There is anecdotal evidence that parts of the public prefer documentaries. Although many are devoted to the Discovery networks and a smaller number turn to Public Broadcasting or Home Box Office, general documentary audiences go to see films made by celebrity documentarians or works about specific subjects that relate to them personally. 2014 saw the wide release of additional important political documentaries. Errol Morris profiles another major politician and architect of war in *The Unknown* about former Secretary of State Donald Rumsfeld. With the artistry of filmmakers like Morris, there is a continued vitality in the form, and perhaps the first decades of the twenty-first century will truly be a "Golden Age" for documentary film.

Notes

1 The term American is used here to describe the Republic and the people of The United States of America with full knowledge that North America is also composed of Canada and Mexico, and that there are many Central American and South American nations.

2 This essay uses the words film, documentary and title interchangeably, except when noted. These words are also used with the full knowledge that film itself is a dead technology that television shows are often the main outlet for documentaries and that diverse delivery methods are appearing rapidly. It also uses the word cinema in one of its traditional senses as the world's historical and contemporary body of films.

3 Figures were taken from the Internet Movie Database http://www.imdb.com/title/tt0361596/business?ref_=tt_dt_bus (accessed on 18 February 2015).

4 These figures were retrieved through Box Office Mojo www.boxofficemojo.com (accessed on 18 February 2015).

5 See Box Office Mojo, http://www.boxofficemojo.com/genres/chart/?id=documentary.htm (accessed on 18 February 2015).

Bibliography

Block, M. (2012) Personal Interview with the Author, Los Angeles, California, 30 August.

Bond, P. (2012) "Investors in Legal Confrontation Over '2016: Obama's America'," *Hollywood Reporter*, 24 October, http://www.hollywoodreporter.com/thr-esq/2016-obamas-america-investors-legal-382884 (accessed on 18 February 2015).

French, P. (2013) "Review: We Steal Secrets," *The Guardian*, 13 July, http://www.theguardian.com/film/2013/jul/14/we-steal-secrets-wikileaks-review (accessed on 18 February 2015).

Gavin, P. (2013) "Alexandra Pelosi Follows Jim McGreevy on Film," *Politico*, 26 March, http://www.politico.com/story/2013/03/alexandra-pelosi-jim-mcgreevey-film-89341.html (accessed 18 February 2015).
Holden, S. (2003) "Revisiting McNamara and the War He Headed," *New York Times*, 11 October, http://www.nytimes.com/2003/10/11/movies/film-festival-review-revisiting-mcnamara-and-the-war-he-headed.html (accessed on 18 February 2015).
Jump Cut (1977) Special Section "Radical Cinema in the '30s: Film and Photo League," *Jump Cut*, 14, March, pp 23–33.
Morfoot, A. (2014) "Right-Wing Documentaries Left in the Dark at Film Festivals," *Variety*, 16 January, http://variety.com/2014/film/spotlight/right-wing-docs-dont-feel-the-fest-love-1201061557/ (accessed on 18 February 2015).
Moving Picture Institute (n.d.) "*The Rubber Room* Synopsis," http://www.thempi.org/films/therubberroom.html (accessed on 18 February 2015).
White, M. (2012) "Obama's America Director Emulates Moore to Boost Movie," *Bloomberg's BusinessWeek*, 24 August, http://www.bloomberg.com/news/articles/2012-08-24/-obama-s-america-director-emulates-moore-to-boost-movie (accessed on 18 February 2015).
White, T. (2009) "American Documentary Showcase Delegate Report: Israel and Jordan," http://www.icus.us/delegations-2009/israel-jordan/ (accessed on 18 February 2015).

37

DOCUMENTING DISSENT

Political documentary in the People's Republic of China

Luke Robinson

Introduction: the emergence of a documentary mode

Contemporary independent Chinese documentary frequently traces its roots to a loosely affiliated group of filmmakers who, in the early 1990s, decided to leave their positions at China Central Television (CCTV), the national broadcaster, and strike out on their own. Once outside the state media system, these filmmakers largely adopted an observational aesthetic, making films that increasingly focused on the socially marginal or engaged in Frederick Wiseman-esque institutional analysis. In the past decade, however, what is sometimes termed the "New Documentary Movement" has diversified considerably. One symptom of this pluralization is the emergence of an explicitly socially and politically engaged strand of filmmaking that takes the early filmmakers' emerging interest in the subaltern in new and often quite radical directions. From the late 1990s, the socially and economically marginal came under sustained scrutiny from independent documentary filmmakers. Feature-length films were made about subcultures of all descriptions – sex workers, drug users, the elderly, homosexuals, migrant workers, migrant children, the mentally ill, the physically disabled, the urban poor – but also, increasingly, about those suffering from various forms of social, economic and political injustice.[1] These documentaries were complemented by cruder footage that directly captured events associated with such oppression.[2] Sometimes these images were then interwoven with other footage to create full-length films, as the directors Hu Jie and Ai Xiaoming did in *Our Children/Women de wawa* (2009). This is a documentary about the investigations conducted by parents of schoolchildren crushed to death in the 2008 Wenchuan earthquake into why their children died; Hu and Ai incorporated material shot by their subjects, on video and on mobile phones, into the final cut. Lastly, the issue of historical trauma raised its head. Certain filmmakers began to record the stories of those who had suffered in the past, particularly during the Maoist era, capturing their testimony on camera. Hu Jie's *Xunzhao Lin Zhao de linghun/Searching for Lin Zhao's Soul* (2004) and *Wo sui siqu/Though I Am Gone* (2007) are textbook cases here, but so is *Minjian jiyi jihua/The Memory Project* (2010–) initiated by Beijing-based filmmaker Wu Wenguang's Caochangdi Studio. In all such examples, despite the continued influence of the observational aesthetic, it is increasingly possible to find sequences that break with the independent Chinese documentary tradition of carefully cultivated 'objectivity'.

Two factors in particular have contributed to the growth of this new documentary mode. First, the diffusion across China at the end of the 1990s of comparatively inexpensive video production and editing technology, particularly the digital camera and laptop editing packages. No longer the exclusive purview of ex-television professionals, but running the full gamut from complete amateurs to internationally acclaimed artists, documentary filmmaking has thus become a genuinely mass activity. The result is material that often differs markedly in both content and perspective from work shot in the early 1990s. Second, China's 2001 entry into the World Trade Organization (WTO), coupled with its hosting of major international events such as the 2008 Beijing Olympics and the 2010 Shanghai Expo, accelerated already growing social inequality between regions, classes, and the city and the countryside, resulting in violent incidents that highlighted such tensions. The rise of a more explicitly engaged independent documentary mode in China could therefore be viewed as a direct response to the reality of the country's ongoing transition to a market economy, coupled with a growing desire among the general populace to capture the consequences and casualties of these changes using newly accessible technologies. It is partly this dynamic that has led Chris Berry and Lisa Rofel (2010) to christen contemporary independent documentary in China an "alternative archive."

Locating the political

While my aim here is to discuss these documentaries as political filmmaking, to assume coherence to this body of work and its politics is potentially controversial. As the elasticity of terms such "socially engaged" and "alternative archive" suggests, this material is heterogeneous in form and content. Few of the films or filmmakers previously mentioned conform to the standard Euro-American blueprint of political filmmaking, that of activist documentary. Only a small number of the works discussed above agitate within a rights-based framework, while almost none of the directors would class themselves as activists, however so defined. The exceptions to this rule are often the most prominent – the aforementioned Ai Xiaoming, Hu Jie and Ai Weiwei, for example – though other less famous figures such as AIDS activist Hu Jia could be included. Yet to reduce politically engaged filmmaking to these characteristics is to ignore the question of how activism manifests in China more broadly. As Peter Ho and Richard Louis Edmonds (2007: 217–218) point out, in a semi-authoritarian state such as China, activism is always "embedded". It is a matter less of conflict than of ongoing negotiation with the state and the Party, precisely because the latter leaves little room for association that stands outside the former. Thus, activism in China does not always manifest in the form of direct legal contestation with the authorities. Indeed, the severity of the potential response to such behaviour means many groups avoid such direct challenges to state power, turning instead to what Ching Kwan Lee and You-tien Hsing (2010: 4) term the "politics of recognition" and the "politics of representation". The former aims to redraw the line between the public and the private, seeking both to publicly articulate, and to get formal acknowledgment of, the identities and needs of particular social groups. The latter engages in "symbolic contestation": challenges to official state discourse expressed through written and audio-visual media. At times the two may be connected, particularly where the state refuses to acknowledge the existence of certain communities, or frames their needs in specific ways. In this sense, a Chinese documentary could be considered actively political if its representational strategies contest or dissent from the official government position on the subject documented, in the process moving the viewer to respond to the condition of that subject, whether affectively, discursively, or through concrete social action. These films could therefore be considered types of "small media" (Sreberny-Mohammadi and Sreberny-Mohammadi 1994: 22), combining form and content in ways that seek to "conscientize, politicize and mobilize" their audiences, if only in limited ways.

What I am terming here political documentary thus covers a broad spectrum of work, from the explicitly activist to the less self-consciously interventionist or engaged. This is not to minimize the differences across such a spectrum, but rather to suggest that these documentaries can be situated on a continuum, and may therefore hold certain concerns in common. Lee and Hsing's framework is one way to understand this continuum; using it, however, requires us to address the significance of a cultural form implicit in their politics: the public. For a politics of recognition to redraw the boundary between public and private necessitates that a normally hidden social identity be made visible: in other words, be performed, articulated or displayed "in public". Here, public is a location, a physical space outside the home where people can gather. It is similar to the coffee shops where citizens could engage in rational debate and discussion in Jurgen Habermas's (1989) classic theorization of the public sphere. Yet at the same time, such a public is clearly discursive. This assumption is explicit in the concept both of a politics of representation and of symbolic contestation; it is also central to the belief that articulating particular subjectivities has the ability to move those witnessing such a performance to an immediate response. Implicit here is Michael Warner's (2002) idea of the public as a social formation that is hailed into being, an entity or entities created through processes of mobilization, rather than one that is free-standing. Although the articulation of a public may be achieved through the exercise of reason, in practice sentiment, emotion and "structures of feeling" (Williams 1977) are often as important. In any case, it is at moments like these that the public as a form of common social experience – the "general social horizon" (Negt and Kluge 1993: 2) – is usually activated, however temporarily.

Using Lee and Hsing's framework to assess the ways in which political documentary in China is political thus requires us to consider how these films engage public space, public discourse and viewing publics as part of their politics. The rest of this chapter builds on this premise. First, it looks at documentary practice, considering how certain directors make use of the filmmaking process to perform marginal social identities in public spaces, soliciting a politics of recognition from those whom they encounter there. Second, it looks at the poetics of these documentaries, considering how the films try to make their subject matter visible, but also how they exploit particular tropes to mobilize publics of sentiment, encouraging the viewer to sympathize with those presented on camera. Finally, it addresses infrastructure: how these films are exhibited, distributed and publicized. These processes are critical to their ability to sustain a public, or a position in public discourse, over time. It is here that Chinese political documentary faces its severest pressures, and these problems, I argue, may in turn feed back into the particular ways in which these films represent their subjects on screen.

Filmmaking as public performance: the political self

If digital technology helped "democratize" the means of independent documentary production in China, it also helped shape documentary practice. In particular, it enabled the development of a more mobile mode of filmmaking. Lightweight cameras emancipated the director from the need for a crew: the documentary-maker Wu Wenguang (2010: 54) commented that, as a result, "I have become an individual with a DV camera, filming anything that I please that happens to wander into my line of vision". This new mobility enabled directors to cover and penetrate space more effectively, resulting in work that accessed domestic interiors for the first time – such spaces were harder to film with larger, more conspicuous equipment.

The consequence was increased concern about the ethics of independent documentary filmmaking and the potential power disparity between those behind and in front of the camera, particularly where the latter were socially marginal subjects in the first place.

For politically engaged filmmakers, however, I would suggest that the mobility of the digital camera presented an opportunity rather than a threat. Specifically, it represented the potential to move *out* into public space as much as move *inwards* into the domestic sphere. Take Fan Popo and David Cheng's *Xin Qianmen dajie/New Beijing, New Marriage* (2009), for example. This documentary short chronicles the performance of a gay wedding at Beijing's Qianmen Street on Valentine's Day 2009. Tracking the participants – one female and one male couple respectively – as they don western-style wedding clothes and make-up, travel by taxi to the venue and have wedding photographs taken in full view of members of the general public, the film then turns its gaze outwards. The directors and participants question this audience on its views of homosexuality; ask whether those watching would accept gay marriage; and finally get people to pose for photographs with the happy couples. The film concludes with a montage of gay wedding stills from around the world, and an appeal for the legal recognition of same sex partnerships in China.

New Beijing, New Marriage finishes with the kind of legal flourish recognizable to many gay rights groups around the world, and in that sense is clearly legible as a form of activist documentary. As important, though, is how the filmmakers exploit the mobility of the camera throughout the short, first to enter public space, then to enact a politics of recognition. Though the documentary starts in private space – a hotel room, where both couples are preparing for their wedding – the camera tracks the couple through the ambiguous public–private hybrid of the taxi out into the entirely public space of Qianmen. The documentary as a totality is therefore structured around a movement outwards from private to public. Second, once they have arrived at Qianmen, the filmmakers do more than simply record the audience. By moving the camera into and around the crowd, and by actively asking questions of these onlookers from behind the camera – questions that mirror those posed by the couples, such as "will you support our same sex wedding?" – the filmmakers clearly align their own identity with that of their subjects. In effect, the filming process serves to double that of the wedding. By performing the ceremony, the brides and grooms seek to make their sexualities public knowledge, while at the same soliciting the support of the general public both for their identities and for their relationships. Through the act of filming the event, the directors actualize their own public identities as gay filmmakers, while in turn challenging those gathered around to accept them as such. Here, the digital camera facilitates the transformation of documentary filmmaking into its own kind of political praxis, one that enables the public articulation of personal and marginal social identities, while at the same time appealing to a broader public for the validation of these identities and the relationships associated with them.

The kind of identity publicly enacted in and through Fan and Cheng's documentary might be specific to one minority community, but the use of documentary filmmaking to construct new public subjectivities in China is not. Ai Weiwei is a case in point. In films such as *Lao ma ti hua/Disturbing the Peace* (2009), Ai exploits the act of filming to publicly enact his identity both as an activist filmmaker and as a citizen of the People's Republic of China (PRC). Using the filmmaking process as a fact-finding mission, Ai's on-camera confrontations with the authorities – particularly the police and the Public Security Bureau – become opportunities to consciously assert his legal rights in public, while at the same time cataloguing the practical abuse of, and limits to, such rights on a day-to-day basis. Filming thus becomes a way in which the documentary director as critical citizen can be brought into being. Participatory "citizen filmmaking" projects, such as Ai Xiaoming's with the Wenchuan earthquake victims' parents, can also use documentary-making as a way of disseminating this identity at a local level. To quote Ai:

> In the past, we felt we could only film with a hidden camera – we felt we had no power to confront the police. But Ai Weiwei and others encouraged the idea of facing the authorities, emphasizing the rights of citizens to film and scrutinize their actions. This was a huge breakthrough, not in terms of content, but in attitude: the documentarian no longer runs away, but instead stands up, insists on filming to the end, facing the opponent's camera.
>
> (*Chang and Qian 2011: 76*)

Here, the act of filming generates the subjectivity of citizenship through the public assertion of citizens' rights – even, indeed particularly, where such filming involves direct conflict with government representatives.

Textual strategies: observationalism, affect and the witnessing public

If documentary filmmaking as a practice may allow for a variety of activist-style interventions, documentary film as product may also constitute an intervention, and a more obviously discursive one. If these films are to be understood as a form of symbolic contestation then the question of how they represent their subject matter is key. This is underlined by the diversification of Chinese documentary filmmaking styles since the late 1990s. As previously noted, the earliest independent filmmakers initially adopted the observational style of American direct cinema. Although this tradition still exerts a strong influence on Chinese independent documentary filmmakers, it is increasingly mixed with other practices. These practices include acknowledgment of the camera by those being filmed; audio-visual recognition of the filmmaker's presence on screen; participatory gestures, including handing the camera over to the documentary subject; montage editing; and the use of extra-diegetic music. All of the above depart from the self-imposed constraints of observational filmmaking. While there are clear institutional reasons for these formal developments – in particular, the increasing interpenetration of the Chinese independent film and contemporary art worlds – here I would like to consider the question of documentary aesthetics in relation to observational practice, politics and the public. This provides a slightly different perspective on why certain directors may choose to retain, or dispense with, filmmaking practices well established in the sphere of Chinese independent documentary production.

One example of a political documentary that demonstrates the continued influence of direct cinema is Wang Wo and Zhu Rikun's *Duihua/The Dialogue* (2014). Shot over a period of several years, this film takes as its subject matter the relationship between China's Han Chinese majority and ethnic minority groups, specifically Tibetans and Uighurs, and focuses on attempts by Chinese intellectual Wang Lixiong and human rights lawyer Teng Biao to engage in dialogue with the Dalai Lama. It starts with a Skype interview between these three figures – an interview that took place in 2010, during which Wang and Teng posed a series of questions to the Dalai, including some which were submitted online by Chinese citizens, and tweeted his responses – before proceeding to chronicle the aftermath of the meeting. The documentary also includes a section with Ilham Tohti, the now-imprisoned Uighur scholar and activist, discussing Han–Uighur relations, and finishes with a lengthy sequence in which Wang Lixiong addresses the camera directly, discoursing on the future of inter-ethnic relations in China.

The Dialogue is shot almost entirely observationally. With the exception of the segment featuring Tohti the camera hardly moves and the presence of the directors barely registers. Instead, we are treated to lengthy, static shots of Wang Lixiong's apartment, taken from a limited number of angles. These shots capture the online discussion as it evolves in real time, and then again, in the film's concluding segment, register with precise detail Wang's analysis of inter-ethnic politics in the PRC. This seems deliberate. *The Dialogue* is as much document as documentary. Its aim is not to treat this discussion creatively, but to act as record for an event that – officially, at any rate – never took place. Its lack of formal sophistication, with regard to both editing and cinematography, reflects this goal. But at the same time, I would argue that in ensuring form does not overwhelm content, Wang Wo and Zhu Rikun are attempting to address as broad a public as possible. Early independent documentary directors tended to use observational filmmaking to engage in the analysis of spaces and institutions, constructing subtle metaphors about the exercise of government power in China through editing. The results, like Duan Jinchuan and Zhang Yuan's *Guangchang/The Square* (1992), were often highly sophisticated but difficult to interpret. In contrast, by simplifying how they represent their chosen subject matter, Wang and Zhu have crafted a formal vehicle that may facilitate the reception and circulation of *The Dialogue*; this in turn means the film can ignite its own discussions and debates, continuing to circulate discursively long after a screening. The directors' record of these discussions ensures that the film's status as both an archive and an act of symbolic contestation is simultaneously underlined and catalyzed.

Contrast this with the following scene from Zhao Liang's *Petition/Shangfang* (2009). Shot over 12 years, *Petition* tracks a group of individuals who have travelled to Beijing from the Chinese provinces, seeking redress from central government for miscarriages of justice suffered in their home towns. This process is known as "petitioning", and those engaged in it as "petitioners": given the sensitivity of the activity, it is something rarely touched on in the mainstream media (Chen 2012: 168). Halfway through the film, the audience is confronted with an arresting sequence. It is set beside a railway: various petitioners mill around in front of the camera, the women keening loudly. "We were all together for petition", one of them cries, as Zhao cuts to a shot of the tracks, the camera zooming in for an extreme close-up of some unidentifiable matter spread across the ground. "Sister, poor older sister", continue the weeping voices on the soundtrack. One elderly woman, beside herself, kneels down by the railway, and has to be dragged backwards to safety as a train rushes past. As this confusion subsides, however, it becomes clear what has just happened. A woman petitioner named Sun Sannü, running to escape from the authorities, has been mown down by a train. Her fellow petitioners have come to the railway tracks in the hope of locating her body. While they walk along the tracks, identifying bits of Sun's corpse, Zhao Liang follows them; as the petitioners find and bag what they can, Zhao captures each moment in extreme close-up. In the process, he replicates the shot from the very beginning of this sequence, providing the viewer with an unobstructed view of what are now very clearly human remains.

Petition's imagery, though extreme, is not unique. It recalls *Though I Am Gone*, in which the protagonist displays the excrement-stained garments his schoolteacher wife was wearing when beaten to death by her students at the start of the Cultural Revolution; the ending of *Searching for Lin Zhao's Soul*, in which Hu Jie caresses locks of his dead subject's hair; even the famous moment in *Disturbing the Peace* when Ai Weiwei presents his face, battered by Chinese law enforcement, to the camera. In all these scenes, the human body is used to materially index the brutality of the Chinese state; in *Petition*, Zhao Liang remains behind the camera throughout this sequence, emphasizing the role the equipment must play in simply capturing this violence. And yet, this scene is far from objective in the sense of distancing. The direct address to camera, the intensity of the petitioners' distress, the location of body parts for the camera, the close-ups: all these elements both register Zhao Liang's presence "as a human witness ... rather than as an indifferent mechanical device" (Li 2010: 40), and engage the viewer in an immediate, emotive, almost excessive manner. To quote Ai Xiaoming once more: "Words can make it easier for us to understand things conceptually, but images mobilize our senses, allowing us to experience with our emotions" (Chang and Qian 2011: 75).

This sequence in *Petition* thus serves not simply to register Zhao Liang's subjectivity on screen or convey the intensity of the emotional trauma that the petitioners are going through, but also to invoke a particular subjective response in the spectator. The visceral qualities of the scene provide a point of entry into the world of the petitioners, a conduit to some briefly held affective commonality, if not a common understanding of their experience. If like *The Dialogue* the documentary functions as an alternative archive, it also does more than that. *Petition* clearly seeks to move the viewer to reassess the plight of the individuals whom Zhao Liang has captured on camera. In doing so, the documentary is not merely making its subjects' lives public, but also *making publics*. The film "hails" its audience both to recognize the identity of the petitioners as a group and to contemplate the moral validity of their individual claims. It does so through highly rhetorical strategies that are based around moments of excess and are clearly intended to provoke a strong emotional and embodied response in the viewer. Such strategies are here clearly intended to produce "witnessing publics", "collectives ... encouraged into an active engagement and responsibility with what they see" (Torchin 2012: 14). It is in this sense that I would argue *Petition* could be classified as political documentary, even if Zhao Liang himself would almost certainly disagree.

The politics of infrastructure

In all the examples discussed above, the publics that underpin the politics of recognition and representation are discursive. They are produced through the act of filmmaking, or encoded as aesthetic appeals that are supposedly activated at the moment of viewing. Consequently, they are bounded in time and space rather than permanent, conditional in part upon systems that enable these films to "navigate the media ecosystem to provide an effective message that is not lost in the noise" (Torchin 2012: 14). While in the age of the digital such navigation no longer requires public space in a physical sense, it does demand an infrastructure: an institutionalized network that allows these films to move across and between spaces, understood both in a material and a cultural sense (Larkin 2008: 5). How political documentary enters the Chinese social imagination, and its consequent ability to expand the boundaries of public discourse in the PRC, is thus intimately bound up with issues of exhibition and distribution.

Although unofficial cinema has long travelled outside China, finding ways to show these films at home has been harder. Two critical forms of infrastructure for independent cinema exhibition in the PRC have been film clubs and independent film festivals. The former emerged in the 1990s, along with VCDs and DVDs. Informal forums in which individuals could gather to watch and discuss cinema that was not theatrically distributed, these clubs started in domestic spaces, but often expanded into more public ones – university classrooms, coffee shops, bars, art galleries – positioned between the state and China's emerging private sector. Independent film festivals began to coalesce around the beginning of the twenty-first century, though some can trace their roots back to these film clubs. Often positioned somewhat euphemistically in Chinese – since film *festivals* (*jie*) have to be formally approved by the government ministry responsible for the film sector, terms such as *zhan* (exhibition) were frequently used to technically bypass this process – they too took place in a similar range of venues to the film clubs, although on a far larger scale. Increasingly structured on the international film festival model, with films 'in competition', prizes, juries and special invited guests, by the second decade of the twenty-first century there were significant annual or biennial festivals occurring in Beijing, Chongqing, Nanjing and Kunming, and many other smaller festivals being staged across the country.

While all these events are location specific, increasingly independent film festivals constitute a national network through which Chinese independent cinema can circulate, while cinephile clubs are co-operating with festivals to screen their programmes. Describing this circuit as a form of public infrastructure, however – particularly for political documentary – is more problematic. First, as events that occupy a legal grey area, independent film festivals are often at risk of being shut down. There is always the possibility that local authorities will step in to halt screenings. Even when negotiations allow these events to continue, conditions are often imposed that are clearly intended to minimize experience of the festival as a public space: in 2013, for example, after an initial intervention the Beijing Independent Film Festival was allowed to reconvene, but only on condition that films were screened at the venue on computers, and to groups of no less than two but no more than five people (Wilkinson 2013). Second, it has sometimes been precisely the programming of these documentaries that has attracted such unwanted attention. In 2007, for example, the Yunnan Multiculture Visual Festival, or Yunfest, was forced to close its biennial festival in Kunming, the provincial capital of Yunnan Province, and move all its events to Dali, a small town to the west of the province. This was connected to controversies surrounding the festival's programming of *Though I Am Gone*, a highly sensitive documentary due to its Cultural Revolution subject matter. The status of these festivals as public events – collective social spaces where publics may be conjured up through screenings – is thus inherently unstable; the presence of political documentary, at least in its most radical forms, only serves to exacerbate this.

One response to these pressures has been the revival of mobile film exhibition practices, popular in the Maoist era. The Beijing Queer Film Festival founded a touring festival in 2008 as a way of bringing films in Beijing to an audience outside the capital. Since this travelling festival does not remain in one place for very long, its format is an effective spatial tactic for evading attempts at state surveillance and control while simultaneously expanding the potential public for the films screened. At the same time, by turning the festival format into a mode of distribution, however temporary, it provides one solution to the problem of circulation. More radical filmmakers, however, have often eschewed the independent film festival circuit entirely, turning to self-distribution as a way of reaching their public. Both DVDs and the internet have been critical here, but so have more established infrastructural systems. Ai Weiwei distributed 20,000 DVDs of *Disturbing the Peace* through the Chinese postal system (Qian 2014: 190). Both he and Ai Xiaoming upload their films: Ai Weiwei has a YouTube channel (Ai Weiwei Studio Documentary). Finally, filmmakers have also taken to the internet to form fan communities and to promote their work: websites like Douban and the now-defunct Fanhall serve as places where discussions of independent cinema can be conducted and disseminated, while Wu Wenguang uses Weibo, the Chinese microblogging service, to promote his Caochangdi Studio and associated projects. In consequence, while it may be difficult to talk of a coordinated infrastructure for the public distribution and exhibition of socially committed documentary in China, it is clear that multiple, partial infrastructures do exist, and that filmmakers exploit them as and when necessary, in a variety of different combinations.

To treat these various mechanisms of publicity as ineffectual would be inaccurate. The different infrastructures touched on above may not be integrated, but the variety of options available allows for constant improvisation in the quest to connect with viewers. As Ai Xiaoming says of Ai Weiwei's tactic of free distribution, "this has encouraged people to discuss, to participate. This experience of public participation is an important step forward" (Chang and Qian 2011: 76). Nonetheless, not only is this infrastructure uneven, but it is no less prone to government intervention than that of the film festival circuit: the temporary closure of Fanhall in December 2009 was apparently connected to debates around *Petition* on the site, while discussion of Zhao Liang's documentary was censored on Douban. This leaves Chinese political documentary in a conflicted position. While the spread of digital technology has made production of such documentary in China a genuinely popular practice, and one that can take place independently of state-run institutions, this development has not yet been replicated at the levels of exhibition, distribution and promotion. The possibilities for intervention at the level of representation and performance have expanded; as yet, however, this has not been systematically matched by the crucial material structures needed to circulate these films systematically through the Chinese mediascape, both activating and sustaining public awareness of the issues that the documentaries address.

I would like to conclude by linking this structural unevenness to the question of aesthetics. As I hope I have made clear, while in some ways the contemporary Chinese independent media ecology is one of abundance, in other ways it remains one of scarcity – or at least, unpredictability. The question of how to bridge this gap remains a troubling one for many independent filmmakers. This is particularly true for those seeking to conscientize their viewers, to move them to contemplate, or even act upon, the social, economic, or political problems that they have captured on screen. In a discussion of Ai Weiwei and Ai Xiaoming's work, Ying Qian (2014: 190–192) has perceptively linked these filmmakers' use of social media for distribution and publicity to the emergence of new forms of seriality in their documentaries. In contrast, I would like to refer back to the two distinct poetics I noted in *Petition* and *The Dialogue*, and link these to the issues of infrastructure. The particular affective, embodied appeals in *Petition* reflect the documentary subjects' experience of violence, both literal and social, and the need to create a sympathetic public at the moment of viewing; in contrast, the artlessness of *The Dialogue* reflects its desire to capture and convey information. But perhaps these two qualities also reflect the potential scarcity of the independent documentary viewing experience, the problems these directors encounter with exhibition and distribution, and thus the structural contingency that characterizes the Chinese independent media scene at most levels. In this context, the urgency of communication is possibly intensified, for who knows when the next opportunity to move your viewer, to create your public, may arise? Even more so than elsewhere, political documentary practice in the PRC is an "unknown journey" (Chang and Qian 2011: 73); navigating the unpredictability of this journey presents particular pleasures, but also exacts its own costs. In their different ways, the two aesthetic and formal approaches to political documentaries that I have outlined here make this plain.

Conclusion

In this chapter I traced the emergence of a newly politicized form of independent documentary in China. While acknowledging the heterogeneity of this form, I have suggested how its politics might still be understood with reference to those of recognition and of representation, as outlined by Ching Kwan Lee and You-tien Hsing. Not only are these terms sensitive to the variety of ways in which the political manifests in the PRC, but they also, perhaps inadvertently, require us to reflect upon the concept of the public – of public space, making public, of viewing publics – and how this cultural form is integral both to Lee and Hsing's political framework, and also, by extension, to this emerging documentary practice. Documentary filmmaking as a spatially mobile process enables the public performance of identity so central to the politics of both representation and recognition. At the same time, two different documentary poetics I identify – and I should stress that these are far from comprehensive or prescriptive, and should not be read as such – can be understood as trying to make public, or make publics, through their textual strategies; they can therefore both be understood as political, though in different ways. Finally, the multiple infrastructures that support the circulation of this cinema are clearly attempts to facilitate its entry into post-socialist China's emerging public culture. Such infrastructures are imperfect, and I have suggested that their instability may in turn feed into the aesthetic strategies previously discussed. However, they are critical to the survival of political documentary filmmaking in the PRC, and deserve further, more detailed consideration. Clearly, the issue of the public in its various manifestations cannot be said to dictate the politics of political documentary in China. Nevertheless, the concept provides a useful point of entry, and a way of connecting issues of documentary practice, form and ecology.

Notes

1 For example, two recent yet distinct genres of independent documentary focus on illegal land appropriations and urban 'demolitions and relocations'. Such films often, though not exclusively, focus on the problems inherent in these processes, ranging from official corruption to forced eviction, and the trauma suffered by those obliged to undergo them.

2 One example would be the video sent to *The Washington Post* in 2005 by farmers from Shengyou, Hebei Province, which documented violent attempts to evict them from their own land to make way for an ash storage facility (Pan 2005).

Bibliography

Berry, C. and Rofel, L. (2010) "Alternative Archives: China's Independent Documentary Culture", in Berry, C., Lü, X. and Rofel, L. (eds) *The New Chinese Documentary Movement: For the Public Record*. Hong Kong: Hong Kong University Press, pp. 135–154.

Chang, T-C. and Qian, Y. (2011) "Ai Xiaoming: The Citizen Camera", *New Left Review*, 72, pp. 63–79.

Chen, X. (2012) *Social Protest and Contentious Authoritarianism in China*. Cambridge: Cambridge University Press.

Habermas, J. (1989) *The Structural Transformation of the Public Sphere: An Enquiry into a Category of Bourgeois Society*. Cambridge: Polity Press.

Ho, P. and Edmonds, R. L. (2007) "Perspectives of Time and Change: Rethinking Green Environmental Activism in China", in Ho, P. and Edmonds, R. L. (eds) *China's Embedded Activism: Opportunities and Constraints of a Social Movement*. Abingdon: Routledge, pp. 216–225.

Larkin, B. (2008) *Signal and Noise: Media, Infrastructure, and Urban Culture in Nigeria*. Durham, NC: Duke University Press.

Lee, C. K. and Hsing, Y-T. (2010) "Social Activism in China: Agency and Possibility", in Lee, C. K. and Hsing, Y-T. (eds) *Reclaiming Chinese Society: The New Social Activism*. Abingdon: Routledge, pp. 1–14.

Li, J. (2010) "Filming Power and the Powerless: Zhao Liang's *Crime and Punishment* (2007) and *Petition* (2009)", *China Perspectives* 81, pp. 35–45.

Negt, A. and Kluge, O. (1993) *Public Sphere and Experience* (trans. Labanyi, P., Daniel, J. O. and Oksiloff, A.). Minneapolis: University of Minnesota Press.

Pan, P. (2005) "Chinese Peasants Attacked in Land Dispute", *Washington Post*, 15 June [Online]. Available at: http://www.washingtonpost.com/wp-dyn/content/article/2005/06/14/AR2005061401542.html (accessed 6 June 2014).

Qian, Y. (2014) "Working with Rubble: Montage, Tweets and the Reconstruction of an Activist Documentary", in Johnson, M., Wagner, K., Yu, T. and Vulpiani, L. (eds) *China's i-Generation: Cinema and Moving Image Culture for the Twenty-First Century*. London: Bloomsbury Academic, pp. 181–196.

Sreberny-Mohammadi, A. and Sreberny-Mohammadi, A. (1994) *Small Media, Big Revolution: Communication, Culture and the Iranian Revolution*. Minneapolis: University of Minnesota Press.
Torchin, L. (2012) *Creating the Witness: Documenting Genocide on Film, Video and the Internet*. Minneapolis: University of Minnesota Press.
Warner, M. (2002) *Publics and Counterpublics*. Cambridge: The MIT Press.
Wilkinson, J. (2013) "Beijing Independent Film Festival Cancelled. Kind of…", *Time Out Beijing*, 24 August [Online]. Available at: http://www.timeoutbeijing.com/features/Blogs_Books__Film_Blogs/22999/Beijing-Independent-Film-Festival-cancelled-Kind-of.html (accessed 6 June 2014).
Williams, R. (1977) *Marxism and Literature*. Oxford: Oxford University Press.
Wu, W. (2010) (trans. Clayton, C.) "DV: Individual Filmmaking", in Berry, C., Lü, X. and Rofel, L. (eds) *The New Chinese Documentary Movement: For the Public Record*. Hong Kong: Hong Kong University Press, pp. 49–54.

38

POLITICS AND INDEPENDENCE

Documentary in Greece during the crisis

Lydia Papadimitriou

The opening film of the Fourteenth Thessaloniki Documentary Festival on March 9, 2012 was Algerian-born French director Tony Gatliff's *Indignados* (2012). A formally hybrid film, it combines re-enacted sequences of an African immigrant crossing the Greek shores on her way to greener pastures in Europe with footage from the Occupy movements in Spain, and extensive quotes from Stephane Hessel's polemical essay *Indignez-vous!/Time for Outrage!* (2010). The choice of this film to open Greece's main non-fiction film festival reflected the pulse of the country at the time.

It had been two and a half years since the disclosure to the Greek public of the country's unsustainable debt by the then newly elected center left government in October 2009; and just over two years since the Greek parliament's approval of the first austerity package measures in February 2010. In the months that followed the country's sovereign debt crisis rapidly transformed into a political and social one too. The decision, in April 2010, to request an international bailout to avoid bankruptcy led to increased austerity measures and a series of strikes and demonstrations. After a year during which the country's credit rating continued to drop and public anxieties intensified, inspired by the Spanish sit-in protests (shown in Gatliff's film), the Greek *aganasktismenoi* – indignant citizens – occupied Syntagma (Constitution) Square in Athens and other city centers, in protest against the austerity measures. The approval of another austerity bill by the parliament in June 2011 culminated in further demonstrations and clashes with the police, while in November 2011 the government fell and an interim technocratic government was put in place by the parliament. Its remit was to facilitate the implementation of the memorandum, that is, the agreements with the European and international lenders, and lead the country to elections. By March 2012, when the aforementioned documentary festival was held in Greece's second largest city, anger and anxiety about the future were widespread in the country.

At a time of extensive availability of digital means for recording, editing, and circulating audiovisual material, it is not surprising that a lot of images and footage, especially of the protests and clashes, were produced, circulated online, and used in different contexts. The media, both in Greece and internationally, widely reported the events, and the crisis brought almost unprecedented notoriety to the country. The reported events have been framed variously depending on the political orientation of the different outfits, ranging from an emphasis on the effects of corruption and state inefficiency, to calls for solidarity towards the victims of neo-liberalism. Within this context, documentary filmmakers, but also independent journalists, benefited from the new, relatively inexpensive, technologies and both produced and circulated films that offered different perspectives on the unfolding of the crisis. Some of these perspectives were explicitly oppositional to mainstream media representations of the crisis, while others tried to offer a more balanced and less openly judgmental approach.

In this chapter I will focus on four independently produced and circulated documentaries that have addressed aspects of the financial and political crisis in Greece as experienced from its outset in 2009 up until the national elections of 2012. While the outcome of these elections (first held in May 2012 but proved inconclusive, and then repeated a month later) did not resolve the crisis or minimize its social impact, it located Greece within a clear path of accepting the terms of its lenders (the so-called 'troika' of the European Union, European Central Bank, and International Monetary Fund), firmly positioning it within the neo-liberal context of international financial dependence. Despite the continuing presence of dissenting voices, the strengthening of the left, but, alas, also of the extreme right, public opposition to the government as expressed via protests and demonstrations subsided. In January 2015, however, new elections brought to power a coalition with a strong anti-austerity mandate led by a left-wing party; as I write, difficult negotiations around the terms of Greece's debt are taking place with uncertain outcomes about the country's position in the Eurozone. Given this state of affairs, it is not surprising that the crisis and its effects have continued to preoccupy documentary filmmakers in Greece, as evidenced, among others, by the significant number of crisis-related films shown at the Thessaloniki Documentary Festival since 2010 (Papadimitriou 2013, 2014). However, arguably reflecting a (temporarily) more resigned public sphere following the 2012 elections, as well as the fact that people tried to find mechanisms of coping with the more immediate consequences of the crisis, the majority of the documentaries on the crisis made till 2014 are not explicitly political, but address issues related to surviving in/with/despite the crisis. They explore its impact on particular agents, and, in many cases, celebrate the people's adaptability and resilience demonstrated in the light of these difficulties.[1] The fewer films that explicitly focus on political issues after 2012 address the rise of the extreme right.[2]

The aim of this chapter is to explore the ways in which the advent of the financial crisis that led to political instability and extensive social upheaval has been addressed through documentary in Greece. It will focus on four case studies that will be examined from both a textual and contextual angle. Each film adopts a different way of addressing, representing, and interpreting the crisis, while the degree of direct political engagement projected also varies. The analysis will examine the films' form and political intent, the ways in which these films came into being, as well as how they circulated and reached audiences. Such an approach is particularly relevant in the light of the fact that they were all independently produced without any financial support by state-related institutions, private profit-orientated companies, or indeed, political parties – they were not just *about* the crisis, but they were products *of* the crisis. As such, this study is both specific to a particular historical moment, but also representative of the broader set of conditions and range of possibilities open to independent documentary filmmakers making socio-political interventions at times of crisis – but in, broadly speaking, liberal environments, that is, without the threat of direct censorship (Kinkle and Toscano 2011).

The four case studies examined represent different combinations of expository, observational and interactive/participatory documentaries (Nichols 1991, 2010). The first case study, Aris Chatzistefanou and Katerina Kitidi's *Debtocracy* (2011), crowdfunded and released freely on the internet, is polemical and didactic, offering a distinctive and highly persuasive interpretation of the financial crisis, and calling for specific action. The second, Yiorgos Pandeleakis' *155 Sold* (2012) foregrounds its status as raw document, but utilizes expository intertitles and editing techniques to underline the police's abuse of power during the suppression of the demonstrations. The third, Nikos Katsaounis' and Nina-Maria Paschalidou's *Krisis* (2012), part of a larger multimedia project under the title *The Prism GR 2011*, is expository and interactive in that it utilizes voice-over and interviews, but unlike the previous two, its aim is to present the crisis from multiple angles rather than to offer a particular reading of it. The fourth, Marco Gastine's *Democracy: The Way of the Cross* (2012) follows four candidates during their election campaign, and, consistent in its commitment to observation, minimizes interaction at the moment of shooting, and avoids editorial interventions that would guide the spectators' thinking.

The four films selected represent the range of options explored by documentary filmmakers in Greece in response to the crisis, in terms of both formal choices and means of dissemination. As opposed to films made after 2012 that offered more in-depth portraits of individuals affected by the crisis, all the films discussed here represent the crisis as a collective problem affecting the people in the streets, the electorate, the nation – but also, in some cases, Europe and the world more broadly. The independent status of the filmmakers and the limited – if any – financial reward from producing and distributing these films guarantees that they were made out of a genuine desire to capture and convey the situation in crisis-ridden Greece. The intentionality, politics, and aesthetic choices adopted vary significantly: from activist journalism that seeks to motivate audiences to adopt a particular political stance; to oppositional observation that encourages a particular reading of the recorded and edited events; to multi-perspectival plurality that avoids political commitment but subtly favors tolerance and multiculturalism; and finally to observational recording that prioritizes documentary ethics over a political message. While the crisis ultimately eludes representation, examining these four films together offers a powerful insight into some of its causes, its effects, and the ways in which independent documentary can express and communicate them.

Activist journalism

Debtocracy was released through an open access website on April 6, 2011.[3] Directed by two journalists, Aris Chatzistefanou and Katerina Kitidi, the film offers an analysis of the Greek debt crisis and calls for popular resistance and refusal of payments. Consisting of a neologism that combines 'debt' with the Greek-derived suffix '-cracy' (from the word for power and state '*kratos*'), its title implicitly juxtaposes 'democracy' to 'debtocracy,' highlighting how contemporary capitalism utilizes economic dependency to create political and financial subjugation. The film was released at a time of intense anxieties about the way in which the Greek debt crisis would be dealt with, as, following the first bailout about a year earlier, the country's fiscal situation and credit rating had continued to rapidly deteriorate, and public opposition to the second bailout was intensifying.

The film utilizes the concept of 'odious debt,' whereby a country should not be obliged to pay off its debts if they were not incurred for the benefit of its people, to argue that the Greeks should not have to make repayments. More specifically, it supports the idea that an audit committee should be formed to check the legitimacy of the debt, and uses as a role model the case of Equador, where such a process was successfully followed. The film functions as an activist tool, using a number of techniques to inform opinion and persuade its audience to reject the bailout deal, clearly positioning itself on the side of the protesters and the *indignados* that were gathering on Syntagma Square. *Debtocracy* is very effective as a rhetorical instrument. Utilizing a relatively fast editing pace, montage sequences with uplifting music, a mix of archival and everyday imagery, cartoons, sketches, and interviews, together with a focused explanatory and caustically humorous voice-over, the film easily manages to maintain the audience's interest for its 75 minutes.

Debtocracy opens with a series of close-ups of the building of the Greek Parliament over which are heard quotes by the 1967–74 Greek dictator George Papadopoulos and the 2007–11 head of the IMF, Dominic Strauss-Kahn, both of whom use metaphors of illness with reference to Greece and/or the economic crisis. This acerbic beginning underlines the polemical intentions of the film, and creates a scathing parallel between two otherwise unrelated leaders and their patronizing views. Aiming to explore the crisis in some depth the film soon raises the question of whether the crisis was systemic to capitalism or symptomatic to Greece (Figure 38.1). In building up a case for the former, it introduces its first animated sequence that combines visuals from American cartoons with interviews with academics Kostas Lapavitsas and David Harvey to illustrate how, especially after the 1970s, debt has been used by capitalism to sustain the necessary for its survival growth. After a section in which more economists and politicians explain the problems caused by the monetary Union – the fact that Greece belongs to the Eurozone – a second animated sequence begins. Presented in mock vintage black-and-white frames, the directors here elaborate on the Greek post-1980s politicians' responsibility for the debt. A section paralleling Greece with Argentina follows, with images from the documentary *The Take* (2004) and interviews with its director, journalist Ari Lewis. The argument that Greece would be better off if it refused to repay the debt, and that this is morally justified, begins to unravel. Images from the protests are used to stress the damaging effects of austerity, while a commentary by Alain Badiou about the use of violence by capitalism to suppress the reaction to unpopular measures provides theoretical backing to this critique. A third animated sequence, this time with hand-drawn sketches, explains the history of odious debt, and introduces the last part of the film, which presents the case of Ecuador, as a positive example of a Latin American country that refused to pay its debts, and ended up greatly benefitting from it. The final section

Figure 38.1 Poignant juxtaposition: 'Eat the Rich' graffiti next to a Greek National Bank cashpoint in *Debtocracy*.

focuses on the action proposal: that an audit committee should be set up (just like in Ecuador) to assess the legitimacy of the debt, which the filmmakers anticipate would lead to its cancellation. As Chatzistefanou puts it in his voice-over – and the interviewees reiterate in different ways in the montage that follows – "even if the debt was legitimate, no government has the right to kill its citizens in order to satisfy its lenders." After shots of demonstrators celebrating in the streets the film concludes with nonagenarian emblematic left-wing politician Manolis Glezos emphasizing the desire to remove financial and political interference, and an ironically used statement by the then still Prime Minister George Papandreou saying "Now is the crucial moment – let's go."

Highly polemical in its message, and expressing the emotional drive – if not, necessarily all the arguments – of the 'anti-memorandum' camp, the film reached 40,000 viewings within the first hours of its release. Approximate viewing figures provided by the director suggest that more than 500,000 people saw it within the first week, and there have been at least 1.5 million viewers internationally so far (Chatzistefanou 2013; Papastathis 2011). Aside from its topicality, these figures can be understood with reference to its makers' professional identity and the particular way in which the crowdfunding campaign for the film developed. *Debtocracy* was an extension of the journalistic activity of Aris Chatzistefanou, whose radio program *Infowar* had been broadcast for a number years by the commercial Greek channel *SKAI*, and which also aired on television for a year (2007–08). Chatzistefanou's brand of political analysis and lively presentation style that used music, jokes, puns, and a fast pace, had gained him a significant audience base. While initially conceived as a short film, the project gradually grew, and with it the financial demands. When self-financing was not possible anymore, the team turned to the public and set up a crowdfunding site for the film. The response was impressive: the required 8,000 euros were collected in just two weeks. Chatzistefanou's media visibility, established brand, and ability to promote through his radio program were crucial for the success of the crowdfunding campaign. And when, four days before the film was uploaded, the broadcaster for which Chatzistefanou worked sacked him as a result of disagreements over salary reductions, more publicity was generated, leading to additional viewings of the film.

Debtocracy, however, was highly controversial. Commentators in the mainstream press objected to its perceived one-sidedness, its improper use of the two Latin American countries as parallel examples, and its lack of positive propositions for an exit from the crisis (Mandravelis 2011; Papastathis 2011). To such objections, the filmmakers responded by asserting that the film did not aim to be objective, but to counterbalance the biased and one-sided representation of mainstream media, with a set of counter-arguments (Moisis 2011). Chatzistefanou has since made two more crowdfunded films: *Catastroika* (2012 – also with Katerina Kitidi) that deals with the catastrophic effects of rapid privatizations, and *Fascism, Inc.* (2014), which explores the rise of the extreme right wing in Greece in relation to the interests of bourgeois capitalism. As the financial pressures on the Greek public intensified, fundraising for these two films was harder, but it still worked. Chatzistefanou and Kitidi's hope for such funds to enable the contributors to be paid for their labor only met with modest success. Having also circulated freely on the internet with a 'creative commons license,' that is with all copyright released, these films have been widely seen and discussed, impacting on the public's understanding of the crisis.

Oppositional observation

Similar in its anti-memorandum political and polemical drive is Yiorgos Pandeleakis' *155 Sold* (2012), a film that focuses on the protests and their brutal suppression by the police on

Syntagma Square in Athens on June 28 and 29, 2011. Unlike Chatzistefanou and Kitidi's journalistic and expository approach, Pandeleakis' film relies almost exclusively on material shot during these two days, and constructs a diaristic account of the events from the perspective of the protesters, without utilizing voice-over or post-dated interviews. The title of the film refers to the number of MPs (155 out of 300) who voted in favor of the second international bailout (the 'Midterm Agreement') on June 29, 2011.

Despite its overall observational approach, Pandeleakis uses a number of expository intertitles that not only situate spatio-temporally the unfolding events, but also frame the film ideologically and assert the director's oppositional approach. This is evident from the start, as consecutive black screens with white text explain his intentions: to support the view that "Greece has been chosen as the first Western European experiment by 'Economy War'…"; to highlight that the Midterm agreement will result in loss of national sovereignty via economic means; to document "the massive participation, the solidarity and the spirit of the people"; to denounce "State and Parastate [sic], along with the police brutality and its extensive use of chemicals…" After such clear declaration of intentions, the final on-screen statement that the film uses "raw footage and minimal commentary" seems somewhat paradoxical.

However, as Pandeleakis claims, the film consists almost exclusively of footage caught in the streets during these two days. The often highly mobile and erratic images testify to the intensity of the confrontations witnessed and convey a strong sense of immediacy. Pandeleakis punctuates his careful selection of material with editorial decisions that guide our attention to what he wants us to notice and how he wants us to feel. For example, in the opening two shots where we see policemen clad in highly protective gear and tear-gas masks standing around Syntagma Square, a woman's voice apparently caught unawares by the microphone is heard saying "the cops [in Greek slang: *batsoi*] are throwing rocks man," thus directing our attention to the back of the shot where a policeman is doing just this (Figure 38.2).

Figure 38.2 Policemen around Syndagma Square in *155 Sold*.

Editorial interventions are more intrusive. For example, in three separate instances where footage shows the police beating up unarmed citizens, Pandeleakis completely removes the sound, creating an eerie silence that enhances the images' emotional impact and underlines the brutal means of suppression. Elsewhere, television footage showing two politicians addressing parliament is used to create meaning through juxtaposition and irony. The first sequence shows the then Minister of Citizen Affairs, Christos Papoutsis, seeking to offer explanations about the footage that showed uniformed policemen offering protection to some tattooed, masked, semi-naked men carrying iron rods, guiding them safely towards the Parliament building. This footage, which is repeatedly shown in the film, is juxtaposed with the sound, and sometimes also image, of the speaking Minister, raising a number of questions about the existence and activities of the so-called 'para-state,' a secret organization that is believed to illegally support the interests of the state. With the Minister's attempted explanation making effectively no sense, Pandeleakis manages, if not to provide any answers, at least to keep the questions about the identity and the role of these people in the riots, alive. His second such intervention is more awkward in its evident lack of sensitivity towards the representation of disability. It consists of a speech by Panagiotis Kouroublis, the only MP of the governing party to vote against the memorandum, and it seems to express the filmmaker's political views. However, the subtitle that provides the politician's name also indicates that he is blind. While this aims to underline the irony that the only man who can see [the truth] is a blind man, in subjugating the physical condition of a particular person to an abstract metaphor, it treads on thin ethical grounds.

While the film's purely observational claims can be easily challenged, *155 Sold* remains a troubling account of the events on Syntagma Square during these two critical days. It conveys effectively the atmosphere in the streets, ranging from the singing and dancing on the night of June 28, to the suffocation felt from the use of tear gas, and the sense of over-powerment and injustice experienced by the demonstrators. As a very low-budget film produced independently by Pandeleakis, it functions as much as a personal testimony as an ideological indictment. The film premiered at the Fourteenth Thessaloniki Documentary Festival, and it also traveled to a number of other documentary festivals in Greece (Patras, Chalkida) and outside Greece (Austria, Turkey, Italy, the Czech Republic).[4] The Greek State Television (ERT) bought the film, but due to its closure in June 2013, the film has not been broadcast. Its politically sensitive nature makes it uncertain whether the new public broadcaster NERIT will show it or not, but political developments since January 2015 may open new paths for it. The filmmaker, however, is legally tied and can neither commercially distribute, nor make the film freely available on the internet (Pandeleakis 2014).

Multi-perspectival plurality

In contrast to the politically positioned films discussed so far, *Krisis* offers a more wide-ranging and impressionistic portrait of Greece at a time of extensive social transformation. Taking its cue from the 2010 near financial collapse, the film explores the ways in which the crisis has been understood and experienced by a broad range of people representing different ideological, educational, regional, generational, ethnic, racial, class, and ability parameters. The pluralistic and ultimately optimistic approach chosen reflects both its mode of production and the position of the directors as relative outsiders. The 62-minute-long film is part of a multimedia project entitled *The Prism GR 2011* that also includes 27 short films and a two language website.[5] Its directors, Nikos Katsaounis and Nina Maria Paschalidou, had been based in the USA, and returned to Greece during the crisis for this project. Their aim was to document a wide range of different topics in high-quality images with as little cost as possible. To do so, they gathered 14 photojournalists who had not previously made films; in exchange for technical training, use of cameras and expenses (and in some cases a small fee) the photojournalists agreed to film two short films each on a crisis-related topic specified by the directors. The collaborative project lasted for five months (November 2010 to April 2011).

For Katsaounis and Paschalidou the overall project (website, short films, feature) was both an aesthetic and a business experiment. High in their priorities was to achieve a technically accomplished result while capturing the multifaceted dimensions of a crisis that manifested itself in the recent events but had been slowly developing for a number of years. The technical possibilities offered by high-resolution DSLR cameras were critical in enabling this ambition, as they facilitated the move from still photography to video for the photojournalists involved. The equipment was partly provided by sponsors,[6] but overall the project was self-funded, and it was important for the directors to keep the cost-per-minute of the finished product as low as possible. While the short films are available on the website for free, the film is on a pay-per-view platform. This differentiates its status as a more complete and desirable product, but also aims to recoup some of the costs – only with modest success so far.

The title of the multimedia project, *The Prism GR 2011*, underlines its multi-perspectival character, alluding to the various reflections and refractions of the phenomenon of the crisis. The short films' subject matter ranges from the topical – the financial crisis (*Crash*), the demonstrations and protests (*Radical Youth*), the partiality of the media (*Media Wars*) – to broader dimensions of social change, such as the impact of immigration (*Battlefield, Westbound, Yinka, Hidden Crescent*), to environmental concerns (*Forbidden Sea, Destroy Athens*), to explorations of urban and rural lifestyles (*From a Distance, 100+, Forgotten, Once Upon a time*). The 62-minute film *Krisis* (alluding to Greece through the use of the Greek letter 'K' instead of 'C') is based on extracts from the shorts. It has a faster pace than these, moving rapidly from topic to topic. While this at times frustrates for its lack of depth, the availability of the shorts allows the keen viewer to explore particular topics in more depth.

The film opens with the directors' voice-over explaining their own distant perspective as Greeks who have been living abroad: this film is a means for them to understand the homeland they had left behind. The voice-over is matched with accelerated shots of Greek landscapes and cityscapes that create a distancing effect in their puppet-like movement. The rest of the film relies on interviews to convey information. The interviewees range from experts and technocrats, to ordinary citizens and activists. The account begins with the Athens Olympic Games of 2004, a moment of peak of national confidence, and then moves to the December 2008 riots that erupted in response to the killing of a youth by a policeman, in many ways presaging the social crisis that was to follow.[7] The views expressed are highly divergent, and avoid an overarching interpretative narrative, aiming to convey the sense that a story can be told from many different perspectives. Some of the interviewees/characters stand out – for example, the dignified figures of the black musician, Yinka, and the law student Asef Farjam, who not only impress with their command of the Greek language, but also come across as thoughtful and inspirational, pointing towards the future of a new multicultural Greece (Figure 38.3). However, the film also gives voice to one of the leading figures of the extreme right-wing party Golden Dawn, who proudly proclaims the party's anti-immigration policy and admits to its racist beliefs. While not explicitly condemning these views, the inclusion of a number of immigrants and their depiction as fully fleshed characters rather than just background figures, indicates the directors' favoring of a multicultural and pluralistic view of Greece.

While the film relies on interviews, it follows a number of its characters in action, and, wherever possible, it includes external shots of distressed cityscapes or sublime landscapes.

Figure 38.3 Multicultural Greece in *Krisis*.

The often beautifully composed images, rapid editing and change of topics, almost continuous musical soundtrack, and speeded-up frames recall techniques akin to advertising. Aesthetically, this counterpoints the subject matter of the crisis, but this is intentional as the overall project aims to convey a sense of optimism – to posit the crisis as an opportunity for renewal – despite the difficult subject matter it communicates. The advantage of this aesthetic is that it can be more widely appealing: for audiences outside Greece in particular, the film offers a non-confrontational introduction to different aspects of its crisis, while providing visual pleasures. The disadvantage is that the visual slickness, musical comfort, and multifocal but ultimately reassuring message softens the effect of the crisis, and reduces the film's impact on the viewer.

Observational recording

Marco Gastine's election documentary *Democracy: The Way of the Cross* (2012) was also collaboratively filmed. However, unlike *Krisis* its thematic focus is very specific – the two-week campaign leading to the elections of May 6, 2012 – and its approach observational. Taking its cue from such landmark direct-cinema election documentaries as *Primary* (Drew, 1960), (Karakasis 2014, 118–122), *Democracy* differentiates itself from films made by journalists that seek to communicate a particular interpretative angle (such as *Debtocracy*) or aim to offer broad exposition and information (see *Krisis*). Keeping the interaction between filmmaker and subject to a minimum, *Democracy* uses no interviews, while anything external to the captured footage – such as voice-over, non-diegetic music or even archival material – is also avoided.

The film follows four candidates during their electoral campaign, focusing on their behind-the-scenes activities and interactions with prospective voters, rather than on their public speeches and political views. Two of the selected candidates represent the parties that had shared power in the last thirty years (center-left PASOK and center-right Nea Dimokratia/New Democracy); one was from the left-wing party SYRIZA and one from the extreme right-wing Golden Dawn. Gastine hired four filmmakers to follow and shoot the individual candidates, while he coordinated and edited the overall project.[8] The film was totally self-funded: Gastine paid the filmmakers/cinematographers himself, with money he had earned from previous work for television. He also gave them a percentage of the rights should the film be bought for broadcasting.

Democracy: The Way of the Cross is not a polemical film. Its aim is to use the observational camera in order to reveal something beyond the official rhetoric of the political parties and its media representations. The film, however, is defined by some objective limitations: it not only adopts a strictly observational mode of shooting, but it is also restricted by a code of ethics towards the consenting four candidates. While the respect towards the filmed subjects is laudable, it also means that the filmmakers were delimited by what the consenting subjects (and their political entourage) allowed them to shoot. The film, therefore, is not in a position – nor does it aim – to expose newsworthy information that will dramatically change the audience's perception of the particular candidates, and/or the political parties they represent. Instead, it is through the subtle observations recorded on camera and foregrounded through editing that meaning is produced. But this meaning is neither analytically coherent nor fixed. The film remains far more open to interpretation than any of the films discussed above, and allows the audience to read the events according to their own ideological baggage.

Just like *155 Sold*, *Democracy* opens with a pre-credit sequence that offers exposition through titles. However, unlike in Pandeleakis' film, the information here is factual: it provides a trimmed-down chronicle of the debt crisis and presents the May 2012 elections as the result of popular pressure following extensive socio-political discontent. The titles are intercut with mobile shots taken from a car driving in Athens and culminate in a shot of the Greek Parliament, while non-diegetic percussive music creates a reflective, slightly dissonant atmosphere. The title of the film marks the transition to a pared-down observational style: crowd noise takes us into the corridors of power. The name of the first candidate (who was, at the time, a government minister) is noted on the screen together with the statistic of his popularity at the previous elections. We then see him address a group of followers defending his party's unpopular political decisions. The remaining three candidates are also introduced in a similar way, but the parallels also highlight differences in approach, personality, and ways of engaging their audience. For example, while the candidates of the parties who had already been in power spoke to their supporters from enclosed and controlled spaces, both the SYRIZA and Golden Dawn candidates were out in the streets addressing people directly and (apparently) spontaneously.

By drawing a portrait of each of the four candidates, the film also highlights, more or less explicitly, their political ideology. The critique is often subtle. For example, the inclusion of a scene where a prospective voter of the center-right candidate asks him for an employment favor highlights the traditional clientelist relationships that have long defined Greek politics (Figure 38.4). On the other hand, the aggressively anti-immigrant language of the Golden Dawn candidate exposes the party's foundation on racist hatred. But it is up to the audience to position themselves ideologically. The proximity of the camera to all four candidates fleshes them out as characters and encourages sympathy. However, to use Murray Smith's terminology, alignment with characters – following their actions – does not necessarily result in allegiance – approving of their actions and beliefs (Smith 1995). It is up to the moral and ideological makeup of the audience to position themselves accordingly, and *Democracy: The Way of the Cross* creates the space for this.

The film takes us past Election Day, when only the candidates of SYRIZA and Golden Dawn were elected, through to the swearing-in of what proved to be a very short-lived parliament. Through shots taken from the ceremony's broadcast on television, the director

Figure 38.4 Clientelism exposed in *Democracy: The Way of the Cross*.

consolidates the themes of the film and illuminates the ambiguous title of the film. On the one hand, the 'cross' refers to the passion of the Christ, metaphorically highlighting the struggle for election; on the other it refers to the electoral system (discussed at various points in the film): the fact that Greeks vote not only for a party but for specific candidates in it – they put a cross next to their name. The film suggests that this aspect of the electorate system creates many distortions, including clientelist relations.

The film's power is its exploration of the dynamic between candidate and voter, the exchange and interaction that is at the heart of the democratic process, however distorted this may have become. But the film does not propose any particular solutions; it has no catharsis, and no happy ending. Even the elections that it recorded were inconclusive, leading to new elections a month later.[9] The film offers no interpretative framework and no answers. Instead, it reinforces a number of painful questions, thus making for difficult viewing. In documenting the elections *of* the crisis, it also suggests how complex and multifaceted this crisis has been.

The four films examined above are all examples of independent documentaries made in response to the crisis in Greece in the first few years of its manifestation. They fulfill different functions – from activism and polemical intervention, to journalistic exploration and information, to reaching *beyond* the surface by paying attention *to* the surface. *Debtocracy* utilized documentary's powers of persuasion to participate into the public debate about how to respond to the crisis; *155 Sold* interpretatively framed raw footage to construct a politically oppositional narrative of events; *Krisis* relied on extensive and broad-ranging interviews to offer often conflicting accounts of the crisis and its causes; and *Democracy: The Way of the Cross* resorted to detached observation to raise the elections as a metaphor for Greece in crisis. The films have circulated differently, reflecting their different aims: the activist film sought the widest possible exposure and disregarded financial rewards, while the others were more mixed in their approach, aiming to combine visibility – through festival showings, websites, and/or television broadcasts – with some financial returns (none of which, however, have been sustainable as models for future production). As a means of expressing opinions and documenting sociopolitical situations differently, independent documentary filmmaking has proved very versatile, creative, and inspirational during the Greek crisis. As a means of providing a sustainable mode of production and circulation, however, it is far more precarious, and its future uncertain.

Acknowledgments

I would like to thank Aris Chatzistefanou, Marco Gastine, Nikos Katsaounis, and Yorgos Pandeleakis for granting me very illuminating interviews and for giving me access to their films.

Notes

1 For example, see *Omorfies kai Dyskolies – Mitchigan/Hardships and Beauties – Michigan* (Tsakiris, 2013), *Little Land* (Dayandas, 2013), I *Tehni tis Krisis: I Periptosi tou Theatrou/The Art of Crisis: Theatre Matters* (Patroni, 2014), *Na Meino I na Fygo?/Should I Stay or should I Go?* (Karamangiolis, 2014), *Gr. Work in Progress* (Zervopoulou, 2014), *Koinoniko Odeio – Notes/ Social Conservatory – Notes* (Malamou and Saliba, 2014), *Ithopoioi: Imerologio Spoudis/ Becoming an Actor* (Koutsiabasakos, 2014), *Sto Farmakeio/ At the Pharmacy* (Tsapa, 2014), *Love in the time of Crisis* (Skarlatos and Kallergis, 2014).

2 See, *Neo- Nazi: To Olokaftoma tis Mnimis/Neo-Nazi: The Holocaust of Memory* (Kouloglou, 2013) and *Fascism, Inc.* (Chatzistefanou, 2014).

3 The website's URL is: http://infowarproductions.com/debtocracy_doc/

4 See Independent Greek Cinema website: http://www.igc.gr/

5 The website's URL is: http://www.theprism.gr

6 For more information see: http://www.theprism.gr/sponsors.html

7 These events are examined in the documentaries *Orgismenos Dekemvris/Enraged December* (Kersanidis and Tzelepi, 2010) and *Children of the Riots* (Georgiou, 2012).

8 The filmmakers/cinematographers were Katerina Patroni, Haris Raftogiannis, Hristoforos Georgoutsos, and Nikolia Apostolou.

9 These elections, as the closing titles indicate, were made without a cross, according to the law for repeat elections.

Bibliography

Chatzistefanou, A. (2013) Personal interview with the author, April 22, 47 mins, Skype.

Hessel, S. (2010) *Indignez-Vous!*, Montpellier: Indigene.

Karakasis, A. (2014) "Election Documentaries Enter Greek Cinema" in *Filmicon: Journal of Greek Film Studies*, 2, pp. 117–132.

Kinkle, J. and Toscano, A. (2011) "Filming the Crisis: A Survey" in *Film Quarterly*, 65.1, pp. 39–51.

Mandravelis, P. (2011) "Psemata, Megala Psemata kai Documentaire"/"Lies, Big Lies and Documentary" in *Kathimerini*, April 17, http://www.kathimerini.gr/724793/opinion/epikairothta/arxeio-monimes-sthles/yemata-megala-yemata-kai-ntokimanter (accessed September 21, 2014).

Moisis, M. (2011) "*Debtocracy*" in *Eleftherotypia*, 26 April, http://www.enet.gr/?i=news.el.article&id=270271 (accessed September 21, 2014).

Nichols, B. (1991) *Representing Reality: Issues and Concepts in Documentary*, Bloomington: Indiana University Press.

Nichols, B. (2010) *Introduction to Documentary*, 2nd edition, Bloomington: Indiana University Press.

Pandeleakis, Y. (2014) Personal communication with the author via email, August 9.

Papadimitriou, L. (2013) "Reaching Audiences: The 15th Thessaloniki Documentary Festival" in *Senses of Cinema*, 67 (July 2013), http://sensesofcinema.com/2013/festival-reports/reaching-audiences-the-15th-thessaloniki-documentary-festival/ (accessed September 21, 2014).

Papadimitriou, L. (2014) "Weathering the Crisis: The Sixteenth Thessaloniki Documentary Festival" in *Journal of Greek Media and Culture*, 1.1 (September), pp. 169–176.

Papastathis, A. (2011) "I *Hreokratia* Anapse Fotia sto Diadiktyo"/"*Debtocracy* Set the Internet on Fire" in *To Vima*, April 17, http://www.tovima.gr/politics/article/?aid=396042 (accessed September 21, 2014).

Smith, M. (1995) *Engaging Characters: Fiction, Emotion and the Cinema*, Oxford: Clarendon Press.

39

SECRET CITY (2012)

A reception diary

Michael Chanan and Lee Salter

Preproduction

Secret City (Chanan and Salter, 2012) is a David and Goliath story. The Corporation of the City of London is at the heart of a lobbying network that spends £93m a year on behalf of finance capital. *Secret City*, which unmasks the Corporation, started out with a zero budget and was completed with university funding of just £7,200 – and no budget at all for marketing and publicity. In two words, an example of 'small media'. It was made over the first nine months of 2012 by a team of four people (two academics and two interns), and then launched with a screening at the House of Commons in October. A year later, it had been screened around ninety times up and down the country, always to full houses, at community, cultural and university venues, alongside independent cinemas. This was only possible by taking an integrated approach to the use of the social media, and it demonstrates the potential of the web to discover an 'audience-in-waiting' that is not served by broadcast media or conventional film distribution – nor the expense of marketing. The parallel outlets provided by the web are vital to creating the presence that produces dissemination through the dynamics of social networking. With non-commercial production sans a marketing and publicity budget, the web becomes the crucial means for making links with cultural, community and campaign groups and thereby organising the public screenings through which the film finds an audience and enters into dialogue with them around the issues. There are many negative things to be said about the forms of sociality found on the web; this is one of the positives. From the first, the film was highly commended as, for example, "a revelatory insight into the Vatican of contemporary finance" (Lustgarten 2012) and "a powerful, fascinating and terrifying documentary" (Ollerton 2013). It was not reviewed in the mainstream press, but took the best documentary award at the London Independent Film Festival 2013. Jasper Sharp, picking his Five Best of 2013 at Midnight Eye, called it "a brilliant example of micro-budget guerrilla film-making that really hits its target" (Sharp 2013). Not the sort of thing that will ever play on TV or in conventional cinemas, he said, it certainly needs to be seen by a lot more people, "but its makers have been doing a wonderful job of bringing it to audiences through the festival circuit and special pop-up screenings" (ibid.).

The origins of *Secret City* go back ten years, when the film's writer and presenter, Lee Salter, worked as a researcher with three people who were petitioning the House of Lords against a bill to 'reform' the City of London's electoral system by securing plural votes for businesses. (The bill was passed and the City of London is now the only place in the country where businesses as well as residents are able to vote for local councillors, see Salter 2004.) They were a curious bunch: the political scientist Maurice Glasman; William Taylor, a vicar and dissenting Common Councillor in the City; and John McDonnell MP. Their efforts were backed by a City entrepreneur, Malcolm Matson, who had been blackballed by the Corporation when he was elected as an Alderman for his ideas about open government and transparency. This unlikely assembly of a Marxist academic, a vicar, a Labour MP and a millionaire businessman, is joined in the film by other academics and campaigners to create a dialogical narrative of interweaving strands: the history of a city that pioneered both capitalism and empire; the impact of this concentration of financial power both at home and abroad; the effect of the City on the wellbeing of those who live in its shadow; the spiritual malaise inflicted by the single interest of financial capitalism; the lack of transparency and the influence held by the City over Parliament.

The film's director, Michael Chanan, a seasoned documentarist since the 1970s, has been working in digital video under academic aegis for about fifteen years, producing both long-form documentaries and a variety of short videos. Some of the latter were made for academic presentation, some as video diaries, others comprise a series of video blogs investigating the protest movement that appeared on the *New Statesman* website over the first three months of 2011 (subsequently gathered together as *Chronicle of Protest* (Chanan, 2011). The lessons of this experience of what is known in academic terminology as practice-as-research (or research-as-practice; we don't quite know the difference) are various. They include, from the practical point of view, the need for the digital documentarist, who is able to work alone at all stages of production, to compensate for their solitude by finding new forms of collaboration to replace the collective creativity of the film crew. *Secret City* provided the opportunity to follow a model that Chanan first employed on *Detroit: Ruin of a City* (2005), where the filmmaker engages in a full-scale collaboration with an academic investigator who brings the initial expertise and knowledge of the subject, conducts the interviews, shares the development and intellectual authorship of the script, and joins in the editing.

Production

The production of *Secret City* answered to opportunity and circumstances, after the Occupy movement took up residence on the steps of St Paul's Cathedral and immediately turned public and media attention on the City. The two of us, being anti-ivory tower academics and scholars of the media, realised that this was not just a pressing topic for academic attention, but also 'a story', and finding ourselves especially well positioned to make it, felt a sense of urgency about doing so.

Changing circumstances redirect attention, open up spaces and change the structure of political opportunity (Tarrow 1998). Habermas's often poorly understood theory of the public sphere noted the propensity for crises to loosen the world as taken-for-granted. It is during such crises that consensus is shaken, and the certainty of accepted presuppositions is suspended (Habermas 1976a: 120). It is in times of crisis that spaces are opened up – or physically occupied to the same effect – where attention turns to neglected questions, new ideas are able to take root, debate and discussion are able to flourish without the usual hegemonic constraints on public debate (Habermas 1976b, 1996). *Secret City* was intended as a contribution to this expanding conceptual space, where the grip of the state and capital on the public sphere was being robustly challenged. The film wants to bring out into the open the secrecy behind the public face of the City of London, and its consequences.

Given our sense of urgency, we considered the option of seeking academic funding only briefly, since that would entail a delay of many months. Lee had already lined up several key interviews, so we just started. We soon had a short pilot to show, and broached the idea of a television sale with a sympathetic independent television documentary producer. Together we quickly reached the conclusion that UK television was an impossible prospect. The BBC, for example, would want it narrated by one of their own people, the commercial sector would want revelations. But there were not any revelations beyond the very scandal of the City's secrecy – you cannot get information about the Corporation's private accounts, for example, from a Freedom of Information request, because it is not a public body like any other local authority.

There was also a third aspect to our decision not to pursue television. The central subject of the film is the Corporation of London, and a question frequently asked at screenings is why we did not include representatives of the Corporation in the film. The question alludes to an expectation embedded in conventional forms of documentary discourse, especially as practised in public service television with its principles of balance, fairness and impartiality – a holy trinity fitting the ethical profile of a liberal patrician ideology. It was not our purpose to produce that kind of account, which all too easily allows an entity like the Corporation to put up a smokescreen. The Corporation of London is a significant node in the global network of power. It has distorting effects, materially on London's built environment, financially on the economy, politically through its influence on government, and ideologically through the plethora of media, including the financial pages of the newspapers, whose accounts of 'economics' are really just accounts of the interests of capital. The interests of the Corporation animate British economic policy, and its voice is heard indirectly through the media all the time. They are so adept at the veiled expression of their ideological self-interest that we were sure we knew what they would say. Indeed, they had already said it in one or two corporate videos we found on the web, which we included in the film to represent their point of view – and throw it into relief. This was not only quicker and easier (as well as cheaper), but these clips took their place alongside a range of archive footage which we used to draw out the history of the representations of the City over the past century. Such representations often jar with the critiques we hear from film's contributors, and the crack that opens between them allows a more adequate comprehension of the relations between the Corporation and those it impacts upon.

Postproduction

For the same reason we decided not to wait around for funding to make the film, we also decided not to wait to get it screened at festivals, especially when one of its contributors, John McDonnell MP, invited us to present a preview at the House of Commons, which took place in October 2012. The fact of this unusual location for a documentary film premiere in itself drew the attention of a good number of political commentators, journalists and campaign organisers who attended and helped to set the film on its way. McDonnell summed up the post-screening discussion at the premiere in the comment that the film came as a "revelation to many of our audience tonight". Several people spoke of it as very educational, one person with an eye to the lingo called it "an excellent piece of knowledge transfer", another called it "a brilliant film, with potentially far-reaching impact in catalysing a new movement for City reform. Activists will see this film and be inspired" (*Secret City* Audience Feedback 2012).

This last piece of praise inadvertently raises a crucial issue, because universities are nowadays required to report on the impact of their research in the process of bidding for research funding. What kind of far-reaching impact did this person mean? There is a fundamental problem in reporting the 'impact' of works of creative practice, like documentary films. Although very occasionally a documentary film might have real-life repercussions, it has always been rare for a film to produce a direct and concrete impact on, say, policy-making, even in the days when television documentaries commanded audiences of several millions. The impact of a film is primarily aesthetic and entirely diffuse, and by its very nature cannot be pinned down or measured. Attempts to do so are always reductive, probably even more so when the work is disseminated horizontally by digital communication, and reception is atomised. But the activist knows that small media, like independent video and other forms of creative practice, can and do contribute to the formation of opinion at a less visible level, the level of communities, both local and now virtual, where it connects with alternative initiatives and campaigning. The type of impact to be achieved in this arena is like all aesthetic experience, of an experiential and existential kind that necessarily falls beneath the bureaucrats' radar.

The impact of an aesthetic work begins in front of it, by enhancing and intensifying the beholder's awareness. It begins in the moment of reception, and a video or performance, say, is created for the purpose of arousing the beholder's immediate response as such, because without it there cannot be any longer-lasting impact. This is the domain of the critic, although films from the margins receive little mainstream critical attention, and only short notices on the web. For example, according to a review by a blogger on *The Independent*, *Secret City*

> is shot over the eerie tune of children singing . . . Oranges and Lemons, and the backing music sets an unnerving tone that is in keeping with the message of the film – that the City of London has a secretive and closely guarded history.
>
> (*Spary 2013*)

For our part, we followed the old practice of independent film since the 1970s where the filmmaker goes out on the road with the film: almost every screening has been attended by one or both of the filmmakers, and is followed by a discussion, so we have our own testimony to the immediate aesthetic impact of the film. But it is not the kind of impact the research bureaucracy is talking about.

Distribution

We have a strong informal impression of the audience the film appealed to. The timing of the production of the film – starting while Occupy London was in full flow – meant that our interviewees not only had a strong interest in the Corporation but many were actively involved in campaigns and thus amenable to participating: each viewed the film as part of their own opportunity structure (Tarrow 1998), that is, they saw their involvement as an extension of their own political objectives, and the Occupy movement and continuing economic crisis made participation in a small media project more attractive than it might have been otherwise. Audiences largely comprised their counterparts and sympathisers, including people with a professional interest, expressing a range of left-of-centre political sentiments. Screenings revealed three key and partly overlapping constituencies: cultural audiences, political audiences and, let's call it, the general public. The first comprises audiences for political documentary in academia and activist cinephile groups like a film co-op in Manchester or a film club in Dublin. The second, audiences for screenings by political groups such as Labour Party branches or activist groups like an Indymedia group in Oxford, This Is Not a Gateway (TINAG) in London, and Transition City in Lancaster. The third is the broader audience at independent cinemas like the Watershed in Bristol, or in London venues like the Frontline Club and DocHouse, which includes media professionals.

The social networks were crucial to getting the film seen: those to which the writer and director were already connected, those that existed around the issues highlighted in the film, and the network that gathered around the film and its participants, were all instrumental in publicising the film and getting screenings arranged. We have anecdotal evidence that word of mouth played its part. Many requests for screenings came though the film's website and Facebook page, with the result that many screenings were organised locally by interested activists, linked to local campaign groups involved in anti-cuts, tax justice and similar activities. Screenings in London at venues like Passing Clouds and the TINAG festival were largely populated by those involved in or close to Occupy London and similar initiatives. The film was tapping into a stratum of active concern which since the autumn of 2010, beginning with the student protests against the brutal rise in university fees, had periodically been taking to the streets in large numbers in protest against the regime of austerity imposed by the Coalition government, which was increasingly perceived as part of an ideologically motivated attack on the welfare state.

While several screenings took place in independent art cinemas, like Bristol's Watershed, Liverpool's Fact and London's Roxy, not all such venues were receptive. The political economy of independent art cinemas (especially in times of recession and cultural devastation) makes them subject to many of the same compulsions as any other kind of locale, with the difference that the cinema chains are programmed centrally. The independent exhibitor uses local knowledge to weigh up films in terms of their ability to generate revenue. Would people come and see a controversial radical documentary they hadn't heard of? Some venues expressed their worry about this and were thus susceptible to persuasion. Others simply did not get back to us.

Impact

Responses to the film invariably begin with the shock of not knowing the things that the film is telling them about how the City is run and rules itself. A typical articulation of this rejoinder is "I'm a well-informed person, and I'm really angry that I didn't know any of this", or less politely, "[expletive deleted], I didn't know that!". As a blog on the screening at the Frontline Club reported, the evening's chair, Joris Luyendijk, started the discussion with the remark, "I think I had a bit of a Jimmy Saville moment, when you see something quite shocking and you realise it's been hiding in plain sight for all this time" (Ashley-Cound 2013). After that, the most common question that audiences begin to ask, not so much of the filmmakers as of each other, is "so what can we do?" This is partly the result of the film's narrative form, which provides a sketch-map of manifold political and economic problems but refrains from proposing a 'solution'. This is a little different from the dominant style of campaign documentaries nowadays available through 'niche market' web distributors like Dogwoof. As political documentaries they provide useful insights into aspects of social problems, while offering the consolation of 'happy chapters' about individual lobbying or initiatives to change particular buying habits which are claimed to make significant changes. But they generally refrain from connecting these campaigns to broader struggles or to issues of class and political economy. Films like these can be both entertaining and worthy, but remain ideologically at sea. *Secret City* is quite explicit in providing a socialist perspective, drawing its analysis from sources such as Marxist analysis and the theology of liberation, but without seeking to suggest what might be done, because we did not think we should anticipate the debate that the film wanted to raise. Indeed, just because we made the film it does not mean we have the solution! The result is that this is the very question on everyone's lips after watching it, and whatever the film's limitations and gaps, it works very well to invite debate.

Secret City situates and positions finance capitalism and the Corporation's role in that system in historical context. This context is not one of discrete historical events but of processes running both diachronically and synchronically. It is embodied on the screen by people whose experience of this context cannot be separated from those processes, and the film is thus partly narrated by people inside the system or closely interacting with it. However, unlike the expectable 'human interest' first-person testimonies of the campaign genre, these are not stories of personal misfortune, but the experiences of people trying to confront an alienating institution which eludes their grasp. Audiences responded to this with complex emotions, like anger and the demand for action at the same time as the realisation that there is no quick fix, no simple 'happy chapter'. The Frontline blog quoted a contribution from an audience member who works in the City, which we like because it is close to our own opinion:

> Most people in the City are not corrupt but there are incentives within the system which cause all the problems that we have. . . . When you're in the City you understand the parameters within which you're working and you never question that and therefore it's only when you step outside and actually look . . . that you begin to question the whole rationale. And it's only when you question the whole rationale that you seen [sic] this is not about bad people or corruption, it's about a system which is clearly not fit for what we need, it dwarfs everything else . . . . It is a system that is designed in such a way that it has certain effects and that's what we need to attack. It's not the people, it's the systemic flaws.
>
> (*Ashley-Cound 2013*)

This is not the kind of feedback the academic bureaucrats are looking for, however. To them, it is merely anecdotal.

Lessons

In formal language, *Secret City* exemplifies the theorised practice of unbudgeted independent video documentary and comprises a critique of the relations of power in contemporary society through an investigation of one of the key institutions in the state. It is situated in the space between social protest in times of economic crisis and the unremitting attack of an ideologically motivated regime of austerity. The reach of the film is achieved through a small-scale but sustained programme of public engagement through the so-called social networks, which generates the web traffic whose efficacy is demonstrated by numerous screenings, locally organised, where the film achieves its immediate impact, the physical encounter where audiences engage in debates about citizenship, economics, politics and culture. But this immediate impact is a very different animal from the category of 'impact' in Research Council parlance and the present account amounts to a critique of the bureaucratic criteria.

First there is the question of the mode of production. The capacity to adequately represent the complex character of an institution like the City is limited by both the material conditions and the subjectivity of the filmmaker; a combination in which subjectivity, in the form of imagination, is able to trump material limitations, and digital videography can come into its own. In these circumstances, subjectivity is a strength, because it allows escape from conventional wisdom. The conditions of production of many liberal-activist films tell of being enmeshed in a system of commercial 'independent' production that is linked in a variety of ways to the 'industry', but the mode of audiovisual production has radically altered with digital video and the internet, and since the turn of the millennium has expanded explosively.

Independent production companies act as providers of the means of sustenance to their mostly precarious workforce. The company itself, in order to pay wages and bills, and to attract funding to make and distribute activist documentaries, interfaces with festival circuits, funding bodies and niche markets through the web and direct sales. Such material relations can constrain to a significant degree the treatment of subject matter in the films that get made. It is part of this habitus (in Bourdieu's terminology) that these relations are incorporated into their conceptualisation of both the film and its 'impact' – they aim to raise awareness about a given issue without disheartening the audience and leaving them feeling debilitated or hopeless. The 'happy chapter' serves to combat this effect, to offer the hope that without too much disruption to their lives, audiences can change their consumption habits to make the problem go away. In contrast, *Secret City* attempts no such closure, it raises questions and proposes discussion – and refrains from making the kind of 'policy proposals' which the bureaucratic 'impact' agenda operates with.

The term 'independent' which we have been using to describe the film's mode of production has always been a slippery one. One of us is able to recall the discussions about this very problem in the late 1970s, in the process of setting up the Independent Filmmakers Association (IFA, later adding video to become the IFVA). People asked, independent of what? Today it has become possible to realise the greatest degree of independence with minimal expenditure as long as you possess your own means and instruments of production, which can nowadays be purchased for less than the price of a small car. Although *Secret City* was made with zero budget – which really means that incidental expenses were paid out of our pockets – the filmmakers were receiving their salaries as academics. This means that we were structured by a dissimilar environment to that of a commercial independent producer, in short, a distinct habitus, where finances operate differently and different ways of thinking prevail. This has a significant impact on the discursive structuring of the film because it means we operate under conditions of academic freedom, without having to answer to any external pressure or criteria.

However, just as commercial independent producers are enmeshed in market relations, so academics are institutionalised in universities. They are managed within institutions and are disciplined through state-licensed bureaucratic structures that managers are paid to enforce. This discursive structure is one in which, as Howard Newby put it when he was head of the Higher Education Funding Council for England and Wales, "It was once the role of Governments to provide for the purposes of universities; it is now the role of universities to provide for the purposes of Governments" (Newby 2004). Those purposes are in a general way to serve the interests of capital, but this can be done is several ways, and much of what is encouraged or allowed depends on what sector of capital is ascendant in the corridors of power. The current expectation for academic activity in film and media in the UK is to engage and 'enhance' the largely commercial 'culture industry', in partnership with local or even big industry. These relations become the basis of the conceptualisation of 'impact' in the state inspection of research performance, the Research Excellence Framework (REF), that binds academics to the system. If a piece of practice-as-research like *Secret City* does not easily fit the required profile, this is partly because the whole exercise has been poorly conceived. In particular, the humanities are badly served by an underlying model which remains that of the sciences, and the results are distorted by the contortions of academic managerialism.

Liberal ideology requires that Government must still be seen to provide for the social benefit of academic activity independent of its contribution to the economy, even if the present one is loath to admit it. Academic research and production is supposed to "benefit individuals, organisations and nations by fostering global economic performance, and specifically the economic competitiveness of the United Kingdom" (Research Councils UK 2014). It is hoped that individuals, organisations and the nation might also benefit from academics "increasing the effectiveness of public services and policy" or "enhancing quality of life, health and creative output" (ibid.). If this system is biased against arts and humanities, consider who is in charge: the government minister responsible for higher education is the Business Secretary. How come? It happened on New Labour's watch, when the first Business Secretary to take charge of universities was Peter Mandelson, who, McDonnell in the film reminds us, declared himself relaxed about the filthy rich. Mandelson represents a managerialist ideology in the interests of commercial and business criteria – criteria essentially alien to the concept and practice of academic freedom. This is the same ideology that is intent on 'reforming' the whole university system in the direction of market values. Anything that cannot be value-costed does not count. Humanist values of inquiry are old hat unless they can be commoditised, or at least conveniently packaged for purposes of cost analysis; hence the new emphasis on 'robust' evidence, that is, hard data: figures and numbers. This approach ineluctably produces gobbledygook, like the warning of a *Guardian* blogger that 'There's still a lot we don't know about the relative quality profile of the output weightings' (Miah 2012). But the policy that demands this data is itself not remotely interested in evidence as the basis for its prescriptions: its agenda is entirely ideological.

Digital critique

As a recent academic blog on the subject puts it, "The Funding Council's overly restrictive 'physical science' view of how research influences policy has created an artificial minefield of pointless obstacles" (Tinkler and Dunleavy 2012). To begin with, a great deal of arts and humanities research – scholarly or creative – produces effects that are not easily measurable: the book that is ignored on first publication but turns out ten years later to have been pioneering; the artful video that circulates on the web without leaving an academic footprint (so it cannot be 'objectively' evaluated) – but that video is situated at the forefront of testing out new possibilities for reaching what the lingo calls the 'beneficiaries.' However, anyone producing work in a field like the digital arts, which engages with non-traditional forms of dissemination and reception, will have to deal with the particular problems inherent in the metrics which measure web usage, which are at best both fuzzy and evanescent – which means they are not 'robust'. According to an early career researcher quoted in a recent newspaper report (Tickle 2012) "It's yet to be seen how grant-awarding bodies will measure the value of social networking", while post-doctoral researcher Shahidha Bari makes the simple observation that "the value of research is not always something you can predict from the outset – that's the point of research" (quoted in Tickle 2012). "Impact", Bari continues, "reads like a policy designed to help universities appease governmental demands for justification of expenditure", but "if you're in the business of producing ideas and culture as you do in arts and humanities research, then you're not producing tangible, measurable effects" (ibid.). There may nonetheless be "non-tangible effects that are no less important". These effects involve factors like aesthetic, moral and political judgement, which are not susceptible to meaningful quantification.

Then there is the question of engagement in the digital sphere, which applies to all scholars in the humanities and is much encouraged – only for the evaluators to turn round and say that blogs, for example, do not count (perhaps because they are not peer reviewed). Part of the problem is in the mythologies of the digital domain, like the unexamined notion of the viral as a measure of impact when numbers alone tell you nothing and the viral is in fact entirely relative. You can use social media and blogging to extend the reach of your work, but this does not produce a measurable indicator of impact. As another blogger puts it, "social media metrics are often poorly calculated and even more poorly understood" (Another Rambler 2012), which does not mean your blogging is not worth the effort (as we ourselves have discovered).

The digital arts face a particular problem, because most of the works produced within the academy inevitably remain marginal, simply because the web is hugely dominated by commercial operators and popular trivia. Nevertheless, it is also very good at letting a thousand flowers bloom in its interstices. Appraising the impact of one these flowers, however, is far from straightforward. Such figures as are provided, for example, by the web platforms that carry the videos are only rough-and-ready guides to dissemination. They may tell you about the distribution of viewers across different countries, but not what kind of viewer they are, even as the video in question is clearly reaching out into the wider world. The reception of streaming video, despite the web's much touted interactivity, remains anonymous. This is connected with sociological and conceptual questions about identity which again place the administrative categories in question. The idea that impact outside the academy can be neatly separated out and measured ignores what has been taught within the academy for many years, that everyone's identity is multiple and shared with others in different groupings. A student shares a video through a social network with family or friends outside it: is she doing so as a student, or as a sister, or as a drinking companion? A university lecturer sends a link to members of his cricket club, some of whom are also academics but in other disciplines: is he doing so as an academic colleague, or a sporting pal, or as a concerned citizen?

The problem is not that targeted funding would improve results but a structural one, in which both intellectual production and social critique are disadvantaged and marginalised. The public sphere is not a homogenous arena but a network of dispersed, unequal and overlapping spaces of communication dominated by the centralised mass media which are now also embedded in the virtual domain of the web. The web is dominated in turn by gigantic players like Google, Facebook, Twitter, Amazon and some others, which serve to extend the reach of pre-existing media while also forcing corporate consolidation in the culture industry, like the 2013 merger of Penguin and Random House, which together control a quarter of world book publishing (see Rankin 2013). But the web, notwithstanding its open and borderless flows, is highly fragmented, and most of the time, rather than overcoming cultural compartmentalisation, it amplifies it. Thus, on the one hand, it reproduces the entrenched anti-intellectual populism of the centralised media, while on the other, it has opened up new spaces for ideas to circulate more or less freely through open and borderless flows, which is not always a good thing. All of which, however, would mean that 'impact' is a specious and entirely ideological concept. In the words of a comment on a leader in the *Times Higher Education Supplement*: a weird dogma to apply to the workings of the intellect, and "an excrescence of an ideology that has temporarily established its domination not only in Britain but in the Western world generally" (*THES 2012*).

The dissemination of *Secret City* is pretty small scale, precisely because it has happened outside the marketplace, an example of a new kind of artisanal cultural production in the age of global cultural monopolies. It has had a modest success that is corroborated by the figures on condition that you know how to interpret them. Of course, you can hardly use a phrase like 'modest success' in a case study where you have to talk it up. Although it is certainly an 'independent production', its fate rests on a network of relations with other organisations, institutions and interests. It is not autonomous but rather belongs in a set of relations between people, social movements, political groups, institutions and the state, no less complex than the subject matter of the film itself. As a public institution the university is not completely autonomous either, and the marketisation and commercialisation of higher education in recent years has pernicious effects on academic freedom (Barnett 2003), especially in relation to media (Salter 2012), arts and humanities. But there are good reasons why the bureaucratic management of academic research cannot be completely controlled by bureaucratic management, and while universities will be cautious about publicising work of a 'political' nature, this is still possible in the interstices of our educational institutions, even though the national research agenda is stacked against it.

Bibliography

Another Rambler (2012) "Social media = academic impact", http:// anotherrambler.wordpress.com/2012/09/29/social-media-academic-impact/ (accessed on 5 December 2014).

Ashley-Cound, S. (2013) "The City's Secrets", *Frontline Bloggers*, 15 January, www.frontlineclub.com/the-citys-secrets (accessed on 5 December 2014).

Barnett, R. (2003) *Beyond All Reason: Living with Ideology in the University*, Milton Keynes: Open University Press.

Habermas, J. (1976a) *Legitimation Crisis* (trans. McCarthy, T.), London: Heinemann.

Habermas, J. (1976b) "What is Universal Pragmatics?" in Habermas, J. *On the Pragmatics of Communication*, London: Polity Press, pp. 21–103.

Habermas, J. (1996) *Between Facts and Norms* (trans. Rehg, W.), London: Polity Press.

Lustgarten, A. (2013) "A Revelatory Insight into the Vatican of Contemporary Finance", http://secretcity-thefilm.com/a-revelatory-insight-into-the-vatican-of-contemporary-finance (accessed on 5 December 2014).

Miah, A. (2012) "Ref2014: What Should Researchers be Concentrating On?", *Guardian High Education Blog*, 21 February, www.theguardian.com/higher-education-network/blog/2012/feb/21/ref2014-what-researchers-concentrating-on?INTCMP=SRCH (accessed on 5 December 2014).

Newby, H. (2004) "Regulation, Planning and the Market in Pursuing Public Purposes in Higher Education", Higher Education Funding Council for England, SHEEO conference, 2004.

Ollerton, D. (2013) "*Secret City* Review – London Independent Film Festival", The London Film Review, 23 April, http://www.thelondonfilmreview.com/film-review/secret-city-review/ (accessed on 18 February 2015).

Rankin, J. (2013) "Plot Thickens for Authors as Penguin and Random House Merger Creates £2.6bn Powerhouse", *The Guardian*, 28 July, www.theguardian.com/books/2013/jul/ 28/penguin-random-house-merger-reactions (accessed on 5 December 2014).

Research Councils UK (2014) "What do Research Councils Mean by 'Impact'?" in Research Councils UK, http://www.rcuk.ac.uk/ke/impacts/meanbyimpact/ (accessed 22 August 2014).

Salter, L. (2004) "Parliament and Parliamentarians: The Worrying Case of the City of London (Ward Elections) Bill" in *The Political Quarterly* 75(2), pp. 155–167.

Salter, L. (2012) "Journalism in the Academy: A MacIntyean Account of the Institutions and Practices of Journalism Education in England" in *Revista Cientifica de Informacion y Comumicacion* 9, pp. 72–102.

Secret City Audience Feedback (2012) http://secretcity-thefilm.com/audience-feedback (accessed 5 December 2014).

Sharp, J. (2013) "Jasper Sharp's Five Best of 2013", www.midnighteye.com/features/midnight-eyes-best-and-worst-of-2013/#sthash.D55Gtgbr.dpuf (accessed 5 December 2014).

Spary, S. (2013) "*Secret City*: Uncovering London's Hidden History" in *The Independent* (blogs), http://blogs.independent.co.uk/2013/01/15/secret-city-uncovering-a-hidden-history-behind-london (accessed on 18 February 2015).

Tarrow, S. (1998) *Power in Movement*, Cambridge: Cambridge University Press.

Tickle, L. (2012) "Must all Postgrad Research Have 'Impact'?", *The Guardian*, 14 November, www.guardian.co.uk/education/2012/nov/14/postgraduates-higher-education (accessed on 5 December 2014).

Times Higher Education Supplement (2012) "Leader: REF Must Ensure Fair Play for All", 11 October, www.timeshighereducation.co.uk/421444.article (accessed on 5 December 2014).

Tinkler, J. and Dunleavy, P. (2012) "REF Advice Notes 3: What will HEFCE Count as 'Under-pinning' Research?", 29 October, http://blogs.lse.ac.uk/impactofsocialsciences/2012/10/29/dunleavy-tinkler-advice-three-research/ (accessed on 5 December 2014).

40

INTERACTIVE DOCUMENTARY

Film and politics in the digital era

James Lyons

Digital communications technologies have served to usher in what John Postill terms the "digitisation of traditional politics as well as the rise of new forms of political life originating in the digital world" (2012: 165). The impact of web 2.0 and social networking in fostering citizen journalism, and helping to mobilize "global and local 'action coalitions'" such as the Occupy movement, attest to Richard Allan's claim that "new technology may fundamentally and irrevocably change the nature of the very processes of political and social interaction" (quoted in Bruns 2008: 362). Discussing the import of 'digital activism' to the events of the Arab Spring, Philip N. Howard and Muzammil M. Hussain argue that the spread of social protest across North Africa and the Middle East was facilitated by "digital media [that] allowed communities to realize that they shared grievances and … nurtured transportable strategies for mobilizing against dictators" (2013: 4). One question we might ask, therefore, is how such developments impact on the documentary, which Bill Nichols has described as "the most explicitly political film form" (1991: x). Writing in 1991, Nichols stated that "documentary remains distinct in its representation of the historical world, the world of power, dominance, and control, the arena of struggle, resistance, and contestation" (115). As that world comes increasingly digital (at least for some), in what ways does documentary adapt to maintain that political function? And what challenges might this new era of digital activism and participatory democracy pose to documentary's own implicit regimes of "power, dominance, and control," as people come to identify increasingly as 'produsers,' – Axel Bruns' term for individuals and communities "which engage in the collaborative creation and extension of information and knowledge" (2008: 2)?

In the following pages I explore these questions, with a specific focus on digital interactive documentary, a burgeoning area of documentary production around which questions of politics, both at the level of representation and participation, are particularly pronounced. Here I draw on the work of Kate Nash, Sandra Gaudenzi, Jon Dovey, and Mandy Rose, all of whom have been at the forefront of critical thinking on digital interactive formats, in order to delineate with some specificity the potentiality and the challenges that interactivity presents for documentary politics. I use a range of examples to help illustrate the scope, in terms of subject matter, objectives, and modes of interaction that the field of production encompasses. While this is an undoubtedly new and rapidly evolving site for the interface between 'film' – as it exists in a post-celluloid era of digital convergence – and 'politics' – as Postill indicates, an ever-more capacious noun – there is the possibility to draw some conclusions about the path forward, albeit provisional and cautiously couched, bearing in mind Bruns' heed to "remain skeptical of ... transformative potential" adumbrated by such technological affordances (2008: 359).

John Corner writes that "documentary has a longstanding, often highly self-conscious and sometimes controversial connection with the portrayal of the 'political'" (2009: 113). From the Griersonian ethos that documentary should be "socially useful storytelling," which, as Patricia Aufderheide notes, left a "large footprint on documentary filmmaking" (2007: 44, 37), the wide spectrum of ways in which documentary has sought to make "an intervention in public debate" (Chanan 2007: 16) is clearly in evidence, from ostensibly sober journalistic inquiry through to agitprop. Moreover, Corner makes clear that:

> This extends from direct attention to core political structures and processes through to indicating the broader manifestations of politicality (that is to say, the various aspects and dimensions of the 'political', ways of being 'political' and of doing 'politics') in everyday life and culture, often involving spaces in which politics has an understated, implicit or even denied presence.
>
> *(2009: 113)*

Michael Chanan, noting the way that documentary "has shifted its ground and become more individual and personal" (2007: 5), speaks to the way that filmmakers have sought to produce works that reveal, either directly or indirectly, the politics of identity. Debra Zimmerman, Executive Director of Women Make Movies, has argued against a narrow definition of political documentary as "films that comment on politics or that profile politicians," stating that "if a film has the power to make someone think about an issue in a different way, to rethink preconceptions or stereotypes, then to me it's political" (2005: 34). There is, arguably, a middle-ground, albeit tentatively drawn, between the direct focus on 'Politics' as manifest in works such as *Primary* (Drew, 1960) or *The War Room* (Pennebaker, 1993), and the politics of the everyday to be found in *Grey Gardens* (Maysles, 1975) or *Tarnation* (Caouette, 2003). Composed of films that Corner terms those that "engage explicitly for a significant part of their length with matters to do with the control of resources ... and the exercising of social power through formal institutions and procedures of regulation" (2009: 113–114), this describes a slew of films that tackle paradigmatic documentary topics, such as poverty, war, racism, the environment, or corporate malfeasance. And significantly, as Kate Nash points out, it is these topics that have very often been the subject of a new wave of digital interactive documentaries, suggesting that alongside some very notable transformations in documentary form, practice, and modes of engagement, we can also point to clear "continuities of purpose" (2012: 197) with traditional documentary film.

There has been a remarkable explosion of digital interactive documentary production over the last ten years. Projects such as MIT's docubase, which serves to curate an ever-expanding collection of digital documentaries, have helped to compose an emerging infrastructure dedicated to its research and development. MIT's Open Documentary Lab, UWE Bristol's i-Docs symposia, Sheffield Doc/Fest Crossover Labs, the IDFA's DocLab, the Tribeca Film Institute Sandbox, and the Sundance Institute's New Frontier Storylab are just a few of the more notable venues leading in this respect. A range of prestigious, well-established producers and commissioners of socially and politically oriented documentary and non-fiction content, such as the National Film Board of Canada, ARTE France, NPR, the *Guardian*, and the *New York Times*, have been in some cases extensively involved in funding digital interactive documentary. And a number of independent production companies, such as Upian (France), Submarine Channel (US and Netherlands), or Honkytonk Films (France), often working in conjunction with the institutions and venues outlined above, have also been at the forefront of developing innovative digital interactive documentaries.

As with many rapidly developing areas of cultural production, issues of terminology and classification are extensively debated. Galloway *et al.*'s often repeated definition of interactive documentary as "any documentary that uses interactivity as a core part of its delivery mechanism" (2009: 330–331) makes clear the potential breadth of the term, admitting gallery installations, DVDs and CD-Roms, 'docu-games,' or even theatrical performances, as in the case of Nathan Pennington's *Choose Your Own Documentary* (2014). Mandy Rose makes the case for this "broader definition" of interactive documentary, one that "opens up to participation … [including] participation in terms of making" (Rose 2014), which would encompass her own work as producer of the landmark BBC participatory media project *Video Nation* (1993–2001). Paramount here is the politics of documentary representation, central to an ethos of collaboration that Nash notes "has long been fundamental to documentary" (2014a: 50). Nichols, in his landmark work of documentary scholarship *Representing Reality*, classifies 'interactive documentary' as one of documentary's four dominant modes of representation, one which seeks to "engage with individuals more directly while not reverting to classic exposition," in which the "veil of illusory absence is shorn away" (1991: 33, 44). As exemplified in the work of Jean Rouch or Emile de Antonio, there is an obvious politics to this strategy – one in which "textual authority shifts towards the social actors recruited" (1991: 44) and that is ideologically congruous with the subject matter of the work. More recent definitions of interactivity in documentary are conceptually distinct from that offered by Nichols, so much so that they largely fail to make any reference to this earlier usage. This distinction is most apparent by considering the emphasis Nichols places upon the social actors' "direct encounter with the filmmaker" (47) – something entirely absent from many, if not most of the digital interactive documentaries considered here. Yet Nichols' consideration of the question of 'textual authority' gains arguably much wider purchase, given that the interaction under scrutiny is no longer restricted to that between filmmaker and documentary subject/social actor, but also encompasses that between documentary interface and viewer, whom, as Gaudenzi notes, should instead be retitled user/participant or 'doer,' while acknowledging that "what type of doer the user becomes depends on the interactivity afforded by the artefact" (2013: 38).

Gaudenzi's work has been important in setting out a taxonomy of the interactive documentary, or i-doc, as it pertains specifically to the use of digital technology. Her approach is intentionally "platform agnostic," focusing instead on the "interactive logic" with which the participant encounters and engages with the documentary (2012: 126). Working with Judith Aston, and invoking Nichols' original 'four dominant modes' model for documentary, Gaudenzi has set out "four dominant understandings of interactivity" (126). As both writers make clear, "each interactive mode creates a different dynamic with the user, the author, the artefact and its context" (128), while all exploit the affordances offered by digital technologies to create distinctive documentary forms and experiences. And each mode raises specific issues as pertains to documentary politics.

Arguably the most prominent mode of interactive documentary at present – so much so that it has somewhat annexed the term 'interactive documentary' in common parlance – is titled 'hypertext' by Gaudenzi and Aston, and works via a series of selections made from options offered by a (typically closed) database. Most hypertext documentaries are designed for the web, and thus are often termed webdocs, and at least some of their predominance lies in their capacity to recreate what Stefano Odorico terms the "'documentary value' proper of the classic non-fiction films" (2011: 236). Certainly, it appears that documentaries made in this mode hew most closely to the tackling of paradigmatic documentary topics. For instance, *Clouds over Cuba* (Tricklebank, 2012), explores the events leading up to the Cuban missile crisis; *The Big Issue* (Bollendorff and Colo, 2009) examines the global 'obesity epidemic'; *Waterlife* (McMahon, 2009) looks at environmental pollution of the Great Lakes; *Gaza/Sderot* (Bechar, 2008) considers life on the Palestine/Israel border; and *Alma: A Tale of Violence* (Dewever-Plana and Fougère, 2012) offers a former member's story of life inside one of Guatemala's most brutal gangs. As Nash points out, the webdoc's use of "many of the representational conventions of film and television documentary," and employment of an "investigative/journalistic goal" suggest clear "continuities of purpose" with traditional documentary (2012: 198).

An instructive example is the webdoc's approach to the 'classic non-fiction' subject of the mining of coal. Coal mining's status as a domain of human activity possessing a prominent political dimension stretches back to the origins of mass extraction, the industrial revolution, and the organization of labor unions in the early nineteenth century. And concerns with environmental pollution and global energy security have reshaped the political discourse around coal production in the twenty-first century. Coal mining was the subject of one the landmark works of the 1930s British documentary movement, *Coal Face* (1935), directed by Alberto Cavalcanti and produced by John Grierson for the GPO Film Unit. Like its celebrated counterpart *Night Mail* (Watt and Wright, 1936), the film poetically eulogizes the journey of a national resource from its point of origin as it traverses the land. Eschewing British coal production as a site of labor politics – the violent Ammanford Anthracite Strike had occurred only a decade previous – *Coal Face* can yet be understood as an emphatically political film, in that it seeks to naturalize Grierson's documentary philosophy through a remarkable blend of sound, dialogue and image – an ultimately optimistic celebration of "industrial workers contributing their share towards a larger collectivity" (Morris 1987: 30).

The acclaimed webdoc *Journey to the End of Coal* (Bollendorff and Ségrétin, 2008), draws implicitly on the legacy established by *Coal Face*, in that it offers up a journey narrative that seeks to capture in synoptic overview the national conditions of coal production. It is framed by an expressly divergent political purpose, namely to expose the labor conditions in China's coalmines from the perspective of international observers (it was produced by the French company Honkytonk Films in partnership with Amnesty International and Reporters without Borders). This is made clear at the outset by means of an intertitle, an established documentary convention, which states that "the race towards economic growth is often uncompromising for those that must suffer the consequences." Yet this is immediately followed by a second intertitle, offering "as a freelance journalist, you have decided to investigate the living conditions of those who are making the 'Chinese miracle' possible." This shift to addressing the viewer in the first person positions them in the simulation of investigative journalism, and the documentary quickly "establishes the terms of the interactive experience" (Nash 2014a: 60) which consists of selecting from a limited range of options offered on each webpage – usually two or three choices of where to go next, with text boxes, photos, or short video interviews. This branching narrative schema affords the viewer an open-ended time frame to visit a finite number of sites (from state-owned mines to private plants) contained within the closed database structure. As Gaudenzi notes, this structure allows for "control of the story" (2013: 52), which has in any case been carefully framed by the opening intertitle and is consistently employed throughout. Although interaction is posited as a mode of 'investigation' its other function is arguably a strategic one, in terms of its rhetoric of persuasion. Selecting from interactive options may well distract users from questioning the tightly framed nature of the argument, one which they have no opportunity to dispute (by contrast Nash cites the webdoc

Prison Valley (Dufresne and Brault, 2009), which saw individuals take to the discussion forum to challenge the documentary makers' argument [2014b, 390]), whilst the miners remain traditional documentary subjects, rather than participants. In offering up material evidence to form an argument about a remote, dangerous but extraordinary world, *Journey to the End of Coal* in fact demonstrates a remarkable degree of continuity with *Coal Face*.

Gaudenzi and Aston term a second interactive mode 'conversational,' wherein the goal is to create an apparently freely navigable and seamless interaction, as in 3D immersive virtual worlds. Arguably the most significant individual working extensively in this mode with the explicit goal of creating political content is Nonny de la Peña, who started out as a correspondent for *Newsweek* before turning to documentary filmmaking to make *Unconstitutional* (2004), which examined the impact of the USA PATRIOT Act on civil liberties (the film's executive producer was Robert Greenwald). A section of the film focused on Guantanamo Bay, and the erosion of habeas corpus rights of detainees in the prison camp. Together with digital artist Peggy Weil, de la Peña recreated the prison in the online virtual world Second Life, naming the virtual installation *Gone Gitmo* (2007–). Whereas Second Life customarily affords the user a free exploration of the virtual world via one's avatar, entry to *Gone Gitmo* required individuals to surrender this liberty, and experience the virtually rendered reality of open-ended incarceration. Upon entering the inside of a C-17 military transport plane, users would click on a spot on the floor and find their avatar immediately bound, and their 3D view restricted to the inside of a black hood. As de la Peña explained,

> this is what it was like for the detainees who were being hooded and then brought shackeled to Camp X-Ray, and when the black hood was removed you would find that you were inside a cage, a replica of Camp X-ray.
>
> (*Art for Justice 2009*)

Clothed in orange overalls, users could rise from a crouching position in an outdoor cell, and upon exiting would be confronted by a video showing real footage of Guantanamo detainees. Further movement would prompt additional video screens of clips from *Unconstitutional.* Other sections of *Gone Gitmo* included another recreation (from original defense department photos of detainees), this time of Camp Delta, in which the user's avatar, confined to a cell, attempted to extract information from a guard by means of a series of click-response questions. The futility of attempting to get answers to questions such as 'what would you do next? – call your parents?, call your lawyer?, ask what you're in here for?' was intended to confront the user powerfully with 'what it means to lose your habeas corpus rights.' Eschewing the simulation of the prison camp's notorious interrogation techniques, Weil stated that "we do not torture your avatar, so rather than a torture chamber, we elected to build a contemplation chamber, a series of spaces to contemplate the practices going on in Guantanamo" (2009). Composed of news stories, photos, audio recordings and poems from detainees, as well as interrogation transcripts read by actors, the chamber functioned as a repository for information on the continuing plight of its detainees, what 'Guantanamo Reports' author Mark Denbeaux described as "a virtual platform where people from around the world can gather together to discuss important social justice issues" (Rikomatic 2007). By contrast de la Peña stressed the experiential dimension afforded by the avatar, stating that the goal was to "make it more real for people," adding that "people get so connected to the digital version of themselves" (Art for Justice 2009).

de la Peña's subsequent projects have developed this interest in crafting emotionally powerful virtual experiences of real world events that have explicit political content. *Hunger in Los Angeles* (2012), employed Unity 3D, a body-tracking system with a head-mounted goggle display, to allow wearers to witness an individual fall into a diabetic coma while in line at a food bank. Using live audio from this actual event, the project confronted individuals with the question of how to react as this distressing event unfolded in front of them in the simulated world. Her most recent work, *Project Syria* (2014), used the Unity 3D system to put people on a street in Aleppo, Syria, during a rocket shell attack causing immediate confusion and chaos, before transporting them to a Syrian refugee camp in Iraq. Again, the audio came from live recordings made by a team sent over by de la Peña, while video and photographs were used to generate the virtual spaces. de la Peña has coined the phrase "immersive journalism" to describe her work, with the objective of putting "the audience 'on scene' and evok[ing] the feeling of 'being there'" (Project Syria 2014). Retaining the term 'audience,' rather than opting for 'user,' speaks to the emphasis on emotionally powerful eye-witnessing, through virtual immersion, rather than interacting with other individuals, or being able to adjust or create content; de la Peña and her production team retain total control over the environment.

One question we might ask is how we judge the political efficacy of de la Peña's work. *Project Syria* was displayed at the 2014 World Economic Forum at the request of Executive Chairman Klaus Schwab, with the purpose of "compelling world leaders to act on this crucial issue" (2014). As bespoke installations only available to those at its physical location (such as my experience of *Project Syria* at Sheffield Doc/Fest), the Unity 3D projects have very limited circulation, with the hope that attention from the right individuals at those locations (policy makers, news agencies, and so forth), can help provoke action. Similar projects, such as Oscar Raby and Katy Morrison's *Assent* (2014), which uses the Oculus Rift VR headset to recreate Raby's father's witnessing of the execution of prisoners captured by the military regime in Chile in 1973, are comparably powerfully immersive, using the technology to fulfill the documentary aim of, in Corner's words, "deliver[ing] the political as both an experience of knowing and of feeling" (2009: 112), but also leaving open the question of how this might translate into efficacy or activism. Drawing on Jane Gaines' work on 'political mimesis,' Corner questions the extent to which films that "make 'visceral appeals that work to rouse audiences (Gaines 1999: 99)' can 'develop from being an individualized experience of emotional alignment to being a behaviour (e.g. joining an organization, changing lifestyle, becoming involved in forms of political activity)'" (Corner 2009: 127). Despite its use of more basic rendering technology, *Gone Gitmo*, widely accessible, and offering a heterogeneous assortment of user generated content to explore, arguably comes closer to enlisting the affordances of new media in the service of active civic participation, which, for a number of commentators, represents one of the most significant potentials of interactive documentary content with stated political objectives.

There appears, at first glance, to be a degree of overlap between projects such as *Hunger in Los Angeles* and *Assent* and those fitting Gaudenzi and Aston's third mode of interactivity, entitled experiential, which brings "digital content into physical space" using GPS, smartphones and other mobile devices to create a "locative documentary" (2012: 127). Yet those works seek to immerse the individual entirely within the virtual world unfolding through the 3D headset, requiring no involvement with the immediate physical environment. Conversely, the growth of locative technologies has helped stimulate a range of innovative projects that blend activist and documentary impulses in relation to events and issues occurring on the ground in specific settings, sharing knowledge and information to achieve often quite explicit political goals. An early example of the potential of this approach is the 2008 partnership between San Francisco PBS television station KQED and Oakland High School, to coincide with the re-release of the landmark civil rights documentary series *Eyes on the Prize* (1987–90). Informed by the issues raised by the series, students went into their neighborhoods to document social justice problems, and then used this content to create narrative accounts tagged to their locations with Google Earth. Handheld GPS devices then geo-tagged these stories so that they could be triggered for playback when individuals found themselves in those specific locations (Eyes on the Prize 2008). Tina Bastajian and Seda Manavoglu's *Coffee Deposits: Topologies of Chance* (2010) is by contrast an instructive example of a locative documentary project that evolved by happenstance into a work foregrounding issues of political and social justice, suggesting how the mode's generative mechanism of eliciting participant testimony can lead in unexpected geographic and discursive directions. Funded by the European Cultural Foundation, and situated in Istanbul, the project set out with the objective of charting "movements, rhythms and dwelling" in the city, "moving through the mode of mobile, in-situ and ad-hoc Turkish coffee encounters" and "introducing GPS and location aware gestures, augmenting these encounters with residual digital traces" (*Coffee Deposits* 2010). Yet this ludic, psychogeographic, digitally augmented dérive halted abruptly when confronted with how the rise of political Islam was impacting on the free movement of certain individuals around the city. For instance, a mobile encounter with the transsexual Deniz revealed a story of escalating harassment and discrimination, and the spurious use of laws aimed at street-vendors to take LGBT individuals into police custody.

Perhaps the most ambitious approach to harnessing the potential of the locative documentary mode to generate testimony shaped around a specific social justice issue is *Quipu Project* (2014–) (http://quipu-project.com/) a partnership between Chaka Films and academics Matthew Brown and Karen Tucker, and funded by the REACT Knowledge Exchange Hub for the Creative Economy in the UK. The aim of the documentary project was to "collect and share the stories of those affected by the sterilization policy which targeted over 300,000 indigenous women without their consent applied in Peru in the late 90s," with the objective to "activate and promote a dialogue around issues of self-empowerment and self-representation" (*Quipu: A Living Documentary*, 2014). Faced with the issue of communities in rural Peru with no access to digital media, the production team used a toll-free telephone number connecting to a bespoke VoIP telephone service to let women record testimonies of their own experiences of sterilization, which they could then replay, and also listen to the accounts of others. Those testimonies were also automatically saved to a dedicated server, for the purpose of uploading to the project website, in order to, in the words of co-director Rosemarie Lerner, help bridge the "digital divide" and enable the women "to communicate with the rest of the world ... for the first time they can actually become part of a wider dialogue" (*Quipu: A Living Documentary*, 2013). The team used the term 'living documentary' (a concept employed, albeit in slightly different ways, in the work of Gaudenzi and Jon Dovey and Mandy Rose), to describe the project, and to identify in particular the fact that, unlike feature documentaries, but also interactive documentaries such as *Journey to the End of Coal, Project Syria* or *Assent*, the objective was not to author an account or recreation, but rather "making the conditions for the story to emerge" (*Quipu: A Living Documentary*, 2013). The producers' ethical and political stance on the sterilization policy was explicit and unequivocal, but so was the importance of designing an interactive mode responsive not just to the issue, but also to addressing the underlying conditions of isolation and disempowerment that allowed the policy to be implemented without active resistance in the first place.

Nash notes that "the potential for participants and audiences to 'speak for themselves' has been at the heart of much of the enthusiasm surrounding interactive documentary" (2014b: 385), and the emphasis placed by Karen Tucker on *Quipu Project* as a "collaborative" documentary, one in which ethical considerations and issues of agency are paramount certainly bears that out (*Quipu: A Living Documentary*, 2013). Yet Nash draws on the work of Nico Carpentier to make an important distinction between participation *in* media, and participation *through* media, pointing out that: "Critical reflection on participation in documentary would focus on the nature of participant contributions, the 'framing' of the invitation to participate and the relationships surrounding production. In contrast, participation through media draws attention to documentary's social dimension" (2014b: 388). As she rightly notes, both types of participation have a longer history within the documentary filmmaking tradition, but the potential of digital technologies to facilitate new forms of collaboration is clear. *Quipu Project* appears to blend elements of the experiential, locative documentary mode, in that it uses a digital technology to enable the recording and replaying of testimony in a physical space, documenting the histories of events which occurred within and around those environs, with strong elements of the participative mode – Gaudenzi and Aston's fourth and final category of interactivity (2012: 126). And the women's' participation in the project can be understood as both *in* the creation of content, and to connect with others affected by the sterilization policy *through* the VoIP telephone service.

Arguably the most frequently cited example of a participative documentary that harnesses the mode's capacity to document a rapidly evolving political event is *18 Days in Egypt* (2011–), the creation of former *New York Times* video-journalist Jigar Mehta and technologist Yasmin Elayat, and described on the project website as "an interactive, crowd-sourced documentary project about the ongoing Egyptian revolution" (*18 Days in Egypt* 2012). Mehta's original inspiration came from watching televised footage of the Egyptian uprising in 2011, and wanting to capitalize on the fact that mobile-phone wielding protestors were clearly documenting their own participation, with footage, photos, and commentary subsequently uploaded to social media sites such as Twitter, Facebook, YouTube, and Flickr (Future of Film Preview 2014). An initial website designed by Mehta sought simply to aggregate such content by linking it with the hashtag #18DaysinEgypt. From there, and with the goal of creating "a more innovative, interesting, complete account of the uprising," Mehta and Elayat designed GroupStream, an interactive platform used to crowd-source, contextualize, and archive photographs, texts, tweets, and video clips, which launched in January 2012, accompanied by a 'call to action' video intended to encourage participation, and which ended with the line "you lived it, you recorded it, now let's write our country's history" (Future of Film Preview 2014).

If Mehta's initial photo-journalist's impulse was to "go to Egypt, find characters, film their experiences, and tell the story through my eyes" (Future of Film Preview 2014), *18 Days in Egypt* was by contrast designed to collate and document participatory experience through an open and evolving database of user-generated content. As Mehta stated, "they really told us what they wanted to share" (Future of Film Preview 2014). And, interestingly, what users shared was occasionally topically removed from the uprising and its political ambit, such as stories from the Japanese Fukushima nuclear disaster. Again, this perhaps raises the question of how we judge the success, in political terms, of *18 Days in Egypt* as a documentary. As with *Quipu Project*, or *Mapping Main Street* (Oehler *et al.* 2009), another participatory documentary that built a user database of photos, images, and stories from the more than 10,000 Main Streets across the US, in order to counter the idea that "when politicians mention Main Street, they evoke one people and one place" (http://www.mappingmainstreet.org/) we are required to think differently about the notion of a documentary argument. Unlike a traditional documentary, it is the interactive format of the response to the initial, and explicitly political catalyst, be it mass sterilization, the rhetoric of unrepresentative homogeneity, or, as in the case of *18 Days in Egypt*, the uprising against an autocratic regime, that *is* the argument. In Mubarak's Egypt, the regulation of state media and the suppression of freedom of speech were, as Howard and Hussain point out, combatted by new digital communication networks which helped make possible "rapid mobilization and collective protest action" (2013: 4). *18 Days in*

Egypt is thus both a reflection on, and a reflection of, the growth of digital activism, and what Howard and Hussain describe as a key tenet of civil society, namely that "no one group can claim to represent the whole of society, and that society is best served by a multitude of groups that contribute in different ways to the dissemination and exchange of information" (4).

If this builds a powerful case for the participatory documentary from the perspective of the contributor, it perhaps still leaves open the issue of what significance these works give to those individuals simply viewing content. As *18 Days in Egypt* built up its database, Mehta turned his attention to the question of "how are we going to engage a larger population with these stories?," stating that the strategy was to try and "move the needle from journalism to cinema," and attempt to "bring these stories together in a cohesive narrative that can stay true to the storyteller" (Future of Film Preview 2014). One approach was to hone in on contributors as 'characters,' whose evolving body of content could be followed. Yet the notion of engaging audiences in cinematic stories of individual characters brings the project clearly in to line with traditional approaches to documentary storytelling, and appears much more directly driven by the producers' understandable desire to sustain the ongoing life of the project, and much less with "the creation of community and . . . fostering civic involvement" (2014: 390–391). It is worth noting that none of the participatory documentaries cited here allow for what Gaudenzi describes as 'open' interactivity, where users can input not only into the content of the documentary, but also into the structure itself (2013: 69). Ingrid Kopp, Head of Digital Initiatives at Tribeca Film Institute (the organization that helped fund *18 Days in Egypt*), makes the point that the "tension between authorship and openness" characterizes many interactive documentary projects (Power to the Pixel 2013). If anything, Mehta's plans for evolution proposed a tighter directorial/curatorial command of structure, searching for the story 'cohesion' to attract a broader audience.

Aufderheide, reflecting on the changes wrought by new forms of participatory media states that "it is clear that interactivity multiplies the ethical challenges" for documentarians, not least in terms of questions of trust in an "emergent ecology ... more characterised by questions than answers, as it is characterised more by experiments than by settled practice" (2014: 243). Nowhere is this more evident than in relation to the issue of data. As she notes, protecting the "privacy of the data that subjects have shared" on interactive platforms is a major test, one amplified dramatically by the political furore provoked by Edward Snowden's leaking of NSA surveillance program documents in 2013. Jon Dovey writes that the "voluntary provision of content and the frequently involuntary provision of data go hand in hand," stating that the "political question here is what rights and responsibilities do we have for the 'biomass' that we produce?" (2014: 25, 27). Documentary's ability to formulate robust answers to these issues of participatory trust, integrity and ethics, without which, as Aufderheide maintains, the work "no longer has documentary status," will define its future as it moves forward into this ever-growing world of interactive and participatory culture.

Bibliography

18 Days in Egypt, available at: http://beta.18daysinegypt.com [accessed 5 September 2014].

"Art for Justice Podcast" (2009), available at: http://www.archive.org/details/ArtForJusticeTalkWPeggyWeilNonnyDeLaPenaAtIntlJusticeCenterIn_715 [accessed 17 July 2014].

Aufderheide, P. (2007) *Documentary Film: A Very Short Introduction*, Oxford: Oxford University Press.

Aufderheide, P. (2014) "Ethical Challenges for Documentarians in a User-Centric Environment," in K. Nash, C. Hight and C. Summerhayes (eds) *New Documentary Ecologies: Emerging Platforms, Practices and Discourses*, London: Palgrave Macmillan, pp. 237–250.

Bruns, A. (2008) *Blogs, Wikipedia, Second Life and Beyond: From Production to Produsage*, New York: Peter Lang.

Chanan, M. (2007) *The Politics of Documentary*, London: British Film Institute.

Coffee Deposits: Topologies of Chance (2010), available at: http://coffeedeposits.nl/ [accessed 5 September 2014].

Corner, J. (2009) "Documenting the Political: Some Issues," *Studies in Documentary Film*, 3(2), pp. 113–129.

Dovey, J. (2014) "Documentary Ecosystems: Collaboration and Exploitation," in K. Nash, C. Hight and C. Summerhayes (eds) *New Documentary Ecologies: Emerging Platforms, Practices and Discourses*, London: Palgrave Macmillan, pp. 11–32.

"Eyes on the Prize" (2008) *Centre for Locative Media*, available at: http://www.locative-media.org/projects/C82/ [accessed 12 June 2013].

"Future of Film Preview: Jigar Mehta on 18 Days in Egypt" (2014), available at: https://www.youtube.com/watch?v=yyANcPaNT7o [accessed 5 September 2014].

Gaines, J. (1999) "Political mimesis," in J. Gaines and M. Renov (eds) *Collecting Visible Evidence*, Minneapolis: University of Minnesota Press, pp 84–102.

Galloway, D., McAlpine, K. and Harris, P. (2009) "From Michael Moore to JFK Reloaded: Towards a Working Model of Interactive Documentary," *Journal of Media Practice*, 8(3), pp. 325–339.

Gaudenzi, S. (2013) *The Living Documentary: From Representing Reality to Co-creating Reality in Digital Interactive Documentary*, Doctoral thesis, Goldsmiths, University of London: Goldsmiths Research Online.

Gaudenzi, S. and Aston, J. (2012) "Interactive Documentary: Setting the Field," *Studies in Documentary Film*, 6(2), pp. 125–139.

Howard, P.N. and Hussain, M.M. (2013) *Democracy's Fourth Wave?: Digital Media and the Arab Spring*, New York: Oxford University Press.

Morris, P. (1987) "Re-Thinking Grierson: The Ideology of John Grierson," in P. Veronneau, M. Dorland and S. Feldman (eds) *Dialogue: Canadian and Quebec Cinema*, Montreal: Mediatexte, pp. 21– 56.

Nash, K. (2012) "Modes of Interactivity: Analysing the Webdoc," *Media, Culture and Society*, 34(2), pp. 195–210.

Nash, K. (2014a) "Clicking on the World: Documentary Representation and Interactivity," in K. Nash, C. Hight and C. Summerhayes (eds) *New Documentary Ecologies: Emerging Platforms, Practices and Discourses*, London: Palgrave Macmillan, pp. 50–66.

Nash, K. (2014b) "What is Interactivity for? The Social Dimension of Web-Documentary Participation," *Journal of Media & Cultural Studies*, 28(3), pp. 383–395.

Nichols, B. (1991) *Representing Reality: Issues and Concepts in Documentary*, Bloomington: Indiana University Press.

Odorico, S. (2011) "Documentary on the Web between Realism and Interaction. A Case Study: From Zero – People Rebuilding Life after the Emergency," *Studies in Documentary Film*, 5(3), pp. 235–246.

Postill, J. (2012) "Digital Politics and Political Engagement," in H. Horst and D. Miller (eds) *Digital Anthropology*, Oxford: Berg, pp. 165–184.

Power to the Pixel (2013) *Experiments in Interactive Design*, [Online Video], 21 November, available at: http://thepixelreport.org/2013/11/21/experiments-in-interactive-documentary-what-robots-coal-miners-and-mobile-phones-have-taught-me-about-storytelling-and-social-change/ [accessed 5 September 2014].

"Project Syria: Premieres at the World Economic Forum" (2014), available at: http://www.immersivejournalism.com/project-syria-premieres-at-the-world-economic-forum/ [accessed 23 January 2014].

Quipu: A Living Documentary (2013), available at: http://www.react-hub.org.uk/future-doc-sandbox/projects/2013/quipu/ [accessed 5 September 2014].

Quipu: A Living Documentary (2014), available at: http://projectquipu.com/?q=node/9 [accessed 5 September 2014].

Rikomatic, 'Virtual Gitmo" to Focus on Legal and Political Issues of US Detention of Alleged Terrorists' (2007) *Rikomatic*, available at: http://www.rikomatic.com/blog/2007/09/seton-hall-laun.html#more [accessed 5 September 2014].

Rose, M. (2014) "Mandy Rose Defines Interactive Documentary," *Open Documentary Lab at MIT*, available at: http://opendoclab.mit.edu/video-interview-mandy-rose-defines-interactive-documentary [accessed 5 September 2014].

Zimmerman, D. (2005) "The Political Documentary in America Today," *Cineaste*, 30(3), pp. 29–36.

INDEX

Note: Foreign-language films are listed under their English title, where given.